Microsoft Excel Pivot Table Data Crunching

Including Dynamic Arrays, Power Query, and Copilot

Bill Jelen

Microsoft Pivot Table Data Crunching: Including Dynamic Arrays, Power Query, and Copilot

Bill Jelen

Published with the authorization of Microsoft Corporation by:

Pearson Education, Inc.

Copyright © 2025 by Pearson Education, Inc.

Hoboken, New Jersey

ISBN-13: 978-0-13-540879-7

ISBN-10: 0-13-540879-2

Library of Congress Control Number: On file

1 2024

Trademarks

Warning and Disclaimer

EDITOR-IN-CHIEF
Brett Bartow

EXECUTIVE EDITOR
Loretta Yates

ASSOCIATE EDITOR
Shourav Bose

DEVELOPMENT EDITOR
Rick Kughen

MANAGING EDITOR
Sandra Schroeder

SENIOR PROJECT EDITOR
Tracey Croom

COPY EDITOR
Rick Kughen

INDEXER
Timothy Wright

PROOFREADER
Jennifer Hinchliffe

TECHNICAL EDITOR
Bob Umlas

EDITORIAL ASSISTANT
Cindy Teeters

COVER DESIGNER
Twist Creative, Seattle

COMPOSITOR
codeMantra

FRONT COVER IMAGE
whiteMocca/Shutterstock

Dedication

To Kim Sekas and Stacie Fuss from my morning workout crew in the Supernatural VR headset. Any time that I started posting irrelevant Excel analyses, they would remind me that I had chapters to update.

—Bill Jelen

Contents at a Glance

Contents

Chapter 4   **Grouping, sorting, and filtering pivot data**   **77**

Chapter 14   Advanced pivot table tips and techniques   395

Acknowledgments

At Microsoft, thanks to the Excel team for always being willing to answer questions about various features. At MrExcel.com, thanks to an entire community of people who are passionate about Excel. Thanks to Bob Umlas for his tech editing of this book and to the Kughens for their project management. Thanks to Mike Alexander for being my co-author on this book through the first four editions. Thanks to Suat Ozgur—the Batcoder—for his review of my code in Chapter 13. Finally, thanks to my wife, Mary Ellen, for her support during the writing process.

About the author

Bill Jelen, Excel MVP and the host of MrExcel.com, has been using spreadsheets since 1985, and he launched the MrExcel.com website in 1998. Bill was a regular guest on *Call for Help* with Leo Laporte and has produced more than 2,600 episodes of his daily video podcast, Learn Excel from MrExcel. He is the author of 69 books about Microsoft Excel and writes the monthly Excel column for *Strategic Finance* magazine. Before founding MrExcel.com, Bill spent 12 years in the trenches, working as a financial analyst for the finance, marketing, accounting, and operations departments of a $500 million public company. He lives in Merritt Island, Florida, with his wife, Mary Ellen.

Introduction

The pivot table is the single most powerful tool in all of Excel. Pivot tables came along during the 1990s, when Microsoft and Lotus were locked in a bitter battle for dominance of the spreadsheet market. The race to continually add enhanced features to their respective products during the mid-1990s led to many incredible features, but none as powerful as the pivot table.

With a pivot table, you can transform one million rows of transactional data into a summary report in seconds. If you can drag a mouse, you can create a pivot table. In addition to quickly summarizing and calculating data, pivot tables enable you to change your analysis on the fly by simply moving fields from one area of a report to another.

No other tool in Excel gives you the flexibility and analytical power of a pivot table. The Power Query tools that debuted between Excel 2013 and Excel 2016 come close to the power of a pivot table. You will see some Power Query examples in Chapter 17, "Pivoting without a pivot table using formulas, Python, or Power Query," and Chapter 18, "Unpivoting in Power Query."

What you will learn from this book

It is widely agreed that close to 60 percent of Excel customers leave 80 percent of Excel untouched—that is, most people do not tap into the full potential of Excel's built-in utilities. Of these utilities, the most prolific by far is the pivot table. Despite the fact that pivot tables have been a cornerstone of Excel for almost 30 years, they remain one of the most underused tools in the entire Microsoft Office suite.

Having picked up this book, you are savvy enough to have heard of pivot tables—and you have perhaps even received them on occasion. You have a sense that pivot tables provide a power that you are not using, and you want to learn how to leverage that power to increase your productivity quickly.

Within the first two chapters, you will be able to create basic pivot tables, increase your productivity, and produce reports in minutes instead of hours. Within the first seven chapters, you will be able to output complex pivot reports with drill-down capabilities and accompanying charts. By the end of the book, you will be able to build a dynamic pivot table reporting system.

What is new in Microsoft Excel's pivot tables

Microsoft introduced two new array functions to make it easier to replicate a pivot table using a formula: PIVOTBY and GROUPBY. One advantage of formulas over pivot tables is that formulas will automatically recalculate when the underlying data changes. There are times when you are creating dashboards for the manager three levels up, and you really can't count on them to know to click the Refresh button on the pivot table menu. In these cases, the PIVOTBY function can make sure your dashboard is up to date.

For several years, Microsoft offered the Analyze Data feature where you could often create a pivot table just by asking a question about your data. The Analyze Data feature is tested and reliable and will always produce a reliable result. For this edition of the book, a brand new Copilot feature is available in Excel. You have to pay extra. It will often produce a report as accurate as the same report as Analyze Data. However, it will sometimes produce the wrong report or an inaccurate report. At the very least, having Copilot on the other side of a paywall should make you appreciate the superior Analyze Data feature that is freely available in Microsoft 365.

You can now create a pivot table while using Excel Online. It does not offer all the features of Excel for Windows, but being able to create a pivot table in Excel Online is a giant leap for the online version of Excel. It was just few years ago that I wrote in the previous edition of this book that Excel Online would never allow you to create pivot tables, and now, they do it. You can't tweak them like you can in Windows, but you can create pivot tables.

Office 365 offers a new Analyze Data feature that is powered by Artificial Intelligence. Select a data set with up to 250,000 cells and ask Excel to analyze the data. Excel will suggest about 30 interesting analyses, including several pivot tables.

The Analyze Data feature allows you to ask a question about your data. There is a fairly high chance that the answer will be provided as a pivot table or a pivot chart. So, Analyze Data and Ask a Question become new entry points for creating pivot tables.

If you missed the 2019 edition of this book, these features were new since Excel 2016:

- You can specify default settings for all future pivot tables.

- The automatic date grouping introduced in Excel 2016 pivot tables can now be turned off. A mix of empty cells and numeric cells will be treated like a numeric column and will default to Sum instead of Count.

- Power Pivot is now included in all Windows versions of Excel 2019 and Office 365.

Case study: Life without pivot tables

Say that your manager asks you to create a one-page summary of a sales database. They would like to see total revenue by region and product. Suppose you do not know how to use pivot tables. You will have to use dozens of keystrokes or mouse clicks to complete this task.

This sample data set (included with the download files for the book—see page xxxii)—has headings in row 1, data in rows 2 through 564, and columns in column A through column I.

First, you have to get a sorted, unique list of products down the left side of the summary report and a sorted, unique list of products across the top. In the past, this might involve an Advanced Filter or the Remove Duplicates command. But today, it is easiest with a formula.

1. Enter =SORT(UNIQUE(B2:B564)) in cell K2. You will have a list of the unique region names spilling to K2:K5.

2. To get a list of unique products across the top of the report, enter =TRANSPOSE (SORT(UNIQUE(C2:C564))) in cell L1.

At this point, with 57 keystrokes, you've built the shell of the final report, but there are no numbers inside yet (see Figure I-1).

	B	C	D	E	F	G	H	I	J	K	L	M	N	O
											Doodads	Gadget	Gizmo	Widget
1	Region	Product	Date	Customer	Quantity	Revenue	COGS	Profit						
2	Midwest	Gizmo	1/1/2029	Ford	1000	22810	10220	12590		Midwest				
3	Northeast	Gadget	1/2/2029	Verizon	100	2257	984	1273		Northeast				
4	South	Gizmo	1/4/2029	Valero Energy	400	9152	4088	5064		South				
5	Midwest	Gadget	1/4/2029	Cardinal Hea	800	18552	7872	10680		West				

FIGURE I-1 It took 57 keystrokes to get to this point.

Next, you need to build a SUMIFS function to total the revenue for each Region and Product. As shown in Figure I-2, the formula =SUMIFS(G2:G564,B2:B564,K2#,C2:C56 4,L1#) does the trick. It takes 40 characters plus the Enter key to finish the formula.

f_x =SUMIFS(G2:G564,B2:B564,K2#,C2:C564,L1#)

K	L	M	N	O
	Doodads	Gadget	Gizmo	Widget
Midwest	6036	544772	652651	537965
Northeast	38860	714009	751724	620019
South	0	839551	918588	844186
West	28663	65382	70057	75349

FIGURE I-2 Before Dynamic Arrays were introduced, the formula in L2 would have needed dollar signs and then been copied to all 16 cells showing numbers.

Enter the heading Total for the total row and for the total column. You can do this in nine keystrokes if you type the first heading, press Ctrl+Enter to stay in the same cell, and then use Copy, select the cell for the second heading, and use Paste.

If you select K1:P6 and press Alt+= (that is, Alt and the equal sign key), you can add the total formula in three keystrokes.

With this method, which takes 110 clicks or keystrokes, you end up with a nice summary report, as shown in Figure I-3. If you could pull this off in 5 or 10 minutes, you would probably be fairly proud of your Excel prowess; there are some good tricks among those 110 operations.

K	L	M	N	O	P
	Gizmo	Gadget	Widget	Doodads	Total
Midwest	652651	544772	537965	6036	1741424
Northeast	751724	714009	620019	38860	2124612
South	918588	839551	844186	0	2602325
West	70057	65382	75349	28663	239451
Total	2393020	2163714	2077519	73559	6707812

FIGURE I-3 A mere 110 operations later, you have a summary report.

You hand the report to your manager. Within a few minutes, they come back with one of the following requests, which will certainly cause a lot of rework:

- Could you put products down the side and regions across the top?

- Could you show me the same report for only the manufacturing customers?

- Could you show profit instead of revenue?

- Could you copy this report for each of the customers?

Invention of the pivot table

When the actual pivot table was invented is in dispute. The Excel team coined the term *pivot table*, which appeared in Excel in 1993. However, the concept was not new. Pito Salas and his team at Lotus were working on the pivot table concept in 1986 and released Lotus Improv in 1991. Before then, Javelin offered functionality similar to that of pivot tables.

The core concept behind a pivot table is that the data, formulas, and data views are stored separately. Each column has a name, and you can group and rearrange the data by dragging field names to various positions on the report.

Case study: Life after pivot tables

Say that you're tired of working so hard to remake reports every time your manager wants a change. You're in luck: You can produce the same report as in the last case study but use a pivot table instead. Excel offers you 10 thumbnails of recommended pivot tables to get you close to the goal. Follow these steps:

1. Click the Insert tab of the ribbon.

2. Click Recommended PivotTables. Scroll through the list of suggested pivot tables, looking for one with Revenue, Product, and Region. You might have to click See All 10 Results below the fourth suggestion. As shown in Figure I-4, you could choose either Revenue By Region And Product or Revenue By Product And Region. Either one is fine. Choose the + Existing Sheet button beneath Revenue By Region And Product.

3. Excel will ask you to specify a starting cell for the pivot table. It is a good idea to leave a blank column to the right of your data and then have the pivot table start in cell K2. The initial pivot table will have both Region and Product in the first column of the pivot table. Your goal is to have the products appear along the top of the pivot table.

4. Drag the Product field from the Rows area to the Columns area (see Figure I-5).

FIGURE I-4 Choose a recommended pivot table that is as close as you will get to the desired report.

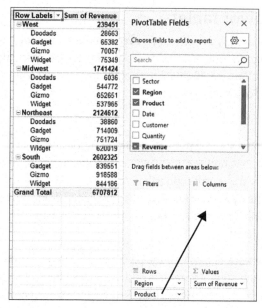

FIGURE I-5 To finish the report, drag the Product heading to the Columns area.

With just a few clicks of the mouse, you have the report shown in Figure I-6.

	Sum of Revenue	Product ▾				
	Region ▾	Doodads	Gadget	Gizmo	Widget	Grand Total
5	West	28663	65382	70057	75349	239451
6	Midwest	6036	544772	652651	537965	1741424
7	Northeast	38860	714009	751724	620019	2124612
8	South	0	839551	918588	844186	2602325
9	Grand Total	73559	2163714	2393020	2077519	6707812

FIGURE I-6 It took a few clicks to create this report.

In addition, when your manager comes back with a request like the ones near the end of the prior case study, you can easily use the pivot table to make the changes. Here's a quick overview of the changes you'll learn to make in the chapters that follow:

- Could you put products down the side and regions across the top? (This change will take you 10 seconds: Drag Product to Rows and Region to Columns.)

- Could you show me the same report for only the manufacturing customers? (15 seconds: Select Insert Slicer | Sector. Then, click OK and click Manufacturing.)

- Could you show profit instead of revenue? (10 seconds: Clear the Revenue check-box and select the Profit checkbox.)

- Could you copy this report for each of the customers? (30 seconds: Move Customer to Report Filter, open the tiny dropdown next to the Options button, choose Show Report Filter Pages, and click OK. For more details, see Tip 17: Use a pivot table to explode a data set to different tabs in Chapter 14).

Creating a pivot table using Artificial Intelligence

The new Analyze Data tool uses artificial intelligence to analyze a data set. You can type a question in natural language, and Excel will create a pivot table.

With one cell in your data set selected, choose the Analyze Data command on the right side of the Home tab. The Analyze Data pane appears with several suggested analyses. In the Ask a Question box at the top, type **Revenue by Product and Region as Table** and press Enter.

Excel will draw a thumbnail of your report. Click +Insert PivotTable at the bottom of the thumbnail.

FIGURE I-7 Slightly more typing, but certainly easier to create.

Who this book is for

This book is a comprehensive-enough reference for hard-core analysts yet relevant to casual users of Excel.

We assume that you are comfortable navigating in Excel and that you have some large data sets that you need to summarize.

How this book is organized

The bulk of the book covers how to use pivot tables in the Excel user interface. Chapter 10, "Unlocking features with the Data Model and Power Pivot," delves into the Power Pivot window. Chapter 13, "Using VBA or TypeScript to create pivot tables," describes how to create pivot tables in Excel's powerful VBA macro language. Chapter 18, "Using Artificial Intelligence and Copilot for Building Pivot Tables, describes using artificial intelligence and Copilot to create analyses. Anyone who has a firm grasp of basics such as preparing data, copying, pasting, and entering simple formulas should not have a problem understanding the concepts in this book.

About the companion content

The download files for this book include all of the data sets used to produce the book, so you can practice the concepts in the book. For access to these companion files, and other resources, visit *MicrosoftPressStore.com/register*, sign in or create a new account, and register ISBN 9780135408797 by December 31, 2027.

System requirements

You need the following software and hardware to build and run the code samples for this book:

You will need Microsoft Excel running on a Windows computer. (Yes, Excel runs on an iPad, on an Android tablet, but none of those are going to support the creation of pivot tables anytime soon.) For people using Excel on a Mac, some of the basic pivot table concepts will apply. Power Query and Power Pivot will not run on a Mac. For people using Excel Online, you can make many of the pivot tables in this book, but you won't be able to do as much formatting.

Compact versus tabular layout

Microsoft changed the default layout of pivot tables in 2007 to something that it calls Compact layout. For various reasons that I will explain here, I am not a fan of Compact layout and have changed settings in Excel options so that my pivot tables are created in Tabular layout. As you work through this book, it will help if you can quickly recognize the contrast between how Compact and Tabular layouts show the same data.

In Figure I-8, columns N:Q show a traditional pivot table in tabular layout. Each of the three row fields appears in a different column with meaningful headings such as Region, Product, and Sector.

In contrast, columns S:T show the same data in compact layout. The meaningful headings from N2:P2 are replaced by a single heading of "Row Labels" in S2. The values for Region, Product, and Sector are intermingled in column S with a different indent level showing if you are looking at a region, product name, or sector name.

	N	O	P	Q	R	S	T
2	Region	Product	Sector	Sum of Revenue		Row Labels	Sum of Revenue
3	⊟West	⊟Widget	Energy	26406		⊟West	239451
4	West	Widget	Financial	13853		⊟Widget	75349
5	West	Widget	Manufacturing	17840		Energy	26406
6	West	Widget	Retail	17250		Financial	13853
7	West	Widget Total		75349		Manufacturing	17840
8	West	⊟Gizmo	Energy	7032		Retail	17250
9	West	Gizmo	Financial	19544		⊟Gizmo	70057
10	West	Gizmo	Manufacturing	25861		Energy	7032
11	West	Gizmo	Retail	17620		Financial	19544
12	West	Gizmo Total		70057		Manufacturing	25861
13	West	⊟Gadget	Energy	20610		Retail	17620
14	West	Gadget	Financial	26484		⊟Gadget	65382
15	West	Gadget	Healthcare	2358		Energy	20610
16	West	Gadget	Manufacturing	11550		Financial	26484
17	West	Gadget	Retail	4380		Healthcare	2358
18	West	Gadget Total		65382		Manufacturing	11550
19	West	⊟Doodads	Healthcare	28663		Retail	4380
20	West	Doodads Total		28663		⊟Doodads	28663
21	West Total			239451		Healthcare	28663
22	⊟Midwest	⊟Gizmo	Consumer Goods	61125		⊟Midwest	1741424
23	Midwest	Gizmo	Healthcare	17728		⊟Gizmo	652651

FIGURE I-8 The Row Labels heading in S2 is the clue that your pivot tables are defaulting to Compact layout.

My irritation with the Compact layout is how Excel mixes Regions, Products, and Sectors in column S. Any human reading the report can tell the difference by noticing the indent levels. But there is no calculation function that can tell the difference between a field indented by eight spaces instead of four spaces.

I know that in many cases, I will be converting the pivot table to values and using the static version of the table for other uses. Those other uses will always need each field in its own column.

If you are following along with the examples in this book and end up with a pivot table in Compact layout, rest assured that the numbers in your pivot table and the numbers in the book are the same, just with different formatting.

You can switch one pivot table to a new layout using the Design tab in the ribbon. Open the Report Layout dropdown and choose between Compact and Tabular.

If you happen to agree that the pivot table shown in columns N:Q of Figure I-8 is superior to the pivot table shown in columns S:T, then follow these steps to change your pivot table defaults on your computer.

1. Open the File menu and choose Excel Options.

2. In the Excel Options dialog, choose the Data category from the left navigation bar.

3. Click the top button for Edit Default Layout next to Make Changes To The Default Layout Of Pivot Tables.

4. Open the Report Layout dropdown and choose Show in Tabular Form.

5. Choose the box next to Repeat All Item Labels.

6. Click the PivotTable Options... button in the lower-right part of the Edit Default Layout dialog. There are five tabs across the top of the PivotTable Options dialog.

7. On the Layout & Format tab, click in the For Empty Cells Show box and type a zero (**0**). Click OK three times to close all of the open dialogs.

Your pivot tables will now default to the format shown on the left side of Figure I.8.

Errata, updates, and book support

We've made every effort to ensure the accuracy of this book and its companion content. You can access updates to this book—in the form of a list of submitted errata and their related corrections—at the following page:

MicrosoftPressStore.com/Excel365pivotdata/errata

If you discover an error that is not already listed, please submit it to us at the same page.

For additional book support and information, please visit:

MicrosoftPressStore.com/Support

Please note that product support for Microsoft software and hardware is not offered through the previous addresses. For help with Microsoft software or hardware, go to *http://support.microsoft.com.*

Stay in touch

Let's keep the conversation going! We're on X:

http://x.com/MicrosoftPress

http://x.com/MrExcel

## CHAPTER 1

Pivot table fundamentals

In this chapter, you will:

- Learn why you should use a pivot table

- Learn when to use a pivot table

- Get to know the anatomy of a pivot table

- Peek at pivot tables behind the scenes

- Examine pivot table backward compatibility

Imagine that Excel is a large toolbox that contains different tools at your disposal. The pivot table is essentially one tool in your Excel toolbox. If a pivot table were indeed a physical tool that you could hold in your hand, a camera zoom lens would most accurately represent it.

When you look through a lens at an object, you see that object differently. You can turn the camera to move around the details of the object. The object itself doesn't change, and it's not connected to the lens. The lens is simply a tool you use to create a unique perspective on an ordinary object.

Think of a pivot table as a zoom lens that is pointed at a data set. When you look at a data set through a pivot table, you can see details in the data that you might not have noticed before. You can zoom out to get a summary view or you can zoom in to study details of one section of the data. Furthermore, you can turn your pivot table to see your data from different perspectives. The data set itself doesn't change, and it's not connected to the pivot table. The pivot table is simply a tool you use to create a unique perspective on your data.

A pivot table enables you to create an interactive view of your data set, called a *pivot table report*. With a pivot table report, you can quickly and easily categorize your data into groups, summarize large amounts of data into meaningful information, and perform a variety of calculations in a fraction of the time it takes by hand. But the real power of a pivot table report is that you can use it to interactively drag and drop fields within your report, dynamically change your perspective, and recalculate totals to fit your current view.

Why you should use a pivot table

As a rule, what you do in Excel can be split into three categories:

- Calculating data

- Shaping (formatting) data

- Filtering to see certain parts of your data

Although many built-in tools and formulas facilitate both tasks, using a pivot table is often the fastest and most efficient way to calculate and shape data. Let's look at one simple scenario that illustrates this point.

You have just given your manager some revenue information by month, and he has predictably asked for more information. He adds a note to the worksheet and emails it back to you. As you can see in Figure 1-1, he would like you to add a line that shows credits by month.

	A	B	C	D	E	F	G	H
1		Jan	Feb	Mar	Apr	May	Jun	Jul
2	Revenues	66,427,076	68,619,453	69,444,496	67,669,316	69,572,075	67,196,220	66,884,7
3		Please add a "credits" line and show the amount of credits for each month						

FIGURE 1-1 Your manager predictably changes his request after you provide the first pass of a report.

To meet this new requirement, you run a query from your legacy system that provides the needed data. As usual, the data is formatted specifically to make you suffer. Instead of data by month, the legacy system provides detailed transactional data by day, as shown in Figure 1-2.

	A	B	C
1	Document Number	In Balance Date	Credit Amount
2	D29210	1/2/2029	(34.54)
3	D15775	1/2/2029	(313.64)
4	D46035	1/2/2029	(389.04)
5	D45826	1/2/2029	(111.56)
6	D69172	1/2/2029	(1630.25)
7	D25388	1/2/2029	(3146.22)

FIGURE 1-2 The data from the legacy system is by day instead of by month.

Your challenge is to calculate the total dollar amount of credits by month and shape the results into an extract that fits the format of the original report. The final extract should look like the data shown in Figure 1-3.

Jan	Feb	Mar	Apr	May	Jun	Jul
-4,298,073	-3,532,412	-4,042,267	-3,561,353	-3,813,290	-3,592,965	-3,163,087

FIGURE 1-3 Your goal is to produce a summary by month and transpose the data to a horizontal format.

Creating the extract manually would require a tricky dynamic array formula:
`=SUM(FILTER(New!$C$2:$C$2616,TEXT(New!$B$2:$B$2616,"MMM")=B2))`.

In contrast, creating the extract with a pivot table would take 8 mouse clicks:

- **Create the pivot table report:** 5 clicks

- **Group dates into months:** 3 clicks

Both methods give you the same extract, which you can paste into the final report, as shown in Figure 1-4.

◢	A	B	C	D	E	F	G	H
1		Jan	Feb	Mar	Apr	May	Jun	Jul
2	Revenues	66,427,076	68,619,453	69,444,496	67,669,316	69,572,075	67,196,220	66,884,772
3	Credits	-4,298,073	-3,532,412	-4,042,267	-3,561,353	-3,813,290	-3,592,965	-3,163,087
4	Adjusted Revenues	62,129,003	65,087,041	65,402,229	64,107,963	65,758,785	63,603,255	63,721,685

FIGURE 1-4 After adding credits to the report, you can calculate the net revenue.

Using a pivot table to accomplish the task just described not only cuts down the complexity by more than half but also reduces the possibility of human error. In addition, using a pivot table allows for the quick-and-easy shaping and formatting of the data.

This example shows that using a pivot table is not just about calculating and summarizing your data. Pivot tables can often help you do a number of tasks faster and better than conventional functions and formulas. For example, you can use pivot tables to instantly transpose large groups of data vertically or horizontally. You can use pivot tables to quickly find and count the unique values in your data. You can also use pivot tables to prepare your data to be used in charts.

The bottom line is that pivot tables can help you dramatically increase your efficiency and decrease your errors on a number of tasks you might have to accomplish with Excel. Pivot tables can't do everything for you, but knowing how to use just the basics of pivot table functionality can take your data analysis and productivity to a new level.

When to use a pivot table

Large data sets, ever-changing impromptu data requests, and multilayered reporting are absolute productivity killers if you have to tackle them by hand. Going into hand-to-hand combat with one of these is not only time-consuming but also opens up the possibility of an untold number of errors in your analysis. So, how do you recognize when to use a pivot table before it's too late?

Generally, a pivot table would serve you well in any of the following situations:

- You have a large amount of transactional data that has become increasingly difficult to analyze and summarize in a meaningful way.

- You need to find relationships and groupings within your data.

- You need to find a list of unique values for one field in your data.

- You need to find data trends using various time periods.

- You anticipate frequent requests for changes to your data analysis.

- You need to create subtotals that frequently include new additions.

- You need to organize your data into a format that's easy to chart.

Anatomy of a pivot table

Because the anatomy of a pivot table is what gives it its flexibility and, indeed, its ultimate functionality, truly understanding pivot tables would be difficult without understanding their basic structure.

A pivot table is composed of four areas:

- Values area

- Rows area

- Columns area

- Filters area

The data you place in these areas defines both the utility and appearance of the pivot table.

You will go through the process of creating a pivot table in the next chapter, and the following sections prepare you for that by taking a closer look at the four pivot table areas and the functionality around them.

Values area

The *Values area* is shown in Figure 1-5. It is a large rectangular area below and to the right of the headings. In this example, the Values area contains a sum of the Revenue field.

The Values area is the area that calculates. This area is required to include at least one field and one calculation on that field. The data fields you drop here are those you want to measure or calculate. The Values area might include Sum Of Revenue, Count Of Units, and Average Of Price.

	A	B	C	D	E	F
1	REGION	(All) ▼				
2						
3	Sum of REVENUE	MONTH ▼				
4	MODEL ▼	January	February	March	April	May
5	2500P	$33,073	$29,104	$25,612	$22,538	$19,834
6	3002C	$35,880	$31,574	$27,785	$24,451	$21,517
7	3002P	$90,258	$79,427	$69,896	$61,508	$54,127
8	4055T	$13,250	$11,660	$10,261	$9,030	$7,946
9	4500C	$100,197	$88,173	$77,593	$68,281	$60,088

FIGURE 1-5 The heart of the pivot table is the Values area. This area typically includes a total of one or more numeric fields.

It is also possible to have the same field dropped in the Values area twice but with different calculations. For example, a marketing manager might want to see Sum Of Revenue, Percentage Of Total Revenue, Rank, and Running Total Of Revenue.

Rows area

The *Rows area*, as shown in Figure 1-6, is composed of the headings that go down the left side of the pivot table.

	A	B	C	D	E	F
1	REGION	(All) ▼				
2						
3	REVENUE	MONTH ▼				
4	MODEL ▼	January	February	March	April	May
5	2500P	$33,073	$29,104	$25,612	$22,538	$19,834
6	3002C	$35,880	$31,574	$27,785	$24,451	$21,517
7	3002P	$90,258	$79,427	$69,896	$61,508	$54,127
8	4055T	$13,250	$11,660	$10,261	$9,030	$7,946
9	4500C	$100,197	$88,173	$77,593	$68,281	$60,088

FIGURE 1-6 The headings down the left side of the pivot table make up the Rows area of the pivot table.

Adding a field into the Rows area displays the unique values from that field down the rows of the left side of the pivot table. The Rows area typically has at least one field, although it is possible to have no fields. The example earlier in the chapter where you needed to produce a one-line report of credits is an example where there are no row fields.

The types of data fields you would drop here include those you want to group and categorize—for example, Products, Names, and Locations.

Columns area

The *Columns area* is composed of headings that stretch across the top of columns in the pivot table. In the pivot table in Figure 1-7, the Month field is in the Columns area.

Dropping fields into the Columns area would display your items in a column-oriented perspective. The Columns area is ideal for showing trends over time. The types of data fields you would drop here include those you want to trend or show side by side—for example, Months, Periods, and Years.

	A	B	C	D	E	F
1	REGION	(All)				
2						
3	Sum of REVENUE	MONTH				
4	MODEL	January	February	March	April	May
5	2500P	$33,073	$29,104	$25,612	$22,538	$19,834
6	3002C	$35,880	$31,574	$27,785	$24,451	$21,517
7	3002P	$90,258	$79,427	$69,896	$61,508	$54,127
8	4055T	$13,250	$11,660	$10,261	$9,030	$7,946
9	4500C	$100,197	$88,173	$77,593	$68,281	$60,088

FIGURE 1-7 The Columns area stretches across the top of the columns. In this example, it contains the unique list of months in your data set.

Filters area

The *Filters area* is an optional set of one or more dropdowns at the top of the pivot table. In Figure 1-8, the Filters area contains the Region field, and the pivot table is set to show all regions.

	A	B	C	D	E	F
1	REGION	(All)				
2						
3	Sum of REVENUE	MONTH				
4	MODEL	January	February	March	April	May
5	2500P	$33,073	$29,104	$25,612	$22,538	$19,834
6	3002C	$35,880	$31,574	$27,785	$24,451	$21,517
7	3002P	$90,258	$79,427	$69,896	$61,508	$54,127
8	4055T	$13,250	$11,660	$10,261	$9,030	$7,946
9	4500C	$100,197	$88,173	$77,593	$68,281	$60,088

FIGURE 1-8 Filter fields are great for quickly filtering a report. The Region dropdown in cell B1 enables you to print this report for one particular region manager.

Dropping fields into the Filters area would enable you to filter the data items in your fields. The Filters area is optional and comes in handy when you need to filter your results dynamically. The types of data fields you would drop here include those you want to isolate and focus on—for example, Regions, Line Of Business, and Employees.

Slicers and Timelines have replaced some of the most common functionality of the Filters area. Technically, a Slicer is not a part of the pivot table. It is an external filter, which allows one slicer to be connected to multiple pivot tables. This is very useful in building dashboards. See "Filtering using slicers and timelines" in Chapter 4 for more details.

Pivot tables behind the scenes

It's important to know that pivot tables come with a few file space and memory implications for your system. To get an idea of what this means, let's look at what happens behind the scenes when you create a pivot table.

When you initiate the creation of a pivot table report, Excel takes a snapshot of your data set and stores it in a *pivot cache*, which is a special memory subsystem where your data source is duplicated for quick access. Although the pivot cache is not a physical object you can see, you can think of it as a container that stores a snapshot of the data source.

 Caution Any changes you make to your data source are not picked up by your pivot table report until you take another snapshot of the data source or "refresh" the pivot cache. Refreshing is easy: Simply right-click the pivot table and click Refresh. You can also click the large Refresh button on the PivotTable Analyze tab.

The benefit of working against the pivot cache and not your original data source is optimization. Any changes you make to the pivot table report, such as rearranging fields, adding new fields, or hiding items, are made rapidly and with minimal overhead.

Pivot table backward compatibility

Nearly every new version of Excel introduces pivot table features that will not work in previous editions of Excel.

- Specific formatting applied to a data point in Microsoft 365 won't work in Excel 2016 or earlier.

- Timelines created in Excel 2013 will not work in Excel 2010 or earlier.

- Slicers created in Excel 2010 or later will not work in Excel 2007 or earlier.

The limits for a pivot table based on a pivot cache have remained the same since Excel 2007. If you need to go beyond these limits, see Chapter 10, "Unlocking features with the Data Model and Power Pivot."

Table 1.1 shows limits for pivot tables.

TABLE 1-1 Pivot table limitations

Feature	Maximum limit
PivotTable reports on a sheet	Limited by available memory
Unique items per field	1,048,576
Row or column fields in a PivotTable report	Limited by available memory
Report filters in a PivotTable report	256 (may be limited by available memory)
Value fields in a PivotTable report	256

TABLE 1-1 *(continued)*

Feature	Maximum limit
Calculated item formulas in a PivotTable report	Limited by available memory
Report filters in a PivotChart report	256 (may be limited by available memory)
Value fields in a PivotChart report	256
Calculated item formulas in a PivotChart report	Limited by available memory
Length of the MDX name for a PivotTable item	32,767
Length for a relational PivotTable string	32,767
Items displayed in filter dropdown lists	10,000

A word about compatibility

Excel provides a tool to identify any problems with backward compatibility. To check compatibility, select File | Info | Check For Issues | Check Compatibility, as shown in Figure 1-9.

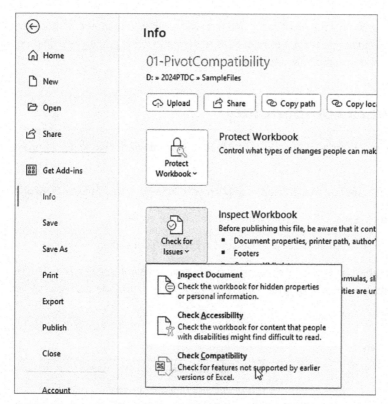

FIGURE 1-9 Open the Check For Issues dropdown to find the Check Compatibility tool.

In the Compatibility Checker dialog, use the Select Versions To Show dropdown to choose which version of Excel your coworkers might be using. The dialog shows issues with your pivot tables (see Figure 1-10). Anything labeled Significant Loss Of Functionality should be corrected. Anything labeled Minor Loss Of Fidelity refers to formatting issues.

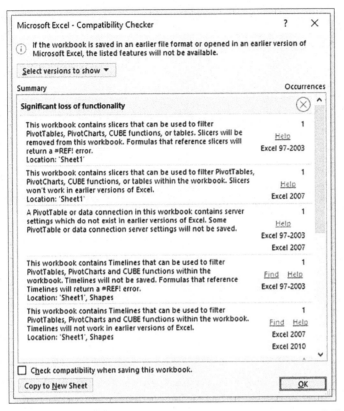

FIGURE 1-10 The Compatibility Checker alerts you about any compatibility issues before you save to a previous version of Excel.

Next steps

In the next chapter, you'll learn how to prepare your data to be used by a pivot table. Chapter 2, "Creating a basic pivot table," also walks through creating your first pivot table report using the Create PivotTable dialog.

Creating a basic pivot table

In this chapter, you will:

- Format your source data before creating a pivot table

- Learn how to create a basic pivot table

- Understand the Recommended PivotTable and the Analyze Data features

- Use slicers to filter your report

- Keep up with changes in the data source

- Share the pivot cache

- Save time with PivotTable tools

When you have a family portrait taken, the photographer takes time to make sure that the lighting is right, the poses are natural, and everyone smiles their best smile. This preparation ensures that the resulting photo is effective in its purpose.

When you create a pivot table report, you're the photographer, taking a snapshot of your data. By taking time to make sure your data looks its best, you can ensure that your pivot table report is effective in accomplishing the task at hand.

One of the benefits of working in a spreadsheet is that you have the flexibility of laying out your data to suit your needs. Indeed, the layout you choose depends heavily on the task at hand. However, many of the data layouts used for presentations are not appropriate when used as the source data for a pivot table report.

> **Tip** As you read the following pages, which discuss preparing your data, keep in mind that pivot tables have only one hard rule pertaining to the data source: The data source must have column headings, which are labels in the first row of the data that describe the information in each column. Without column headings, you cannot create a pivot table report.

However, just because a pivot table report is created successfully does not mean that it's effective. A host of things can go wrong as a result of bad data preparation—from inaccurate reporting to problems with grouping and sorting.

Format your source data before creating a pivot table

Let's look at a few of the steps you can take to ensure that you end up with a viable pivot table report.

Ensuring that data is in a Tabular layout

A perfect layout for the source data in a pivot table is a Tabular layout. In Tabular layout, there are no blank rows or columns. Every column has a heading. Every field has a value in every row in most cases. Columns do not contain repeating groups of data.

Figure 2-1 shows an example of data structured properly for a pivot table. There are headings for each column. Even though the values in D2:D6 are all the same model, the model number appears in each cell. Month data is organized down the page instead of across the columns.

	A	B	C	D	E	F
1	REGION	MARKET	STORE	MODEL	MONTH	REVENUE
2	North	Great Lakes	65061011	4055T	April	$2,354
3	North	Great Lakes	65061011	4055T	February	$3,040
4	North	Great Lakes	65061011	4055T	January	$3,454
5	North	Great Lakes	65061011	4055T	March	$2,675
6	North	Great Lakes	65061011	4055T	May	$2,071
7	North	New England	2105015	2500P	April	$11,851
8	North	New England	2105015	2500P	February	$15,304
9	North	New England	2105015	2500P	January	$17,391
10	North	New England	2105015	2500P	March	$13,468
11	North	New England	2105015	2500P	May	$10,429
12	North	New England	22022012	3002C	April	$256
13	North	New England	22022012	3002C	February	$330
14	North	New England	22022012	3002C	January	$375
15	North	New England	22022012	3002C	March	$300

FIGURE 2-1 This data is structured properly for use as a pivot table source.

Tabular layouts are *database-centric*, meaning you would most commonly find these types of layouts in databases. These layouts are designed to store and maintain large amounts of data in a well-structured, scalable format.

Tip You might work for a manager who demands that the column labels be split into two rows. For example, they might want the heading Gross Margin to be split, with Gross in row 1 and Margin in row 2. Because pivot tables require a unique heading one row high, your manager's preference can be problematic. To overcome this problem, start typing your heading; for example, type **Gross**. Before leaving the cell, press Alt+Enter and then type **Margin**. The result is a single cell that contains two lines of data.

Avoiding storing data in section headings

Examine the data in Figure 2-2. This spreadsheet shows a report of sales by month and a model for the North region of a company. Because the data in rows 2 through 24 pertains to the North region, the author of the worksheet entered the title North as a single cell in C1. This approach is effective for displaying the data, but it's not effective for a pivot table data source.

Also, in Figure 2-2, the author was very creative with the model information. The data in rows 2 through 6 applies to Model 2500P, so the author entered this value once in A2 and then applied a fancy vertical format combined with Merge Cells to create an interesting look for the report. Again, although this is a cool format, it is not useful for pivot table reporting.

	A	B	C	
1			North	
2	Model 2500P	January	33,073	
3		February	35,880	
4		March	90,258	
5		April	13,250	
6		May	100,197	
7				
8	Model 3002P	January	29,104	
9		February	31,574	
10		March	79,427	
11		April	11,660	
12		May	88,173	
13				
14	Model 4055 T	January	35,880	
15		February	25,612	
16		March	27,785	
17		April	69,896	
18		May	10,261	
19				
20	Model 4500 T	January	33,073	
21		February	25,612	
22		March	27,785	
23		April	69,896	
24		May	10,261	

FIGURE 2-2 Region and model data are not formatted properly in this data set.

In addition, the worksheet in Figure 2-2 is missing column headings. You can guess that column A is Model, column B is Month, and column C is Sales. However, for Excel to create a pivot table, this information must be included in the first row of the data.

Avoiding repeating groups as columns

The format shown in Figure 2-3 is common. A time dimension is presented across several columns. Although it is possible to create a pivot table from this data, this format is not ideal.

	A	B	C	D	E	F	G	H
1								
2	North	MODEL	JANUARY	FEBRUARY	MARCH	APRIL	MAY	JUNE
3		4054T	$2,789	$2,454	$2,160	$1,901	$1,673	$1,472
4		4500C	$32,605	$28,692	$25,249	$22,219	$19,553	$17,207
5		3002P	$52,437	$46,145	$40,607	$35,734	$31,446	$27,673
6		2500P	$17,391	$15,304	$13,468	$11,851	$10,429	$9,178
7		4055T	$2,468	$2,172	$1,911	$1,682	$1,480	$1,302
8		3002C	$375	$330	$290	$256	$225	$198

FIGURE 2-3 This matrix format is common but not effective for pivot tables. The Month field is spread across several columns of the report.

The problem is that the headings spread across the top of the table pull double duty as column labels and actual data values. In a pivot table, this format would force you to manage and maintain six fields, each representing a different month.

Eliminating gaps and blank cells in the data source

Delete all empty columns within your data source. An empty column in the middle of your data source causes your pivot table to fail on creation because the blank column, in most cases, does not have a column name.

Delete all empty rows within your data source. Empty rows may cause you to inadvertently leave out a large portion of your data range, making your pivot table report incomplete.

Fill in as many blank cells in your data source as possible. Although filling in cells is not required to create a workable pivot table, blank cells are generally errors waiting to happen. A good practice is to represent missing values with some logical missing value code wherever possible.

Note Although eliminating gaps and blank cells might seem like a step backward for those of you who are trying to create a nicely formatted report, it pays off in the end. When you are able to create a pivot table, there will be plenty of opportunities to apply some pleasant formatting.

Note In Chapter 3, "Customizing a pivot table," you'll discover how to apply style formatting to your pivot tables.

Applying appropriate type formatting to fields

Formatting fields appropriately helps you avoid a whole host of possible issues, from inaccurate reporting to problems with grouping and sorting.

Make certain that any fields to be used in calculations are explicitly formatted as a number, currency, or any other format appropriate for use in mathematical functions. Fields containing dates should also be formatted as any one of the available date formats.

Summary of good data source design

The attributes of an effective tabular design are as follows:

- The first row of your data source is made up of field labels or headings that describe the information in each column.

- Each column in your data source represents a unique category of data.

- Each row in your data source represents individual items in each column.

- None of the column names in your data source double as data items that will be used as filters or query criteria (that is, names of months, dates, years, names of locations, or names of employees).

Case study: Cleaning up data for pivot table analysis

The worksheet shown in Figure 2-4 is a great-looking report. However, it cannot be effectively used as a data source for a pivot table. Can you identify the problems with this data set?

	A	B	C	D	E	F
1	Sector	Customer		Jan	Feb	Mar
2	Associations	IMA Houston Chapter		0	0	0
3		Association for Computers & Taxation		30094	0	0
4						
5	Consultants	Andrew Spain Consulting		89581	114596	112012
6		Data2Impact		21730	0	0
7		Cambia Factor		0	0	0
8		Fintega Financial Modelling		21015	0	0
9		Excelerator BI		0	0	0
10		Construction Intelligence & Analytics, Inc.		22104	0	2484
11						
12	Professional	Serving Brevard Realty		0	7152	24224
13		WM Squared Inc.		0	0	0
14		Juliet Babcock-Hyde CPA, PLLC		0	0	0
15						
16	Retail	Hartville MarketPlace and Flea Market		34132	40608	12427

FIGURE 2-4 Someone spent a lot of time formatting this report to look good, but what problems prevent it from being used as a data source for a pivot table?

These are the three problems with the data set and the fixes needed to get the data set pivot table ready:

- There are blank rows and columns in the data. Column C should be deleted. The blank rows between sectors (such as rows 4, 11, and 15) also should be deleted.

- Blank cells present the data in an outline format. The person reading this worksheet would probably assume that cells A6:A10 fall into the Consultants sector. These blank cells need to be filled in with the values from above.

- The worksheet presents the data for each month in several columns (one column per month). Columns D through O need to be reformatted as two columns. Place the month name in one column and the units for that month in the next column.

Cleaning this data used to require some VBA code or a bunch of manual steps in Excel. The Get & Transform tools that debuted in Excel 2016 will make it very easy to clean this data. Follow these steps:

1. Select the entire range of data. In the sample file, it would be A1:O33.

2. Click in the Name box and type a one-word name, such as **UglyData**. Press Enter to name the range.

3. On the Data tab, in the Get & Transform Data group, choose From Table/Range (see Figure 2-5).

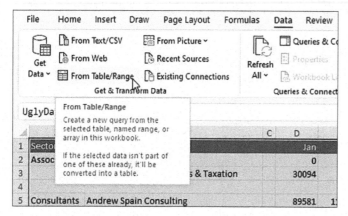

FIGURE 2-5 Originally called Power Query but later rebranded as Get & Transform Data, these new tools that appeared on the Data tab in 2016 are amazing.

The Power Query Editor will open. Notice you have ribbon tabs for Home, Transform, Add Column, and View. Follow these steps in the Power Query Editor.

4. The formerly blank column C now has a heading of Column 3. Click that heading and choose Remove Columns from the Home tab (see Figure 2-6).

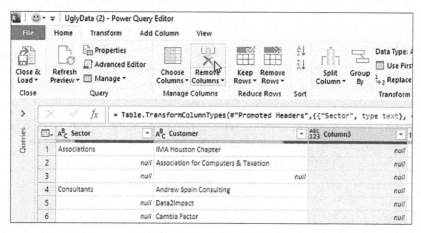

FIGURE 2-6 The Power Query Editor offers tools that are often better than their Excel equivalents.

5. Click the Customer heading. Choose Home | Remove Rows | Remove Blank Rows (see Figure 2-7).

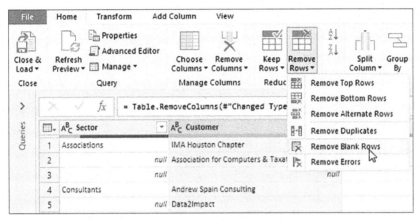

FIGURE 2-7 Deleting blank rows is a built-in command in Power Query.

6. Select the Sector column header. From the Transform tab, choose Fill | Down (see Figure 2-8). This amazing command will replace all the null cells with the value from above.

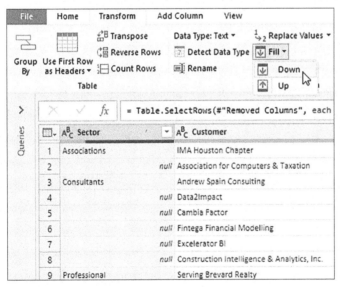

FIGURE 2-8 Fill Down replaces Home | Find & Select | Go To Special | Blanks | OK, and then entering =A2 and pressing Ctrl+Enter. It is far easier to remember one command instead of many obscure commands strung together.

7. Select both the Sector and Customer headings.

8. Open the Unpivot Columns dropdown on the Transform tab and choose Unpivot Other Columns. The result is shown in Figure 2-9. Pause for a moment to admire the sheer simplicity of steps 5 through 8. Those are three new tools that replace far more complicated tasks in Excel. Although the data could be returned to Excel at this point, there are a few simple clean-up steps left.

	AᴮC Sector	AᴮC Customer	AᴮC Attribute	1.2 Value
1	Associations	IMA Houston Chapter	Jan	0
2	Associations	IMA Houston Chapter	Feb	0
3	Associations	IMA Houston Chapter	Mar	0
4	Associations	IMA Houston Chapter	Apr	14004
5	Associations	IMA Houston Chapter	May	0
6	Associations	IMA Houston Chapter	Jun	4060
7	Associations	IMA Houston Chapter	Jul	0
8	Associations	IMA Houston Chapter	Aug	0
9	Associations	IMA Houston Chapter	Sep	18072
10	Associations	IMA Houston Chapter	Oct	0
11	Associations	IMA Houston Chapter	Nov	15104
12	Associations	IMA Houston Chapter	Dec	0
13	Associations	Association for Computers & Taxation	Jan	30094
14	Associations	Association for Computers & Taxation	Feb	0

fx = Table.UnpivotOtherColumns(#"Filled Down", {"Sector", "Customer"},

FIGURE 2-9 At this point, you could return the data to Excel for pivoting.

9. Right-click the Value column. Choose Rename and type **Revenue**.

10. Open the Filter dropdown for Revenue. Unselect 0 to remove all the zero values.

11. Select the Attribute Column. On the Add Column tab, choose Column From Example. The first row in your data might read "Apr." If this data applies to the year 2029, type a value of **Apr 1, 2029** in the new column. Power Query fills in the remaining rows and offers a Merged heading. Click OK (see Figure 2-10).

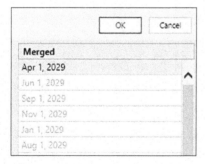

FIGURE 2-10 Add Column From Example is similar to Flash Fill in Excel, but it actually creates a formula that can be reused.

12. Right-click the heading for the new Merged column. Choose Rename and type **Date** as the heading name.

13. With the Date column selected, click the Transform tab. Open the Date Type dropdown and choose Date. The text dates are converted to real dates.

14. You no longer need the month abbreviations shown in the Attribute column. Choose the Attribute column and then Home | Remove Columns. Before you return to Excel, look at the right side of the Power Query window for the list of Applied Steps. This is the world's greatest Undo stack. You can click any step and see what the data looked like at that point. If you made a mistake several steps ago, you can click that step and make a correction. If you want to be more impressed, select the View tab and choose Advanced Editor. All that code is a programming language called "M." By doing steps 4 through 13, you successfully wrote a program that can be reused the next time you download similar data from the IT department.

15. Select Home | Close | Load. Your original data stays on Sheet1, and a new Sheet2 is added to the workbook (see Figure 2-11). The cleaned data is narrow and tall. In general, narrow and tall data sets are better for pivoting.

	A	B	C	D
1	Sector	Customer	Revenue	Date
2	Associations	IMA Houston Chapter	24004	4/1/2029
3	Associations	IMA Houston Chapter	4060	6/1/2029
4	Associations	IMA Houston Chapter	18072	9/1/2029
5	Associations	IMA Houston Chapter	15104	11/1/2029
6	Associations	Association for Computers & Taxation	30094	1/1/2029
7	Associations	Association for Computers & Taxation	4270	8/1/2029
8	Consultants	Andrew Spain Consulting	89581	1/1/2029
9	Consultants	Andrew Spain Consulting	114596	2/1/2029
10	Consultants	Andrew Spain Consulting	112012	3/1/2029
11	Consultants	Andrew Spain Consulting	67408	4/1/2029
12	Consultants	Andrew Spain Consulting	84383	5/1/2029

FIGURE 2-11 Just 11 steps in Power Query quickly cleaned the ugly data.

Not only is Power Query fast, it makes it easy to redo the data cleansing. Go back to Sheet1 and change any number in the original data. Go to Sheet2. Expand the Queries & Connections panel so you can click the Refresh icon on the far right of the UglyData query. Power Query repeats all the steps and updates the result.

How to create a basic pivot table

Now that you have a good understanding of the importance of a well-structured data source, let's walk through creating a basic pivot table.

Note The sample data set used throughout this book is available for download at www.microsoftpressstore.com/ExcelPivotTable/downloads.

To ensure that the pivot table captures the range of your data source by default, click any single cell in your data source. Next, select the Insert tab and find the Tables group. In the Tables group, select PivotTable and then choose From Table/Range from the dropdown. Figure 2-12 demonstrates how to start a pivot table.

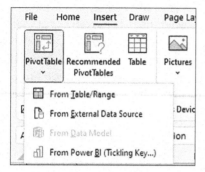

FIGURE 2-12 Start a pivot table by selecting PivotTable from the Insert tab.

Choosing these options activates the Create PivotTable dialog, shown in Figure 2-13.

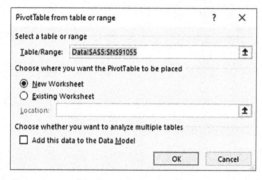

FIGURE 2-13 The Create PivotTable dialog.

Tip You can also press the shortcut to start a pivot table: Press and release Alt, press and release N, and then press and release V.

As you can see in Figure 2-13, the Create PivotTable dialog asks you only two fundamental questions:

- Where's the data that you want to analyze?

- Where do you want to put the pivot table?

Here's how you handle these two sections of the dialog:

- **Choose The Data That You Want To Analyze**—In this section, you tell Excel where your data set is. You can specify a data set that is located within your workbook, or you can tell Excel to look for an external data set. As you can see in Figure 2-13, Excel is smart enough to read your data set and fill in the range for you. However, you should always take note of the range Excel selects to ensure that you are capturing all your data.

- **Choose Where You Want The PivotTable Report To Be Placed**—In this section, you tell Excel where you want your pivot table to be placed. This is set to New Worksheet by default, meaning that your pivot table will be placed in a new worksheet within the current workbook. You will rarely change this setting because there are relatively few times you'll need your pivot table to be placed in a specific location.

Note   Note the presence of another option in the Create PivotTable dialog shown in Figure 2-13: the Add This Data To The Data Model option. You would select this option if you were trying to consolidate multiple data sources into a single pivot table.

The Add This Data To The Data Model option is covered in detail in Chapter 7, "Analyzing disparate data sources with pivot tables," and in Chapter 10, "Unlocking features with the Data Model and Power Pivot."

In this chapter, we'll keep it basic by covering the steps to create a pivot table by using a single source, which means you can ignore this particular option.

After you have answered the two questions in the Create PivotTable dialog, simply click the OK button. At this point, Excel adds a new worksheet that contains an empty pivot table report. Next to that is the PivotTable Fields list, shown in Figure 2-14. This pane helps you build your pivot table.

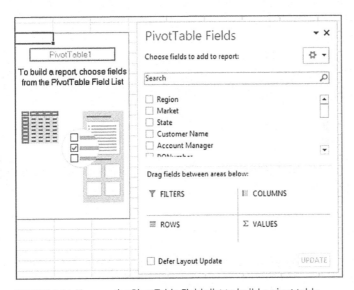

FIGURE 2-14 You use the PivotTable Fields list to build a pivot table.

Caution The icons for Columns and Rows in Figure 2-14 are reversed. A summer intern at Microsoft inadvertently reversed the icons several versions ago, and no one noticed. After Bill pointed this out to the correct project manager, Microsoft pledged to restore the icons to the correct location. The dark-gray portion of the icon is supposed to show where the data will be displayed when you drop a field here. Any data dropped into the Columns area will display across the top of the report (as illustrated in the icon currently in the Rows area). It feels sort of goofy to show the wrong icons in this book on pivot tables, but that's the way it appears to us at press time.

Tip   Finding the PivotTable Fields list

The PivotTable Fields list is your main work area in Excel. This is the place where you add fields and make changes to a pivot table report. By default, this pane pops up when you place your cursor anywhere inside a pivot table. However, if you explicitly close this pane, you override the default and essentially tell the pane not to activate when you are in the pivot table.

If clicking on the pivot table does not activate the PivotTable Fields list, you can manually activate it by right-clicking anywhere inside the pivot table and selecting Show Field list. You can also click anywhere inside the pivot table and then choose the large Fields List icon on the Analyze tab under PivotTable Tools in the ribbon.

Adding fields to a report

You can add the fields you need to a pivot table by using the four "areas" found in the PivotTable Fields list: Filters, Columns, Rows, and Values. These areas, which correspond to the four areas of the pivot table, are used to populate your pivot table with data:

- **Filters**—Adding a field to the Filters area enables you to filter on its unique data items. In previous versions of Excel, this area was known as the Report Filters area.

- **Columns**—Adding a field into the Columns area displays the unique values from that field across the top of the pivot table.

- **Rows**—Adding a field into the Rows area displays the unique values from that field down the left side of the pivot table.

- **Values**—Adding a field into the Values area includes that field in the Values area of your pivot table, allowing you to perform a specified calculation using the values in the field.

Note   Review Chapter 1, "Pivot table fundamentals," for a refresher on the four areas of a pivot table.

Fundamentals of laying out a pivot table report

Now, let's pause a moment and go over some fundamentals of laying out a pivot table report. This is generally the point where most new Excel customers get stuck. How do you know which field goes where?

Before you start dropping fields into the various areas, answer two questions:

- "What am I measuring?"
- "How do I want to see it?"

The answer to the first question tells you which fields in your data source you need to work with, and the answer to the second question tells you where to place the fields.

Let's say you wanted to measure the dollar sales by region. This would automatically tell you that you need to work with the Sale Amount and Region fields. How do you want to see it? You want regions to go down the left side of the report and the sales amount to be calculated next to each region.

To achieve this effect, you need to add the Region field to the Rows area and add the Sale Amount field to the Values area.

Find the Region field in the PivotTable Fields list and select the checkbox next to it. As you can see in Figure 2-15, not only is the field automatically added to the Rows area, but also your pivot table is updated to show the unique region names.

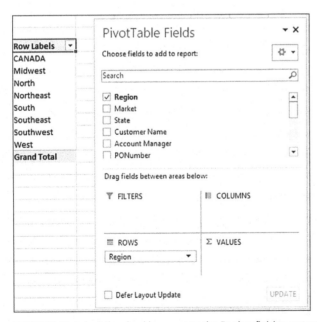

FIGURE 2-15 Select the checkbox next to the Region field to automatically add that field to your pivot table.

> **Tip** If you see a region that is repeated in the Rows area, it usually means that there are one or more trailing spaces after some of the rows for that region. You should find those cells, delete the trailing spaces, and then Refresh the pivot table.

Now that you have regions in your pivot table, it's time to add in the dollar sales. To do that, simply find the Sale Amount field and select the checkbox next to it. As Figure 2-16 shows, the Sale Amount field is automatically added to the Values area, and your pivot table report now shows the total dollar sales for each region.

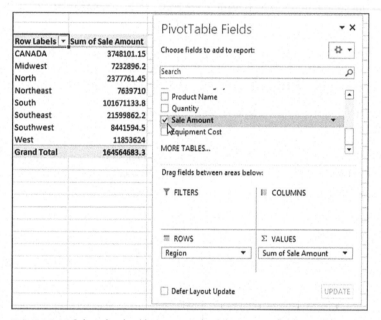

FIGURE 2-16 Select the checkbox next to the Sale Amount field to add data to your pivot table report.

At this point, you have already created your first pivot table report!

> **Tip How does Excel know where your fields go?**
>
> As you've just experienced, the PivotTable Fields list interface enables you to add fields to your pivot table by simply selecting the checkbox next to each field name. Excel automatically adds the selected fields to the pivot table. But how does Excel know which area to use for a field you select? The answer is that Excel doesn't really know which area to use, but it makes a decision based on data type. Here's how it works: When you select a checkbox next to a field, Excel evaluates the data type for that field. If the data type is numeric, Excel places the field in the Values area; otherwise, Excel places the field in the Rows area. This placement obviously underlines the importance of correctly assigning the data types for your fields.

> **Note** Blank cells in your numeric columns previously caused the column to be treated as text. A change in early 2018 for Office 365 subscribers changed this behavior. Now, a column with a mix of numbers and empty cells will be treated as values, and the field will go to the Values area with a default calculation of Sum.
>
> If you have someone who clears out cells by mashing down the spacebar several times instead of using the Delete key, Excel will treat those spaces as text. A mix of numbers and text in a column will cause Excel to default to counting the column instead of summing.

Adding layers to a pivot table

Now, you can add another layer of analysis to your report. Say that now you want to measure the amount of dollar sales each region earned by product category. Because your pivot table already contains the Region and Sales Amount fields, all you have to do is select the checkbox next to the Product Category field. As you can see in Figure 2-17, your pivot table automatically added a layer for the Product Category and refreshed the calculations to include subtotals for each region. Because the data is stored efficiently in the pivot cache, this change took less than a second.

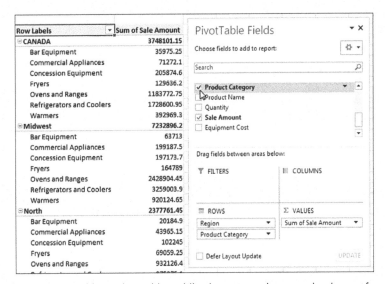

FIGURE 2-17 Without pivot tables, adding layers to analyses requires hours of work and complex formulas.

Rearranging a pivot table

Suppose that the view you've created doesn't work for your manager. He wants to see Product Categories across the top of the pivot table report. To make this change, simply drag the Product Category field from the Rows area to the Columns area, as illustrated in Figure 2-18.

> **Note** You don't have to move your fields into an area to be able to drag them around. You can actually drag fields directly from the list of fields in the PivotTable Fields list to the desired area. You can also move a field into an area by using that field's context menu: Click the black triangle next to the field name and then select the desired area.

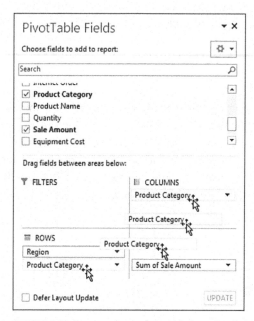

FIGURE 2-18 Rearranging a pivot table is as simple as dragging fields from one area to another.

The report is instantly restructured, as shown in Figure 2-19.

Sum of Sale Amount	Column Labels			
Row Labels	Bar Equipment	Commercial Appliances	Concession Equipment	Fryers
CANADA	35975.25	71272.1	205874.6	129636.2
Midwest	63713	199187.5	197173.7	164789
North	20184.9	43965.15	102245	69059.25
Northeast	68407.1	285103.35	258557.4	190152.4
South	1191742.35	5923096.6	6971902.45	2420745
Southeast	283902.15	1525894.3	1569948.6	452579.35
Southwest	73528.5	289526.5	355845.45	268554.85
West	68684.65	296291.55	422201.2	276443.05
Grand Total	1806137.9	8634337.05	10083748.4	3971959.1

FIGURE 2-19 Your product categories are now column-oriented.

Tip   Longing for drag-and-drop functionality?

In Excel 2003 and previous versions, you could drag and drop fields directly onto the pivot table layout. This functionality is allowed only within the PivotTable Fields list (dragging into areas). However, Microsoft has provided the option of working with a classic pivot table layout, which enables drag-and-drop functionality.

To activate the classic pivot table layout, right-click anywhere inside the pivot table and select PivotTable Options. In the PivotTable Options dialog, select the Display tab and select the checkbox next to Classic PivotTable Layout, as demonstrated in Figure 2-20. Click the OK button to apply the change.

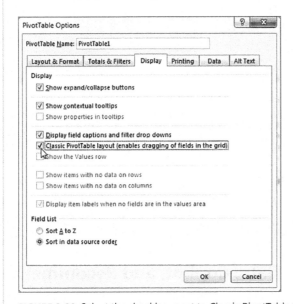

FIGURE 2-20 Select the checkbox next to Classic PivotTable Layout.

At this point, you can drag and drop fields directly onto your pivot table layout. If you always want your pivot tables to be in Classic layout, follow these steps:

1. Select File | Options. A new Data category is added along the left panel starting in 2017 for Microsoft 365 subscribers.

2. In the Data category, the first setting is Make Changes To The Default Layout Of Pivot-Tables. Click Edit Default Layout.

3. The Edit Default Layout dialog offers a few common choices. Apparently, Classic layout did not make it to the top few choices. Click the PivotTable Options button in the Edit Default Layout dialog. You will see a dialog similar to Figure 2-20. Choose the Display tab and the Classic PivotTable Layout. Click OK three times to close each of the open dialogs. All future pivot tables can be built in Classic mode.

Creating a report filter

You might be asked to produce different reports for particular regions, markets, or products. Instead of building separate pivot table reports for every possible analysis scenario, you can use the Filter field to create a report filter. For example, you can create a region-filtered report by simply dragging the Region field to the Filters area and the Product Category field to the Rows area. This way, you can analyze one particular region at a time. Figure 2-21 shows the totals for just the North region.

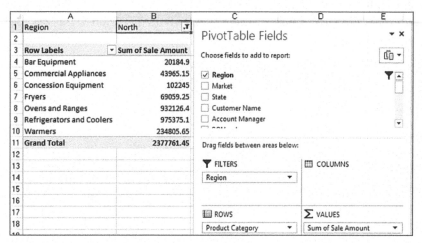

FIGURE 2-21 With this setup, you not only can see revenues by product clearly, but also can click the Region dropdown to focus on one region.

Understanding the Analyze Data, Copilot, and Recommended PivotTable features

As this book is being written in the summer of 2024, the Artificial Intelligence industry is moving at the speed of sound. At this point, Copilot is still in preview and will be coming out to General Availability later in 2024.

At this moment, the Analyze Data feature is the mature option for creating pivot tables and pivot charts using Artificial Intelligence. In 2024, Microsoft changed the legacy Recommended PivotTable functionality to use the same algorithm as the Analyze Data. Looking forward, the ability for Copilot to create a pivot table has been trained using the existing Analyze Data feature.

The Analyze Data feature uses artificial intelligence to analyze up to 250,000 cells of your data. It offers descriptive pivot tables and then offers far more advanced analyses. The Analyze Data feature often produces over 30 choices. Figures 2-22 and 2-23 show some results available from it.

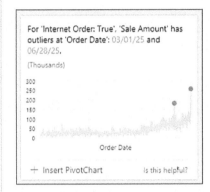

FIGURE 2-22 Artificial Intelligence detected a pair of outliers in this segment of the data.

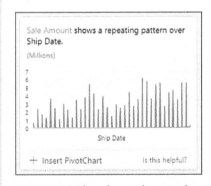

FIGURE 2-23 Ideas detected a repeating pattern. This might indicate some weekly or monthly seasonality.

Unfortunately, customers who purchased a perpetual license to Excel 2021 or Excel 2024 will not have the feature in either location. Microsoft's stance is that if you are not continuing to pay a monthly subscription fee, you cannot make use of the Office intelligent services.

In late 2019, a second iteration of artificial intelligence was added that allows you to ask a natural-language question about your data. See Figure 7 in the Introduction for an example.

Using slicers to filter your report

With Excel 2010, Microsoft introduced a feature called *slicers*. Slicers enable you to filter your pivot table in much the same way as Filter fields filter a pivot table. The difference is that slicers offer a user-friendly interface that enables you to easily see the current filter state, even when multiple items are selected.

Creating a standard slicer

To understand the concept behind slicers, place your cursor anywhere inside your pivot table and then select the Insert tab on the ribbon. Click the Slicer icon (see Figure 2-24).

FIGURE 2-24 Inserting a slicer.

The Insert Slicers dialog, shown in Figure 2-25, opens. The idea is to select the dimensions you want to filter. In this example, the Region and Market slicers are selected.

FIGURE 2-25 Select the dimensions for which you want to create slicers.

After the slicers are created, you can simply click the filter values to filter your pivot table. As you can see in Figure 2-26, clicking Midwest in the Region slicer filters your pivot table, and also the Market slicer responds by highlighting the markets that belong to the Midwest region.

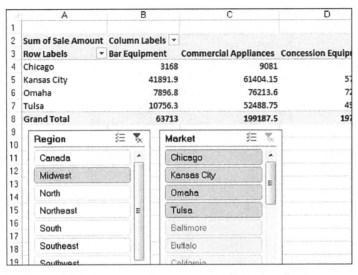

	A	B	C	D
1				
2	Sum of Sale Amount	Column Labels ▾		
3	Row Labels ▾	Bar Equipment	Commercial Appliances	Concession Equipm
4	Chicago	3168	9081	
5	Kansas City	41891.9	61404.15	5
6	Omaha	7896.8	76213.6	7
7	Tulsa	10756.3	52488.75	4
8	Grand Total	63713	199187.5	19

Region slicer: Canada, Midwest, North, Northeast, South, Southeast, Southwest

Market slicer: Chicago, Kansas City, Omaha, Tulsa, Baltimore, Buffalo, California

FIGURE 2-26 Select the dimensions you want to filter using slicers.

> **Tip** You can select multiple values by holding down the Ctrl key on your keyboard while selecting the needed filters. Alternatively, you can enable the Multi-Select toggle next to the filter icon at the top of the slicer.

In Figure 2-27, the Multi-Select toggle was enabled and then Baltimore, California, Charlotte, and Chicago were selected. Note that Excel highlights the selected markets in the Market slicer and also highlights their associated regions in the Region slicer.

Another advantage you gain with slicers is that you can tie each slicer to more than one pivot table. In other words, any filter you apply to your slicer can be applied to multiple pivot tables.

To connect a slicer to more than one pivot table, simply right-click the slicer and select Report Connections. The Report Connections dialog, shown in Figure 2-28, opens. Select the checkbox next to any pivot table that you want to filter using the current slicer.

At this point, any filter applied via the slicer is applied to all the connected pivot tables. Again, slicers have a unique advantage over Filter fields in that they can control the filter state of multiple pivot tables. Filter fields can control only the pivot table in which they live.

Note that the choices in Figure 2-28 are the pivot tables that rely on the same pivot table cache. If you want to use a slicer to control data coming from two different data sets, see "Tip 22 – Slicer to control data from two different data sets" in Chapter 14.

The Multi-Select Toggle

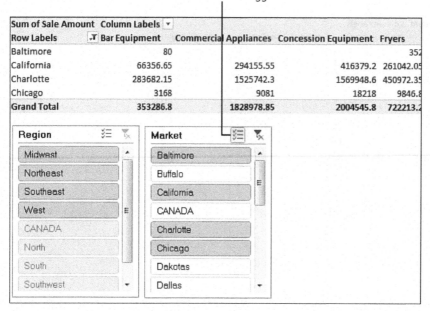

Sum of Sale Amount	Column Labels			
Row Labels	Bar Equipment	Commercial Appliances	Concession Equipment	Fryers
Baltimore	80			352
California	66356.65	294155.55	416379.2	261042.05
Charlotte	283682.15	1525742.3	1569948.6	450972.35
Chicago	3168	9081	18218	9846.8
Grand Total	353286.8	1828978.85	2004545.8	722213.2

FIGURE 2-27 The fact that they enable you to see the current filter state gives slicers a unique advantage over the Filter field.

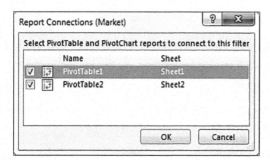

FIGURE 2-28 Choose the pivot tables you want to filter using this slicer.

Tip Notice that in Figure 2-28, the list of pivot tables is a bit ambiguous (PivotTable1, PivotTable2). Excel automatically gives your pivot tables these generic names, which it uses to identify them. You can imagine how difficult it would be to know which pivot table is which when working with more than a handful of pivots. Therefore, you might want to consider giving your pivot tables user-friendly names so you can recognize them in dialogs, such as the one you see in Figure 2-28.

You can easily change the name of a pivot table by placing your cursor anywhere inside the pivot table, selecting the PivotTable Analyze tab, and entering a friendly name in the PivotTable Name input box found on the far left.

Creating a Timeline slicer

The Timeline slicer (introduced with Excel 2013) works in the same way as a standard slicer in that it lets you filter a pivot table using a visual selection mechanism instead of the old Filter fields. The difference is that the Timeline slicer is designed to work exclusively with date fields, and it provides an excellent visual method to filter and group the dates in a pivot table.

> **Note** In order to create a Timeline slicer, your pivot table must contain a field where *all* the data is formatted as dates. This means that your source data table must contain at least one column where all the values are formatted as valid dates. If even only one value in the source date column is blank or not a valid date, Excel does not create a Timeline slicer.

To create a Timeline slicer, place your cursor anywhere inside your pivot table, select the Insert tab on the ribbon, and then click the Timeline icon.

The Insert Timelines dialog opens, showing you all the available date fields in the chosen pivot table. Here, you select the date fields for which you want to create slicers.

After your Timeline slicer is created, you can filter the data in your pivot table by using this dynamic data-selection mechanism. As you can see in Figure 2-29, clicking the April slicer filters the data in the pivot table to show only April data.

Row Labels ▾	Sum of Sale Amount
Buffalo	42638
California	102981
CANADA	32459
Charlotte	373468.3
Chicago	4637
Dakotas	9274
Dallas	47749.4

Ship Date — Apr 2007 — MONTHS ▾
2006 2007
DEC JAN FEB MAR APR MAY JUN

FIGURE 2-29 Click a date selection to filter your pivot table.

Figure 2-30 demonstrates how you can expand the slicer range with the mouse to include a wider range of dates in your filtered numbers.

Row Labels ▾	Sum of Sale Amount
Buffalo	335113
California	543023
CANADA	147187.7
Charlotte	1178225.2
Chicago	6878
Dakotas	27353.8
Dallas	469309.15
Denver	291211

Ship Date — Feb - Apr 2007 — MONTHS ▾
2006 2007
DEC JAN FEB MAR APR MAY JUN

FIGURE 2-30 You can expand the range on the Timeline slicer to include more data in the filtered numbers.

Want to quickly filter your pivot table by quarters? Well, you can easily do it with a Timeline slicer. Click the time period dropdown and select Quarters. As you can see in Figure 2-31, you also can select Years, Months, or Days, if needed.

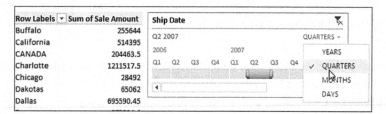

FIGURE 2-31 Quickly switch between filtering by years, quarters, months, and days.

Note Be aware that Timeline slicers are not backward compatible with Excel 2010 or earlier.

Case study: Analyzing activity by market

Your organization has 18 markets that sell 7 types of products. You have been asked to build a report that breaks out each market and highlights the dollar sales for each product. You are starting with an intimidating transaction table that contains more than 91,000 rows of data. To start your report, do the following:

1. Place your cursor inside the data set, select the Insert tab, and click PivotTable.

2. When the Create PivotTable dialog appears, click the OK button. At this point, you should see an empty pivot table with the PivotTable Fields list.

3. Find the Market field in the PivotTable Fields list and select the checkbox next to it.

4. Find the Sale Amount field in the PivotTable Fields list and select the checkbox next to it.

5. To get the product breakouts, find the Product Category field in the PivotTable Fields list and drag it into the Columns area.

In five easy steps, you have calculated and designed a report that satisfies the requirements. After a little formatting, your pivot table report should look similar to the one shown in Figure 2-32.

Lest you lose sight of the analytical power you just harnessed, keep in mind that your data source has more than 91,000 rows and 14 columns, which is a hefty set of data by Excel standards. Despite the amount of data, you produced a relatively robust analysis in a matter of minutes.

Sum of Sale Amount	Column Labels			
Row Labels	Bar Equipment	Commercial Appliances	Concession Equipment	Fryer
Baltimore	80			
Buffalo	37397.9	237297.85	187711	127
California	66356.65	294155.55	416379.2	2610
CANADA	35975.25	71272.1	205874.6	129
Charlotte	283682.15	1525742.3	1569948.6	4509
Chicago	3168	9081	18218	9
Dakotas	3386.5	7287.05	30619.2	180
Dallas	59580.3	255146	306037	151
Denver	34558.85	70068.8	75712.8	1200
Florida	1132162.05	5667950.6	6665865.45	2269
Great Lakes	16798.4	36678.1	71625.8	51
Kansas City	41891.9	61404.15	57300.7	50
Knoxville	220	152		

FIGURE 2-32 This summary can be created in less than a minute.

Keeping up with changes in the data source

Let's go back to the family portrait analogy. As years go by, your family will change in appearance and might even grow to include some new members. The family portrait that was taken years ago remains static and no longer represents the family today. So, another portrait needs to be taken.

As time goes by, your data might change and grow with newly added rows and columns. However, the pivot cache that feeds your pivot table report is disconnected from your data source, so it cannot represent any of the changes you make to your data source until you take another snapshot.

The action of updating your pivot cache by taking another snapshot of your data source is called *refreshing* your data. There are two reasons you might have to refresh your pivot table report:

- Changes have been made to your existing data source.

- Your data source's range has been expanded with the addition of rows or columns.

The following sections explain how to keep your pivot table synchronized with the changes in your data source.

Dealing with changes made to the existing data source

If a few cells in your pivot table's source data have changed due to edits or updates, you can refresh your pivot table report with a few clicks. Simply right-click inside your pivot table report and select Refresh. This selection takes another snapshot of your data set, overwriting your previous pivot cache with the latest data.

Note You can also refresh the data in a pivot table by selecting the Refresh icon on the PivotTable Analyze tab or Refresh All on the Data tab.

> **Tip** Clicking anywhere inside a pivot table activates the PivotTable tabs in the ribbon.

Dealing with an expanded data source range due to the addition of rows or columns

When changes have been made to your data source that affect its range (for example, if you've added rows or columns), you have to update the range being captured by the pivot cache.

To do this, click anywhere inside the pivot table and then select the PivotTable Analyze tab in the ribbon. From here, select Change Data Source. This selection triggers the dialog shown in Figure 2-33.

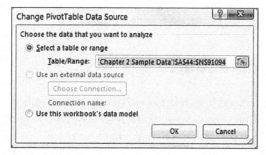

FIGURE 2-33 The Change PivotTable Data Source dialog enables you to redefine the source data for your pivot table.

All you have to do here is update the range to include new rows and columns. After you have specified the appropriate range, click the OK button.

Note that if you format your pivot table source data as a table by choosing Home | Format As Table; Insert | Table; or pressing Ctrl+T, the Pivot Table Source range will automatically expand as the data grows. You will still have to click Refresh to pick up the new rows.

Sharing the pivot cache or creating a new cache

You quite often need to analyze the same data set in multiple ways. In most cases, this process requires you to create separate pivot tables from the same data source. Keep in mind that every time you create a pivot table, you are storing a snapshot of the entire data set in a pivot cache. Every pivot cache that is created increases your memory usage and file size. For this reason, you should consider sharing your pivot cache.

> **Note** In situations where you need to create multiple pivot tables from the same data source, you can use the same pivot cache to feed multiple pivot tables. By using the same pivot cache for multiple pivot tables, you gain a certain level of efficiency when it comes to memory usage and file size.

In legacy versions of Excel, when you created a pivot table using a data set that was already being used in another pivot table, Excel actually gave you the option of using the same pivot cache. However, Excel today does not give you such an option.

Instead, each time you create a new pivot table in Excel, Excel automatically shares the pivot cache. Most of the time, this is beneficial: You can link as many pivot tables as you want to the same pivot cache with a negligible increase in memory and file size.

On the flip side, when you group one pivot table by month and year, all the pivot tables are grouped similarly. If you want one pivot table by month and another pivot table by week, you have to force a separate pivot cache. You can force Excel to create a separate pivot cache by taking the following steps:

1. Select one cell in your original data set.

2. Press and release Alt+D, and then press P to launch the PivotTable Wizard.

3. Click the Next button to get past the first screen of the wizard.

4. On the second screen, select the range for your pivot table and click the Next button.

5. Excel displays a wordy message saying that you can use less memory if you click Yes. Instead, click No.

6. On the next screen, click the Finish button.

At this point, you have a blank pivot table that pulls from its own pivot cache.

> **Tip** If you already have an existing pivot table, you can use an alternative method for creating a separate pivot cache: Copy and paste the existing table to a new workbook and then copy and paste the pivot table back to a new sheet in the original workbook.

Side effects of sharing a pivot cache

It's important to note that there are a few side effects to sharing a pivot cache. For example, suppose you have two pivot tables using the same pivot cache. Certain actions affect both pivot tables, each of which is discussed further in Chapter 5, "Performing calculations in pivot tables":

- **Refreshing your data**—You cannot refresh one pivot table and not the other. Refreshing affects both tables.

- **Adding a calculated field**—If you create a calculated field in one pivot table, your newly created calculated field shows up in the PivotTable Fields list of the other pivot table.

- **Adding a calculated item**—If you create a calculated item in one pivot table, it shows in the other as well.

- **Grouping or ungrouping fields**—Any grouping or ungrouping you perform affects both pivot tables. For instance, suppose you group a date field in one pivot table to show months. The same date field in the other pivot table is also grouped to show months.

Although none of these side effects are critical flaws in the concept of sharing a pivot cache, it is important to keep them in mind when determining whether using a pivot table as your data source is the best option for your situation.

Saving time with PivotTable tools

Microsoft has invested a lot of time and effort in the overall pivot table experience. The results of these efforts are tools that make pivot table functionality more accessible and easier to use. The following sections look at a few of the tools that help you save time when managing pivot tables.

Deferring layout updates

The frustrating part of building a pivot table from a large data source is that each time you add a field to a pivot area, you are left waiting while Excel crunches through all that data. This can become a maddeningly time-consuming process if you have to add several fields to your pivot table.

Excel offers some relief for this problem by providing a way to defer layout changes until you are ready to apply them. You can activate this option by selecting the relatively inconspicuous Defer Layout Update checkbox in the PivotTable Fields list, as shown in Figure 2-34.

Here's how this feature works: With the Defer Layout Update checkbox selected, you prevent your pivot table from making real-time updates as you move your fields around without your pivot table. When you are ready to apply your changes, click the Update button on the lower-right corner of the PivotTable Fields list.

FIGURE 2-34 Select the Defer Layout Update checkbox to prevent your pivot table from updating while you add fields.

Note Remember to clear the checkmark from the Defer Layout Update checkbox when you are done building your pivot table. Leaving it selected results in your pivot table remaining in a state of manual updates, preventing you from using other features of the pivot table, such as sorting, filtering, and grouping.

Tip Incidentally, the Defer Layout Update option is available through VBA. It can help improve the performance of any macro that automates the creation of pivot tables.

Note For detailed information on how to use VBA to create pivot tables, refer to Chapter 13, "Using VBA or TypeScript to create pivot tables."

Starting over with one click

Often, you might want to start from scratch when working with your pivot table layouts. Excel provides a simple way to essentially start over without deleting your pivot cache. Select the PivotTable Analyze tab and select the Clear dropdown. As you can see in Figure 2-35, this command enables you to either clear your entire pivot table layout or remove any existing filters you might have applied in your pivot table.

FIGURE 2-35 The Clear command enables you to clear your pivot table fields or remove the applied filters from your pivot table.

Relocating a pivot table

You might find that after you have created a pivot table, you need to move it to another location. It might be in the way of other analyses on the worksheet, or you might simply need to move it to another worksheet. Although there are several ways to move a pivot table, the easiest is Excel's no-frills way: Select Move PivotTable from the PivotTable Analyze tab in the ribbon. This icon activates the Move PivotTable dialog, shown in Figure 2-36. All you have to do here is specify where you want your pivot table moved.

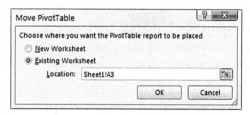

FIGURE 2-36 The Move PivotTable dialog enables you to quickly move your pivot table to another location.

Show Details for any cell in the values area

You've produced a pivot table and sent it to your manager, who takes one look at it and says, "This can't be right! There is no way we sold $205K of Concession Equipment to Canada!"

Any time someone questions one of the numbers in the values area of your pivot table, simply select the cell containing the value. On the PivotTable Tools tab, click Show Details (see Figure 2-37).

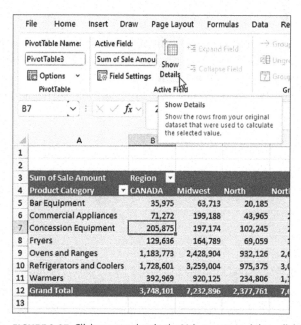

FIGURE 2-37 Click any number in the Values area and then click Show Details.

Excel will insert a new sheet to the left of the current sheet. This sheet will contain a title indicating what cell was active when Show Details was clicked. There will be a blank row 2 and then all of the rows from the original data set that make up the selected number, as shown in Figure 2-38.

Before 2024, you could achieve this Show Details report by double-clicking any cell in the pivot table Values area. In 2024, Microsoft added the Show Details button to the ribbon and improved the result by adding the title.

⬚	A	B	C	D	E	F
1	Details for Sum of Sale Amount - Product Category: Concession Equipment, Region: CANADA					
2						
3	Region ▾	Market ▾	State ▾	Customer Name ▾	Account Manager ▾	PONumber ▾ O
4	CANADA	CANADA	NB	ATLANT Corp.	Faxon Mundy	47980
5	CANADA	CANADA	NB	ATLANT Corp.	Faxon Mundy	50203
6	CANADA	CANADA	NB	ATLANT Corp.	Faxon Mundy	53527
7	CANADA	CANADA	NB	ATLANT Corp.	Faxon Mundy	71841

FIGURE 2-38 Excel inserts a new worksheet to the left of the active sheet with all of the rows that make up the selected number.

If you use Show Details on the total number at the intersection of the Grand Total row and the Grand Total column, the Show Details report will be an exact copy of the entire original data set.

You can use Show Details over and over. Each time will create a new worksheet to the left of the active sheet. If you don't need these worksheets, you can press Ctrl+Z to undo; Excel will remove the new sheet.

Next steps

In Chapter 3, you'll learn how to enhance your pivot table reports by customizing your fields, changing field names, changing summary calculations, applying formats to data fields, adding and removing subtotals, and using the Show As setting.

Customizing a pivot table

In this chapter, you will:

- Make common cosmetic changes

- Make report layout changes

- Customize a pivot table's appearance with styles and themes

- Change summary calculations

- Change the calculation in a value field

- Add and remove subtotals

Although pivot tables provide an extremely fast way to summarize data, sometimes the pivot table defaults are not exactly what you need. In such cases, you can use many powerful settings to tweak pivot tables. These tweaks range from making cosmetic changes to changing the underlying calculation used in the pivot table.

Many of the changes in this chapter can be customized for all future pivot tables using the new pivot table default settings. If you find yourself always making the same changes to a pivot table, consider making that change in the pivot table defaults.

In Excel, you find controls to customize a pivot table in myriad places: the PivotTable Analyze tab, Design tab, Field Settings dialog, Data Field Settings dialog, PivotTable Options dialog, and context menus.

Rather than cover each set of controls sequentially, this chapter covers the following functional areas in making pivot table customizations:

- **Minor cosmetic changes**—Change blanks to zeros, adjust the number format, and rename a field. If you find yourself making the same changes to each pivot table, see "Tip 5: Use pivot table defaults to change behavior of all future pivot tables" in Chapter 14.

- **Layout changes**—Compare three possible layouts, show/hide subtotals and totals, and repeat row labels.

- **Major cosmetic changes**—Use pivot table styles to format a pivot table quickly.

- **Summary calculations**—Change from Sum to Count, Min, Max, and more.

- **Advanced calculations**—Use settings to show data as a running total, percent of total, rank, percent of parent item, and more.

- **Other options**—Review some of the obscure options found throughout the Excel interface.

Making common cosmetic changes

You need to make a few changes to almost every pivot table to make it easier to understand and interpret. Figure 3-1 shows a typical pivot table. To create this pivot table, open the Chapter 3 data file. Select Insert | Pivot Table | OK. Select the checkboxes for the Sector, Customer, and Revenue fields and drag the Region field to the Columns area.

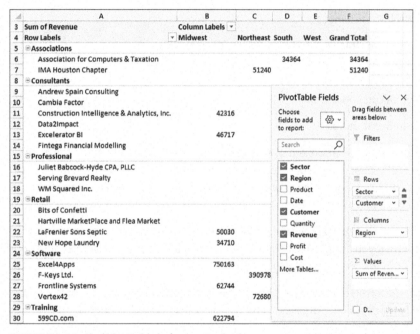

FIGURE 3-1 A typical pivot table before customization.

This default pivot table contains several annoying items that you might want to change quickly:

- The default table style uses no gridlines, which makes it difficult to follow the rows and columns across and down.

- Numbers in the Values area are in a general number format. There are no commas, currency symbols, and so on.

- For sparse data sets, many blanks appear in the Values area. The blank cell in E5 indicates that there were no Associations sales in the Midwest. Most people prefer to see zeros instead of blanks.

- Excel renames fields in the Values area with the unimaginative name Sum Of Revenue. You can change this name.

You can correct each of these annoyances with just a few mouse clicks. The following sections address each issue.

> **Tip** Excel MVP Debra Dalgleish sells a Pivot Power Premium add-in that fixes most of the issues listed here. Debra's add-in offers a few more features than the new PivotTable Defaults. This add-in is great if you will be creating pivot tables frequently. For more information, visit http://mrx.cl/pivpow16.

Applying a table style to restore gridlines

The default pivot table layout contains no gridlines and is rather plain. Fortunately, you can apply a table style. Any table style that you choose is better than the default.

Follow these steps to apply a table style:

1. Make sure that the active cell is in the pivot table.

2. From the ribbon, select the Design tab. Three arrows appear on the right side of the PivotTable Style gallery.

3. Click the bottom arrow to open the complete gallery, which is shown in Figure 3-2.

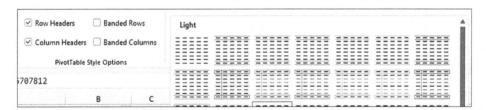

FIGURE 3-2 The gallery contains 85 styles to choose from.

4. Choose any style other than the first style from the dropdown. Styles toward the bottom of the gallery tend to have more formatting.

5. Select the checkbox for Banded Rows to the left of the PivotTable Styles gallery. This draws gridlines in light styles and adds row stripes in dark styles.

It does not matter which style you choose from the gallery; any of the 84 other styles are better than the default style.

> **Note** For more details about customizing styles, see "Customizing a pivot table's appearance with styles and themes" later in this chapter.

Changing the number format to add thousands separators

If you have gone to the trouble of formatting your underlying data, you might expect that the pivot table will capture some of this formatting. Unfortunately, it does not. Even if your underlying data fields were formatted with a certain numeric format, the default pivot table presents values formatted with a general format. As a sign of some progress, when you create pivot tables from Power Pivot, you can specify the number format for a field before creating the pivot table. This functionality has not come to regular pivot tables yet.

> **Note** For more about Power Pivot, read Chapter 10, "Unlocking features with the Data Model and Power Pivot."

For example, in the figures in this chapter, the numbers are in the thousands or tens of thousands. At this level of sales, you would normally have a thousands separator and probably no decimal places. Although the original data had a numeric format applied, the pivot table routinely formats your numbers in an ugly general style.

What is the fastest way to change the number format? It depends if you have a single value field or multiple value fields.

In Figure 3-3, the pivot table Values area contains Revenue. There are many columns in the pivot table because Product is in the Columns area. In this case, right-click any number and choose Number Format.

	A	B	C	D	E	F
3	Revenue	Product ▾				
4	Region ▾	Doodads	Gadget	Gizmo	Widget	Grand Total
5	Midwest	60:	Calibri ▾ 11 ▾ A̅ A̅ $ ▾ % ﹐			741424
6	Northeast	3886	B I ≡ ⬠ ▾ A̅ ▾ ⊞ ▾ ⬩.0 .00 ⬦			124612
7	South					502325
8	West	2866?	55?0?	700F?	75?49	239451
9	Grand Total	7355	📋 Copy		519	6707812
10			⊞ Format Cells...			
11			Number Format...			
12			🗋 Refresh			
13						
14			Sort ▸			

FIGURE 3-3 For a single value field, right-click any number and choose Number Format.

In contrast to Figure 3-3, the pivot table in Figure 3-4 contains three fields in the Values area: Revenue, Cost, and Profit. Rather than applying the Number Format to each individual column, you can format the entire pivot table by following these steps:

1. Select from the first numeric cell to the last numeric cell, including the Grand Total row or column if it is present.

2. Press Ctrl+1 to display the Format Cells dialog.

3. Choose the Number tab across the top of the dialog.

4. Select a number format.

5. Click OK.

Until a coding change in Excel 2010, the preceding steps would not change the number format in cases where the pivot table became taller. However, provided you include the Grand Total in your selection, these steps will change the number format for all the fields in the Values area.

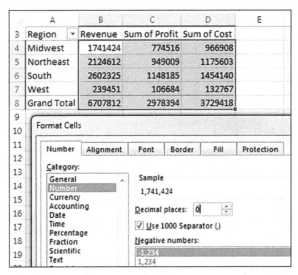

FIGURE 3-4 With multiple fields in the Values area, select all number cells as shown here and change the format using the Format Cells dialog.

Replacing blanks with zeros

One of the elements of good spreadsheet design is that you should never leave blank cells in a numeric section of a worksheet.

A blank tells you that there were no sales for a particular combination of labels. In the default view, an actual zero is used to indicate that there was activity, but the total sales were zero. This value might mean that a customer bought something and then returned it, resulting in net sales of zero. Although there are limited applications in which you need to differentiate between having no sales and having net zero sales, this seems rare. In 99 percent of the cases, you should fill in the blank cells with zeros.

Follow these steps to change this setting for the current pivot table:

1. Right-click any cell in the pivot table and choose PivotTable Options.

2. On the Layout & Format tab in the Format section, type **0** next to the field labeled For Empty Cells Show (see Figure 3-5). Alternatively, you can unselect the For Empty Cells Show option. Or you can type anything here, such as a dash or even **zip**, **nada**, or **nothing**.

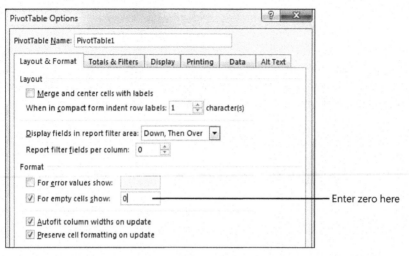

FIGURE 3-5 Enter a zero in the For Empty Cells Show box to replace the blank cells with zero.

3. Click OK to accept the change.

The result is that the pivot table is filled with zeros instead of blanks, as shown in Figure 3-6.

	A	B	C	D	E	F
1						
2						
3	Sum of Revenue	Column Labels ▾				
4	Row Labels ▾	Midwest	Northeast	South	West	Grand Total
5	⊟Associations	$0	$51,240	$34,364	$0	$85,604
6	Association for Computers & Taxation	$0	$0	$34,364	$0	$34,364
7	IMA Houston Chapter	$0	$51,240	$0	$0	$51,240
8	⊟Consultants	$89,033	$0	$926,970	$115,132	$1,131,135
9	Andrew Spain Consulting	$0	$0	$869,454	$0	$869,454
10	Cambia Factor	$0	$0	$57,516	$0	$57,516
11	Construction Intelligence & Analytics, Inc.	$42,316	$0	$0	$0	$42,316
12	Data2Impact	$0	$0	$0	$59,881	$59,881
13	Excelerator BI	$46,717	$0	$0	$0	$46,717
14	Fintega Financial Modelling	$0	$0	$0	$55,251	$55,251
15	⊟Professional	$0	$0	$437,695	$39,250	$476,945
16	Juliet Babcock-Hyde CPA, PLLC	$0	$0	$31,369	$0	$31,369
17	Serving Brevard Realty	$0	$0	$406,326	$0	$406,326
18	WM Squared Inc.	$0	$0	$0	$39,250	$39,250
19	⊟Retail	$84,740	$0	$704,359	$31,021	$820,120

FIGURE 3-6 Your report is now a solid contiguous block of non-blank cells.

Changing a field name

Every field in a final pivot table has a name. Fields in the row, column, and filter areas inherit their names from the heading in the source data. Fields in the values section are given names such as Sum Of Revenue. In some instances, you might prefer to print a different name in the pivot table. You might prefer Total Revenue instead of the default name. In these situations, the capability to change your field names comes in quite handy.

To change a field name in the Values area, follow these steps:

1. Select a cell in the pivot table that contains the appropriate type of value. You might have a pivot table with both Sum Of Quantity and Sum Of Revenue in the Values area. Choose a cell that contains a Sum Of Revenue value.

2. Go to the PivotTable Analyze tab in the ribbon. A Pivot Field Name text box appears below the heading Active Field. Currently, the box contains Sum Of Revenue.

3. Type a new name in the box, as shown in Figure 3-7. Click a cell in your pivot table to complete the entry and have the heading in A3 change. The name of the field title in the Values area also changes to reflect the new name.

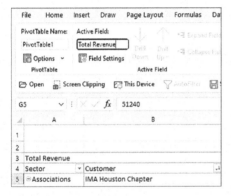

FIGURE 3-7 The name typed in the Custom Name box appears in the pivot table. Although names should be unique, you can trick Excel into accepting a name that's similar to an existing name by adding a space to the end of it.

Tip   When you can see the value field name, such as "Sum Of Revenue," in the Excel worksheet, you can directly type a new value to rename the field. For example, in Figure 3-7, you could type **Sales** in cell A3 to rename the field.

Note   One common frustration occurs when you would like to rename Sum Of Revenue to Revenue. The problem is that this name is not allowed because it is not unique; you already have a Revenue field in the source data. To work around this limitation, you can name the field and add a space to the end of the name. Excel considers "Revenue " (with a space) to be different from "Revenue" (with no space). Because this change is only cosmetic, the readers of your spreadsheet do not notice the space after the name.

Making report layout changes

Excel offers three report layout styles. The Excel team continues to offer the Compact layout as the default report layout. If you prefer a different layout, change it using the default settings for pivot tables.

If you consider three report layouts and the ability to show subtotals at the top or bottom, plus choices for blank rows and Repeat All Item Labels, you have 16 different layout possibilities available.

Layout changes are controlled in the Layout group of the Design tab, as shown in Figure 3-8. This group offers four icons:

- **Subtotals**—Moves subtotals to the top or bottom of each group or turns them off.

- **Grand Totals**—Turns the grand totals on or off for rows and columns.

- **Report Layout**—Uses the Compact, Outline, or Tabular forms. Offers an option to repeat item labels.

- **Blank Rows**—Inserts or removes blank lines after each group.

Note You mathematicians in the audience might think that 3 layouts × 2 repeat options × 2 subtotal location options × 2 blank row options would be 24 layouts. However, choosing Repeat All Item Labels does not work with the Compact layout, thus eliminating 4 of the combinations. In addition, Subtotals At The Top Of Each Group does not work with the Tabular layout, eliminating another 4 combinations.

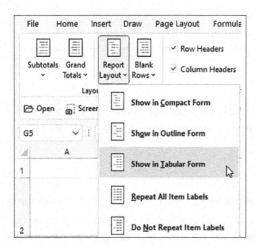

FIGURE 3-8 The Layout group on the Design tab offers different layouts and options for totals.

Using the Compact layout

By default, all new pivot tables use the Compact layout that you saw in Figure 3-6. In this layout, multiple fields in the row area are stacked in column A. Note in the figure that the Consultants sector and the Andrew Spain Consulting customer are both in column A.

The Compact form is suited for using the Expand and Collapse icons. If you select one of the Sector value cells, such as Associations in A5, and then click the Collapse Field icon on the Analyze tab, Excel hides all the customer details and shows only the sectors, as shown in Figure 3-9.

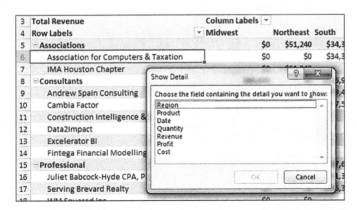

FIGURE 3-9 Click the Collapse Field icon to hide levels of detail.

After a field is collapsed, you can show detail for individual items by using the plus icons in column A, or you can click Expand Field on the PivotTable Analyze tab to see the detail again.

Tip If you select a cell in the innermost row field and click Expand Field on the Options tab, Excel displays the Show Detail dialog, as shown in Figure 3-10, to enable you to add a new innermost row field.

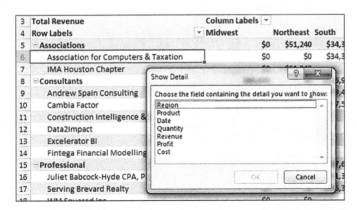

FIGURE 3-10 When you attempt to expand the innermost field, Excel offers to add a new innermost field.

Using the Outline layout

When you select Design | Layout | Report Layout | Show In Outline Form, Excel puts each row field in a separate column. The pivot table shown in Figure 3-11 is one column wider, with revenue values starting in C instead of B. This is a small price to pay for allowing each field to occupy its own column. Soon, you will find out how to convert a pivot table to values so you can further sort or filter. When you do this, you will want each field in its own column.

The Excel team added the Repeat All Item Labels option to the Report Layout tab starting in Excel 2010. This alleviated a lot of busy work because it takes just two clicks to fill in all the blank cells along the outer row fields. Choosing to repeat the item labels causes values to appear in cells A6:A7, A9:A14, as shown in Figure 3-11.

Figure 3-11 shows the same pivot table from before, now in Outline form and with labels repeated.

Caution This layout is suitable if you plan to copy the values from the pivot table to a new location for further analysis. Although the Compact layout offers a clever approach by squeezing multiple fields into one column, it is not ideal for reusing the data later.

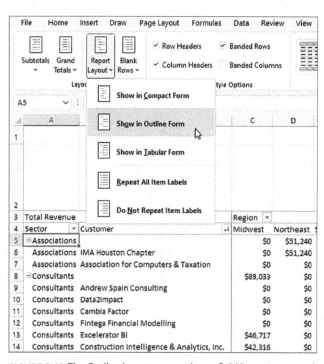

FIGURE 3-11 The Outline layout puts each row field in a separate column.

By default, both the Compact and Outline layouts put the subtotals at the top of each group. You can use the Subtotals dropdown on the Design tab to move the totals to the bottom of each group, as shown in Figure 3-12. In Outline view, this causes a not-really-useful heading row to appear at the top of each group. Cell A5 contains "Associations" without any additional data in the columns to the right. Consequently, the pivot table occupies 44 rows instead of 37 rows because each of the 7 sector categories has an extra header.

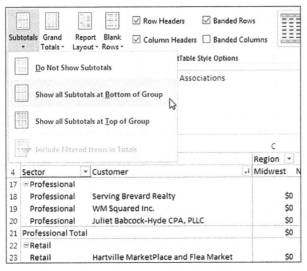

FIGURE 3-12 With subtotals at the bottom of each group, the pivot table occupies several more rows.

Using the traditional Tabular layout

Figure 3-13 shows the Tabular layout. This layout is similar to the one that has been used in pivot tables since their invention through Excel 2003. In this layout, the subtotals can never appear at the top of the group. Repeat All Item Labels works with this layout, as shown in Figure 3-13.

	A	B	C	D	E
3	Revenue		Region		
4	Sector	Customer	Midwest	Northeast	South
5	⊟Associations	IMA Houston Chapter	$0	$51,240	$0
6	Associations	Association for Computers & Taxation	$0	$0	$34,364
7	Associations Total		$0	$51,240	$34,364
8	⊟Consultants	Andrew Spain Consulting	$0	$0	$869,454
9	Consultants	Data2Impact	$0	$0	$0
10	Consultants	Cambia Factor	$0	$0	$57,516
11	Consultants	Fintega Financial Modelling	$0	$0	$0
12	Consultants	Excelerator BI	$46,717	$0	$0
13	Consultants	Construction Intelligence & Analytics, Inc.	$42,316	$0	$0
14	Consultants Total		$89,033	$0	$926,970
15	⊟Professional	Serving Brevard Realty	$0	$0	$406,326
16	Professional	WM Squared Inc.	$0	$0	$0
17	Professional	Juliet Babcock-Hyde CPA, PLLC	$0	$0	$31,369
18	Professional Total		$0	$0	$437,695
19	⊟Retail	Hartville MarketPlace and Flea Market	$0	$0	$704,359

FIGURE 3-13 The Tabular layout is similar to pivot tables in legacy versions of Excel.

The Tabular layout is the best layout if you expect to use the resulting summary data in a subsequent analysis. If you wanted to reuse the table in Figure 3-13, you would do additional "flattening" of the pivot table by choosing Subtotals | Do Not Show Subtotals And Grand Totals | Off For Rows And Columns.

Case study: Converting a pivot table to values

Say that you want to convert the pivot table shown in Figure 3-13 to a regular data set that you can sort, filter, chart, or export to another system. You don't need the Sectors totals in rows 7, 14, 18, and so on. You don't need the Grand Total at the bottom. Depending on your future needs, you might want to move the Region field from the Columns area to the Rows area. This would allow you to add Cost and Profit as new columns in the final report.

Finally, you want to convert from a live pivot table to static values. To make these changes, follow these steps:

1. Select any cell in the pivot table.

2. From the Design tab, select Grand Totals | Off For Rows And Columns.

3. Select Design | Subtotals | Do Not Show Subtotals.

4. Drag the Region tile from the Columns area in the PivotTable Fields list. Drop this field between Sector and Customer in the Rows area.

5. Check Profit and Cost at the top of the PivotTable Fields list. Because both fields are numeric, they move to the Values area and appear in the pivot table as new columns. Rename both fields using the Active Field box on the PivotTable Analyze tab. The report is now a contiguous solid block of data, as shown in Figure 3-14.

	A	B	C	D	E	F
1						
2						
3	Sector	Region	Customer	Total Revenue	Total Profit	Total Cost
4	Associations	Northeast	IMA Houston Chapter	$51,240	22824	28416
5	Associations	South	Association for Computers & Taxation	$34,364	15576	18788
6	Consultants	Midwest	Construction Intelligence & Analytics, Inc.	$42,316	18764	23552
7	Consultants	Midwest	Excelerator BI	$46,717	19961	26756
8	Consultants	South	Andrew Spain Consulting	$869,454	382170	487284
9	Consultants	South	Cambia Factor	$57,516	26765	30751
10	Consultants	West	Data2Impact	$59,881	25913	33968
11	Consultants	West	Fintega Financial Modelling	$55,251	24632	30619
12	Professional	South	Juliet Babcock-Hyde CPA, PLLC	$31,369	13730	17639
13	Professional	South	Serving Brevard Realty	$406,326	178585	227741

FIGURE 3-14 The pivot table now contains a solid block of data.

6. Select one cell in the pivot table. Press Ctrl+* to select all the data in the pivot table.

7. Press Ctrl+C to copy the data from the pivot table.

8. Right-click a blank section of a worksheet and notice that to the right of the words "Paste Special" is a greater-than sign that leads to a flyout with 14 ways to Paste Special. Choose Paste Values And Number Formatting, as shown in Figure 3-15. Excel pastes a static copy of the report to the worksheet.

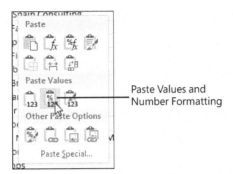

FIGURE 3-15 Use Paste Values And Number Formatting to create a static version of the data.

9. If you no longer need the original pivot table, select the entire pivot table and press the Delete key to clear the cells from the pivot table and free up the area of memory that was holding the pivot table cache. One way to select the entire pivot table is to use the Select dropdown on the PivotTable Analyze tab and choose Entire PivotTable.

The result is a solid block of summary data. These 27 rows are a summary of the 500+ rows in the original data set, but they also are suitable for exporting to other systems.

Controlling blank lines, grand totals, and other settings

Additional settings on the Design tab enable you to toggle various elements.

The Blank Rows dropdown offers the Insert Blank Line After Each Item choice. This setting applies only to pivot tables with two or more row fields. Blank rows are not added after each item in the inner row field. You see a blank row after each group of items in the outer row fields. As shown in Figure 3-16, the blank row after each sector makes the report easier to read. However, if you remove Sector from the report, you have only Customer in the row fields, and no blank rows appear (see Figure 3-17).

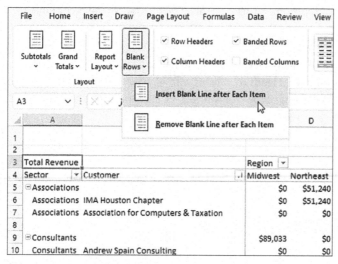

FIGURE 3-16 The Blank Rows setting makes the report easier to read.

	A	B	C	D
3	Total Revenue	Region ▼		
4	Customer	Midwest	Northeast	South
5	Andrew Spain Consulting	$0	$0	$869,454
6	Excel4Apps	$750,163	$0	$0
7	Hartville MarketPlace and Flea Market	$0	$0	$704,359
8	599CD.com	$622,794	$0	$0
9	MySpreadsheetLab	$0	$613,514	$0
10	CPASelfStudy.com	$0	$568,851	$0
11	MyOnlineTrainingHub.com	$0	$0	$498,937
12	LearnExcelBooks.com	$0	$427,349	$0
13	Serving Brevard Realty	$0	$0	$406,326

FIGURE 3-17 Blank rows will not appear when there is only one item in the row field.

Grand totals can appear at the bottom of each column and/or at the end of each row, or they can be turned off altogether. Settings for grand totals appear in the Grand Totals dropdown of the Layout group on the Design tab. The wording in this dropdown is a bit confusing, so Figure 3-18 shows what each option provides. The default is to show grand totals for rows and columns.

If you want a grand total column but no grand total at the bottom, choose On For Rows Only, as shown at the top of Figure 3-18. To me, this seems backward. To keep the grand total column, you have to choose to turn on grand totals for rows only. I guess the rationale is that each cell in F5:F8 is a grand total of the row to the left of the cell. Hence, you are showing the grand totals for all the rows but not for the columns. Perhaps someday Microsoft will ship a version of Excel in English-Midwest where this setting would be called "Keep the Grand Total Column." But for now, it remains confusing.

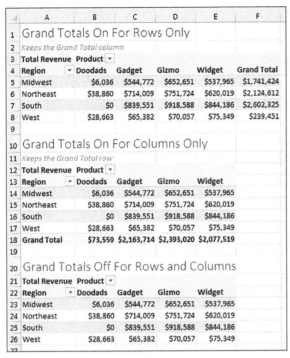

	A	B	C	D	E	F
1	Grand Totals On For Rows Only					
2	*Keeps the Grand Total column*					
3	Total Revenue	Product				
4	Region	Doodads	Gadget	Gizmo	Widget	Grand Total
5	Midwest	$6,036	$544,772	$652,651	$537,965	$1,741,424
6	Northeast	$38,860	$714,009	$751,724	$620,019	$2,124,612
7	South	$0	$839,551	$918,588	$844,186	$2,602,325
8	West	$28,663	$65,382	$70,057	$75,349	$239,451
9						
10	Grand Totals On For Columns Only					
11	*Keeps the Grand Total row*					
12	Total Revenue	Product				
13	Region	Doodads	Gadget	Gizmo	Widget	
14	Midwest	$6,036	$544,772	$652,651	$537,965	
15	Northeast	$38,860	$714,009	$751,724	$620,019	
16	South	$0	$839,551	$918,588	$844,186	
17	West	$28,663	$65,382	$70,057	$75,349	
18	Grand Total	$73,559	$2,163,714	$2,393,020	$2,077,519	
19						
20	Grand Totals Off For Rows and Columns					
21	Total Revenue	Product				
22	Region	Doodads	Gadget	Gizmo	Widget	
23	Midwest	$6,036	$544,772	$652,651	$537,965	
24	Northeast	$38,860	$714,009	$751,724	$620,019	
25	South	$0	$839,551	$918,588	$844,186	
26	West	$28,663	$65,382	$70,057	$75,349	
27						

FIGURE 3-18 The wording is confusing, but you can toggle off the grand total column, row, or both.

Similarly, to show a grand total row but no grand total column, you open the Grand Totals menu and choose On For Columns Only. Again, in some twisted version of the English language, cell B18 is totaling the cells in the column above it.

The final choice, Off For Rows And Columns, is simple enough. Excel shows neither a grand total column nor a grand total row.

> **Tip** You can abandon these confusing menu choices by using the right-click menu. If you right-click on any cell containing the words "Grand Total," you can choose Remove Grand Total.

Back in Excel 2003, pivot tables were shown in Tabular layout, and logical headings such as Region and Product would appear in the pivot table, as shown in the top pivot table in Figure 3-19. When the Excel team switched to Compact form, they replaced those headings with Row Labels and Column Labels. These add nothing to the report. To toggle off those headings, look on the far-right side of the PivotTable Analyze tab for the Field Headers icon and click it to remove Row Labels and Column Labels from your pivot tables in Compact form.

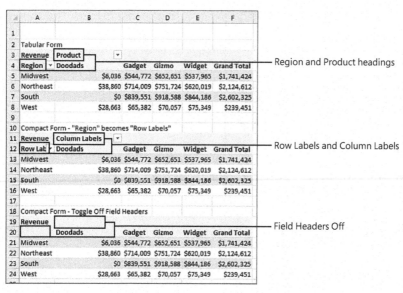

Region and Product headings

Row Labels and Column Labels

Field Headers Off

FIGURE 3-19 The Compact form replaces useful headings with Row Labels. You can turn these off.

Caution When you arrange several pivot tables vertically, as in Figure 3-19, you'll notice that changes in one pivot table change the column widths for the entire column, often causing #### to appear in the other pivot tables. By default, Excel changes the column width to AutoFit the pivot table but ignores anything else in the column. To turn off this default behavior, right-click each pivot table and choose PivotTable Options. In the first tab of the Options dialog, the second-to-last checkbox is AutoFit Column Widths On Update. Clear this checkbox. This is another setting that you might want to adjust in Pivot Table Defaults. See Tip 5 - Use pivot table defaults to change the behavior of all future pivot tables in Chapter 14.

Customizing a pivot table's appearance with styles and themes

You can quickly apply color and formatting to a pivot table report by using the 85 built-in styles in the PivotTable Styles gallery on the Design tab. These 85 styles are further modified by the four checkboxes to the left of the gallery. Throw in the 48 themes on the Page Layout tab, and you have 65,280 easy ways to format a pivot table. If none of those provide what you need, you can define a new style.

Start with the four checkboxes in the PivotTable Style Options group of the Design tab of the ribbon. You can choose to apply special formatting to the row headers, column headers, banded rows, or banded columns. My favorite choice here is banded rows because it makes it easier for the reader's eye to follow a row across a wide report. You should choose from these settings first because the choices here will modify the thumbnails shown in the Styles gallery.

As mentioned earlier, the PivotTable Styles gallery on the Design tab offers 85 built-in styles. Grouped into 28 styles each of Light, Medium, and Dark, the gallery offers variations on the accent colors used in the current theme. In Figure 3-20, you can see which styles in the gallery truly support banded rows and which just offer a bottom border between rows.

True banded rows

1				
2	Tabular Form			
3	Product ▾	Sector ▾	Revenue	Sum of Profit
4	Doodads	Consultants	$6,036	2716
5	Doodads	Retail	$28,663	12761
6	Doodads	Software	$38,860	16996
7	Doodads Total		$73,559	32473
8				
9	Gadget	Associations	$22,334	9840
10	Gadget	Consultants	$397,088	174168
11	Gadget	Professional	$150,638	64944
12	Gadget	Retail	$222,030	98400
13	Gadget	Software	$370,856	166296
14	Gadget	Training	$1,000,768	448704
15	Gadget Total		$2,163,714	962352

Medium

Borders between items

FIGURE 3-20 The styles are shown here with accents for row headers, column headers, and alternating colors in the columns.

> **Tip** Note that you can modify the thumbnails for the 85 styles shown in the gallery by using the four checkboxes in the PivotTable Style Options group.

The Live Preview feature in Excel works in the Styles gallery. As you hover your mouse cursor over style thumbnails, the worksheet shows a preview of the style.

Customizing a style

You can create your own pivot table styles, and the new styles are added to the gallery for the current workbook only. To use the custom style in another workbook, copy and temporarily paste the formatted pivot table to the other workbook. After the pivot table has been pasted, apply the custom style to an existing pivot table in your workbook and then delete the temporary pivot table.

Say that you want to create a pivot table style in which the banded colors are three rows high. Follow these steps to create the new style:

1. Find an existing style in the PivotTable Styles gallery that supports banded rows. Right-click the style in the gallery and select Duplicate. Excel displays the Modify PivotTable Quick Style dialog.

2. Choose a new name for the style. Excel initially appends a 2 to the existing style name, which means you have a name such as PivotStyleDark3 2. Type a better name, such as **Greenbar**.

3. In the Table Element list, click First Row Stripe. A new section called Stripe Size appears in the dialog.

4. Select 3 from the Stripe Size dropdown, as shown in Figure 3-21.

5. To change the stripe color, click the Format button. The Format Cells dialog appears. Click the Fill tab and then choose a fill color. If you want to be truly authentic, choose More Colors | Custom and use Red=200, Green=225, and Blue=204 to simulate 1980s-era greenbar paper. Click OK to accept the color and return to the Modify PivotTable Quick Style dialog.

6. In the Table Element List, click Second Row Stripe. Select 3 from the Stripe Size dropdown. Modify the format to use a lighter color, such as white.

7. If you plan on creating more pivot tables in this workbook, choose the Set As Default Pivot-Table Style For This Document checkbox in the lower left.

8. Optionally, edit the colors for Header Row and Grand Total Row.

9. Click OK to finish building the style. Strangely, Excel doesn't automatically apply this new style to the pivot table. After you put in a few minutes of work to tweak the style, the pivot table does not change.

10. Your new style should be the first thumbnail visible in the Styles gallery. Click that style to apply it to the pivot table.

Tip If you have not added more than seven custom styles, the thumbnail should be visible in the closed gallery, so you can choose it without reopening the gallery.

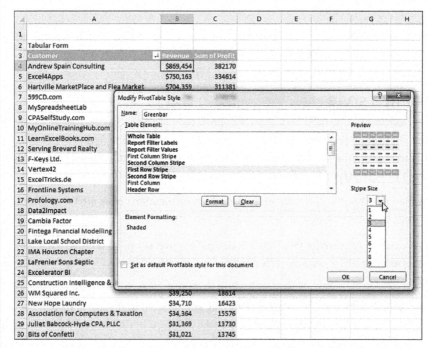

FIGURE 3-21 Customize the style in the Modify PivotTable Style dialog.

Modifying styles with document themes

The formatting options for pivot tables in Excel are impressive. The 84 styles combined with 16 combinations of the Style options make for hundreds of possible format combinations.

In case you become tired of these combinations, you can visit the Themes dropdown on the Page Layout tab, where many built-in themes are available. Each theme has a new combination of accent colors, fonts, and shape effects.

To change a document theme, open the Themes dropdown on the Page Layout tab. Choose a new theme, and the colors used in the pivot table change to match the theme.

 Caution Changing the theme affects the entire workbook. It changes the colors and fonts and affects all charts, shapes, tables, and pivot tables on all worksheets of the active workbook. If you have several other pivot tables in the workbook, changing the theme will apply new colors to all the pivot tables.

 Tip Some of the themes use unusual fonts. You can apply the colors from a theme without changing the fonts in your document by using the Colors dropdown next to the Themes menu, as shown in Figure 3-22.

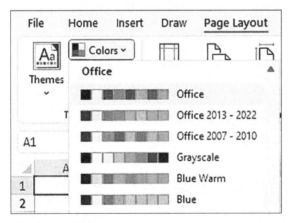

FIGURE 3-22 Choose new colors from the Colors menu.

Case study: Excel pivot table archaeology

At Microsoft, a great person named Howie Dickerman has been in charge of pivot tables for the last few years. Howie was an architect of Power Pivot and was always happy to engage the MVPs when we had some crazy pivot table idea. Occasionally, we would find a pivot table oddity, and Howie would dig into the code to try to figure out why. He called this Excel Archaeology. Howie retired in 2021, and his willingness to go deep into the Excel code base on archaeological expeditions will be missed.

This oddity would have been right up his alley. Excel MVP Wyn Hopkins from Access Analytic recently uncovered a feature in pivot tables that allows you to quickly apply a border to several sections inside the pivot table.

Say that you have a pivot table such as the one in Figure 3-23. Leave a blank row and column on each side of the pivot table, but then completely surround the pivot table with a border. The border shown in Figure 3-23 has a different style on each side to illustrate how each side of the border will be translated to the pivot table.

Total Revenue	Region					
Sector	▾	Midwest	Northeast	South	West	Grand Total
Associations		$0	$51,240	$34,364	$0	$85,604
Consultants		$89,033	$0	$926,970	$115,132	$1,131,135
Professional		$0	$0	$437,695	$39,250	$476,945
Retail		$84,740	$0	$704,359	$31,021	$820,120
Software		$812,907	$463,658	$0	$0	$1,276,565
Training		$754,744	$1,609,714	$498,937	$54,048	$2,917,443
Grand Total		$1,741,424	$2,124,612	$2,602,325	$239,451	$6,707,812

FIGURE 3-23 A relatively plain pivot table with a border just outside the pivot table.

To transfer the outer border to the pivot table, right-click any cell in the pivot table and choose Refresh. The borders from outside the pivot table are applied to various sections inside the pivot table, as shown in Figure 3-24.

In a very specific pattern, the border styles used in the outer border are applied throughout the pivot table. The dashed border used above row 2 is applied above rows 3 and 4 and above cell C11. The dotted border used below row 12 is applied in the pivot table below row 11. A similar pattern happens with the left border being applied to most vertical lines in the pivot table. The right border is applied to the right edge of the pivot table.

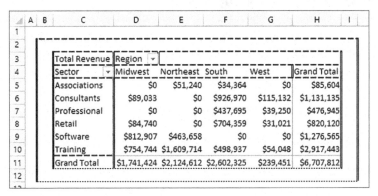

Total Revenue	Region				
Sector	Midwest	Northeast	South	West	Grand Total
Associations	$0	$51,240	$34,364	$0	$85,604
Consultants	$89,033	$0	$926,970	$115,132	$1,131,135
Professional	$0	$0	$437,695	$39,250	$476,945
Retail	$84,740	$0	$704,359	$31,021	$820,120
Software	$812,907	$463,658	$0	$0	$1,276,565
Training	$754,744	$1,609,714	$498,937	$54,048	$2,917,443
Grand Total	$1,741,424	$2,124,612	$2,602,325	$239,451	$6,707,812

FIGURE 3-24 The border styles from the outer border are applied to the pivot table.

Why is this feature in Excel? It had to pre-date the Formatting Gallery. It must have been a way to build your own Pivot Table Styles before there were styles.

Changing summary calculations

When you create a pivot table report, by default Excel summarizes the data by either counting or summing the items. Instead of Sum or Count, you might want to choose functions such as Min, Max, and Count Numeric. In all, 11 options are available.

The Excel team fixed the Count Of Revenue bug

In early 2018, Microsoft fixed a bug that caused many pivot tables to provide a count of revenue instead of a sum. If a data column contains all numbers, Excel will default to Sum as the calculation. If a column contains text, the pivot table will default to Count. But up until 2018, a bug appeared if you had a mix of numbers and empty cells. An empty cell would cause your pivot table to Count instead of Sum.

One Excel customer wrote a letter to the Excel team describing this bug: "Why are you treating empty cells as text? Treat them like any other formula would treat them and consider them to be zero. A mix of numbers and zeroes should not cause a Count of that field."

Without a single vote on *feedbackportal.microsoft.com*, someone on the Excel team patched the bug. If you have a mix of numbers and blank cells, you will no longer get a Count Of Revenue. This is a nice improvement.

Changing the calculation in a value field

The Value Field Settings dialog offers 11 options on the Summarize Values As tab and 15 main options on the Show Values As tab. The options on the first tab are the basic Sum, Average, Count, Max, and Min options that are ubiquitous throughout Excel; the 15 options under Show Values As are interesting ones, such as % of Total, Running Total, and Ranks.

There are several ways to open the Value Field Settings dialog:

- If you have multiple fields in the Values area, double-click the heading for any value field.

- Choose any number in the Values area and click the Field Settings button in the PivotTable Analyze tab of the ribbon.

- In the PivotTable Fields list, open the dropdown for any item in the Values area. The last item will be Value Field Settings.

- If you right-click any number in the Values area, you have a choice for Value Field Settings, plus two additional flyout menus offering 6 of the 11 choices for Summarize Values By and most of the choices for Show Values As (see Figure 3-25).

The following examples show how to use the various calculation options. To contrast the settings, you can build a pivot table where you drag the Revenue field to the Values area nine separate times. Each one shows up as a new column in the pivot table. Over the next several examples, you will see the settings required for the calculations in each column.

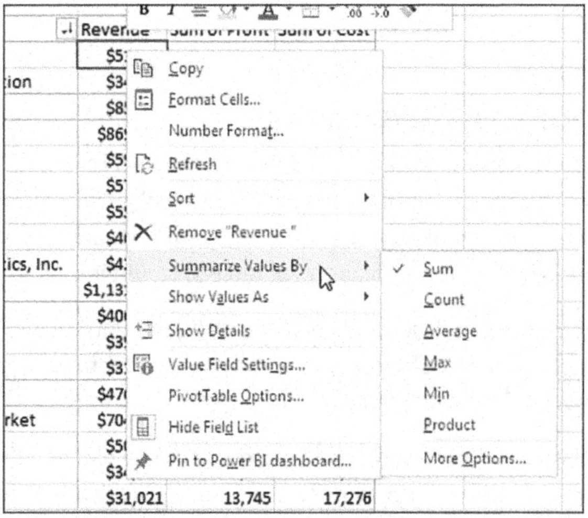

FIGURE 3-25 The right-click menu for any number in the Values area offers a flyout menu with the popular calculation options.

The following examples show how to use the various calculation options. To contrast the settings, you can build a pivot table where you drag the Revenue field to the Values area nine separate times.

Each one shows up as a new column in the pivot table. Over the next several examples, you will see the settings required for the calculations in each column.

To change the calculation for a field, select one Value cell for the field and click the Field Settings button on the PivotTable Analyze tab of the ribbon. The Value Field Settings dialog is similar to the Field Settings dialog, but it has two tabs. The first tab, Summarize Values By, contains Sum, Count, Average, Max, Min, Product, Count Numbers, StdDev, StdDevP, Var, and VarP. You can choose 1 of these 11 calculation options to change the data in the column. In Figure 3-26, columns B through D show various settings from the Summarize Values By tab.

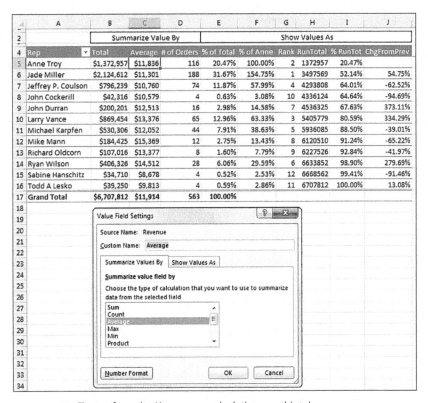

Rep	Total	Average	# of Orders	% of Total	% of Anne	Rank	RunTotal	% RunTot	ChgFromPrev
Anne Troy	$1,372,957	$11,836	116	20.47%	100.00%	2	1372957	20.47%	
Jade Miller	$2,124,612	$11,301	188	31.67%	154.75%	1	3497569	52.14%	54.75%
Jeffrey P. Coulson	$796,239	$10,760	74	11.87%	57.99%	4	4293808	64.01%	-62.52%
John Cockerill	$42,316	$10,579	4	0.63%	3.08%	10	4336124	64.64%	-94.69%
John Durran	$200,201	$12,513	16	2.98%	14.58%	7	4536325	67.63%	373.11%
Larry Vance	$869,454	$13,376	65	12.96%	63.33%	3	5405779	80.59%	334.29%
Michael Karpfen	$530,306	$12,052	44	7.91%	38.63%	5	5936085	88.50%	-39.01%
Mike Mann	$184,425	$15,369	12	2.75%	13.43%	8	6120510	91.24%	-65.22%
Richard Oldcorn	$107,016	$13,377	8	1.60%	7.79%	9	6227526	92.84%	-41.97%
Ryan Wilson	$406,326	$14,512	28	6.06%	29.59%	6	6633852	98.90%	279.69%
Sabine Hanschitz	$34,710	$8,678	4	0.52%	2.53%	12	6668562	99.41%	-91.46%
Todd A Lesko	$39,250	$9,813	4	0.59%	2.86%	11	6707812	100.00%	13.08%
Grand Total	$6,707,812	$11,914	563	100.00%					

FIGURE 3-26 Choose from the 11 summary calculations on this tab.

Column B is the default Sum calculation. It shows the total of all records for a given market. Column C shows the average order for each item by market. Column D shows a count of the records. You can change the heading to # Of Orders, # Of Records, or whatever is appropriate. Note that the count is the actual count of records, not the count of distinct items.

> **Note** Counting distinct items has been difficult in pivot tables but is now easier using PowerPivot. See "Unlocking hidden features with the Data Model" in Chapter 10 for more details.

Far more interesting options appear on the Show Values As tab of the Value Field Settings dialog, as shown in Figure 3-27. Fifteen options appear in the dropdown. Depending on the option you choose, you might need to specify either a base field or a base field and a base item. Columns E through J in Figures 3-26 and 3-27 show some of the calculations possible using Show Values As.

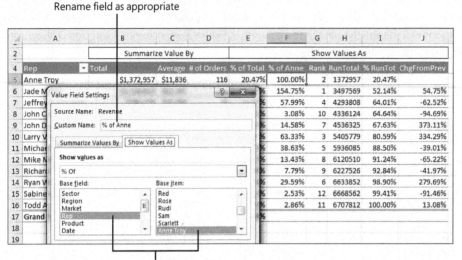

FIGURE 3-27 Fifteen different ways to show that data is available on this tab.

Table 3-1 summarizes the Show Values As options.

TABLE 3-1 Calculations in Show Values As

Show Values As	Additional Required Information	Description
No Calculation	None	–
% of Grand Total	None	Shows percentages so all the detail cells in the pivot table total 100%.
% of Column Total	None	Shows percentages that total up and down the pivot table to 100%.
% of Row Total	None	Shows percentages that total across the pivot table to 100%.
% of Parent Row Total	None	With multiple row fields, a percentage of the parent item's total row is shown.
% of Parent Column Total	None	With multiple column fields, a percentage of the parent column's total is shown.
Index	None	Calculates the relative importance of items. For an example, see Figure 3-31.
% of Parent Total	Base Field only	With multiple row and/or column fields, a cell's percentage of the parent item's total is calculated.

TABLE 17-1 *(continued)*

Show Values As	Additional Required Information	Description
Running Total In	Base Field only	Calculates a running total.
% Running Total In	Base Field only	Calculates a running total as a percentage of the total.
Rank Smallest to Largest	Base Field only	Provides a numeric rank, with 1 as the smallest item.
Rank Largest to Smallest	Base Field only	Provides a numeric rank, with 1 as the largest item.
% of	Base Field and Base Item	Expresses the values for one item as a percentage of another item.
Difference From	Base Field and Base Item	Shows the difference of one item compared to another item or to the previous item.
% Difference From	Base Field and Base Item	Shows the percentage difference of one item compared to another item or to the previous item.

The capability to create custom calculations is another example of the unique flexibility of pivot table reports. With the Show Values As setting, you can change the calculation for a particular data field to be based on other cells in the Values area.

The following sections illustrate a number of Show Values As options.

Showing percentage of total

In Figure 3-26, column E shows % Of Total. Jade Miller, with $2.1 million in revenue, represents 31.67% of the $6.7 million total revenue. Column E uses % Of Column Total on the Show Values As tab. Two other similar options are % Of Row Total and % Of Grand Total. Choose one of these based on whether your text fields are going down the report, across the report, or both down and across.

Using % Of to compare one line to another line

The % Of option enables you to compare one item to another item. For example, in the current data set, Anne was the top sales rep in the previous year. Column F shows everyone's sales as a percentage of Anne's. Cell F7 in Figure 3-28 shows that Jeff's sales were almost 58% of Anne's sales.

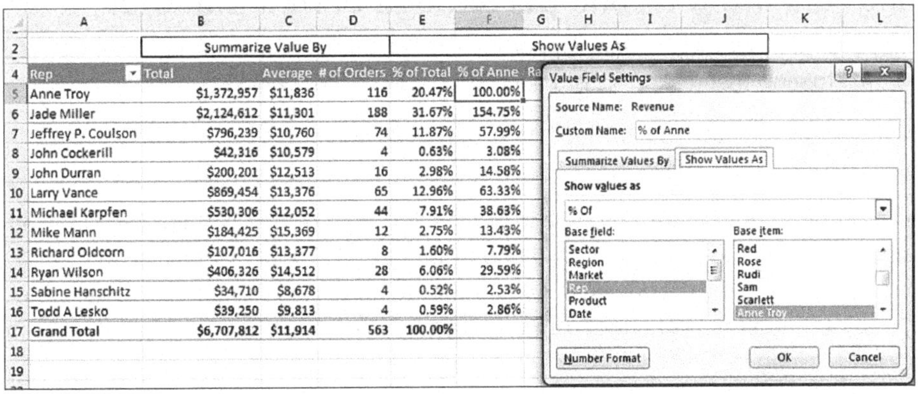

FIGURE 3-28 This report is created using the % Of option with Anne Troy as the Base Item.

To set up this calculation, choose Show Values As, % Of. For Base Field, choose Rep because this is the only field in the Rows area. For the Base Item, choose Anne Troy. The result is shown in Figure 3-29.

Showing rank

Two ranking options are available. Column G in Figure 3-29 shows Rank Largest To Smallest. Jade Miller is ranked #1, and Sabine Hanschitz is #12. A similar option is Rank Smallest To Largest, which would be good for the pro golf tour.

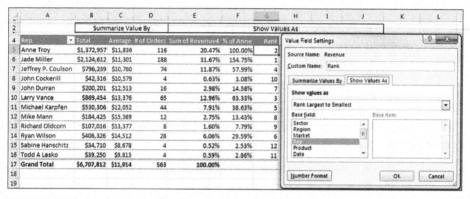

FIGURE 3-29 The Rank options will rank ascending or descending.

To set up a rank, choose Value Field Settings | Show Values As | Rank Largest To Smallest. You are required to choose Base Field. In this example, because Rep is the only row field, it is the selection under Base Field.

These rank options show that pivot tables have a strange way of dealing with ties. I say *strange* because they do not match any of the methods already established by the Excel functions =RANK(), =RANK.AVG(), and =RANK.EQ(). For example, if the top two markets have a tie, they are both assigned a rank of 1, and the third market is assigned a rank of 2.

Tracking running total and percentage of running total

Running total calculations are common in reports where you have months running down the column or when you want to show that the top N customers make up N% of the revenue.

In Figure 3-30, cell I8 shows that the top four sales reps account for 76.97% of the total sales.

> **Note** To produce this figure, you have to use the Sort feature, which is discussed in depth in Chapter 4, "Grouping, sorting, and filtering pivot data." To create a similar analysis with the sample file, go to the dropdown in A4 and choose More Sort Options, Descending, By Total. Also note that the % Change From calculation shown in the next example is not compatible with sorting.

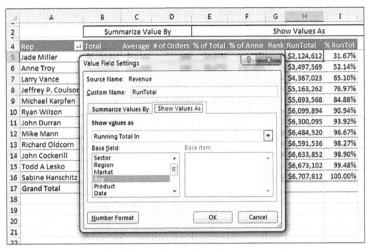

FIGURE 3-30 Show running totals or a running percentage of total.

To specify Running Total In (as shown in Column H) or % Running Total In (Column I), select Field Settings | Show Values As | Running Total In. You have to specify a Base Field, which, in this case, is the Row Field: Rep.

Displaying a change from a previous field

Figure 3-31 shows the % Difference From setting. This calculation requires a Base Field and Base Item. You could show how each market compares to Anne Troy by specifying Anne Troy as the Base Item. This would be similar to Figure 3-26, except each market would be shown as a percentage of Anne Troy.

FIGURE 3-31 The % Difference From options enable you to compare each row to the previous or next row.

With date fields, it would make sense to use % Difference From and choose (Previous) as the base item. Note that the first cell will not have a calculation because there is no previous date in the pivot table.

Tracking the percentage of a parent item

The legacy % Of Total settings always divides the current item by the grand total. In Figure 3-32, cell E4 says that Chicago is 2.75% of the total data set. A common question at the MrExcel.com message board is how to calculate Chicago's revenue as a percentage of the Midwest region total. This was possible but difficult in older versions of Excel. Starting in Excel 2010, though, Excel added the % Of Parent Row, % Of Parent Column, and % Of Parent Total options.

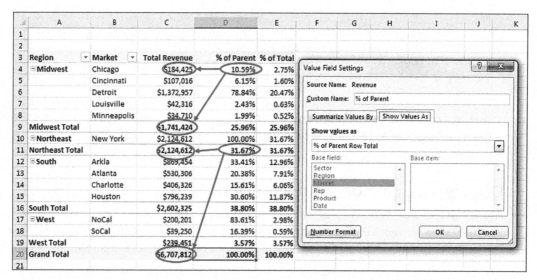

FIGURE 3-32 An option in Excel enables you to calculate a percentage of the parent row.

To set up this calculation in Excel, use Field Settings, Show Values As, % Of Parent Row Total. Cell D4 in Figure 3-32 shows that Chicago's $184,425 is 10.59% of the Midwest total of $1,741,424.

Although it makes sense, the calculation on the subtotal rows might seem confusing. D4:D8 shows the percentage of each market as compared to the Midwest total. The values in D9, D11, D16, and D19 compare the region total to the grand total. For example, the 31.67% in D11 says that the Northeast region's $2.1 million is a little less than a third of the $6.7 million grand total.

Tracking relative importance with the Index option

The final option of the 11 calculations is Index. It creates a somewhat obscure calculation. Microsoft claims that this calculation describes the relative importance of a cell within a column. In Figure 3-33, Georgia peaches have an index of 2.55, and California peaches have an index of 0.50. This shows that if the peach crop is wiped out next year, it will be more devastating to Georgia fruit production than to California fruit production.

	A	B	C	D	E	F	G	H	I
1	Sum of Sales	State ▾						GA Peach	180
2	Crop ▾	California	Georgia		Ohio Grand Total			/ GA Total	210
3	Apple	100	10	30	140			A = Worth of Peaches to GA	0.86
4	Banana	200	10	1	211				
5	Kiwi	200	10	1	211			Peach Total	285
6	Peach	100	180	5	285			/ Total	847
7	Grand Total	600	210	37	847			B = Worth of Peaches	0.34
8									
9								Index is A/B	2.55
10	Index	State ▾							
11	Crop ▾	California	Georgia		Ohio Grand Total				
12	Apple	1.01	0.29	4.91	1.00				
13	Banana	1.34	0.19	0.11	1.00				
14	Kiwi	1.34	0.19	0.11	1.00				
15	Peach	0.50	2.55	0.40	1.00				
16	Grand Total	1.00	1.00	1.00	1.00				

For rows 11 area (right side), the equation shown:

$$= \frac{GeorgiaPeach \div GeorgiaTotal}{PeachTotal \div Total}$$

FIGURE 3-33 Using the Index function, Excel shows that peach sales are more important in Georgia than in California.

Here is the exact calculation:

1. First, divide Georgia peaches by the Georgia total. This is 180/210, or 0.857.

2. Next, divide total peach production (285) by total fruit production (847). This shows that peaches have an importance ratio of 0.336.

3. Now, divide the first ratio by the second ratio: 0.857/0.336.

In Ohio, apples have an index of 4.91, so an apple blight would be bad for the Ohio fruit industry.

I have to admit that even after writing about this calculation for 10 years, there are parts I don't quite comprehend. What if a state like Hawaii relied on the production of lychees, but lychees were nearly immaterial to US fruit production? If lychees were half of Hawaii's fruit production but just 0.001 of US fruit production, the Index calculation would skyrocket to 500.

Adding and removing subtotals

Subtotals are an essential feature of pivot table reporting. Sometimes, you might want to suppress the display of subtotals, and other times, you might want to show more than one subtotal per field.

Suppressing subtotals with many row fields

When you have many row fields in a report, subtotals can obscure your view. For example, in Figure 3-34, there is no need to show subtotals for each market because there is only one sales rep for each market.

3	Region	Market	Rep	Sum of Revenue
4	⊟Midwest	⊟Chicago	Mike Mann	184425
5		Chicago Total		184425
6		⊟Cincinnati	Richard Oldcorn	107016
7		Cincinnati Total		107016
8		⊟Detroit	Anne Troy	1372957
9		Detroit Total		1372957
10		⊟Louisville	John Cockerill	42316
11		Louisville Total		42316
12		⊟Minneapolis	Sabine Hanschitz	34710
13		Minneapolis Total		34710
14	Midwest Total			1741424
15	⊟Northeast	⊟New York	Jade Miller	2124612
16		New York Total		2124612
17	Northeast Total			2124612
18	⊟South	⊟Arkla	Larry Vance	869454
19		Arkla Total		869454

FIGURE 3-34 Sometimes, you do not need subtotals at every level.

If you used the Subtotals dropdown on the Design tab, you would turn off all subtotals, including the Region subtotals and the Market subtotals. The Region subtotals are still providing good information, so you want to use the Subtotals setting in the Field Settings dialog. Choose one cell in the Market column. On the PivotTable Analyze tab, choose Field Settings. Change the Subtotals setting from Automatic to None (see Figure 3-35).

FIGURE 3-35 Use the Subtotals setting in the Field list to turn off subtotals for one field.

To remove subtotals for the Market field, click the Market field in the bottom section of the PivotTable Fields list. Select Field Settings. In the Field Settings dialog, select None under Subtotals, as shown in Figure 3-35. Alternatively, right-click a cell that contains a Market and remove the checkmark from Subtotal Market.

Adding multiple subtotals for one field

You can add customized subtotals to a row or column label field. Select the Region field at the bottom of the PivotTable Fields list, and select Field Settings.

In the Field Settings dialog for the Region field, select Custom and then select the types of subtotals you would like to see. In Figure 3-36, five custom subtotals are selected for the Region field. It is rare to see pivot tables use this setting. It is not perfect. Note that the count of 211 records in cell D25 automatically gets a currency format like the rest of the column, even though this is not a dollar figure. Also, the average of $12,333 for South is an average of the detail records, not an average of the individual market totals.

	A	B	C	D	E	F	G	H
19	Northeast Min			$1,741	Field Settings			
20	South	Arkla	Larry Vance	$869,454				
21		Atlanta	Michael Karpfen	$530,306	Source Name: Region			
22		Charlotte	Ryan Wilson	$406,326	Custom Name: Region			
23		Houston	Jeffrey P. Coulson	$796,239				
24	South Sum			$2,602,325	Subtotals & Filters	Layout & Print		
25	South Count			$211	Subtotals			
26	South Average			$12,333	Automatic			
27	South Max			$25,350	None			
28	South Min			$1,740	Custom			
29	West	NoCal	John Durran	$200,201	Select one or more functions:			
30		SoCal	Todd A Lesko	$39,250	Sum / Count / Average / Max / Min / Product			
31	West Sum			$239,451				
32	West Count			$20				
33	West Average			$11,973	Filter			
34	West Max			$21,730	Include new items in manual filter			
35	West Min			$2,358				

FIGURE 3-36 By selecting the Custom option in the Subtotals section, you can specify multiple subtotals for one field.

Tip If you need to calculate the average of the four regions, you can do it with the DAX formula language and Power Pivot. See Chapter 10.

Formatting one cell is new in Microsoft 365

In the summer of 2018, a new trick appeared for Microsoft 365 customers. You can format a cell in a pivot table, and the formatting will move with that position.

For example, in Figure 3-37, a white font on dark fill has been applied to Revenue for Doodads sales to the Software sector.

If you rearrange the pivot table, the dark formatting will follow the cell in the pivot table. While cell B9 was formatted in Figure 3-37, the formatting has moved to D5 in Figure 3-38.

Note that the formatting will persist if you remove the cell with a filter. If you unselect Software from the Slicer and then reselect Software, the formatting will return.

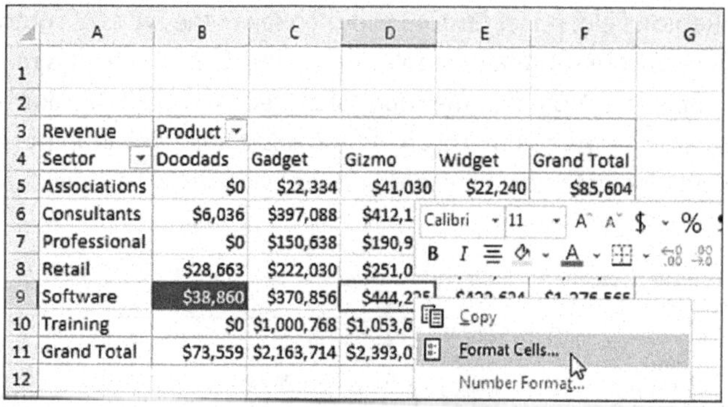

Revenue	Product				
Sector	Doodads	Gadget	Gizmo	Widget	Grand Total
Associations	$0	$22,334	$41,030	$22,240	$85,604
Consultants	$6,036	$397,088	$412,1		
Professional	$0	$150,638	$190,9		
Retail	$28,663	$222,030	$251,0		
Software	$38,860	$370,856	$444,2		
Training	$0	$1,000,768	$1,053,6		
Grand Total	$73,559	$2,163,714	$2,393,0		

FIGURE 3-37 A new Format Cells option appears in the right-click context menu.

However, if you remove Sector, Product, or Revenue from the pivot table, the individual cell formatting will be lost.

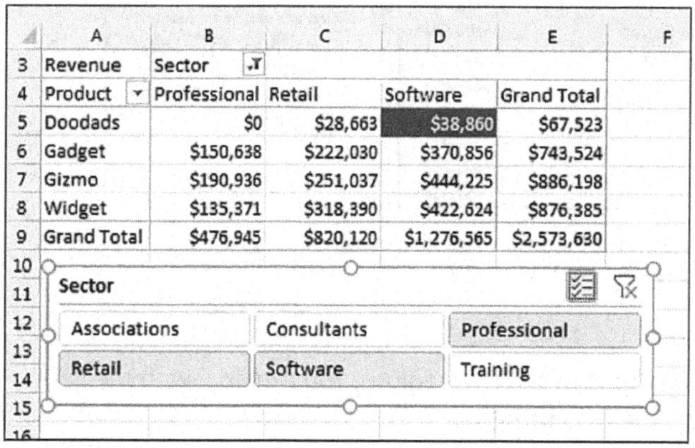

Revenue	Sector			
Product	Professional	Retail	Software	Grand Total
Doodads	$0	$28,663	$38,860	$67,523
Gadget	$150,638	$222,030	$370,856	$743,524
Gizmo	$190,936	$251,037	$444,225	$886,198
Widget	$135,371	$318,390	$422,624	$876,385
Grand Total	$476,945	$820,120	$1,276,565	$2,573,630

FIGURE 3-38 Rearrange the pivot table and the formatting moves so that revenue for Doodads sales to the Software sector stays formatted.

In Figure 3-39, a Customer field has been added as the inner-row field. The dark formatting applied to Doodads sales of Software is now expanded to C5:C8 to encompass all four customers in this group. Note that in cell C9, the subtotal for Doodads sold to the Software sector is not formatted.

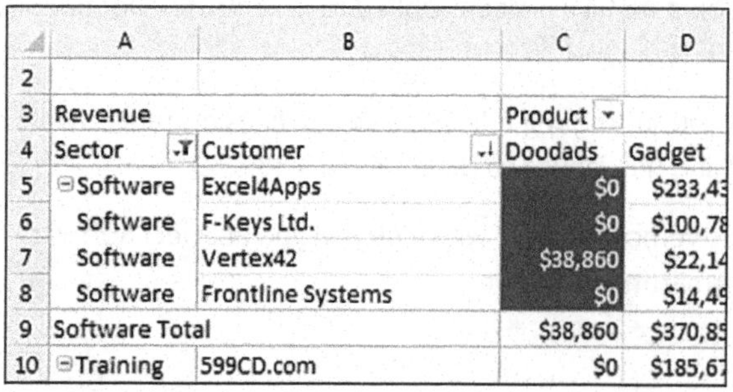

Revenue		Product	
Sector	Customer	Doodads	Gadget
Software	Excel4Apps	$0	$233,4
Software	F-Keys Ltd.	$0	$100,7
Software	Vertex42	$38,860	$22,14
Software	Frontline Systems	$0	$14,4
Software Total		$38,860	$370,8
Training	599CD.com	$0	$185,6

FIGURE 3-39 If you add an inner-row field, the formatting will expand to encompass all customers for Doodads in the Software sector.

Next Steps

Note that the following pivot table customizations are covered in Chapter 4, "Grouping, sorting, and filtering pivot data," and Chapter 5, "Performing calculations in pivot tables":

- **Chapter 4**
  - Sorting a pivot table
  - Filtering records in a pivot table
  - Grouping daily dates up to months or years
  - Using data visualizations and conditional formatting in a pivot table

- **Chapter 5**
  - Adding new calculated fields

Grouping, sorting, and filtering pivot data

In this chapter, you will:

- Use the PivotTable Fields pane

- Sort in a pivot table

- Filter a pivot table

- Use filters for row and column fields

- Filter using the Filters area

- Group and create hierarchies in a pivot table

First, a quick overview of the PivotTable Fields. Then, a detailed look at sorting, filtering, and grouping a pivot table.

Using the PivotTable Fields pane

The entry points for sorting and filtering are spread throughout the Excel interface. It is worth taking a closer look at the row header dropdowns and the PivotTable Fields pane before diving into sorting and filtering.

As you've seen in these pages, I rarely use the Compact form for a pivot table. I use Pivot Table Defaults to make sure my pivot tables start in a Tabular layout instead of a Compact layout. Although there are many good reasons for this, one is illustrated in Figures 4-1 and 4-2.

In Figure 4-1, a Region dropdown appears in A3, and a Customer dropdown appears in B3. Each of these separate dropdowns offers great settings for sorting and filtering.

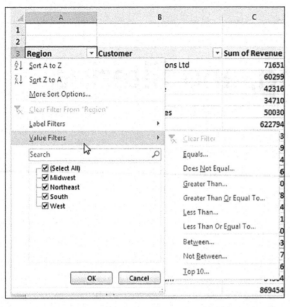

FIGURE 4-1 The dropdown in B3 for Customer is separate from the dropdown for Region.

When you leave the pivot table in the Compact form, there are no separate headings for Region and Customer. Both fields are crammed into column A, with the silly heading, Row Labels. This means the dropdown always offers sorting and filtering options for Region. Every time you go back to the A3 dropdown with hopes of filtering or sorting the Customer field, you have to reselect Customer from a dropdown at the top of the menu. This is an extra click. If you are making five changes to the Customer field, you are reselecting Customer over and over and over and over and over. This should be enough to convince you to abandon the Compact layout as shown in Figure 4.2.

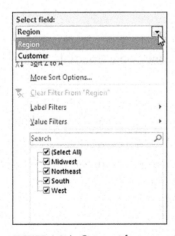

FIGURE 4-2 In Compact form, one single dropdown tries to control sorting and filtering for all the row fields.

If you decide to keep the Compact layout and get frustrated with the consolidated Row Labels dropdown, you can directly access the invisible dropdown for the correct field by using the PivotTable

Fields pane, which contains a visible dropdown for every field in the areas at the bottom. Those visible dropdowns do not contain the sorting and filtering options.

The good dropdowns are actually at the top of the Fields pane, but you have to hover over the field to see them. After you hover as shown in Figure 4-3, you can directly access the same customer dropdown shown in Figure 4-1.

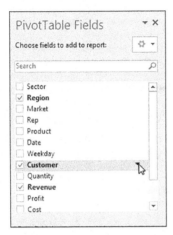

FIGURE 4-3 Hover over the field at the top of the Fields pane to directly access the sorting and filtering settings for that field.

Docking and undocking the PivotTable Fields pane

The PivotTable Fields pane starts out docked on the right side of the Excel window. Hover over the PivotTable Fields heading in the pane, and the mouse pointer changes to a four-headed arrow. Drag to the left to enable the pane to float anywhere in your Excel window.

After you have undocked the PivotTable Fields pane, you might find that it is difficult to redock it on either side of the screen. To redock the Fields pane, you must grab the title bar and drag until at least 85 percent of the Fields pane is off the edge of the window. Pretend that you are trying to remove the floating Fields pane completely from the screen. Eventually, Excel gets the hint and redocks it. Note that you can dock the PivotTable Fields pane on either the right side or the left side of the screen.

Minimizing the PivotTable Fields pane

In 2020, a new feature appeared that was designed to minimize the space taken up by multiple task panes. If you get into a situation where you have two or more task panes displayed, Excel will show a dock along the right side of the screen. The active pane will be visible, and the others will be reduced to an icon on the task pane dock.

There is no way to invoke this dock until you've displayed two task panes at the same time. Here is an easy way to get two task panes open: With a text cell in your pivot table selected, go to the Review tab and choose Smart Lookup. Excel will display a task pane where you can see that the PivotTable Fields pane is reduced to an icon, as shown in Figure 4-4.

PivotTable Fields collapsed ⌐

Search pane is active ⌐

FIGURE 4-4 A new Task Pane dock tries to avoid the situation where four open task panes cover most of the grid.

What if you really want two task panes displayed at the same time? Display the PivotTable Fields pane, follow the previous instructions to undock it, and then dock it off the left side of the screen. Anything docked to the left side will not participate in the task pane docking panel.

Rearranging the PivotTable Fields pane

As shown in Figure 4-5, a small gear-wheel icon appears near the top of the PivotTable Fields pane. Select this dropdown to see its five possible arrangements. Although the default is to have the Fields section at the top of the list and the Areas section at the bottom of the list, four other arrangements are possible. Other options let you control whether the fields in the list appear alphabetically or in the same sequence that they appeared in the original data set.

Microsoft's Howie Dickerman, who ran the pivot table team for many years, said that the arrangement shown in Figure 4-5 is his favorite. It allows more room to see all of the fields and room for the four areas.

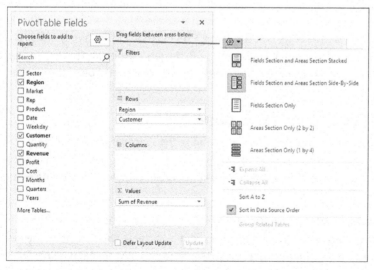

FIGURE 4-5 Use this dropdown to rearrange the PivotTable Fields pane.

The final three arrangements offered in the dropdown are rather confusing. If someone changes the PivotTable Fields pane to show only the Areas section, you cannot see new fields to add to the pivot table.

If you ever encounter a version of the PivotTable Fields pane with only the Areas section or only the Fields section, remember that you can return to a less confusing view of the data by using the arrangement dropdown.

Using the Areas section dropdowns

As shown in Figure 4-6, every field in the Areas section has a visible dropdown arrow. When you select this dropdown arrow, you see four categories of choices:

- The first four choices enable you to rearrange the field within the list of fields in that area of the pivot table. You can accomplish this by dragging the field up or down in the area.

- The next four choices enable you to move the field to a new area. You could also accomplish this by dragging the field to a new area.

- The next choice enables you to remove the field from the pivot table. You can also accomplish this by dragging the field outside the Fields pane.

- The final choice displays the Field Settings dialog for the field.

FIGURE 4-6 Use this dropdown to rearrange the fields in your pivot table.

Sorting in a pivot table

Items in the row area and column area of a pivot table are sorted in ascending order by any custom list first. This allows weekday and month names to be sorted into Monday, Tuesday, Wednesday, ... instead of the alphabetical order Friday, Monday, Saturday, ..., Wednesday.

If the items do not appear in a custom list, they will be sorted in ascending order. This is fine, but in many situations, you want the customer with the largest revenue to appear at the top of the list. When you sort in descending order using a pivot table, you are setting up a rule that controls how that field is sorted, even after new fields are added to the pivot table.

> **Tip** Excel includes four custom lists by default, but you can add your own custom list to control the sort order of future pivot tables. See "Using a custom list for sorting" later in this chapter.

Sorting customers into high-to-low sequence based on revenue

Three pivot tables appear in Figure 4-7. The first pivot table shows the default sort for a pivot table: Customers are arranged alphabetically, starting with Adaept, Calleia, and so on.

In the second pivot table, the report is sorted in descending sequence by Total Revenue. This pivot table was sorted by selecting cell E3 and choosing the ZA icon in the Data tab of the ribbon. Although that sounds like a regular sort, it is better. When you sort inside a pivot table, Excel sets up a rule that will be used after you make additional changes to the pivot table.

	A	B	C	D	E	F	G	H
1	Customers AZ is default			Sort descending by revenue			After adding fields, sort rule remains	
2								
3	Customer	Total $		Customer	Total $			Total $
4	Adaept Information Mana	498937		MySpreadsheetLab	869454		⊟Consulting	2555333
5	Calleia Company	406326		Surten Excel	750163		Surten Excel	750163
6	Excel Design Solutions Ltd	71651		SkyWire, Inc.	704359		NetCom Computer	613514
7	Excel Learning Zone	72680		SpringBoard	622794		Adaept Information N	498937
8	Excel4Apps	91320		NetCom Computer	613514		Calleia Company	406326
9	Excel-Translator.de	42316		St. Peter's Prep	568851		Excel Design Solution	71651
10	F-Keys Ltd.	34710		Adaept Information Mana	498937		Yesenita	62744
11	JEVS Human Services	50030		The Salem Ohio Historical	427349		Symons	55251
12	LearnExcelBooks.com	34364		Calleia Company	406326		JEVS Human Services	50030
13	MyExcelOnline.com	54048		MyOnlineTrainingHub.cor	390978		Spain Enterprises	46717
14	MyOnlineTrainingHub.con	390978		Excel4Apps	91320		⊟Museums	427349
15	MySpreadsheetLab	869454		Excel Learning Zone	72680		The Salem Ohio Histo	427349

FIGURE 4-7 When you override the default sort, Excel remembers the sort as additional fields are added.

The pivot table in columns G:H shows what happens after you add Sector as a new outer row field. Within each sector, the pivot table continues to sort the data in descending order by revenue. Within Consulting, Surten Excel appears first, with $750K, followed by NetCom, with $614K.

You could remove Customer from the pivot table, make more adjustments, and then add Customer back to the column area, and Excel would remember that the customers should be presented from high to low.

If you could see the entire pivot table in G3:H35 in Figure 4-7, you would notice that the sectors are sorted alphabetically. It might make more sense, though, to put the largest sectors at the top. The following tricks can be used for sorting an outer row field by revenue:

- You can select cell G4 and then use Collapse Field on the PivotTable Analyze tab to hide the customer details. When you have only the sectors showing, select H4 and click ZA to sort descending. Excel understands that you want to set up a sort rule for the Sector field.

- You can temporarily remove Customer from the pivot table, sort descending by revenue, and then add Customer back.

- You can use More Sort Options, as described in the following paragraphs.

To sort the Sector field, you should open the dropdown for the Sector field. If your pivot table is in Compact Form, finding the dropdown arrow is super confusing. Find the Sector field in the PivotTable Fields pane. When you hover the mouse over the Sector field, a secret dropdown arrow appears. Click that arrow, and the menu shown in Figure 4-8 will appear.

This is just one more reason why I prefer Tabular or Outline form. In either of those, a dropdown arrow will always be visible on the word "Sector" in the pivot table.

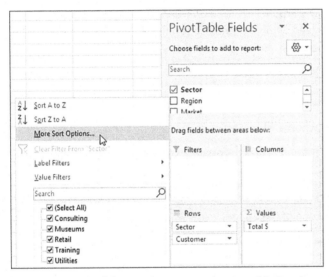

FIGURE 4-8 For explicit control over sort order, open this dropdown.

Inside the dropdown, choose More Sort Options to open the Sort (Sector) dialog. In this dialog, you can choose to sort the Sector field in Descending order by Total $ (see Figure 4-9).

The Sort (Sector) dialog shown in Figure 4-9 includes a More Options button in the lower left. If you click this button, you arrive at the More Sort Options dialog (Figure 4-10), in which you can specify a custom list to be used for the first key sort order. You can also specify that the sorting should be based on a column other than Grand Total.

FIGURE 4-9 Choose to sort Sector based on the Total $ field.

In Figure 4-11, the pivot table includes Product in the column area. If you wanted to sort the customers based on total gadget revenue instead of total revenue, for example, you could do so with the More Sort Options dialog by following these steps:

1. Open the Customer heading dropdown in A4.

2. Choose More Sort Options.

3. In the Sort (Customer) dialog, choose More Options.

4. In the More Sort Options (Customer) dialog, choose the Sort By Values In Selected Column option (see Figure 4-10).

5. Click in the reference box and then click cell C5. Note that you cannot click the Gadget heading in C4; you have to choose one of the Gadget value cells.

6. Click OK twice to return to the pivot table.

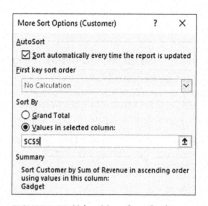

FIGURE 4-10 Using More Sort Options, you can sort by a specific pivot field item.

If your pivot table has only one field in the Rows area, you can set up the "Sort by Doodads" rule by doing a simple sort using the Data tab. Select any cell in B5:B30 and choose Data, ZA. The pivot table will be sorted with the largest Doodads customers at the top (see Figure 4-11). Note that you cannot sort from the Doodads heading in B4. Sorting from there will sort the product columns by revenue.

	A	B	C	D	E
3	Total $	Product			
4	Customer	Doodads	Gadget	Gizmo	Widget
5	Excel Learning Zone	38860	22140	11680	0
6	Excel4Apps	28663	20115	30068	12474
7	Excel-Translator.de	6036	18552	17728	0
8	JEVS Human Services	0	30104	4614	15312
9	MySpreadsheetLab	0	304198	288409	276847
10	Adaept Information Management	0	182755	173770	142412

FIGURE 4-11 Sort from cell B5 to sort by Doodads.

Using a manual sort sequence

The Sort dialog offers something called a *manual sort*. Rather than using the dialog, you can invoke a manual sort in a surprising way.

Note that the products in Figure 4-11 are in the following order: Doodads, Gadget, Gizmo, and Widget. It appears that the Doodads product line is a minor product line and probably would not fall first in the product list.

Place the cell pointer in cell E4 and type **Doodads**. When you press Enter, Excel figures out that you want to move the Doodads column to be last. All the values for this product line move from column B to column E. The values for the remaining products shift to the left.

One unintended consequence is that the customers re-sort based on the product that moved to column B: Gadget. This is because the "Sort by Doodads" rule was actually a "Sort by whatever is in column B" rule.

In Figure 4-12, note the numbers in row 17 and compare them to the numbers in row 5 in Figure 4-11. The values followed the change in headings.

This behavior is completely unintuitive. You should never try this behavior with a regular (non-pivot table) data set in Excel. You would never expect Excel to change the data sequence just by moving the labels. Figure 4-12 shows the pivot table after a new column heading has been typed in cell E4.

If you prefer to use the mouse, you can drag and drop the column heading to a new location. Select a column heading. Hover over the edge of the active cell border until the mouse changes to a four-headed arrow. Drag the cell to a new location, as shown in Figure 4-13. When you release the mouse, all the value settings move to the new column.

A	B	C	D	E	F
3 Total $	Product ▾				
4 Customer	↓ Gadget	Gizmo	Widget	Doodads	Grand Total
5 St. Peter's Prep	367915	200936	0	0	568851
6 MySpreadsheetLab	304198	288409	276847	0	869454
7 Surten Excel	233435	235761	280967	0	750163
8 NetCom Computer	204234	205758	203522	0	613514
9 SpringBoard	185675	245491	191628	0	622794
10 SkyWire, Inc.	185286	224935	294138	0	704359
11 Adaept Information Management	182755	173770	142412	0	498937
12 The Salem Ohio Historical Society	178254	149551	99544	0	427349
13 Calleia Company	133009	159354	113963	0	406326
14 MyOnlineTrainingHub.com	100784	165727	124467	0	390978
15 IFVS Human Services	30104	4614	15312	0	50030
16 Vertex42	26484	19544	13853	0	59881
17 Excel Learning Zone	22140	11680	0	38860	72680
18 Excel Design Solutions Ltd	20950	41066	9635	0	71651
19 MyExcelOnline.com	20610	7032	26406	0	54048
20 Excel4Apps	20115	30068	12474	28663	91320
21 Spain Enterprises	19520	25378	1819	0	46717

FIGURE 4-12 Simply type a heading in E4 to rearrange the columns.

A	B	C	D	E	F
3 Total $	Product ▾			D4:D31	
4 Customer	↓ Gadget	Gizmo	Widget	Doodads	Grand Total
5 St. Peter's Prep	367915	200936	0	0	568851
6 MySpreadsheetLab	304198	288409	276847	0	869454
7 Surten Excel	233435	235761	280967	0	750163
8 NetCom Computer	204234	205758	203522	0	613514
9 SpringBoard	185675	245491	191628	0	622794
10 SkyWire, Inc.	185286	224935	294138	0	704359

FIGURE 4-13 Use drag and drop to move a column to a new position.

> **Caution**   After you use a manual sort, any new products you add to the data source are automatically added to the end of the list rather than appearing alphabetically.

Using a custom list for sorting

Another way to permanently change the order of items along a dimension is to set up a custom list. All future pivot tables created on your computer will automatically respect the order of the items in a custom list.

The pivot table at the top of Figure 4-14 includes weekday names. The weekday names were added to the original data set by using =TEXT(F2,"DDD") and copying it down. Excel automatically puts Sun first and Sat last, even though this is not the alphabetical sequence of these words, because Excel ships with four custom lists to control the days of the week, months of the year, and the three-letter abbreviations for both.

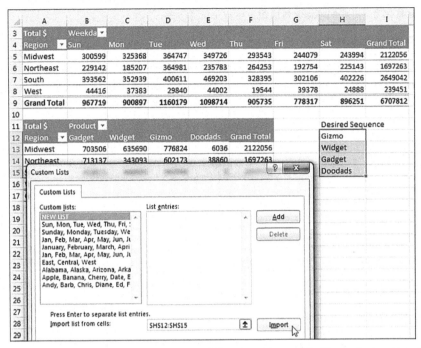

	A	B	C	D	E	F	G	H	I
3	Total $	Weekda							
4	Region	Sun	Mon	Tue	Wed	Thu	Fri	Sat	Grand Total
5	Midwest	300599	325368	364747	349726	293543	244079	243994	2122056
6	Northeast	229142	185207	364981	235783	264253	192754	225143	1697263
7	South	393562	352939	400611	469203	328395	302106	402226	2649042
8	West	44416	37383	29840	44002	19544	39378	24888	239451
9	Grand Total	967719	900897	1160179	1098714	905735	778317	896251	6707812
10									
11	Total $	Product						Desired Sequence	
12	Region	Gadget	Widget	Gizmo	Doodads	Grand Total		Gizmo	
13	Midwest	703506	635690	776824	6036	2122056		Widget	
14	Northeast	713137	343093	602173	38860	1697263		Gadget	

Custom Lists

Custom Lists

Custom lists: List entries:

NEW LIST
Sun, Mon, Tue, Wed, Thu, Fri, :   Add
Sunday, Monday, Tuesday, We
Jan, Feb, Mar, Apr, May, Jun, Ju   Delete
January, February, March, Apri
Jan, Feb, Mar, Apr, May, Jun, Ju
East, Central, West
Alabama, Alaska, Arizona, Arka
Apple, Banana, Cherry, Date, E
Andy, Barb, Chris, Diane, Ed, F

Press Enter to separate list entries.
Import list from cells: $H$12:$H$15   Import

FIGURE 4-14 The weekday names in B4:H4 follow the order specified in the Custom Lists dialog.

> **Note** Pivot tables will also automatically sort quarters that are entered as **JFM**, **AMJ**, **JAS**, and **OND**, where JFM is an abbreviation for January, February, and March. This special sorting routine is hard-coded into Excel and only works for English month names. I reached out to the elders from the Excel team, and there is some recollection that the logic was added in the 1990s, likely at the request of a particular customer. It was recently discovered when a new coworker named Jas (perhaps short for Jasmine?) started sorting to the top of the pivot table.

You can define your own custom list to control the sort order of pivot tables. Follow these steps to set up a custom list:

1. In an out-of-the-way section of the worksheet, type the products in their desired sequence. Type one product per cell, going down a column.

2. Select the cells containing the list of regions in the proper sequence.

3. Click the File tab and select Options.

4. Select the Advanced category in the left navigation bar. Scroll down to the General group and click the Edit Custom Lists button. In the Custom Lists dialog, your selection address is entered in the Import text box, as shown in Figure 4-14.

5. Click Import to bring the products in as a new list.

6. Click OK to close the Custom Lists dialog, and then click OK to close the Excel Options dialog.

The custom list is now stored on your computer and is available for all future Excel sessions. All future pivot tables will automatically show the product field in the order specified in the custom list. Figure 4-15 shows a new pivot table created after the custom list was set up.

	A	B	C	D	E	F
3	Sum of Profit	Product ⌄				
4	Market ⌄	Gizmo	Widget	Gadget	Doodads	Grand Total
5	New York	273896	150766	318020	16996	759678
6	Arkla	124684	123662	133824	0	382170
7	Atlanta	81760	64372	87576	0	233708
8	Charlotte	71540	49973	57072	0	178585

FIGURE 4-15 After you define a custom list, all future pivot tables will follow the order in the list.

To sort an existing pivot table by the newly defined custom list, follow these steps:

1. Open the Product header dropdown and choose More Sort Options.

2. In the Sort (Product) dialog, choose More Options.

3. In the More Sort Options (Product) dialog, clear the AutoSort checkbox.

4. As shown in Figure 4-16, in the More Sort Options (Product) dialog, open the First Key Sort Order dropdown and select the custom list with your product names.

5. Click OK twice.

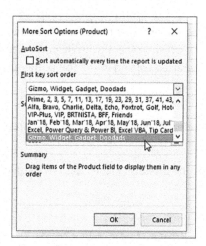

FIGURE 4-16 Choose to sort by the custom list.

Caution Items in a custom list will automatically sort to the top of all future pivot tables. If you have a pivot table of people using their first names, people with names like Jan, May, and April will automatically appear before other names. Names that appear in any list, even across several custom lists, will be sorted in the wrong sequence. To turn off this behavior for one pivot table, right-click one cell in the pivot table and choose PivotTable options. On the Totals & Filters tab, deselect Use Custom Lists When Sorting. If you want to turn this off for all pivot tables, change the Pivot Table Defaults by choosing File | Options | Data | Edit Default Layout | PivotTable Options.

Filtering a pivot table: An overview

Excel provides dozens of ways to filter a pivot table. Figure 4-17 shows some of the filters available. These methods—and the best way to use each one—are discussed in the following sections.

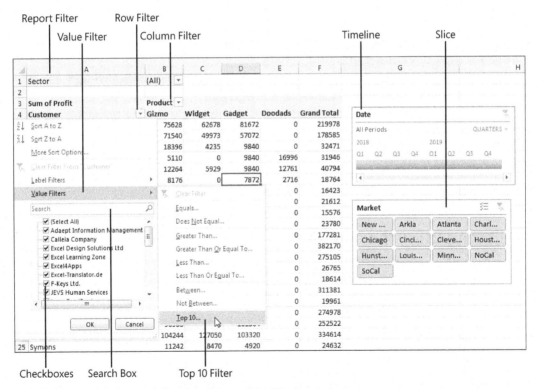

FIGURE 4-17 This figure shows a fraction of the available filtering choices.

There are many ways to filter a pivot table, as shown in Figure 4-17:

- The Date Timeline filter in G4:H10 was introduced in Excel 2013.

- The Market filter in G12:H19 is an example of the slicer introduced in Excel 2010.

- A dropdown in B1 offers what were known as "page filters" in Excel 2003, "report filters" in Excel 2010, and now simply "filters."

- Cell G4 offers the top-secret AutoFilter location.

- Dropdowns in A4 and B3 lead to even more filters.

- You see the traditional checkbox filters for each pivot item.

- A Search box filter was introduced in Excel 2010.

- A flyout menu has Label filters.

- Depending on the field type, you might see a Value Filters flyout menu, including the powerful Top 10 filter, which can do Top 10, Bottom 5, Bottom 3%, Top $8 Million, and more.

- Depending on the field type, you might see a Date Filters flyout menu with 37 virtual filters, such as Next Month, Last Year, and Year to Date.

Using filters for row and column fields

If you have a field (or fields) in the row or column area of a pivot table, a dropdown with filtering choices appears on the header cell for that field. In Figure 4-17—shown in the previous section—a Customer dropdown appears in A4, and a Product dropdown appears in B3. The pivot table in that figure uses a Tabular layout. If your pivot tables use a Compact layout, you see a dropdown on the cell with Row Labels or Column Labels.

If you have multiple row fields, it is just as easy to sort using the invisible dropdowns that appear when you hover over a field at the top of the PivotTable Fields pane.

Filtering using the checkboxes

You might have a few annoying products appear in a pivot table. In the present example, the Doodads product line is a specialty product with very little sales. It might be an old legacy product that is out of line, but it still gets an occasional order from the scrap bin. Every company seems to have these orphan sales that no one really wants to see.

The checkbox filter provides an easy way to hide these items. Open the Product dropdown and clear the Doodads checkbox. The product is hidden from view (see Figure 4-18).

What if you need to clear hundreds of items' checkboxes in order to leave only a few items selected? You can toggle all items off or on by using the Select All checkbox at the top of the list. You can then select the few items that you want to show in the pivot table.

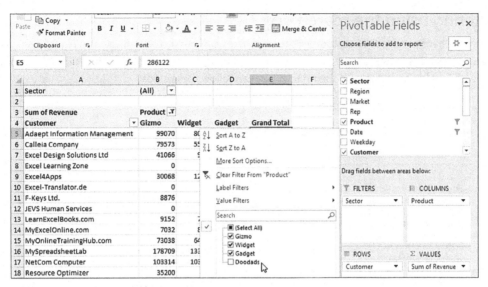

FIGURE 4-18 Open the Product filter and clear the Doodads checkbox.

In Figure 4-19, Select All turned off all customers, and then two clicks reselected Excel4Apps and F-Keys Ltd.

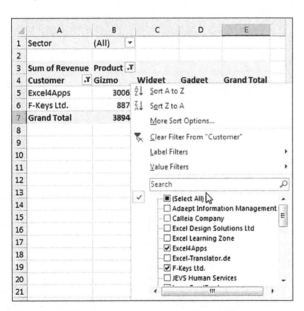

FIGURE 4-19 Use Select All to toggle all items off or on.

The checkboxes work great in this tiny data set with 26 customers. In real life, with 500 customers in the list, it will not be this easy to filter your data set by using the checkboxes.

Filtering using the search box

When you have hundreds of customers, the search box can be a great timesaver. In Figure 4-20, the database includes consultants, trainers, and other companies. If you want to narrow the list to companies with *Excel* or *spreadsheet* in their name, you can follow these steps:

1. Open the Customer dropdown.

2. Type **Excel** in the search box (see Figure 4-20).

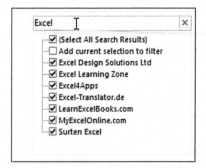

FIGURE 4-20 Select the results of the first search.

3. By default, Select All Search Results is selected. Click OK.

4. Open the Customer dropdown again.

5. Type **spreadsheet** in the search box.

6. Choose Add Current Selection to Filter, as shown in Figure 4-21. Click OK.

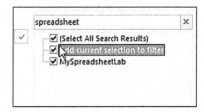

FIGURE 4-21 For the second search, add these results to the existing filter.

You now have all customers with either "Excel" or "spreadsheet" in the name.

 Caution Filters applied with the search box are single-use filters. If you add more data to the underlying data and refresh the pivot table, this filter will not be reevaluated.

If you need to reapply the filter, it would be better to use the Label filters as discussed in the following section. Label filters would work to find every customer with Excel in the name. It would not find "Excel or spreadsheet."

Filtering using the Label Filters option

What if you want to find all the Lotus 1-2-3 consultants and turn those off? There is an unintuitive way to toggle all search results to off. However, most people will find it easier to use the Label filters. The Label Filters option enables you to handle queries such as "select all customers that do not contain 'Lotus'."

Text fields offer a flyout menu called Label Filters. To filter out all of the Insurance customers, you can apply a Does Not Contain filter (see Figure 4-22). In the next dialog, you can specify that you want customers that do not contain Excel, Exc, or Exc*.

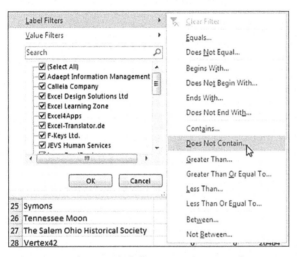

FIGURE 4-22 Choose Label Filters, Does Not Contain.

While choosing Labels Filters | Does Not Contain makes sense, there is a potentially faster way to exclude all items that say Excel. I will describe the four steps, but I have to admit that they are so unintuitive I have to come back to this page in the book every time I want to try them.

To remove all items that contain a word, such as "excel," follow these steps:

1. Open the filter dropdown for Customer. Type **excel** in the search box. Excel will show all of the customers that contain the words "excel", "Excel", or "EXCEL". All of the customers will be selected, as shown in Figure 4-23.

2. Unselect Select All Search Results. This will toggle all of the visible entries below the search box to Off.

3. Select Add Current Selection To Filter. This unintuitive step will apply the current unselected state of the seven visible customers to the filter.

4. Click OK. The filter will hide all of the matching customers.

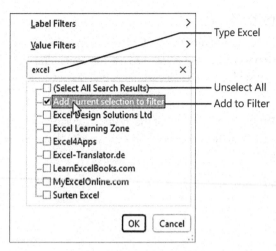

FIGURE 4-23 Three unintuitive steps to toggle matching customers to be hidden.

Note that label filters are not additive. You can only apply one label filter at a time. If you take the data in Figure 4-22 and apply a new label filter between D and Fzzz, some Excel customers that were filtered out reappear, as shown in Figure 4-24.

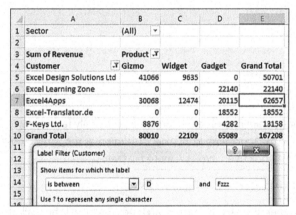

FIGURE 4-24 Note that a second label filter does not get added to the previous filter. Excel is back in.

Filtering a Label column using information in a Values column

The Value Filters flyout menu enables you to filter customers based on information in the Values columns. Perhaps you want to see customers who had between $20,000 and $30,000 of revenue. You can use the Customer heading dropdown to control this. Here's how:

1. Open the Customer dropdown.

2. Choose Label Filters.

3. Choose Between (see Figure 4-25).

4. Type the values **20000** and **30000**, as shown in Figure 4-26.

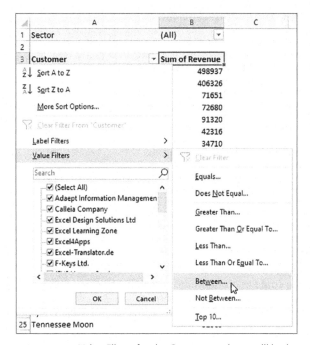

FIGURE 4-25 Value Filters for the Customer column will look at values in the Revenue field.

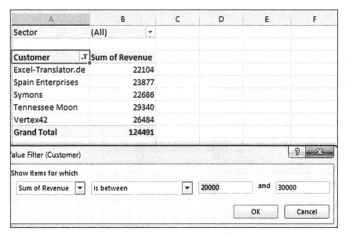

FIGURE 4-26 Choose customers between 20000 and 30000, inclusive.

5. Click OK.

The results are inclusive; if a customer had exactly $20,000 or exactly $30,000, they are returned along with the customers between $20,000 and $30,000.

 Note Choosing a Value filter clears out any previous Label filters.

Creating a top-five report using the Top 10 filter

One of the more interesting value filters is the Top 10 filter. If you are sending a report to the VP of Sales, they will not want to see hundreds of pages of customers. One short summary of the top customers is almost more than the VP's attention span can handle. Here's how to create it:

1. Go to the Customer dropdown and choose Value Filters, Top 10.

2. In the Top 10 Filter dialog, which enables you to choose Top or Bottom, leave the default Top setting.

3. In the second field, enter any number of customers: 10, 5, 7, 12, or something else.

4. In the third dropdown on the dialog, select Items, Percent, or Sum. You could ask for the top 10 items. You could ask for the top 80 percent of revenue (which the theory says should be 20 percent of the customers). Or you could ask for enough customers to reach a sum of $5 million (see Figure 4-27).

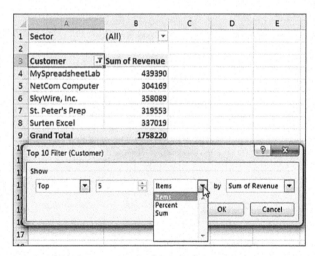

FIGURE 4-27 Create a report of the top five customers.

The $1,758,220 total shown in cell B9 in Figure 4-27 is the revenue of only the visible customers. It does not include the revenue for the remaining customers. You might want to show the grand total of all customers at the bottom of the list. You have a few options:

- A setting on the Design tab, under the Subtotals dropdown, enables you to include values from filtered items in the totals. This option is available only for OLAP data sets and data sets where you choose Add This Data To The Data Model when creating the pivot table.

Note See Chapter 10, "Unlocking features with the Data Model and Power Pivot," for more information on working with Power Pivot.

- You can remove the grand total from the pivot table in Figure 4-28 and build another one-row pivot table just below this data set. Hide the heading row from the second pivot table, and you will appear to have the true grand total at the bottom of the pivot table.

- If you select the blank cell to the right of the last heading (C3 in Figure 4-27), you can turn on the filter on the Data tab. This filter is not designed for pivot tables and is usually unavailable ("grayed out"). After you've added the regular filters, open the drop-down in B3. Choose Top 10 Filter and ask for the top six items, as shown in Figure 4-28, which returns the top five customers and the grand total from the data set.

Caution Be aware that this method is taking advantage of a bug in Excel. Normally, the Filter found on the Data tab is not allowed in a pivot table. If you use this method and later refresh the pivot table, the Excel team will not update the filter for you. As far as they know, the option to filter is grayed out when you are in a pivot table.

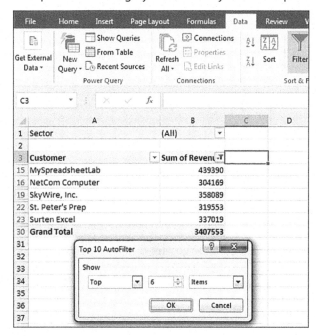

FIGURE 4-28 You are taking advantage of a hole in the fabric of Excel to apply a regular AutoFilter to a pivot table.

Filtering using the Date filters in the Label dropdown

If your label field contains all dates, Excel replaces the Label Filter flyout with a Date Filters flyout. These filters offer many virtual filters, such as Next Week, This Month, Last Quarter, and so on (see Figure 4-29).

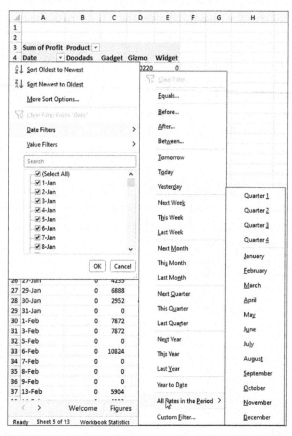

FIGURE 4-29 The Date Filters menu offers various virtual date periods.

You can specify a date or a range of dates if you choose Equals, Before, After, or Between.

Options for the current, past, or next day, week, month, quarter, or year occupy 15 options. Combined with Year To Date, these options change day after day. You can pivot a list of projects by due date and always see the projects that are due in the next week by using this option. When you open the workbook on another day, the report recalculates.

> **Tip** A week runs from Sunday through Saturday. If you select Next Week, the report always shows a period from the next Sunday through the following Saturday.

When you select All Dates In The Period, a new flyout menu offers options such as Each Month and Each Quarter.

> **Caution** If your date field contains dates and times, the Date Filters might not work as expected. You might ask for dates equal to 4/15/2022, and Excel will say that no records are found. The problem is that 6 p.m. on 4/15/2022 is stored internally as 44666.75, with the ".75" representing the 18 hours elapsed in the day between midnight and 6 p.m. If you want to return all records that happened at any point on April 15, select the Whole Days checkbox in the Date Filter dialog.

Filtering using the Filters area

Pivot table veterans remember the old Page area section of a pivot table. This area has been renamed the Filters area and still operates basically the same as in legacy versions of Excel. Microsoft did add the capability to select multiple items from the Filters area. Although the Filters area is not as showy as slicers, it is still useful when you need to replicate your pivot table for every customer.

Adding fields to the Filters area

The pivot table in Figure 4-30 is a perfect ad-hoc reporting tool to give to a high-level executive. He can use the dropdowns in B1:B4 and E1:E4 to find revenue quickly for any combination of Sector, Region, Market, Rep, Customer, Product, Date, or Weekday. This is a typical use of filters.

	A	B	C	D	E
1	Sector	(All) ▾		Customer (All) ▾	
2	Region	(All) ▾		Product Gizmo ⊤	
3	Market	(All) ▾		Date (All) ▾	
4	Rep	(All) ▾		Weekday Fri ⊤	
5					
6	Sum of Revenue	Sum of Profit			
7	274860	122640			

FIGURE 4-30 With multiple fields in the Filters area, this pivot table can answer many ad-hoc queries.

To set up the report, drag Revenue and Profit to the Values area and then drag as many fields as desired to the Filters area.

If you add many fields to the Filters area, you might want to use one of the obscure pivot table options settings. Click Options on the PivotTable Analyze tab. On the Layout & Format tab of the PivotTable Options dialog, change Report Filter Fields per Column from 0 to a positive number. Excel rearranges the Filter fields into multiple columns. Figure 4-30 shows the filters with four fields per column. You can also change Down, Then Over to Over, Then Down to rearrange the sequence of the Filter fields.

Choosing one item from a filter

To filter the pivot table, click any dropdown in the Filters area of the pivot table. The dropdown always starts with (All) but then lists the complete unique set of items available in that field.

Choosing multiple items from a filter

At the bottom of the Filters dropdown is a Select Multiple Items checkbox. If you select it, Excel adds a checkbox next to each item in the dropdown. This enables you to select multiple items from the list.

In Figure 4-31, the pivot table is filtered to show revenue from multiple sectors, but it is impossible to tell which sectors are included.

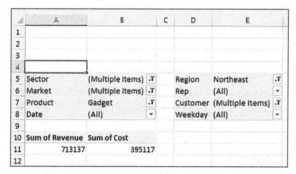

	A	B	C	D	E
1					
2					
3					
4					
5	Sector	(Multiple Items)		Region	Northeast
6	Market	(Multiple Items)		Rep	(All)
7	Product	Gadget		Customer	(Multiple Items)
8	Date	(All)		Weekday	(All)
9					
10	Sum of Revenue	Sum of Cost			
11	713137	395117			
12					

FIGURE 4-31 You can select multiple items, but after the Filter dropdown closes, you cannot tell which items were selected.

> **Tip** Selecting multiple items from the filter leads to a situation where the person reading the report will not know which items are included. Slicers solve this problem.

Replicating a pivot table report for each item in a filter

Although slicers are now the darlings of the pivot table report, the good old-fashioned report filter can still do one trick that slicers cannot do. Say you have created a report that you would like to share with the industry managers. You have a report showing customers with revenue and profit. You would like each industry manager to see only the customers in their area of responsibility.

Follow these steps to quickly replicate the pivot table:

1. Make sure the formatting in the pivot table looks good before you start. You are about to make several copies of the pivot table, and you don't want to format each worksheet in the workbook, so double-check the number formatting and headings now.

2. Add the Sector field to the Filters area. Leave the Sector filter set to (All).

3.   Select one cell in the pivot table so that you can see the PivotTable Analyze tab in the ribbon.

4.   Find the Options button on the left side of the PivotTable Analyze tab. Next to the Options tab is a dropdown. Don't click the big Options button. Instead, open the dropdown (see Figure 4-32).

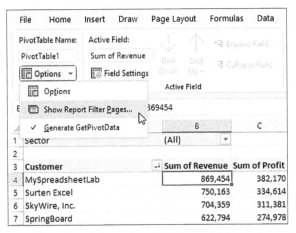

FIGURE 4-32 Click the tiny dropdown arrow next to the Options button.

5.   Choose Show Report Filter Pages. In the Show Report Filter Pages dialog, you see a list of all the fields in the report area. Because this pivot table has only the Sector field, this is the only choice (see Figure 4-33).

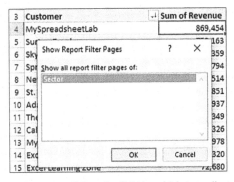

FIGURE 4-33 Select the field by which to replicate the report.

6.   Click OK and stand back.

Excel inserts a new worksheet for every item in the Sector field. On the first new worksheet, Excel chooses the first sector as the filter value for that sheet. Excel renames the worksheet to match the sector. Figure 4-34 shows the new Consulting worksheet, with neighboring tabs that contain Museums, Retail, Training, and Utilities.

Tip If the underlying data changes, you can refresh all of the Sector worksheets by using Refresh on one Sector pivot table. After you refresh the Consulting worksheet, all the pivot tables refresh.

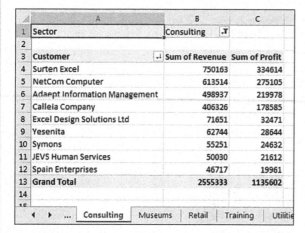

	A	B	C
1	Sector	Consulting	
2			
3	Customer	Sum of Revenue	Sum of Profit
4	Surten Excel	750163	334614
5	NetCom Computer	613514	275105
6	Adaept Information Management	498937	219978
7	Calleia Company	406326	178585
8	Excel Design Solutions Ltd	71651	32471
9	Yesenita	62744	28644
10	Symons	55251	24632
11	JEVS Human Services	50030	21612
12	Spain Enterprises	46717	19961
13	Grand Total	2555333	1135602
14			

Consulting | Museums | Retail | Training | Utilitie

FIGURE 4-34 Excel quickly adds one worksheet per sector.

Filtering using slicers and timelines

Slicers are graphical versions of the Report Filter fields. Rather than hiding the items selected in the filter dropdown behind a heading such as (Multiple Items), the slicer provides a large array of buttons that show at a glance which items are included or excluded.

To add slicers, click the Insert Slicer icon on the PivotTable Analyze tab. Excel displays the Insert Slicers dialog. Choose all the fields for which you want to create graphical filters, as shown in Figure 4-35.

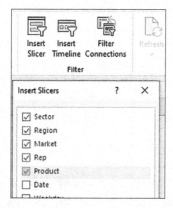

FIGURE 4-35 Choose fields for slicers.

Initially, Excel chooses one-column slicers of similar color in a cascade arrangement (see Figure 4-36). However, you can change these settings by selecting a slicer and using the Slicer Tools Options tab in the ribbon.

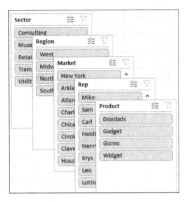

FIGURE 4-36 The slicers appear with one column each.

You can add more columns to a slicer. If you have to show 50 two-letter state abbreviations, that will look much better as 5 rows of 10 columns than as 50 rows of 1 column. Click the slicer to get access to the Slicer Tools PivotTable Analyze tab. Use the Columns spin button to increase the number of columns in the slicer. Use the resize handles in the slicer to make the slicer wider or shorter. To add visual interest, choose a different color from the Slicer Styles gallery for each field.

After formatting the slicers, arrange them in a blank section of the worksheet, as shown in Figure 4-37.

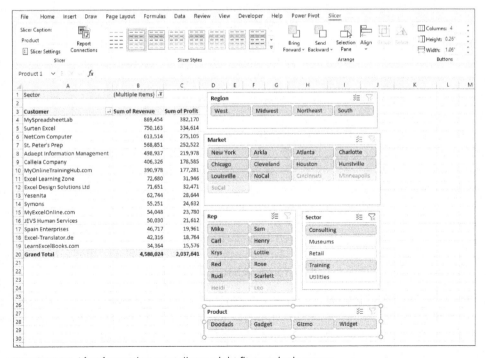

FIGURE 4-37 After formatting, your slicers might fit on a single screen.

Three colors might appear in a slicer. The dark color indicates items that are selected. Gray boxes often mean the item has no records because of other slicers. White boxes indicate items that are not selected.

Note that you can control the heading for the slicer and the order of items in the slicer by using the Slicer Settings icon on the Slicer Tools Options tab of the ribbon. Just as you can define a new pivot table style, you can also right-click an existing slicer style and choose Duplicate. You can change the font, colors, and so on.

A new icon that appears as three checkmarks debuted in Excel 2016 in the slicer's top bar. When you select it, you can select multiple items from the slicer without having to hold down the Ctrl key.

Using timelines to filter by date

After slicers were introduced in Excel 2010, there was some feedback that using slicers was not an ideal way to deal with date fields. You might end up adding some fields to your original data set to show (perhaps) a decade and then use the group feature for year, quarter, and month. You would end up with a whole bunch of slicers, all trying to select a time period, as shown in Figure 4-38.

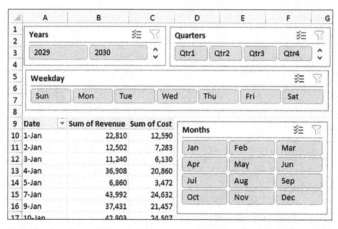

FIGURE 4-38 Four different slicers are necessary to filter by date.

For Excel 2013, Microsoft introduced a new kind of filter called a *timeline slicer*. To use one, select one cell in your pivot table and choose Insert Timeline from the PivotTable Analyze tab. Timeline slicers can only apply to fields that contain dates. Excel gives you a list of date fields to choose from, although in most cases, there is only one date field from which to choose.

Figure 4-39 shows a Timeline slicer. Perhaps the best part of a Timeline slicer is the dropdown that lets you repurpose the timeline for days, months, quarters, or years. This works even if you have not grouped your daily dates up to months, quarters, or years.

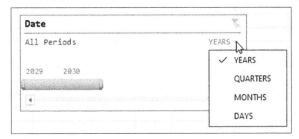

FIGURE 4-39 A single Timeline slicer can filter your pivot table by day, month, quarter, or year.

Driving multiple pivot tables from one set of slicers

Chapter 12, "Enhancing pivot table reports with macros," includes a tiny macro that lets you drive two pivot tables with one set of filters. This has historically been difficult to do unless you used a macro.

Now, one set of slicers or timelines can be used to drive multiple pivot tables or pivot charts. In Figure 4-40, the Market slicer is driving three elements. It drives the pivot table in the top left with revenue by sector and product. It drives two pivot tables created for the top-right and lower-left charts.

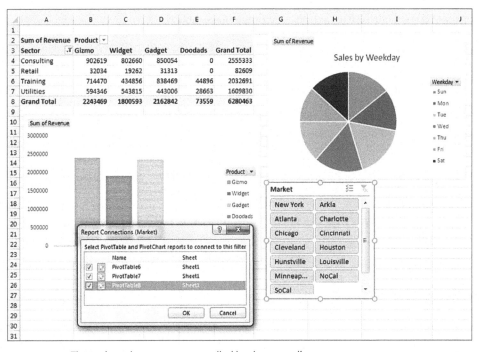

FIGURE 4-40 Three pivot elements are controlled by the same slicer.

Note For more information about how to create pivot charts, refer to Chapter 6, "Using pivot charts and other visualizations."

The following steps show you how to create three pivot tables that are tied to a single slicer:

1. Create your first pivot table.

2. Select a cell in the first pivot table. Choose Insert Slicer. Choose one or more fields to be used as a slicer. Alternatively, insert a Timeline slicer for a date field.

3. Select the entire pivot table.

4. Copy with Ctrl+C or the Copy command.

5. Select a new blank area of the worksheet.

6. Paste. Excel creates a second pivot table that shares the pivot cache with the first pivot table. In order for one slicer to run multiple pivot tables, they must share the same pivot cache.

7. Change the fields in the second pivot table to show some other interesting analysis.

8. Repeat steps 3–7 to create a third copy of the pivot table.

The preceding steps require you to create the slicer after you create the first pivot table but before you make copies of the pivot table.

If you already have several existing pivot tables and need to hook them up to the same slicer, follow these steps:

1. Click the slicer to select it. When the slicer is selected, the Slicer Tools Design tab of the ribbon appears.

2. Select the Slicer tab and choose Report Connections. Excel displays the Report Connections (Market) dialog. Initially, only the first pivot table is selected.

3. As shown in Figure 4-41, choose the other pivot tables in the dialog and click OK.

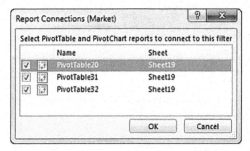

FIGURE 4-41 Choose to hook this slicer up to the other pivot tables.

4. If you created multiple slicers and/or timelines, repeat steps 1 through 3 for the other slicers.

The result is a dashboard in which all of the pivot tables and pivot charts update in response to selections made in the slicer (see Figure 4-42).

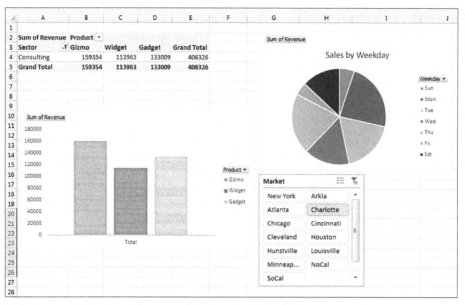

FIGURE 4-42 All of the pivot charts and pivot tables update when you choose from the slicer.

> **Tip** The worksheet in Figure 4-42 would be a perfect worksheet to publish to SharePoint or your OneDrive. You can share the workbook with coworkers and allow them to interact with the slicers. They won't need to worry about the underlying data or enter any numbers; they can just click on the slicer to see the reports update.

Grouping and creating hierarchies in a pivot table

Pivot tables can do roll-ups in memory. You can roll daily dates up to weeks, months, quarters, or years. Time can roll up to minutes or hours. Numbers can be grouped into equal-sized buckets. Text entries can be grouped into territories.

You can use the Power Pivot grid to define a hierarchy so you can quickly drill down on a pivot table or chart.

Grouping numeric fields

The Grouping dialog for numeric fields enables you to group items into equal ranges. This can be useful for creating frequency distributions. The pivot table in Figure 4-43 is quite the opposite of anything you've seen so far in this book. The numeric field—Revenue—is in the Rows area. A text field—Customer—is in the Values area. When you put a text field in the Values area, you get a count of how many records match the criteria. In its present state, this pivot table is not that fascinating; it tells you that exactly one record in the database has a total revenue of $23,990.

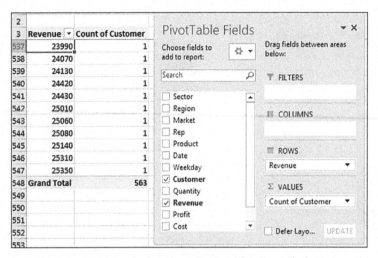

FIGURE 4-43 Nothing interesting here—just lots of order totals that appear exactly one time in the database.

Select one number in column A of the pivot table. Select Group Field from the PivotTable Analyze tab of the ribbon. Because this field is not a date field, the Grouping dialog offers Starting At, Ending At, and By fields. As shown in Figure 4-44, you can choose to show amounts from 0 to 30,000 in groups of 5,000.

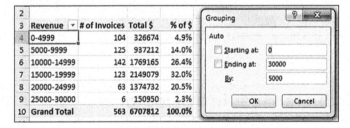

FIGURE 4-44 Create a frequency distribution by grouping the order size into $5,000 buckets.

After grouping the order size into buckets, you might want to add additional fields, such as Revenue and % Of Revenue shown as a percentage of the total.

Note The Grouping dialog requires all groups to be the same size. I have heard questions where people want to group into 0–100K, 200K–500K, but this is not possible using the Grouping feature. You would have to add a new column to the source data in order to create these groupings.

Case study: Grouping text fields for redistricting

Say that you get a call from the VP of Sales. The Sales Department is secretly considering a massive reorganization of the sales regions. The VP would like to see a report showing revenue after redistricting. You have been around long enough to know that the proposed regions will change several times before the reorganization happens, so you are not willing to change the Region field in your source data quite yet.

First, build a report showing revenue by market. The VP of Sales is proposing eliminating two regional managers and redistricting the country into three super-regions. While holding down the Ctrl key, highlight the five regions that will make up the new West region. Figure 4-45 shows the pivot table before the first group is created.

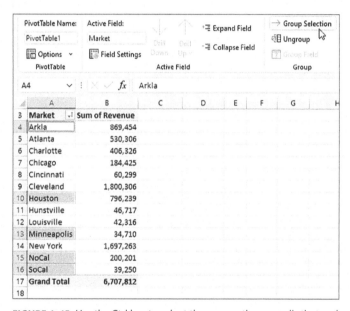

FIGURE 4-45 Use the Ctrl key to select the noncontiguous cells that make up the new region.

From the PivotTable Analyze tab, click Group Selection. Excel adds a new field called Market2. The five selected regions are arbitrarily rolled up to a new territory called Group1. In Figure 4-46, the Group1 label in A4 is the first item in the new Market2 virtual field. The other items in the Market2 field include Atlanta in A10, Charlotte in A12, and so on. The similar items in A11 and A13 are items in the original Market field. Use care while holding down the Ctrl key to select the unbolded markets for the South region: Atlanta in row 11, Charlotte in row 13, Huntsville in row 20, and Louisville in row 22.

Click Group Selection to group the markets in the proposed Southeast region. Repeat to group the remaining regions into the proposed Northeast region. Figure 4-47 shows what it looks like when you have grouped the markets into new regions. Five things need further adjustment: the names of Group1, Group2, Group3, and Market2, and the lack of subtotals for the outer row field.

Market2	Market	Sum of Revenue
Group1	Arkla	869,454
Group1	Houston	796,239
Group1	Minneapolis	34,710
Group1	NoCal	200,201
Group1	SoCal	39,250
Group1 Total		1,939,854
Atlanta	Atlanta	530,306
Atlanta Total		530,306
Charlotte	Charlotte	406,326
Charlotte Total		406,326
Chicago	Chicago	184,425
Chicago Total		184,425
Cincinnati	Cincinnati	60,299
Cincinnati Total		60,299
Cleveland	Cleveland	1,800,306
Cleveland Total		1,800,306
Hunstville	Hunstville	46,717
Hunstville Total		46,717
Louisville	Louisville	42,316
Louisville Total		42,316
New York	New York	1,697,263
New York Total		1,697,263
Grand Total		6,707,812

FIGURE 4-46 The first super-region is arbitrarily called Group1.

Market2	Market	Sum of Revenue
Group1	Arkla	869,454
Group1	Houston	796,239
Group1	Minneapolis	34,710
Group1	NoCal	200,201
Group1	SoCal	39,250
Group1 Total		1,939,854
Group2	Atlanta	530,306
Group2	Charlotte	406,326
Group2	Hunstville	46,717
Group2	Louisville	42,316
Group2 Total		1,025,665
Group3	Chicago	184,425
Group3	Cincinnati	60,299
Group3	Cleveland	1,800,306
Group3	New York	1,697,263
Group3 Total		3,742,293
Grand Total		6,707,812

FIGURE 4-47 The markets are grouped, but you have to do some cleanup.

If you are not seeing Group1 Total, Group2 Total, and Group3 Total in your pivot table, right-click Market2 in A2 and choose Field Settings. In the Field Settings dialog, change from None to Automatic. Cleaning up the report takes only a few moments:

1. Select cell A4. Type **West** to replace the arbitrary name Group1.

2. Select cell A10. Type **Southeast** to replace the arbitrary name Group2.

3. Select A15. Type **Northeast** to replace Group3.

4. Select any outer heading in A4, A10, or A15. Click Field Settings on the PivotTable Analyze tab.

5. In the Field Settings dialog, replace the Custom Name of Market2 with Proposed Region.

Figure 4-48 shows the pivot table that results, which is ready for the VP of Sales.

	A	B	C
3	Proposed Region ▾	Market ▾	Sum of Revenue
4	⊟West	Arkla	869,454
5	West	Houston	796,239
6	West	Minneapolis	34,710
7	West	NoCal	200,201
8	West	SoCal	39,250
9	**West Total**		**1,939,854**
10	⊟Southeast	Atlanta	530,306
11	Southeast	Charlotte	406,326
12	Southeast	Hunstville	46,717
13	Southeast	Louisville	42,316
14	**Southeast Total**		**1,025,665**
15	⊟Northeast	Chicago	184,425
16	Northeast	Cincinnati	60,299
17	Northeast	Cleveland	1,800,306
18	Northeast	New York	1,697,263
19	**Northeast Total**		**3,742,293**
20	**Grand Total**		**6,707,812**

FIGURE 4-48 It is now easy to see that these regions are heavily unbalanced.

You can probably predict that the Sales Department needs to shuffle markets to balance the regions. To go back to the original regions, select one of each of the Proposed Region cells in A4, A10, and A15 and choose Ungroup. You can then start over, grouping regions in new combinations.

Grouping date fields manually

As of late 2024, Microsoft has once again turned on automatic date grouping in pivot tables. I recommend that you turn this feature off and manually group dates when you need dates to be grouped.

To turn off automatic data grouping, go to File | Options | Data. The fifth checkbox is Disable Automatic Grouping Of Date/Time Columns In Pivot Tables. Select this box to prevent automatic date grouping.

I am not a fan of letting Microsoft's algorithm determine how to group because the grouping seems unpredictable. If your data spans an entire year, the pivot table is grouped a certain way. But what if your company did not produce any invoices on the New Year's holiday? If there were no invoices for January 1, then your data does not span the entire year and Microsoft will group a different way. Rather than leave the grouping to chance, it is easier to turn off the automatic grouping and then apply the grouping as you need it to be.

Excel provides a straightforward way to group date fields. Select any date cell in your pivot table. On the PivotTable Analyze tab, click Group Field in the Group option.

When your field contains date information, the date version of the Grouping dialog appears. By default, the Months option is selected. You have choices to group by Seconds, Minutes, Hours, Days, Months, Quarters, and Years. It is possible—and usually advisable—to select more than one field in the Grouping dialog. In this case, select Months and Years, as shown in Figure 4-49.

There are several interesting points to note about the resulting pivot table. First, notice that two virtual fields called Years (Date) and Months (Date) have been added to the PivotTable Fields pane. Your source data is not changed to include the new fields. Instead, these fields are now part of your pivot cache in memory.

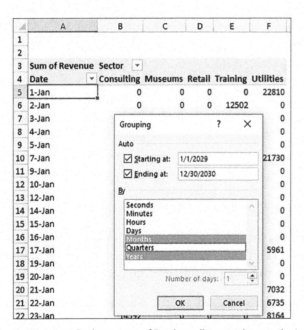

FIGURE 4-49 Business users of Excel usually group by months (or quarters) and years.

Another interesting point is that, by default, the Months (Date) and Years (Date) fields are automatically added to the same area as the original date field in the pivot table layout, as shown in Figure 4-50. Although this happens automatically, you are free to pivot months and years onto the opposite axis of the report. This is a quick way to create a year-over-year sales report.

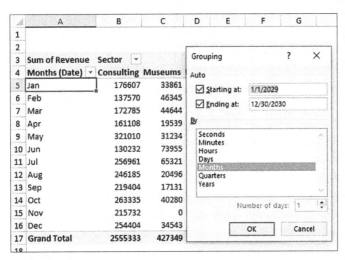

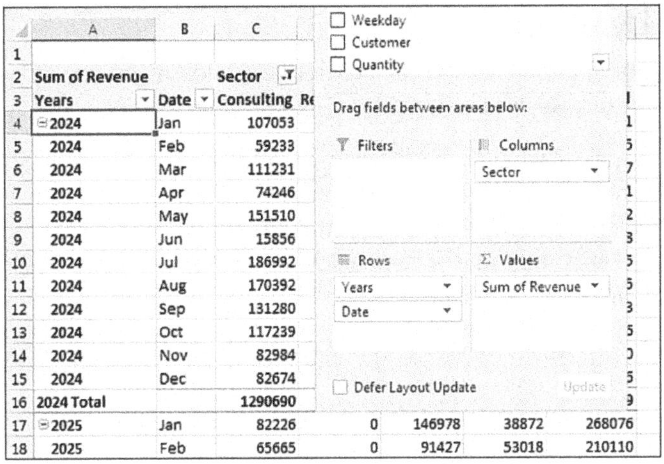

⚠	A	B	C		☐ Weekday			
1					☐ Customer			
2	Sum of Revenue		Sector ⫪		☐ Quantity			▾
3	Years ▾	Date ▾	Consulting Re		Drag fields between areas below:			
4	⊟2024	Jan	107053					1
5	2024	Feb	59233		▼ Filters	� Columns		5
6	2024	Mar	111231			Sector	▾	7
7	2024	Apr	74246					1
8	2024	May	151510					2
9	2024	Jun	15856					3
10	2024	Jul	186992		☰ Rows	Σ Values		5
11	2024	Aug	170392		Years ▾	Sum of Revenue ▾		5
12	2024	Sep	131280		Date ▾			3
13	2024	Oct	117239					5
14	2024	Nov	82984					⊃
15	2024	Dec	82674		☐ Defer Layout Update	Update		5
16	2024 Total		1290690					⇂
17	⊟2025	Jan	82226	0	146978	38872	268076	
18	2025	Feb	65665	0	91427	53018	210110	

FIGURE 4-50 By default, Excel adds the new grouped date field to your pivot table layout.

Finally, the newly grouped fields include the original column name in parentheses. This can be helpful when your original data has multiple date columns. For example, you might have an Order Date and a Ship Date. If you group both of those up to Months and Years, you will see the newly grouped fields with names such as Months (Order Date) and Months (Ship Date).

Including years when grouping by months

Although this point is not immediately obvious, it is important to understand that if you group a date field by month, you also need to include the year in the grouping. If your data set includes January 2029 and January 2030, selecting only months in the Grouping dialog will result in both January 2029 and January 2030 being combined into a single row called Jan (see Figure 4-51).

⚠	A	B	C	D	E	F	G
1							
2							
3	Sum of Revenue	Sector ▾		Grouping		? ✕	
4	Months (Date) ▾	Consulting	Museums	Auto			
5	Jan	176607	33861	☑ Starting at:	1/1/2029		
6	Feb	137570	46345	☑ Ending at:	12/30/2030		
7	Mar	172785	44644	By			
8	Apr	161108	19539				
9	May	321010	31234	Seconds			
10	Jun	130232	73955	Minutes Hours			
11	Jul	256961	65321	Days			
12	Aug	246185	20496	Months Quarters			
13	Sep	219404	17131	Years			
14	Oct	263335	40280				
15	Nov	215732	0	Number of days:	1 ⇅		
16	Dec	254404	34543				
17	Grand Total	2555333	427349	OK	Cancel		
18							

FIGURE 4-51 If you fail to include the Year field in the grouping, the report mixes sales from last Jan and this Jan into a single row called Jan.

Grouping date fields by week

The Grouping dialog offers choices to group by second, minute, hour, day, month, quarter, and year. It is also possible to group on a weekly or biweekly basis.

The first step is to find either a paper calendar or an electronic calendar, such as the Calendar feature in Outlook, for the year in question. If your data starts on January 1, 2029, it is helpful to know that January 1 is a Monday that year. You need to decide if the weeks should start on Sunday or Monday or any other day. For example, you can check the paper or electronic calendar to learn that the nearest starting Sunday is December 31, 2028.

Select any date heading in your pivot table. Then select Group Field from the PivotTable Analyze tab. In the Grouping dialog, clear all the By options and select only the Days field. This enables the Number of Days spin box. To produce a report by week, increase the number of days from 1 to 7.

Next, you need to set up the Starting At date. If you were to accept the default of starting on January 1, 2029, all your weekly periods would run from Monday through Sunday. By checking a calendar before you begin, you know that you want the first group to start on December 31, 2028, to have weeks that run Sunday through Monday. Figure 4-52 shows the settings in the Grouping dialog and the resulting report.

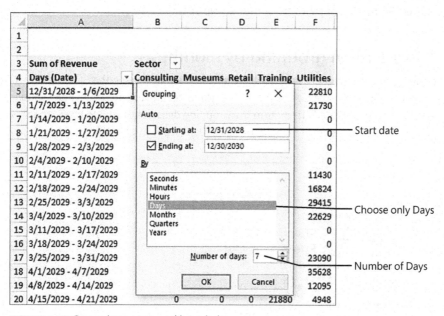

FIGURE 4-52 Group dates up to weekly periods.

Caution If you choose to group by week, none of the other grouping options can be selected. You cannot group this or any field by month, quarter, or year. You cannot add calculated items to the pivot table.

Creating an easy year-over-year report

You can use date grouping to easily create a year-over-year report. You can either manually group the dates to years or use the AutoGroup.

Follow these steps:

1. Create a pivot table with Years in the Columns area and Months in the Rows area. Drag Revenue to the Values area.

2. By default, the pivot table will offer a Grand Total column. Right-click the Grand Total heading and choose Remove Grand Total. Your pivot table will look like Figure 4-53.

3. Drag Revenue a second time to the Values area.

4. In the Columns area, drag Years so it is below Values. You will have the pivot table shown in Figure 4-54.

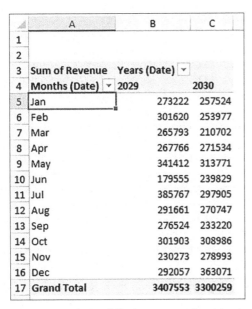

	A	B	C
1			
2			
3	Sum of Revenue	Years (Date) ▾	
4	Months (Date) ▾	2029	2030
5	Jan	273222	257524
6	Feb	301620	253977
7	Mar	265793	210702
8	Apr	267766	271534
9	May	341412	313771
10	Jun	179555	239829
11	Jul	385767	297905
12	Aug	291661	270747
13	Sep	276524	233220
14	Oct	301903	308986
15	Nov	230273	278993
16	Dec	292057	363071
17	Grand Total	3407553	3300259

FIGURE 4-53 Group daily dates to months and years. Drag Years to go across the report.

	A	B	C	D	E
3		Values	Years (Date)	▾	
4		Sum of Revenue		Sum of Revenue2	
5	Months (Date) ▾	2029	2030	2029	2030
6	Jan	273222	257524	273222	257524
7	Feb	301620	253977	301620	253977
8	Mar	265793	210702	265793	210702
9	Apr	267766	271534	267766	271534
10	May	341412	313771	341412	313771
11	Jun	179555	239829	179555	239829
12	Jul	385767	297905	385767	297905
13	Aug	291661	270747	291661	270747
14	Sep	276524	233220	276524	233220
15	Oct	301903	308986	301903	308986
16	Nov	230273	278993	230273	278993
17	Dec	292057	363071	292057	363071
18	Grand Total	3407553	3300259	3407553	3300259

FIGURE 4-54 This year and last year appear twice across the top of the report.

5. Double-click the Sum of Revenue2 heading in cell D4 to display the Value Field Settings dialog.

6. In the Value Field Settings dialog, change the Custom Name to % Change. Select the Show Values As tab. In the Show Values As dropdown, choose % Difference From. In the Base Field list, choose Years (Date). In the Base Item, choose (Previous), as shown in Figure 4-55.

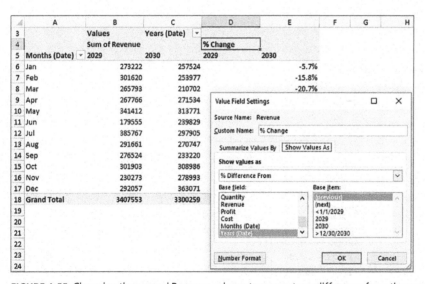

FIGURE 4-55 Changing the second Revenue column to percentage difference from the previous year.

7. Close the Value Field Settings dialog. Column E will show the percentage change from the first year to the last year. Column D will be blank because the pivot table has no data from 2028 to compare to 2029.

8. Hide column D.

9. Select the 2030 heading in E5. Press Ctrl+1 for Format Cells. On the Number tab, choose Custom. Type a format of `;;; "% Change "`.

You have a report showing the year 2029 versus the year 2030 and a percentage change. You can easily remove the Months from column A and insert Region, Market, or Product to see the year-over-year change. Figure 4-56 shows a year-over-year report for Regions.

	A	B	C	E
3		**Values**	**Years (Date)** ▾	
4		**Sum of Revenue**		
5	**Region** ▾	**2029**	**2030**	**% Change**
6	West	127,340	112,111	-12.0%
7	Midwest	972,790	1,149,266	18.1%
8	Northeast	897,378	799,885	-10.9%
9	South	1,410,045	1,238,997	-12.1%
10	Grand Total	3,407,553	3,300,259	-3.1%

FIGURE 4-56 Once you have the year-over-year report set up, you can swap any field into column A.

Creating hierarchies

If you build your pivot table using the Data Model, you can use the Diagram View in Power Pivot to create a formal hierarchy.

Using hierarchies is so rarely used that Microsoft removed the Drill Down and Drill Up buttons from the PivotTable Analyze tab of the ribbon in order to make room for the new Show Details icon. Hierarchies are cool and should be used more often. If you try them, you will have to customize the Quick Access Toolbar or the ribbon to add the Drill Down and Drill Up icons.

Here are the steps to add Drill Down and Drill Up icons to the PivotTable Analyze tab of the ribbon.

1. Right-click the ribbon and choose Customize Ribbon. Excel displays the Excel Options dialog, opened to the Customize Ribbon category.

2. In the top-right dropdown, change from Main Tabs to Tool Tabs.

3. In the right list box, find the entry for PivotTable Analyze. Click the > icon to the left of the entry to expand the list of icons on this tab.

4. Click on the PivotTable group just under the PivotTable Analyze entry. Below the right-side list box, choose New Group. A new group called New Group (Custom) appears after the Pivot Table entry.

5. With New Group (Custom) selected, click the Rename box just below the right-side list box. Type **Drill** as the new Display Name. It is not important to choose an icon. Click OK to close the Rename dialog.

6. In the top left dropdown, change from Popular Commands to All Commands.

7. In the left list box, scroll down until you see three entries for Drill Down, Drill Up, and Drill Up with a flyout menu. Choose the Drill Down item and click the Add>> button in the center of the dialog. Repeat for the first Drill Up item.

8. Click OK to close Excel Options. You should see Drill Down and Drill Up icons on the PivotTable Analyze tab of the ribbon. This is shown later in Figures 4-60 and 4-61.

Alternatively, you could add these icons to the Quick Access Toolbar.

Consider the pivot table and pivot chart shown in Figure 4-57. The pivot table is built using the Data Model; when you choose Insert Pivot Table, make sure to choose Add This Data To The Data Model. The pivot table has regions in the Rows area and Products in the Columns area. The pivot chart shows a stacked column chart.

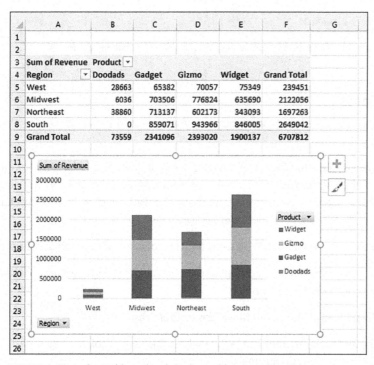

FIGURE 4-57 A pivot table and a pivot chart without any hierarchy.

Follow these steps to add a hierarchy below Region:

1. Click the Manage icon in the Power Pivot tab of the ribbon.

2. On the Home tab of the Power Pivot for Excel window, click Diagram View.

3. Resize the Range table so you can see all the fields.

4. Click on the top field for the hierarchy: Region. Ctrl+click the remaining members of the hierarchy: Market and Rep.

5. Right-click Region and choose Create Hierarchy (see Figure 4-58).

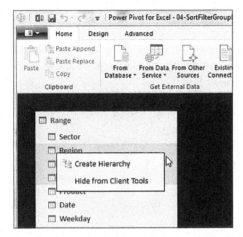

FIGURE 4-58 Select Region, Market, and Rep. Right-click and choose Create Hierarchy.

6. Hierarchy1 will appear at the bottom of the table. Right-click the name and choose Rename. Type a meaningful name such as Geography (see Figure 4-59).

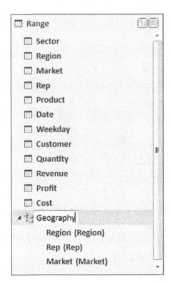

FIGURE 4-59 The hierarchy is shown at the bottom of the table.

7. Carefully review the sequence of the hierarchy. In Figure 4-59, Rep is appearing before Market. This is incorrect. Right-click Market and choose Move Up.

8. Close the Power Pivot window and return to Excel. After a brief pause, the PivotTable Fields pane will show the table name (Range), the hierarchy name (Geography), and something called More Fields.

9. Remove Region from the Rows area. Choose the Geography hierarchy from the PivotTable Fields pane. As shown in Figure 4-60, you have something very similar to Figure 4-57. However, note that Drill Down is now enabled in the ribbon.

FIGURE 4-60 Plus signs appear next to each region. The Drill Down icon is enabled.

10. Select cell A7 for South. Click on Drill Down. The pivot table and pivot chart will change to show the markets in the South region (see Figure 4-61).

You can keep using Drill Down or Drill Up to travel through the hierarchy.

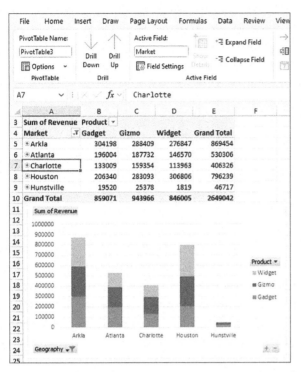

FIGURE 4-61 After drilling down on the South region, the markets in the South appear. The Drill Up icon is now enabled.

Next steps

In Chapter 5, "Performing calculations in pivot tables," you'll learn how to use pivot table formulas to add new virtual fields to a pivot table.

## CHAPTER 5

Performing calculations in pivot tables

In this chapter, you will:

- Be introduced to calculated fields and calculated items
- Create a calculated field
- Create a calculated item
- Understand the rules and shortcomings of pivot table calculations
- Manage and maintain pivot table calculations

Introducing calculated fields and calculated items

When analyzing data with pivot tables, you will often need to expand your analysis to include data based on calculations that are not in your original data set. Excel provides a way to perform calculations within a pivot table through calculated fields, measures, and calculated items.

A *calculated field* is a data field you create by executing a calculation against existing fields in the pivot table. Think of a calculated field as a virtual column added to your data set. This column takes up no space in your source data, contains the data you define with a formula, and interacts with your pivot data as a field—just like all the other fields in your pivot table.

A *measure* is a calculated field created in a Data Model pivot table using the Data Analysis Expressions (DAX) formula language. In many cases, measures run circles around calculated fields. In order to create a measure, you have to choose Add This Data To The Data Model when creating the pivot table. Measures are discussed in length in Chapter 10, "Unlocking features with the Data Model and Power Pivot." Refer to "Creating Median in a pivot table using DAX measures," "Reporting text in the Values area," and "Using time intelligence" in Chapter 10. Measures are also used in the case study at the end of this chapter: "Case study: Using DAX measures instead of calculated fields."

A *calculated item* is a data item you create by executing a calculation against existing items within a data field. Think of a calculated item as a virtual row of data added to your data set. This virtual row takes up no space in your source data and contains summarized values based on calculations performed on other rows in the same field. Calculated items interact with your pivot data as data items—just like all the other items in your pivot table.

With calculated fields and calculated items, you can insert a formula into a pivot table to create your own custom field or data item. Your newly created data becomes a part of your pivot table, interacting with other pivot data, recalculating when you refresh, and supplying you with a calculated metric that does not exist in your source data.

The example in Figure 5-1 demonstrates how a basic calculated field can add another perspective to your data. Your pivot table shows the total sales amount and contracted hours for each market. A calculated field that shows your average dollar per hour enhances this analysis and adds another dimension to your data.

	A	B	C	D
1				
2	Row Labels	Sales_Amount	Contracted Hours	Avg Dollar Per Hour
3	BUFFALO	$450,478	6,864	$65.63
4	CALIFORNIA	$2,254,735	33,014	$68.30
5	CANADA	$776,245	12,103	$64.14
6	CHARLOTTE	$890,522	14,525	$61.31
7	DALLAS	$467,089	6,393	$73.06
8	DENVER	$645,583	8,641	$74.71
9	FLORIDA	$1,450,392	22,640	$64.06
10	KANSASCITY	$574,899	8,547	$67.26
11	MICHIGAN	$678,705	10,744	$63.17
12	NEWORLEANS	$333,454	5,057	$65.94
13	NEWYORK	$873,581	14,213	$61.46
14	PHOENIX	$570,255	10,167	$56.09
15	SEATTLE	$179,827	2,889	$62.25
16	TULSA	$628,405	9,583	$65.57
17	Grand Total	$10,774,172	165,380	$65.15

FIGURE 5-1 Avg Dollar per Hour is a calculated field that adds another perspective to your data analysis.

Now, you might look at Figure 5-1 and ask, "Why go through all the trouble of creating calculated fields or calculated items? Why not just use formulas in surrounding cells or even add the calculation directly into the source table to get the information needed?"

To answer these questions, in the next sections we will look at the three different methods you can use to create the calculated field in Figure 5-1:

- Manually add the calculated field to your data source.

- Use a formula outside your pivot table to create the calculated field.

- Insert a calculated field directly into your pivot table.

Method 1: Manually add a calculated field to the data source

If you manually add a calculated field to your data source, the pivot table can pick up the field as a regular data field (see Figure 5-2). On the surface, this option looks simple, but this method of precalculating metrics and incorporating them into your data source is impractical on several levels.

	N	O	P	Q	R
1	Sales_Amount	Contracted Hours	Sales_Period	Sales_Rep	Avg Dollar Per Hour
2	$197.95	2	P08	5060	$98.98
3	$197.95	2	P08	5060	$98.98
4	$191.28	3	P08	5060	$63.76
5	$240.07	4	P11	44651	$60.02
6	$147.22	2	P08	160410	$73.61
7	$163.51	2	P02	243	$81.76
8	$134.01	3	P02	243	$44.67
9	$134.01	3	P02	243	$44.67
10	$134.01	3	P02	243	$44.67
11	$239.00	3	P01	4244	$79.67
12	$215.87	4	P02	5030	$53.97
13	$180.57	4	P02	64610	$45.14
14	$240.07	4	P02	213	$60.02

FIGURE 5-2 Precalculating calculated fields in your data source is both cumbersome and impractical.

If the definitions of your calculated fields change, you have to go back to the data source, recalculate the metric for each row, and refresh your pivot table. If you have to add a metric, you have to go back to the data source, add a new calculated field, and then change the range of your pivot table to capture the new field.

Method 2: Use a formula outside a pivot table to create a calculated field

You can add a calculated field by performing the calculation in an external cell with a formula. In the example shown in Figure 5-3, the Avg Dollar Per Hour column was created with formulas referencing the pivot table.

D3			f_x	=B3/C3	
	A	B	C		D
1					
2	Row Labels	Sales_Amount	Contracted Hours		Avg Dollar Per Hour
3	BUFFALO	$450,478	6,864		$65.63
4	CALIFORNIA	$2,254,735	33,014		$68.30
5	CANADA	$776,245	12,103		$64.14
6	CHARLOTTE	$890,522	14,525		$61.31
7	DALLAS	$467,089	6,393		$73.06
8	DENVER	$645,583	8,641		$74.71
9	FLORIDA	$1,450,392	22,640		$64.06
10	KANSASCITY	$574,899	8,547		$67.26
11	MICHIGAN	$678,705	10,744		$63.17
12	NEWORLEANS	$333,454	5,057		$65.94
13	NEWYORK	$873,581	14,213		$61.46
14	PHOENIX	$570,255	10,167		$56.09
15	SEATTLE	$179,827	2,889		$62.25
16	TULSA	$628,405	9,583		$65.57
17	Grand Total	$10,774,172	165,380		$65.15

FIGURE 5-3 Typing a formula next to your pivot table essentially gives you a calculated field that refreshes when your pivot table is refreshed.

Although this method gives you a calculated field that updates when your pivot table is refreshed, any changes in the structure of your pivot table have the potential to render your formula useless.

As you can see in Figure 5-4, moving the Market field to the Filters area changes the structure of your pivot table—and exposes the weakness of makeshift calculated fields that use external formulas.

	A	B	C	D
1	Market	(All) ▾		
2				Avg Dollar Per Hour
3	Sales_Amount	Contracted Hours		#VALUE!
4	$10,774,172	165,380		#DIV/0!
5				#DIV/0!
6				#DIV/0!
7				#DIV/0!
8				#DIV/0!
9				#DIV/0!
10				#DIV/0!
11				#DIV/0!
12				#DIV/0!
13				#DIV/0!
14				#DIV/0!
15				#DIV/0!
16				#DIV/0!
17				#DIV/0!

FIGURE 5-4 External formulas can cause errors when the pivot table structure is changed.

Method 3: Insert a calculated field directly into a pivot table

Inserting a calculated field directly into a pivot table is the best option. Going this route eliminates the need to manage formulas, provides for scalability when your data source grows or changes, and allows for flexibility in the event that your metric definitions change.

Another huge advantage of this method is that you can alter your pivot table's structure and even measure different data fields against your calculated field without worrying about errors in your formulas or losing cell references.

The pivot table report shown in Figure 5-5 is the same one you saw in Figure 5-1, except it has been restructured to show the average dollar per hour by market and product.

	A		B	C	D	E
1						
2	Market ▾		Product_Description ▾	Sales_Amount	Contracted Hours	Avg Dollar Per Hour
3	⊟ BUFFALO		Cleaning & Housekeeping Services	$66,845	982	$68.07
4			Facility Maintenance and Repair	$69,570	821	$84.74
5			Fleet Maintenance	$86,460	1,439	$60.08
6			Green Plants and Foliage Care	$34,831	490	$71.08
7			Landscaping/Grounds Care	$65,465	1,172	$55.86
8			Predictive Maintenance/Preventative Maintenance	$127,307	1,960	$64.95
9	BUFFALO Total			$450,478	6,864	$65.63
10	⊟ CALIFORNIA		Cleaning & Housekeeping Services	$37,401	531	$70.44
11			Facility Maintenance and Repair	$281,198	3,103	$90.62
12			Fleet Maintenance	$337,225	5,737	$58.78
13			Green Plants and Foliage Care	$830,413	11,900	$69.78
14			Landscaping/Grounds Care	$248,343	3,421	$72.59
15			Predictive Maintenance/Preventative Maintenance	$520,156	8,322	$62.50
16	CALIFORNIA Total			$2,254,735	33,014	$68.30

FIGURE 5-5 Your calculated field remains viable even when your pivot table's structure changes to accommodate new dimensions.

The bottom line is that there are significant benefits to integrating your custom calculations into a pivot table, including the following:

- Elimination of potential formula and cell reference errors

- Ability to add or remove data from your pivot table without affecting your calculations

- Ability to auto-recalculate when your pivot table is changed or refreshed

- Flexibility to change calculations easily when your metric definitions change

- Ability to manage and maintain your calculations effectively

Note If you move your data to PowerPivot, you can use the DAX formula language to create more powerful calculations. See Chapter 10, "Unlocking features with the Data Model and Power Pivot," to get a concise look at the DAX formula language.

Creating a calculated field

Before you create a calculated field, you must first have a pivot table, so build the pivot table shown in Figure 5-6.

	A	B	C
1			
2	**Market**	**Sales_Amount**	**Contracted Hours**
3	BUFFALO	$450,478	6,864
4	CALIFORNIA	$2,254,735	33,014
5	CANADA	$776,245	12,103
6	CHARLOTTE	$890,522	14,525
7	DALLAS	$467,089	6,393
8	DENVER	$645,583	8,641
9	FLORIDA	$1,450,392	22,640
10	KANSASCITY	$574,899	8,547
11	MICHIGAN	$678,705	10,744
12	NEWORLEANS	$333,454	5,057
13	NEWYORK	$873,581	14,213
14	PHOENIX	$570,255	10,167
15	SEATTLE	$179,827	2,889
16	TULSA	$628,405	9,583
17	**Grand Total**	**$10,774,172**	**165,380**

FIGURE 5-6 Create the pivot table shown here.

Once you have a pivot table, it's time to create your first calculated field. To do this, you must activate the Insert Calculated Field dialog. Select PivotTable Analyze and then select Fields, Items, & Sets from the Calculations group. Selecting this option activates a dropdown from which you can select Calculated Field, as demonstrated in Figures 5-7 and 5-8.

Note Normally, the fields in the Values area of Figure 5-6 would be called Sum Of Sales_ Amount and Sum Of Contracted Hours. After creating the default pivot table, click in cell B2 and type a new name of `Sales_Amount` followed by a space. Similarly, rename C2 from Sum Of Contracted Hours to **Contracted Hours** followed by a space.

FIGURE 5-7 Start the creation of your calculated field by selecting Calculated Field.

After you select Calculated Field, Excel activates the Insert Calculated Field dialog, as shown in Figure 5-8.

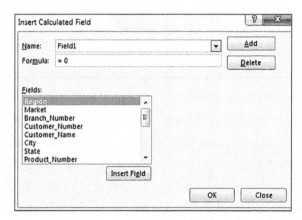

FIGURE 5-8 The Insert Calculated Field dialog assists you in creating a calculated field in a pivot table.

Notice the two input boxes—Name and Formula—at the top of the dialog. The objective here is to give your calculated field a name and then build the formula by selecting the combination of data fields and mathematical operators that provide the metric that you are looking for.

As you can see in Figure 5-9, you first give your calculated field a descriptive name—that is, a name that describes the utility of the mathematical operation. In this case, enter **Avg Dollar Per Hour** in the Name input box.

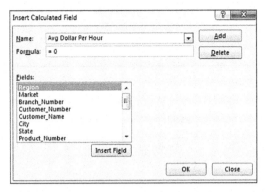

FIGURE 5-9 Give your calculated field a descriptive name.

Next, go to the Fields list and double-click the Sales_Amount field. Enter **/** to let Excel know you plan to divide the Sales_Amount field by something.

Caution   By default, the Formula input box in the Insert Calculated Field dialog contains = 0. Ensure that you delete the zero before continuing with your formula.

At this point, your dialog should look similar to the one shown in Figure 5-10.

FIGURE 5-10 Start your formula with = Sales_Amount/.

Next, double-click the Contracted Hours field to finish your formula, as illustrated in Figure 5-11. Finally, select Add and then click OK to create the new calculated field.

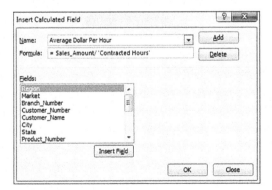

FIGURE 5-11 The full formula, =Sales_Amount/'Contracted Hours', gives you the calculated field you need.

Note The resulting values from a calculated field are not formatted. You can easily apply any desired formatting by using some of the techniques from Chapter 3, "Customizing a pivot table."

Does this mean you have just added a column to your data source? The answer is no.

Calculated fields are similar to the pivot table's default subtotal and grand total calculations in that they are all mathematical functions that recalculate when the pivot table changes or is refreshed. Calculated fields merely mimic the hard fields in your data source; you can drag them, change field settings, and use them with other calculated fields.

Take a moment and take another close look at Figure 5-11. Notice that the formula entered there is in a format similar to the one used in the standard Excel formula bar. The obvious difference is that instead of using hard numbers or cell references, you are referencing pivot data fields to define the arguments used in this calculation. If you have worked with formulas in Excel before, you will quickly grasp the concept of creating calculated fields.

As you can see in Figure 5-12, the pivot table creates a new field called Sum Of Avg Dollar Per Hour. Note that in addition to adding your calculated field to the pivot table, Excel also adds your new field to the PivotTable Fields list.

	A	B	C	D
1				
2	Market	Sales_Amount	Contracted Hours	Sum of Avg Dollar Per Hour
3	BUFFALO	$450,478	6,864	65.62911859
4	CALIFORNIA	$2,254,735	33,014	68.29634034
5	CANADA	$776,245	12,103	64.13660002
6	CHARLOTTE	$890,522	14,525	61.30963787
7	DALLAS	$467,089	6,393	73.06264195
8	DENVER	$645,583	8,641	74.71164101
9	FLORIDA	$1,450,392	22,640	64.06325088
10	KANSASCITY	$574,899	8,547	67.26324675
11	MICHIGAN	$678,705	10,744	63.1706022
12	NEWORLEANS	$333,454	5,057	65.93902511
13	NEWYORK	$873,581	14,213	61.46351298
14	PHOENIX	$570,255	10,167	56.08882561
15	SEATTLE	$179,827	2,889	62.24548633
16	TULSA	$628,405	9,583	65.57495878
17	Grand Total	$10,774,172	165,380	65.14797303

FIGURE 5-12 You can change the settings on your new calculated field—for example, field name, number format, and color—just as you would on any other field.

Case study: Summarizing next year's forecast

All the branch managers in your company have submitted their initial revenue forecasts for next year. Your task is to take the first-pass numbers they submitted and create a summary report that shows the following:

- Total revenue forecast by market
- Total percentage growth over last year
- Total contribution margin by market

Because these numbers are first-pass submissions and you know they will change over the next two weeks, you decide to use a pivot table to create the requested forecast summary.

Start by building the initial pivot table, shown in Figure 5-13, to include Revenue Last Year and Forecast Next Year for each market. After creating the pivot table, you will see that by virtue of adding the Forecast Next Year field in the data area, you have met your first requirement: to show the total revenue forecast by market.

MARKET	Revenue Last Year	Forecast Next Year
BUFFALO	$450,478	$411,246
CALIFORNIA	$2,254,735	$2,423,007
CANADA	$776,245	$746,384
CHARLOTTE	$890,522	$965,361
DALLAS	$467,089	$510,635
DENVER	$645,583	$722,695
FLORIDA	$1,450,392	$1,421,507
KANSASCITY	$574,899	$607,226
MICHIGAN	$678,705	$870,447
NEWORLEANS	$333,454	$366,174
NEWYORK	$873,581	$953,010
PHOENIX	$570,255	$746,721
SEATTLE	$179,827	$214,621
TULSA	$628,405	$661,726
Grand Total	**$10,774,172**	**$11,620,760**

FIGURE 5-13 The initial pivot table is basic, but it provides the data for your first requirement: show total revenue forecast by market.

The next metric you need is percentage growth over last year. To get this data, you need to add a calculated field that calculates the following formula:

```
(Forecast Next Year / Revenue Last Year) - 1
```

To achieve this, do the following:

1. Activate the Insert Calculated Field dialog, and name your new field **Percent Growth** (see Figure 5-14).

2. Delete the 0 in the Formula input box.

3. Enter **(** (an opening parenthesis).

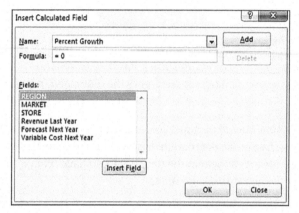

FIGURE 5-14 Name your new field Percent Growth.

4. Double-click the Forecast Next Year field.

5. Enter **/** (a division sign).

6. Double-click the Revenue Last Year field.

7. Enter **)** (a closing parenthesis).

8. Enter **–** (a minus sign).

9. Enter the number **1**.

At this point, the formula looks like this:

```
= ( 'Forecast Next Year'/'Revenue Last Year')-1
```

Tip You can use any constant in your pivot table calculations. Constants are static values that do not change. In this example, the number 1 is a constant. While the value of Revenue Last Year or Forecast Next Year will almost certainly change based on the available data, the number 1 will always have the same value.

10. After you have entered the full formula, your dialog should look like the one shown in Figure 5-15.

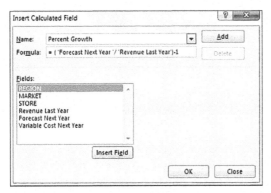

FIGURE 5-15 With just a few clicks, you have created a variance formula!

11. With your formula typed in, you can now click OK to add your new field. After changing the format of the resulting values to percentages, you have a nicely formatted Percent Growth calculation in your pivot table. At this point, your pivot table should look like the one shown in Figure 5-16.

3	MARKET	Revenue Last Year	Forecast Next Year	Sum of Percent Growth
4	BUFFALO	$450,478	$411,246	-8.7%
5	CALIFORNIA	$2,254,735	$2,423,007	7.5%
6	CANADA	$776,245	$746,384	-3.8%
7	CHARLOTTE	$890,522	$965,361	8.4%
8	DALLAS	$467,089	$510,635	9.3%
9	DENVER	$645,583	$722,695	11.9%
10	FLORIDA	$1,450,392	$1,421,507	-2.0%
11	KANSASCITY	$574,899	$607,226	5.6%
12	MICHIGAN	$678,705	$870,447	28.3%
13	NEWORLEANS	$333,454	$366,174	9.8%
14	NEWYORK	$873,581	$953,010	9.1%
15	PHOENIX	$570,255	$746,721	30.9%
16	SEATTLE	$179,827	$214,621	19.3%
17	TULSA	$628,405	$661,726	5.3%
18	Grand Total	$10,774,172	$11,620,760	7.9%

FIGURE 5-16 You have added a Percent Growth calculation to your pivot table.

12. With this newly created view into your data, you can easily see that three markets need to resubmit their forecasts to reflect positive growth over last year (see Figure 5-17).

Now it's time to focus on your last requirement, which is to find the total contribution margin by market. The original data set includes a column for Variable Cost Next Year, where the values are stored as negative values. To get this data, you need to add a calculated field that calculates the following formula:

```
Forecast Next Year + Variable Cost Next Year
```

	A	B	C	D
1				
2				
3	MARKET	Revenue Last Year	Forecast Next Year	Sum of Percent Growth
4	BUFFALO	$450,478	$411,246	-8.7%
5	CALIFORNIA	$2,254,735	$2,423,007	7.5%
6	CANADA	$776,245	$746,384	-3.8%
7	CHARLOTTE	$890,522	$965,361	8.4%
8	DALLAS	$467,089	$510,635	9.3%
9	DENVER	$645,583	$722,695	11.9%
10	FLORIDA	$1,450,392	$1,421,507	-2.0%
11	KANSASCITY	$574,899	$607,226	5.6%

FIGURE 5-17 You can already discern some information from the calculated field, which identifies three problematic markets.

Note A quick look at Figure 5-17 confirms that the Variable Cost Next Year field is not displayed in the pivot table report. Can you build pivot table formulas with fields that are currently *not even in* the pivot table? The answer is yes; you can use any field available to you in the PivotTable Fields list, even if the field is not shown in the pivot table.

To create this field, do the following:

1. Activate the Insert Calculated Field dialog and name your new field: Contribution Margin.

2. Delete the 0 in the Formula input box.

3. Double-click the Forecast Next Year field.

4. Enter + (a plus sign).

5. Double-click the Variable Cost Next Year field.

After you have entered the full formula, your dialog should look like the one shown in Figure 5-18.

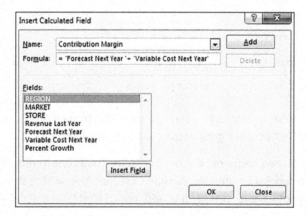

FIGURE 5-18 With just a few clicks, you have created a formula that calculates the contribution margin.

Now that you have created the Contribution Margin calculation, this report is ready to be formatted and delivered (see Figure 5-19).

	A	B	C	D	E
1					
2					
3	MARKET	Revenue Last Year	Forecast Next Year	Sum of Percent Growth	Sum of Contribution Margin
4	BUFFALO	$450,478	$411,246	-8.7%	($169,546)
5	CALIFORNIA	$2,254,735	$2,423,007	7.5%	$1,152,641
6	CANADA	$776,245	$746,384	-3.8%	$118,415
7	CHARLOTTE	$890,522	$965,361	8.4%	$360,343
8	DALLAS	$467,089	$510,635	9.3%	($908,021)
9	DENVER	$645,583	$722,695	11.9%	($697,393)
10	FLORIDA	$1,450,392	$1,421,507	-2.0%	$865,700
11	KANSASCITY	$574,899	$607,226	5.6%	($328,773)
12	MICHIGAN	$678,705	$870,447	28.3%	($92,813)
13	NEWORLEANS	$333,454	$366,174	9.8%	($586,405)
14	NEWYORK	$873,581	$953,010	9.1%	$506,335
15	PHOENIX	$570,255	$746,721	30.9%	$318,496
16	SEATTLE	$179,827	$214,621	19.3%	($163,738)
17	TULSA	$628,405	$661,726	5.3%	($1,193,984)
18	Grand Total	$10,774,172	$11,620,760	7.9%	($818,743)

FIGURE 5-19 Contribution Margin is now a data field in your pivot table report, thanks to your calculated field.

With this pivot table report, you can easily analyze any new forecast submissions by refreshing your report with the new updates.

Creating a calculated item

As you learned at the beginning of this chapter, a calculated item is a virtual data item you create by executing a calculation against existing items within a data field. Calculated items come in especially handy when you need to group and aggregate a set of data items.

For example, the pivot table in Figure 5-20 gives you sales amount by sales period. Imagine that you need to compare the average performance of the most recent six sales periods to the average of the prior seven periods. That is, you want to take the average of P01–P07 and compare it to the average of P08–P13.

Note Watch the Grand Total amount through the next several examples. The $10.77 million shown in Figure 5-20 is the correct amount.

	M	N
3	Sales_Period ▾	Sum of Sales_Amount
4	P01	$681,865
5	P02	$1,116,916
6	P03	$657,611
7	P04	$865,498
8	P05	$925,802
9	P06	$868,930
10	P07	$640,587
11	P08	$1,170,262
12	P09	$604,552
13	P10	$891,253
14	P11	$949,605
15	P12	$887,665
16	P13	$513,625
17	**Grand Total**	**$10,774,172**
18		

FIGURE 5-20 You want to compare the most recent six sales periods to the average of the prior seven periods.

Caution Calculated Items are always added to one specific field in the pivot table. In this case, you are calculating new totals along the Sales_Period field. Thus, you must select one of the Sales_Period cells before selecting Calculated Item from the Fields, Items, and Sets dropdown.

Follow these steps to compare the most recent six sales periods to the average of the prior seven periods:

1. Place your cursor on any data item in the Sales_Period field, and then select Fields, Items, & Sets from the Calculations group.

2. Next, select Calculated Item, as shown in Figure 5-21. Selecting this option opens the Insert Calculated Item dialog. A quick glance at Figure 5-22 shows you that the top of the dialog identifies which field you are working with. In this case, it is the Sales_Period field. In addition, notice that the Items list box is automatically filled with all the items in the Sales_Period field.

3. You need to give your calculated item a name and then build its formula by selecting the combination of data items and operators that provides the metric you are looking for.

4. In this example, name your first calculated item **Avg P1-P7 Sales**, as shown in Figure 5-23.

5. Next, you can build your formula in the Formula input box by selecting the appropriate data items from the Items list. In this scenario, you want to create the following formula:

=Average(P01, P02, P03, P04, P05, P06, P07)

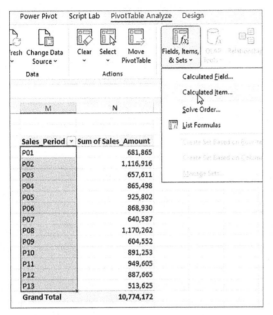

FIGURE 5-21 Start the creation of your calculated item by selecting one cell that represents a sales period and then selecting Calculated Item.

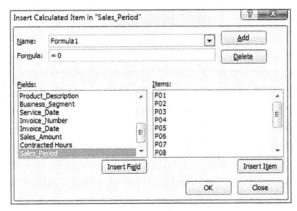

FIGURE 5-22 The Insert Calculated Item dialog is automatically populated to reflect the field with which you are working.

6. Enter the formula shown in Figure 5-23 into the Formula input box.

7. Click OK to activate your new calculated item. As you can see in Figure 5-24, you now have a data item called Avg P1-P7 Sales.

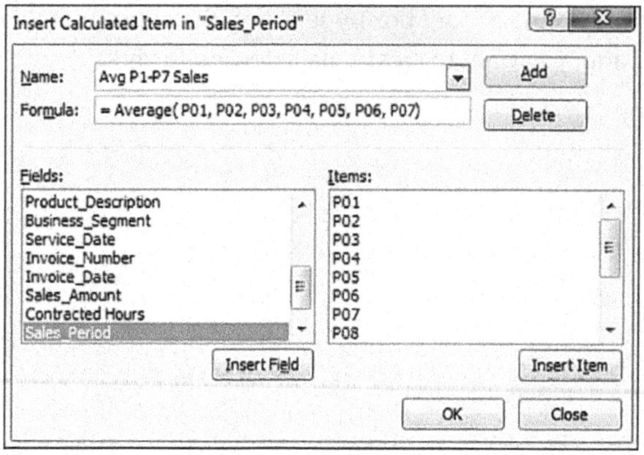

FIGURE 5-23 Enter a formula that gives you the average of P01–P07.

	A	B
1		
2		
3	**Row Labels** ▼	**Sum of Sales_Amount**
4	P01	$681,865
5	P02	$1,116,916
6	P03	$657,611
7	P04	$865,498
8	P05	$925,802
9	P06	$868,930
10	P07	$640,587
11	P08	$1,170,262
12	P09	$604,552
13	P10	$891,253
14	P11	$949,605
15	P12	$887,665
16	P13	$513,625
17	Avg P1-P7 Sales	$822,458
18	**Grand Total**	**$11,596,630**

FIGURE 5-24 You have successfully added a calculated item to row 17 of your pivot table, although the Grand Total is now incorrect.

There is an oddity in the formula language for calculated items. In the previous formula, you explicitly called out Period 1 using the P01 name of the field. If, for some reason, you weren't sure if this was going to be called P01 or M01 or something else, you could refer to the item using an index number in square brackets. Sales_Period[1] would be the way to refer to the first sales period shown in the pivot table.

This would lengthen the formula to

```
=AVERAGE(Sales_Period[1], Sales_Period[2], Sales_Period[3], Sales_Period[4],
Sales_Period[5], Sales_Period[6], Sales_Period[7])
```

It is also possible to use a relative index number. To refer to the sales period five items after the calculated item, you could use =Sales_Period[+5]. Oddly, the relative index number can only be positive, making it impossible to point to the previous item in the list using a relative index.

You can use any worksheet function in both a calculated field and a calculated item. The only restriction is that the function you use cannot reference external cells or named ranges. In effect, this means you can use any worksheet function that does not require cell references or defined names to work (such as COUNT, AVERAGE, IF, and OR).

Create a calculated item to represent the average sales for P08–P13, as shown in Figure 5-25.

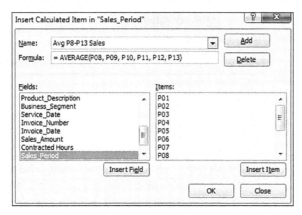

FIGURE 5-25 Create a second calculated item.

Now, you can hide the individual sales periods so that the report shows only the two calculated items. As shown in Figure 5-26, after a little formatting, your calculated items allow you to compare the average performance of the six most recent sales periods to the average of the prior seven periods.

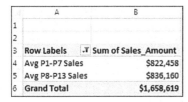

	A	B
1		
2		
3	Row Labels	Sum of Sales_Amount
4	Avg P1-P7 Sales	$822,458
5	Avg P8-P13 Sales	$836,160
6	Grand Total	$1,658,619

FIGURE 5-26 You can now compare the six most recent sales periods to the average of the prior seven periods.

Caution It is often prudent to hide the data items you used to create your calculated item. In Figure 5-26, notice that all periods have been hidden. This prevents any grand totals and subtotals from showing incorrect aggregations. One could argue that the sum of two averages shown in the Grand Total row is meaningless. Remove the Grand Total by choosing PivotTable Tools | Design, Grand Totals, Off For Rows And Columns.

Understanding the rules and shortcomings of pivot table calculations

There is no better way to integrate your calculations into a pivot table than by using calculated fields and calculated items. However, calculated fields and calculated items do come with their own set of drawbacks. It's important you understand what goes on behind the scenes when you use pivot table calculations, and it's even more important to be aware of the boundaries and limitations of calculated fields and calculated items to avoid potential errors in your data analysis.

The following sections highlight the rules related to calculated fields and calculated items that you will most likely encounter when working with pivot table calculations.

Remembering the order of operator precedence

Just as in a spreadsheet, you can use any operator in your calculation formulas—meaning any symbol that represents a calculation to perform (+, -, *, /, %, ^). Moreover, just as in a spreadsheet, calculations in a pivot table follow the order of operator precedence. In other words, when you perform a calculation that combines several operators, as in (2+3) * 4/50%, Excel evaluates and performs the calculation in a specific order. Excel's order of operations is as follows:

- Evaluate items in parentheses.

- Evaluate ranges (:).

- Evaluate intersections (spaces).

- Evaluate unions (,).

- Perform negation (-).

- Convert percentages (%).

- Perform exponentiation (^).

- Perform multiplication (*) and division (/), which are of equal precedence.

- Perform addition (+) and subtraction (-), which are of equal precedence.

- Evaluate text operators (&).

- Perform comparisons (=, <, >, <>, <=, >=).

 Note Operations that are equal in precedence are performed from left to right.

Consider this basic example. The correct answer to (2+3)*4 is 20. However, if you leave off the parentheses so that you have 2+3*4, Excel performs the calculation like this: 3*4 = 12 + 2 = 14. The order of operator precedence mandates that Excel perform multiplication before addition. Entering

2+3*4 gives you the wrong answer. Because Excel evaluates and performs all calculations in parentheses first, placing 2+3 inside parentheses ensures the correct answer.

Here is another widely demonstrated example. If you enter 10^2, which represents the exponent 10 to the second power as a formula, Excel returns 100 as the answer. If you enter –10^2, you expect –100 to be the result, but instead, Excel returns 100 yet again. The reason is that Excel performs negation before exponentiation, which means Excel converts 10 to –10 before doing the exponentiation, effectively calculating –10*–10, which indeed equals 100. When you use parentheses in the formula, –(10^2), Excel calculates the exponent before negating the answer, giving you –100.

Understanding the order of operations helps you avoid miscalculating your data.

Using cell references and named ranges

When you create calculations in a pivot table, you are essentially working in a vacuum. The only data available to you is the data that exists in the pivot cache. Therefore, you cannot reach outside the confines of the pivot cache to reference cells or named ranges in your formula.

Using worksheet functions

When you build calculated fields or calculated items, Excel enables you to use any worksheet function that accepts numeric values as arguments and returns numeric values as the result. Some of the many functions that fall into this category are COUNT, AVERAGE, IF, AND, NOT, and OR.

Some examples of functions you cannot use are VLOOKUP, INDEX, SUMIF, COUNTIF, LEFT, and RIGHT. Again, these are all impossible to use because they either require cell array references or return textual values as the result.

Using constants

You can use any constant in your pivot table calculations. Constants are static values that do not change. For example, in the formula [Units Sold]*5, 5 is a constant. Though the value of Units Sold might change based on the available data, 5 always has the same value.

Referencing totals

Your calculation formulas cannot reference a pivot table's subtotals or the grand total, meaning you cannot use the result of a subtotal or grand total as a variable or an argument in a calculated field. Measures created using the DAX formula language can overcome this limitation.

Rules specific to calculated fields

Calculated fields will not work in all cases. Sometimes, it is better to add the intermediate calculation to the original data set.

Consider the very simple data set shown in Figure 5-27. You had two sales of apples in Q1. The first was five cases at $20 and then five cases at $25. The total Q1 sales should be $225 derived by calculating =SUM(5*20,5*25).

	A	B	C	D	E	F	G
1	Qtr	Product	Units	Price		Total Q1 Apple	
2	1	Apple	5	20		100	
3	1	Apple	5	25		125	
4	1	Banana	3	28		225	
5	1	Banana	2	33			
6	1	Cherry	3	42			

FIGURE 5-27 The total sales for apples in Q1 should be $225.

The pivot table will get this calculation wrong on several levels. Cell L2 in Figure 5-28 adds the two unit prices together, producing a meaningless answer of $45. The calculated field in M2 then takes the correct total of 10 cases of apples times the incorrect price of $45 to arrive at $450 as the total Q1 revenue for apples. Recall that the correct answer from Figure 5-27 should have been $225. The problem gets worse at the Q1 total of $9,424 versus a correct answer of $1,192. The issues continue to escalate. Not shown in the figure, at the Grand Total level, the pivot table shows $137,372 versus a correct answer of $4,257.

Based on the example in Figure 5-28, you would think that the rule is that pivot tables are summing first, and then the calculated field is multiplying the summary numbers. But this is not always true.

	I	J	K	L	M
1	Qtr ▼	Product ▼	Total Units	Total Price	Calc: Units Times Price M
2		⊟1 Apple	10	45	450
3		1 Banana	5	61	305
4		1 Cherry	5	89	445
5		1 Dill	11	109	1199
6	1 Total		31	304	9424
7		⊟2 Apple	7	39	273

FIGURE 5-28 This pivot table was wrong before it got to the calculated field in column M.

Based on Figure 5-28, the rule seems to be that the pivot table will perform the aggregation first and then use the formulas in the Calculated Field. However, look at a different example from the same data set. Your manager wants to know the lowest price for apples, the highest price for apples, and the difference between those.

Drag Price to the Values area two more times. Double-click the heading in N1 and change the calculation to Min. Double-click the heading in O1 and change the calculation to Max. The numbers in columns N and O are correct.

But then add a calculated field with MAX(Price) - MIN(Price), as shown in Figure 5-29. If Excel is doing the aggregation first, the answer to this formula should be 25–20 or 5. But the answer is zero. This indicates that Excel is reaching back and doing this math: =SUM(MAX(D2)-MIN(D2),MAX(D3)-MIN(D3)). Why does the calculation engine change methods? If you worked on the Excel team in Redmond, you could do some Excel archaeology in the code base to figure it out, but the easier method is to switch from calculated fields to measures, as described in the following case study.

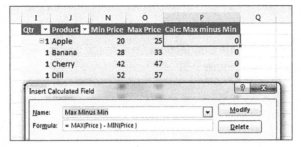

FIGURE 5-29 Min and Max work fine, but the Max Minus Min fails as a calculated field.

Case study: Using DAX measures instead of calculated fields

You can correctly solve this using a combination of Power Query, the Data Model, and a DAX measure:

1. Select one cell in your data and use Home, Format As Table.

2. On the Table Tools Design tab, change the name of your table from Table1 to OriginalData.

3. From the Data tab, choose From Table/Range in the Get & Transform Data group.

4. In the Power Query editor, select Add Column | Custom Column. Define Revenue as `=[Units]*[Price]` (see Figure 5-30).

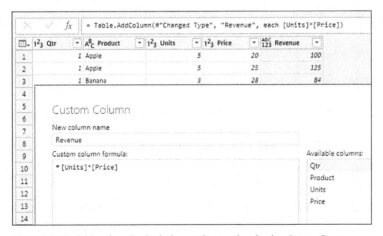

FIGURE 5-30 Add a virtual calculation at the row level using Power Query.

5. Select your new Revenue column in Power Query. On the Transform tab, open the Data Type dropdown and choose Currency.

6. In the top right of the Power Query Editor, change the Name from OriginalData to DataWithRevenue.

7. In Power Query, open the Close & Load dropdown on the Home tab. Choose Close and Load To.

8. In the Import Data dialog, choose Only Create Connection. Choose the box for Add This Data To The Data Model and click OK (see Figure 5-31).

FIGURE 5-31 Load the query to the Data Model as a Connection.

9. Insert a new blank worksheet in the workbook.

10. From the blank worksheet, select Insert | PivotTable | From Data Model (see Figure 5-32).

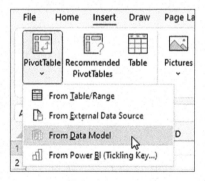

FIGURE 5-32 Choose to create a pivot table from the Data Model.

11. In the Create PivotTable From Data Model dialog, click OK (see Figure 5-33).

FIGURE 5-33 When you specify the pivot table should be built from the Data Model, the only question left is, "Where do you want the pivot table?"

12. In the PivotTable Fields list, you will see two tables: OriginalData and DataWithRevenue. Expand the DataWithRevenue table. Drag Qtr and Product to the Rows area. Drag Units and Revenue to the Values area. At this point, the Revenue in Column D is correct. The next steps will attempt to show the Min, Max, and Delta of the unit prices.

13. Drag Price to the Values area twice.

14. Double-click the heading for the first price and change the calculation to Min. Change the field name to **Min Price**.

15. Double-click the heading for the second price. Change the calculation to Max. Change the field name to **Max Price**.

> **Caution** If you listen to the Power Pivot pros, such as my good friend Rob Collie at P3Adaptive.com, he will tell you that steps 14 and 15 have created a pair of evil "implicit measures." Rob will ominously warn you never to use implicit measures. I generally believe that Rob must have really had a bad experience with implicit measures in his adolescent years on the Power Pivot team. I am sure Rob has a reason that is way above my head for saying they are evil. But here is my confession: I've now heard Rob say this for 15 years, and for 15 years, I have ignored Rob and used implicit measures all the time. No evil has befallen me in those 15 years. None. My hair is a bit grayer, but it is not because of these implicit measures.
>
> Now, I know that Rob is super busy running around the country doing Power Pivot seminars, and I know he will never have time to read this book, specifically this page.
>
> But do me a favor: If you ever run into Rob Collie in a dark alley, please don't tell him that I am encouraging you to use implicit measures. Let's keep that between us.

16. In the PivotTable Fields list, right-click the DataWithRevenue heading and choose Add Measure.

17. In the Measure dialog, type the Measure Name as **Max Minus Min**.

18. Move to the Formula box. Type an equal sign and then the left square bracket: `=[`. This will bring up a list of all fields. Choose `[Max of Price]` from the list. Type a minus sign and another left square bracket: `-[`. Choose `[Min of Price]` (see Figure 5-34). Optionally, use the Category list box to classify the calculation as Currency with 0 decimal places.

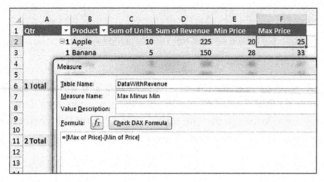

FIGURE 5-34 Create a measure using DAX.

Click OK to finish adding the measure. Wait. Wait some more. Nothing happens to your pivot table. I get tripped up by this every single time. You would think that Excel would add the new measure to the pivot table automatically, but it doesn't. Instead, the new Max Minus Min appears with an *fx* logo in the PivotTable Fields list (see Figure 5-35). This makes me think, "Why did I go to the trouble of adding this measure if I didn't want to add it to the pivot table?" But look, I appreciate the Excel team and the Pivot Table team, and I would never say those thoughts out loud.

FIGURE 5-35 You've defined the measure, but Excel does not automatically add it to the pivot table.

19. Choose the Max Minus Min field in the PivotTable Fields list. It will automatically move to the Values area.

The result is shown in Figure 5-36. The calculation for Max Minus Min is correct at all levels. Examine the Q1 total line in row 6. The Min price for the quarter is Apples at $20. The Max price is Dill at $57. The Max Minus Min in G6 is $37.

	A	B	C	D	E	F	G	H
1	Qtr ▼	Product ▼	Units	Revenue	Min Price	Max Price	Max Minus Min	
2		⊟1 Apple	10	225	20	25	$5	
3		1 Banana	5	150	28	33	$5	
4		1 Cherry	5	220	42	47	$5	
5		1 Dill	11	597	52	57	$5	
6	1 Total		31	1192	20	57	$37	
7		⊟2 Apple	7	134	17	22	$5	
8		2 Banana	12	306	23	28	$5	
9		2 Cherry	9	353	37	42	$5	
10		2 Dill	5	260	50	55	$5	
11	2 Total		33	1053	17	55	$38	
12		⊟3 Apple	6	105	15	20	$5	
13		3 Banana	8	172	19	24	$5	
14		3 Cherry	6	243	38	43	$5	
15		3 Dill	7	386	53	58	$5	
16	3 Total		27	906	15	58	$43	
17		⊟4 Apple	8	180	20	25	$5	
18		4 Banana	7	218	29	34	$5	
19		4 Cherry	6	213	33	38	$5	
20		4 Dill	10	495	47	52	$5	
21	4 Total		31	1106	20	52	$32	
22	Grand Total		122	4257	15	58	$43	
23								

FIGURE 5-36 Using a DAX measure, the Max Minus Min calculation works.

I don't want to disparage the regular pivot table calculated fields, but every time I run into something that a pivot table cannot do, I find that a few DAX measures can solve the problem.

Note The real reason that Excel does not add your new measure to the pivot table is simple: Many people will build complex calculations in steps. Only the final measure is used in the pivot table.

Note To learn more about DAX, check out Rob Collie's book *Power Pivot and Power BI* (ISBN 978-1-61547-062-4) or Matt Allington's *Supercharge Power BI 3rd Edition* (ISBN 978-1-61547-069-3).

Rules specific to calculated items

To use calculated items effectively, it is important that you understand a few ground rules:

- You cannot use calculated items in a pivot table that uses averages, standard deviations, or variances. Conversely, you cannot use averages, standard deviations, or variances in a pivot table that contains a calculated item.

- You cannot use a filter field to create a calculated item, nor can you move any calculated item to the report filter area.

- You cannot add a calculated item to a report that has a grouped field, nor can you group any field in a pivot table that contains a calculated item.

- When building your calculated item formula, you cannot reference items from a field other than the one you are working with.

As you think about the pages you have just read, don't be put off by these shortcomings of pivot tables. Despite the clear limitations highlighted, the capability to create custom calculations directly into your pivot table remains a powerful and practical feature that can enhance your data analysis.

Now that you are aware of the inner workings of pivot table calculations and understand the limitations of calculated fields and items, you can avoid the pitfalls and use these features with confidence.

Managing and maintaining pivot table calculations

In your dealings with pivot tables, you will find that sometimes you don't keep a pivot table for more than the time it takes to say, "Copy, Paste Values." Other times, however, it will be more cost-effective to keep a pivot table and all its functionality intact.

When you find yourself maintaining and managing pivot tables through changing requirements and growing data, you might find the need to maintain and manage your calculated fields and calculated items as well.

Editing and deleting pivot table calculations

When a calculation's parameters change, or you no longer need a calculated field or calculated item, you can activate the appropriate dialog to edit or remove the calculation.

Simply activate the Insert Calculated Field or Insert Calculated Item dialog and select the Name dropdown, as demonstrated in Figure 5-37.

As you can see in Figure 5-38, after you select a calculated field or item, you have the option of deleting the calculation or modifying the formula.

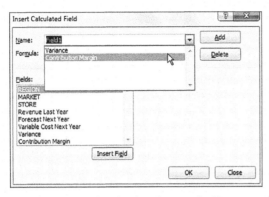

FIGURE 5-37 Opening the dropdown under Name reveals all the calculated fields or items in the pivot table.

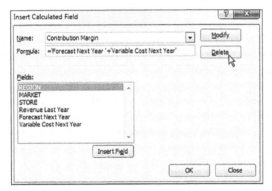

FIGURE 5-38 After you select the appropriate calculated field or item, you can either delete or modify the calculation.

Changing the solve order of calculated items

If the value of a cell in your pivot table is dependent on the results of two or more calculated items, you have the option of changing the solve order of the calculated items. That is, you can specify the order in which the individual calculations are performed.

To specify the order of calculations, you need the Solve Order dialog. To get there, place your cursor anywhere in the pivot table, select Fields, Items, & Sets from the Calculations group, and then select Solve Order.

The Solve Order dialog, shown in Figure 5-39, lists all the calculated items that currently exist in the pivot table. The order in which the formulas are listed here is the order in which the pivot table will perform the operations. To make changes to this order, select any of the calculated items you see and then click Move Up, Move Down, or Delete, as appropriate.

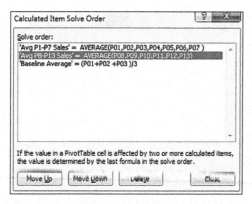

FIGURE 5-39 After you identify the calculated item you are working with, simply move the item up or down to change the solve order. You also have the option of deleting items in this dialog.

Documenting formulas

Excel provides a nice little function that lists the calculated fields and calculated items used in a pivot table, along with details on the solve order and formulas. This feature comes in especially handy if you need to quickly determine what calculations are being applied in a pivot table and which fields or items those calculations affect.

To list your pivot table calculations, simply place your cursor anywhere in the pivot table, select Fields, Items, & Sets, and then select List Formulas. Excel creates a new tab in your workbook that lists the calculated fields and calculated items in the current pivot table. Figure 5-40 shows an example of a tab created by the List Formulas command.

Calculated Field		
Solve Order	Field	Formula
Calculated Item		
Solve Order	Item	Formula
1	'Avg P1-P7 Sales'	= AVERAGE(P01,P02,P03,P04,P05,P06,P07)
2	'Avg P8-P13 Sales'	= AVERAGE(P08,P09,P10,P11,P12,P13)
3	'Baseline Average'	=(P01+P02 +P03)/3
Note:	When a cell is updated by more than one formula,	
	the value is set by the formula with the last solve order.	
	To change formula solve orders,	
	use the Solve Order command on the Pivot Formulas drop down menu.	

FIGURE 5-40 The List Formulas command documents the details of your pivot table calculations quickly and easily.

Next steps

In Chapter 6, "Using pivot charts and other visualizations," you will discover the fundamentals of pivot charts and the basics of representing your pivot data graphically. You'll also get a firm understanding of the limitations of pivot charts and alternatives to using pivot charts.

Using pivot charts and other visualizations

In this chapter, you will:

- Learn about pivot charts

- Create a pivot chart

- Keep pivot chart rules in mind

- Examine alternatives to using pivot charts

- Use conditional formatting with pivot tables

- Create custom conditional formatting rules

What is a pivot chart...really?

When sharing your analyses with others, you will quickly find that there is no getting around the fact that people want charts. Pivot tables are nice, but they show a lot of pesky numbers that take time to absorb. Charts, on the other hand, enable people to make split-second determinations about what the data is actually revealing. Charts offer instant gratification, allowing people to immediately see relationships, point out differences, and observe trends. The bottom line is that managers today want to absorb data as fast as possible, and nothing delivers that capability faster than a chart. This is where pivot charts come into play. Whereas pivot tables offer the analytical, pivot charts offer the visual.

A common definition of a pivot chart is a graphical representation of the data in a pivot table. Although this definition is technically correct, it somehow misses the mark on what a pivot chart truly does.

When you create a standard chart from data that is not in a pivot table, you feed the chart a range made up of individual cells holding individual pieces of data. Each cell is an individual object with its own piece of data, so your chart treats each cell as an individual data point and thus charts each one separately.

However, the data in a pivot table is part of a larger object. The pieces of data you see inside a pivot table are not individual pieces of data that occupy individual cells. Rather, they are items inside a larger pivot table object that is occupying space on your worksheet.

When you create a chart from a pivot table, you are not feeding it individual pieces of data inside individual cells; you are feeding it the entire pivot table layout. Indeed, a *pivot chart* is a chart that uses a PivotLayout object to view and control the data in a pivot table.

Using the PivotLayout object allows you to interactively add, remove, filter, and refresh data fields inside a pivot chart, just like in a pivot table. The result of all this action is a graphical representation of the data you see in a pivot table.

Creating a pivot chart

There are (at least) five different ways to create a pivot chart:

- On the Insert tab, to the right of regular charts, a PivotChart dropdown offers the first two methods: PivotChart and PivotChart & PivotTable, as shown in Figure 6-1. The odd thing is that both of these options do the exact same thing—insert a blank pivot table and a blank pivot chart. The PivotTable Fields pane is now called PivotChart Fields. The Columns area is renamed as Legend (Series), and the Rows area is called Axis (Categories). As you start to add fields to the pivot table, Excel automatically starts creating a Clustered Column chart. If you wish to use a different chart type, you have to go to the Design tab in the ribbon and choose Change Chart Type. (For those of you counting, I could use these two icons as two different methods for creating a pivot chart, even though both icons appear to do the same thing.)

- You can use the Analyze Data tool on the Home tab. Most charts suggested in the Analyze Data pane offer a button to Insert PivotChart. While these charts are often Pie, Bar, or Column charts, you are still somewhat limited to the chart types that the algorithm happens to offer.

- The fourth method is to create any pivot table. With one cell in the pivot table selected, go to the Insert tab in the ribbon and choose a valid chart type. The resulting chart will be a pivot chart.

- The fifth method is the only way to create a pivot chart without an accompanying pivot table. If you add your data to the Data Model as described in Chapter 10, "Unlocking features with the Data Model and Power Pivot," you can use the Data Model window and choose to add a Pivot Chart. This creates a pivot chart without the underlying pivot table.

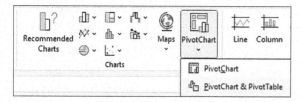

FIGURE 6-1 Using the PivotChart icon always leads to a clustered column chart. It seems simpler to create a pivot table and then convert it to a pivot chart.

Note In Chapter 9, "Using cube formulas with the Data Model or OLAP data," you will find out how to create pivot charts that are completely decoupled from any pivot table.

For the first pivot chart in this chapter, you will start with a pivot table and then add a pivot chart.

The pivot table in Figure 6-2 provides a simple view of the revenue by market. The Business_Segment field in the report filter area lets you parse out revenue by line of business.

Note The pivot table in Figure 6-2 is shown in Tabular layout. The Sum Of Sales_Amount heading in B3 has been replaced by typing **Sales Amount** in B3.

	A	B	C
1	Business_Segment	(All)	
2			
3	**Market**	**Sales Amount**	
4	CALIFORNIA	$2,254,735	
5	FLORIDA	$1,450,392	
6	MICHIGAN	$678,705	
7	BUFFALO	$450,478	
8	CANADA	$776,245	
9	CHARLOTTE	$890,522	
10	DALLAS	$467,089	
11	DENVER	$645,583	
12	KANSASCITY	$574,899	
13	NEWORLEANS	$333,454	
14	NEWYORK	$873,581	
15	PHOENIX	$570,255	
16	SEATTLE	$179,827	
17	TULSA	$628,405	
18	**Grand Total**	**$10,774,172**	
19			

FIGURE 6-2 This basic pivot table shows revenue by market and allows for filtering by line of business.

Creating a pivot chart from this data would not only allow for an instant view of the performance of each market but would also permit you to retain the ability to filter by line of business.

To start the process, place your cursor anywhere inside the pivot table and click the Insert tab on the ribbon. On the Insert tab, you can see the Charts group displaying the various types of charts you can create. Here, you can choose the chart type you would like to use for your pivot chart. For this example, click the Column chart icon and select the first 2-D column chart.

Figure 6-3 shows the chart Excel creates after you choose a chart type.

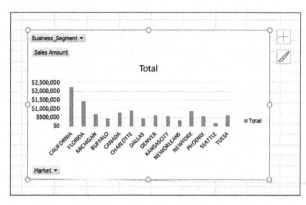

FIGURE 6-3 Excel creates your pivot chart on the same sheet as your pivot table.

Tip Notice that pivot charts are now, by default, placed on the same sheet as the source pivot table. If you long for the days when pivot charts were located on their own chart sheets, you are in luck. All you have to do is place your cursor inside a pivot table and then press F11 to create a pivot chart on its own sheet.

You can easily change the location of a pivot chart by right-clicking the chart (outside the plot area) and selecting Move Chart. This activates the Move Chart dialog, in which you can specify the new location.

You now have a chart that is a visual representation of your pivot table. More than that, because the pivot chart is tied to the underlying pivot table, changing the pivot table in any way changes the chart. For example, as Figure 6-4 illustrates, adding the Region field to the pivot table adds a region dimension to your chart.

FIGURE 6-4 The pivot chart displays the same fields that the underlying pivot table displays.

Note The pivot chart in Figure 6-4 does not display the subtotals shown in the pivot table. When creating a pivot chart, Excel ignores subtotals and grand totals.

In addition, filtering a business segment not only filters the pivot table but also the pivot chart. All this behavior comes from the fact that pivot charts use the same pivot cache and pivot layout as their corresponding pivot tables. This means that if you add or remove data from the data source and refresh the pivot table, the pivot chart updates to reflect the changes.

Take a moment to think about the possibilities. You can essentially create a fairly robust interactive reporting tool on the power of one pivot table and one pivot chart—no programming necessary.

Understanding pivot field buttons

In Figure 6-4, notice the gray buttons and dropdowns on the pivot chart. These are called pivot field buttons. By using these buttons, you can dynamically rearrange the chart and apply filters to the underlying pivot table.

The Expand Entire Field (+) and Collapse Entire Field (-) buttons are automatically added to any pivot chart that contains nested fields. Figure 6-4 shows these buttons in the lower-right corner of the chart.

Clicking Collapse Entire Field (-) on the chart collapses the data series and aggregates the data points. For example, Figure 6-5 shows the same chart collapsed to the Region level. You can click Expand Entire Field (+) to drill back down to the Market level. These new buttons enable customers to interactively drill down or roll up the data shown in pivot charts.

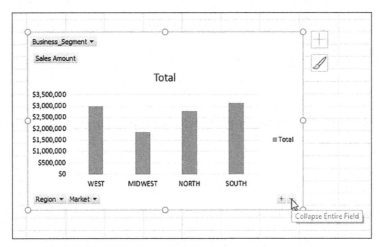

FIGURE 6-5 The new Expand Entire Field (+) and Collapse Entire Field (-) buttons allow for dynamic drill down and grouping of chart series.

Tip Keep in mind that pivot field buttons are visible when you print a pivot table. If you aren't too keen on showing the pivot field buttons directly on your pivot charts, you can remove them by clicking your chart and then selecting the PivotChart Analyze tab. On the PivotChart Analyze tab, you can use the Field Buttons dropdown to hide some or all the pivot field buttons.

 Tip Did you know you can also use slicers with pivot charts? Simply click a pivot chart, select the PivotChart Analyze tab, and then click the Insert Slicer icon to take advantage of all the benefits of slicers with your pivot chart!

 Note See "Using slicers to filter your report" in Chapter 2, "Creating a basic pivot table," to get a quick refresher on slicers.

Keeping pivot chart rules in mind

As with other aspects of pivot table technology, pivot charts come with their own set of rules and limitations. The following sections give you a better understanding of the boundaries and restrictions of pivot charts.

Changes in the underlying pivot table affect a pivot chart

The primary rule you should always be cognizant of is that a pivot chart that is based on a pivot table is merely an extension of the pivot table. If you refresh, move a field, add a field, remove a field, hide a data item, show a data item, or apply a filter, the pivot chart reflects your changes.

The placement of data fields in a pivot table might not be best suited for a pivot chart

One common mistake people make when using pivot charts is assuming that Excel places the values in the column area of the pivot table on the x-axis of the pivot chart.

For instance, the pivot table in Figure 6-6 is in a format that is easy to read and comprehend. The structure chosen shows Sales_Period in the column area and Region in the row area. This structure works fine in the pivot table view.

▲	A	B	C	D	E	F
1	Business_Segment (All) ▼					
2						
3	Sales Amount	Sales_Period ▼				
4	Region ▼	P01	P02	P03	P04	P05
5	MIDWEST	$109K	$207K	$102K	$155K	$159K
6	NORTH	$181K	$261K	$183K	$215K	$235K
7	SOUTH	$198K	$334K	$189K	$256K	$283K
8	WEST	$193K	$315K	$183K	$240K	$248K
9	Grand Total	$682K	$1,117K	$658K	$865K	$926K
10						

FIGURE 6-6 The placement of the data fields works for a pivot table view.

Suppose you decide to create a pivot chart from this pivot table. You would instinctively expect to see fiscal periods across the x-axis and lines of business along the y-axis. However, as you can see in Figure 6-7, the pivot chart comes out with Region on the x-axis and Sales_Period on the y-axis.

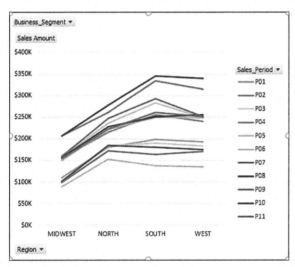

FIGURE 6-7 Creating a pivot chart from your nicely structured pivot table does not yield the results you were expecting.

So, why does the structure in the pivot table not translate to a clean pivot chart? The answer has to do with the way pivot charts handle the different areas of a pivot table.

In a pivot chart, both the x-axis and y-axis correspond to specific areas in your pivot table:

- **Axis (Categories)**—Corresponds to the row area in a pivot table and makes up the x-axis of a column chart.

- **Legend (Series)**—Corresponds to the column area in a pivot table. Each item here is a different series in the pivot chart.

Given this information, look again at the pivot table in Figure 6-6. This structure says that the Sales_Period field will be treated as the Legend because it is in the column area. Meanwhile, the Region field will be treated as the x-axis because it is in the row area.

Now, suppose you were to rearrange the pivot table to show fiscal periods in the row area and lines of business in the column area, as shown in Figure 6-8.

	A	B	C	D	E	F
1	Business_Segment (All)					
2						
3	Sales Amount	Region				
4	Sales_Period	MIDWEST	NORTH	SOUTH	WEST	Grand Total
5	P01	$109K	$181K	$198K	$193K	$682K
6	P02	$207K	$261K	$334K	$315K	$1,117K
7	P03	$119K	$207K	$215K	$209K	$750K
8	P04	$170K	$242K	$274K	$266K	$953K
9	P05	$166K	$234K	$302K	$261K	$962K
10	P06	$152K	$241K	$248K	$250K	$891K
11	P07	$158K	$238K	$271K	$262K	$929K
12	P08	$170K	$248K	$289K	$281K	$988K
13	P09	$147K	$226K	$226K	$242K	$841K
14	P10	$160K	$241K	$294K	$264K	$959K
15	P11	$171K	$249K	$292K	$271K	$982K
16	P12	$121K	$211K	$197K	$192K	$720K
17	Grand Total	$1,849K	$2,779K	$3,141K	$3,005K	$10,774K
18						

FIGURE 6-8 This format makes for slightly more difficult reading in a pivot table view but allows a pivot chart to give you the effect you are looking for.

This arrangement generates the pivot chart shown in Figure 6-9.

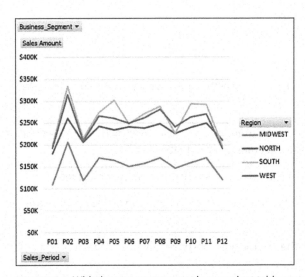

FIGURE 6-9 With the new arrangement in your pivot table, you get a pivot chart that makes sense.

A few formatting limitations still exist in Excel

With versions of Excel prior to Excel 2007, many people avoided using pivot charts because of their many formatting limitations. These limitations included the inability to resize or move key components of the pivot chart, the loss of formatting when underlying pivot tables were changed, and the inability to use certain chart types. Because of these limitations, most people viewed pivot charts as being too clunky and impractical to use.

Over the last few versions of Excel, Microsoft introduced substantial improvements to the pivot chart functionality. Today, the pivot charts in Excel look and behave very much like standard charts. However, a few limitations persist in Excel that you should keep in mind:

- You still cannot use XY (scatter), bubble, stock, map, waterfall, treemap, sunburst, histogram, funnel, or box and whisker charts when creating a pivot chart.

- Applied trend lines can be lost when you add or remove fields in the underlying pivot table.

- The chart titles in the pivot chart cannot be resized.

Tip Although you cannot resize the chart titles in a pivot chart, you can make the font bigger or smaller to indirectly resize a chart title. Alternatively, you can opt to create your own chart title by simply adding a text box that will serve as the title for your chart. To add a text box, select the Text Box command on the Insert tab and then click on your pivot chart. The resulting text box will be fully customizable to suit your needs.

Case study: Creating an interactive report showing revenue by product and time period

You have been asked to provide both region and market managers with an interactive reporting tool that will allow them to easily see revenues across products for a variety of time periods. Your solution needs to give managers the flexibility to filter out a region or market if needed, as well as give managers the ability to dynamically filter the chart for specific periods.

Given the amount of data in your source table and the possibility that this will be a recurring exercise, you decide to use a pivot chart. Follow these steps:

1. Start by building the pivot table shown in Figure 6-10.

▲	A	B
1	Region	(All) ▾
2	Market	(All) ▾
3		
4	Product_Description ▾	Sales Amount
5	Cleaning & Housekeeping Services	$1,139K
6	Facility Maintenance and Repair	$2,361K
7	Fleet Maintenance	$2,628K
8	Green Plants and Foliage Care	$1,277K
9	Landscaping/Grounds Care	$1,191K
10	Predictive Maintenance/Preventative Maintenance	$2,179K
11	Grand Total	$10,774K
12		

FIGURE 6-10 The initial pivot table meets all the data requirements.

2. Next, place your cursor anywhere inside the pivot table and click Insert. On the Insert tab, you can see the Charts menu displaying the various types of charts you can create. Choose the Column chart icon and select the first 2-D column chart. You immediately see a chart like the one in Figure 6-11.

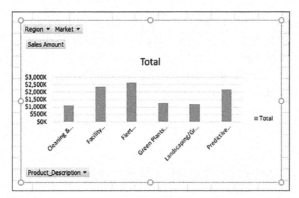

FIGURE 6-11 Your raw pivot chart needs some formatting to meet requirements.

3. Notice that the legend along the right side of the chart with the word Total is pointless in this chart. Regular Excel charts stopped adding single-entry legends in Excel 2013, yet they persist in pivot charts. Click the legend to select it and press the Delete key.

4. Next, click the newly created chart and select Insert Timeline from the PivotTable Analyze tab under PivotChart Tools (see Figure 6-12).

FIGURE 6-12 Insert a Timeline slicer.

Excel opens the Insert Timelines dialog, shown in Figure 6-13, which lists the available date fields in the pivot table.

FIGURE 6-13 Insert a Timeline slicer for Invoice_Date.

5. From the list, select Invoice_Date. You have created a slicer that aggregates and filters the pivot chart by time-specific periods (see Figure 6-14).

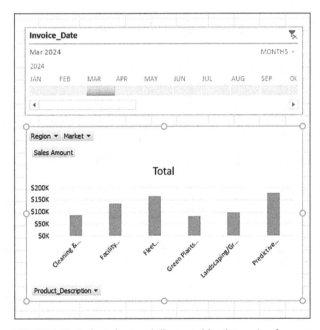

FIGURE 6-14 A pivot chart and slicer combination makes for a powerful reporting mechanism.

Note   See "Using slicers to filter your report" in Chapter 2 to get a quick refresher on Timeline slicers.

At this point, you can remove any superfluous pivot field buttons from the chart. In this case, the only buttons you need are the Region and Market dropdowns, which give your people an interactive way to filter the pivot chart. The other gray buttons you see on the chart are not necessary.

You can remove superfluous pivot field buttons by clicking the chart and selecting the PivotChart Analyze tab in the ribbon. You can then use the Field Buttons dropdown to choose the field buttons you want to be visible in the chart. In this case, you want only the Report filter field buttons to be visible, so select only that option (see Figure 6-15).

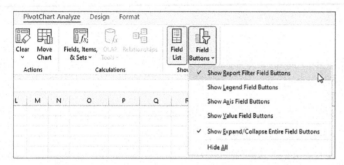

FIGURE 6-15 Use the Field Buttons dropdown to hide any unwanted pivot field buttons on the chart.

Your final pivot chart should look like the one in Figure 6-16.

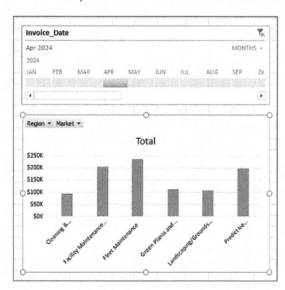

FIGURE 6-16 Your final report meets all the requirements of content and interactivity.

You now have a pivot chart that enables a manager to interactively review revenue by product and time period. This pivot chart also gives anyone using this report the ability to filter by region and market.

Examining alternatives to using pivot charts

There are generally two reasons you would need an alternative to using pivot charts:

- You do not want the overhead that comes with a pivot chart.

- You want to avoid some of the formatting limitations of pivot charts.

In fact, sometimes you might create a pivot table simply to summarize and shape data in preparation for charting. In these situations, you don't plan on keeping the source data, and you definitely don't want a pivot cache taking up memory and file space.

The example in Figure 6-17 shows a pivot table that summarizes revenue by quarter for each product.

	A	B	C	D	E	F
1						
2	Sum of Sales_Amount	Invoice_Date				
3	Product_Description	Qtr1	Qtr2	Qtr3	Qtr4	Grand Total
4	Cleaning & Housekeeping Services	$257,218	$290,074	$297,251	$294,049	$1,138,593
5	Facility Maintenance and Repair	$563,799	$621,715	$600,810	$574,834	$2,361,158
6	Fleet Maintenance	$612,496	$691,440	$674,592	$649,269	$2,627,798
7	Green Plants and Foliage Care	$293,194	$325,276	$329,787	$328,527	$1,276,783
8	Landscaping/Grounds Care	$288,797	$310,670	$303,086	$288,363	$1,190,915
9	Predictive Maintenance/Preventative Maintenance	$533,127	$567,391	$552,380	$526,027	$2,178,925
10	Grand Total	$2,548,631	$2,806,566	$2,757,906	$2,661,069	$10,774,172

FIGURE 6-17 This pivot table was created to summarize and chart revenue by quarter for each product.

Keep in mind that you need this pivot table only to summarize and shape data for charting. You don't want to keep the source data, nor do you want to keep the pivot table with all its overhead.

Caution If you try to create a chart using the data in the pivot table, you'll inevitably create a pivot chart. This effectively means you have all the overhead of the pivot table looming in the background. Of course, this could be problematic if you do not want to share your source data with end users or if you don't want to inundate them with unnecessarily large files.

The good news is you can use a few simple techniques to create a chart from a pivot table but not end up with a pivot chart. Any one of the following four methods does the trick:

- Turn the pivot table into hard values.

- Delete the underlying pivot table.

- Distribute a picture of the pivot chart.

- Use cells linked back to the pivot table as the source data for the chart.

Details about how to use each of these methods are discussed in the next sections.

Method 1: Turn the pivot table into hard values

After you have created and structured a pivot table appropriately, select the entire pivot table and copy it. Then select Paste Values from the Home tab, as demonstrated in Figure 6-18. This action essentially deletes your pivot table, leaving you with the last values that were displayed in the pivot table. You can subsequently use these values to create a standard chart.

Note This technique effectively disables the dynamic functionality of your pivot chart—that is, the pivot chart becomes a standard chart that cannot be interactively filtered or refreshed. This is also true with methods 2 and 3, which are outlined in the following sections.

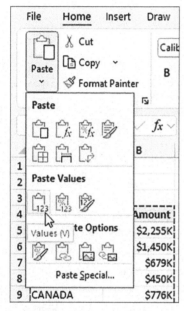

FIGURE 6-18 The Paste Values functionality is useful when you want to create hard-coded values from pivot tables.

Method 2: Delete the underlying pivot table

If you have already created a pivot chart, you can turn it into a standard chart by simply deleting the underlying pivot table. To do this, select the entire pivot table and press the Delete key on the keyboard. Keep in mind that with this method, unlike with method 1, you are left with none of the values that made up the source data for the chart. In other words, if anyone asks for the data that feeds the chart, you will not have it.

> **Tip**   Here is a handy tip to keep in the back of your mind: If you ever find yourself in a situation where you have a chart, but the data source is not available, activate the chart's Data Table. One quick way is to select the chart, click the Plus icon at the top-right corner of the chart, and select Data Table. The Data Table lets you see the data values that feed each series in the chart.

Method 3: Distribute a picture of the pivot chart

Now, it might seem strange to distribute pictures of a pivot chart, but this is an entirely viable method of distributing your analysis without a lot of overhead. In addition to very small file sizes, you also get the added benefit of controlling what your clients can see.

To use this method, right-click the chart itself (outside the plot area) and select Save as Picture. Select the picture type you prefer from (.png, .jpg, .gif, .tif, or .svg). A picture of your pivot chart is saved to your computer.

> **Caution**   If you have pivot field buttons on your chart, they will also show up in the copied picture. This will not only be unsightly but might leave your audience confused because the buttons don't work. Be sure to hide all pivot field buttons before copying a pivot chart as a picture. You can remove them by clicking on your chart and then selecting the PivotChart Analyze tab. On the PivotChart Analyze tab, you can use the Field Buttons dropdown and choose Hide All.

Method 4: Use cells linked back to the pivot table as the source data for the chart

Many Excellers shy away from using pivot charts solely based on the formatting restrictions and issues they encounter when working with them. Often, these people give up the functionality of a pivot table to avoid the limitations of pivot charts.

However, if you want to retain key functionality in your pivot table, such as report filters and top 10 ranking, you can link a standard chart to your pivot table without creating a pivot chart.

In the example in Figure 6-19, a pivot table shows the top 10 markets by contracted hours, along with their total revenue. Notice that the report filter area allows you to filter by business segment so you can see the top 10 market segments.

Suppose you want to turn this view into an XY scatter chart to be able to point out the relationship between the contracted hours and revenues.

	A	B	C
1	Business_Segment (All)		
2			
3	Market	Contracted Hours	Sales_Amount
4	CALIFORNIA	33,014	$2,254,735
5	FLORIDA	22,640	$1,450,392
6	CHARLOTTE	14,525	$890,522
7	NEWYORK	14,213	$873,581
8	CANADA	12,103	$776,245
9	MICHIGAN	10,744	$678,705
10	PHOENIX	10,167	$570,255
11	TULSA	9,583	$628,405
12	DENVER	8,641	$645,583
13	KANSASCITY	8,547	$574,899
14	Grand Total	144,177	$9,343,323

FIGURE 6-19 This pivot table allows you to filter by business segment to see the top 10 markets by total contracted hours and revenue.

Well, a pivot chart is definitely out because you can't build pivot charts with XY scatter charts. The techniques outlined in methods 1, 2, and 3 are also out because those methods disable the interactivity you need.

So, what's the solution? Use the cells around the pivot table to link back to the data you need, and then chart those cells. In other words, you can build a mini data set that feeds your standard chart. This data set links back to the data items in your pivot table, so when your pivot table changes, so does your data set.

Click your cursor in a cell next to your pivot table, as demonstrated in Figure 6-20, and reference the first data item that you need to create the range you will feed to your standard chart.

When you build the formula in E4, make sure to type =B4 without using the mouse or arrow keys to point to B4. If you use the mouse or arrow keys, Excel will insert the GETPIVOTDATA function instead of your formula.

Now copy the formula you just entered and paste that formula down and across to create your complete data set. At this point, you should have a data set that looks like the one shown in Figure 6-21.

	A	B	C	D	E
1	Business_Segment (All)				
2					
3	Market	Contracted Hours	Sales_Amount		
4	CALIFORNIA	33,014	$2,254,735		=B4
5	FLORIDA	22,640	$1,450,392		
6	CHARLOTTE	14,525	$890,522		
7	NEWYORK	14,213	$873,581		
8	CANADA	12,103	$776,245		
9	MICHIGAN	10,744	$678,705		
10	PHOENIX	10,167	$570,255		
11	TULSA	9,583	$628,405		
12	DENVER	8,641	$645,583		
13	KANSASCITY	8,547	$574,899		
14	Grand Total	144,177	$9,343,323		

FIGURE 6-20 Start your linked data set by referencing the first data item you need to capture.

	A	B	C	D	E	F
1	Business_Segment (All)					
2						
3	Market	Contracted Hours	Sales_Amount		Contracted Hours	Sales_Amount
4	CALIFORNIA	33,014	$2,254,735		33,014	2,254,735
5	FLORIDA	22,640	$1,450,392		22,640	1,450,392
6	CHARLOTTE	14,525	$890,522		14,525	890,522
7	NEWYORK	14,213	$873,581		14,213	873,581
8	CANADA	12,103	$776,245		12,103	776,245
9	MICHIGAN	10,744	$678,705		10,744	678,705
10	PHOENIX	10,167	$570,255		10,167	570,255
11	TULSA	9,583	$628,405		9,583	628,405
12	DENVER	8,641	$645,583		8,641	645,583
13	KANSASCITY	8,547	$574,899		8,547	574,899
14	Grand Total	144,177	$9,343,323			

FIGURE 6-21 Copy the formula and paste it down and across to create your complete data set.

When your linked data set is complete, you can use it to create a standard chart. In this example, you are creating an XY scatter chart with this data. You could never do this with a pivot chart.

Figure 6-22 demonstrates how this solution offers the best of both worlds. You can filter out a particular business segment using the page field, and you also have all the formatting freedom of a standard chart without any of the issues related to using a pivot chart.

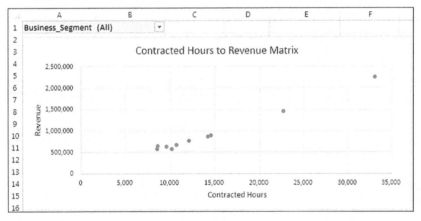

FIGURE 6-22 This solution allows you to continue using the functionality of your pivot table without any of the formatting limitations you would have with a pivot chart.

Using conditional formatting with pivot tables

In the next sections, you'll learn how to leverage the magic combination of pivot tables and conditional formatting to create interactive visualizations that serve as an alternative to pivot charts.

An example of using conditional formatting

To start the first example, create the pivot table shown in Figure 6-23.

	A	B	C
1			
2	Market	Sum of Sales_Amount	Sum of Sales_Amount2
3	BUFFALO	$450,478	450,478
4	CALIFORNIA	$2,254,735	2,254,735
5	CANADA	$776,245	776,245
6	CHARLOTTE	$890,522	890,522
7	DALLAS	$467,089	467,089
8	DENVER	$645,583	645,583
9	FLORIDA	$1,450,392	1,450,392
10	KANSASCITY	$574,899	574,899
11	MICHIGAN	$678,705	678,705
12	NEWORLEANS	$333,454	333,454
13	NEWYORK	$873,581	873,581
14	PHOENIX	$570,255	570,255
15	SEATTLE	$179,827	179,827
16	TULSA	$628,405	628,405
17	Grand Total	$10,774,172	10,774,172

FIGURE 6-23 Create this pivot table.

Suppose you want to create a report that enables your managers to see the performance of each sales period graphically. You could build a pivot chart, but you decide to use conditional formatting. In this example, you'll go the easy route and quickly apply some data bars.

Select all the Sum Of Sales_Amount2 values in the Values area but not the Grand Total. After you have highlighted the revenue for each Sales_Period, click the Home tab and select Conditional Formatting in the Styles group. Then select Data Bars and select one of the Solid Fill options, as shown in Figure 6-24.

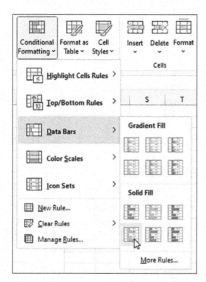

FIGURE 6-24 Apply data bars to the values in your pivot table.

You immediately see data bars in your pivot table, along with the values in the Sum Of Sales_ Amount2 field. You want to hide the actual value and show only the data bar. To do this, follow these steps:

1. Click the Conditional Formatting dropdown on the Home tab and select Manage Rules.

2. In the Rules Manager dialog, select the data bar rule you just created and select Edit Rule.

3. Select the Show Bar Only checkbox (see Figure 6-25).

As you can see in Figure 6-26, you now have a set of bars that correspond to the values in your pivot table. This visualization looks like a sideways chart, doesn't it? What's more impressive is that as you filter the markets in the report filter area, the data bars dynamically update to correspond with the data for the selected market.

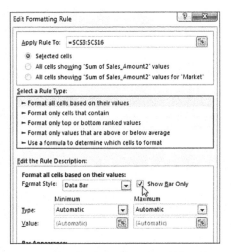

FIGURE 6-25 Check the Show Bar Only option to get a clean view of just the data bars.

	A	B	C
1			
2	**Market**	**Sum of Sales_Amount**	**Sum of Sales_Amount2**
3	BUFFALO	$450,478	
4	CALIFORNIA	$2,254,735	
5	CANADA	$776,245	
6	CHARLOTTE	$890,522	
7	DALLAS	$467,089	
8	DENVER	$645,583	
9	FLORIDA	$1,450,392	
10	KANSASCITY	$574,899	
11	MICHIGAN	$678,705	
12	NEWORLEANS	$333,454	
13	NEWYORK	$873,581	
14	PHOENIX	$570,255	
15	SEATTLE	$179,827	
16	TULSA	$628,405	
17	**Grand Total**	**$10,774,172**	10,774,172

FIGURE 6-26 You have applied conditional data bars with just three easy clicks!

Preprogrammed scenarios for condition levels

In the previous example, you did not have to trudge through a dialog to define the condition levels. How can that be? Excel has a handful of preprogrammed scenarios that you can leverage when you want to spend less time configuring your conditional formatting and more time analyzing your data.

For example, to create the data bars you've just employed, Excel uses a predefined algorithm that takes the largest and smallest values in the selected range and calculates the condition level for each bar.

Other examples of preprogrammed scenarios include the following:

- Top N Items
- Top N %
- Bottom *N* Items
- Bottom N %
- Above Average
- Below Average

As you can see, Excel makes an effort to offer the conditions that are most commonly used in data analysis.

Note To remove the applied conditional formatting, place your cursor inside the pivot table, click the Home tab, and select Conditional Formatting in the Styles group. From there, select Clear Rules | Clear Rules From This PivotTable.

Creating custom conditional formatting rules

It's important to note that you are by no means limited to the preprogrammed scenarios mentioned in the previous section. You can still create your own custom conditions.

To see how this works, you need to begin by creating the pivot table shown in Figure 6-27.

In this scenario, you want to evaluate the relationship between total revenue and dollars per hour. The idea is that some strategically applied conditional formatting helps identify opportunities for improvement.

Place your cursor in the Sales_Amount column. Click the Home tab and select Conditional Formatting | New Rule. This activates the New Formatting Rule dialog, shown in Figure 6-28. In this dialog, you need to identify the cells where the conditional formatting will be applied, specify the rule type to use, and define the details of the conditional formatting.

	A	B	C	D
1	Product_Description (All)			
2				
3	Market	Sales_Amount	Contracted Hours	Dollars Per Hour
4	BUFFALO	$450,478	6,864	$65.63
5	CALIFORNIA	$2,254,735	33,014	$68.30
6	CANADA	$776,245	12,103	$64.14
7	CHARLOTTE	$890,522	14,525	$61.31
8	DALLAS	$467,089	6,393	$73.06
9	DENVER	$645,583	8,641	$74.71
10	FLORIDA	$1,450,392	22,640	$64.06
11	KANSASCITY	$574,899	8,547	$67.26
12	MICHIGAN	$678,705	10,744	$63.17
13	NEWORLEANS	$333,454	5,057	$65.94
14	NEWYORK	$873,581	14,213	$61.46
15	PHOENIX	$570,255	10,167	$56.09
16	SEATTLE	$179,827	2,889	$62.25
17	TULSA	$628,405	9,583	$65.57
18	Grand Total	$10,774,172	165,380	$65.15

FIGURE 6-27 This pivot table shows Sales_Amount, Contracted_Hours, and a calculated field that calculates Dollars Per Hour.

First, you must identify the cells where your conditional formatting will be applied. You have three choices:

- **Selected Cells**—This selection applies conditional formatting to only the selected cells. In the image below, it would apply only to cell B4, which would not be useful.

- **All Cells Showing "Sales_Amount" Values**—This selection applies conditional formatting to all values in the Sales_Amount column, including all subtotals and grand totals. This selection is ideal for use in analyses using averages, percentages, or other calculations where a single conditional formatting rule makes sense for all levels of analysis.

- **All Cells Showing "Sales_Amount" Values for "Market"**—This selection applies conditional formatting to all values in the Sales_Amount column at the Market level only. (It excludes subtotals and grand totals.) This selection is ideal for use in analyses using calculations that make sense only within the context of the level being measured.

Note The words "Sales_Amount" and "Market" are not permanent fixtures of the New Formatting Rule dialog. These words change to reflect the fields in your pivot table. Sales_Amount is used here because the cursor is in that column. "Market" is used because the active data items in the pivot table are in the Market field.

FIGURE 6-28 The New Formatting Rule dialog.

In this example, the third selection (All Cells Showing "Sales_Amount" Values for "Market") makes the most sense, so click that radio button, as shown in Figure 6-29.

FIGURE 6-29 Click the radio button next to All Cells Showing "Sales_Amount" Values for "Market."

Next, in the Select A Rule Type section, you must specify the rule type you want to use for the conditional format. You can select one of five rule types:

- **Format All Cells Based On Their Values**—This selection enables you to apply conditional formatting based on some comparison of the actual values of the selected range; that is, the values in the selected range are measured against each other. This selection is ideal when you want to identify general anomalies in your data set.

- **Format Only Cells That Contain**—This selection enables you to apply conditional formatting to cells that meet specific criteria you define. Keep in mind that the values in your range are not measured against each other when you use this rule type. This selection is useful when you are comparing your values against a predefined benchmark.

- **Format Only Top Or Bottom Ranked Values**—This selection enables you to apply conditional formatting to cells that are ranked in the top or bottom Nth number or percentage of all the values in the range.

- **Format Only Values That Are Above Or Below Average**—This selection enables you to apply conditional formatting to values that are mathematically above or below the average of all values in the selected range.

- **Use A Formula To Determine Which Cells To Format**—This selection enables you to specify your own formula and evaluate each value in the selected range against that formula. If the values evaluate to true, the conditional formatting is applied. This selection comes in handy when you are applying conditions based on the results of an advanced formula or mathematical operation.

> **Note** You can use data bars, color scales, and icon sets only when the selected cells are formatted based on their values. This means that if you want to use data bars, color scales, and icon sets, you must select the Format All Cells Based On Their Values rule type.

In this scenario, you want to identify problem areas using icon sets; therefore, you want to format the cells based on their values, so select Format All Cells Based On Their Values.

Finally, you need to define the details of the conditional formatting in the Edit The Rule Description section. Again, you want to identify problem areas using the slick icon sets that Excel offers. Therefore, select Icon Sets from the Format Style drop down.

After selecting Icon Sets, select a style appropriate to your analysis. The style selected in Figure 6-30 is ideal in situations in which your pivot tables cannot always be viewed in color.

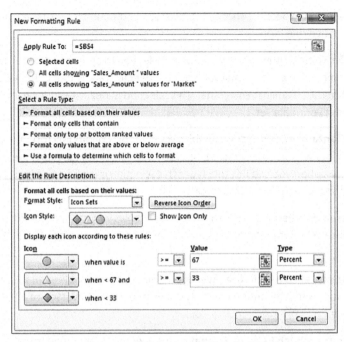

FIGURE 6-30 Select Icon Sets from the Format Style dropdown.

With this configuration, Excel applies the sign icons based on the percentile bands >=67, >=33, and <33. Keep in mind that you can change the actual percentile bands based on your needs. In this scenario, the default percentile bands are sufficient. Fun fact: three equal-sized bands are called *tertiles*.

Click the OK button to apply the conditional formatting. As you can see in Figure 6-31, you now have icons that enable you to quickly determine where each market falls in relation to other markets in terms of revenue.

	A	B	C	D
1	Product_Description (All) ▼			
2				
3	**Market** ▼	**Sales_Amount**	**Contracted Hours**	**Dollars Per Hour**
4	BUFFALO	◇ $450,478	6,864	$65.63
5	CALIFORNIA	○ $2,254,735	33,014	$68.30
6	CANADA	◇ $776,245	12,103	$64.14
7	CHARLOTTE	△ $890,522	14,525	$61.31
8	DALLAS	◇ $467,089	6,393	$73.06
9	DENVER	◇ $645,583	8,641	$74.71
10	FLORIDA	△ $1,450,392	22,640	$64.06
11	KANSASCITY	◇ $574,899	8,547	$67.26
12	MICHIGAN	◇ $678,705	10,744	$63.17
13	NEWORLEANS	◇ $333,454	5,057	$65.94
14	NEWYORK	△ $873,581	14,213	$61.46
15	PHOENIX	◇ $570,255	10,167	$56.09
16	SEATTLE	◇ $179,827	2,889	$62.25
17	TULSA	◇ $628,405	9,583	$65.57
18	**Grand Total**	**$10,774,172**	**165,380**	**$65.15**

FIGURE 6-31 You have applied your first custom conditional formatting!

Now apply the same conditional formatting to the Dollars Per Hour field. When you are done, your pivot table should look like the one shown in Figure 6-32.

	A	B	C	D
1	Product_Description (All) ▾			
2				
3	Market ▾	Sales_Amount	Contracted Hours	Dollars Per Hour
4	BUFFALO	◇ $450,478	6,864 △	$65.63
5	CALIFORNIA	◯ $2,254,735	33,014 △	$68.30
6	CANADA	◇ $776,245	12,103 △	$64.14
7	CHARLOTTE	△ $890,522	14,525 ◇	$61.31
8	DALLAS	◇ $467,089	6,393 ◯	$73.06
9	DENVER	◇ $645,583	8,641 ◯	$74.71
10	FLORIDA	△ $1,450,392	22,640 △	$64.06
11	KANSASCITY	◇ $574,899	8,547 △	$67.26
12	MICHIGAN	◇ $678,705	10,744 △	$63.17
13	NEWORLEANS	◇ $333,454	5,057 △	$65.94
14	NEWYORK	△ $873,581	14,213 ◇	$61.46
15	PHOENIX	◇ $570,255	10,167 ◇	$56.09
16	SEATTLE	◇ $179,827	2,889 △	$62.25
17	TULSA	◇ $628,405	9,583 △	$65.57
18	Grand Total	$10,774,172	165,380	$65.15

FIGURE 6-32 You have successfully created an interactive visualization.

Take a moment to analyze what you have here. With this view, a manager can analyze the relationship between total revenue and dollars per hour. For example, the Dallas market manager can see that they are in the bottom tertile for revenue but in the top tertile for dollars per hour. With this information, the manager immediately sees that their dollar-per-hour rates might be too high for his market. Conversely, the New York market manager can see that they are in the middle tertile for revenue but in the bottom tertile for dollars per hour. This tells the manager that their dollar-per-hour rates might be too low for their market.

Remember that this is an interactive report. Each manager can view the same analysis by product by simply filtering the report filter area!

Case study: Create a pivot chart without a pivot table

Most pivot charts have an accompanying pivot table. There is one way to make a pivot chart that is not connected to any pivot table.

1. Start with any data set. Select Home | Format As Table to convert the data set to a table.

2. If you do not see a Power Pivot tab in the ribbon, go to the Data tab in the Data Tools group, open the Data Model dropdown, and choose Manage Data Model. This takes you to the Power Pivot window. When you close the Power Pivot window and save the workbook, the Power Pivot tab should appear in the ribbon.

3. With one cell in your data set selected, go to the Power Pivot tab and choose Add To Data Model. The Power Pivot for Excel window opens, showing a copy of your data.

4. On the Home tab in the Power Pivot window, open the PivotTable dropdown and choose PivotChart, as shown in Figure 6-33. This will insert a new pivot chart in Excel without an associated pivot table.

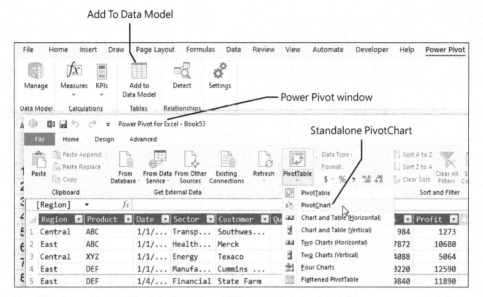

FIGURE 6-33 The Power Pivot window offers a way to create one or more pivot charts without an associated pivot table.

Next steps

In Chapter 7, "Analyzing disparate data sources with pivot tables," you will find out how to bring together disparate data sources into one pivot table. You will create a pivot table from multiple data sets and learn the basics of creating pivot tables from other pivot tables.

Analyzing disparate data sources with pivot tables

In this chapter, you will:

- Use the Data Model

- Build a pivot table using external data sources

- Leverage Power Query to extract and transform data

Up to this point, you have been working with one local table located in the worksheet within which you are operating. Indeed, it would be wonderful if every data set you came across was neatly packed in one easy-to-use Excel table. Unfortunately, the business of data analysis does not always work out that way.

The reality is that some of the data you encounter will come from disparate data sources—sets of data that are from separate systems, stored in different locations, or saved in a variety of formats. In an Excel environment, disparate data sources generally fall into one of two categories:

- **External data**—External data is exactly what it sounds like—data that is not located in the Excel workbook in which you are operating. Some examples of external data sources are text files, access tables, SQL Server tables, and other Excel workbooks.

- **Multiple ranges**—Multiple ranges are separate data sets located in the same workbook but separated either by blank cells or by different worksheets. For example, if your workbook has three tables on three different worksheets, each of your data sets covers a range of cells. Therefore, you are working with multiple ranges.

A pivot table can be an effective tool when you need to summarize data that is not neatly packed into one table. With a pivot table, you can quickly bring together either (or both) data found in an external source or data found in multiple tables within your workbook. In this chapter, you'll discover various techniques for working with external data sources and data sets located in multiple ranges within a workbook.

Using the Data Model

Excel 2013 introduced a new in-memory analytics engine called the Data Model that is based on the Power Pivot engine. Every workbook has one Data Model that enables you to work with and analyze disparate data sources like never before.

The idea behind the Data Model is simple. Let's say you have two tables: a Customers table and an Orders table. The Orders table contains basic information about invoices (customer number, invoice date, and revenue). The Customers table contains information such as customer number, customer name, and state. If you want to analyze revenue by state, you have to join the two tables and aggregate the Revenue field in the Orders table by the State field in the Customers table.

In the past, in order to do this, you would have had to go through a series of gyrations involving using VLOOKUP, SUMIF, or other functions. With the new Data Model, however, you can simply tell Excel how the two tables are related (they both have customer numbers) and then pull them into the Data Model. The Excel Data Model then builds an analytical cube based on that customer number relationship and exposes the data through a pivot table. With the pivot table, you can create the aggregation by state with a few mouse clicks.

Note The Data Model uses the Power Pivot data engine. Starting with Excel 2019, every Windows version of Excel includes full access to the Power Pivot tools. See Chapter 10, "Unlocking features with the Data Model and Power Pivot."

Building out your first Data Model

Imagine that you have the Transactions table shown in Figure 7-1. On another worksheet, you have the Employees table shown in Figure 7-2. Both of these tables have been formatted as a table by choosing Home | Format As Table.

Using Format As Table creates names like "Table 1" and "Table 2." After formatting as a table, visit the Table Design tab and assign new names, such as "Transactions" and "Employees."

	A	B	C	D
1	Sales_Rep	Invoice_Date	Sales_Amount	Contracted Hours
2	4416	1/5/2029	111.79	2
3	4416	1/5/2029	111.79	2
4	160006	1/5/2029	112.13	2
5	6444	1/5/2029	112.13	2
6	160006	1/5/2029	145.02	3
7	52661	1/5/2029	196.58	4
8	6444	1/5/2029	204.20	4
9	51552	1/5/2029	225.24	3
10	55662	1/6/2029	86.31	2

FIGURE 7-1 This table shows transactions by sales rep number.

	A	B	C	D
1	Employee_Number	Last_Name	First_Name	Job_Title
2	21	SIOCAT	ROBERT	SERVICE REPRESENTATIVE 3
3	42	BREWN	DONNA	SERVICE REPRESENTATIVE 3
4	45	VAN HUILE	KENNETH	SERVICE REPRESENTATIVE 2
5	104	WIBB	MAURICE	SERVICE REPRESENTATIVE 2
6	106	CESTENGIAY	LUC	SERVICE REPRESENTATIVE 2
7	113	TRIDIL	ROCH	SERVICE REPRESENTATIVE 2
8	142	CETE	GUY	SERVICE REPRESENTATIVE 3
9	145	ERSINEILT	MIKE	SERVICE REPRESENTATIVE 2
10	162	GEBLE	MICHAEL	SERVICE REPRESENTATIVE 2
11	165	CERDANAL	ALAIN	SERVICE REPRESENTATIVE 3
12	201	GEIDRIOU	DOMINIC	TEAMLEAD 1

FIGURE 7-2 This table provides information on employees: first name, last name, and job title.

You need to create an analysis that shows sales by job title. This would normally be difficult, given the fact that sales and job titles are in two separate tables. But with the new Data Model, you can follow these simple steps:

1. Go to the Data tab of the ribbon. In the Data Tools group, open the Data Model dropdown and choose Relationships.

2. In the Relationships dialog, click New.

3. In the Create Relationships dialog, the primary table is the Transactions table. The Column (Foreign) is Sales_Rep. On the next row of the dialog, specify Employees as the Related Table and Employee Number as the Related Column (Primary Key). (See Figure 7-3.)

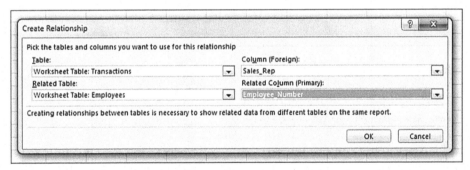

FIGURE 7-3 Define a relationship between the two tables.

The importance of primary keys

In Figure 7-3, the Related Column (Primary) dropdown appears at the lower right. In this case, the term "Primary" means that the Data Model uses this field from the associated table as the primary key.

A *primary key* is a field that contains only unique non-null values (no duplicates or blanks). Primary key fields are necessary in the Data Model to prevent aggregation errors and duplications. Every relationship you create must have a field designated as the primary key.

In the scenario in Figure 7-2, the Employees table must have all unique values in the Employee_Number field, with no blanks or null values. This is the only way Excel can ensure data integrity when joining multiple tables.

4. Click OK to create the relationship. This process might take a bit of time because this is the point where the two tables are added to the Data Model.

5. Click OK to close the Relationships dialog.

6. Insert a new blank worksheet in the workbook.

7. From the blank worksheet, select Insert | PivotTable | From Data Model. Notice the PivotTable Fields list in Figure 7-4. This is the Data Model version. At the top are two tabs: Active and All. Each table appears in the field well, and both are initially collapsed, so you cannot see the fields inside.

FIGURE 7-4 Each table appears in the PivotTable Fields panel.

8. Use the Greater-Than icon next to each table to expand the table. Drag Job_Title from the Employees table to Rows. Drag Sales_Amount from the Transactions table to Values.

After you create the relationship, you have a single pivot table that effectively uses data from both tables to create the analysis you need. Figure 7-5 illustrates that using the Excel Data Model, you have achieved the goal of showing sales by job title.

FIGURE 7-5 You have achieved your goal of showing sales by job title.

Managing relationships in the Data Model

After you assign tables to the Data Model, you might need to adjust the relationships between the tables. To make changes to the relationships in a Data Model, activate the Manage Relationships dialog.

Click the Data tab in the ribbon, open the Data Model dropdown, and select the Relationships command. The dialog shown in Figure 7-6 appears.

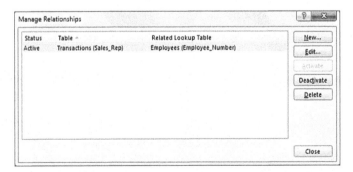

FIGURE 7-6 The Manage Relationships dialog enables you to make changes to the relationships in the Data Model.

The Manage Relationships dialog offers the following buttons:

- **New**—Create a new relationship between two tables in the Data Model.

- **Edit**—Alter the selected relationship.

- **Activate**—Enforce the selected relationship; that is, tell Excel to consider the relationship when aggregating and analyzing the data in the Data Model.

- **Deactivate**—Turn off the selected relationship; that is, tell Excel to ignore the relationship when aggregating and analyzing the data in the Data Model.

- **Delete**—Remove the selected relationship.

Adding a new table to the Data Model

You can add a new table to the Data Model by using Home | Format As Table. Until you define a relationship to the table, it might be shown in the All tab of the PivotTable Fields list instead of the Active tab.

Although you can hunt down the new table on the All tab, it is best to define a new relationship using Data | Data Model | Relationships before adding the field to the pivot table. Defining a relationship will move the table to the Active tab.

Limitations of the Data Model

As with most things in Excel, the Data Model does have limitations. Table 7-1 highlights the maximum and configurable limits for the Excel Data Model.

TABLE 7-1 Data Model limitations

Object	Specification
Data Model size	In 32-bit environments, Excel workbooks are subject to a 2GB limit. This includes the in-memory space shared by Excel, the Data Model, and add-ins that run in the same process. In 64-bit environments, there are no hard limits on file size. Workbook size is limited only by available memory and system resources.
Characters in a table or column name	100 characters
Number of tables in the Data Model	2,147,483,647
Number of rows in each table in the Data Model	The limit is 1,999,999,997 rows.
Number of columns and calculated columns in each table in the Data Model	2,147,483,647
Number of distinct values in a column	The limit is 1,999,999,997 values.
String length in each field	The limit is 536,870,912 bytes (512MB), which is equivalent to 268,435,456 Unicode characters (256 mega-characters).

Building a pivot table using external data sources

Excel is certainly good at processing and analyzing data. In fact, pivot tables themselves are a testament to the analytical power of Excel. However, despite all its strengths, Excel makes for a poor relational data management platform, primarily for three reasons:

- A data set's size has a significant effect on performance, making for less efficient data crunching. The reason for this is the fundamental way Excel handles memory. When you open an Excel file, the entire file is loaded into RAM to ensure quick data processing and access. The drawback to this behavior is that Excel requires a great deal of RAM to process even the smallest change in a spreadsheet (and typically gives you a "Calculating" indicator in the status bar). Although Excel offers more than 1 million rows and more than 16,000 columns, creating and managing large data sets causes Excel to slow down considerably, making data analysis a painful endeavor.

- The lack of a relational data structure forces the use of flat tables that promote redundant data. This also increases the chance of errors.

- There is no way to index data fields in Excel to optimize performance when you're attempting to retrieve large amounts of data.

In smart organizations, the task of data management is not performed by Excel; rather, it is primarily performed by relational database systems such as Microsoft Access and SQL Server. These databases are used to store millions of records that can be rapidly searched and retrieved. The effect of this separation in tasks is that you have a data management layer (your database) and a presentation layer (Excel). The trick is to find the best way to get information from your data management layer to your presentation layer for use by your pivot table.

Managing your data is the general idea behind building a pivot table using an external data source. Building pivot tables from external systems enables you to leverage environments that are better suited to data management. This means you can let Excel do what it does best: analyze and create a presentation layer for your data. The following sections walk you through several techniques for building pivot tables using external data.

Building a pivot table with Microsoft Access data

Often Access is used to manage a series of tables that interact with each other, such as a Customers table, an Orders table, and an Invoices table. Managing data in Access provides the benefit of a relational database where you can ensure data integrity, prevent redundancy, and easily generate data sets via queries.

Most Excel customers use an Access query to create a subset of data and then import that data into Excel. From there, the data can be analyzed with pivot tables. The problem with this method is that it forces the Excel workbook to hold two copies of the imported data sets: one on the spreadsheet and one in the pivot cache. Obviously, holding two copies causes the workbook to be twice as big as it needs to be, and it introduces the possibility of performance issues.

In Excel 2024 and Microsoft 365, Microsoft is encouraging everyone to use Power Query instead of the legacy Get External Data tools. For this chapter, you will use the legacy tools. Before you can do that, you need to bring the icons back to the ribbon.

Choose File | Options | Data. At the bottom of the Excel Options dialog, choose From Access (Legacy) and click OK. Close your workbook and reopen it. You can now find the From Access (Legacy) has been revealed by choosing Data | Get Data | Legacy Wizards (see Figure 7-7).

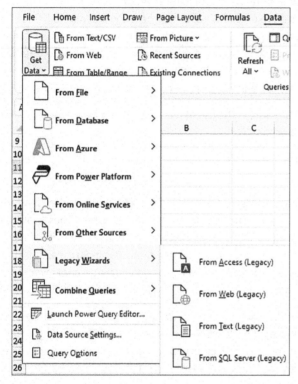

FIGURE 7-7 You have to use Excel Options to bring the legacy wizards back.

To try out this functionality, create a blank workbook in Excel.

1. Choose Data | Get Data | Legacy Wizards | From Access (Legacy).

2. Clicking the From Access button activates a dialog, asking you to select the database you want to work with. Select your database.

3. After your database has been selected, the dialog shown in Figure 7-8 appears. This dialog lists all the tables and queries available. In this example, select the query called Sales_By_Employee and click the OK button.

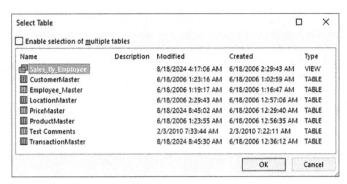

FIGURE 7-8 Select the table or query you want to analyze.

Note In Figure 7-8, notice that the Select Table dialog contains a column called Type. There are two types of Access objects you can work with: views and tables. View indicates that the data set listed is an Access query, and Table indicates that the data set is an Access table.

In this example, notice that Sales_By_Employee is actually an Access query. This means that you import the results of the query. This is true interaction at work: Access does all the back-end data management and aggregation, and Excel handles the analysis and presentation!

4. Next, you see the Import Data dialog, where you select the format in which you want to import the data. As you can see in Figure 7-9, you have the option of importing the data as a table, as a pivot table, or as a pivot table with an accompanying pivot chart. You also have the option to tell Excel where to place the data.

5. Select the radio button next to PivotTable Report and click the OK button.

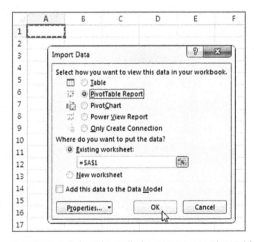

FIGURE 7-9 Select the radio button next to PivotTable Report.

At this point, you should see the PivotTable Fields list shown in Figure 7-10. From here, you can use this pivot table just as you normally would.

The wonderful thing about this technique is that you can refresh the data simply by refreshing the pivot table. When you refresh, Excel takes a new snapshot of the data source and updates the pivot cache.

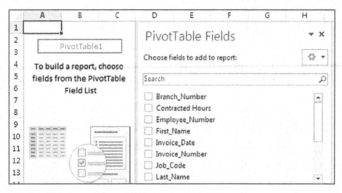

FIGURE 7-10 Your pivot table is ready to use.

Caution   If you create a pivot table that uses an Access database as its source, you can refresh that pivot table only if the table or view is available. That is to say, deleting, moving, or renaming the database used to create the pivot table destroys the link to the external data set, thus destroying your ability to refresh the data. Deleting or renaming the source table or query has the same effect.

Following that reasoning, any clients using your linked pivot table cannot refresh the pivot table unless the source is available to them. If you need your clients to be able to refresh, you might want to make the data source available via a shared network directory.

Building a pivot table with SQL Server data

In the spirit of collaboration, Excel vastly improves your ability to connect to transactional databases such as SQL Server. With the connection functionality found in Excel, creating a pivot table from SQL Server data is as easy as ever.

Before you can use the legacy SQL Server tools, go to File, Options, Data. At the bottom of the panel, choose From SQL Server (Legacy). Create a new Excel workbook, and you will find the command has been added to the Data tab, as described next.

Start on the Data tab and select Get Data | Legacy Wizards | From SQL Server (Legacy), as shown in Figure 7-11.

Selecting this option activates the Data Connection Wizard, as shown later in Figure 7-12. The idea here is to configure your connection settings so Excel can establish a link to the server.

Note There is no sample file for this example. The essence of this demonstration is the interaction between Excel and a SQL server data source. The actions you take to connect to your particular database are the same as demonstrated here.

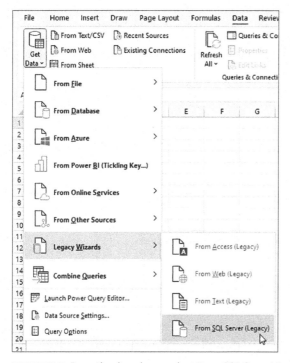

FIGURE 7-11 From the dropdown, select From SQL Server (Legacy).

You need to provide Excel with some authentication information. As you can see in Figure 7-12, you enter the name of your server, as well as your username and password.

FIGURE 7-12 Enter your authentication information and click the Next button.

Note If you are typically authenticated via Windows Authentication, you simply select the Use Windows Authentication option.

Next, you select the database with which you are working from a dropdown containing all available databases on the specified server. As you can see in Figure 7-13, a database called AdventureWorks2012 has been selected in the dropdown. Selecting this database causes all the tables and views in it to be exposed in the list of objects below the dropdown. All that is left to do in this dialog is to choose the table or view you want to analyze and then click the Next button.

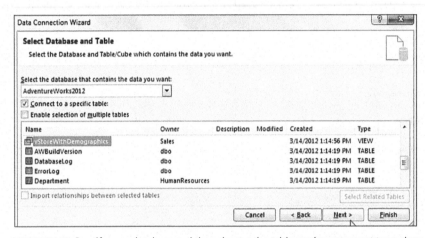

FIGURE 7-13 Specify your database and then choose the table or view you want to analyze.

The next screen in the wizard, shown in Figure 7-14, enables you to enter some descriptive information about the connection you've just created.

FIGURE 7-14 Enter descriptive information for your connection.

Note All the fields in the dialog shown in Figure 7-14 are optional edits only. That is, if you bypass this screen without editing anything, your connection works fine.

Here are the fields you'll use most often:

- **File Name**—In the File Name input box, you can change the file name of the .odc (Office Data Connection) file generated to store the configuration information for the link you just created.

- **Save Password in File**—Under the File Name input box, you have the option of saving the password for your external data in the file itself (via the Save Password In File checkbox). Selecting this checkbox actually enters your password in the file. Keep in mind that this password is not encrypted, so anyone interested enough could potentially get the password for your data source simply by viewing your file with a text editor.

- **Description**—In the Description field, you can enter a plain description of what this particular data connection does.

- **Friendly Name**—The Friendly Name field enables you to specify your own name for the external source. You typically enter a name that is descriptive and easy to read.

When you are satisfied with your descriptive edits, click the Finish button to finalize your connection settings. You immediately see the Import Data dialog, shown previously in Figure 7-9. In it you select a pivot table and then click the OK button to start building your pivot table.

Leveraging Power Query to extract and transform data

Every day, millions of people manually pull data from some source location, manipulate that data, and integrate it into their pivot table reporting.

This process of extracting, manipulating, and integrating data is called ETL. It refers to the three separate functions typically required to integrate disparate data sources: extraction, transformation, and loading. The extraction function involves reading data from a specified source and extracting a desired subset of data. The transformation function involves cleaning, shaping, and aggregating data to convert it to the desired structure. The loading function involves actually importing or using the resulting data.

In an attempt to empower Excel analysts to develop robust and reusable ETL processes, Microsoft created Power Query. Power Query enhances the ETL experience by offering an intuitive mechanism to extract data from a wide variety of sources, perform complex transformations on that data, and then load the data into a workbook or the Data Model.

In the following sections, you'll see how Power Query works and discover some of the innovative ways you can use it to help save time and automate the steps for importing clean data into your pivot table reporting models.

Power Query: It is already in your Excel

Before Excel 2016, Power Query was an add-in that had to be installed. Since Excel 2016, the Power Query tools are in your Excel, found in the Get & Transform group on the left side of the Data tab. Starting in 2023, a limited version of Power Query is available in Excel for the Mac.

Power Query basics

Although Power Query is relatively intuitive, it's worth taking the time to walk through a basic scenario to understand its high-level features. To start this basic look at Power Query, you need to import data from a website. For this example, I've chosen a simple table from my MrExcel.com website. As shown in the following example, the Get & Transform group of the Data tab contains all the commands you need to start this query.

To start your query, follow these steps:

1. Select the From Web icon in the Get & Transform Data group of the Data tab of the ribbon (see Figure 7-15).

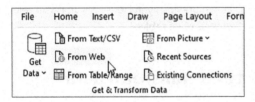

FIGURE 7-15 Starting a Power Query web query.

2. In the dialog that appears (see Figure 7-16), enter the URL for the data you need—in this case, *https://www.mrexcel.com/misc/product-list.html*.

FIGURE 7-16 Enter the target URL containing the data you need.

3. Power Query sometimes asks if you need a password to sign in to the website. You can choose Anonymous access or enter your authentication information.

4. After a bit of gyrating, the Navigator pane shown in Figure 7-17 appears. Here, you select the data source you want extracted. You can click on each table to see a preview of the data. In this case, Table 1 holds the data you need, so click on Table 1 and then click the Transform Data button.

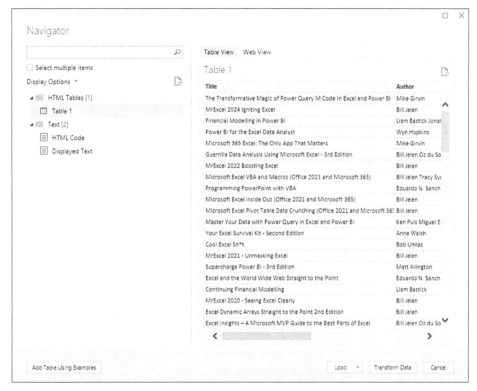

FIGURE 7-17 Select the correct data source and then click the Edit button.

Note You may have noticed that the Navigator pane shown in Figure 7-17 offers a Load button (to the left of the Transform Data button). The Load button allows you to skip any editing and import your targeted data as is. If you are sure you will not need to transform or shape your data in any way, you can opt to click the Load button to import the data directly into the Data Model or a spreadsheet in your workbook.

Note Excel used to offer a web scraping tool that was also called From Web. This has been removed from the ribbon. You can add it back by choosing File | Options | Data and then choosing From Web (Legacy). After reopening your workbook, the command will be found under Data | Get Data | Legacy Wizards.

When you click the Transform Data button, Power Query activates a new Power Query Editor window, which contains its own ribbon and a preview pane that shows a preview of the data (see Figure 7-18). Here, you can apply certain actions to shape, clean, and transform the data before importing.

Formula bar   Preview pane   Applied Steps

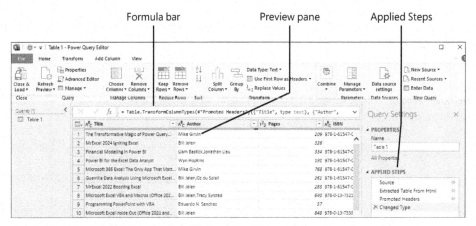

FIGURE 7-18 The Query Editor window allows you to shape, clean, and transform data.

Caution   The formula bar is not displayed by default, but it should be. If you aren't seeing the formula bar, make sure you are in the Power Query Editor and select View, Formula Bar.

The idea is to work with each column shown in the Power Query Editor, applying the necessary actions that will give you the data and structure you need.

In Figure 7-18, some records have multiple authors. Let's say you would like each author to be on its own row so you can produce a summary by author later. Select the Author heading. On the Home tab of the Power Query Editor, choose Split Column | By Delimiter, as shown in Figure 7-19.

It is helpful to know that the Power Query tool was not built by the Excel team. It was built by the SQL Server Analysis Services team at Microsoft. It is very common to see commands in Power Query that seem similar to Excel but with different names. For example, Delete Column in Excel is similar to Remove Column in Power Query. In this example, Split Column in Power Query seems very similar to Text to Columns in Excel. But as you will see, while both commands perform similar actions, the Power Query version is often more powerful.

5.   For the delimiter, change Space to Comma. One benefit of Power Query is that the Power Query editor makes an intelligent guess at the Delimiter. There are not enough records with commas for Power Query to guess correctly this time, but it usually guesses correctly. Also note that there are choices to split at the first delimiter, last delimiter, or each delimiter. In this case, leave the setting at each delimiter. But in many cases, you might want to make sure that a column only splits once.

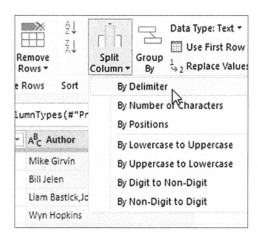

FIGURE 7-19 The goal is to split each author so that each appears on a new row.

6. Open Advanced Options and locate the Split Into option. Change from Commas to Rows. This amazing setting will insert new rows for each co-author and copy the remaining columns into the new row. (See Figure 7-20.)

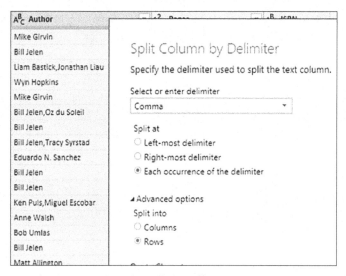

FIGURE 7-20 Split Column by Delimiter offers more choices than Excel's Text to Columns.

7. There is a date field at the end of each row. You can easily convert the date to a year. Select the heading for Published On. Using the Transform tab, go to Date | Year | Year. The daily dates will be converted to a four-digit year. (See Figure 7-21.)

FIGURE 7-21 Use the Date dropdown to convert a date to Start Of Year, End Of Month, Week, Year Number, or more.

8. Like many data sets on the web, there is some garbage data in this table. While most of the products are books, there are a few DVD-ROM videos and an Excel Function Clock. Browsing through the data, you can see that removing anything with a page count less than 10 would eliminate the nonbooks. Select the column header for Pages. Use the Filter dropdown. Choose Number Filters | Greater Than. Type **10** and click OK. Power Query will remove anything that is not a book. At this point, it is tempting to pull the remaining data into Excel and start summarizing with a pivot table. However, it is possible to do further summarizing in Power Query. Let's say you want to see the average page length by author and year.

9. Select the Authors heading. Ctrl+Select the Published On Column to add the Year column to the selection. On the left side of the Transform tab, choose Grouping. Power Query chooses to group by Author and Year. Fill in the aggregation column as shown in Figure 7-22.

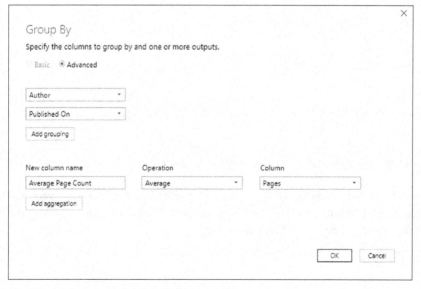

FIGURE 7-22 Summarize the data by Author and Year.

10. When you've finished cleaning and summarizing the data using the Power Query editor, click Home | Close & Load.

Note Alternatively, you can open the Close & Load dropdown and choose Load To. You can choose to output the results to the Data Model. Or you can choose to save the query as a query connection only, which means you will be able to use the query in various in-memory processes without needing to actually output the results anywhere.

At this point, you will have a table similar to the one shown in Figure 7-23.

	A	B	C
1	Author	Published On	Average Page Count
2	Mike Girvin	2024	209
3	Bill Jelen	2024	326
4	Liam Bastick	2022	334
5	Jonathan Liau	2022	334
6	Wyn Hopkins	2022	191
7	Mike Girvin	2022	768
8	Bill Jelen	2022	394.6666667
9	Oz du Soleil	2022	261
10	Tracy Syrstad	2022	640

FIGURE 7-23 Your final query pulled from the Internet—transformed, put into an Excel table, and ready to use in a pivot table.

Take a moment to appreciate what Power Query allowed you to do just now. With a few clicks, you searched the Internet, found some data, shaped the data to keep only the columns you needed, and even manipulated that data to split and summarize the base data. This is what Power Query is about: enabling you to easily extract, filter, and reshape data without the need for any programmatic coding skills.

Understanding Applied Steps

Power Query uses its own formula language (known as the "M" language) to codify your queries. As with macro recording, each action you take when working with Power Query results in a line of code being written into the Applied Steps list box. Query steps are embedded M code that allows your actions to be repeated each time you refresh your Power Query data.

To get back into your query, right-click the Query name in the Queries & Connections pane and choose Edit.

Note If the Queries & Connections pane is not showing, choose Data | Queries & Connections. The first time you display the pane, it is not wide enough. If you don't see a Refresh icon to the right of the query, drag the left side of the pane to the left to make it wider.

The applied steps appear along the right side of the screen (see Figure 7-24). Click any applied step to see how the data looked at that point in the process. The formula bar shows what action happened at that step.

FIGURE 7-24 Query steps can be viewed and managed in the Applied Steps section of the Query Settings pane.

Each query step represents an action you took to get to a data table. You can click on any step to see the underlying M code in the Power Query formula bar. For example, clicking the step called Extracted Year Errors reveals the code for that step in the formula bar.

You can right-click on any step to see a menu of options for managing your query steps. Figure 7-25 illustrates the following options:

- **Edit Settings**—Edit the arguments or parameters that define the selected step.

- **Rename**—Give the selected step a meaningful name.

- **Delete**—Remove the selected step. Be aware that removing a step can cause errors if subsequent steps depend on the deleted step.

- **Delete Until End**—Remove the selected step and all the following steps.

- **Insert Step After**—Insert a new step after this step.

- **Move Before**—Move the selected step up in the order of steps.

- **Move After**—Move the selected step down in the order of steps.

- **Extract Previous**—Extracts the steps before the selected step into a new query. You will be asked to give the new query a name.

- **View Native Query**—Show the underlying SQL behind a Source step.

- **Properties**—Add a description to any step. The description will be added as a comment in your M code. View the full M code using View | Advanced Editor.

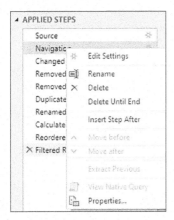

FIGURE 7-25 Right-click on any query step to edit, rename, delete, or move the step.

Viewing the Advanced Query Editor

Power Query gives you the option of viewing and editing a query's embedded M code directly. While in the Power Query Editor window, click the View tab of the ribbon and select Advanced Editor. You will see the M code created as you performed various steps (see Figure 7-26).

If you read Ken Puls's book on Power Query, *Master Your Data* (ISBN 978-1-61547-058-7), you might occasionally be told to type some code directly into the advanced editor.

As Power Query becomes mature, more people start with the Advanced Editor and type code from scratch. One book that covers this approach is Mike Girvin's *The Transformative Magic of Power Query M Code in Excel and Power BI* (ISBN 978-1-61547-083-9).

```
Advanced Editor                                                      □   ×

Table 1                                          Display Options ▾   ❓

1  let
2      Source = Web.BrowserContents("https://www.mrexcel.com/misc/product-list.html"),
3      #"Extracted Table From Html" = Html.Table(Source, {{"Column1", "TABLE[id='mrexcel-product-list'] > * > TR > :nth-child(1)"
4      #"Promoted Headers" = Table.PromoteHeaders(#"Extracted Table From Html", [PromoteAllScalars=true]),
5      #"Changed Type" = Table.TransformColumnTypes(#"Promoted Headers",{{"Title", type text}, {"Author", type text}, {"Pages", I
6      #"Split Column by Delimiter" = Table.ExpandListColumn(Table.TransformColumns(#"Changed Type", {{"Author", Splitter.SplitTe
7      #"Changed Type1" = Table.TransformColumnTypes(#"Split Column by Delimiter",{{"Author", type text}}),
8      #"Extracted Year" = Table.TransformColumns(#"Changed Type1",{{"Published On", Date.Year, Int64.Type}}),
9      #"Filtered Rows" = Table.SelectRows(#"Extracted Year", each [Pages] > 10),
10     #"Grouped Rows" = Table.Group(#"Filtered Rows", {"Author", "Published On"}, {{"Average Page Count", each List.Average([Pag
11 in
12     #"Grouped Rows"
```

FIGURE 7-26 View the M code created by your steps of cleaning the data.

Refreshing Power Query data

The best part of Power Query comes on the second day that you have to run your report. After using the Power Query Editor to clean your data on the first day, the next time you need to run the report, you simply open your workbook and refresh the data. Power Query will go back to the original source and reperform all the steps.

If you choose to load your Power Query results to an Excel table in the existing workbook, you can manually refresh by right-clicking the table and selecting the Refresh option.

For queries that are loaded directly to the Data Model, open the Queries & Connections pane by using Data | Queries & Connections. Right-click any query and choose Refresh.

Power Query connection types

Microsoft has invested a great deal of time and resources in ensuring that Power Query can connect to a wide array of data sources. Whether you need to pull data from an external website, a text file, a database system, or a web service, Power Query can accommodate most, if not all, your source data needs.

You can see all the available connection types by clicking on the New Query dropdown on the Data tab. Power Query offers the ability to pull from a wide array of data sources:

- **From File**—Pull data from a specified Excel file, text file, CSV file, XML file, JSON folder, PDF, or SharePoint folder.

- **From Database**—Pull data from SQL Server, Microsoft Access, Analysis Services, Oracle, IBM DB2, MySQL, PostgreSQL, Sybase, Teradata, or SAP HANA.

- **From Azure**—Pull data from Azure SQL database, Synapse analytics, HDInsight, Blog storage, Table storage, Data Lake storage, or Azure Data Explorer.

- **From Online Services**—Pull data from SharePoint Online List, Microsoft Exchange Online, Dynamics 365 Online, Salesforce Objects, or Salesforce Reports.

- **From Other Sources**—Pull data from a wide variety of sources, such as Table/Range, Web, Microsoft Query, SharePoint List, OData Feed, Hadoop File, Active Directory, Microsoft Exchange, ODBC, and OLEDB.

- **From Sheet**—Query data from a defined Excel table or named range within the current worksheet.

- **Combine Queries**—Lets you append two queries of similar data (perhaps last year and this year) or merge two queries, essentially doing an XLOOKUP between two queries.

Case study: Transposing a data set with Power Query

In Chapter 2, "Creating a basic pivot table," you learned that the Tabular layout is the perfect layout for the source data in a pivot table. Tabular layout is a particular table structure where there are no blank rows or columns, every column has a heading, every field has a value in every row, and columns do not contain repeating groups of data.

Unfortunately, you often encounter data sets like the one shown in Figure 7-27. The problem here is that the month headings are spread across the top of the table, doing double duty as column labels and actual data values. In a pivot table, this format would force you to manage and maintain 12 fields, each representing a different month.

⬚	A	B	C	D	E	F
1	Market	Product_Description	Jan	Feb	Mar	Apr
2	BUFFALO	Cleaning & Housekeeping Se	6,220	4,264	5,386	6,444
3	BUFFALO	Facility Maintenance and Re|	3,256	9,490	4,409	4,958
4	BUFFALO	Fleet Maintenance	5,350	8,925	6,394	6,522
5	BUFFALO	Green Plants and Foliage Car	2,415	2,580	2,402	2,981
6	BUFFALO	Landscaping/Grounds Care	5,474	4,501	5,324	5,706

FIGURE 7-27 You need to convert this matrix-style table to a Tabular data set so it can be used in a pivot table.

You can leverage Power Query to easily transform this matrix-style data set to one that is appropriate for use with a pivot table. Follow these steps:

1. Select one cell inside your data. Select Data | From Table/Range. Excel will ask you to confirm that your data has headers. Click OK. The Power Query Editor appears.

2. In the Power Query Editor, hold down the Ctrl key as you select the Market and Product_ Description fields (which are the fields you do not want to transpose).

3. Go to the Transform tab on the Power Query Editor ribbon, select the Unpivot Columns dropdown, and then select Unpivot Other Columns (see Figure 7-28). All the month names now fall under a column called Attributes.

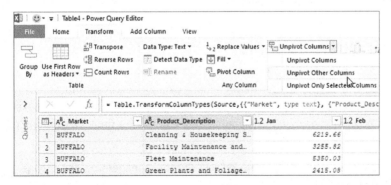

FIGURE 7-28 Power Query's Unpivot transformation makes quick work of tricky transpose operations.

4. Rename the Attributes column Month. Rename the Values column Revenue.

5. Click the Home tab on the Power Query Editor ribbon and select the Close & Load command to send the results to a new worksheet in the current workbook.

Amazingly, that is it! If all went well, you should now have a table similar to the one shown in Figure 7-29.

	A	B	C	D
1	Market	Product Description	Month	Revenue
2	BUFFALO	Cleaning & Housekeeping Services	Jan	6219.66
3	BUFFALO	Cleaning & Housekeeping Services	Feb	4263.92
4	BUFFALO	Cleaning & Housekeeping Services	Mar	5386.12
5	BUFFALO	Cleaning & Housekeeping Services	Apr	6443.99
6	BUFFALO	Cleaning & Housekeeping Services	May	4360.14
7	BUFFALO	Cleaning & Housekeeping Services	Jun	5097.46
8	BUFFALO	Cleaning & Housekeeping Services	Jul	7566.19
9	BUFFALO	Cleaning & Housekeeping Services	Aug	4263.92
10	BUFFALO	Cleaning & Housekeeping Services	Sep	7245.64
11	BUFFALO	Cleaning & Housekeeping Services	Oct	3847.15
12	BUFFALO	Cleaning & Housekeeping Services	Nov	6540.21
13	BUFFALO	Cleaning & Housekeeping Services	Dec	5610.45
14	BUFFALO	Facility Maintenance and Repair	Jan	3255.82
15	BUFFALO	Facility Maintenance and Repair	Feb	9490
16	BUFFALO	Facility Maintenance and Repair	Mar	4409.23

FIGURE 7-29 Your data is now ready for use in a pivot table.

In just a few clicks, you were able to transpose your data set in preparation for use in a pivot table. Even better, this query can be refreshed! As new month columns or rows are added to the source table, Power Query will rerun your steps and automatically include any new data in the resulting table.

The new Power Query functionality is an exciting addition to Excel. In the past, it was a chore to import and clean external data in preparation for pivot table reporting. Now with Power Query, you can create automated extraction and transformation procedures that traditionally would require personnel and skillsets found only in the IT department.

One more Power Query example

For 17 years, I performed 35 live seminars a year, traveling around the country and showing off Excel tips and tricks. I always walked around the room beforehand, looking for Excel questions. Recently, I ran into a beleaguered accountant who had a manager who kept sending workbooks that looked like Figure 7-30. Each project occupied one row. The expenses were entered in a single cell, using Alt+Enter to separate each line.

Obviously, this is not how you should set up data in Excel. But the manager wouldn't change. He has been doing it this way for 28 years and only has two more years until retirement and wants the total to appear in column C. Impossible, right?

Power Query is improving every month. Luckily, just a month before I ran into this data set, Microsoft added the ability to split text at each delimiter and to generate new rows for anything after each delimiter.

Take the data into Power Query. Select the Expenses Column. On the Home tab, choose Split Column, By Delimiter. In the Split Column By Delimiter dialog, choose Advanced Options. Change the Split Into from Columns to Rows. Clear out the dash that was entered in the Custom Delimiter box. At the bottom, use Insert Special Character and Line Feed. Figure 7-31 shows the dialog.

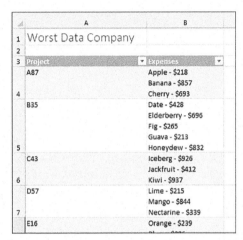

FIGURE 7-30 Each cell in B4:B8 is about as useful as putting the data in Microsoft Word.

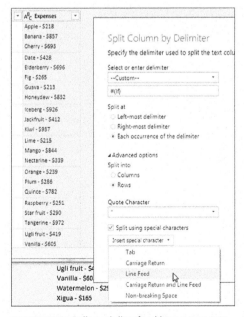

FIGURE 7-31 Split each line feed into a new row.

Look at Figure 7-32. The Apple, Banana, Cherry entry was split into three rows. For the two new rows, the Project was copied to the new rows. If you have more data in columns C through J, all that data will be replicated for the new rows.

Initially, the data in Figure 7-32 had Apple – $218 in one column. You can easily split the data at the dash by selecting Split Column | By Delimiter and clicking OK.

Right now, you would likely be thrilled to take this data back to Excel. But let's go even further.

	AᵇC Project	AᵇC Expenses.1	$ Expenses.2
1	A87	Apple	218
2	A87	Banana	857
3	A87	Cherry	693
4	B35	Date	428
5	B35	Elderberry	696
6	B35	Fig	265
7	B35	Guava	213

FIGURE 7-32 Using Split Column twice solves the problem of the bad data.

Delete the products in the Expenses.1 column. Select the Project column and choose Group By. In the Group By dialog, choose Group By Project and create a new column called TotalExpense that is a Sum Of Expense.2. This will produce a table with one row per project. Each row will list the total expense for that project.

When you choose Close And Load, Excel will insert a new worksheet with a new table. Each project occurs once with the total expense. A simple VLOOKUP from the original table brings the totals back next to the horrible data (see Figure 7-33).

The only tricky part left was to teach the manager to click Data | Refresh All after making any edits.

C4		fx	=VLOOKUP([@Project],Table6_2,2,0)		
	A	B	C	D	E
1	Worst Data Company				
2					
3	Project	Expenses	Total From Power Query		
4	A87	Apple - $218 Banana - $857 Cherry - $693	1768		
5	B35	Date - $428 Elderberry - $696 Fig - $265 Guava - $213 Honeydew - $832	2434		
6	C43	Iceberg - $926 Jackfruit - $412 Kiwi - $937	2275		
7	D57	Lime - $215 Mango - $844 Nectarine - $339	1398		

FIGURE 7-33 A VLOOKUP returns the Power Query answer back to the original data set.

Every time that I think that I am going to have to reach for VBA, I am amazed that Power Query saves the day.

Next steps

Chapter 8, "Sharing dashboards with Power BI," covers the ins and outs of sharing pivot tables with the world. In that chapter, you will find out how you can distribute your pivot tables through the web.

Sharing dashboards with Power BI

In this chapter, you will:

- Get started with Power BI Desktop

- Build interactive reports

- Publish to Power BI

- Design a workbook as an interactive web page

Power BI Desktop is an application that lets you share interactive dashboards based on your Excel data. Authoring dashboards is quick—you are basically building pivot charts by dragging fields to a Pivot-Table Fields list.

Charts are automatically interactive—if you select something in one chart, all the other charts will filter to the selected item. You can create hierarchies to allow people to drill down into the data.

With a monthly subscription, you can publish your dashboards to the Power BI servers. You can invite others in your company to consume your reports on their computers or mobile devices.

Getting started with Power BI Desktop

Getting started with Power BI Desktop is free. You will need a work email account—Hotmail or Gmail will not qualify. Start at *PowerBI.Microsoft.com*. Sign up and download Power BI Desktop for free.

When you first open Power BI, you will sign in with the account credentials that you created. You are then presented with a start screen with a number of tutorials, as shown in Figure 8-1.

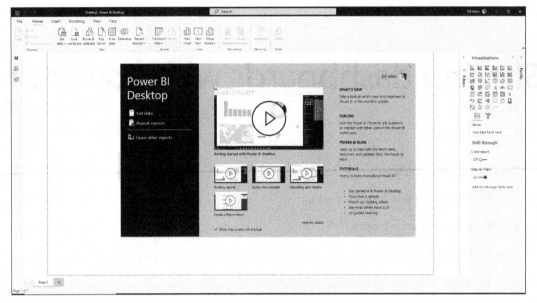

FIGURE 8-1 Power BI Desktop is the authoring tool for Power BI.

Preparing data in Excel

Before you can use Power BI, you need to prepare the data you want to use in it. To do this, build an Excel workbook with each of your data sets formatted as a table. Using the sample files for this book, you would perform the following steps to create a data model in PowerBIData.xlsx:

1. Select each of the three data sets and format them as tables using Ctrl+T.

2. Name the tables "Sales," "Geography," and "Calendar."

3. Define a relationship using Data, Relationship, Create from Sales | Customer to Geography | Customer.

4. Define a second relationship from Sales | Date to Calendar | Date.

Tip If you already have queries and relationships defined in your Excel file, you should use File, Import, Excel Workbook Contents as described next instead of Get Data, Excel.

Importing data to Power BI

The most obvious way to get Excel data into Power BI is not the best. If you choose Home, Get Data, From Excel, you can import the data, but any queries, relationships, KPIs, and synonyms will be lost.

Click File | Import | Power Query | Power Pivot | Power View. Browse to and select your Excel workbook.

An oddly old message appears, reading, "We don't work directly with Excel workbooks, but we know how to extract the useful content from them." Click Start.

At the end, a message will show you the migration is complete and report what has been imported (see Figure 8-2).

Note Power BI Desktop offers a full version of Power Query. Use the Home, Edit button to launch Power Query.

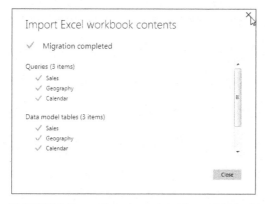

FIGURE 8-2 Power BI can import queries and tables from Excel.

Getting oriented to Power BI

Power BI guides you to Build Visuals With Your Data. It tells you to Select Or Drag Fields From The Fields Pane Onto The Report Canvas. Let's take a look at various elements in the Power BI screen. At the top right are the Visualizations and Fields panels (see Figure 8-3).

The Fields panel is essentially like the top part of the PivotTable Field list. While you start out seeing table names Calendar, Geography, and Sales, you can use the greater-than icon to expand any table and see the fields in that table.

The Visualizations panel starts with about 39 built-in data visualizations. You can add more visualizations using the icon with three dots. Below the panel of visualizations is the Values area. This is like the bottom half of the PivotTable Fields list. You will drag fields here to create a visualization. The Paint Roller icon leads to various formatting choices that are available for a visualization.

FIGURE 8-3 Create new visualizations using these tools in the top right.

In the lower left of the Power BI Desktop screen is a tab labeled Page 1 and a plus sign to add more pages (see Figure 8-4). These are like worksheet tabs in Excel. You can build a report with multiple pages of dashboards.

FIGURE 8-4 Add more pages in the lower left.

In the top left of the screen, there are three icons for Report, Data, and Relationships (see Figure 8-5). The Report view is where you will build your dashboard. The Data view shows you the data loaded in Power BI and is very similar to the Manage Data Model screen in Power Pivot. The Relationships view is similar to the Diagram view in Power Pivot.

FIGURE 8-5 Where is your data? Click the second icon along the left.

Preparing data in Power BI

To create effective reports in Power BI, you want to create some relationships and further customize your data.

Click on the Relationships icon (see the bottom icon on the left in Figure 8-6).

In the Relationships view, you will see that Power BI Desktop automatically detected a relationship between the Sales table and the Geography table. Hover over the line between the tables and Power BI Desktop will show you that the Customer field is used to create the relationship in both tables.

If you resize the tables, you will see the Sigma icon next to Quantity, Revenue, COGS, and Profit. This is correct and means that Power BI will summarize those fields.

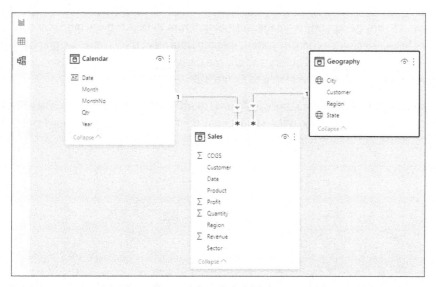

FIGURE 8-6 Power BI Desktop detected the relationship between Sales and Geography.

If you need to define a relationship between two tables, you simply drag from the key field in one table to the corresponding field in another table to create the relationship. Follow these steps if Power BI has a Sigma icon next to any fields that should not be summarized (for example, a customer number):

1. Click the Data icon (the second of three icons along the left side of the screen). In the Data view, you will see the values from one of your tables. To switch to another table, select the table from the Fields panel on the right side of the screen. As an Excel pro, looking on the right side of the screen seems foreign. You would think that there should be tabs at the bottom of the screen for the three data tables.

2. Click on the heading for the field that should not be summarized to select that column.

3. Go to the Column Tools tab in Power BI. Change the Summarization from Sum to Don't Summarize (see Figure 8-7).

4. Repeat Steps 2 and 3 for any other numeric columns that should not be summarized.

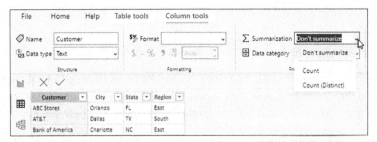

FIGURE 8-7 By default, Power BI Desktop wants to sum any field that is completely numeric. Override this behavior for item numbers, account numbers, and so on.

Assign categories to any geography or image URL fields. Power BI Desktop can plot your data on a map if you have fields like city, zip code, or state. Using the Data view, display the Geography table. Click each heading for City, State, and Country and choose the appropriate data type using the Data Category dropdown on the Column Tools tab (see Figure 8-8).

If you want to display images in your report, include a column with the URL for each image. Choose the Image URL category for that column. When you display the field in a table, the image from that URL will appear.

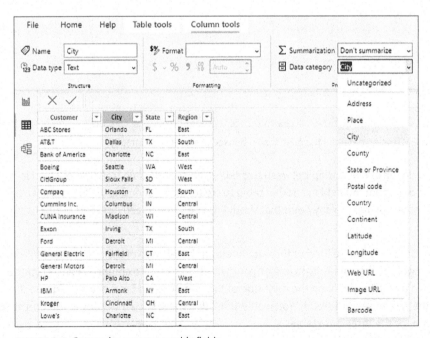

FIGURE 8-8 Categorize any geographic fields.

Defining synonyms in Power BI Desktop

Your company might have specific terms that are used. As an example, I worked in accounting for a company that made handheld computers. While I had a field in the database called COGS (for Cost Of Goods Sold), everyone in this company called this "MLO" (which stood for Material Labor and Overhead).

One of the cool features of Power BI is the ability to type natural language queries. If you define synonyms, Power BI will recognize that MLO is referring to the COGS field in the data.

Select the Model icon (it is the third icon along the left side of the screen). In the Home tab of the ribbon, choose Q&A Setup. Click Field Synonyms. Expand the appropriate table. Use the Add+ button to add new synonyms. Figure 8-9 shows that COGS could be called COG, Cost, or mlo.

FIGURE 8-9 Define synonyms to improve natural-language queries.

Building an interactive report with Power BI Desktop

Now that your data has been set up in Power BI Desktop, it is time to begin creating charts and tables that will appear in the dashboard.

Building your first visualization

Click the Report icon (this is the top of the three icons along the left side of Power BI Desktop). The large, empty white canvas appears in the center of your screen.

Look in the Visualizations panel. There are many built-in tools available. To get your feet wet, choose the first item—a stacked bar chart (see Figure 8-10).

Notice that the field areas change from Values to Axis, Legend, Values, Small Multiples, and Tooltips. Every time that you choose a visualization type, the list of field types will change.

FIGURE 8-10 To start, choose any visualization from the Visualizations panel

When you choose a bar chart from the Visualizations panel, a tile placeholder appears on the canvas, as shown in Figure 8-11. You can resize this tile using any of the eight resize handles. Or drag by the Title Bar area to move it to a different location.

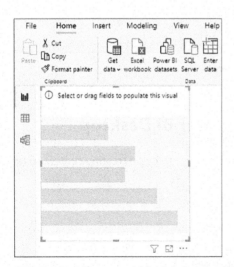

FIGURE 8-11 Before you add fields to it, a visualization starts as a blank tile.

To add fields to the visualization, choose Revenue from the Sales table. Choose Region from the Geography table. Region will move to the Axis drop zone, and Revenue will move to the Values drop zone (see Figure 8-12).

FIGURE 8-12 Choose fields for the chart.

At the top of the drop zones, there is a paint roller icon. Click that to find formatting options for the chart. These options will be different depending on the type of visualization.

In Figure 8-13, the Data Labels have been turned on. The remaining options in the figure let you customize the appearance of the data labels.

FIGURE 8-13 Use the Paint Roller section to format your chart.

You might experiment with the Show Background options. You can color the tile with any theme color and set the transparency for the color.

The third icon is the Analysis icon. This looks like a search box with a chart trend line in the magnifying glass. For the Bar Chart visualization, the only choice is to add a Constant Line. Some companies might need to show a line at an arbitrary position. In Figure 8-14, the settings to draw a dashed line at $1.5 Million are shown.

FIGURE 8-14 Set up a constant line.

With the settings in Figures 8-12 through 8-14, you will get the chart shown in Figure 8-15.

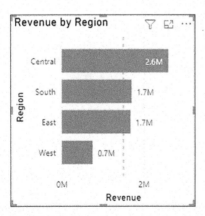

FIGURE 8-15 A bar chart with data labels and a constant line at $1.5 Million.

There are four different ways to sort this chart. Use the Three Dots icon in the top right of the chart to choose if regions should be sorted alphabetically or by revenue and ascending or descending (see Figure 8-16).

To the left of the Ellipsis icon is a Full Screen icon. Instead, you can use the Spotlight selection in the menu, which causes all other charts to fade in the background and keeps the focus on the current chart.

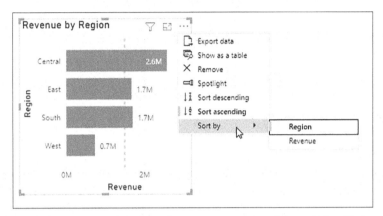

FIGURE 8-16 Settings for the chart are in a menu accessed through the ellipsis.

Building your second visualization

This will seem very simple, but it trips me up every time. In order to create a second tile in your report, you must click away from the first tile. It is easy...click anywhere into the white nothingness of the report canvas.

But if you forget to click away and click the Column Chart visualization, you will change the current chart from a bar chart to a column chart. I don't know why I constantly forget this step, but I constantly forget this step.

Click into the white space of the report. Choose a Column chart from the Visualization panel. Drag Revenue to the Values area. Drag Customer to the Axis area. Drag Product to the Legend area.

The result shown in Figure 8-17 is a column chart with customers along the bottom. The three product lines are stacked for each column. In this particular data set, there are ten big customers and a whole bunch of tiny customers. You could resize the column chart to be very wide and show the long tail of small customers. But you can also drag the right edge of the chart in to show only the ten largest customers. A scrollbar would let someone drag over to see the small customers.

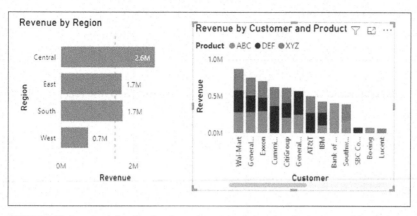

FIGURE 8-17 A second visualization is a column chart showing Customer and Product.

Cross-filtering charts

Here is where the magic of Power BI starts to kick in. Let's face it: you could have created both previous charts in Excel. The Constant Line would have required some Andy Pope-style charting tricks, but it could have been done. The magic is how every chart in Power BI can filter the other charts.

Click the Central region bar in the first chart. The second chart will be updated. Central region customers will stay bright, while other customers fade to a lighter color (see Figure 8-18).

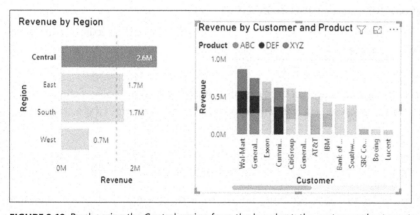

FIGURE 8-18 By choosing the Central region from the bar chart, the customer chart reacts.

Creating a drill-down hierarchy

Interactive hierarchies are very easy to set up in Power BI Desktop. Click the first bar chart to select it. Display the Fields section in the Visualizations panel. The Axis contains the Region field. Drag three more fields from the geography table and drop them beneath Region: State, City, and Customer (see Figure 8-19).

Nothing appears to change in the chart, but you have set up a cool drill-down feature.

FIGURE 8-19 Stack four fields in the Axis area to create a drill-down.

Once the hierarchy has been created, a new Drill Down icon appears in the top right of the chart. Click the icon shown in Figure 8-20 to enable drill-down mode.

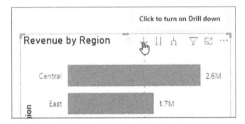

FIGURE 8-20 Click the icon of a down arrow to turn on drill down mode.

Once drill-down mode is active, click on Central in the bar chart to see a new chart of all the states in the Central region.

Notice how the column chart updates to show only customers in the Central region (see Figure 8-21).

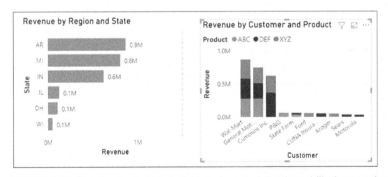

FIGURE 8-21 Click the Central bar in the bar chart, and the chart drills down to show states in the Central region.

From Figure 8-21, you could continue to click on Arkansas and drill down to Bentonville. Click on Bentonville and drill down to Wal-Mart. However, because that is not very interesting, click the Drill Up icon in the top left of the chart to return to all regions.

Click South, followed by Texas. The results in Figure 8-22 show the city level: Dallas, Irving, and Houston.

The choices from the point shown in Figure 8-22 are very subtle. You could click on one of the three cities to show the customers in that city. Or you could decide you want to see all the customers in any of the three cities. The second icon in the top left is two down-arrows. Click that icon to move one level down the hierarchy without any further filtering. You will see Exxon, AT&T, Southwest, SBC, and Compaq.

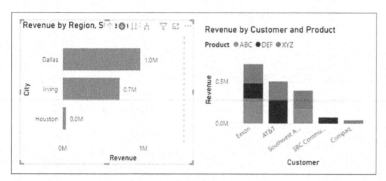

FIGURE 8-22 Drill down to the city level.

To return to the region level, click the Drill Up icon several times.

Importing a custom visualization

You can add new visualizations to Power BI Desktop. The last icon in the Visualizations area is three dots. Click those dots and choose Get More Visuals.

You can browse a variety of free visualizations. In Figure 8-23, click the Add button next to Enlighten Aquarium.

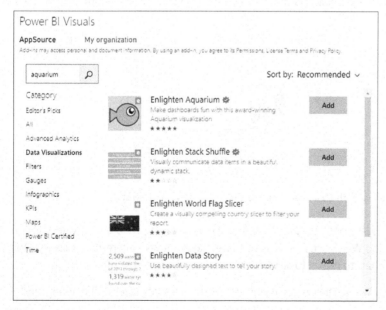

FIGURE 8-23 Power BI visualizations are open source, so you will find a wide array of useful and not-so-useful visualizations.

After adding the Enlighten Aquarium visualization, you will see a new fish icon in the Visualizations panel (see Figure 8-24).

FIGURE 8-24 Installing new visualizations from the Marketplace is a hassle-free experience.

Click in a blank area of your report canvas. Add a new visualization by clicking the Fish icon in the Visualizations panel.

The field drop zones are now labeled Fish and Fish Size. Drag Customer to the Fish area and Revenue to the Fish Size.

An aquarium appears in your report with various-sized fish swimming back and forth (see Figure 8-25). Click on the biggest fish—it will stop swimming, and an information panel appears with Wal-Mart and 869,454.

The aquarium will respond to cross-filtering. If you filter the bar chart to just South, only the five fish from the South region will be swimming.

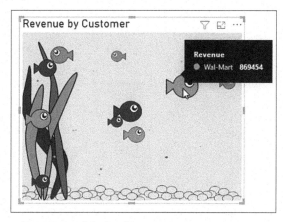

FIGURE 8-25 A fish chart in Power BI.

Publishing to Power BI

Now that your data has been set up in Power BI Desktop, you can share it with others by publishing to Power BI.

Power BI runs in any modern browser. There are dedicated apps for the iPad, iPhone, and Android phones. The default report is designed for a computer screen.

Designing for the mobile phone

If your report will be consumed by people on mobile phones, you can specify how the tiles should be arranged on the phone.

In Power BI Desktop, go to View | Mobile Layout. You can rearrange and resize the visualization tiles, as shown in Figure 8-26.

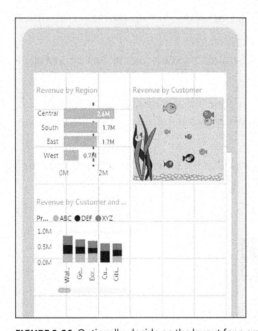

FIGURE 8-26 Optionally, decide on the layout for a smartphone.

Publishing to a workspace

On the Home tab in Power BI, choose Publish. The Publish to Power BI dialog will ask you which work-space to use (see Figure 8-27).

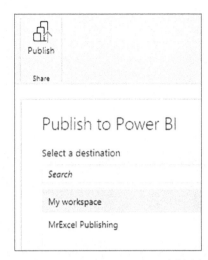

FIGURE 8-27 A report must be published to a workspace.

After publishing, you can choose to view it in Power BI or to see Insights. Figure 8-28 shows your report running in the Chrome browser.

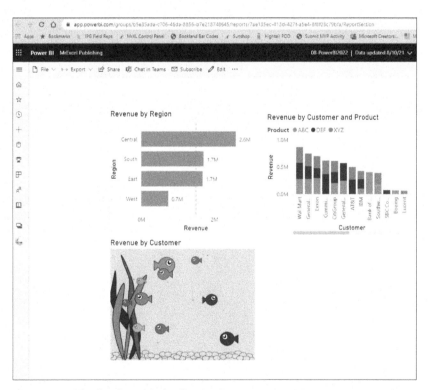

FIGURE 8-28 Viewing the report in a browser.

Next steps

Chapter 9, "Using cube formulas with the Data Model or OLAP data," returns to Excel and shows you how you can analyze external data in Excel pivot tables. Check out the section at the end of Chapter 9 on using Cube functions to break out of the traditional format of pivot tables.

Using cube formulas with the Data Model or OLAP data

In this chapter, you will:

- Be introduced to OLAP

- Connect to an OLAP cube

- Understand the structure of an OLAP cube

- Understand the limitations of OLAP pivot tables

- Create an offline cube

- Break out of the pivot table mold with cube functions

- Add calculations to OLAP pivot tables

There is a great technique with pivot tables where you convert the pivot table to a series of cube formulas. Originally, this technique was only relevant for someone who had SQL Service Analysis Services installed. But today, one click of the Add This Data To The Data Model option moves your data set to the Power Pivot engine, and Power Pivot stores data in an OLAP engine. Thus, you can use cube formulas simply by moving your data to the Data Model.

I have some non-scientific rationale: If I am doing one of my Power Excel seminars and there are 100 people in the room who use pivot tables, only three to five of those people have ever heard of SQL Server Analysis Services. I have been the co-author of this book for 18 years and seven editions. When this chapter was about OLAP tools, I skipped over it every time because I knew that I did not have SQL Server Analysis Services installed.

So, I am changing the focus of the chapter to start with the cube formulas that everyone can use if you simply select the checkbox for Add This Data To The Data Model.

If you have Excel 2013 or newer on a Windows computer, you can use the examples in the first section of this chapter. After seeing how cool cube formulas are, you are free to skip to Chapter 10 once you get to the OLAP material.

Converting your pivot table to cube formulas

You might have encountered the GETPIVOTDATA function to extract cells from a pivot table based on a pivot cache. Cube formulas are a more powerful function that only works when the pivot table is based on an OLAP cube. When you select the Add This Data To The Data Model checkbox, Excel converts your data to a cube. Thus, the cube formulas will work.

Why are cube formulas more powerful? The GETPIVOTDATA function refers to an existing pivot table and extracts cells that already exist in the pivot table to another location. In contrast, cube formulas can completely replace a pivot table. Cube formulas reach into the data store and pull summary data into Excel even if you don't have that data in a pivot table yet.

The easiest way to get started with cube formulas is to let Excel convert an existing pivot table to cube formulas.

Before you get started with your pivot table, format the underlying data with Ctrl+T. Excel uses a name such as Table1. It is important to edit that name before you begin. You will be typing this name frequently, so make the name meaningful but short. For this example, I will use the name CustData.

Select one cell in your data. Choose Insert | PivotTable | From Table Or Range. Choose Add This Data To The Data Model and click OK. Build a pivot table with Customers in the Rows, Revenue in the Values, and Sector as a Slicer (see Figure 9-1).

	A	B	C	D
3	Customer ▼	Sum of Revenue		
4	Adaept Information Management	498937	Sector	
5	Calleia Company	406326		
6	Excel Design Solutions Ltd	71651	Consulting	
7	Excel Learning Zone	72680	Museums	
8	Excel4Apps	91320		
9	Excel-Translator.de	42316	Retail	
10	F-Keys Ltd.	34710	Training	
11	JEVS Human Services	50030		
12	LearnExcelBooks.com	34364	Utilities	

FIGURE 9-1 Start with a pivot table based on the Data Model.

With one cell in the pivot table selected, go to the PivotTable Analyze tab in the ribbon. Select OLAP Tools | Convert To Formulas, as shown in Figure 9-2.

Your entire pivot table is replaced with a series of standalone formulas. The pivot table no longer exists. The CUBEVALUE and CUBEMEMBER formulas are reaching into the Data Model to retrieve summary results (see Figure 9-3).

These formulas are standalone formulas. You can rearrange them. If you ever wanted to insert blank rows in your pivot table, you can do it now; this report has no pivot table limitations because it is no longer a pivot table.

If you need to grab just the Excel4Apps revenue and put it in a dashboard, you can use one single CUBEVALUE formula to do that.

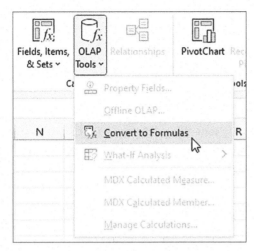

FIGURE 9-2 Excel offers to convert your pivot table to cube formulas.

B4	fx	=CUBEVALUE("ThisWorkbookDataModel",$A4,B$3,Slicer_Sector)								

	A	B	C	D	E	F	G	H	I	J	K
3	Customer	Sum of Revenue		B4							
4	Adaept Information Management	498937		=CUBEVALUE("ThisWorkbookDataModel",$A4,B$3,Slicer_Sector)							
5	Calleia Company	406326		B3							
6	Excel Design Solutions Ltd	71651		=CUBEMEMBER("ThisWorkbookDataModel","[Measures].[Sum of Revenue]")							
7	Excel Learning Zone	72680		A10							
8	Excel4Apps	91320		=CUBEMEMBER("ThisWorkbookDataModel","[CustData].[Customer].&[F-Keys Ltd.]")							
9	Excel-Translator.de	42316									
10	F-Keys Ltd.	34710									
11	JEVS Human Services	50030									

FIGURE 9-3 The former pivot table is converted to a series of formulas.

The primary cube function is CUBEVALUE. The syntax requires the name of the connection and then a series of member_expressions. For pivot tables based on the Data Model, the connection name is always "ThisWorkbookDataModel."

For the member_expressions, the formula in B4 points to Adaept Information Management in A4, the words "Sum Of Revenue" in B3, and the name of the slicer: Slicer_Sector. Had there been more slicers associated with the pivot table, there would have been additional member_expressions for each slicer. The formula in B4 is as follows:

```
=CUBEVALUE("ThisWorkbookDataModel",$A4,B$3,Slicer_Sector)
```

You need to be particularly careful with this point: The formula is pointing to A4, which appears to contain the words "Adaept Information Management." But it is not using the text that we can see in cell A4. In fact, if you would change the formula to the following, it would stop working:

```
=CUBEVALUE("ThisWorkbookDataModel","Adaept Information
Management",B$3,Slicer_Sector)
```

The CUBEVALUE formula is making use of the actual formula text in A4 and B3. Those cells contain CUBEMEMBER functions.

The syntax is:

```
CUBEMEMBER(Connection, Member_Expression, [Caption])
```

The formula to return the words "Sum Of Revenue" to cell B3 is the following:

```
=CUBEMEMBER("ThisWorkbookDataModel","[Measures].[Sum of Revenue]")
```

The optional caption argument allows you to display something different in the cell other than the words "Sum Of Revenue." For example, if you wanted to put the word "Revenue" in the cell, you could use a caption of "Revenue." Regular pivot tables would not let you reuse the word revenue, but it is not a problem here.

So far, everything is great, but the next part of the Convert To Cube Formulas results is going to be a problem down the road. For the customer name cells in A4 to A29, Excel created formulas like this:

```
=CUBEMEMBER("ThisWorkbookDataModel","[CustData].[Customer].&[Adaept Information
Management]")
```

Hard coding the customer name in the formula is not efficient. Customers are going to come and go. Next year, Adaept Information Management might not even be a customer, and other customers will appear.

You don't have to wait for the underlying data to change in order to be disappointed. If you choose Consulting from the Slicer, the CUBEVALUE formulas in column B update to show only consulting results. However, the list of customers in column A does not change, leaving many empty cells in column B (see Figure 9-4).

	A	B	C	D
3	Customer	Sum of Revenue		Sector
4	Adaept Information Management	498937		Consulting
5	Calleia Company	406326		
6	Excel Design Solutions Ltd	71651		Museums
7	Excel Learning Zone			Retail
8	Excel4Apps			
9	Excel-Translator.de			Training
10	F-Keys Ltd.			Utilities
11	JEVS Human Services	50030		

FIGURE 9-4 Choose from the slicer. The formulas in B4:B29 update correctly, but the list of customers in A4:A29 does not update.

We are going to pull out some tricks to make these cube formulas more robust. The first is from Rob Collie at PowerPivotPro.com. Collie says the CUBESET function is useless by itself. It can return a list of all the customers in the underlying data set. It won't display those customers for you, but it forms the basis that allows later formulas to list those customers. Here is the syntax:

```
CUBESET(connection, set_expression, [caption], [sort_order], [sort_by])
```

- **Connection**—This will always be "ThisWorkbookDataModel" for pivot tables based on the Data Model.

- **Set_expression**—Rather than return a single member like CUBEMEMBER, CUBESET returns a whole set of values. There are many different ways to represent a set, but the most common way is <ColumnName>.children, which returns all unique values of that column. For our current example, the table name is [CustData]. The field name is [Customer]. You would use "[CustData].[Customer].children" in quotation marks as the second argument.

- **Caption**—This is optional. Excel won't display the members of the cube set in this cell, so specifying a caption allows you to visually see that there is something in the cell. Power Pivot Pros love to put "" here, but I hate that because then I can't ever find the cell that contains the formula. You could put a caption of "Hey Bill, the CUBESET function is here," but "All Customers" might be less geeky and actually serve to help you remember what is going on when you revisit this workbook months or years from now.

- **Sort_order** (optional)—An integer from 0 to 7, representing:
  - No Sorting
  - Sort Ascending
  - Sort Descending
  - Alpha Ascending
  - Alpha Descending
  - DB order ascending
  - DB order descending

- **Sort_by** (optional)—The measure you want to sort by. You would use [Measures].[Customer] instead of [Range].[Customer]. This argument is ignored unless you specify 1 or 2 for sort_order (1 for ascending or 2 descending).

Figure 9-5 shows the formula returning an "All Customers" caption. The fourth and fifth arguments specify that the customers should be arranged in descending order by Sum of Revenue. To sort the customers alphabetically, change the 2 to a 3, and leave off the fifth argument. The formula is as follows:

```
=CUBESET("ThisWorkbookDataModel",
        " [CustData].[Customer].children",
        "All Customers",
        2,
        " [Measures].[Sum of Revenue] ")
```

At this point, cell E3 contains a list of all customers, but you can't see them. You can use CUBERANKED-MEMBER to extract those customers to cells in the worksheet.

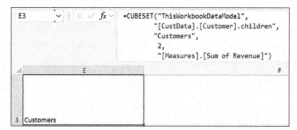

FIGURE 9-5 The cell reads "All Customers," but it actually contains a pointer to the complete set of customers.

To get the first customer, you would use the following:

```
=CUBERANKEDMEMBER("ThisWorkbookDataModel",$E$3,1)
```

The 1 as the third argument says that you want the first customer from the set stored in E3.

It would be better to return the complete list of customers. In the sample data, there are 26 customers, so you could successfully use:

```
=CUBERANKEDMEMBER("ThisWorkbookDataModel",$E$3,SEQUENCE(26))
```

However, this will fail when you have a new customer or lose a customer. There is a function to return the count of members in a cube set. Use =CUBESETCOUNT(E3) to get the number of items in the cube set. Thus, this will provide a complete list of customers in the cube set:

```
=CUBERANKEDMEMBER("ThisWorkbookDataModel",$E$3,SEQUENCE(CUBESETCOUNT(E3)))
```

Figure 9-6 shows a CUBESET function in E3 to connect to the list of customers and use a label of Customers. A CUBEMEMBER in F3 returns a pointer to the Sum Of Revenue and calls it Revenue. A single dynamic array formula in E4 returns all the customer names. To get the revenue in F4, use a CUBEVALUE function that refers to the customer in E4 and revenue in F3 and to the slicer.

E4			*fx*	=CUBERANKEDMEMBER("ThisWorkbookDataModel",$E$3,SEQUENCE(CUBESETCOUNT(E3)))

	E	F	G	H
				E3 =CUBESET("ThisWorkbookDataModel",
				"[CustData].[Customer].children",
				"Customers",
				2,
3	Customers	Revenue		"[Measures].[Sum of Revenue]")
4	MySpreadsheetLab	869,454		F3 =CUBEMEMBER("ThisWorkbookDataModel","[Measures].[Sum of Revenue]","Revenue")
5	Surten Excel	750,163		E4 =CUBERANKEDMEMBER("ThisWorkbookDataModel",$E$3,SEQUENCE(CUBESETCOUNT(E3)))
6	SkyWire, Inc.	704,359		F4 =CUBEVALUE("ThisWorkbookDataModel",E4,$F$3,Slicer_Sector)
7	SpringBoard	622,794		
8	NetCom Computer	613,514		
9	St. Peter's Prep	568,851		
10	Adaept Information Management	498,937		
11	The Salem Ohio Historical Society	427,349		

FIGURE 9-6 The CUBERANKEDMEMBER retrieves the customers from the set in E3.

The setup is closer to your goal, but there are still problems. When the number of customers changes, the formula in column F must be copied to rows, more or less.

Your first reaction might be to refer to E4# in the formula in F4. However, this seems to violate the "Excel can't calculate an array of arrays" limitation and does not work.

There is an elegant solution, first proposed by Chris Webb. It uses several brand-new functions, such as MAKEARRAY, LET, SWITCH, and LAMBDA. Here is a brief introduction to MAKEARRAY:

The MAKEARRAY function will make a two-dimensional array. You tell Excel how many rows and columns and then provide the logic to create the array using a LAMBDA function.

Let's say you are creating a 5-row by 3-column array. The MAKEARRAY function will call the LAMBDA function 15 times. The first time, it will call it for row 1, column 1. Next, it will call the LAMBA for row 1, column 2. Then, it will call row 1, column 3, and so on. The first two arguments for the LAMBDA are the variable names for row and column. In this example, you are using r for row and c for column. The third argument of the LAMBDA is the logic to fill each cell given the r and c values.

In Figure 9-7, a single formula in A2 returns 5 rows and 3 columns. The calculation for each position in the array is the word "Row" followed by the row of the array, a pipe (|), and then the word "Col" followed by the column number of the array. The formula is:

```
=MAKEARRAY(5,3,LAMBDA(r,c, "Row "&r&" | Col "&c))
```

This is a simple example of MAKEARRAY because every cell of the array uses the same logic. The second example in the figure adds some complexity, which will be discussed below.

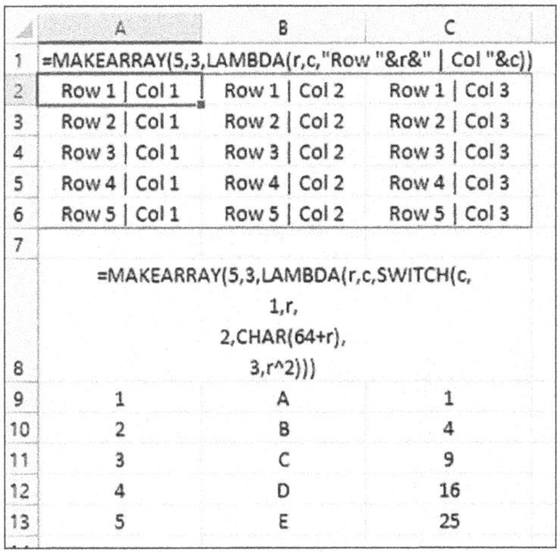

	A	B	C
1	=MAKEARRAY(5,3,LAMBDA(r,c,"Row "&r&" | Col "&c))		
2	Row 1	Col 1	Row 1	Col 2	Row 1	Col 3
3	Row 2	Col 1	Row 2	Col 2	Row 2	Col 3
4	Row 3	Col 1	Row 3	Col 2	Row 3	Col 3
5	Row 4	Col 1	Row 4	Col 2	Row 4	Col 3
6	Row 5	Col 1	Row 5	Col 2	Row 5	Col 3
7			
8	=MAKEARRAY(5,3,LAMBDA(r,c,SWITCH(c, 1,r, 2,CHAR(64+r), 3,r^2)))		
9	1	A	1
10	2	B	4
11	3	C	9
12	4	D	16
13	5	E	25

FIGURE 9-7 The new MAKEARRAY function lets you build logic for each intersection of row and column in a new array.

The second example in Figure 9-7 changes the logic in each of the three columns of the array by using the SWITCH function. In English, here is the logic of the SWITCH:

- You will make a decision based on the value stored in c.

- If c is 1, then simply use the row number stored in r.

- If c is 2, then return capital letters A, B, C by using =CHAR(64+r).

- If c is 3, then return r times itself.

The formula in cell A9 is

```
=MAKEARRAY(5,3,LAMBDA(r,c,SWITCH(c,1,r,2,CHAR(64+r),3,r^2)))
```

Note that the MAKEARRAY function must have a LAMBDA as the third argument. With this simple example, you can see how MAKEARRAY with LAMBDA and SWITCH allows you to create a single array with different logic for each column.

Let's apply the MAKEARRAY function to the problem of returning the entire table using cube functions.

In Figure 9-8, a single formula in A3 returns all customers and revenue. Here is the formula:

```
=MAKEARRAY(CUBESETCOUNT(A2),2,
LAMBDA(r,c,SWITCH(c,
1,CUBERANKEDMEMBER("ThisWorkbookDataModel",A2,r),
2,CUBEVALUE("ThisWorkbookDataModel",
    CUBERANKEDMEMBER("ThisWorkbookDataModel",A2,r),B2,Slicer_Sector))))
```

Here is how this formula works:

- MAKEARRAY creates an array that is two columns wide and has enough rows to accommodate the count of items in the Customer cubeset.

- The SWITCH function handles different logic for the two columns.

FIGURE 9-8 There is still an issue with customers that were removed by the slicer still appearing.

- For column 1, use the CUBERANKEDMEMBER function for row r. This is similar to the formulas in A4 in Figure 9-4.

- For column 2, use the CUBEVALUE to get revenue for the customer in this row of the array.

The formula in Figure 9-8 is inefficient because it calculates the customer name twice for each row. The new LET function would allow you to calculate that once for each row.

In the formula in Figure 9-9, the LET function creates a variable called ThisCust and stores the results of CUBERANKEDMEMBER for this row. The later calculations can refer to ThisCust.

```
=MAKEARRAY(CUBESETCOUNT(A2),2,
LAMBDA(r,c,
LET(ThisCust,CUBERANKEDMEMBER("ThisWorkbookDataModel",A2,r),
SWITCH(c,
1,ThisCust,
2,CUBEVALUE("ThisWorkbookDataModel",ThisCust,B2,Slicer_Sector)))))
```

FIGURE 9-9 The formulas update in response to the slicer, but the non-consulting customers remain.

Before you think everything is perfect, go back to your slicer and choose any sector. The numbers update, but the CUBESET is still returning all customers, regardless of whether they are in the slicer selections.

The FILTER function will handle this, provided you enter the results in a new range. You can't wrap the current function in FILTER because it creates an array of an array and will not calculate.

In Figure 9-10, the formula in D4 is: =FILTER(A4#,INDEX(A4#,,2)<>""). It successfully returns the customers who are part of the sectors selected by the slicer.

The cube functions, in collaboration with a Data Model pivot table, open an interesting set of possibilities for reusing pivot table data in dashboards and other reports. The rest of this chapter dives into OLAP and SQL Server Analysis Services.

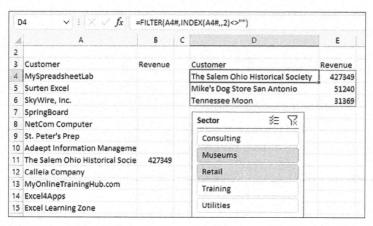

FIGURE 9-10 The new FILTER function prevents you from having to dive into the MDX.

Introduction to OLAP

Online analytical processing (OLAP) is a category of data warehousing that enables you to mine and analyze vast amounts of data with ease and efficiency. Unlike other types of databases, OLAP databases are designed specifically for reporting and data mining. In fact, there are several key differences between standard transactional databases, such as Access and SQL Server, and OLAP databases.

Records within a transactional database are routinely added, deleted, and updated. OLAP databases, on the other hand, contain only snapshots of data. The data in an OLAP database is typically archived data stored solely for reporting purposes. Although new data may be appended regularly, existing data is rarely edited or deleted.

Another difference between transactional databases and OLAP databases is structure. Transactional databases typically contain many tables; each table usually contains multiple relationships with other tables. Indeed, some transactional databases contain so many tables that it can be difficult to determine how each table relates to another.

However, in an OLAP database, all the relationships between the various data points have been predefined and stored in an *OLAP cube*, which already contains the relationships and hierarchies you need to easily navigate the data within. Consequently, you can build reports without needing to know how the data tables relate to one another.

The biggest difference between OLAP and transactional databases is the way the data is stored. The data in an OLAP cube is rarely stored in raw form. Typically, OLAP cubes store data in views that are already organized and aggregated; that is, grouping, sorting, and aggregations are predefined and ready to use. This makes querying and browsing for data far more efficient than in a transactional database, where you have to group, aggregate, and sort records on the fly.

Note An OLAP database is typically set up and maintained by the database administrator in your IT department. If your organization does not use OLAP databases, you might want to speak with your database administrator about the possibility of using some OLAP reporting solutions.

Connecting to an OLAP cube

Before you can browse OLAP data, you must establish a connection to an OLAP cube. Start on the Data tab and select Get Data | From Database | From Analysis Services (see Figure 9-11).

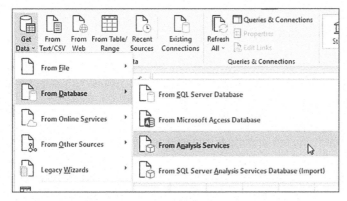

FIGURE 9-11 Select the Data Connection Wizard.

Selecting this option activates the Data Connection Wizard shown in Figure 9-12. The idea here is that you configure your connection settings so Excel can establish a link to the server.

 Note The examples in this chapter have been created using the Analysis Services Tutorial cube that comes with SQL Server Analysis Services 2017. The actions you take to connect to and work with your OLAP database are the same as demonstrated here because the concepts are applicable to any OLAP cube you are using.

Here are the steps to follow:

1. Provide Excel with authentication information. Enter the name of your server, as well as your username and password, as demonstrated in Figure 9-12. Click Next.

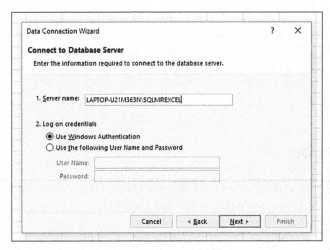

FIGURE 9-12 Enter your authentication information and click Next.

> **Note** If you are typically authenticated via Windows Authentication, you simply select the Use Windows Authentication option.

2. Select the database with which you are working from the dropdown. As Figure 9-13 illustrates, the Analysis Services Tutorial database is selected for this scenario. Selecting this database causes all the available OLAP cubes to be exposed in the list of objects below the dropdown. Choose the cube you want to analyze and then click Next.

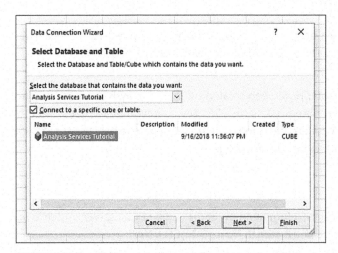

FIGURE 9-13 Specify your database and then choose the OLAP cube you want to analyze.

3. On the next screen, shown in Figure 9-14, enter some descriptive information about the connection you've just created.

Note All the fields in the screen shown in Figure 9-14 are optional. That is, you can bypass this screen without editing anything, and your connection will work fine.

4. Click the Finish button to finalize your connection settings. You immediately see the Import Data dialog, as shown in Figure 9-15.

5. In the Import Data dialog, select PivotTable Report and then click the OK button to start building your pivot table.

FIGURE 9-14 Edit descriptive information for your connection.

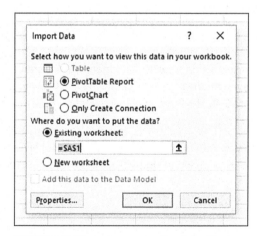

FIGURE 9-15 When your connection is finalized, you can start building your pivot table.

Understanding the structure of an OLAP cube

When a pivot table is created, you might notice that the PivotTable Fields pane looks somewhat different from that of a standard pivot table. The reason is that the PivotTable Fields pane for an OLAP pivot table is arranged to represent the structure of the OLAP cube you are connected to.

To effectively browse an OLAP cube, you need to understand the component parts of OLAP cubes and how they interact. Figure 9-16 illustrates the basic structure of a typical OLAP cube.

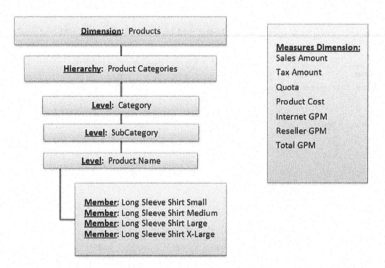

FIGURE 9-16 The basic structure of an OLAP cube.

As you can see, the main components of an OLAP cube are dimensions, hierarchies, levels, members, and measures:

- **Dimensions**—Major classifications of data that contain the data items that are analyzed. Some common examples of dimensions are the Products, Customer, and Employee dimensions. Figure 9-16 shows the Products dimension.

- **Hierarchies**—Predefined aggregations of levels within a particular dimension. A hierarchy enables you to pivot and analyze multiple levels at one time without having any knowledge of the relationships between the levels. In Figure 9-16, the Products dimension has three levels aggregated into one hierarchy called Product Categories.

- **Levels**—Categories of data that are aggregated within a hierarchy. You can think of levels as data fields that can be queried and analyzed individually. In Figure 9-16, three levels are shown: Category, Subcategory, and Product Name.

- **Members**—The individual data items within a dimension. Members are typically accessed via the OLAP structure of dimension, hierarchy, level, and member. In the example shown in Figure 9-16, the members you see belong to the Product Name level. The other levels have their own members and are not shown here.

■ **Measures**—The data values within the OLAP cube. Measures are stored within their own dimension, appropriately called the *Measures dimension*. The idea is that you can use any combination of dimension, hierarchy, level, and member to query the measures. This is called *slicing the measures.*

Now that you understand how the data in an OLAP cube is structured, take a look at the PivotTable Fields pane in Figure 9-17, and the arrangement of the available fields should begin to make sense.

FIGURE 9-17 The PivotTable Fields pane for an OLAP pivot table.

As you can see, the measures are listed first under the Sigma icon. These are the only items you can drop in the Values area of the pivot table. Next, you see dimensions represented next to the table icon. In this example, you see the Product dimension. Under the Product dimension, you see the Product Categories hierarchy that can be drilled into. Drilling into the Product Categories hierarchy enables you to see the individual levels.

The cool thing is that you can browse the entire cube structure by simply navigating through your PivotTable Fields pane! From here, you can build your OLAP pivot table report just as you would build a standard pivot table.

Understanding the limitations of OLAP pivot tables

When working with OLAP pivot tables, you must remember that the source data is maintained and controlled in the Analysis Services OLAP environment. This means that every aspect of the cube's behavior—from the dimensions and measures included in the cube to the ability to drill into the details of a dimension—is controlled via Analysis Services. This reality translates into some limitations on the actions you can take with your OLAP pivot tables.

When your pivot table report is based on an OLAP data source, keep in mind the following:

- You cannot place any field other than measures into the Values area of the pivot table.

- You cannot change the function used to summarize a data field.

- The Show Report Filter Pages command is disabled.

- The Show Items With No Data option is disabled.

- The Subtotal Hidden Page Items setting is disabled.

- The Background Query option is not available.

- Using Show Details returns only the first 1,000 records of the pivot cache.

- The Optimize Memory checkbox in the PivotTable Options dialog is disabled.

Creating an offline cube

With a standard pivot table, the source data is typically stored on your local drive. This way, you can work with and analyze your data while you're disconnected from the network. However, this is not the case with OLAP pivot tables. With an OLAP pivot table, the pivot cache is never brought to your local drive. This means that while you are disconnected from the network, your pivot table is out of commission. You can't even move a field while disconnected.

If you need to analyze your OLAP data while disconnected from your network, you need to create an offline cube. An *offline cube* is essentially a file that acts as a pivot cache, locally storing OLAP data so that you can browse that data while disconnected from the network.

To create an offline cube, start with an OLAP-based pivot table. Place your cursor anywhere inside the pivot table and click the OLAP Tools dropdown button on the PivotTable Analyze tab and select Offline OLAP, as shown in Figure 9-18.

Selecting this option activates the Offline OLAP Settings dialog (see Figure 9-19), where you click the Create Offline Data File button. The Create Cube File wizard shown in Figure 9-20 appears. Click Next to start the process.

FIGURE 9-18 Select the Offline OLAP option to start the creation of an offline cube.

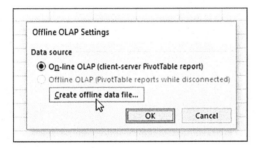

FIGURE 9-19 Start the Create Cube File wizard.

As you can see in Figure 9-20, you first select the dimensions and levels you want to be included in your offline cube. Your selections tell Excel which data you want to import from the OLAP database. The idea is to select only the dimensions that you need available to you while you're disconnected from the server. The more dimensions you select, the more disk space your offline cube file takes up.

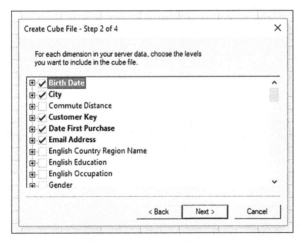

FIGURE 9-20 Select the dimensions and level you want to be included in your offline cube.

Clicking Next moves you to the next dialog, shown in Figure 9-21. Here, you are given the opportunity to filter out any members or data items you do not want to be included. For instance, the Extended Amount measure is not needed, so its checkbox has been cleared. Clearing this box ensures that this measure will not be imported and, therefore, will not take up unnecessary disk space.

The final step is to specify a name and location for your cube file. In Figure 9-22, the cube file is named MyOfflineCube.cub, and it will be placed in a directory called c:\aaa\.

 Note The file name extension for all offline cubes is .cub.

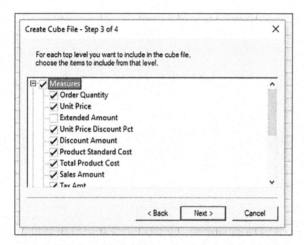

FIGURE 9-21 Clear the checkboxes for any members you do not need to see offline.

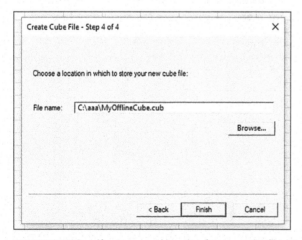

FIGURE 9-22 Specify a name and location for your cube file.

After a few moments of crunching, Excel outputs your offline cube file to your chosen directory. To test it, simply double-click the file to automatically generate an Excel workbook that is linked to the offline cube via a pivot table.

After creating your offline cube file, you can distribute it to others and use it while disconnected from the network.

> **Tip** You can open your offline cube file and refresh the pivot table within when you're connected to the network. This automatically refreshes the data in the cube file. The idea is that you can use the data within the cube file while you are disconnected from the network and can refresh the cube file while a data connection is available. Any attempt to refresh an offline cube while disconnected causes an error.

Breaking out of the pivot table mold with cube functions

Cube functions are Excel functions that can be used to access OLAP data outside a pivot table object. In pre-2010 versions of Excel, you could find cube functions only if you installed the Analysis Services add-in. In Excel 2010, cube functions were brought into the native Excel environment. To fully understand the benefit of cube functions, take a moment to walk through an example.

Exploring cube functions

One of the easiest ways to start exploring cube functions is to allow Excel to convert your OLAP-based pivot table into cube formulas. Converting a pivot table to cube formulas is a delightfully easy way to create a few cube formulas without doing any of the work yourself. The idea is to tell Excel to replace all cells in the pivot table with a formula that connects to the OLAP database. Figure 9-23 shows a pivot table connected to an OLAP database.

Gender	F				
Sales Amount	**Calendar Year**				
Model Name	**2011**	**2012**	**2013**	**2014**	**Grand Total**
All-Purpose Bike Stand				$21,147	$1,113	$22,260
Bike Wash				$3,244	$239	$3,482
Classic Vest				$15,939	$1,524	$17,463
Cycling Cap				$9,341	$476	$9,817
Fender Set - Mountain				$21,518	$1,429	$22,947
Half-Finger Gloves				$15,967	$980	$16,947
Hitch Rack - 4-Bike				$17,040	$1,440	$18,480
HL Mountain Tire				$22,750	$1,540	$24,290
HL Road Tire				$13,496	$880	$14,377
Hydration Pack				$19,137	$1,045	$20,181
LL Mountain Tire				$9,121	$1,000	$10,121
LL Road Tire				$10,466	$838	$11,304
Long-Sleeve Logo Jersey				$41,042	$2,849	$43,891
ML Mountain Tire				$15,205	$1,410	$16,614
ML Road Tire				$10,871	$650	$11,520
Mountain Bottle Cage				$9,481	$549	$10,030

FIGURE 9-23 A normal OLAP pivot table.

You can convert any OLAP pivot table into a series of cube formulas with just a few clicks. Place the cursor anywhere inside the pivot table and click the OLAP Tools dropdown button on the PivotTable Analyze tab. Select Convert To Formulas, as shown in Figure 9-24.

If your pivot table contains a report filter field, the dialog shown in Figure 9-25 appears. This dialog gives you the option of converting your filter dropdown selectors to cube formulas. If you select this option, the dropdown selectors are removed, leaving a static formula. If you need to have your filter dropdown selectors intact so that you can continue to change the selections in the filter field interactively, leave the Convert Report Filters checkbox cleared.

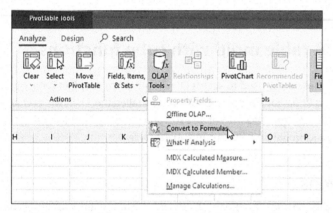

FIGURE 9-24 Select the Convert To Formulas option to convert your pivot table to cube formulas.

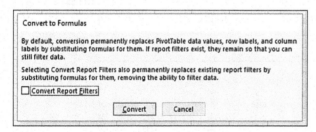

FIGURE 9-25 Excel gives you the option of converting your report filter fields.

Note If you are working with a pivot table in Compatibility mode, Excel automatically converts the filter fields to formulas.

After a second or two, the cells that used to house a pivot table are now homes for cube formulas. Note that, as shown in Figure 9-26, any styles you have applied are removed.

So, why is this capability useful? Well, now that the values you see are no longer part of a pivot table object, you can

■ Insert rows and columns

- Add your own calculations

- Combine the data with other external data

- Modify the report in all sorts of ways by simply moving the formulas around

D5				f_x	=CUBEVALUE("LAPTOP-U21M363N_SQLMREXCEL Analysis Services Tutorial",$B$1,$A$3,$A5,D$4)					
	A	B	C	D	E	F	G	H	I
1	Gender	F							
2									
3	Sales Amount	Calendar Year							
4	Model Name	2011	2012	2013	2014	Grand Total			
5	All-Purpose Bike Stand			21147	1113	22260			
6	Bike Wash			3243.6	238.5	3482.1			
7	Classic Vest			15938.5	1524	17462.5			
8	Cycling Cap			9340.61	476.47	9817.08			
9	Fender Set - Mountain			21518.42	1428.7	22947.12			
10	Half-Finger Gloves			15967.48	979.6	16947.08			
11	Hitch Rack - 4-Bike			17040	1440	18480			
12	HL Mountain Tire			22750	1540	24290			
13	HL Road Tire			13496.4	880.2	14376.6			
14	Hydration Pack			19136.52	1044.81	20181.33			
15	LL Mountain Tire			9121.35	999.6	10120.95			
16	LL Road Tire			10465.63	838.11	11303.74			
17	Long-Sleeve Logo Jersey			41041.79	2849.43	43891.22			
18	ML Mountain Tire			15204.93	1409.53	16614.46			
19	ML Road Tire			10870.65	649.74	11520.39			
20	Mountain Bottle Cage			9480.51	549.45	10029.96			

FIGURE 9-26 Note that these cells are now a series of cube formulas in the formula bar!

Adding calculations to OLAP pivot tables

In Excel 2010 and earlier, OLAP pivot tables were limited in that you could not build your own calculations within OLAP pivot tables. This means you could not add the extra layer of analysis provided by the calculated fields and calculated items functionality in standard pivot tables.

> **Note** Calculated fields and calculated items are covered in Chapter 5, "Performing calculations in pivot tables." If you haven't read it already, you might find it helpful to read that chapter first in order to build the foundation for this section.

Excel 2013 changed that with the introduction of the new OLAP tools—calculated measures and calculated members. With these two tools, you are no longer limited to just using the measures and members provided through the OLAP cube by the database administrator. You can add your own analysis by building your own calculations.

In this section, you'll explore how to build your own calculated measures and calculated members.

A word about MDX

When you are using a pivot table with an OLAP cube, you are sending MDX (multidimensional expressions) queries to the OLAP database. MDX is an expression language that is used to return data from multidimensional data sources (that is, OLAP cubes).

As your OLAP pivot table is refreshed or changed, subsequent MDX queries are passed to the OLAP database. The results of the query are sent back to Excel and displayed through the pivot table. This is how you can work with OLAP data without having a local copy of a pivot cache.

When building calculated measures and calculated members, you need to use MDX syntax. This is the only way the pivot table can communicate your calculation to the back-end OLAP database.

The examples in this book use basic MDX constructs in order to demonstrate the calculated measures and calculated members' functionality. If you need to create complex calculated measures and calculated members, you will want to invest some time learning more about MDX.

That being said, the topic of MDX is robust and beyond the scope of this book. If, after reading this section, you have a desire to learn more about MDX, consider picking up *MDX Solutions* (by George Spofford et al.), an excellent guide to MDX that is both easy to understand and comprehensive.

Creating calculated measures

A *calculated measure* is essentially the OLAP version of a calculated field. When you create a calculated measure, you basically create a new data field based on some mathematical operation that uses the existing OLAP fields.

In the example shown in Figure 9-27, an OLAP pivot table contains products along with their respective quantities and revenues. Say that you want to add a new measure that calculates the average sales price per unit.

Place your cursor anywhere in the pivot table and select the PivotTable Analyze tab. Then select MDX Calculated Measure, as shown in Figure 9-28. This activates the New Calculated Measure dialog, as shown in Figure 9-29.

	A	B	C
1	Model Name	Order Quantity	Sales Amount
2	All-Purpose Bike Stand	249	$39,591
3	Bike Wash	908	$7,219
4	Classic Vest	562	$35,687
5	Cycling Cap	2,190	$19,688
6	Fender Set - Mountain	2,121	$46,620
7	Half-Finger Gloves	1,430	$35,021
8	Hitch Rack - 4-Bike	328	$39,360
9	HL Mountain Tire	1,396	$48,860
10	HL Road Tire	858	$27,971
11	Hydration Pack	733	$40,308
12	LL Mountain Tire	862	$21,541
13	LL Road Tire	1,044	$22,436
14	Long-Sleeve Logo Jersey	1,736	$86,783
15	ML Mountain Tire	1,161	$34,818

FIGURE 9-27 You want to add a calculation to this OLAP pivot table to show the average sales price per unit.

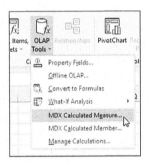

FIGURE 9-28 Choose the MDX Calculated Measure command.

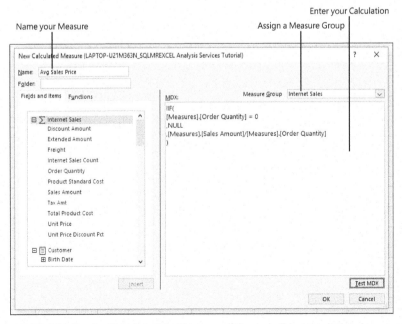

FIGURE 9-29 Use the New Calculated Measure dialog to build your calculated measure.

In the New Calculated Measure dialog, take the following actions:

1. Give your calculated measure a name by entering it in the Name input box.

2. Choose a measure group where Excel should place your calculated measure. If you don't choose one, Excel automatically places your measure in the first available measure group.

3. Enter the MDX syntax for your calculation in the MDX input box. To save a little time, you can use the list on the left to choose the existing measures you need for your calculation. Simply double-click the measures needed, and Excel pops them into the MDX input box. In this example, the calculation for the average sales price is:

```
IIF([Measures].[Order Quantity] = 0,NULL,[Measures].[Sales Amount]/[Measures].
[Order Quantity]).
```

4. Click OK.

> **Tip** Notice the Test MDX button in the New Calculated Measure dialog shown in Figure 9-29. You can click this to ensure that the MDX you entered is well-formed. Excel lets you know via a message box if your syntax contains any errors.

After you have built your calculated measure, you can go to the PivotTable Fields pane and select your newly created calculation (see Figure 9-30).

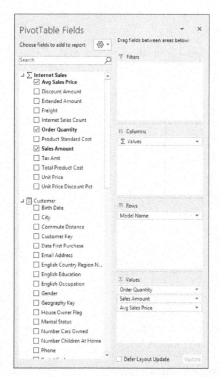

FIGURE 9-30 Add your newly created calculation to your pivot table via the PivotTable Fields pane.

As you can see in Figure 9-31, your calculated measure adds a meaningful layer of analysis to the pivot table.

	A	B	C	D
1	Model Name	Order Quantity	Sales Amount	Avg Sales Price
2	All-Purpose Bike Stand	249	$39,591	$159.00
3	Bike Wash	908	$7,219	$7.95
4	Classic Vest	562	$35,687	$63.50
5	Cycling Cap	2,190	$19,688	$8.99
6	Fender Set - Mountain	2,121	$46,620	$21.98
7	Half-Finger Gloves	1,430	$35,021	$24.49
8	Hitch Rack - 4-Bike	328	$39,360	$120.00
9	HL Mountain Tire	1,396	$48,860	$35.00
10	HL Road Tire	858	$27,971	$32.60
11	Hydration Pack	733	$40,308	$54.99
12	LL Mountain Tire	862	$21,541	$24.99
13	LL Road Tire	1,044	$22,436	$21.49
14	Long-Sleeve Logo Jersey	1,736	$86,783	$49.99
15	ML Mountain Tire	1,161	$34,818	$29.99

FIGURE 9-31 Your pivot table now contains your calculated measure!

> **Note** It's important to note that it exists in your workbook only when you create a calculated measure. In other words, you are not building your calculation directly in the OLAP cube on the server. This means no one else connected to the OLAP cube will be able to see your calculations unless you share or distribute your workbook.

Creating calculated members

A *calculated member* is essentially the OLAP version of a calculated item. When you create a calculated member, you basically create a new data item based on some mathematical operation that uses the existing OLAP members.

In the example shown in Figure 9-32, an OLAP pivot table contains sales information for each quarter in the year. Let's say you want to aggregate quarters 1 and 2 into a new data item called First Half of Year. You also want to aggregate quarters 3 and 4 into a new data item called Second Half of Year.

	A	B	C	D
1	Calendar Quarter	Order Quantity	Sales Amount	Avg Sales Price
2	1	12,601	$5,749,853	$456.30
3	2	14,441	$6,840,488	$473.69
4	3	15,557	$7,670,590	$493.06
5	4	17,799	$9,097,746	$511.14
6	Grand Total	60,398	$29,358,677	$486.09

FIGURE 9-32 You want to add new calculated members to aggregate the four quarters into First Half of Year and Second Half of Year.

Place your cursor anywhere in the pivot table, select the PivotTable Analyze tab, and then select MDX Calculated Member, as shown in Figure 9-33. The New Calculated Member dialog opens (see Figure 9-34).

FIGURE 9-33 Choose the MDX Calculated Member command.

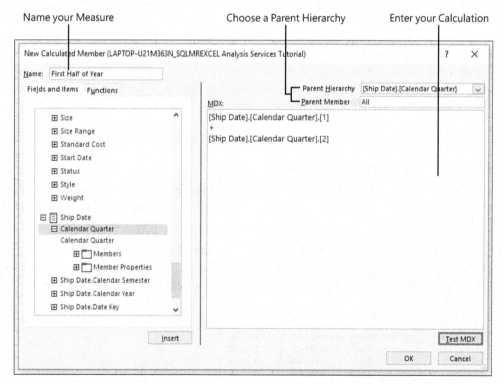

FIGURE 9-34 Use the New Calculated Member dialog to build your calculated member.

In the New Calculated Member dialog, take the following actions:

1. Give your calculated member a name by entering it in the Name input box.

2. Choose the parent hierarchy for which you are creating new members. Be sure to leave Parent Member set to All. This ensures that Excel takes into account all members in the parent hierarchy when evaluating your calculation.

3. Enter the MDX syntax for your calculation in the MDX input box. To save a little time, you can use the list on the left to choose the existing members you need for your calculation. Simply double-click the member needed, and Excel pops them into the MDX input box. In the example in Figure 9-34, you are adding quarter 1 and quarter 2:

`[Ship Date].[Calendar Quarter].[1] + [Ship Date].[Calendar Quarter].[2].`

4. Click OK.

As soon as you click OK, Excel shows your newly created calculated member in the pivot table. As you can see in Figure 9-35, your calculated member is included with the other original members of the pivot field.

	A	B	C	D
1	Calendar Quarter	Order Quantity	Sales Amount	Avg Sales Price
2	1	12,601	$5,749,853	$456.30
3	2	14,441	$6,840,488	$473.69
4	3	15,557	$7,670,590	$493.06
5	4	17,799	$9,097,746	$511.14
6	First Half of Year	27,042	$12,590,341	$465.58
7	Grand Total	60,398	$29,358,677	$486.09

FIGURE 9-35 Excel immediately adds your calculated member to your pivot field.

Figure 9-36 shows how you repeat the process to calculate the Second Half Of Year member.

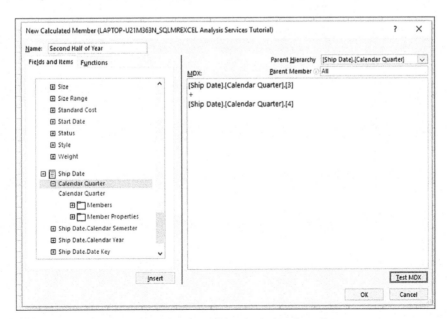

FIGURE 9-36 Repeat the process for any additional calculated members.

Notice in Figure 9-37 that Excel does not attempt to remove any of the original members. In this case, you see that quarters 1 through 4 are still in the pivot table. This might be fine for your situation, but you will likely hide these members to avoid confusion in most scenarios.

	A	B	C	D
1	Calendar Quarter	Order Quantity	Sales Amount	Avg Sales Price
2	1	12,601	$5,749,853	$456.30
3	2	14,441	$6,840,488	$473.69
4	3	15,557	$7,670,590	$493.06
5	4	17,799	$9,097,746	$511.14
6	First Half of Year	27,042	$12,590,341	$465.58
7	Second Half of Year	33,356	$16,768,337	$502.71
8	Grand Total	60,398	$29,358,677	$486.09

FIGURE 9-37 Excel shows your final calculated members along with the original members. It is a best practice to remove the original members to avoid confusion.

Note   Remember that your calculated member exists in your workbook only. No one else connected to the OLAP cube can see your calculations unless you share or distribute your workbook.

Caution   If the parent hierarchy or parent member is changed in the OLAP cube, your calculated member ceases to function. You must re-create the calculated member.

Managing OLAP calculations

Excel provides an interface for managing the calculated measures and calculated members in an OLAP pivot table. Simply place your cursor anywhere in the pivot table, select the PivotTable Analyze tab, and then select Manage Calculations, as shown in Figure 9-38.

FIGURE 9-38 Activate the Manage Calculations dialog.

The Manage Calculations dialog, shown in Figure 9-39, appears, offering three commands:

- **New**—Create a new calculated measure or calculated member.

- **Edit**—Edit the selected calculation.

- **Delete**—Permanently delete the selected calculation.

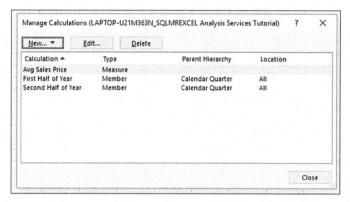

FIGURE 9-39 The Manage Calculations dialog enables you to create a new calculation, edit an existing calculation, or delete an existing calculation.

Performing what-if analysis with OLAP data

Another piece of functionality that Microsoft introduced in Excel 2013 is the ability to perform what-if analysis with the data in OLAP pivot tables. With this functionality, you can actually edit the values in a pivot table and recalculate your measures and members based on your changes. You can even publish your changes back to the OLAP cube.

To make use of the what-if analysis functionality, create an OLAP pivot table and then go to the Pivot-Table Analyze tab. Once there, select What-If Analysis | Enable What-If Analysis, as shown in Figure 9-40.

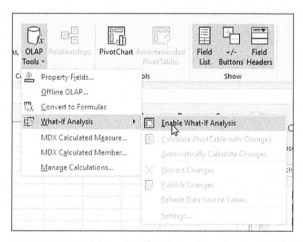

FIGURE 9-40 Enabling what-if analysis allows you to change the values in a pivot table.

At this point, you can edit the values in your pivot table. After you have made changes, you can right-click any of the changed values and choose Calculate PivotTable With Change (see Figure 9-41). This forces Excel to reevaluate all the calculations in the pivot table based on your edits—including your calculated members and measures.

	A	B	C	D
1	Model Name	Order Quantity	Sales Amount	Avg Sales Price
2	All-Purpose Bike Stand	249	$39,591	$159.00
3	Bike Wash	908	$7,219	$7.95
4	Classic Vest	562	$35,687	$63.50
5	Cycling Cap	2,190	$19,688	$8.99
6	Fender Set - Mountain	4,432	$46,620	$21.98
7	Half-Finge	Value has been changed	$35,021	$24.49
8	Hitch Rack		$39,360	$120.00
9	HL Mounta	Data source value: (click to retrieve)	$48,860	$35.00
10	HL Road Ti	Calculate PivotTable with Change	$27,971	$32.60
11	Hydration	Discard Change	$40,308	$54.99
12	LL Mounta	What-If Analysis Settings	$21,541	$24.99

FIGURE 9-41 Choose Calculate PivotTable With Change to reevaluate all your calculations.

The edits you make to your pivot table while using what-if analysis are, by default, local edits only. If you are committed to your changes and would like to actually make the changes on the OLAP server, you can tell Excel to publish your changes. To do this, in the PivotTable Analyze tab, select What-If Analysis | Publish Changes (see Figure 9-42). This triggers a "write-back" to the OLAP server, meaning the edited values are sent to the source OLAP cube.

Note You need adequate server permissions to publish changes to the OLAP server. Your database administrator can guide you through the process of getting write access to your OLAP database.

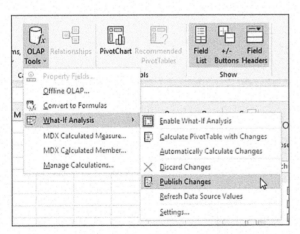

FIGURE 9-42 Excel lets you publish your changes to the source OLAP cube!

Case study: Used sets and editing MDX to show sum for each Product and average at total level only

The goal is to show a pivot table with Sum of Sales for each Product, a total Sum of Sales, and then a Total Average of Sales without showing averages for each item. In Figure 9-43, the goal is to hide rows 9 through 13 automatically.

⬙	A	B	C	D	E	F
1	Product ▾	Sales ▾				
2	Elderberry	867				
3	Banana	864		Values	Product ▾	
4	Apple	5541		Sum of Sales	Apple	47,323
5	Banana	825			Banana	4,440
6	Dill	162			Cherry	2,878
7	Dill	296			Dill	1,627
8	Dill	169			Elderberry	4,570
9	Apple	5298		Average of Sales	Apple	3,640
10	Apple	341			Banana	740
11	Elderberry	642			Cherry	480
12	Apple	625			Dill	271
13	Banana	970			Elderberry	762
14	Banana	518		Total Sum of Sales		60,838
15	Apple	8288		Total Average of Sales		1,644

FIGURE 9-43 Show product detail for the Sum of Sales section but hide product detail for Average of Sales.

To get to the starting pivot table shown above, follow these steps:

1. Make your original data in columns A and B into a table using Home | Format as Table.

2. On the Power Pivot tab in the ribbon, choose Add to Data Model. Close the Power Pivot window and return to Excel.

3. From cell D3, select Insert | Pivot Table | From Data Model.

4. Drag Product to the Rows area. Drag Sales to the Values area twice.

5. Double-click the Sum of Sales2 heading. Change the calculation to Average. Change the heading to Average of Sales.

6. Drag the Σ Values field from Columns and drop it as the first field in Rows.

7. When a pivot table is based on the Data Model, there is a built-in way to hide rows or columns in the pivot table. Select one of the product cells. From the PivotTable Analyze tab, choose Fields, Items, & Sets | Create Set Based On Row Items, as shown in Figure 9-44.

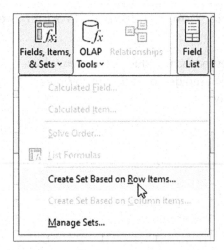

FIGURE 9-44 Choose Create Set Based On Row Items.

8. The New Set dialog appears. You should click next to the first Average of Sales items and then remove it from the set using the Delete Row icon. In Figure 9-45, the last product for Average of Sales is about to be removed.

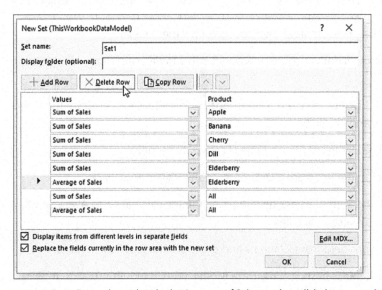

FIGURE 9-45 For each product in the Average of Sales section, click the row and then press Delete Row.

At first glance, Figure 9-46 shows what appears to be a successful result. However, think about what will happen when new products are added to the data set. Someone will have to remember that there is a set and edit the definition to add the new products to the Sum of Sales or remove products from the Average of Sales.

Values	Product	
Sum of Sales	Apple	47,323
	Banana	4,440
	Cherry	2,878
	Dill	1,627
	Elderberry	4,570
Total Sum of Sales		60,838
Total Average of Sales		1,644

FIGURE 9-46 Success? This pivot table looks correct.

You can improve this pivot table by using MDX:

1. Go to the Fields, Items, & Sets dropdown on the PivotTable Analyze tab. Choose Manage Sets.

2. In the Manage Sets dialog, choose Set 1 and then click Edit.

3. In the Modify Set dialog, choose Edit MDX from the lower-right corner. As shown in Figure 9-47, Excel displays an ominous warning that once you modify the MDX, future changes will have to be made to the MDX. This is okay because once you make these changes, you won't need to make any additional changes.

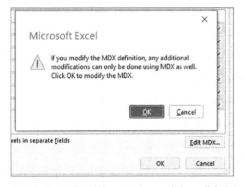

FIGURE 9-47 Read the warning and then click OK.

Without any knowledge of MDX, you can see there are lines in the Set Definition for each product (Apple, Banana, Cherry, Dill, and Elderberry), as shown in Figure 9-48. A better way to create this definition is discussed below.

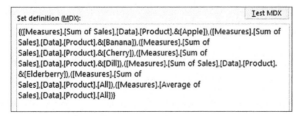

FIGURE 9-48 The MDX created for the set has one line of code for each line in the final pivot table.

The solution is to replace most of the definitions with a single line that asks for the children of the Product field. As shown in Figure 9-49, paste the following MDX code in the Set Definition:

```
{
([Measures].[Sum of Sales],[Data].[Product].Children),
([Measures].[Sum of Sales],[Data].[Product].[All]),
([Measures].[Average of Sales],[Data].[Product].[All])
}
```

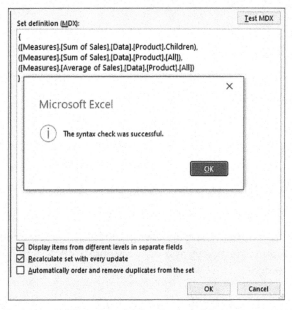

FIGURE 9-49 All the code in the previous figures is replaced with three lines of MDX code.

Assuming this is your first time writing MDX, there is a tedious order of curly braces and parentheses. It is easy to get it wrong. Click the Test MDX button at the top right. You should see the message in Figure 9-50 indicating that the MDX is successful.

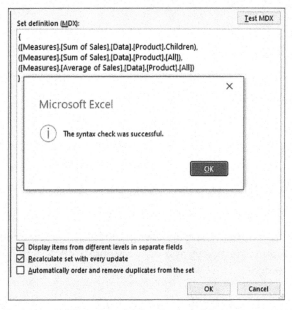

FIGURE 9-50 The syntax check was successful.

After clicking the Test MDX button, you get a The Syntax Check Was Successful message.

To test the MDX, you can replace a few items in the original data set. In Figure 9-51, the products in A7 & A8 have been replaced with a new product called Cranberry. Click in the pivot table and Refresh the pivot table. The new Cranberry product is inserted in the correct alphabetical sequence.

	A	B	C	D	E	F
1	Product	Sales				
2	Elderberry	867				
3	Banana	864		Values	Product	
4	Apple	5541		Sum of Sales	Apple	47,323
5	Banana	825			Banana	4,440
6	Dill	162			Cherry	2,878
7	Cranberry	2961			Cranberry	4,507
8	Cranberry	1546			Dill	1,162
9	Apple	5298			Elderberry	4,570
10	Apple	341		Total Sum of Sales		64,880
11	Elderberry	642		Total Average of Sales		1,754
12	Apple	625				

FIGURE 9-51 Cranberry is added to the original data set. After a refresh, the pivot table inserts the new product in the correct location alphabetically.

This case study introduces two fairly obscure concepts: Sets and editing the MDX. However, Sets and MDX combine to create a robust pivot table that will react to new products being added.

Next steps

In Chapter 10, "Unlocking features with the Data Model and Power Pivot," you'll find out how to use Power Pivot to create powerful reporting models that can process and analyze millions of rows of data in a single pivot table.

Unlocking features with the Data Model and Power Pivot

In this chapter, you will:

- Replace XLOOKUP with the Data Model

- Unlock hidden features with the Data Model

- Process big data with Power Query

- Use advanced Power Pivot techniques

- Overcome limitations of the Data Model

When I first saw the Power Pivot add-in in 2008, I thought the big news was the ability to handle 100 million rows in Excel. As time passes, and I realize that I frequently don't have anywhere near a million rows of data, I have started to appreciate the other powerful features that become available when you choose the box Add This Data To The Data Model.

The phrase "Add this data to the Data Model" is very boring. During the era of Excel 2013 and Excel 2016, Microsoft was slowly incorporating more of the Power Pivot tools into the core Excel.

At the same time, Microsoft was trying to convince customers to pay an extra $2 every month for Power Pivot. You can see where Excel 2013's goal was to make the phrase "Add this data to the Data Model" sound pretty boring. If no one selected the box, then people might think they had to pay the extra $2 a month.

However, given that Excel includes the full Power Pivot feature set, there is no reason for Microsoft to be so cagey. When you see "Data Model," you should think "Power Pivot."

> **Note** As I am writing this in 2024, Microsoft seems to have lost interest in the Data Model. Because of competitive pressures from Google Sheets, Microsoft is intent on making Excel Online the leading version of Excel. This is completely out of step with the rest of the world outside of Redmond, who perceive Excel Online as a non-starter. However, since the Data Model will never run in Excel Online, the Excel team is forced to make the unfortunate decision not to invest any further engineering resources in the Data Model or Power Pivot. Microsoft will continue to support people using Windows versions of Excel, so all of the amazing goodness that comes from the Data Model is still safe to use in Windows.

Replacing XLOOKUP with the Data Model

Some people describe Power Pivot as being able to do Access in Excel. This is true to a point: Power Pivot and the Data Model let you create a relationship between two tables.

Consider the two tables shown in Figures 10-1 and 10-2. The first data set—located on Sheet1—is a transactional data set. There are columns for Date, Invoice Number, Product, Quantity, Revenue, and Profit.

Note the formatting in Figure 10-1. Use either Home, Format As Table, or press Ctrl+T to format the data as a table. The formatting is not the important part. Making the data into a table is important if you will be joining two data sets in Excel.

When you press Ctrl+T, Excel will name the data set Table1. Press Ctrl+T on another data set, and that table will be named Table2. These are horrible names, so take the time to go to the Table Design tab of the ribbon and type a new name. In Figure 10-1, the table is called "Data." The SQL Server professional would call this table "Fact." I prefer "Data" just to differentiate myself from the SQL Server people.

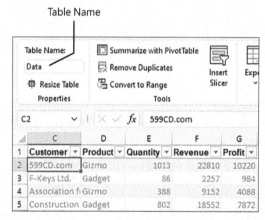

FIGURE 10-1 Press Ctrl+T to format your data as a table. Give the table a meaningful name.

While there are hundreds or thousands of invoices in the Data table, the second table is much smaller. It contains one row for each customer and maps the customer name to a sector and a region.

In most legacy situations, if you needed to create a report showing the revenue from the Data table and the region from the Lookup table, you would knock out a column or two of XLOOKUP functions and bring the Region data into the first table.

But with the Data Model, you do not have to do the XLOOKUP. Simply leave the two data sets on Sheet1 and Sheet2. You do want to take the extra step of defining the lookup table as a table using Ctrl+T. As Figure 10-2 shows, you can rename the table "Lookup," "CustomerLookup," or anything that is meaningful to you.

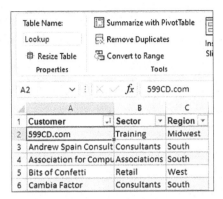

FIGURE 10-2 Define the lookup data as a table using Ctrl+T. Rename the table.

There are many ways to get your two tables into the Data Model.

- If you need to perform any transformations on the data in the table, you can use Power Query. In the final step, choose Close & Load To | Add This Data To The Data Model.

- If you see the Power Pivot tab in the ribbon, you can click the Add To Data Model icon from each of the tables to add to the Data Model. This tab is not always displayed. Excel MVP Wyn Hopkins offers this quick tip for adding the Power Pivot tab: Go to the Data tab in the ribbon and click Manage Data Model. In the Data Model screen, click File | Close. This step will cause the Power Pivot tab to display immediately and in the future.

- You can create a pivot table from the Data table and click the box for Add This Data To The Data Model.

- You can define a relationship between the tables, which automatically adds them to the Data Model.

- If you use the Diagram View in Manage Data Model, you can create relationships by dragging a line between two fields in two tables.

Because we need a relationship between the two tables, you can easily get the data loaded to the Data Model by creating a new relationship. Follow these steps.

1. From the Data tab, find the Data Model dropdown in the Data Tools group dropdown and choose Relationships.

2. In the Manage Relationships dialog, click New. The Create Relationship dialog appears with four dropdowns.

3. From the Table dropdown, choose the Data table.

4. From the Column (Foreign) dropdown, choose Customer.

5. From the Related Table dropdown, choose Lookup.

6. From the Related Column (Primary) dropdown, choose Customer, as shown in Figure 10-3.

7. Click OK to create the relationship.

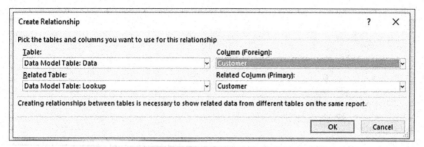

FIGURE 10-3 Creating a relationship between two tables automatically adds both tables to the Data Model.

 Note Some lookup tables might require you to match based on two fields, such as Cost Center and Account. There is a case study at the end of this chapter that shows how to use Power Query for this type of relationship.

To create the pivot table, select any blank area of your worksheet. Select Insert, PivotTable, From Data Model. Excel asks if you want to create the pivot table in a new worksheet or an existing worksheet. Click OK.

You will notice that the two tables appear in the PivotTable Fields pane in a collapsed state. As shown in Figure 10-4, you see only Data and Lookup. Click the greater than symbol (>) to the left of either table to see a list of fields in the table.

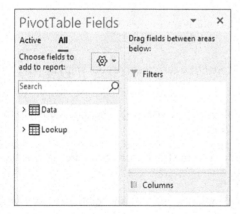

FIGURE 10-4 A pivot table based on the Data Model offers multiple tables.

Click the lookup table to reveal the Customer, Sector, and Region fields. Drag the Sector field to the Columns area. Drag the Region field to the Rows area. Click the Data table and drag the Revenue field to the Values area. As shown in Figure 10-5, you will have a pivot table that is drawing data from two different tables without a single XLOOKUP.

The results in Figure 10-5 are fairly groundbreaking. You just had Excel do a database join between data on two worksheets and didn't have to know how to do a VLOOKUP or XLOOKUP.

Even if you know and love XLOOKUP, when you get to a data set with 100,000 records and a lookup table with 12 columns, you don't want to build 1,200,000 XLOOKUP formulas to join those data sets together. Power Pivot and the Data Model scale perfectly.

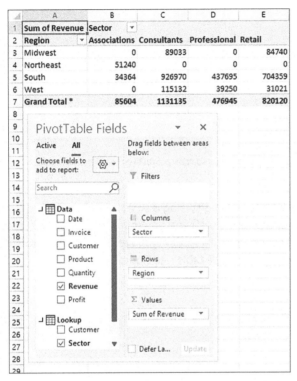

FIGURE 10-5 Excel joined the data and lookup tables in memory and reported the results using both tables.

For me, joining two tables in a single pivot table is the number-one benefit of Power Pivot and the Data Model. But there are many more powerful features unlocked when you select the Data Model checkbox while creating a pivot table.

Unlocking hidden features with the Data Model

I have done live Excel seminars for many years. I hear a variety of Excel questions in those seminars. Some questions are common enough that they pop up a couple of times a year. When my answer starts with, "Have you ever noticed the Add This Data To The Data Model box?" people can't believe that the answer has been right there, hiding in Excel. A typical reaction from the audience member is, "How was anyone supposed to know that 'Add This Data To The Data Model' means that I can create a median in a pivot table?"

The following examples use a single data set with no relationships. The fastest way to get the single data set into the Data Model is to select one cell in the data and choose Insert | PivotTable | From Table/Range, as shown in Figure 10-6. Note that you don't have to format the range as a Table with Ctrl+T. Excel will call your data with the "Range" name.

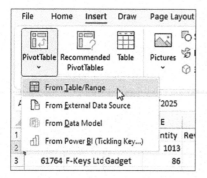

FIGURE 10-6 With only a single table, there are no relationships to create. Start to create a pivot table, but then do one extra step in Figure 10-7.

Near the bottom of the PivotTable From Table Or Range dialog is an Add This Data To The Data Model checkbox. The heading above this checkbox indicates that you should select it if you want to analyze multiple tables. But for all of the techniques in this section, you are choosing the Data Model to unlock pivot table functionality that is useful with a single table (see Figure 10-7).

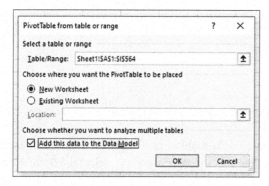

FIGURE 10-7 The box for Add This Data To The Data Model does not fully explain all the cool functionality that gets unlocked.

Count Distinct in a pivot table

Consider the three pivot tables shown in Figure 10-8. The question is: "How many unique customers are in each sector?" The pivot table in columns A and B allows you to figure out the answer. You can mentally count that there are two customers (B4 and B5) in the Associations sector. There are six customers listed in the Consultants sector.

But how would you present the top-left pivot table to your manager? You would have to grab some paper and jot down "Associations: 2, Consultants: 6, Professional: 3," and so on.

When you try to build a pivot table to answer the question, you might get the wrong results shown in D3:E10. This pivot table says it is calculating a "Count Of Customer," but this is actually the number of invoices in each sector. The trick to solving the problem is to add your data to the Data Model.

The pivot table in D13:E20 in Figure 10-8 somehow reports the correct number of unique customers in each sector.

A regular pivot table offers 11 calculations that have not changed in 33 years: Sum, Count, Average, Max, Min, Product, Count Numbers, StdDev, StdDevP, Var, and VarP.

However, if you create your pivot table and select the Add This Data To The Data Model checkbox, a new calculation option appears at the end of the Value Field Settings dialog: Distinct Count.

An ugly solution in A:B has a pivot table with Sector and Customer in the row area. You have to count how many rows are in each sector. When you drag Customer to the Values area, the heading reads "Count Of Customer," but the numbers are much higher than they should be. It is really a count of records. The following paragraphs will explain how the pivot table in D13:E20 reports the correct answer.

	A	B	C	D	E
1					
2				Regular Pivot Table	
3	Sector	Customer		Sector	Count of Customer
4	Association	Association for Computers & Taxation		Associations	8
5	Association	IMA Houston Chapter		Consultants	85
6	Associations Total			Professional	36
7	Consultant	Andrew Spain Consulting		Retail	78
8	Consultant	Cambia Factor		Software	104
9	Consultant	Construction Intelligence & Analytics, Inc.		Training	252
10	Consultant	Data2Impact		Grand Total	563
11	Consultant	Excelerator BI			
12	Consultant	Fintega Financial Modelling		Data Model	
13	Consultants Total			Sector	Unique Customer
14	Profession	Juliet Babcock-Hyde CPA, PLLC		Associations	2
15	Profession	Serving Brevard Realty		Consultants	6
16	Profession	WM Squared Inc.		Professional	3
17	Professional Total			Retail	4
18	Retail	Bits of Confetti		Software	4
19	Retail	Hartville MarketPlace and Flea Market		Training	8
20	Retail	LaFrenier Sons Septic		Grand Total	27
21	Retail	New Hope Laundry			
22	Retail Total				

FIGURE 10-8 By using the Data Model pivot table, you get the correct answer of two unique customers in the Associations sector.

Drag Customer to the Values area and double-click the Count Of Customer heading. Choose Distinct Count, change the title, and you have the solution shown in Figure 10-8. Figure 10-9 shows the Value Field Settings dialog.

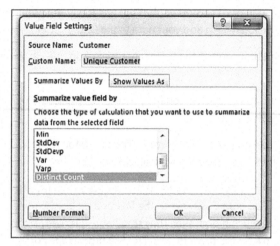

FIGURE 10-9 Distinct Count appears in Data Model pivot tables.

Note One oddity: The Product calculation is missing from the Value Field Settings for the Data Model. I've never met anyone who actually used the Product calculation. But if you were a person who loved Product, then having Excel swap out Product to make room for Distinct Count will not be popular. You can add a new measure with =PRODUCT([Revenue]) to replicate the Product calculation. See the creating a median example later in this chapter.

Including filtered items in totals

Excel pivot tables offer an excellent filtering feature called Top 10. This feature is very flexible: It can be Top 10 Items, Bottom 5 Items, Top 80%, or Top Records To Get To $4 Million In Revenue.

Shortening a long report to show only the top 5 items is great for a dashboard or a summary report, but there is an annoyance when you use any of the filters.

In Figure 10-10, the top pivot table occupies rows 3 through row 31. Revenue is shown both as Revenue and as a % of Total. The largest customer is Andrew Spain Consulting, with 869K. In the top pivot table, the Grand Total is $6.7 Million, and Andrew Spain is 12.96% of that total.

In the same figure, rows 34:40 show the same pivot table with the Top 5 selected in the Top 10 filter. The Grand Total now shows only $3.56 Million. Andrew Spain is 24% of the smaller total number, which is wrong. Andrew Spain Consulting should be 12.96% of the total—not 24%.

	A	B	C
3	Customer	Sum of Revenue	% of Total
25	CPASelfStudy.com	568,851	8.48%
26	MySpreadsheetLab	613,514	9.15%
27	599CD.com	622,794	9.28%
28	Hartville MarketPlace and Flea Market	704,359	10.50%
29	More4Apps	750,163	11.18%
30	Andrew Spain Consulting	869,454	12.96%
31	Grand Total	6,707,812	100.00%
32			
33	Values Filters, Top 10, Top 5 Items		
34	Customer	Sum of Revenue	% of Total
35	MySpreadsheetLab	613,514	17.23%
36	599CD.com	622,794	17.49%
37	Hartville MarketPlace and Flea Market	704,359	19.78%
38	More4Apps	750,163	21.07%
39	Andrew Spain Consulting	869,454	24.42%
40	Grand Total	3,560,284	100.00%

FIGURE 10-10 Using the Top 10 Filter can change the Percentage Of Total calculation.

On January 30, 2007, Microsoft released Excel 2007. A new feature was added to Excel called Include Filtered Items In Subtotals, which would solve the problem in Figure 10-10. But as you can see in Figure 10-11, the feature is unavailable. It has been unavailable since January 30, 2007. I can attest to that because I check every day to see if it is enabled.

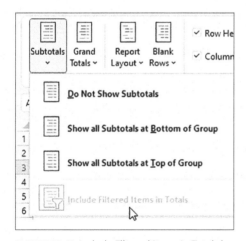

FIGURE 10-11 Include Filtered Items In Totals is grayed out.

You can solve this problem by choosing Add This Data To The Data Model as you create the pivot table. This enables the choice. The asterisk on the Grand Total in cell A49 means that rows hidden from the pivot table are included in the totals.

More importantly, the % of Column calculation is still reporting the correct 12.96% for Andrew Spain Consulting (see Figure 10-12).

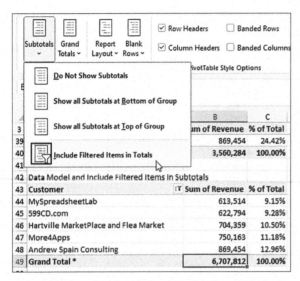

	B	C
3	um of Revenue	% of Total
39	869,454	24.42%
40	3,560,284	100.00%
41		
42 Data Model and Include Filtered Items In Subtotals		
43 Customer	Sum of Revenue	% of Total
44 MySpreadsheetLab	613,514	9.15%
45 599CD.com	622,794	9.28%
46 Hartville MarketPlace and Flea Market	704,359	10.50%
47 More4Apps	750,163	11.18%
48 Andrew Spain Consulting	869,454	12.96%
49 Grand Total *	6,707,812	100.00%

FIGURE 10-12 By choosing the Data Model, the calculation is correct.

Creating median in a pivot table using DAX measures

Pivot tables still do not support the median calculation. But when you add the data to the Data Model, you can build any calculation supported by the DAX formula language. Between Excel 2016 and Excel 2019, the DAX formula language was expanded to include a median calculation.

Calculations made with DAX are called *measures*. Figure 10-13 shows different ways to start a DAX calculation. You can right-click the table name in the PivotTable Fields pane and choose Add Measure, or you can use the Measures dropdown on the PowerPivot tab in Excel. Using the Measures dropdown is slightly better because any new measures are automatically added to the Values area of a pivot table.

Figure 10-14 shows the Measure dialog. There are several fields:

- The Table Name will be filled in automatically for you.

- Type a meaningful name for the new calculation in the Measure Name box.

- You can leave the Description box empty.

- The *fx* button lets you choose a function from a list.

- The Check Formula button will look for syntax errors.

- Type **=Median(Range[Revenue])** as the formula.

- In the lower-left, choose a number format.

As you type the formula, something that feels like AutoComplete will offer tooltips on how to build the formula. When you finish typing the formula, click the Check Formula button. You want to see the No Errors In Formula result, as shown in Figure 10-14.

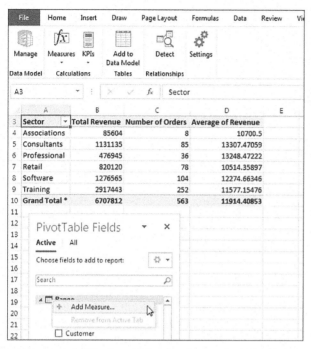

FIGURE 10-13 Build a pivot table using the Data Model and then add a measure.

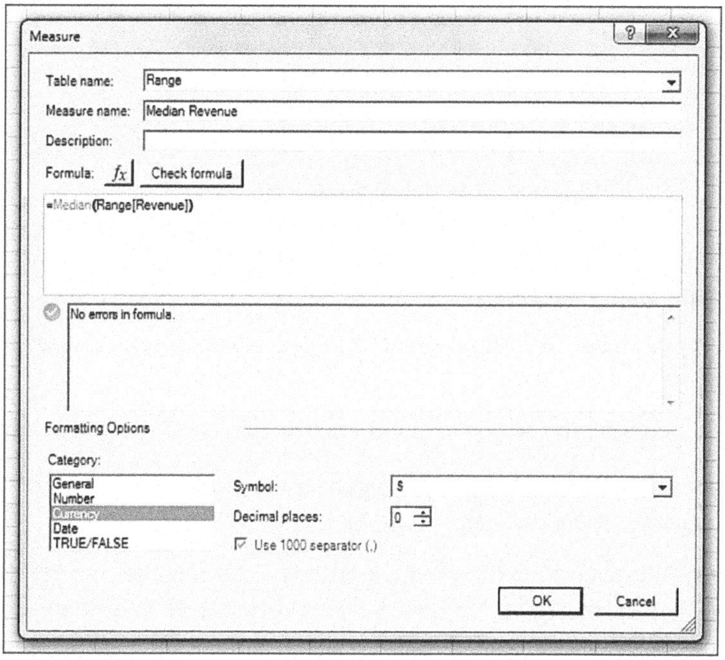

FIGURE 10-14 Build a measure to calculate the median.

Click OK. Median Revenue will appear in the Fields pane. Choose the field in the Fields pane, and it will be added to your pivot table. Column E in Figure 10-15 shows the median for each sector.

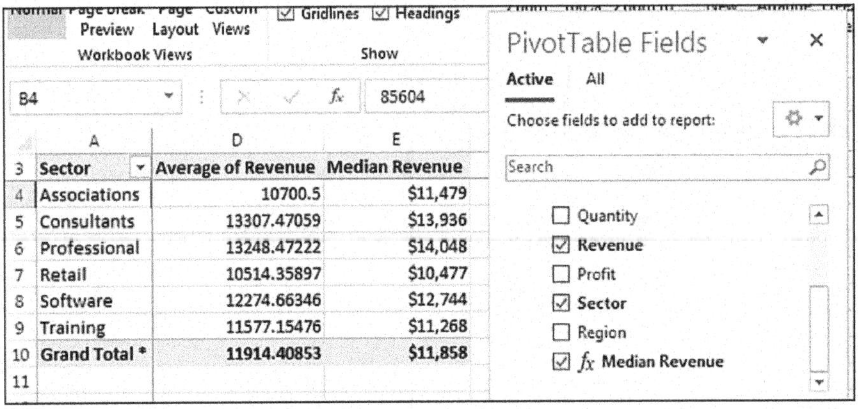

FIGURE 10-15 A pivot table with medians.

Calculations created by measures are easy to reuse. Change the pivot table from Figure 10-15 to show Regions in A instead of Sector. The measure is reused and starts calculating the median by Region (see Figure 10-16).

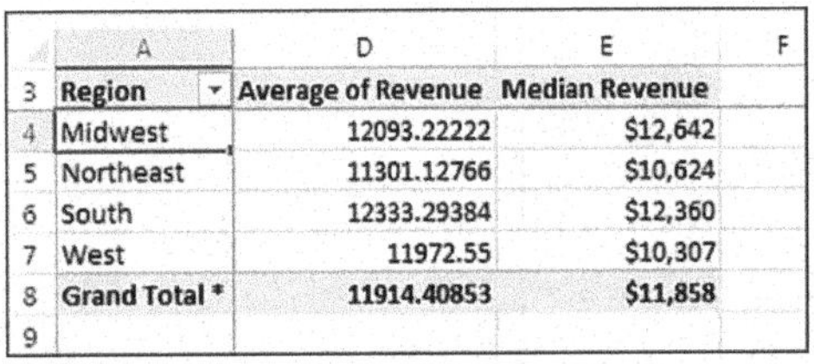

FIGURE 10-16 The measure keeps working if you change the shape of the pivot table.

Reporting text in the Values area

Pivot tables are great at reporting numbers. But you've never really been able to display text answers in the Values area of a pivot table.

The new DAX calculation for CONCATENATEX will return a text value to each value in the pivot table.

In Figure 10-17, the original data is shown in columns A:C. Each customer is assigned a team of three staff members: a sales rep, a manager, and a customer service rep.

You would like to build a report with Customers down the side and Roles across the top. In each Values area, list the names of the people assigned. The pivot table shown in Figure 10-17 uses the CONCATENATEX function to produce the report.

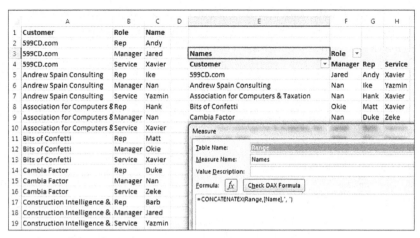

FIGURE 10-17 This narrow data set is pivoted to show text going across.

Tip The formula in Figure 10-17 might show duplicate values multiple times in a pivot table cell. To prevent those duplicates, change the formula to =CONCATENATEX(Values(Table1[Code]), Table1[Code],", ").

Processing big data with Power Query

You might have been excited when Excel moved from 65,536 rows in Excel 2003 to 1,048,576 rows in Excel 2007. But what if you have more than 1.1 million rows of data?

The 10-BigData.txt file included with the sample files has 1.8 million rows of data. How can you analyze this data in Excel?

You can use the Power Query tools in the Get & Transform group of the Data tab of the ribbon. There are several different strategies:

- **Edit the file using Power Query**—Try to remove the unnecessary records. You might not need sales from the outlet store or anything before 2005. If you can get the 1.8 million rows below 1,048,576 records, you can load directly to the Excel grid.

- **Group the file using Power Query**—Maybe you know that you will not ever care about daily data. You can add a formula in Power Query to calculate monthly dates from the daily dates. Group the data by Store, Category, and Month, summing the quantity and revenue. If that data is under 1,048,576 rows, you can load it to the Excel grid.

- **Skip the Excel grid and load directly to the Data Model using Power Pivot**—You can still add calculated columns in the Power Pivot grid.

- **Use a hybrid approach**—Use Power Query to remove sales through the outlet store, but then load to the Data Model.

When you load directly to the Data Model, you lose the ability to do any analysis other than a pivot table. But you will have a much smaller file size. 65 MB of data in a text file will often become 4 MB of data in the Data Model. The following paragraphs will outline the hybrid approach.

To load a text file using Power Query, choose From Text/CSV in the Data tab's Get & Transform Data group (see Figure 10-18).

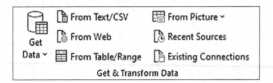

FIGURE 10-18 The Get & Transform Data group makes up the Power Query tools.

In the next dialog, browse to and locate your text file. This dialog is not shown. After you click OK, the preview in Figure 10-19 appears. If the file is under 1,048,575 rows and if you don't have to edit the query at all, you can click Load. I've never been able to click Load. I always choose Transform Data.

After you choose Transform Data, the first 1,000 rows from the file will appear in the Power Query editor. Tools are spread across the Home, Transform, and Add Column tabs.

In the current example, you want to remove four store IDs. If you open the Filter dropdown for StoreID, the choices are based on the first 1,000 rows. The outlet stores that you need to remove are deep in the file, not in the Filter dropdown. Instead, choose Value Filters | Does Not Equal.

StoreID	Date	Division	Units	Revenue
340001	1/1/2000	Handbags	4	780
340001	1/1/2000	Belts	8	392
340001	1/1/2000	Watches	6	270
340001	1/1/2000	Eyewear	8	400
340001	1/1/2000	Jewelry	40	880
340001	1/1/2000	Luggage	3	525
340001	1/1/2000	Shoes	4	600
340002	1/1/2000	Handbags	6	1170
340002	1/1/2000	Belts	6	294
340002	1/1/2000	Watches	4	180
340002	1/1/2000	Eyewear	7	350
340002	1/1/2000	Jewelry	34	748
340002	1/1/2000	Luggage	3	525
340002	1/1/2000	Shoes	4	600
340003	1/1/2000	Handbags	6	1170
340003	1/1/2000	Belts	10	490
340003	1/1/2000	Watches	6	270
340003	1/1/2000	Eyewear	8	400
340003	1/1/2000	Jewelry	38	836
340003	1/1/2000	Luggage	4	700

10-BigData.txt

File Origin: 1252: Western European (Windows)
Delimiter: Comma
Data Type Detection: Based on first 200 rows

The data in the preview has been truncated due to size limits.

Load | Transform Data | Cancel

FIGURE 10-19 Make sure the preview is pointing to the correct file, and then click Transform Data.

The dialog shown in Figure 10-20 appears. Type the first store number to remove. Click OK. Repeat for the other three stores.

In Figure 10-20, there is an Advanced version of the Filter and an option to specify a second store by choosing And or Or. Each pass through this dialog gets recorded as a different row in the Applied Steps pane. You might want the filters to be four separate lines so you can easily duplicate one later when a new outlet store is added.

If you have four stores to remove, repeat the steps in Figure 10-20 three more times.

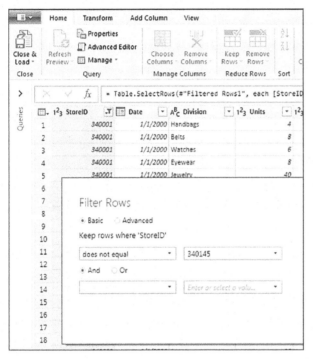

FIGURE 10-20 Choose a store to remove during import. This particular store is an outlet mall that is not usually included in the report.

Adding a new column using Power Query

The text file includes a date field. You want to add new columns for Year, Month Name, and Month Number. The function language in Power Query is annoyingly different from the functions in Excel. Plus, the language is case-sensitive. In Excel, you could use =YEAR(A2), =year(a2), =Year(A2), or =yEaR(A2). But in Power Query, you would have to type =Date.Year([Date]) to do the same calculation. It had to be typed exactly that way. =date.year([date]) would return an error.

In the summer of 2018, Microsoft introduced the Column From Examples feature. This feature is similar to Flash Fill in Excel with one massive improvement: Column From Examples will insert the correct formula in the query so that the step can be reused on a newer version of the text file.

I am a big fan of Column From Examples because every time I built a formula in Power Query, I knew that the process would involve the following:

1. Find the online Power Query function reference.

2. Search to try to find the syntax.

3. Copy the syntax without really learning anything.

4. Make a resolution to one day learn these new functions as well as I know Excel.

5. Never follow up with step #4.

Today, with Column From Examples, I know that I will never need to learn the Power Query functions.

Here are the steps to add a calculated Year field to your text file as it is imported.

1. In the Power Query editor, click the Date heading to select that column.

2. On the Add Column tab, open the Column From Examples dropdown and choose From Selection, as shown in Figure 10-21.

A new cell will appear on the right edge of the query window. Type the correct value for this year. In this case, you would type **2000**.

In response to typing **2000**, a menu appears with the choices shown in Figure 10-22. Look at that list. I just wanted a year, but they are offering all sorts of amazing things, such as End Of Quarter From Date or End Of Year From Date. Those might come in handy someday, but today, you just want the year, so choose 2000 (Year From Date).

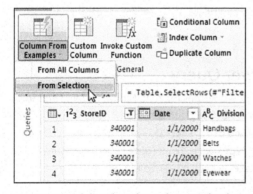

FIGURE 10-21 Select the column that contains the source data.

By clicking this option, Power Query adds a new column with a Year heading and the correct formula. You can look in the formula bar and see `Date.Year([Date])`, so there is an opportunity to learn the function language.

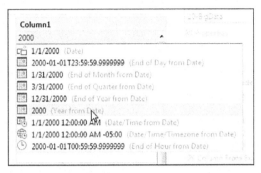

FIGURE 10-22 Type 2000, and Power Query offers all sorts of formulas.

You can keep adding custom columns from examples. Check the sample files to see the Month, Name, and Day.

Power Query is like the Macro Recorder but better

As you perform steps in Power Query, a list of steps appears in the Applied Steps panel on the right side. Think of this list as the world's greatest visible undo stack:

- You can click any item in the list and see what the data looked like at that point.

- You can click the Gear icon next to any step and see the dialog that was used at that step.

- You can remove the last step using the X icon. You can remove other steps as well, but you will likely screw up the query until you edit the Power Query code.

- To see the Power Query code you created by doing the steps in Power Query (the language is called the M language), go to View | Advanced Editor.

How is this different from the VBA Macro Recorder? The code recorded by Power Query will work the next time. If you get a new text file with 50,000 new records, the Power Query code will have no problem adapting the code to more or fewer records. In the VBA Macro Recorder, having more records would almost always make a recorded macro stop working.

See the Applied Steps from this example in Figure 10-23.

FIGURE 10-23 Power Query documents the transformations needed for a file.

Avoiding the Excel grid by loading to the Data Model

In the current example, you have a 1.8 million-row file that is now 1.7 million rows after you deleted the outlet stores. This is too big for the Excel grid. But even if you trimmed the file to 600,000 rows, you should still consider loading the file directly to the Data Model.

The Data Model uses a compression algorithm that frequently trims a 56 MB file to 4 MB in memory. This is a 14:1 compression ratio. If your plan is to create pivot tables from the data, loading straight to the Data Model is the way to save memory.

To skip loading to the Excel grid, go to the Power Query Home tab. Use the dropdown at the bottom of Close & Load and choose Close & Load To, as shown in Figure 10-24.

FIGURE 10-24 Avoid loading to the Excel grid by choosing Close & Load To.

In the Import Data dialog, choose Only Create Connection and also choose Add This Data To The Data Model (see Figure 10-25).

FIGURE 10-25 Choose to load the results of Power Query to the Data Model.

When you click OK, Excel will actually load the 1.7 million rows into your workbook. You will watch the row counter in the Queries & Connections panel count up. This will take as long as it will take. Excel doesn't have any magic way to load the data from disk. But as Microsoft is loading that data, it is being organized and vertically compressed. From here on, the pivot tables will be very fast.

When the import is finished, the Queries & Connections panel will report how many rows were loaded (see Figure 10-26).

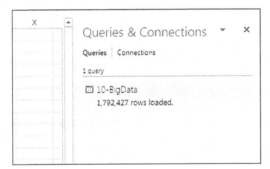

FIGURE 10-26 1.8 million rows are loaded to an Excel workbook and are ready for pivoting.

Adding a linked table

The database pros who created your text file are smart. They knew it would take a lot of space to include a 20-character store name on 1.8 million rows of text. Instead, they used a Store ID.

You probably have a small worksheet that maps the store number to the store name and other information. This workbook probably already exists somewhere in your company.

The worksheet shown in Figure 10-27 is a subset of a real StoreInfo workbook that gets a lot of use at my friend's company. In real life, there are columns for Manager Name, Phone Number, and so on.

Compared to the 1.8 million-row text file, this tiny 175-row worksheet is really small. To add this worksheet to the Data Model, follow these steps:

1. Insert a new worksheet in your workbook that contains the 1.8-million-row import.

2. Copy the Store Info to the new worksheet.

3. Select one cell in the data set and press Ctrl+T to define the data as a table.

4. Make sure My Data Has Headers is selected. Click OK.

5. Go to the Table Tools Design tab and replace the name Table1 with StoreInfo.

6. With one cell in the table selected, go to the Power Pivot tab in the Excel ribbon. Choose Add To Data Model.

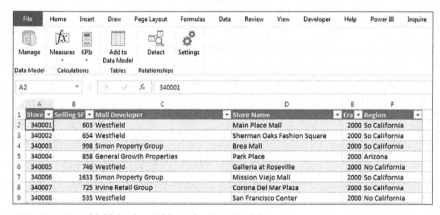

FIGURE 10-27 Add this lookup table to the Data Model.

Defining a relationship between two tables using Diagram View

An alternate way to create the relationship is the Diagram View in the Power Pivot window. Drag an arrow from StoreID to Store (see Figure 10-28).

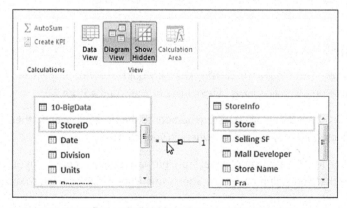

FIGURE 10-28 Define a relationship in the Power Pivot window.

Adding calculated columns in the Power Pivot grid

In addition to adding calculations with Power Query, you can add calculated columns in the Power Pivot grid. Instead of the Diagram View shown in Figure 10-28, switch back to the Data View shown in Figure 10-29. Click an empty column and type the correct formula in the formula bar.

The functions in the Power Pivot window are very similar to the functions you already know and love in Excel. For example, the =YEAR() function in Excel is =YEAR(). The =MONTH() function in Excel is =MONTH(). So far, so good, right? There are two annoying differences:

- The =TEXT() function in Excel is =FORMAT() in Power Pivot. If you wanted to create the Month Name column in Power Pivot, you would use =FORMAT([Date],"MMMM") instead of =TEXT(B2,"MMMM") in Excel. Why did this function change? Remember that the Excel team did not write Power Pivot; the SQL Server Analysis Services team wrote it. Excel has TEXT. SQL Server has FORMAT. The second argument in FORMAT offers more choices than TEXT, so the team chose to go with FORMAT instead. That was a fine choice.

- The VLOOKUP() function in Excel is =RELATED() in Power Pivot. At this point, you have defined a relationship between the 1.8-million-row table and the StoreInfo lookup. If you needed to refer to Selling Square Feet in a calculation in the data table, you would use something like: = [Revenue]/RELATED(StoreInfo[Selling SF]). RELATED is superior to VLOOKUP in every way. Why should you care whether Selling Square Feet is the second column in the lookup table? Why do you have to know the arcane =VLOOKUP(A2,Sheet2!A1:F175,2,False)? When I type **RELATED**, it says to me, "Hey Excel—just go figure this out. I've given you all the information you need to know what I am talking about."

In Figure 10-29, after you press Enter, the formula is copied down to all 1.8 million rows. That is great. The annoying thing is that the new column will be called Column1. You have to right-click the heading, choose Rename, and then type a meaningful name. Or, you can double-click the heading and type the new name.

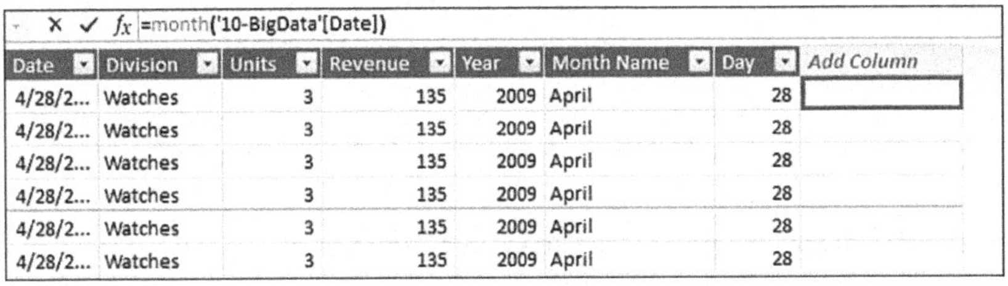

Date	Division	Units	Revenue	Year	Month Name	Day	Add Column
4/28/2...	Watches	3	135	2009	April	28	
4/28/2...	Watches	3	135	2009	April	28	
4/28/2...	Watches	3	135	2009	April	28	
4/28/2...	Watches	3	135	2009	April	28	
4/28/2...	Watches	3	135	2009	April	28	
4/28/2...	Watches	3	135	2009	April	28	

fx =month('10-BigData'[Date])

FIGURE 10-29 Build a formula in the formula bar in the Power Pivot grid.

Sorting one column by another column

The Data Model is better than Excel pivot tables in almost every way. But there is one annoying exception.

Say that your data has a month column with Jan, Feb, Mar, Apr, May, and Jun. If you add that to a pivot table in Excel, the data will be sorted by Jan, Feb, Mar, and so on.

But in Power Pivot, the resulting pivot table will have the months appear as Apr, Aug, Dec, Feb. Why? That is the alphabetic sequence for the months.

When I wrote *Power Pivot for the Data Analyst* in 2010, I complained about this bug. I suggested that Power Pivot should automatically sort by the Custom Lists, just as Excel would do.

In later versions of Power Pivot, the team solved this differently. If you choose the Month Name column in the Power Pivot window and select Home | Sort By Column, you can specify that the Month Name column should be sorted by the data in the Month Number column (see Figure 10-30).

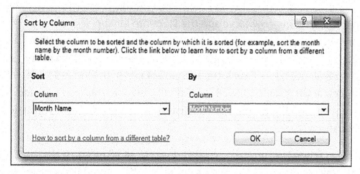

FIGURE 10-30 Specify that Month Number should sort the Month Name.

TIP Changing the sort sequence using the dialog in Figure 10-30 will also ensure that any slicers are in the proper sequence. This makes the Sort By Column method better than using More Sort Options in the Pivot Table.

Creating a pivot table from the Data Model

Now that you have two tables loaded to Power Pivot with a relationship, it is time to create your pivot table. Start from any blank cell on a blank worksheet. Choose Insert | PivotTable | From Data Model.

The Power Pivot version of the Fields pane appears. You have choices at the top for Active and All. The pivot table in Figure 10-31 reports revenue from the data table and region from the lookup table.

FIGURE 10-31 The resulting pivot table combined 1.8 million rows of a text file with an Excel lookup table.

Using advanced Power Pivot techniques

So far, you've seen a simple relationship between a data table and a lookup table. In real life, you might need to join two data tables, so this section covers complicated relationships and time intelligence functions.

Handling complicated relationships

Relationships in the Data Model need to be one-to-many. You cannot have a many-to-many relationship in Power Pivot.

Figure 10-32 shows a 54-row budget table and a 2000-row actuals table register. Both tables have Region, Date, and Product in common. Let's say you would like to report the total budget and actuals for each product or region.

While you can't directly relate Budget to Actuals, you can add three very small tables between the two tables. For example, the Product table contains one row for each product. You define a relationship from Budget to Product. This is a valid one-to-many relationship. Then, define a relationship from Actuals to Product. Again, this is a valid one-to-many relationship.

In your pivot table, the Values area will contain numbers from the budget and actuals table, but any time you need to report Product, Region, or Date in your pivot table, use the field from the tiny joiner table.

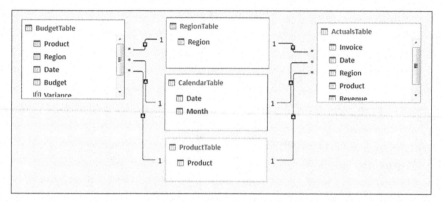

FIGURE 10-32 Use tiny joiner tables between tables to overcome the many-to-many limitation.

Figure 10-33 shows the two data tables and the three tiny joiner tables.

	A	B	C	D	E	F	G	H	I	J	K	L	M	N	O	P	Q
1	Budget - Top Level					"Joiners"							Invoice Detail				
2																	
3	Product	Region	Date	Budget		Product	Region		Date	Month		Invoice	Date	Region	Product	Revenue	
4	Widget	East	1/31/2018	10,300		Gadget	Central		1/2/2018	2018-01		1001	1/2/2018	Central	Gadget	1572	
5	Widget	East	2/28/2018	10,600		Whatsit	East		1/5/2018	2018-01		1002	1/5/2018	Central	Widget	1534	
6	Widget	East	3/31/2018	10,900		Widget	West		1/6/2018	2018-01		1003	1/5/2018	Central	Whatsit	1608	
7	Widget	East	4/30/2018	11,200					1/7/2018	2018-01		1004	1/5/2018	Central	Widget	2369	
8	Widget	East	5/31/2018	11,500					1/8/2018	2018-01		1005	1/5/2018	East	Widget	1509	
9	Widget	East	6/30/2018	11,800					1/9/2018	2018-01		1006	1/5/2018	Central	Widget	2376	
10	Widget	Central	1/31/2018	15,450					1/12/2018	2018-01		1007	1/6/2018	East	Gadget	1602	
11	Widget	Central	2/28/2018	15,900					1/13/2018	2018-01		1008	1/6/2018	West	Widget	1962	

FIGURE 10-33 Use the joiner table fields in your rows and columns of the pivot table.

Using time intelligence

Typically, Excel stores dates as serial numbers. When you enter 2/17/2029 in a cell, Excel only knows that this date is 47,166 days after December 31, 1899. Power Pivot adds time intelligence. When you have a date such as 2/17/2029 in Power Pivot, there are time intelligence functions that know that year-to-date means 1/1/2029 through 2/17/2029. The time intelligence functions know that the month-to-date from the prior year is 2/1/2028 through 2/17/2028.

Each value cell in a pivot table is a result of filters imposed by the slicers and by the row and column fields. Cell D28 in Figure 10-34 is being filtered to 2001 by the slicer and further filtered to January 25, 2001, by the row field in B28. But that cell needs to break free of the filter in order to add all of the sales from January 1, 2001, through January 25, 2001. The CALCULATE function helps you solve this problem.

In many ways, the DAX CALCULATE function is like a supercharged version of the Excel SUMIFS function. =CALCULATE(Field,Filter,Filter,Filter,Filter) is the syntax. However, any Filter argument could actually un-apply a filter that's being imposed by a slicer or a row field.

DATESMTD([Date]) returns all the dates used to calculate the month-to-date total for the cell. For January 25, 2001, the DATESMTD function will return January 1 through 25, 2001. When you use DATESMTD as the filter in the CALCULATE function, it breaks the chains of the 1/25/2001 filter and reapplies a new filter of January 1–25, 2001. The DAX formula for MTDSales is as follows:

```
=CALCULATE([Sum of Revenue],DATESMTD('10-BigData'[Date]))
```

	B	C	D	E	F	G	H	I
3	Row Labels ▼	Sum of Revenue	MTDSales	LYSales				
22	1/19/2001	$133,915	$1,741,562	$21,021				
23	1/20/2001	$119,718	$1,861,280	$25,600				
24	1/21/2001	$107,216	$1,968,496	$39,502				
25	1/22/2001	$70,332	$2,038,828	$36,266		Date (Year)		
26	1/23/2001	$71,239	$2,110,067	$30,938				
27	1/24/2001	$71,003	$2,181,070	$21,255		2000	2001	
28	1/25/2001	$84,855	$2,265,925	$20,574		2002	2003	
29	1/26/2001	$134,513	$2,400,438	$21,057				
30	1/27/2001	$120,091	$2,520,529	$24,342		2004	2005	
31	1/28/2001	$105,613	$2,626,142	$39,923				
32	1/29/2001	$70,722	$2,696,864	$34,319		2006	2007	
33	1/30/2001	$69,773	$2,766,637	$31,409				
34	1/31/2001	$69,804	$2,836,441	$20,941		2008	2009	
35	2/1/2001	$85,800	$85,800	$21,131				
36	2/2/2001	$131,516	$217,316	$21,367				

FIGURE 10-34 Time intelligence lets you calculate MTD or Prior Year sales.

The measure in column E requires two filter arguments. First, you need to tell DAX to ignore the Years filter. Use ALL([Years]) to do this. Then, you need to point to one year ago. Use DATEADD([Date],-1,YEAR) to move backward one year from January 25, 2002, to January 25, 2001. Therefore, this is the formula for LYSales:

```
CALCULATE([Sum of Revenue],
All('10-BigData'[Date (Year)]),
DATEADD('10-BigData'[Date],-1,YEAR))
```

Other time intelligence functions include DATESQTD and DATESYTD.

Creating a Flattened Pivot Table

Once your data is in the Data Model, you can use the Manage Data Model command to open the Power Pivot for Excel window. The PivotTable dropdown in the Power Pivot window offers eight different choices for creating various combinations of pivot tables and pivot charts. The last item in the list is a Flattened PivotTable. This is a pivot table with all the settings needed to create a summary data set, which is easily reused as a new data set.

Figure 10-35 shows where to find the Flattened PivotTable choice.

Manage Data Model

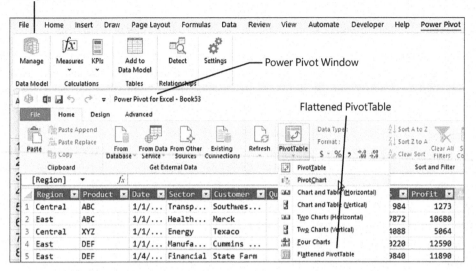

FIGURE 10-35 The Power Pivot window offers a flattened pivot table.

The resulting pivot table will be in a tabular layout. Repeat All Item Labels is turned on. Subtotals are turned off. The pivot table in Figure 10-36 is perfect for reuse as a new data set.

	B	C	D	E	F
3	Region	Product	Sum of Revenue	Sum of COGS	Sum of Profit
4	Central	ABC	766448	339719	426729
5	Central	DEF	773927	344815	429112
6	Central	XYZ	751457	333414	418043
7	East	ABC	879321	389631	489690
8	East	DEF	1078118	476832	601286
9	East	XYZ	839771	377669	462102
10	West	ABC	644219	285628	358591
11	West	DEF	519482	232293	287189
12	West	XYZ	455069	198393	256676
13					

FIGURE 10-36 A flattened pivot table is perfect for reuse as a new data set.

Overcoming limitations of the Data Model

When you use the Data Model, you transform your regular Excel data into an OLAP model. There are annoying limitations and some benefits available to pivot tables built on OLAP models. Here are some of the limitations and the workarounds:

- **Less grouping**—You cannot use the Group feature of pivot tables to create territories or to group numeric values into bins. Instead, you will have to add calculated fields to your data with the grouping information.

- **Product is not a built-in calculation**—I've never created a pivot table where I had to multiply all the rows together. That is the calculation that happens when you change Sum to Product. If you need to do this calculation, you can add a new measure using the PRODUCT function in DAX.

- **Pivot tables won't automatically sort by custom lists**—It takes eight annoying clicks to force a field to sort by a custom list:

  1. Open the field dropdown.
  2. Choose More Sort Options.
  3. In the Sort Options dialog, click More Options.
  4. In the More Sort Options dialog, clear Sort Automatically.
  5. Open the First Key Sort Order.
  6. Choose your Custom List.
  7. Click OK to close the More Sort Options dialog.
  8. Click OK to close the Sort dialog.

- **Strange drill-down**—Usually, you can double-click a cell in a pivot table and see the rows that make up that cell. This does work with the Data Model, but only for the first 1,000 rows.

- **No calculated fields or calculated items**—This is not a big deal because DAX measures run circles around calculated items.

- **No support for arrow keys in formula creation**—In the Excel interface, you might build a formula with =<LeftArrow>*<LeftArrow><LeftArrow><Enter>. This is not supported in Power Pivot. You will have to reach for the mouse to click on the columns that you want to reference.

- **Refresh will be slow**—The Refresh button on the Analyze tab forces Excel to update the data in the pivot table. Think before you do this in Excel today. In the current example, refreshing forces Excel to go out and import the 1.8 million-row data set again.

- **February 29, 1900 does not exist in Power Pivot**—There was no February 29 in 1900. Lotus 1-2-3 had a bug: The date algorithms assumed that 1900 was a leap year. As Excel was battling for market share, they had to produce the same results as Lotus, so Excel repeated the February 29, 1900 bug. The SQL Server Analysis Team refused to perpetuate this bug and did not recognize February 29, 1900. In Excel, day 1 is January 1, 1900. In Power Pivot, day 1 is December 31, 1899. None of this matters unless you have sales that happened from January 1, 1900, through February 28, 1900. In that case, the two pivot tables will be off by a day. No one has data going back that far, right? It will never be an issue, right? Well, in 2018, I met a guy who had a column of quantities. He had values like 30, 42, and 56, but that column was accidentally imported as a date. All the quantities were off by one.

- **32-bit Excel is not enough**—I meet people who complain Excel is slow, even though they added more memory to their machine. Unfortunately, the 32-bit version of Excel can only access 3 GB of memory on your machine. To really use Power Pivot and the Data Model with millions of rows of data, you will need to install 64-bit Excel. This does not cost anything extra.

It does likely involve some pleading with the I.T. department. Also, some old add-ins do not run in 64-bit Excel. If you happen to be using that add-in, you have to choose whether you want faster performance or the old add-in.

> **Note** Excel MVP Charles Williams has documented a way for Data Models in 32-bit Excel to use an extra 1 GB of memory. Read more at *https://fastexcel.wordpress.com/2016/11/27/ excel-memory-checking-tool-using-laa-to-increase-useable-excel-memory/.*

Enjoying other benefits of Power Pivot

Nothing in the previous list is a dealbreaker. In the interest of fairness, here are several more benefits that come from using Power Pivot and the Data Model:

- You can hide or rename columns. If your database administrator thinks TextS1sRepNbr is a friendly name, you can change it to Sales Rep Number. Or, if your data tables are littered with useless fields, you can hide them from the PivotTable Fields pane. In the Power Pivot window, right-click any column heading and choose Hide From Client Tools.

- You can assign categories such as Geography, Image URL, and Web URL to fields. Select the column in the Power Pivot window. Choose a column. On the Advanced tab, choose a Data Category.

- You can define key performance indicators or hierarchies. See "Creating hierarchies" in Chapter 4, "Grouping, sorting, and filtering pivot data."

Create all future pivot tables using the Data Model

If you decide that all future pivot tables that you create should use the Data Model, there is now a setting for that.

Go to File | Options | Data and choose Prefer The Excel Data Model When Creating PivotTables, Query Tables And Data Connections (see Figure 10-37).

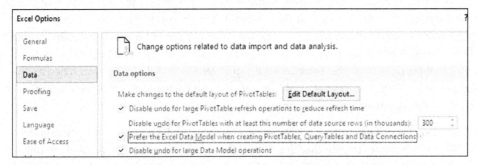

FIGURE 10-37 Change this option to have all future pivot tables default to the Data Model.

Learning more

Power Pivot and Power Query are powerful tools that are completely new for most Excellers. These are my favorite books to learn more:

- For Power Query, read *Master Your Data Is For Data Monkey* by Ken Puls and Miguel Escobar (ISBN 978-1-61547-034-1).

- For DAX formulas in Power Pivot, read *Supercharge Power BI 3rd Edition* by Matt Allington (ISBN 978-1-61547-069-3).

- For Advanced Power Pivot, read *Power Pivot and Power BI* by Rob Collie (ISBN 978-1-61547-039-6).

Case study: Joining tables using multiple fields with Power Query

Say that you need to join tables based on multiple fields. You can do this using a Merge query in Power Query and then load the results to the Data Model. The process involves defining each table to Power Query first and then doing the Merge.

Make sure that both tables have been formatted as a table. Change the table names on the Table Tools ribbon to something meaningful, such as Sales and Rates. See Figure 10-38.

	A	B	C	D	E	F	G	H	I
1	Sales Register - Table Name is Sales						Commission Rate Table - Rates		
2									
3	Invoice	Product	Sales Rep	Qty	Revenue		Name	Product	Rate
4	1001	Apple	Morgan	125	625		Andy	Apple	5.0%
5	1002	Apple	Eddy	145	725		Andy	Banana	6.0%
6	1003	Banana	Zeke	145	725		Barb	Apple	6.0%
7	1004	Apple	Xavier	100	500		Barb	Banana	3.0%
8	1005	Banana	Morgan	115	575		Chris	Apple	6.0%
9	1006	Banana	Yazmin	85	425		Chris	Banana	7.0%
10	1007	Banana	Raul	105	525		Diane	Apple	4.0%
11	1008	Banana	Kim	50	250		Diane	Banana	5.0%
12	1009	Apple	Eddy	125	625		Eddy	Apple	7.0%

FIGURE 10-38 Join these two tables based on name and product.

1. Select one cell in the Sales table. From the Data tab, choose From Table/Range. The Power Query editor will open. Without making any changes, Open the Close And Load drop-down and choose Close and Load To. Choose Only Create A Connection and Click OK. This preliminary step lets Power Query know that Sales refers to this table.

2. Repeat step 1 for the Rates table. The Queries & Connections pane should show two Connection Only queries in the workbook (see Figure 10-39).

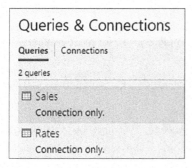

FIGURE 10-39 Setting up the connections to the tables is required before the join.

3. Select Data | Get Data | Combine Queries | Merge Query. Excel will display the Merge dialog.

4. In the Merge dialog, choose Sales from the top dropdown.

5. Choose Rates from the second dropdown.

6. Do this step very carefully in this particular order. In the preview for the Sales table, click the Product heading, hover over the Sales Rep heading, and press Ctrl+Click. After adding the second field, you should see a tiny "1" to the right of the product heading and a tiny "2" to the right of the Sales Rep heading.

7. In the preview for the Rates table, carefully click first on the Product heading. Then hover over the name heading and press Ctrl+Click. The small "2" should appear on the first column, and then the small "1" should appear on the second column. (See Figure 10-40.)

FIGURE 10-40 Make sure the "1" and "2" to the right of the key fields is correct.

8.   Click OK to create the Merge query. The Power Query editor will show all of the fields from the Sales table and a single column for the Rates table with the word "Table" in each cell. The heading for Rates has an Expand icon—two bent arrows facing away from each other.

9.   Click the Expand icon in the heading for the Rates column. Unselect Name and Product since those fields are already in the Product table. This leaves only Rate as the field to add. To prevent a silly Rates.Rate heading, unselect the box for Use Original Column Name As Prefix (see Figure 10-41).

FIGURE 10-41 Choose which fields from the Rates table should be included.

10.   This step is optional. Use the Add Column | Custom Column command to add a new column to calculate Commission payment. The formula is =[Revenue]*[Rate]. After adding the field, choose the Commision column. On the Transform tab, choose the Decimal Number as the Data Type.

11.   On the Power Query Editor Home tab, open the Close And Load dropdown and choose Close And Load To.

12.   In the Close And Load dialog, choose Only Create A Connection and choose Add This Data To The Data Model.

13.   From any blank area of the workbook, choose Insert | PivotTable | From Data Model. The PivotTable Fields pane will show three tables: Sales, Rates, and Merge. Build your pivot table using the fields from the Merge table. Figure 10-42 shows a sample pivot table with Sales Rep, Revenue, and Commission.

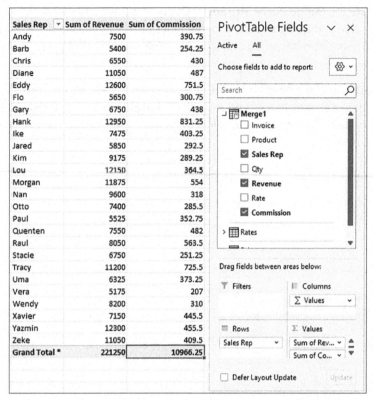

Sales Rep	Sum of Revenue	Sum of Commission
Andy	7500	390.75
Barb	5400	254.25
Chris	6550	430
Diane	11050	487
Eddy	12600	751.5
Flo	5650	300.75
Gary	6750	438
Hank	12950	831.25
Ike	7475	403.25
Jared	5850	292.5
Kim	9175	289.25
Lou	12150	364.5
Morgan	11875	554
Nan	9600	318
Otto	7400	285.5
Paul	5525	352.75
Quenten	7550	482
Raul	8050	563.5
Stacie	6750	251.25
Tracy	11200	725.5
Uma	6325	373.25
Vera	5175	207
Wendy	8200	310
Xavier	7150	445.5
Yazmin	12300	455.5
Zeke	11050	409.5
Grand Total *	221250	10966.25

FIGURE 10-42 A pivot table calculated from two tables joined with multiple fields.

Next steps

The 3D Map feature lets you animate your data on a globe. Chapter 11, "Analyzing geographic data with 3D Map," introduces 3D Map.

CHAPTER 11

Analyzing geographic data with 3D Map

In this chapter, you will:

- Prepare data for 3D Map

- Build a column chart in 3D Map

- Explore 3D Map settings

- Animate data over time

Analyzing geographic data with 3D Map

3D Map allows you to build a pivot table on a three-dimensional globe of the Earth. Provided that your data has any geographic field such as Street, City, State, or Zip Code, you can plot the data on a map.

Once the data is on the map, you can fly through the data, zooming in to study a city or zooming back out to a 50,000-foot view. You can either use 3D Map to interactively study the data or build a tour from various scenes and render that tour as a video for distribution to people who do not have 3D Map.

> **Note** The 3D Map feature was known as an add-in called Power Map in Excel 2013 and also formerly known as GeoFlow. If you have previously used Power Map or GeoFlow, you can find that functionality in Excel as 3D Map.
>
> 3D Map is a feature only found in Windows editions of Excel. It will never be available on the Mac, Excel Online, or Excel for Mobile because it uses the Data Model. In late 2024, Microsoft made the unusual decision to move the 3D Map icon from the Tours group of the Insert tab to a Data Model dropdown on the Data tab. This is an unusual place to move the feature since most people have no idea that the 3D Map feature uses the Data Model. Microsoft explained that they needed to make room for the Checkbox feature on the Insert tab and that 3D Map was the least used icon, so it had to be moved. Someone more cynical might think that the move to the Data Model dropdown is designed to make sure that no one newly discovers the feature.

Preparing data for 3D Map

Although 3D Map uses the Power Pivot Data Model, there is no need to load your data into Power Pivot. You can just select one cell from a data set with a geographic field such as Country, State, County, City, Street, or Zip Code.

For Microsoft 365, you will choose 3D Map from the Data Map dropdown on the right side of the Data tab, as shown in Figure 11-1. For previous versions of Excel, look in the Tours group, just to the right of the Chart choices on the Insert tab.

3D Map converts the current data set to a table and loads it to the Power Pivot Data Model before launching 3D Map. This step might take 10 to 20 seconds as Power Pivot is loaded in the background.

3D Map converts the data to latitude and longitude by using Bing Maps. If your data is outside the United States, you should include a field for country code. Otherwise, Paris will show up in Kentucky, and Melbourne will show up on the east coast of Florida.

There are three special types of geographic data that 3D Map can consume:

- 3D Map can deal with latitude and longitude as two separate fields. Note that west and south values should be negative.

- It is possible to plot the data—not on a globe but on a custom map, such as the floor plan for an airport or a store. In this case, you need to provide x and y data. Remember, x runs across the map, starting with 0 at the left edge, and y runs up the map, starting at 0 at the bottom edge.

- 3D Map now allows for custom shapes. You need to have a KML or SHP file describing the shapes. The names in your data set should match the values in the KML file.

Although you don't have to preload the data into the Power Pivot Data Model, you can take that extra step if you need to define relationships between tables.

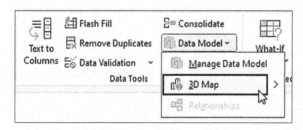

FIGURE 11-1 3D Map appears on the Data tab, hidden under the Data Model dropdown.

Geocoding data

The process of locating points on a map is called *geocoding*. When you first launch 3D Map, Excel attempts to detect your geographic fields. If you've used meaningful headings such as City or State, 3D Map auto-detects these fields, and they are pre-populated into the Location section of 3D Map. If Excel fails to detect a geographic field, use the Add Field choice at the bottom of the Location box.

Excel assigns a geography level for each field. You can use the dropdown to change the geography level (see Figure 11-2).

> **Tip** Fields such as "123 Main Street" should be marked as Street. Fields such as "123 Main Street, Akron, OH" should be marked as Full Address. Marking "123 Main Street" as an address will lead to most of your data points being placed in the wrong state.

Choose one of your geographic fields as the map level. If you choose State, you will get one point per state. If you choose Address, you will get one point for each unique address.

After you've chosen the geographic fields, click Next in the lower-right corner.

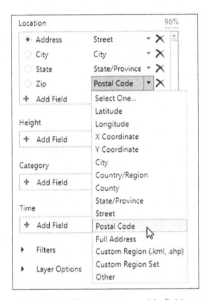

FIGURE 11-2 Choose geographic fields.

It takes a short while for 3D Map to complete the geocoding process. When it is finished, a percentage appears at the top of the PivotTable Fields list. Click this percentage to see a list of data points that could not be mapped (see Figure 11-3). Items with a red X will not appear on the map. Items with a yellow exclamation mark will appear at the address shown in the Result column.

> **Note** When an address is not found, there is currently no tool to place that data point on the map. Other mapping tools, such as MapPoint, would give you choices such as using a similar address or even adding the point to the center of the zip code. But 3D Map currently simply advises you to add more geographic fields to the original data set.

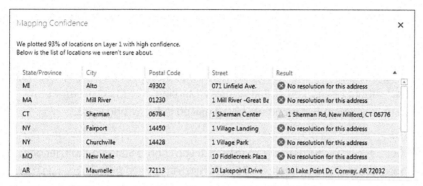

FIGURE 11-3 3D Map indicates which addresses could not be found.

Building a column chart in 3D Map

3D Map offers five types of layers: Stacked Column, Clustered Column, Bubble, Heat Map, and Region. The processes for building Stacked Column and Clustered Column layers are similar:

1. Choose either the Clustered Column or Stacked Column icon in the bottom half of the Layer pane. Height, Category, and Time areas appear.

2. Drag a numeric field to the Height area. Use the dropdown arrow at the right edge of the field to choose Sum, Average, Count Not Blank, Count Distinct, Max, Min, or No Aggregation.

3. If you want the columns to be different colors, drag a field to the Category area. A large legend covers up the map. Click the legend, and resize handles appear. Right-click the legend and choose Edit to control the font, size, and color.

4. To animate the map over time, drag a date or time field to the Time area. Right-click the large time legend and customize how the dates and times appear.

Figure 11-4 shows an initial map using a clustered column chart.

Navigating through the map

Initially, the zoom level is set to show all of your data points. You might discover that a few outliers cause the map to be zoomed out too far. For example, if you are analyzing customer data for an auto repair shop, you might find a few customers who stopped in for a repair while they were driving through on vacation. Suppose 98 percent of your customers are near Charlotte, North Carolina, but three or four New York and California customers are in the data set. In that case, the map will show everything from New York to California.

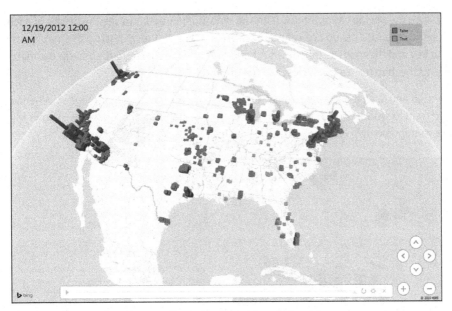

FIGURE 11-4 One column appears for each street address in the data.

You can zoom in or out by using the + or – icons in the lower-right part of the map. You can use the mouse wheel to zoom in or out quickly.

As you start to zoom in, you might realize that you are zooming in on the wrong section of the map. Click and drag the map to re-center it. Or double-click any white space on the map to center it at that point while zooming in. Figure 11-5 shows a map zoomed in to show Florida.

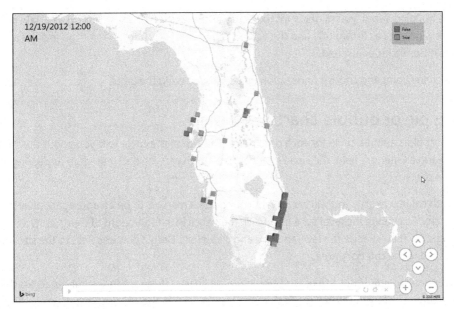

FIGURE 11-5 Zoom in to show Florida.

By default, you usually look straight down on the map, but it is easier to see the height of each column if you tip the map. Use the up arrow and down arrow icons on the map to tip the map up or down. Or use the Alt key and the mouse: Hold down Alt and drag the mouse straight up to tip the map so that you are viewing the map from a point closer to the ground.

Hold down Alt and drag the mouse straight down to move the vantage point higher. When you hold down Alt and drag the mouse left or right, you rotate the view left or right. Figure 11-6 shows Miami from a lower vantage point, as you would see the points from the Atlantic Ocean.

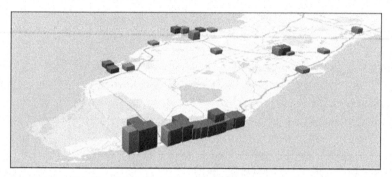

FIGURE 11-6 Alt+drag the mouse to tip or rotate the view.

Labeling individual points

In many data sets, you see unusual data points. To see the details about a particular data point, hover over the point's column, and a tooltip appears, with identifiers for the data point. When you move away from the column, the tooltip is hidden.

If you are building a tour, you might want to display an annotation or a text box on a certain point. An annotation includes a custom title and the value of any fields you choose—or it can include a picture. A text box includes just text.

Right-click any point and choose Annotation or Text Box to build the label.

Building pie or bubble charts on a map

A bubble chart plots a single circle for each data point. The size of the circle tells you about the data point. If you add a Category field, the circle changes to a pie chart, with each category appearing as a wedge in the pie chart.

Unlike with column charts, you will likely want your bubble markers to be an aggregate of all points in a state or city. To change the level for a map, click the Pencil icon to the right of Geography at the top of the Layer pane. Then change the level to State and click Next. Drag a numeric field to the size area. Drag a text field to the category area.

You might need to adjust the size of the bubbles or pie charts. There are four symbols across the top of the Layer pane. The fourth symbol is a Settings gear icon. Click it and choose Layer Options. Slicers appear that let you change the opacity, size, thickness, and colors used (see Figure 11-7).

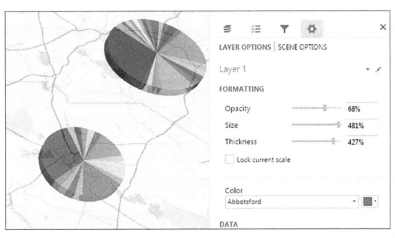

FIGURE 11-7 Use the Layer Options tab of the Layer pane to change the size of the bubbles.

Using heat maps and region maps

3D Map also offers heat maps and shaded region maps. A heat map is centered on an individual point and shows varying shades of green, yellow, and red to show intensity. A region map fills an outline with the same color and is useful for showing data by country, state, or county.

Figure 11-8 shows a map with two layers: One layer is a region map by state, and the other layer is a heat map by city.

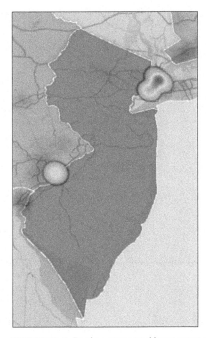

FIGURE 11-8 Region maps and heat maps are combined in a single map.

You might want to create region maps for shapes other than state or country. There are many free SHP or KML files available on the Internet. You can have 3D Map import these custom regions and then shade those areas on the map. To import a custom region, use Import Regions from the 3D Map ribbon.

Exploring 3D Map settings

There are a number of useful settings in 3D Map. Here are some of my favorites:

- **Aerial Photography Map**—If you will be zooming in to the city level, you can show an aerial photograph over the map. Use the Themes dropdown in 3D Map and choose the second theme.

- **Add Map Labels**—Click the Map Labels icon in the ribbon to add labels to the map. If you are zoomed completely out, the labels will be country names. As you zoom in, the labels change to states, cities, and even street names. Note that labels are an all-or-nothing proposition. You cannot easily show some labels and not others.

- **Flat Map**—If you want to see the entire Earth at one time, use the Flat Map icon in the 3D Map ribbon.

Figure 11-9 shows a flat map with labels added.

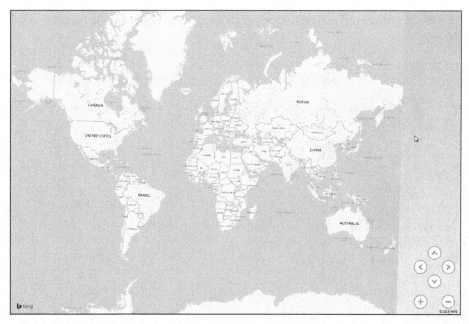

FIGURE 11-9 See the whole Earth with a flat map.

Fine-tuning 3D Map

There are situations where the defaults used by 3D Map are not the best. Here are troubleshooting methods for various situations.

By default, each column in a column chart takes up a fair amount of space on the map. For example, if you plot every house on your street, each column takes about one city block. You won't be able to make out the details for each house. Click the Settings gear icon and then Layer Options. Change the Thickness setting to 5% or 10%. 3D Map makes each column very narrow (see Figure 11-10).

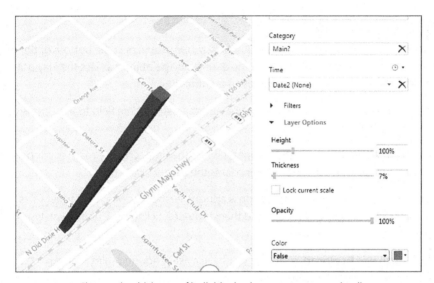

FIGURE 11-10 Change the thickness of individual columns to see more detail.

3D Map looks great on a huge 1080p monitor. If you are stuck on a tiny laptop, though, you should hide the Tour and Layer panes by using the icons in the 3D Map ribbon.

Most legends start out way too large. You can either resize them or right-click and choose Hide to remove them altogether.

The Funnel icon in the Layer pane allows you to add filters to any field. 3D Map cannot render 5,000 checkboxes, so you might have to use the Search utility within the filters to find items to show or hide.

When you hover over a data point, the resulting tooltip is called a data card. You can customize what appears in the card by selecting Layer Options from the gear menu and then clicking the icon below Customize Data Card.

Combining two data sets

If you want to combine two data sets, you need to do some pre-work. First, convert each data set to a table using Home | Format As Table. Then, from each data set, use Power Pivot | Add To Data Model.

If you are stuck in Excel 2013 or 2016 without the Power Pivot tab, you can create a fake pivot table from each data set and select the checkbox for Add This Data To The Data Model to load the data to the Data Model. Alternatively, you could use the Power Query tools to edit a table. After viewing the data in the Power Query Editor, use Home | Close And Load To | Add This Data To The Data Model.

To combine different map types, add a layer using the Add Layer icon. Each layer can be shown in a different geography. You might have a column chart by city on Layer 1 and a region chart by state on Layer 2. The Layer Manager allows you to show and hide various layers.

Animating data over time

You can add a date or time field to any map layer. A time scrubber appears at the bottom of the map. Grab the scrubber and drag it left or right to show the data at any point in time. Use the Play button on the left side of the scrubber to have 3D Map animate the entire time period.

A small clock icon appears above the field when you add the date or time field to the Time area. There are three choices in this dropdown:

- **Data Shows For An Instant**—The data appears when the time scrubber reaches this date, but then the data disappears once the scrubber passes the date.

- **Date Accumulates Over Time**—This option is appropriate for showing how ticket sales happened. If you sold 10 tickets on Monday and then another 5 tickets on Tuesday, you would want the map to show 15 tickets on Tuesday.

- **Data Stays Until It Is Replaced**—Say that you have a list of housing sales for the past 30 years. If a house sold for $200,000 in 2001 and then for $225,000 in 2005, you would want to show $200,000 for all points from 2001 until the end of 2004.

To control the speed of the animation, click the gear icon in the Layer pane and choose Scene Options. The Speed slider in the Time section controls how fast the time will change. Watch the Scene Duration setting at the top of this panel to see how long it will take to animate through the entire period covered by the data set.

You can use the Start Date and End Date dropdowns to limit the animation to just a portion of the time period.

Building a tour

You can use a tour in 3D Map to tell a story. Each scene in the tour can focus on a section of the map, and 3D Map will automatically fly from one scene to the next.

As you have been experimenting with 3D Map, you have been working on Scene 1 in the Tour pane. If you click the gear icon and then Scene Options, you will see that the default scene duration is 10 seconds, with a default transition duration of 3 seconds. Therefore, when you play a tour, this first scene lasts 10 seconds. The time to fly to the next scene takes 3 seconds.

Once you have the timing correct for the first scene, you can add a second scene by selecting Home | New Scene | Copy Scene 1. Customize the second scene to zoom in on a different country section or show a different view of the map.

Say that you want to have the first scene show the data accumulated over time, and then you want the next three scenes to zoom in to three interesting parts of the country. You have to remove the Time field from the Layer pane at the start of Scene 2, or the entire timeline will animate again.

Alternatively, perhaps you want to zoom in on an area at a particular part of the timeline. In this example, you might have these scenes:

- You start with an establishing shot that shows the whole country at the beginning of the time period. Use the Scene Options and set both the start and end date to the earliest date in the data set. By using the same date for start and end, the opening scene will not animate over time.

- You then have a scene that animates over part of the timeline, perhaps from 1971 to 1995.

- Next is a scene that zooms in to Florida in 1995. Use Scene Options to set the start and end date to December 31, 1995, to prevent the data from re-animating.

- Finally, you have a scene that is a copy of Scene 2 but with the date range changed from 1996 to 2018.

> **Tip** Note that annotations and text boxes will appear throughout one scene and through the transition to the next scene. If you have a 6-second scene and a 20-second transition, the text box will appear for all 26 seconds. You might want to go to the extra effort to break this up as a 6-second scene with the text box and a 0-second transition, followed by a 1-second scene with no text box and a 20-second transition.

To have the map constantly moving, change the Effect dropdown to something other than No Effect. For example, with Circle or Figure 8, the camera flies in an arc above the scene. Depending on how long the scene lasts, you may not get a complete circle. Adjust the Effect speed to increase the chances of finishing the circle.

Click Play Tour to hide all panels and play the tour in full-screen mode. Drag the mouse over the tour to reveal Play and Pause buttons at the bottom of the screen. Press the Esc key to go back to 3D Map.

Creating a video from 3D Map

To share a tour with others, you can use 3D Map to render a video. Build a tour first, and then click Create Video. You can choose from three video resolutions and add a soundtrack.

> **Note** Rendering a several-minute tour in full HD resolution can take more than an hour on a fast PC.

Case study: Using a store map instead of a globe

Say that you have a database of sales in a retail mall. For each day, you have sales for each of several stores in the mall. You would like to animate how sales unfold during the business day in the mall. For example, items located near the coffee bar might sell best in the morning, while high-ticket items might sell best in the evening:

1. Find a drawing or an image of the store map. Figure out the height and width of the image. In this case, say that the image is 800 pixels wide and 366 pixels tall.

2. Build a table in Excel with a unique list of store names. (You could also use a unique list of departments or categories.)

3. Figure out the x and y location for each unique store name. Remember that x measures the number of pixels across the image, starting at the left edge. In Figure 11-11, the image is inserted into Excel. It fills columns E:U. Because the total width is 800, each column represents about 47 pixels. Sears is about 620 pixels from the left edge. For the y value, remember to start at the bottom. Since the image is 366 pixels tall and fills 29 rows, each row is about 12.62 pixels tall. Cell C15 shows that the word Sears falls at about 176 pixels from the bottom edge.

> **Caution** The first time I tried finding x and y locations, I used the cursor location in Photoshop. It was fast and easy. But then I realized that Photoshop measures the y location starting at the top edge instead of the bottom edge. This initially seemed like a bad mistake, but because the data was keyed into Excel, a helper column with a formula of =366-F2 quickly corrected the Y values.

4. Create a table from your sales data by using Ctrl+T. Add the data to the Data Model.

5. Create a table from your location data by using Ctrl+T. Add the data to the Data Model.

6. In Power Pivot, create a relationship between the two tables.

7. From a blank cell in Excel, choose Data | Data Model | 3D Map. 3D Map shows you the fields from the Data Model.

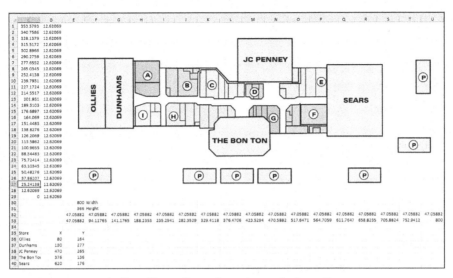

FIGURE 11-11 Locate the X and Y coordinates for each store in the mall map.

8. In the Choose Geography section of the Layer pane, choose X and Y.

9. In the Geography and Map Level section, assign X as X Coordinate. Assign Y as Y Coordinate. 3D Map now asks you a question: Change To A Custom Map? (see Figure 11-12).

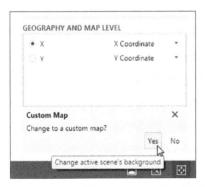

FIGURE 11-12 When you choose X and Y, 3D Map asks about using a custom map.

10. Click Yes to choose a custom map. In the Change Map Type dialog, choose New Custom Map.

11. In the Custom Map Options dialog, click the Picture icon next to Browse for the Background Picture. Select the same picture used for step 3. As shown in Figure 11-13, the dialog starts out with Min and Max values for X and Y that represent the data in your data set. Because no data points are falling at the 0,0 coordinate or at the 800,366 coordinate, these estimates will always be incorrect.

12. Change the Min for X and the Min for Y to 0. Change the Max for X to the picture width. Change the Max for Y to the picture height. Click Apply to see your data on the picture. Click Done when everything looks correct.

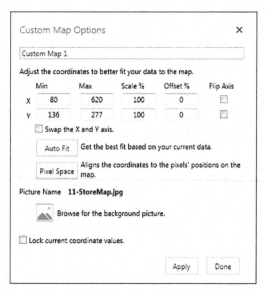

FIGURE 11-13 The Min and Max for X and Y will always be incorrect in real life.

13. In the 3D Map Layer pane, click Next.

Your data is now plotted on a custom map of the mall, as shown in Figure 11-14. You can use 3D Map navigation to tip, rotate, and zoom the map.

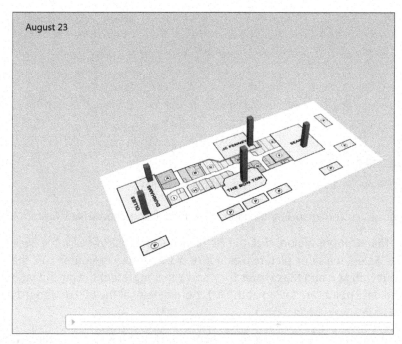

FIGURE 11-14 Sales are plotted on a custom map.

Next steps

Chapter 12, "Enhancing pivot table reports with macros," introduces you to simple macros you can use to enhance your pivot table reports.

Enhancing pivot table reports with macros

In this chapter, you will:

- Use macros with pivot table reports

- Record a macro

- Create a user interface with form controls

- Alter a recorded macro to add functionality

Using macros with pivot table reports

Imagine that you could be in multiple locations at one time, with multiple clients at one time, helping them with their pivot table reports. Suppose you could help multiple clients refresh their data, extract the top 20 records, group by months, or sort by revenue—all at the same time. The fact is you can do just that by using Excel macros.

In its broadest sense, a *macro* is a sequence of instructions that automates an aspect of Excel so that you can work more efficiently and with fewer errors. Macros can be created by recording and saving a series of keystrokes. Once saved, a macro can be played back on demand. In other words, you can record your actions in a macro, save the macro, and then allow your clients to play back your actions with the click of a button or by pressing a keyboard shortcut. It would be as though you were right there with them! This functionality is especially useful when you're distributing pivot table reports.

For example, suppose that you want to give your clients the option of grouping their pivot table report by month, quarter, or year. Although anyone can perform the process of grouping, some of your clients might not have a clue how to do it. In this case, you could record a macro to group by month, a macro to group by quarter, and a macro to group by year. Then, you could create three buttons, one for each macro. In the end, your clients who have little experience with pivot tables need only to click a button to group their pivot table reports.

A major benefit of using macros with your pivot table reports is the power you can give your clients to easily perform pivot table actions that they would not normally be able to perform on their own, empowering them to more effectively analyze the data you provide.

While macros have traditionally been written in VBA using the Excel Macro Recorder, the new Power Query tools can also produce a macro using the M programming language. When someone refreshes the Power Query results, Excel runs the macro on new data. Given that Power Query gives you the ability to pivot your data, this chapter will include a Power Query example to load all Excel files from a single folder.

Recording a macro

Look at the pivot table in Figure 12-1. You know that you can refresh this pivot table by right-clicking inside the pivot table and selecting Refresh Data. Now, if you were to record your actions with a macro while you refreshed this pivot table, you or anyone else could replicate your actions and refresh this pivot table by running the macro.

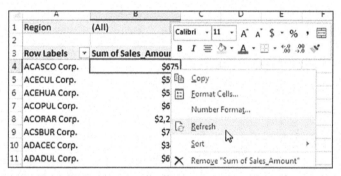

FIGURE 12-1 You can easily refresh this basic pivot table by right-clicking and selecting Refresh, but if you recorded your actions with a macro, you could also refresh this pivot table simply by running the macro.

The first step in recording a macro is to initiate the Record Macro dialog. Select the Developer tab on the ribbon and then select Record Macro.

> **Tip** Can't find the Developer tab on the ribbon? Right-click the ribbon and choose Customize The Ribbon. In the list box to the far right, select the checkbox next to Developer. Selecting the check mark next to this option enables the Developer tab.

When the Record Macro dialog activates, you can fill in a few key pieces of information about the macro:

- **Macro Name**—Enter a name for your macro. You should generally enter a name that describes the action being performed.

- **Shortcut Key**—You can enter any letter into this input box. That letter becomes part of a set of keys on your keyboard that can be pressed to play back the macro. This is optional. If you do choose a letter, avoid the shortcut keys you already use, such as Ctrl+x, Ctrl+c, Ctrl+v, and anything else you rely on. If you assign a macro to Ctrl+c, then you won't be able to use Ctrl+c to copy after changing the macro shortcut to Ctrl+c.

- **Store Macro In**—Specify where you want the macro to be stored. If you are distributing your pivot table report, you should select This Workbook to make the macro available to your clients.

- **Description**—In this input box, you can enter a few words that give more detail about the macro.

Because this macro refreshes your pivot table when it is played, name your macro RefreshData, as shown in Figure 12-2. Also, assign the shortcut key as a capital R. Notice that, based on this, the dialog gives you the Ctrl+Shift+R key combination. Keep in mind that you use the key combination to play your macro after it is created. Be sure to store the macro in This Workbook. Click OK to continue.

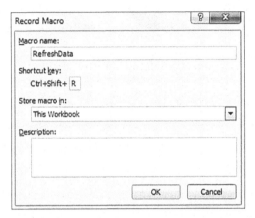

FIGURE 12-2 Fill in the Record Macro dialog as shown here and then click OK to continue.

When you click OK in the Record Macro dialog, you initiate the recording process. At this point, any action you perform is recorded by Excel. In this case, you want to record the process of refreshing your pivot table.

Right-click anywhere inside the pivot table and select Refresh Data. After you have refreshed your pivot table, you can stop the recording process by going up to the Developer tab and selecting the Stop Recording button.

Congratulations! You have just recorded a macro. You can now play your macro by pressing Ctrl+Shift+R on your keyboard at the same time.

A word on macro security

You should be aware that when you record a macro yourself, your macro runs on your PC with no security restrictions. However, when you distribute workbooks that contain macros, your clients have to let Excel know that your workbook is not a security risk in order to allow your macros to run.

Indeed, you will note that the sample file that comes with this chapter does not run unless you tell Excel to enable the macros within.

The best way to do this is to use the workbook in a *trusted location*, a directory that is deemed a safe zone where only trusted workbooks are placed. A trusted location allows you and your clients to run a macro-enabled workbook with no security restrictions as long as the workbook is in that location.

To set up a trusted location, follow these steps:

1. Select the Macro Security button on the Developer tab. This activates the Trust Center dialog.

2. From the left navigation bar, choose Trusted Locations.

3. Select Add New Location.

4. Click Browse and then specify the directory to be considered a trusted location.

After you specify a trusted location, all workbooks opened from that location are, by default, opened with macros enabled.

Note In Excel 2013, Microsoft enhanced the security model to remember files that you've deemed trustworthy. That is to say, when you open an Excel workbook and click the Enable button, Excel remembers that you trusted that file. Each time you open the workbook after that, Excel automatically trusts it.

Caution Starting in 2023, Microsoft added an extra layer of security to Excel workbooks that arrive via email or are downloaded from the web. By default, macros are blocked from running. Once you download the workbook to your computer, follow these steps to unblock the macro.

1. Locate the workbook in Windows Explorer.

2. Right-click the workbook and choose Properties.

3. In the Properties dialog, at the bottom of the General tab, look for a message reading "This File Came From Another Computer And Might Be Blocked To Help Protect This Computer." To the right of that message, choose Unblock.

4. Click OK to close the Properties dialog.

5. Open the Excel workbook. You will still have to choose to enable macros.

Creating a user interface with form controls

Allowing your clients to run your macro with shortcut keys such as Ctrl+Shift+R can be a satisfactory solution if you have only one macro in your pivot table report. However, suppose you want to allow your clients to perform several macro actions. In this case, you should give your clients a clear and easy way to run each macro without having to remember a gaggle of shortcut keys.

A basic user interface provides the perfect solution. A *user interface* is a set of controls such as buttons, scrollbars, and other devices that allow users to run macros with a simple click of the mouse. In fact, Excel offers a set of controls designed specifically for creating user interfaces directly on a spreadsheet. These controls are called *form controls*. The general idea behind form controls is that you can place one on a spreadsheet and then assign a macro to it—meaning a macro you have already recorded. After a macro is assigned to the control, that macro is executed (played) when the control is clicked.

You can find form controls in the Controls group on the Developer tab. To get to the form controls, simply select the Insert icon in the Controls group, as shown in Figure 12-3.

FIGURE 12-3 To see the available form controls, click Insert in the Controls group on the Developer tab.

 Note Notice that there are Form controls and ActiveX controls. Although they look similar, they are quite different. Form controls, with their limited overhead and easy configuration settings, are designed specifically for use on a spreadsheet. Meanwhile, ActiveX controls are typically used on Excel user forms. As a general rule, you should use form controls when working on a spreadsheet.

Here, you can select the control that best suits your needs. In this example, you want your clients to be able to refresh their pivot table with the click of a button. Click the Button control to select it, and then drop the control onto your spreadsheet by clicking the location where you would like to place the button.

After you drop the button control onto your spreadsheet, the Assign Macro dialog, shown in Figure 12-4, opens and asks you to assign a macro to this button. Select the macro you want to assign to the button—in this case, RefreshData—and then click OK.

FIGURE 12-4 Select the macro you want to assign to the button and then click OK. In this case, you want to select RefreshData.

Note Keep in mind that all the controls in the Forms toolbar work in the same way as the command button: you assign a macro to run when the control is selected.

As you can see in Figure 12-5, you can assign each macro in your workbook to a different form control and then name the controls to distinguish between them. To edit the text on a button, right-click the button and choose Edit Text. Use any of the eight resize handles on the button to resize the button.

Region	(All)	
Row Labels	**Sum of Sales_Amount**	Refresh Pivot Table
ACASCO Corp.	$675	
ACECUL Corp.	$593	See Top 20 Customers
ACEHUA Corp.	$580	
ACOPUL Corp.	$675	See Bottom 20 Customers
ACORAR Corp.	$2,232	
ACSBUR Corp.	$720	Reset Pivot Table
ADACEC Corp.	$345	
ADADUL Corp.	$690	
ADANAS Corp.	$345	
ADCOMP Corp.	$553	

FIGURE 12-5 You can create a different button for each of your macros.

As you can see in Figure 12-6, when you have all the controls you need for your pivot table report, you can format the controls and surrounding spreadsheet to create a basic interface.

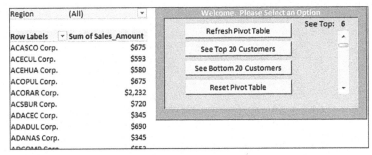

FIGURE 12-6 You can easily create the feeling of an interface by adding a handful of macros, a few form controls, and a little formatting.

Altering a recorded macro to add functionality

When you record a macro, Excel creates a module that stores the recorded steps of your actions. These recorded steps are actually lines of VBA code that make up your macro. You can add some interesting functionality to pivot table reports by tweaking a macro's VBA code to achieve various effects.

To get a better understanding of how this process works, start by creating a new macro that extracts the top five records by customer. Go to the Developer tab and select Record Macro. Set up the Record Macro dialog, as shown in Figure 12-7. Name your new macro TopNthCusts and specify This Workbook as the place where you want to store the macro. Click OK to start recording.

FIGURE 12-7 Name your new macro and specify where you want to store it.

After you have started recording, right-click the Customer field and select Filter. Then select Top 10. Selecting this option opens the Filter dialog, where you specify that you want to see the top five customers by sales amount. Enter the settings shown in Figure 12-8 and then click OK.

FIGURE 12-8 Enter the settings you see here to get the top five customers by revenue.

After you record the steps to extract the top five customers by revenue, select Stop Recording from the Developer tab.

You now have a macro that, when played, filters your pivot table to the top five customers by revenue. The plan is to tweak this macro to respond to a scrollbar; that is, you force the macro to base the number used to filter the pivot table on the number represented by a scrollbar in your user interface. In other words, a user can get the top 5, top 8, or top 32 simply by moving a scrollbar up or down.

Inserting a scrollbar form control

To get a scrollbar onto your spreadsheet, select the Insert icon on the Developer tab. Next, select the scrollbar control from the form controls and place the scrollbar control onto your spreadsheet. You can change the dimensions of the scrollbar to an appropriate length and width by clicking and dragging the corners.

Right-click the scrollbar and select Format Control. This activates the Format Control dialog, in which you make the following setting changes: Set the Minimum Value to 1 so the scrollbar cannot go below 1; set the Maximum Value to 200 so the scrollbar cannot go above 200; and set Cell Link to $M$2, so that the number represented by the scrollbar will output to cell M2. After you have completed these steps, your dialog should look like the one shown in Figure 12-9.

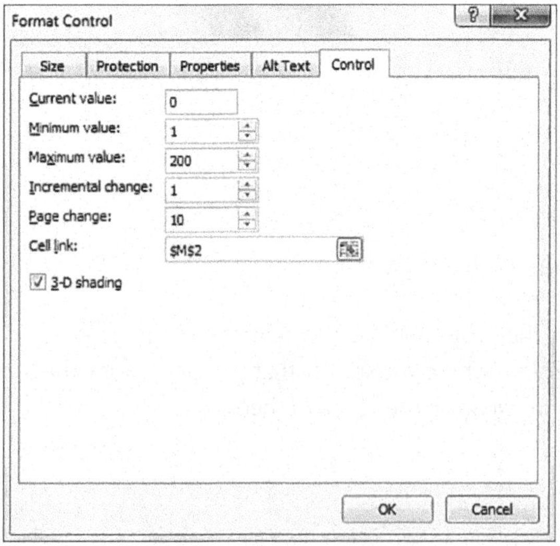

FIGURE 12-9 After you have placed a scrollbar on your spreadsheet, configure the scrollbar as shown here.

Next, you need to assign the TopNthCusts macro you just recorded to your scrollbar. To do this, right-click the scrollbar and select Assign Macro. Select the TopNthCusts macro from the list shown in Figure 12-10, and then click OK. Assigning this macro ensures that it plays each time the scrollbar is clicked.

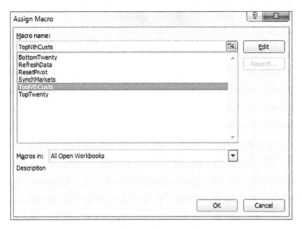

FIGURE 12-10 Select the macro from the list.

At this point, test your scrollbar by clicking it. Two things should happen when you click your scrollbar: The TopNthCusts macro should play, and the number in cell M2 should change to reflect your scrollbar's position. The number in cell M2 is important because that is the number you are going to reference in your TopNthCusts macro.

The only thing left to do is tweak your macro to respond to the number in cell M2, effectively tying it to your scrollbar. To do this, you have to get to the VBA code that makes up the macro. You have several ways to get there, but for this example, go to the Developer tab and select Macros. Selecting this option opens the Macro dialog, exposing several options. From here, you can run, delete, step into, or edit a selected macro. To get to the VBA code that makes up your macro, select the macro and then click Edit, as shown in Figure 12-11.

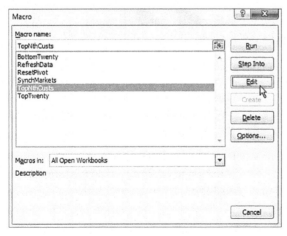

FIGURE 12-11 To get to the VBA code that makes up the TopNthCusts macro, select the macro and then select Edit.

The Visual Basic Editor opens with a detailed view of all the VBA code that makes up this macro (see Figure 12-12). Notice that the number 5 is hard-coded as part of your macro. The reason is that you originally recorded your macro to filter the top five customers by revenue. Your goal here is to replace the hard-coded number 5 with the value in cell M2, which is tied to your scrollbar.

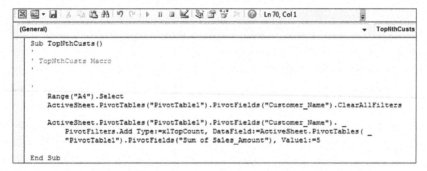

FIGURE 12-12 Your goal is to replace the hard-coded number 5, as specified when you originally recorded your macro, with the value in cell M2.

Therefore, you need to delete the number 5 and replace it with the following:

```
ActiveSheet.Range("M2").Value
```

Your macro's code should now look like the code shown in Figure 12-13.

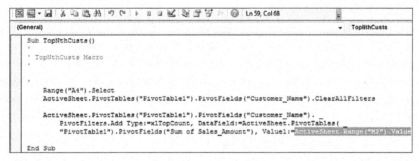

FIGURE 12-13 Simply delete the hard-coded number 5 and replace it with a reference to cell M2.

Close the Visual Basic Editor to get back to your pivot table report. Test your scrollbar by setting it to 11. Your macro should play and filter out the top 11 customers by revenue, as shown in Figure 12-14.

You could improve the buttons shown in Figure 12-14 by creating a formula to change See Top 20 Customers and See Bottom 20 Customers to reflect the value selected in the scrollbar.

The formula has to be entered in a cell somewhere on the worksheet. Perhaps use this formula in Z1: ="See Top "&M1&" Customers". Right-click the button to select it. Click in the formula bar, type **=Z1**, and press Enter. Repeat in Z2 to create a See Bottom 11 Customers caption.

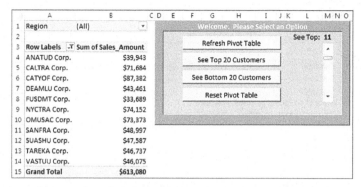

FIGURE 12-14 After a little formatting, you have a clear and easy way for your clients to get the top customers by revenue.

Creating a macro using Power Query

In the previous examples, you would record a macro with the VBA Macro Recorder and then have to tweak the VBA code to have it work. That is normal with the VBA Macro Recorder; it is difficult to record a macro that will work with a larger data set.

I've written plenty of books on VBA, but here is the secret: Anymore, most of my automated tasks are done using Power Query instead of VBA. Power Query is easier and more reliable, and you rarely have to "tweak" any code.

For the example in this chapter, you have a series of similar workbooks, each with a single worksheet containing invoice information for one month. Of course, each month's workbook has a different number of rows, but since the file is generated by some enterprise system somewhere, the columns remain constant from month to month.

Your manager would like to see a report showing revenue by product, by month. He wants products down the side and months across the top.

You've set up a folder called C:\InvoiceRegisters\ and have six monthly workbooks in it (see Figure 12-15).

FIGURE 12-15 Every month, a new workbook is added to this folder.

All the workbooks look similar to Figure 12-16.

⚄	A	B	C	D	E	F	G	H	I
1	Sector	Region	Product	Date	Customer	Quantity	Revenue	Profit	Cost
2	Training	Midwest	Gizmo	1/1/2030	599CD.com	1000	22810	10220	12590
3	Software	Northeast	Gadget	1/2/2030	F-Keys Ltd.	100	2257	984	1273
4	Associations	South	Gizmo	1/4/2030	Association for Computers & Taxation	400	9152	4088	5064
5	Consultants	Midwest	Gadget	1/4/2030	Construction Intelligence & Analytics, Inc.	800	18552	7872	10680
6	Consultants	West	Gadget	1/7/2030	Data2Impact	1000	21730	9840	11890
7	Software	Midwest	Widget	1/7/2030	More4Apps	400	8456	3388	5068
8	Software	Midwest	Widget	1/9/2030	More4Apps	800	16416	6776	9640
9	Consultants	South	Gizmo	1/10/2030	Andrew Spain Consulting	900	21438	9198	12240

FIGURE 12-16 Each workbook has the same columns but different number of rows.

Start with a blank workbook with one worksheet. Select Data | Get Data | From File | From Folder, as shown in Figure 12-17.

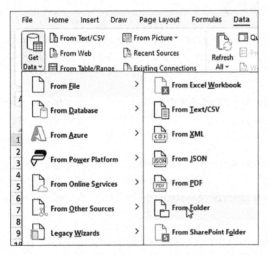

FIGURE 12-17 Specify that you want data from a folder.

Power Query asks you to browse for your folder. Find `C:\InvoiceRegisters\` and click OK. Power Query shows you a list of files. Open the Combine dropdown and choose Combine & Transform Data (see Figure 12-18).

The Combine Files dialog appears. Initially, you see "No Item Selected For Preview" on the dialog's right side. You must choose a file and a worksheet before you can see a preview of your data.

By default, the Sample File is set to First File. If the First File is not representative of most data files, you can choose a different workbook as the sample workbook. In Figure 12-19, there is only one worksheet available in the sample file. Click Sheet1 to see a preview appear on the right side. Click OK.

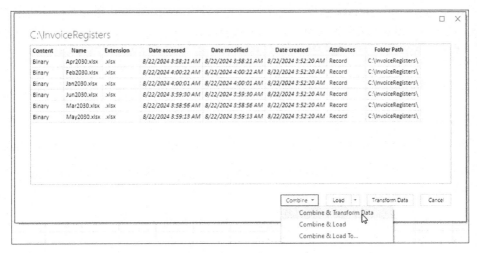

FIGURE 12-18 Choose to combine the files.

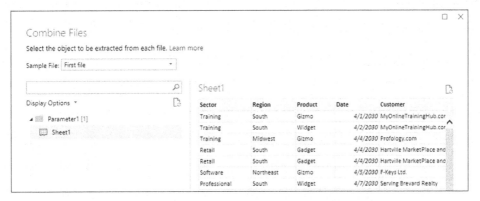

FIGURE 12-19 Power Query shows you a preview of one of the workbooks.

The Power Query editor appears. A new column has been added to the left of your data with the Source.Name heading (see Figure 12-20), showing you which column the row came from. That might be nice to know one day, but it is not needed for this project.

```
fx    = Table.TransformColumnTypes(#"Expanded Table Column1",{{"Source.Name", type text}
```

	ABC Source.Name	ABC Sector	ABC Region	ABC Product
1	Apr2030.xlsx	Training	South	Gizmo
2	Apr2030.xlsx	Training	South	Widget
3	Apr2030.xlsx	Training	Midwest	Gizmo
4	Apr2030.xlsx	Retail	South	Gadget
5	Apr2030.xlsx	Retail	South	Gadget
6	Apr2030.xlsx	Software	Northeast	Gizmo
7	Apr2030.xlsx	Professional	South	Widget
8	Apr2030.xlsx	Training	Northeast	Widget

FIGURE 12-20 A preview shows the first 1,000 records.

The goal is to produce a report with Product, Month, and Revenue columns. Click the Product heading, and then Ctrl+click the Date and Revenue column headings so that all three columns are selected. Right-click and choose Remove Other Columns (see Figure 12-21).

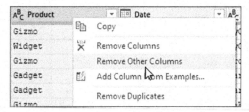

FIGURE 12-21 Select the columns that you want to keep and then remove the other columns.

Choosing Remove Other Columns is a better option than removing each column because one day—perhaps five years from now—your IT department will add an extra column for something. By choosing Remove Other Columns, you ensure that the new column is deleted.

In this example, the invoice files had daily dates, so you need to convert them to month-ending dates. Select the Date column, right-click the heading, and choose Transform | Month | End Of Month, as shown in Figure 12-22.

At this point, you have Product, Date, Revenue, and End Of Month columns selected. Right-click Date and choose Remove Column.

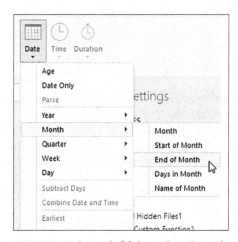

FIGURE 12-22 Instead of Column From Examples, an End Of Month transform is available.

Sort End Of Month in ascending order by using the AZ button on the Home tab. You will notice a few rows marked with null all the way across. These appear as null because there are blank rows in each invoice file. Open the Filter icon for End Of Month and deselect the Null option.

Stop and consider what has happened so far. You have combined records from all six workbooks. You've deleted unnecessary columns. You've done a calculation to convert Date to End Of Month.

At this point, you could choose Close, then Load, and do the final pivot table in Excel. But you can also do the pivot action right here in Power Query. Select the Product column. On the Transform tab, choose Pivot Column (see Figure 12-23).

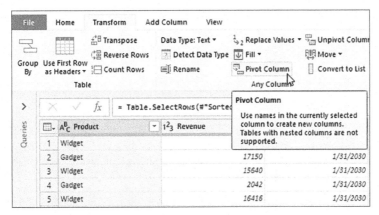

FIGURE 12-23 Choose Product before choosing Pivot Column.

Pivoting in Power Query is a bit different than in regular Excel. Specify the Values column as Revenue. Any other columns in the data set will become Row fields. If you open the Advanced Options, the Aggregate Value Function dropdown allows you to specify how Revenue should be aggregated. The default of Sum works in this case (see Figure 12-24).

Pivot Column

Use the names in column "Product" to create new columns.

Values Column ⓘ

Revenue

▲ Advanced options

Aggregate Value Function

Sum

Learn more about Pivot Column

FIGURE 12-24 Specify how to create the pivoted report.

In this particular data set, there is a product called Doodads. These are not sold every month, and there are some months where the total sales of Doodads are reported as null.

Choose the Doodads column. On the Home tab, choose Replace Values. In the Value To Find box, type the word **null**. In the Replace With box, type **0** (zero), as shown in Figure 12-25.

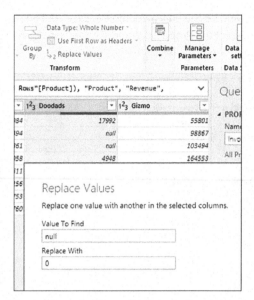

FIGURE 12-25 Replace null cells in the Doodads column with zeroes.

At this point, the report is working great. But the last step is only replacing nulls with zeroes in the Doodads column. What if, many years in the future, your company starts selling a new product—perhaps Doodads Plus? You can't predict what the future columns will be called. Can you make the query flexible?

If you look in the formula bar in Power Query, you will see these lines of code:

```
= Table.ReplaceValue(#"Pivoted Column",null,0,Replacer.ReplaceValue,{"Doodads"})
```

The final argument here is applying the ReplaceValue to the Doodad column. It would be more useful to apply the change to all of the columns. You can't do this (as of today) using the Power Query interface. But you could edit the formula shown in the formula bar to apply ReplaceValue to any product in the future. Replace {"Doodads"} in the formula bar with `Table.ColumnNames(#"Pivoted Column")`.

This change to the formula in Power Query uses the `Table.ColumnNames` function from the Power Query M language to dynamically insert a list of columns in the `Table.ReplaceValue` function.

The results look great, and you will see those in a moment. But just getting the report from this first day of data is not the important part. Study the Applied Steps on the right side of the screen (see Figure 12-26). This is a list of everything you did to produce the report. Click any item to see the data as it appears at that step. Click any Gear icon to see the choices you made at that step.

Are these steps the macro? No. Go to the View tab in Power Query and choose Advanced Editor. This is the macro, which is written in a language called M (see Figure 12-27).

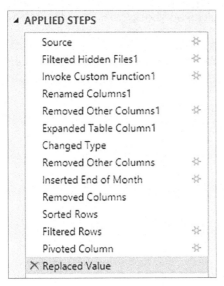

APPLIED STEPS

Source
Filtered Hidden Files1
Invoke Custom Function1
Renamed Columns1
Removed Other Columns1
Expanded Table Column1
Changed Type
Removed Other Columns
Inserted End of Month
Removed Columns
Sorted Rows
Filtered Rows
Pivoted Column
✕ Replaced Value

FIGURE 12-26 Power Query tracks the Applied Steps in a panel.

Advanced Editor

InvoiceRegisters

Display Options ▾ ❓

```
1  let
2      Source = Folder.Files("C:\InvoiceRegisters"),
3      #"Filtered Hidden Files1" = Table.SelectRows(Source, each [Attributes]?[Hidden]? <> true),
4      #"Invoke Custom Function1" = Table.AddColumn(#"Filtered Hidden Files1", "Transform File", each #"Transform File"([Content]
5      #"Renamed Columns1" = Table.RenameColumns(#"Invoke Custom Function1", {"Name", "Source.Name"}),
6      #"Removed Other Columns1" = Table.SelectColumns(#"Renamed Columns1", {"Source.Name", "Transform File"}),
7      #"Expanded Table Column1" = Table.ExpandTableColumn(#"Removed Other Columns1", "Transform File", Table.ColumnNames(#"Trans
8      #"Changed Type" = Table.TransformColumnTypes(#"Expanded Table Column1",{{"Source.Name", type text}, {"Sector", type text},
9      #"Removed Other Columns" = Table.SelectColumns(#"Changed Type",{"Product", "Date", "Revenue"}),
10     #"Inserted End of Month" = Table.AddColumn(#"Removed Other Columns", "End of Month", each Date.EndOfMonth([Date]), type da
11     #"Removed Columns" = Table.RemoveColumns(#"Inserted End of Month",{"Date"}),
12     #"Sorted Rows" = Table.Sort(#"Removed Columns",{{"End of Month", Order.Ascending}}),
13     #"Filtered Rows" = Table.SelectRows(#"Sorted Rows", each ([End of Month] <> null)),
14     #"Pivoted Column" = Table.Pivot(#"Filtered Rows", List.Distinct(#"Filtered Rows"[Product]), "Product", "Revenue", List.Sum
15     #"Replaced Value" = Table.ReplaceValue(#"Pivoted Column",null,0,Replacer.ReplaceValue,Table.ColumnNames(#"Pivoted Column")
16  in
17     #"Replaced Value"
```

✓ No syntax errors have been detected.

Done   Cancel

FIGURE 12-27 As you cleaned the data, Excel wrote the macro.

Figure 12-28 shows the result of pivoting the data.

⬚	A	B	C	D	E
1	End of Month ▾	Widget ▾	Gadget ▾	Gizmo ▾	Doodads ▾
2	1/31/2030	130984	68445	55801	17992
3	2/28/2030	107494	95259	98867	0
4	3/31/2030	70861	91438	103494	0
5	4/30/2030	57058	41207	164553	4948
6	5/31/2030	130611	127128	83673	0
7	6/30/2030	76256	76250	27049	0

FIGURE 12-28 This report summarizes an entire folder of Excel workbooks.

From the Home tab, click Close & Load to load the resulting workbook to a new worksheet in your workbook.

You have choices for running the macro in the future. You can click the Refresh icon at the bottom of the Queries & Connections panel, as shown in Figure 12-29.

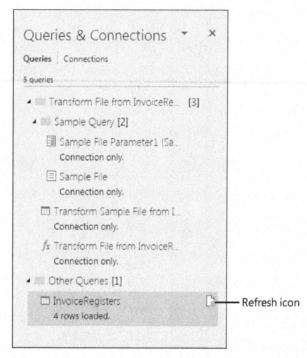 ———— Refresh icon

FIGURE 12-29 One way to rerun the macro is to click Refresh.

But here is the thing: If you are producing this report for your manager, you cannot trust them to click the Refresh button. Here is a better way: Right-click the `InvoiceRegisters` query and choose Properties. In the Query Properties dialog, choose Refresh Data When Opening The File (see Figure 12-30).

Two months later, your folder of `InvoiceRegisters` now has eight workbooks. When you open the workbook, the Power Query steps will run, and your report will be updated to include July and August (see Figure 12-31). This is fairly impressive.

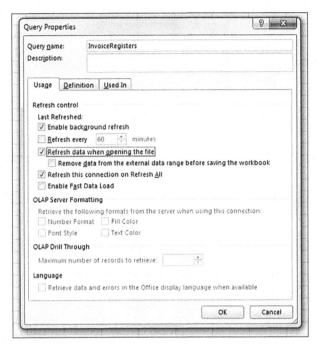

FIGURE 12-30 Choose to run the Power Query macro when the workbook is opened.

	A	B	C	D	E
1	End of Month ▼	Gadget ▼	Widget ▼	Doodads ▼	Gizmo ▼
2	1/31/2030	68445	130984	17992	55801
3	2/28/2030	95259	107494	0	98867
4	3/31/2030	91438	70861	0	103494
5	4/30/2030	41207	57058	4948	164553
6	5/31/2030	127128	130611	0	83673
7	6/30/2030	76250	76256	0	27049
8	7/31/2030	117410	78753	0	189604
9	8/31/2030	67859	73760	17856	132186
10					

FIGURE 12-31 After adding July and August to your folder, the workbook reflects the new months.

Next steps

In the next chapter, you'll go beyond recording macros. Chapter 13, "Using VBA or TypeScript to create pivot tables," shows how to use Visual Basic for Applications to create powerful, behind-the-scenes processes and calculations using pivot tables.

Using VBA or TypeScript to create pivot tables

In this chapter, you will:

- Enable VBA in your copy of Excel

- Use a file format that enables macros

- Use the Visual Basic Editor

- Discover Visual Basic Tools

- Use the macro recorder

- Understand object-oriented code

- Learn tricks of the trade

- Understand versions

- Build a pivot table in Excel VBA

- Deal with limitations of pivot tables

- Create a report showing revenue by category

- Calculate with a pivot table

- Use advanced pivot table techniques

- Use the Data Model in Excel

- Examine TypeScript Code for Creating Pivot Tables in Excel Online

Version 5 of Excel introduced a powerful new macro language called Visual Basic for Applications (VBA). Every copy of Excel shipped since 1993 has had a copy of the powerful VBA language hiding behind the worksheets. VBA enables you to perform steps that you normally perform in Excel quickly and flawlessly. I have seen a VBA program change a process that would take days each month into a single-click operation that now takes a minute of processing time.

Do not be intimidated by VBA. The VBA macro recorder tool gets you 90 percent of the way to a useful macro, and I get you the rest of the way, using examples in this chapter.

Enabling VBA in your copy of Excel

By default, VBA is disabled in Excel. Before you can start using VBA, you need to enable macros in the Trust Center. Follow these steps:

1. Click the File menu to show the Backstage view.

2. In the left navigation pane, select Options. The Excel Options dialog displays.

3. In the left navigation pane of Excel Options, select Customize Ribbon.

4. In the list box on the right, choose the Developer tab from the list of main tabs available in Excel. Click OK to close Excel Options and include the Developer tab in the ribbon.

5. Click the Developer tab in the ribbon. As shown in Figure 13-1, the Code group on the left side of the ribbon includes the Visual Basic Editor, Macros, Macro Recorder, and Macro Security icons.

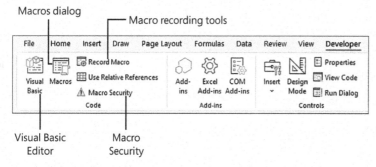

FIGURE 13-1 Enable the Developer tab to access the VBA tools.

6. Click the Macro Security icon. Excel opens the Trust Center.

7. In the Trust Center, choose one of the four options:

   - **Disable VBA Macros with Notification**—When you open a workbook that contains macros, a message appears alerting you that macros are in the workbook. If you expect macros to be in the workbook, you can enable the macros. This is the safest setting because it forces you to explicitly enable macros in each workbook.

   - **Enable VBA Macros**—This setting is not recommended because potentially dangerous code can run. Because it can enable rogue macros to run in files that are sent to you by others, Microsoft recommends that you not use this setting.

   - **Disable VBA Macros Without Notification**—Your macros will not be able to run, and, as the option says, you will not be notified that they're not running. You don't want to choose this option.

- **Disable VBA Macros Except Digitally Signed Macros**—You would have to buy a digital code signing certificate from a third party in order to use this option. This is a waste of money if you are building macros for you and your coworkers.

Using a file format that enables macros

The default Excel file format is initially the Excel workbook (.xlsx). This workbook is defined to disallow macros. You can build a macro in an .xlsx workbook, but it won't be saved with the workbook.

You have several options for saving workbooks that enable macros:

- **Excel Macro-Enabled Workbook (.xlsm)**—This uses the XML-based method for storing workbooks and enables macros. I prefer this file type because it is compact and less prone to becoming corrupt.

- **Excel Binary Workbook (.xlsb)**—This is a binary format and always enables macros.

- **Excel 97-2003 Workbook (.xls)**—Although this legacy file type supports macros, it doesn't support a lot of handy newer features. You lose access to slicers, new filters, rows 65537 through 1048576, columns IW through XFD, and other pivot table improvements.

When you create a new workbook, you can use File | Save As to choose the appropriate file type.

Unblock workbooks from the web

Any workbook that arrives in an e-mail or is downloaded from the web is automatically blocked from running macros. To allow macros to run, follow these steps:

1. Find the workbook in Windows Explorer.

2. Right-click the file and choose Properties.

3. In the lower-right corner of the Properties dialog, choose Unblock.

4. Click OK to close the Properties dialog.

Visual Basic Editor

From Excel, press Alt+F11 or select Developer | Visual Basic to open the Visual Basic Editor, as shown in Figure 13-2.

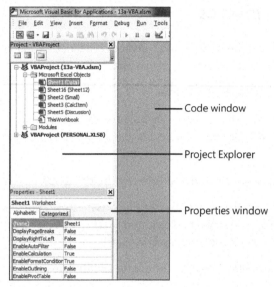

Code window

Project Explorer

Properties window

FIGURE 13-2 The Visual Basic Editor window is lurking behind every copy of Excel shipped since 1993.

The three main sections of the VBA Editor are described here. If this is your first time using VBA, some of these items might be disabled. Follow the instructions in the following list to make sure that each is enabled:

- **Project Explorer**—This pane displays a hierarchical tree of all open workbooks. Expand the tree to see the worksheets, code modules, user forms, and class modules present in the workbook. If the Project Explorer is not visible, enable it by pressing Ctrl+R.

- **Properties window**—The Properties window is important when you begin to program user forms. It has some use when you are writing normal code, so enable it by pressing F4.

- **Code window**—This is the area where you write your code. Code is stored in one or more code modules attached to your workbook. To add a code module to a workbook, select Insert | Module from the VBA menu.

Visual Basic tools

Visual Basic is a powerful development environment. Although this chapter cannot offer a complete course on VBA, if you are new to VBA, you should take advantage of these important tools:

- **AutoComplete**—As you begin to type code, Excel might offer a dropdown with valid choices. This feature, known as AutoComplete, enables you to type code faster and eliminate typing mistakes.

- **Excel Help**—For assistance on any keyword, put the cursor in the keyword and press F1. Excel Help displays a help topic regarding the keyword.

- **Comments**—Excel checks each line of code as you finish it. Lines in error appear in red. Comments appear in green. You can add a comment by typing a single apostrophe before the comment. Use lots of comments so you can remember what each section of code is doing.

- **Debugging**—Despite the aforementioned error-checking, Excel might still encounter an error at runtime. If this happens, click the Debug button. The line that caused the error is highlighted in yellow. Hover your mouse cursor over any variable to see the current value of the variable. When you are in Debug mode, use the Debug menu to step line by line through the code. If you have a wide monitor, try arranging the Excel window and the VBA window side by side. This way, you can see the effect of running a line of code on the worksheet.

Other great debugging tools are breakpoints, the Watch window, the Object Browser, and the Immediate window. Read about these tools in the Excel Help menu.

The macro recorder

Excel offers a macro recorder that is about 90 percent perfect. Unfortunately, the last 10 percent is frustrating. Code that you record to work with one data set is hard-coded to work only with that data set. This behavior might work fine if your transactional database occupies cells A1:L87601 every single day, but if you are pulling in a new invoice register every day, it is unlikely that you will have the same number of rows each day. Given that you might need to work with other data, it would be a lot better if Excel could record selecting cells using the End key. This is one of the shortcomings of the macro recorder.

In reality, Excel pros use the macro recorder to record code but then expect to have to clean up the recorded code.

Understanding object-oriented code

VBA is an object-oriented language. Most lines of VBA code follow the *Noun.Verb* syntax. However, in VBA, it is called `Object.Method`. Examples of objects are workbooks, worksheets, cells, and ranges of cells. Methods can be typical Excel actions such as `.Copy`, `.Paste`, and `.PasteSpecial`.

Many methods allow adverbs—parameters you use to specify how to perform the method. If you see a construct with a colon and an equal sign (`:=`), you know that the macro recorder is describing how the method should work.

You also might see code in which you assign a value to the adjectives of an object. In VBA, adjectives are called *properties*. If you set `ActiveCell.Value = 3`, you are setting the value of the active cell to 3. Note that when you are dealing with properties, there is only an = (equal sign), not a := (colon and equal sign). Examples of properties are `ThisWorkbook.Path`, `Sheet1.Name`, and `UserForm1.Caption`.

Learning tricks of the trade

This section explains a few simple techniques you need to master in order to write efficient VBA code. These techniques help you make the jump to writing effective code.

Writing code to handle a data range of any size

The macro recorder hard-codes the fact that your data is in a range such as A1:L87601. Although this hard-coding works for today's data set, it might not work as you get new data sets. You need to write code that can deal with data sets of different sizes.

The macro recorder uses syntax such as `Range("H12")` to refer to a cell. However, it is more flexible to use `Cells(12, 8)` to refer to the cell in row 12, column 8. Similarly, the macro recorder refers to a rectangular range as `Range("A1:L87601")`. However, it is more flexible to use the `Cells` syntax to refer to the upper-left corner of the range and then use the `Resize()` syntax to refer to the number of rows and columns in the range. The equivalent way to describe the preceding range is `Cells(1, 1).Resize(87601,12)`. This approach is more flexible because you can replace any of the numbers with a variable.

In the Excel user interface, you can use Ctrl+any arrow on the keyboard to jump to the edge of a range of data. If you move the cell pointer to the final row on the worksheet and press the Ctrl+up arrow key, the cell pointer jumps to the last row with data. The equivalent of doing this in VBA is to use the following code:

```
Range("A1048576").End(xlUp).Select
```

> **Caution** The arguments for the `End` property are XLUP, XLDOWN, XLTOLEFT, and XLTORIGHT. Using these properties is equivalent to pressing Ctrl plus the up, down, left, or right arrow keys. Because the VBA Editor shows XLUP as xlUp, many people think the argument contains the number *one* instead of the letter *L*. Think of how "XL" sounds like "Excel." Why did Microsoft add the word To in XLToLeft and XLToRight? Because XLLeft and XLRight were already defined as constants for aligning text in cells.

You do not need to select this cell; you just need to find the row number that contains the last row. The following code locates this row and saves the row number to a variable named `FinalRow`:

```
FinalRow = Range("A1048576").End(xlUp).Row
```

There is nothing magical about the variable name `FinalRow`. You could call this variable x, y, or even your dog's name. However, because VBA enables you to use meaningful variable names, you should use something such as `FinalRow` to describe the final row:

```
FinalRow = Cells(Rows.Count, 1).End(xlUp).Row
```

> **Note** Excel offers 1,048,576 rows and 16,384 columns for a regular workbook. If the workbook opens in Compatibility mode, you have only 65,536 rows and 256 columns. To make your code flexible enough to handle either situation, you can use `Rows.Count` to learn the total number of rows in the current workbook. The preceding code can then be generalized like so:
>
> ```
> FinalRow = Cells(Rows.Count, 1).End(xlUp).Row
> ```

You can also find the final column in a data set. If you are relatively sure that the data set begins in row 1, you can use the End key in combination with the left-arrow key to jump from cell XFD1 to the last column with data. However, if there is any chance that the code will ever run in an XLS workbook, there will not be an XFD column, since XLS workbooks end at column IV. To ensure that the code can run in legacy versions of Excel, you can use the following code:

```
FinalCol = Cells(1, Columns.Count).End(xlToLeft).Column
```

End+Down arrow versus End+Up arrow

You might be tempted to find the final row by starting in cell A1 and using the End key in conjunction with the down-arrow key. Avoid this approach. Data coming from another system is imperfect. If your program imports 500,000 rows from a legacy computer system every day for the next five years, a day will come when someone manages to key a null value into the data set. This value will cause a blank cell or even a blank row to appear in the middle of the data set. Using `Range("A1").End(xlDown)` stops prematurely just above the blank cell instead of including all the data. This blank cell causes that day's report to miss thousands of rows of data, which is a potential disaster that calls into question the credibility of your report. Take the extra step of starting at the last row in the worksheet to greatly reduce the risk of problems.

Using super-variables: Object variables

In typical programming languages, a variable holds a single value. You might use x = 4 to assign the value 4 to the variable x.

Think about a single cell in Excel. Many properties describe a cell. A cell might contain a value such as 4, but the cell also has a font size, a font color, a row, a column, possibly a formula or a comment, a list of precedents, and more. It is possible in VBA to create a super-variable that contains all the information about a cell or about any object. A statement to create a typical variable such as x = Range("A1") assigns the current value of A1 to the variable x.

However, you can use the Set keyword to create an object variable:

```
Set x = Range("A1")
```

You have now created a super-variable that contains all the properties of the cell. Instead of having a variable with only one value, you have a variable in which you can access the values of many properties associated with that variable. You can reference x.Formula to learn the formula in A1 or x.Font.ColorIndex to learn the color of the cell.

> **Note** The examples in this chapter frequently set up an object variable called PT to refer to the entire pivot table. This way, when the code would generally refer to ActiveSheet. PivotTables("PivotTable1"), you can specify PT to avoid typing the longer text.

Using With and End With to shorten code

You will frequently find that you repeatedly make certain changes to a pivot table. Although the following code is explained later in this chapter, all these lines of code are for changing settings in a pivot table:

```
PT.NullString = 0
PT.RepeatAllLabels xlRepeatLabels
PT.ColumnGrand = False
PT.RowGrand = False
PT.RowAxisLayout xlTabularRow
PT.TableStyle2 = "PivotStyleMedium10"
PT.TableStyleRowStripes = True
```

For all these lines of code, the VBA engine has to figure out what you mean by PT. Your code executes faster if you refer to PT only once. Add the initial line With PT. Then, all the remaining lines do not need to start with PT. Any line that starts with a period is assumed to be referring to the object in the With statement. Finish the code block by using an End With statement:

```
With PT
  .NullString = 0
  .RepeatAllLabels xlRepeatLabels
  .ColumnGrand = False
  .RowGrand = False
  .RowAxisLayout xlTabularRow
  .TableStyle2 = "PivotStyleMedium10"
  .TableStyleRowStripes = True
End With
```

Understanding versions

Pivot tables have been evolving. They were introduced in Excel 5 and perfected in Excel 97. In Excel 2000, pivot table creation in VBA was dramatically altered. Some new parameters were added in Excel 2002. A few new properties, such as PivotFilters and TableStyle2, were added in Excel 2007. Slicers and new choices for Show Values As were added in Excel 2010. Timelines and the Power Pivot Data Model were added in Excel 2013. The AutoGroup method was added in Excel 2016. Because of all the changes over the years, you need to be extremely careful when writing code in Excel today that might be run in older versions of Excel. If you use code for a new feature, the code works in the current version, but it crashes in previous versions of Excel:

- Microsoft 365 allows you to set defaults for all future pivot tables. These settings are stored in various properties under Application.DefaultPivotTableLayoutOptions. Record a macro that changes any one setting, and the recorded macro will list all of the available settings.

- Excel 2016 introduced the AutoGroup functionality for dates in pivot tables. To perform the equivalent action in VBA, use the AutoGroup method.

- Excel 2013 introduced the Power Pivot Data Model. You can add tables to the Data Model, create a relationship, and produce a pivot table. This code does not run in Excel 2010 or earlier. The function xlDistinctCount was new in Excel 2013, as were timelines.

- Excel 2010 introduced slicers, Repeat All Item Labels, named sets, and several new calculation options: xlPercentOfParentColumn, xlPercentOfParentRow, xlPercentRunningTotal, xlRankAscending, and xlRankDescending. These do not work in Excel 2007 or earlier.

- Excel 2007 introduced ConvertToFormulas, xlCompactRow layout, xlAtTop for the subtotal location, TableStyles, and SortUsingCustomLists. Macros that include this code fail in previous versions.

Building a pivot table in Excel VBA

This chapter does not mean to imply that you use VBA to build pivot tables to give to your clients. Instead, the purpose of this chapter is to remind you that you can use pivot tables as a means to an end. You can use a pivot table to extract a summary of data and then use that summary elsewhere.

Note   This chapter's code listings are available for download at *microsoftpressstore.com/ ExcelPivotTable/downloads*.

Caution   Beginning with Excel 2007, the user interface used new names for the various pivot table sections. Even so, VBA code continues to refer to the old names. Although the four sections of a pivot table in the Excel user interface are Filters, Columns, Rows, and Values, VBA continues to use the old terms of page fields, column fields, row fields, and data fields. If Microsoft hadn't made this decision, millions of lines of code would have stopped working in Excel 2007 when they referred to a page field instead of a filter field.

In Excel 2000 and newer, you first build a pivot cache object to describe the input area of the data:

```
Dim WSD As Worksheet
Dim PTCache As PivotCache
Dim PT As PivotTable
Dim PRange As Range
Dim FinalRow As Long
Dim FinalCol As Long
Set WSD = Worksheets("Data")

' Delete any prior pivot tables
For Each PT In WSD.PivotTables
  PT.TableRange2.Clear
Next PT

' Define input area and set up a Pivot Cache
FinalRow = WSD.Cells(Rows.Count, 1).End(xlUp).Row
FinalCol = WSD.Cells(1, Columns.Count).End(xlToLeft).Column
Set PRange = WSD.Cells(1, 1).Resize(FinalRow, FinalCol)
Set PTCache = ActiveWorkbook.PivotCaches.Create(SourceType:=xlDatabase, _
  SourceData:=PRange)
```

After defining the pivot cache, use the CreatePivotTable method to create a blank pivot table based on the defined pivot cache:

```
Set PT = PTCache.CreatePivotTable(TableDestination:=WSD.Cells(2, _
  FinalCol + 2), TableName:="PivotTable1")
```

In the CreatePivotTable method, you specify the output location and optionally give the table a name. After running this line of code, you have a strange-looking blank pivot table, like the one shown in Figure 13-3. You now have to use code to drop fields onto the table.

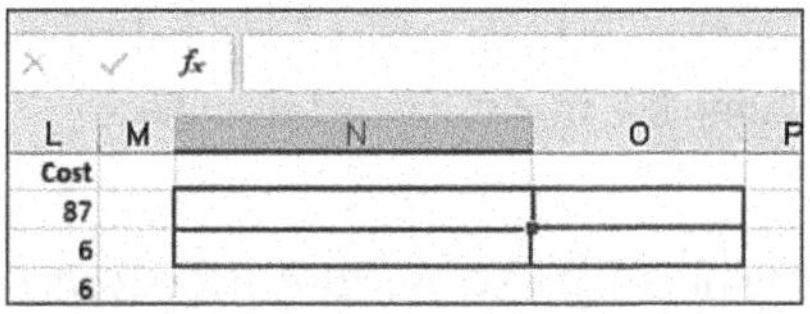

FIGURE 13-3 Immediately after you use the CreatePivotTable method, Excel gives you a four-cell blank pivot table that is not useful.

Now, you can run through the steps needed to lay out the pivot table. In the AddFields method, you can specify one or more fields that should be in the row, column, or filter area of the pivot table.

The RowFields parameter enables you to define fields that appear in the Rows area of the PivotTable Fields list. The ColumnFields parameter corresponds to the Columns layout area. The PageFields parameter corresponds to the Filters layout area.

The following line of code populates a pivot table with two fields in the Rows area and one field in the Columns area:

```
' Set up the row & column fields
PT.AddFields RowFields:=Array("Category", "Product"), _
 ColumnFields:="Region"
```

> **Note** If you are adding a single field, such as the Region field, to the Columns area, you only need to specify the name of the field in quotes. If you are adding two or more fields, you have to include that list inside the array function.

Although the pivot table's row, column, and filter fields can be handled with the AddFields method, it is best to add fields to the data area using the code described in the next section.

Adding fields to the data area

When you add fields to the data area of a pivot table, it is better for you to have control than to let Excel's IntelliSense decide for many settings.

Say that you are building a report with revenue. You likely want a sum of the revenue. If you do not explicitly specify the calculation, Excel scans through the values in the underlying data. If 100 percent of the revenue cells are numeric, Excel sums. If one cell is blank or contains text, Excel decides to count the revenue. This produces confusing results.

Because of this possible variability, you should never use the DataFields argument in the AddFields method. Instead, change the property of the field to xlDataField. You can then specify the function to be xlSum.

While you are setting up the data field, you can change several other properties within the same With...End With block.

The Position property is useful when adding multiple fields to the data area. Specify 1 for the first field, 2 for the second field, and so on.

By default, Excel renames a Revenue field to something strange like Sum Of Revenue. You can use the Name property to change that heading back to something normal. Note that you cannot reuse the word Revenue as a name, but you can use "Revenue " (with a trailing space).

You are not required to specify a number format, but doing so can make the resulting pivot table easier to understand and takes only one extra line of code:

```
' Set up the data fields
With PT.PivotFields("Revenue")
 .Orientation = xlDataField
 .Function = xlSum
 .Position = 1
 .NumberFormat = "#,##0"
 .Name = "Revenue"
End With
```

The preceding block of code adds the Revenue field to the Values area of the pivot table with a new name and a number format.

Formatting the pivot table

Microsoft introduced the Compact layout for pivot tables in Excel 2007. This means that three layouts are available in Excel (Compact, Tabular, and Outline). When a pivot table is created with VBA, Excel usually defaults to using the Tabular layout, which is good because the Tabular view is the one that makes the most sense. It cannot hurt, though, to add one line of code to ensure that you get the desired layout:

```
PT.RowAxisLayout xlTabularRow
```

In the Tabular layout, each field in the row area is in a different column. Subtotals always appear at the bottom of each group. This is the layout that has been around the longest and is most conducive to reusing a pivot table report for further analysis.

The Excel user interface frequently defaults to Compact layout. In this layout, multiple column fields are stacked up into a single column on the left side of the pivot table. To create this layout, use the following code:

```
PT.RowAxisLayout xlCompactRow
```

> **Tip** The one limitation of the Tabular layout is that you cannot show the totals at the top of each group. If you need to do this, you'll want to switch to the Outline layout and show totals at the top of the group:
>
> ```
> PT.RowAxisLayout xlOutlineRow
> PT.SubtotalLocation xlAtTop
> ```

Your pivot table inherits the table style settings selected as the default on whatever computer happens to run the code. If you would like control over the final format, you can explicitly choose a table style. The following code applies banded rows and a medium table style:

```
' Format the pivot table
PT.ShowTableStyleRowStripes = True
PT.TableStyle2 = "PivotStyleMedium10"
```

At this point, you have given VBA all the settings required to generate the pivot table correctly. You will have a complete pivot table, like the one shown in Figure 13-4.

Revenue		Region
Category ▼	Product ▼	Midwest
– Bar Equipment	Bar Cover	1,328
	Cocktail Shaker 28 Oz	4,607
	Commercial Bar Blender	1,704
	Garnish Center	455
	Glass Rimmers Triple Brushes	8,760
	Glass Rimmers Twin Brushes	1,278
	High Power Blender Easy-To-Clean Electronic Membrane	1,500
	High Power Blender With Paddle Switches	1,125
	One Gallon Blender	16,540
	Speed Rail 10 Quart/Liter Bottle Capacity	753
	Speed Rail 5 Quart/Liter Bottle Capacity	989
	Speed Rail 8 Quart/Liter Bottle Capacity	
	Spindle Drink Mixer Single Spindle $ 275.00	1,650
	Spindle Drink Mixers 32 Oz. S/S Containe	1,428
	Spindle Drink Mixers 48 Oz. Poly. Container	21,505
Bar Equipment Total		63,621
– Commercial Applianc	2½ Qt. Cap. Batch Bowl	3,520

FIGURE 13-4 Fewer than 50 lines of code create this pivot table in less than a second.

Listing 13-1 shows the complete code used to generate this pivot table.

LISTING 13-1   Code to generate the pivot table shown in Figure 13-4

```
Sub CreatePivot()
    '
    Dim WBO As Workbook
    Dim WSD As Worksheet
    Dim PT As PivotTable
    Dim FinalRow As Long
    Dim FinalCol As Long
    Dim PRange As Range
    Dim PTCache As PivotCache

    Set WBO = ActiveWorkbook
    Set WSD = WBO.Worksheets("Data")
    WSD.Select

    ' Delete any prior pivot tables
    For Each PT In WSD.PivotTables
        PT.TableRange2.Clear
    Next PT
    ' Delete any previously generated content
    WSD.Range("N1:AZ1").EntireColumn.Clear

    ' Define input area and set up a Pivot Cache
    FinalRow = WSD.Cells(Application.Rows.Count, 1).End(xlUp).Row
    FinalCol = WSD.Cells(1, Application.Columns.Count). _
        End(xlToLeft).Column
    Set PRange = WSD.Cells(1, 1).Resize(FinalRow, FinalCol)
    Set PTCache = WBO.PivotCaches.Add(SourceType:= _
        xlDatabase, SourceData:=PRange.Address)
```

```
' Create the Pivot Table from the Pivot Cache
Set PT = PTCache.CreatePivotTable(TableDestination:=WSD. _
    Cells(2, FinalCol + 2), TableName:="PivotTable1")

' Set up the row & column fields
PT.AddFields RowFields:=Array("Category", "Product"), _
    ColumnFields:="Region"

' Set up the data fields
With PT.PivotFields("Revenue")
    .Orientation = xlDataField
    .Function = xlSum
    .Position = 1
    .NumberFormat = "#,##0"
    .Name = "Revenue "
End With

' Format the pivot table
With PT
    .RowAxisLayout RowLayout:=xlTabularRow
    .ShowTableStyleRowStripes = True
    .TableStyle2 = "PivotStyleMedium10"
End With

    WSD.Cells(2, FinalCol + 2).Select
End Sub
```

Dealing with the limitations of pivot tables

As with pivot tables in the user interface, Microsoft maintains tight control over a live pivot table. You need to be aware of these issues as your code is running on a sheet with a live pivot table.

Filling blank cells in the data area

It is a bit annoying that Excel puts blank cells in the data area of a pivot table. For example, in Figure 13-4, the Midwest region had no sales of a Speed Rail 8 Quart/Liter, so that cell (P15) appears blank instead of containing a zero.

You can override this in the Excel interface by using the For Empty Cells Show setting in the PivotTable Options dialog. The equivalent code is shown here:

```
PT.NullString = "0"
```

> **Note** The Excel macro recorder always wraps that zero in quotation marks. Regardless of whether you specify "0" or just 0, the blank cells in the data area of the pivot table have numeric zeros.

Filling blank cells in the row area

Excel 2010 added a much-needed setting to fill in the blank cells along the left columns of a pivot table. This problem happens any time that you have two or more fields in the row area of a pivot table. Rather than repeat a label such as "Bar Equipment" in cells N5:N18 in the pivot table shown previously in Figure 13-4, Microsoft traditionally has left those cells blank. To solve this problem in Excel, use the following line of code:

```
PT.RepeatAllLabels xlRepeatLabels
```

Preventing errors from inserting or deleting cells

You cannot use many Excel commands inside a pivot table. Inserting rows, deleting rows, and cutting and pasting parts of a pivot table are all against the rules.

Let's say you tried to delete the Grand Total column from column W in a pivot table. If you try to delete or clear column W, the macro comes to a screeching halt with a 1004 error, as shown in Figure 13-5.

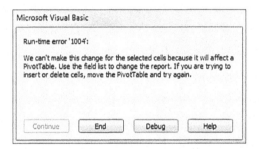

FIGURE 13-5 You cannot delete part of a pivot table.

There are two strategies for getting around this limitation. The first is to find if there is already an equivalent command in the pivot table interface. For example, you want to determine whether there is code to perform any of these actions:

- Remove the grand total column

- Remove the grand total row

- Add blank rows between each section

- Suppress subtotals for outer row fields

The second strategy is to convert the pivot table to values. You can then insert, cut, and clear as necessary.

Both strategies are discussed in the following sections.

Controlling totals

The default pivot table includes a grand total row and a grand total column. You can choose to hide one or both of these elements.

To remove the grand total column from the right side of the pivot table, use this:

```
PT.RowGrand = False
```

To remove the grand total row from the bottom of the pivot table, use this:

```
PT.ColumnGrand = False
```

Turning off the subtotal rows is surprisingly complex. This issue comes up when you have multiple fields in the row area. Excel automatically turns on subtotals for the outermost row fields.

> **Tip** Did you know that you can have a pivot table showing multiple subtotal rows? I have never seen anyone actually do this, but you can use the Field Settings dialog to specify that you want to see Sum, Average, Count, Max, Min, and so on. Figure 13-6 shows the Custom setting where you set this.
>
>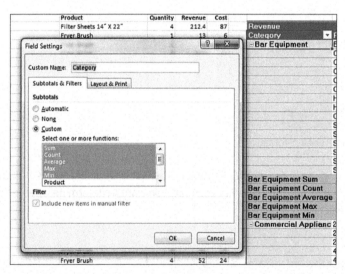
>
> **FIGURE 13-6** The Custom setting is rarely used, but the fact that you can specify multiple types of subtotals for a single field complicates the VBA code for suppressing subtotals.

To suppress the subtotals for a field, you must set the Subtotals property equal to an array of 12 False values. The first False turns off automatic subtotals, the second False turns off the Sum subtotal, the third False turns off the Count subtotal, and so on. This line of code suppresses the Category subtotal:

```
PT.PivotFields("Category").Subtotals = Array(False, False, False, False, _
    False, False, False, False, False, False, False, False)
```

A different technique is to turn on the first subtotal. This method automatically turns off the other 11 subtotals. You can then turn off the first subtotal to make sure all subtotals are suppressed:

```
PT.PivotFields("Category").Subtotals(1) = True
PT.PivotFields("Category").Subtotals(1) = False
```

> **Note** You might be wondering about the Distinct Count option introduced in Excel 2013. Does it force a twelfth position in the array? No. The Custom subtotals option is unavailable for pivot tables that use the Data Model, so you won't ever be able to choose Sum and Distinct Count together.

See "Using the Data Model in Excel" later in this chapter for an example of using Distinct Count.

Converting a pivot table to values

If you plan on converting a live pivot table to values, you need to copy the entire pivot table. How much space it will take might be tough to predict. For example, if you summarize transactional data every day, you might find that you do not have sales from one region on any given day. This can cause your table to be perhaps seven columns wide on some days and only six columns wide on other days.

Excel provides two range properties that you can use to refer to a pivot table. The TableRange2 property includes all the pivot table rows, including any Filter dropdowns at the top of the pivot table. The TableRange1 property starts just below the filter fields. It often includes the unnecessary row with Sum Of Revenue at the top of the pivot table.

If your goal is to convert a pivot table to values and not move the pivot table to a new place, you can use this code:

```
PT.TableRange2.Copy
PT.TableRange2.PasteSpecial xlPasteValuesAndNumberFormats
```

If you want to copy only the data section of the pivot table to a new location, you frequently use the Offset property to start one row lower than the top of TableRange2, like so:

```
PT.TableRange2.Offset(1,0).Copy
```

This reference skips the first row of headings since that row usually only contains the value field and column field names. It copies the remaining headings, the data, and one blank row.

Notice in Figure 13-7 that using Offset without .Resize causes one extra row to be copied. However, because that row is always blank, there is no need to use Resize to not copy the extra blank row.

The code copies PT.TableRange2 and uses PasteSpecial on a cell six rows below the current pivot table.

39	⊟Southwest	Bar Equipment	73,471	33,408
40	Southwest	Commercial Appliances	289,527	130,744
41	Southwest	Concession Equipment	355,845	159,486
42	Southwest	Fryers	267,408	120,208
43	Southwest	Ovens and Ranges	3,011,743	1,360,228
44	Southwest	Refrigerators and Coolers	3,233,297	1,459,587
45	Southwest	Warmers	1,154,938	522,652
46	⊟West	Bar Equipment	68,555	31,130
47	West	Commercial Appliances	296,216	133,680
48	West	Concession Equipment	421,420	189,303
49	West	Fryers	275,557	123,535
50	West	Ovens and Ranges	3,633,635	1,642,191
51	West	Refrigerators and Coolers	5,393,086	2,429,377
52	West	Warmers	1,715,528	776,228
53				
54				

Copied range includes extra row

FIGURE 13-7 An intermediate result of the macro. The pivot table plus one blank row has been copied.

You can then eliminate the pivot table by applying the Clear method to the entire table. If your code does additional formatting, you should remove the pivot cache from memory by setting PTCache equal to Nothing.

The code in Listing 13-2 uses a pivot table to summarize the underlying data. More than 80,000 rows are reduced to a tight 50-row summary. The resulting data is properly formatted for additional filtering, sorting, and so on. The pivot table is copied to static values at the end of the code, and the pivot table is cleared.

LISTING 13-2 Code to produce a static summary from a pivot table

```
Sub UsePivotToCreateValues()
    Dim WBO As Workbook
    Dim WSD As Worksheet
    Dim PT As PivotTable
    Dim FinalRow As Long
    Dim FinalCol As Long
    Dim PRange As Range
    Dim PTCache As PivotCache
    Dim StartRow As Long

    Set WBO = ActiveWorkbook
    Set WSD = WBO.Worksheets("Data")
    WSD.Select

    ' Delete any prior pivot tables
    For Each PT In WSD.PivotTables
        PT.TableRange2.Clear
    Next PT
    WSD.Range("N1:AZ1").EntireColumn.Clear

    ' Define input area and set up a Pivot Cache
    FinalRow = WSD.Cells(Application.Rows.Count, 1).End(xlUp).Row
```

```
    FinalCol = WSD.Cells(1, Application.Columns.Count). _
        End(xlToLeft).Column
    Set PRange = WSD.Cells(1, 1).Resize(FinalRow, FinalCol)
    Set PTCache = WBO.PivotCaches.Add(SourceType:= _
        xlDatabase, SourceData:=PRange.Address)

    ' Create the Pivot Table from the Pivot Cache
    Set PT = PTCache.CreatePivotTable(TableDestination:=WSD. _
        Cells(2, FinalCol + 2), TableName:="PivotTable1")

    ' Set up the row & column fields
    PT.AddFields RowFields:=Array("Region", "Category"), _
        ColumnFields:="Data"

    ' Set up the data fields
    With PT.PivotFields("Revenue")
        .Orientation = xlDataField
        .Function = xlSum
        .Position = 1
        .NumberFormat = "#,##0"
        .Name = "Revenue "
    End With

    With PT.PivotFields("Cost")
        .Orientation = xlDataField
        .Function = xlSum
        .Position = 2
        .NumberFormat = "#,##0"
        .Name = "COGS"
    End With

    ' Settings to create a solid block of data
    With PT
        .NullString = 0
        .RepeatAllLabels Repeat:=xlRepeatLabels
        .ColumnGrand = False
        .RowGrand = 0
        .PivotFields("Region").Subtotals(1) = True
        .PivotFields("Region").Subtotals(1) = False
    End With

    ' Copy the pivot table as values below the pivot table
    PT.TableRange2.Offset(1, 0).Copy
    PT.TableRange1.Cells(1, 1).Offset(PT.TableRange1.Rows.Count + 4, 0).PasteSpecial
xlPasteValuesAndNumberFormats
    StartRow = PT.TableRange1.Cells(1, 1).Offset(PT.TableRange1.Rows.Count + 5, 0).Row

    PT.TableRange1.Clear
    Set PTCache = Nothing

    WSD.Cells(StartRow, FinalCol + 2).Select
End Sub
```

The code in Listing 13-2 creates the pivot table. It then copies the results as values and pastes them below the original pivot table. In reality, you probably want to copy this report to another worksheet or another workbook. Examples later in this chapter introduce the code necessary for this.

So far, this chapter has walked you through building the simplest of pivot table reports. Pivot tables offer far more flexibility, though. Read on for more complex reporting examples.

Pivot table 201: Creating a report showing revenue by category

A typical report might provide a list of markets by category with revenue by year. This report could be given to product line managers to show them which markets are selling well. The report in Figure 13-8 is not a pivot table, but the macro to create the report used a pivot table to summarize the data. Regular Excel commands such as Subtotal finish off the report.

	A	B	C	D	E	F
1	**Revenue by Category & Region**					
2						
3	Category	Region	2029	2030	2031	Grand Total
4	Ovens and Ranges	South	15,672K	13,796K	8,284K	37,752K
5	Ovens and Ranges	Southeast	2,639K	2,745K	1,418K	6,802K
6	Ovens and Ranges	West	519K	1,520K	1,594K	3,634K
7	Ovens and Ranges	Southwest	572K	1,335K	1,104K	3,012K
8	Ovens and Ranges	Northeast	662K	1,146K	801K	2,609K
9	Ovens and Ranges	Midwest	290K	1,379K	760K	2,429K
10	Ovens and Ranges	North	247K	421K	263K	931K
11	**Ovens and Ranges Total**		20,602K	22,342K	14,225K	57,169K
12	Refrigerators and Coolers	South	4,855K	4,659K	12,093K	21,606K
13	Refrigerators and Coolers	West	1,957K	348K	3,088K	5,393K
14	Refrigerators and Coolers	Southeast	929K	1,311K	2,062K	4,302K

FIGURE 13-8 This report started as a pivot table but finished as a regular data set.

In this example, you want to show the markets in descending order by revenue, with years going across the columns. A sample pivot table report is shown in Figure 13-9.

Sum of Revenue		Years (De ▾)			
Category ▾	Region ▾	2029	2030	2031	Grand Total
⊟ Ovens and F	South	15,672K	13,796K	8,284K	37,752K
Ovens and F	Southeast	2,639K	2,745K	1,418K	6,802K
Ovens and F	West	519K	1,520K	1,594K	3,634K
Ovens and F	Southwest	572K	1,335K	1,104K	3,012K
Ovens and F	Northeast	662K	1,146K	801K	2,609K
Ovens and F	Midwest	290K	1,379K	760K	2,429K
Ovens and F	North	247K	421K	263K	931K
⊟ Refrigerators	South	4,855K	4,659K	12,093K	21,606K
Refrigerators	West	1,957K	348K	3,088K	5,393K

FIGURE 13-9 During the macro to create Figure 13-8, you will have this intermediate result as a pivot table.

There are some tricky issues involved in creating this pivot table:

- You have to roll the daily dates in the original data set up to years.

- You want to control the sort order of the row fields.

- You want to fill in blanks throughout the pivot table, use a better number format, and suppress the subtotals for the Category field.

The key to quickly producing this data is to use a pivot table. The default pivot table has some quirky problems that you can correct in the macro. To start, use VBA to build a pivot table with Category and Region as the row fields. Add Date as a column field. Add Revenue as a data field. Here's the code to do all this:

```
PT.AddFields RowFields:=Array("Category", "Region"), ColumnFields:="Date"

' Set up the data fields
With PT.PivotFields("Revenue")
    .Orientation = xlDataField
    .Function = xlSum
    .Position = 1
    .NumberFormat = "#,##0"
End With
```

Figure 13-10 shows the default pivot table created with these settings.

⊿	N	O	P	Q	R	S	T
2	Sum of Revenu		Date	▾			
3	Category ▾	Region ▾	1/2/2029	1/3/2029	1/4/2029	1/5/2029	1/6/2029
4	⊟ Bar Equipme	West					
5		Midwest					
6		North					
7		Northeast					
8		South					
9		Southeast					
10		Southwest					
11	Bar Equipment Total						
12	⊟ Commercial	West	829				829
13		Midwest	838				

FIGURE 13-10 By default, the initial report has many problems.

Here are just a few of the annoyances that most pivot tables present in their default state:

- The outline view is horrible. In Figure 13-10, the value Bar Equipment appears in the product column only once and is followed by six blank cells. Thankfully, Excel offers the RepeatAllLabels method to correct this problem. If you intend to repurpose the data, you need the row labels to be repeated on every row.

- Because the original data set contains daily dates, the default pivot table has more than 1,000 columns of daily data. No one can process this report. You need to roll those daily dates up to years. Pivot tables make this easy.

- The report contains blank cells instead of zeros. In Figure 13-10, the entire visible range of Bar Equipment is blank. These cells should contain zeros instead of blanks.

- The title is boring. Most people would agree that Sum Of Revenue is an annoying title.

- Some captions are extraneous. The word "Date" floating in cell P2 of Figure 13-10 does not belong in a report.

- The default alphabetical sort order is rarely useful. Product line managers will want the top markets at the top of the list. It would be helpful to have the report sorted in descending order by revenue.

- The borders are ugly. Excel draws in myriad borders that make the report look awful.

- Pivot tables offer no intelligent page break logic. If you want to produce one report for each product line manager, there is no fast method for indicating that each product should be on a new page.

- Because of the page break problem, you might find it easier to do away with the pivot table's subtotal rows and have the Subtotal method add subtotal rows with page breaks. You need a way to turn off the pivot table subtotal rows offered for Category in Figure 13-10. These rows show up automatically whenever you have two or more row fields. If you had four row fields, you would want to turn off the automatic subtotals for the three outermost row fields.

Even with all these problems in default pivot tables, default pivot tables are still the way to go. You can overcome each complaint by using special settings within the pivot table or by entering a few lines of code after the pivot table is created and then copied to a regular data set.

Ensuring that Tabular layout is used

In legacy versions of Excel, multiple row fields appeared in multiple columns. Three layouts are now available. The Compact layout squeezes all the row fields into a single column. The Compact layout is the default when a pivot table is created in the Excel interface. Currently, when you create a pivot table in VBA, the default is the Tabular layout. However, Microsoft will correct this discrepancy in some future version, so get in the habit of explicitly changing the layout to a Tabular layout with this code:

```
PT.RowAxisLayout xlTabularRow
```

Rolling daily dates up to years

With transactional data, you often find your date-based summaries having one row per day. Although daily data might be useful to a plant manager, many people in the company want to see totals by month, quarter, or year.

The great news is that Excel handles the summarization of dates in a pivot table with ease. If you have ever had to use the arcane formula =A2+1-Day(A2) to change daily dates into monthly dates, you will appreciate the ease with which you can group transactional data into months or quarters.

Creating a date group with VBA is a bit quirky. The Group method can be applied to only a single cell in the pivot table, and that cell must contain a date or the Date field label.

In Figure 13-10, you would have to select either the Date heading in cell P2 or one of the dates in cells P3:AOZ3. Selecting one of these specific cells is risky, particularly if the pivot table later starts being created in a new column. Two other options are more reliable.

First, if you will never use a different number of row fields, you can assume that the Date heading is in row 1, column 3 of the area known as TableRange2. The following line of code selects this cell:

```
PT.TableRange2.Cells(1, 3).Select
```

You should probably add a comment that you need to edit the 3 in that line to another number any time you change the number of row fields.

Another solution is to use the LabelRange property for the Date field. The following code always selects the cell containing the Date heading:

```
PT.PivotFields("Date").LabelRange.Select
```

To group the daily dates up to yearly dates, you should define a pivot table with Date in the row field. Turn off ManualUpdate to enable the pivot table to be drawn. You can then use the LabelRange property to locate the date label.

You use the Group method on the date label cell. You specify an array of seven Boolean values for the Periods argument. The seven values correspond to seconds, minutes, hours, days, months, quarters, and years. For example, to group by years, you would use this:

```
PT.PivotFields("Date"),LabelRange.Cells(2,1).Group _
    Periods:=(False, False, False, False, False, False, True)
```

After you have grouped by years, the field is still called Date. This differs from the results when you group by multiple fields. To group by months, quarters, and years, you would use this:

```
PT.PivotFields("Date"),LabelRange.Cells(2,1).Group _
    Periods:=(False, False, False, False, True, True, True)
```

After you have grouped up to months, quarters, and years, the Date field starts referring to months. Two new virtual fields are available in the pivot table: Quarters and Years.

To group by weeks, you choose only the Day period and then use the By argument to group into seven-day periods:

```
PT.PivotFields("Date"),LabelRange.Cells(2,1).Group By:=7_
    Periods:=(False, False, False, True, False, False, False)
```

In Figure 13-10, the goal is to group the daily dates up to years, so the following code is used:

```
PT.PivotFields("Date"),LabelRange.Cells(2,1).Group _
    Periods:=(False, False, False, False, False, False, True)
```

Figure 13-11 shows the pivot table after grouping the daily dates up to years.

	N	O	P	Q	R	S
2	Sum of Revenu		Years (Date) ▾			
3	Category ▾	Region ▾	2029	2030	2031	Grand Total
4	⊟ Bar Equipme	West		1,337	67,218	68,555
5		Midwest		22,113	41,508	63,621
6		North		5,950	14,195	20,145
7		Northeast		30,683	37,622	68,305
8		South		667,438	523,901	1,191,339
9		Southeast		165,241	118,655	283,896
10		Southwest		18,652	54,819	73,471
11	Bar Equipment Total			911,416	857,917	1,769,332
12	⊟ Commercial	West	9,182	58,739	228,295	296,216

FIGURE 13-11 Daily dates have been rolled up to years by using the Group method.

Eliminating blank cells

The blank cells in a pivot table are annoying. You will want to fix two kinds of blank cells. Blank cells occur in the Values area when there are no records for a particular combination. For example, in Figure 13-11, the company did not sell bar equipment in 2029, so all cells P4:P11 are blank. Most people would prefer to have zeros instead of those blank cells.

Blank cells also occur in the Row Labels area when you have multiple row fields. The words "Bar Equipment" appear in cell N4, but then cells N5:N10 are blank.

To replace blanks in the Values area with zeros, use this:

```
PT.NullString = "0"
```

> **Note** Although the preceding code appears to use a zero inside quotation marks, Excel actually puts a numeric zero in the empty cells.

To fill in the blanks in the label area in Excel, use this:

```
PT.RepeatAllLabels xlRepeatLabels
```

The RepeatAllLabels code fails in Excel 2007 and earlier. The only solution in legacy versions of Excel is to convert the pivot table to values and then set the blank cells to a formula that grabs the value from the row above, like this:

```
Dim FillRange As Range
Set PT = ActiveSheet.PivotTables("PivotTable1")
' Locate outer row column
Set FillRange = PT.TableRange1.Resize(' 1)
' Convert entire table to values
PT.TableRange2.Copy
PT.TableRange2.PasteSpecial xlPasteValues
' Fill Special Cells Blanks with the value from above
```

```
FillRange.SpecialCells(xlCellTypeBlanks).FormulaR1C1 = _
    "=R[-1]C"
' Convert those formulas to values
FillRange.Value = FillRange.Value
```

Controlling the sort order with AutoSort

The Excel user interface offers an AutoSort option to sort a field in descending order based on revenue. The equivalent code in VBA to sort the region and category fields by descending revenue uses the AutoSort method:

```
PT.PivotFields("Region").AutoSort Order:=xlDescending, _
    Field:="Sum of Revenue"
PT.PivotFields("Category").AutoSort Order:=xlDescending, _
    Field:="Sum of Revenue"
```

Changing the default number format

Numbers in the Values area of a pivot table need to have a suitable number format applied. You cannot count on the numeric format of the underlying field carrying over to the pivot table.

To show the Revenue values with zero decimal places and a comma, use this:

```
PT.PivotFields("Sum of Revenue").NumberFormat = "#,##0"
```

Some companies have customers who typically buy thousands or millions of dollars' worth of goods. You can display numbers in thousands by using a single comma after the number format. To do this, you would include a K abbreviation to indicate that the numbers are in thousands:

```
PT.PivotFields("Sum of Revenue").NumberFormat = "#,##0,K"
```

Local custom dictates the thousands abbreviation. Suppose you are working for a relatively young computer company where everyone uses K for the thousands separator. In that case, you are in luck because Microsoft makes it easy to use this abbreviation. However, if you work at a more than 100-year-old soap company where you use M for thousands and MM for millions, you have a few more hurdles to jump. You must prefix the M character with a backslash to have it work:

```
PT.PivotFields("Sum of Revenue").NumberFormat = "#,##0,\M"
```

Alternatively, you can surround the M character with double quotation marks. To put double quotation marks inside a quoted string in VBA, you must use two sequential quotation marks. To set up a format in tenths of millions that use the #,##0.0,,"MM" format, you would use this line of code:

```
PT.PivotFields("Sum of Revenue").NumberFormat = "#,##0.0,,""M"""
```

Here, the format is quotation mark, pound, comma, pound, pound, zero, period, zero, comma, comma, quotation mark, quotation mark, M, quotation mark, quotation mark, quotation mark. The three quotation marks at the end are correct. You use two quotation marks to simulate typing one quotation mark in the custom number format box and a final quotation mark to close the string in VBA.

Figure 13-12 shows the pivot table blanks filled in, numbers shown in thousands, and category and region sorted in descending order.

	N	O	P	Q	R	S
2	Sum of Revenu		Years (Date) ▾			
3	Category ↓	Region ↓	2029	2030	2031	Grand Total
4	⊟Ovens and F	South	15,672K	13,796K	8,284K	37,752K
5	Ovens and F	Southeast	2,639K	2,745K	1,418K	6,802K
6	Ovens and F	West	519K	1,520K	1,594K	3,634K
7	Ovens and F	Southwest	572K	1,335K	1,104K	3,012K
8	Ovens and F	Northeast	662K	1,146K	801K	2,609K
9	Ovens and F	Midwest	290K	1,379K	760K	2,429K
10	Ovens and F	North	247K	421K	263K	931K
11	Ovens and Ranges Total		20,602K	22,342K	14,225K	57,169K
12	⊟Refrigerators	South	4,855K	4,659K	12,093K	21,606K

FIGURE 13-12 After filling in blanks and sorting, you have only a few extraneous totals and labels to remove.

Suppressing subtotals for multiple row fields

As soon as you have more than one row field, Excel automatically adds subtotals for all but the inner-most row field. That extra row field can get in the way if you plan on reusing the pivot table results as a new data set for some other purpose.

In the current example, you have taken 80,000 rows of data and produced a tight 50-row summary of yearly sales by category and region. That new data set would be interesting for sorting, filtering, and charting if you could remove the total row and the category subtotals.

To remove the subtotal, you first set the Subtotals(1) property to True to turn off the other 10 possible subtotals. You can then turn off the first subtotal to make sure that all subtotals are suppressed:

```
PT.PivotFields("Category").Subtotals(1) = True
PT.PivotFields("Category").Subtotals(1) = False
```

To remove the grand total row, use this:

```
PT.ColumnGrand = False
```

Figure 13-13 shows the first section of the pivot table with the subtotals removed.

	N	O	P	Q	R	S
2	Sum of Revenu		Years (Date) ▾			
3	Category ↓	Region ↓	2029	2030	2031	Grand Total
4	⊟Ovens and F	South	15,672K	13,796K	8,284K	37,752K
5	Ovens and F	Southeast	2,639K	2,745K	1,418K	6,802K
6	Ovens and F	West	519K	1,520K	1,594K	3,634K
7	Ovens and F	Southwest	572K	1,335K	1,104K	3,012K
8	Ovens and F	Northeast	662K	1,146K	801K	2,609K
9	Ovens and F	Midwest	290K	1,379K	760K	2,429K
10	Ovens and F	North	247K	421K	263K	931K
11	⊟Refrigerators	South	4,855K	4,659K	12,093K	21,606K

FIGURE 13-13 Remove the subtotal rows from column A.

Copying a finished pivot table as values to a new workbook

If you plan to repurpose the results of a pivot table, you need to convert the table to values. This section shows you how to copy a pivot table to a brand-new workbook.

To make the code more portable, assign object variables to the original workbook, the new workbook, and the first worksheet in the new workbook. At the top of the procedure, add these statements:

```
Dim WSR As Worksheet
Dim WSD As Worksheet
Dim WBO As Workbook
Dim WBN As Workbook
Set WBO = ActiveWorkbook
Set WSD = Worksheets("Data")
```

After the pivot table has been successfully created, build a blank report workbook with this code:

```
' Create a New Blank Workbook with one Worksheet
Set WBN = Workbooks.Add(xlWorksheet)
Set WSR = WBN.Worksheets(1)
WSR.Name = "Report"
' Set up Title for Report
With WSR.Range("A1")
    .Value = "Revenue by Category, Region and Year"
    .Style = "Title"
End With
```

There are a few remaining annoyances in the pivot table. The borders are annoying, and there are stray labels such as Sum Of Revenue and Date in the first row of the pivot table. You can solve these problems by excluding the first row(s) of PT.TableRange2 from the Copy method and then using PasteSpecial(xlPasteValuesAndNumberFormats) to copy the data to the report sheet.

In the current example, the TableRange2 property includes only one row to eliminate, row 2, as shown in Figure 13-13. If you had a more complex pivot table with several column fields and/or one or more page fields, you would have to eliminate more than just the first row of the report. It helps to run your macro to this point, look at the result, and figure out how many rows you need to delete. You can effectively not copy these rows to the report by using the Offset property. Then copy the TableRange2 property, offset by one row.

Purists will note that this code copies one extra blank row from below the pivot table, but this really does not matter because the row is blank. After copying, you can erase the original pivot table and destroy the pivot cache like this:

```
' Copy the Pivot Table data to row 3 of the Report sheet
' Use Offset to eliminate the title row of the pivot table
PT.TableRange2.Offset(1, 0).Copy
WSR. Range("A3").PasteSpecial Paste:=xlPasteValuesAndNumberFormats
PT.TableRange1.Clear
Set PTCache = Nothing
```

> **Tip** Note that you use the Paste Special option to paste just values and number formats. This gets rid of both borders and the pivot nature of the table. You might be tempted to use the All Except Borders option under Paste, but that keeps the data in a pivot table, and you will not be able to insert new rows in the middle of the data.

Handling final formatting

The last steps for the report involve some basic formatting tasks and the addition of the subtotals. You can bold and right-justify the headings in row 3. Set up rows 1–3 so that the top three rows print on each page:

```
' Do some basic formatting
' Autofit columns, format the headings , right-align
Range("A3").EntireRow.Style = "Heading 4"
Range("A3").CurrentRegion.Columns.AutoFit
Range("A3").EntireRow.HorizontalAlignment = xlRight
Range("A3:B3").HorizontalAlignment = xlLeft
  ' Repeat rows 1-3 at the top of each page
WSR.PageSetup.PrintTitleRows = "$1:$3"
```

Adding subtotals to get page breaks

The Data tab offers a powerful feature: subtotals. Figure 13-14 shows the Subtotal dialog. Note the Page Break Between Groups option. You can apply them in one command using the Subtotal method rather than looping through records to add a page break after each category manually.

If you were sure that you would always have three years and a total, you could use the following code to add subtotals for each line-of-business group:

```
' Add Subtotals by Category.
' Be sure to add a page break at each change in category
Selection.Subtotal GroupBy:=1, Function:=xlSum, _
    TotalList:=Array(3, 4, 5, 6), PageBreaks:=True
```

However, this code fails if you have more or less than three years. The solution is to use the following convoluted code to dynamically build a list of the columns to total, based on the number of columns in the report:

```
Dim TotColumns()
Dim I as Integer
FinalCol = Cells(3, Columns.Count).End(xlToLeft).Column
ReDim Preserve TotColumns(1 To FinalCol - 2)
For I = 3 To FinalCol
    TotColumns(i-2) = i
Next i
Selection.Subtotal GroupBy:=1, Function:=xlSum, TotalList:=TotColumns,_
    Replace:=True, PageBreaks:=True, SummaryBelowData:=True
```

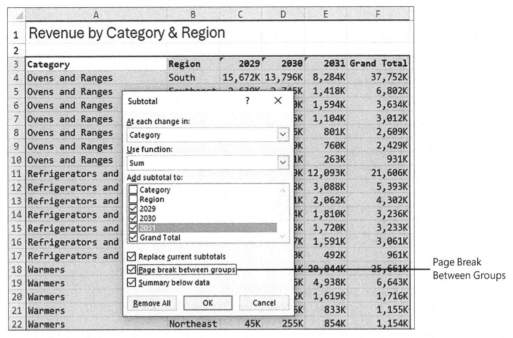

FIGURE 13-14 Using automatic subtotals enables you to add a page break after each category. Using this feature ensures that each category manager has a clean report with only their data in it.

Finally, with the new totals added to the report, you need to AutoFit the numeric columns again with this code:

```
Dim GrandRow as Long
' Make sure the columns are wide enough for totals
GrandRow = Cells(Rows.Count, 1).End(xlUp).Row
Cells(3, 3).Resize(GrandRow- 2, FinalCol- 2).Columns.AutoFit
Cells(GrandRow, 3).Resize(1, FinalCol- 2).NumberFormat = "#,##0,K"
' Add a page break before the Grand Total row, otherwise
' the manager for the final category will have two totals
WSR.hPageBreaks.Add Before:=Cells(GrandRow, 1)
```

Putting it all together

Listing 13-3 produces the product line manager reports in a few seconds. Figure 13-15 shows the report produced by this code.

LISTING 13-3   Code that produces the category report in Figure 13-15

```
Sub CategoryRegionReport()
    ' Category and Region as Row
    ' Years as Column
    Dim WBO As Workbook
    Dim WSD As Worksheet
    Dim PT As PivotTable
```

```vba
Dim FinalRow As Long
Dim FinalCol As Long
Dim PRange As Range
Dim PTCache As PivotCache
Dim TotColumns()
Dim WSR As Worksheet
Dim WBN As Workbook
Dim i As Long
Dim GrandRow As Long

Set WBO = ActiveWorkbook
Set WSD = WBO.Worksheets("Data")
WSD.Select

' Delete any prior pivot tables
For Each PT In WSD.PivotTables
    PT.TableRange2.Clear
Next PT
WSD.Range("N1:XFD1").EntireColumn.Clear

' Define input area and set up a Pivot Cache
FinalRow = WSD.Cells(Application.Rows.Count, 1).End(xlUp).Row
FinalCol = WSD.Cells(1, Application.Columns.Count). _
    End(xlToLeft).Column
Set PRange = WSD.Cells(1, 1).Resize(FinalRow, FinalCol)
Set PTCache = WBO.PivotCaches.Add(SourceType:= _
    xlDatabase, SourceData:=PRange.Address)

' Create the Pivot Table from the Pivot Cache
Set PT = PTCache.CreatePivotTable(TableDestination:=WSD. _
    Cells(2, FinalCol + 2), TableName:="PivotTable1")

' Set up the row fields
PT.AddFields RowFields:=Array("Category", _
    "Region"), ColumnFields:="Date"

' Set up the data fields
With PT.PivotFields("Revenue")
    .Orientation = xlDataField
    .Function = xlSum
    .Position = 1
    .NumberFormat = "#,##0"
End With

' Ensure tabular layout is used
PT.RowAxisLayout xlTabularRow

PT.PivotFields("Date").LabelRange.Group _
    Periods:=Array(False, False, False, False, False, False, True)

' Change number format of Revenue
PT.PivotFields("Sum of Revenue").NumberFormat = "#,##0,K"
```

```
' Fill in blank cells
PT.NullString = "0"
PT.RepeatAllLabels xlRepeatLabels

' Sort both label fields by descending revenue
PT.PivotFields("Category").AutoSort Order:=xlDescending, _
    field:="Sum of Revenue"
PT.PivotFields("Region").AutoSort Order:=xlDescending, _
    field:="Sum of Revenue"

' Suppress Category totals
PT.PivotFields("Category").Subtotals(1) = True
PT.PivotFields("Category").Subtotals(1) = False
PT.ColumnGrand = False

' Create a New Blank Workbook with one Worksheet
Set WBN = Workbooks.Add(xlWorksheet)
Set WSR = WBN.Worksheets(1)
WSR.Name = "Report"
' Set up Title for Report
With WSR.[A1]
    .Value = "Revenue by Category & Region"
    .Style = "Title"
End With

' Copy the Pivot Table data to row 3 of the Report sheet
' Use Offset to eliminate the title row of the pivot table
PT.TableRange2.Offset(1, 0).Copy
WSR.[A3].PasteSpecial Paste:=xlPasteValuesAndNumberFormats
PT.TableRange2.Clear
Set PTCache = Nothing

' Do some basic formatting
' Autofit columns, bold the headings, right-align
WSR.Range("A3").EntireRow.Style = "Heading 4"
WSR.Range("A3").CurrentRegion.Columns.AutoFit
WSR.Range("A3").EntireRow.HorizontalAlignment = xlRight
WSR.Range("A3:B3").HorizontalAlignment = xlLeft

' Repeat rows 1-3 at the top of each page
WSR.PageSetup.PrintTitleRows = "$1:$3"

' Add subtotals
FinalCol = WSR.Cells(3, 255).End(xlToLeft).Column
ReDim Preserve TotColumns(1 To FinalCol - 2)
For i = 3 To FinalCol
    TotColumns(i - 2) = i
Next i
WSR.Range("A3").CurrentRegion.Subtotal GroupBy:=1, Function:=xlSum, _
    TotalList:=TotColumns, Replace:=True, _
    PageBreaks:=True, SummaryBelowData:=True
```

```
' Make sure the columns are wide enough for totals
GrandRow = WSR.Cells(Rows.Count, 1).End(xlUp).Row
WSR.Cells(3, 3).Resize(GrandRow - 2, FinalCol - 2).Columns.AutoFit
WSR.Cells(GrandRow, 3).Resize(1, FinalCol - 2).NumberFormat = "#,##0,K"
' Add a page break before the Grand Total row, otherwise
' the product manager for the final Line will have two totals
WSR.HPageBreaks.Add Before:=Cells(GrandRow, 1)
End Sub
```

	A	B	C	D	E	F
1	Revenue by Category & Region					
2						
3	Category	Region	2029	2030	2031	Grand Total
4	Ovens and Ranges	South	15,672K	13,796K	8,284K	37,752K
5	Ovens and Ranges	Southeast	2,639K	2,745K	1,418K	6,802K
6	Ovens and Ranges	West	519K	1,520K	1,594K	3,634K
7	Ovens and Ranges	Southwest	572K	1,335K	1,104K	3,012K
8	Ovens and Ranges	Northeast	662K	1,146K	801K	2,609K
9	Ovens and Ranges	Midwest	290K	1,379K	760K	2,429K
10	Ovens and Ranges	North	247K	421K	263K	931K
11	**Ovens and Ranges Total**		20,602K	22,342K	14,225K	57,169K
12	Refrigerators and Coolers	South	4,855K	4,659K	12,093K	21,606K
13	Refrigerators and Coolers	West	1,957K	348K	3,088K	5,393K
14	Refrigerators and Coolers	Southeast	929K	1,311K	2,062K	4,302K
15	Refrigerators and Coolers	Midwest	882K	544K	1,810K	3,236K
16	Refrigerators and Coolers	Southwest	1,071K	443K	1,720K	3,233K
17	Refrigerators and Coolers	Northeast	1,043K	427K	1,591K	3,061K
18	Refrigerators and Coolers	North	369K	100K	492K	961K
19	**Refrigerators and Coolers Total**		11,105K	7,833K	22,856K	41,794K
20	Warmers	South	456K	5,161K	20,044K	25,661K

FIGURE 13-15 Converting 80,000 rows of transactional data to this useful report takes less than 2 seconds if you use the code that produced this example. Without pivot tables, the code would be far more complex.

You have now seen the VBA code to produce useful summary reports from transactional data. The next section deals with additional features in pivot tables.

Calculating with a pivot table

So far in this chapter, the pivot tables have presented a single field in the Values area, and that field has always shown as a Sum calculation. You can add more fields to the Values area. You can change from Sum to any of 11 functions or alter the Sum calculation to display running totals, percentage of total, and more. You can also add new calculated fields or calculated items to the pivot table.

Addressing issues with two or more data fields

It is possible to have multiple fields in the Values section of a pivot report. For example, you might have Quantity, Revenue, and Cost in the same pivot table.

The value fields go across the columns when you have two or more data fields in an Excel pivot table that you built in the Excel interface. However, VBA builds the pivot table with the Values fields going down the innermost row field. This creates a bizarre-looking table like the one shown in Figure 13-16.

	N	O	P
1			
2	State	Data	Total
3	AL	Sum of Revenue	752,789.55
4		Sum of Cost	337,502.00
5		Sum of Quantity	1,890
6	AR	Sum of Revenue	134,244.75
7		Sum of Cost	59,499.00
8		Sum of Quantity	130
9	AZ	Sum of Revenue	3,687,831.25
10		Sum of Cost	1,665,417.00
11		Sum of Quantity	6,950
12	CA	Sum of Revenue	11,322,124.25
13		Sum of Cost	5,108,375.00

FIGURE 13-16 This ugly view was banished in the Excel interface after Excel 2003, but VBA still produces it by default.

To correct this problem, you should specify that a virtual field called Data is one of the column fields.

Note In this instance, note that Data is not a column in your original data; it is a special name used to indicate the orientation of the multiple Values fields.

To have multiple Values fields go across the report, use this code:

```
PT.AddFields RowFields:="State", ColumnFields:="Data"
```

After adding a column field called Data, you then define multiple data fields:

```
' Set up the data fields
With PT.PivotFields("Revenue")
    .Orientation = xlDataField
    .Function = xlSum
    .Position = 1
    .NumberFormat = "#,##0.00"
End With

With PT.PivotFields("Cost")
    .Orientation = xlDataField
    .Function = xlSum
    .Position = 2
    .NumberFormat = "#,##0.00"
End With

With PT.PivotFields("Quantity")
    .Orientation = xlDataField
```

```
      .Function = xlSum
      .Position = 3
      .NumberFormat = "#,##0"
   End With
```

This code produces the pivot table shown in Figure 13-17.

	N	O	P	Q
1				
2		Data		
3	State	Sum of Revenue	Sum of Cost	Sum of Quantity
4	AL	752,789.55	337,502.00	1,890
5	AR	134,244.75	59,499.00	130
6	AZ	3,687,831.25	1,665,417.00	6,950
7	CA	11,322,124.25	5,108,375.00	14,585
8	CO	1,280,417.15	580,449.00	1,730
9	FL	65,272,493.30	29,399,753.00	103,763
10	GA	27,955,642.10	12,582,085.00	48,897
11	IA	816,462.00	368,449.00	950

FIGURE 13-17 When you specify the virtual field Data as a column field, multiple values go across the report.

Using calculations other than Sum

So far, all the pivot tables in this chapter have used the Sum function to calculate. There are 11 functions available, including Sum. To specify a different calculation, specify one of these values as the Function property:

- **xlAverage**—Average

- **xlCount**—Count

- **xlCountNums**—Count numeric values only

- **xlMax**—Maximum

- **xlMin**—Minimum

- **xlProduct**—Multiply

- **xlStDev**—Standard deviation, based on a sample

- **xlStDevP**—Standard deviation, based on the whole population

- **xlSum**—Sum

- **xlVar**—Variation, based on a sample

- **xlVarP**—Variation, based on the whole population

Although Count Distinct was added in Excel 2013, you cannot create Count Distinct in a regular pivot-cache pivot table. See "Using the Data Model in Excel" at the end of this chapter.

> **Tip** Note that when you add a field to the Values area of the pivot table, Excel modifies the field name with the function name and the word *of.* For example, `Revenue` becomes `Sum Of Revenue`, and `Cost` might become `StdDev Of Cost`. If you later need to refer to those fields in your code, you need to do so using the new name, such as `Average Of Quantity`.

You can improve the look of your pivot table by changing the `Name` property of the field. If you do not want `Sum Of Revenue` appearing in the pivot table, change the `Caption` property to something like `Total Revenue`. This sounds less awkward than `Sum Of Revenue`. Remember that you cannot have a name that exactly matches an existing field name in the pivot table, so `Revenue` is not suitable as a name. However, `Revenue ` (with a trailing space) is fine to use as a name.

For text fields, the only function that makes sense is a count. You will frequently count the number of records by adding a text field to the pivot table and using the `COUNT` function.

The following code fragment calculates total revenue, a count of records by counting a text field, and average quantity:

```
With PT.PivotFields("Revenue")
     .Orientation = xlDataField
     .Function = xlSum
     .Position = 1
     .NumberFormat = "$#,##0.00"
     .Name = "Revenue"
End With

With PT.PivotFields("Customer")
     .Orientation = xlDataField
     .Function = xlCount
     .Position = 2
     .NumberFormat = "#,##0"
     .Name = "# of Records"
End With

With PT.PivotFields("Revenue")
     .Orientation = xlDataField
     .Function = xlAverage
     .Position = 3
     .NumberFormat = "#,##0.00"
     .Name = "Average Revenue"
End With
' Ensure that we get zeros instead of blanks in the data area
PT.NullString = "0"
PT.TableStyle2 = "PivotStyleMedium3"
```

Figure 13-18 shows the pivot table this code creates.

FIGURE 13-18 You can change the function used to summarize columns in the Values area of the pivot table.

Using calculated data fields

Pivot tables offer two types of formulas. The most useful type defines a formula for a calculated field. This adds a new field to the pivot table. Calculations for calculated fields are always done at the summary level.

To set up a calculated field, use the Add method with the CalculatedFields object. You have to specify a field name and a formula, like so:

```
PT.CalculatedFields.Add Name:="GrossProfit", Formula:="=Revenue-Cost"
PT.CalculatedFields.Add "GP_Pct", "=GrossProfit/Revenue"
```

After you define the field, add it as a data field:

```
With PT.PivotFields("GrossProfit")
    .Orientation = xlDataField
    .Function = xlSum
    .Position = 3
    .NumberFormat = "$#,##0"
    .Caption = "Gross Profit"
End With
With PT.PivotFields("GP_Pct")
    .Orientation = xlDataField
    .Function = xlSum
    .Position = 4
    .NumberFormat = "0.0%"
    .Caption = "GP%"
End With
```

Figure 13-19 shows the Gross Profit calculated field.

FIGURE 13-19 A calculated field adds Gross Profit to the pivot table.

A calculated field can be referenced in subsequent calculated fields. The following code uses the Gross Profit field to calculate `Gross Profit Percent`. Although the `Caption` property renamed the field to Gross Profit (with a space in the middle), the field name in the preceding code is `GrossProfit` (without a space). Use the field name in the following calculation:

```
PT.CalculatedFields.Add "GP_Pct", "=GrossProfit/Revenue", True
With PT.PivotFields("GP_Pct")
    .Orientation = xlDataField
    .Function = xlSum
    .Position = 4
    .NumberFormat = "0.0%"
    .Caption = "GP%"
End With
```

Figure 13-20 shows a report with GP%.

Category	Data			
	Sum of Revenue	Sum of Cost	Gross Profit	GP%
Bar Equipment	$1,769,332	$799,967	$969,365	54.8%
Commercial Appliances	$8,562,837	$3,848,608	$4,714,229	55.1%
Concession Equipment	$9,876,342	$4,436,685	$5,439,657	55.1%
Fryers	$3,835,963	$1,723,930	$2,112,033	55.1%
Ovens and Ranges	$57,168,593	$25,787,407	$31,381,186	54.9%
Refrigerators and Coolers	$41,793,565	$18,828,219	$22,965,346	54.9%
Warmers	$37,482,133	$16,876,630	$20,605,503	55.0%
Grand Total	$160,488,764	$72,301,446	$88,187,318	54.9%

FIGURE 13-20 GP% is based on a field in the data set and another calculated field.

Using calculated items

Calculated items have the potential to produce incorrect results in a pivot table. Say that you have a report of sales by nine states. You want to show a subtotal of four of the states. A calculated item would add a ninth item to the state column. Although the pivot table gladly calculates this new item, it causes the grand total to appear overstated.

Figure 13-21 shows a pivot table with these nine states. The total revenue is $10 million. When a calculated item provides a subtotal of four states (see Figure 13-22), the grand total increases to $15 million. This means that the items that make up the calculated item are included in the total twice. If you like restating numbers to the Securities and Exchange Commission, feel free to use calculated items.

Revenue	
State	Total
Arizona	$550,550
California	$3,165,104
Colorado	$616,097
Louisiana	$814,431
Nevada	$1,170,320
New Mexico	$322,168
Oklahoma	$186,715
Texas	$2,559,021
Utah	$632,897
Grand Total	$10,017,303

FIGURE 13-21 This pivot table adds up to $10 million.

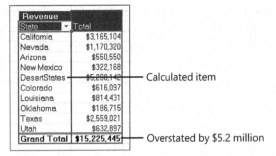

Calculated item

Overstated by $5.2 million

FIGURE 13-22 Add a calculated item, and the total is overstated.

The code to produce the calculated item is shown here. Calculated items are added as the final position along the field, so this code changes the `Position` property to move the `DesertStates` item to the proper position:

```
PT.PivotFields("State").CalculatedItems.Add _
    Name:="DesertStates", _
    Formula:="=California +Nevada +Arizona +'New Mexico'"
PT.PivotFields("State").PivotItems("California").Position = 1
PT.PivotFields("State").PivotItems("Nevada").Position = 2
PT.PivotFields("State").PivotItems("Arizona").Position = 3
PT.PivotFields("State").PivotItems("New Mexico").Position = 4
PT.PivotFields("State").PivotItems("DesertStates").Position = 5
```

If you hope to use a calculated item, you should either remove the grand total row or remove the four states that go into the calculated item. This code hides the four states, and the resulting pivot table returns to the correct total, as shown in Figure 13-23:

```
PT.PivotFields("State").CalculatedItems.Add _
    Name:="DesertStates", _
    Formula:="=California +Nevada +Arizona +'New Mexico'"
' Hide the items included in the new subtotal
With PT.PivotFields("State")
    .PivotItems("California").Visible = False
    .PivotItems("Nevada").Visible = False
    .PivotItems("Arizona").Visible = False
    .PivotItems("New Mexico").Visible = False
End With
```

Revenue	
State	Total
DesertStates	$5,208,142
Colorado	$616,097
Louisiana	$814,431
Oklahoma	$186,715
Texas	$2,559,021
Utah	$632,897
Grand Total	$10,017,303

FIGURE 13-23 One way to use a calculated item is to remove any elements that went into it.

A better solution, which is discussed in the next section, is to skip calculated items and use text grouping.

Calculating groups

If you need to calculate subtotals for certain regions, a better solution is to use text grouping to define the groups. If you group the four states, Excel adds a new field to the row area of the pivot table. Although this process requires some special handling, it is worthwhile and creates a nice-looking report.

To group four states in the Excel interface, you select the cells that contain those four states and select Group Selection from the PivotTable Tools Options tab. This immediately does several things:

- The items in the group are moved together in the row area.

- A new field is added to the left of the state field. If the original field was called State, the new field is called State2.

- Annoyingly, the subtotals property for the new State2 field is set to None instead of Automatic.

- A subtotal for the selected items is added with the Group1 name.

- Any items that are not in a group have a new subtotal added to State2 with the state name repeated.

In VBA, it is somewhat tricky to select the cells that contain the proper states. The following code uses the LabelRange property to point to the cells and then uses the Union method to refer to the four noncontiguous cells:

```
Set R1 = PT.PivotFields("State").PivotItems("California").LabelRange
Set R2 = PT.PivotFields("State").PivotItems("Arizona").LabelRange
Set R3 = PT.PivotFields("State").PivotItems("New Mexico").LabelRange
Set R4 = PT.PivotFields("State").PivotItems("Nevada").LabelRange
Union(R1, R2, R3, R4).Group
```

After setting up the first group, rename the newly created States2 field to have a suitable name:

```
PT.PivotFields("State2").Caption = "State Group"
```

Then, change the name of this region from Group1 to the desired group name:

```
PT.PivotFields("State Group").PivotItems("Group1").Caption = "Desert States"
```

Change the Subtotals property from None to Automatic:

```
PT.PivotFields("State Group").Subtotals(1) = True
```

After you have set up the first group, you can define the remaining groups with this code:

```
Set R1 = PT.PivotFields("State").PivotItems("Utah").LabelRange
Set R2 = PT.PivotFields("State").PivotItems("Colorado").LabelRange
Union(R1, R2).Group
PT.PivotFields("State Group").PivotItems("Group2").Caption = "Rockies"

Set R1 = PT.PivotFields("State").PivotItems("Texas").LabelRange
Set R2 = PT.PivotFields("State").PivotItems("Louisiana").LabelRange
Set R3 = PT.PivotFields("State").PivotItems("Oklahoma").LabelRange
Union(R1, R2, R3).Group
PT.PivotFields("State Group").PivotItems("Group3").Caption = "Oil States"
```

The result is a pivot table with new virtual groups, as shown in Figure 13-24.

Revenue		
State Group ▾ State ▾		Total
▭ Desert State Arizona		$550,550
	California	$3,165,104
	Nevada	$1,170,320
	New Mexico	$322,168
Desert States Total		$5,208,142
▭ Rockies	Colorado	$616,097
	Utah	$632,897
Rockies Total		$1,248,994
▭ Oil States	Louisiana	$814,431
	Oklahoma	$186,715
	Texas	$2,559,021
Oil States Total		$3,560,167
Grand Total		$10,017,303

FIGURE 13-24 Grouping text fields allows for reporting by territories that are not in the original data.

Using Show Values As to perform other calculations

The Show Values As tab in the Value Field Settings dialog offers 15 calculations, allowing you to change from numbers to percentage of total, running totals, ranks, and more.

You change the calculation by using the Calculation option for the pivot field.

> **Note** The Calculation property works with the BaseField and BaseItem properties. Depending on the selected calculation, you might be required to specify a base field and base item, or sometimes only a base field, or sometimes neither of them.

Some calculations, such as % of Column and % of Row, need no further definition; you do not have to specify a base field. Here is code that shows revenue as a percentage of total revenue:

```
With PT.PivotFields("Revenue")
    .Orientation = xlDataField
    .Function = xlSum
```

```
        .Calculation = xlPercentOfTotal
        .Position = 2
        .NumberFormat = "0.0%"
        .Name = "% of Total"
End With
```

Other calculations need a base field. If you are showing revenue and ask for the descending rank, you can specify that the base field is the State field. In this case, you are asking for this state's rank based on revenue:

```
With PT.PivotFields("Revenue")
        .Orientation = xlDataField
        .Calculation = xlRankDescending
        .BaseField = "State"
        .Position = 3
        .NumberFormat = "0%"
        .Name = "RankD"
End With
```

A few calculations require both a base field and a base item. If you want to show every state's revenue as a percentage of California revenue, you have to specify % Of as the calculation, State as the base field, and California as the base item:

```
With PT.PivotFields("Revenue")
        .Orientation = xlDataField
        .Calculation = xlPercentOf
        .BaseField = "State"
        .BaseItem = "California"
        .Position = 4
        .NumberFormat = "0%"
        .Name = "% of CA"
End With
```

Some of the calculation fields were new in Excel 2010. In Figure 13-25, column I uses the new % of Parent calculation, and column H uses the old % of Total calculation. In both columns, Desert States is 52% of the Grand Total (cells H8 and I8). However, cell I5 shows that California is 60.8% of Desert States, whereas cell H5 shows that California is 31.6% of the grand total.

Notice that the Rank field is specified to use State as a base field. The states are ranked within each State Group. There does not appear to be a way to have the states ranked overall unless you remove the State Group column from the pivot table.

Table 13-1 shows the complete list of Calculation options. The second column indicates whether the calculations are compatible with previous versions of Excel. The third column indicates whether you need a base field and base item.

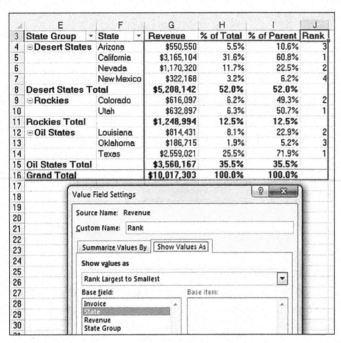

FIGURE 13-25 % of Parent in column I was new in Excel 2010.

TABLE 13-1 Calculation options available in Excel VBA

Calculation	Version	Base Field/Base Item?
XlDifferenceFrom	All	Both required
xlIndex	All	Neither
xlNoAdditionalCalculation	All	Neither
xlPercentDifferenceFrom	All	Both required
xlPercentOf	All	Both required
xlPercentOfColumn	All	Neither
xlPercentOfParent	2010 and later	Base field only
xlPercentOfParentColumn	2010 and later	Both required
xlPercentOfParentRow	2010 and later	Both required
xlPercentOfRow	All	Neither
xlPercentOfTotal	All	Neither
xlPercentRunningTotal	2010 and later	Base field only
xlRankAscending	2010 and later	Base field only
xlRankDescending	2010 and later	Base field only
xlRunningTotal	All	Base field only

Using advanced pivot table techniques

Even if you are a pivot table pro, you might never have run into some of the really advanced techniques available with pivot tables. The following sections discuss such techniques.

Using AutoShow to produce executive overviews

If you are designing an executive dashboard utility, you might want to spotlight the top five markets. This setting lets you select either the top or bottom *n* records based on any data field in the report.

The code to use AutoShow in VBA uses the `AutoShow` method:

```
' Show only the top 5 Markets
PT.PivotFields("Market").AutoShow Top:=xlAutomatic, Range:=xlTop, _
    Count:=5, Field:= "Sum of Revenue"
```

When you create a report using the `AutoShow` method, it is often helpful to copy the data and then go back to the original pivot report to get the totals for all markets. In Listing 13-4, this is achieved by removing the Market field from the pivot table and copying the grand total to the report. The code in Listing 13-4 produces the report shown in Figure 13-26.

	A	B	C
1	Top 5 Markets		
2			
3	Market	Bar Equipment	Commercial Appliances
4	Florida	1,131,779	5,667,799
5	Charlotte	283,676	1,525,742
6	California	66,233	294,080
7	Dallas	59,560	255,146
8	Buffalo	37,366	237,298
9	Top 5 Total	1,578,614	7,980,064
10			
11	Total Company	1,769,332	8,562,837
12			

FIGURE 13-26 The Top 5 Markets report contains two pivot tables.

LISTING 13-4   Code used to create the Top 5 Markets report

```
Sub Top5Markets()
    ' Figure 13.26
    ' Produce a report of the top 5 markets
    Dim WBO As Workbook
    Dim WSD As Worksheet
    Dim PT As PivotTable
    Dim FinalRow As Long
    Dim FinalCol As Long
    Dim PRange As Range
    Dim PTCache As PivotCache
    Dim WSR As Worksheet
```

```vba
Dim WBN As Workbook
Dim LastRow As Long

Set WBO = ActiveWorkbook
Set WSD = WBO.Worksheets("Data")
WSD.Select

' Delete any prior pivot tables
For Each PT In WSD.PivotTables
    PT.TableRange2.Clear
Next PT
WSD.Range("M1:Z1").EntireColumn.Clear

' Define input area and set up a Pivot Cache
FinalRow = WSD.Cells(Application.Rows.Count, 1).End(xlUp).Row
FinalCol = WSD.Cells(1, Application.Columns.Count). _
    End(xlToLeft).Column
Set PRange = WSD.Cells(1, 1).Resize(FinalRow, FinalCol)
Set PTCache = WBO.PivotCaches.Add(SourceType:= _
    xlDatabase, SourceData:=PRange.Address)

' Create the Pivot Table from the Pivot Cache
Set PT = PTCache.CreatePivotTable(TableDestination:=WSD. _
    Cells(2, FinalCol + 2), TableName:="PivotTable1")

' Set up the row fields
PT.AddFields RowFields:="Market", ColumnFields:="Category"

' Set up the data fields
With PT.PivotFields("Revenue")
    .Orientation = xlDataField
    .Function = xlSum
    .Position = 1
    .NumberFormat = "#,##0"
    .Name = "Total Revenue"
End With

' Ensure that we get zeroes instead of blanks in the data area
PT.NullString = "0"

' Sort markets descending by sum of revenue
PT.PivotFields("Market").AutoSort Order:=xlDescending, _
    field:="Total Revenue"

' Show only the top 5 markets
PT.PivotFields("Market").AutoShow Type:=xlAutomatic, Range:=xlTop, _
    Count:=5, field:="Total Revenue"

' Create a new blank workbook with one worksheet
Set WBN = Workbooks.Add(xlWorksheet)
Set WSR = WBN.Worksheets(1)
WSR.Name = "Report"
' Set up Title for Report
With WSR.[A1]
```

```
        .Value = "Top 5 Markets"
        .Font.Size = 14
    End With

    ' Copy the pivot table data to row 3 of the report sheet
    ' Use offset to eliminate the title row of the pivot table
    PT.TableRange2.Offset(1, 0).Copy
    WSR.[A3].PasteSpecial Paste:=xlPasteValuesAndNumberFormats
    LastRow = WSR.Cells(Rows.Count, 1).End(xlUp).Row
    WSR.Cells(LastRow, 1).Value = "Top 5 Total"

    ' Go back to the pivot table to get totals without the AutoShow
    PT.PivotFields("Market").Orientation = xlHidden
    PT.TableRange2.Offset(2, 0).Copy
    WSR.Cells(LastRow + 2, 1).PasteSpecial Paste:=xlPasteValuesAndNumberFormats
    WSR.Cells(LastRow + 2, 1).Value = "Total Company"

    ' Clear the pivot table
    PT.TableRange2.Clear
    Set PTCache = Nothing

    ' Do some basic formatting
    ' Autofit columns, bold the headings, right-align
    WSR.Range(WSR.Range("A3"), WSR.Cells(LastRow + 2, 9)).Columns.AutoFit
    Range("A3").EntireRow.Font.Bold = True
    Range("A3").EntireRow.HorizontalAlignment = xlRight
    Range("A3").HorizontalAlignment = xlLeft

    WSR.Range("A2").Select
    MsgBox "CEO Report has been Created"
End Sub
```

The Top 5 Markets report actually contains two snapshots of a pivot table. After using the AutoShow feature to grab the top five markets with their totals, the macro goes back to the pivot table, removes the AutoShow option, and grabs the total of all markets to produce the Total Company row.

Using ShowDetail to filter a data set

Open any pivot table in the Excel user interface. Double-click any number in the pivot table. Excel inserts a new sheet in the workbook and copies all the source records that represent that number. This is a great way to perform a drill-down query into a data set in the Excel user interface.

The equivalent VBA property is ShowDetail. By setting this property to True for any cell in a pivot table, you generate a new worksheet with all the records that make up that cell:

```
PT.TableRange1.Offset(2, 1).Resize(1, 1).ShowDetail = True
```

Listing 13-5 produces a pivot table with the total revenue for the top three stores and ShowDetail for each of those stores. This is an alternative method to using the Advanced Filter report. The results of this macro are three new sheets. Figure 13-27 shows the first sheet created.

⬚	A	B	C	D	E	F	G
1	Detail for SUASHU Corp. (Store Rank: 1)						
2							
3	Details for Total Revenue - Customer: SUASHU Corp.						
4							
5	Region ▾	Market ▾	State ▾	Customer ▾	Rep ▾	Date ▾	Internet Order ▾
6	South	Florida	GA	SUASHU Corp.	Tory Hanlon	12/30/2031	Yes
7	South	Florida	GA	SUASHU Corp.	Tory Hanlon	12/30/2031	Yes
8	South	Florida	GA	SUASHU Corp.	Tory Hanlon	12/30/2031	Yes
9	South	Florida	GA	SUASHU Corp.	Tory Hanlon	12/30/2031	Yes

FIGURE 13-27 Pivot table applications are incredibly diverse. This macro created a pivot table of the top three stores and then used the ShowDetail property to retrieve the records for each of those stores.

LISTING 13-5   Code used to create a report for each of the top three customers

```
Sub RetrieveTop3CustomerDetail()
    ' Figure 13.27
    ' Retrieve Details from Top 3 Customers
    Dim WBO As Workbook
    Dim WSD As Worksheet
    Dim PT As PivotTable
    Dim FinalRow As Long
    Dim FinalCol As Long
    Dim PRange As Range
    Dim PTCache As PivotCache
    Dim i As Long

    Set WBO = ActiveWorkbook
    Set WSD = WBO.Worksheets("Data")
    WSD.Select

    ' Delete any prior pivot tables
    For Each PT In WSD.PivotTables
        PT.TableRange2.Clear
    Next PT
    WSD.Range("M1:Z1").EntireColumn.Clear

    ' Define input area and set up a Pivot Cache
    FinalRow = WSD.Cells(Application.Rows.Count, 1).End(xlUp).Row
    FinalCol = WSD.Cells(1, Application.Columns.Count). _
        End(xlToLeft).Column
    Set PRange = WSD.Cells(1, 1).Resize(FinalRow, FinalCol)
    Set PTCache = WBO.PivotCaches.Add(SourceType:= _
        xlDatabase, SourceData:=PRange.Address)

    ' Create the Pivot Table from the Pivot Cache
    Set PT = PTCache.CreatePivotTable(TableDestination:=WSD. _
        Cells(2, FinalCol + 2), TableName:="PivotTable1")

    ' Set up the row fields
    PT.AddFields RowFields:="Customer", ColumnFields:="Data"
```

```
' Set up the data fields
With PT.PivotFields("Revenue")
    .Orientation = xlDataField
    .Function = xlSum
    .Position = 1
    .NumberFormat = "#,##0"
    .Name = "Total Revenue"
End With

' Sort Stores descending by sum of revenue
PT.PivotFields("Customer").AutoSort Order:=xlDescending, _
    field:="Total Revenue"

' Show only the top 3 stores
PT.PivotFields("Customer").AutoShow Type:=xlAutomatic, Range:=xlTop, _
    Count:=3, field:="Total Revenue"

' Ensure that we get zeroes instead of blanks in the data area
PT.NullString = "0"

' Produce summary reports for each customer
For i = 1 To 3
    PT.TableRange2.Offset(i + 1, 1).Resize(1, 1).ShowDetail = True
    ' The active sheet has changed to the new detail report
    ' Add a title
    ActiveSheet.Range("A1:A2").EntireRow.Insert
    ActiveSheet.Range("A1").Value = "Detail for " & _
        PT.TableRange2.Offset(i + 1, 0).Resize(1, 1).Value & _
        " (Store Rank: " & i & ")"
Next i

MsgBox "Detail reports for top 3 stores have been created."
End Sub
```

Creating reports for each region or model

A pivot table can have one or more filter fields. A filter field goes in a separate set of rows above the pivot report. It can serve to filter the report to a certain region, model, or combination of region and model. In VBA, filter fields are called *page fields*.

You might create a pivot table with several filter fields to allow someone to do ad-hoc analyses. However, it is more likely that you will use the filter fields in order to produce reports for each region.

To set up a filter in VBA, add the PageFields parameter to the AddFields method. The following line of code creates a pivot table with Region in the Filters area:

```
PT.AddFields RowFields:= "Product", ColumnFields:= "Data", PageFields:= "Region"
```

The preceding line of code sets up the Region filter with the value (A11), which returns all regions. To limit the report to just the North region, use the CurrentPage property:

```
PT.PivotFields("Region").CurrentPage = "North"
```

One use of a filter is to build a user form in which someone can select a particular region or particular product. You then use this information to set the `CurrentPage` property and display the results of the user form.

One amazing trick is to use the Show Pages feature to replicate a pivot table for every item in one filter field dropdown. After creating and formatting a pivot table, you can run this single line of code. If you have eight regions in the data set, eight new worksheets are inserted in the workbook, one for each region. The pivot table appears on each worksheet, with the appropriate region chosen from the dropdown:

```
PT.ShowPages PageField:=Region
```

> **Caution** Be careful with `ShowPages`. If you use `ShowPages` on the Customer field and you have 1,000 customers, Excel attempts to insert 1,000 worksheets in the workbook, each with a pivot table. All of those pivot tables share the same pivot cache in order to minimize memory usage. However, you will eventually run out of memory, and the program will end with a debug error when no additional worksheets will fit in available memory.
>
> The other problem with `ShowPages` is that it creates the individual reports as worksheets in a single workbook. In real life, you probably want separate workbooks for each region so that you can email the reports to the appropriate office. You can loop through all `PivotItems` and display them one at a time in the page field. You can quickly produce top 10 reports for each region using this method.

To determine how many regions are available in the data, use `PT.PivotFields("Region").PivotItems.Count`. Either of these loops would work:

```
For i = 1 To PT.PivotFields("Region").PivotItems.Count
    PT.PivotFields("Region").CurrentPage = _
    PT.PivotFields("Region").PivotItems(i).Name
    PT.Update
Next i

For Each PivItem In PT.PivotFields("Region").PivotItems
    PT.PivotFields("Region").CurrentPage = PivItem.Name
    PT.Update
Next PivItem
```

Of course, in both loops, the three region reports fly by too quickly to see them. In practice, you would want to save each report while it is displayed.

So far in this chapter, you have been using `PT.TableRange2` when copying the data from the pivot table. The `TableRange2` property includes all rows of the pivot table, including the page fields.

There is also a `TableRange1` property, which excludes the page fields. You can use either of these statements to get the detail rows:

```
PT.TableRange2.Offset(3, 0)
PT.TableRange1.Offset(1, 0)
```

> **Caution** Which statement you use is your preference, but if you use `TableRange2`, you will not have problems when you try to delete the pivot table with `PT.TableRange2.Clear`. If you were to accidentally attempt to clear `TableRange1` when there are page fields, you would end up with the dreaded "Cannot move or change part of a pivot table" error.

Listing 13-6 produces a new workbook for each region, as shown in Figure 13-28.

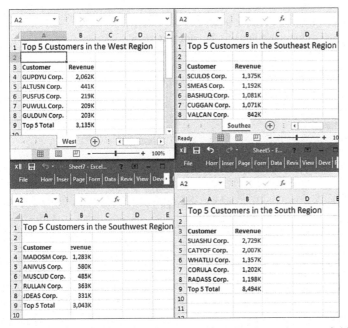

FIGURE 13-28 By looping through all items found in the Region page field, the macro produced one worksheet for each regional manager.

LISTING 13-6 Code that creates a new worksheet for each region

```
Sub Top5ByRegionReport()
    ' Figure 13.28
    ' Produce a report of top 5 customers for each region
    Dim WBO As Workbook
    Dim WSD As Worksheet
    Dim PT As PivotTable
    Dim FinalRow As Long
    Dim FinalCol As Long
    Dim PRange As Range
```

```vba
Dim PTCache As PivotCache
Dim PivItem As PivotItem
Dim WSR As Worksheet
Dim WBN As Workbook
Dim Ctr As Integer
Dim LastRow As Long

Set WBO = ActiveWorkbook
Set WSD = WBO.Worksheets("Data")
WSD.Select

' Delete any prior pivot tables
For Each PT In WSD.PivotTables
    PT.TableRange2.Clear
Next PT
WSD.Range("M1:Z1").EntireColumn.Clear

' Define input area and set up a Pivot Cache
FinalRow = WSD.Cells(Application.Rows.Count, 1).End(xlUp).Row
FinalCol = WSD.Cells(1, Application.Columns.Count). _
    End(xlToLeft).Column
Set PRange = WSD.Cells(1, 1).Resize(FinalRow, FinalCol)
Set PTCache = WBO.PivotCaches.Add(SourceType:= _
    xlDatabase, SourceData:=PRange.Address)

' Create the Pivot Table from the Pivot Cache
Set PT = PTCache.CreatePivotTable(TableDestination:=WSD. _
    Cells(2, FinalCol + 2), TableName:="PivotTable1")

' Set up the row fields
PT.AddFields RowFields:="Customer", ColumnFields:="Data", _
    PageFields:="Region"

' Set up the data fields
With PT.PivotFields("Revenue")
    .Orientation = xlDataField
    .Function = xlSum
    .Position = 1
    .NumberFormat = "#,##0,K"
    .Name = "Total Revenue"
End With

' Sort stores descending by sum of revenue
PT.PivotFields("Customer").AutoSort Order:=xlDescending, _
    field:="Total Revenue"

' Show only the top 5 stores
PT.PivotFields("Customer").AutoShow Type:=xlAutomatic, Range:=xlTop, _
    Count:=5, field:="Total Revenue"

' Ensure that we get zeroes instead of blanks in the data area
PT.NullString = "0"
```

```
    Ctr = 0

    ' Loop through each region
    For Each PivItem In PT.PivotFields("Region").PivotItems
        Ctr = Ctr + 1
        PT.PivotFields("Region").CurrentPage = PivItem.Name

        ' Create a new blank workbook with one worksheet
        Set WBN = Workbooks.Add(xlWorksheet)
        Set WSR = WBN.Worksheets(1)
        WSR.Name = PivItem.Name
        ' Set up Title for Report
        With WSR.[A1]
            .Value = "Top 5 Customers in the " & PivItem.Name & " Region"
            .Font.Size = 14
        End With

        ' Copy the pivot table data to row 3 of the report sheet
        ' Use offset to eliminate the page & title rows of the pivot table
        PT.TableRange2.Offset(3, 0).Copy
        WSR.[A3].PasteSpecial Paste:=xlPasteValuesAndNumberFormats
        LastRow = WSR.Cells(65536, 1).End(xlUp).Row
        WSR.Cells(LastRow, 1).Value = "Top 5 Total"

        ' Do some basic formatting
        ' Autofit columns, bold the headings, right-align
        WSR.Range(WSR.Range("A2"), WSR.Cells(LastRow, 3)).Columns.AutoFit
        WSR.Range("A3").EntireRow.Font.Bold = True
        WSR.Range("A3").EntireRow.HorizontalAlignment = xlRight
        WSR.Range("A3").HorizontalAlignment = xlLeft
        WSR.Range("B3").Value = "Revenue"

        WSR.Range("A2").Select

    Next PivItem

    ' Clear the pivot table
    PT.TableRange2.Clear
    Set PTCache = Nothing

    MsgBox Ctr & " Region reports have been created"

End Sub
```

Manually filtering two or more items in a pivot field

In addition to setting up a calculated pivot item to display the total of a couple of products that make up a dimension, you can manually filter a particular pivot field.

For example, say that you have one client who sells shoes. In the report showing sales of sandals, they want to see just the stores that are in warm-weather states. This is the code to hide a particular store:

```
PT.PivotFields("Store").PivotItems("Minneapolis").Visible = False
```

 Caution   You must be very careful never to set all items to `False` because doing so causes the macro to end with an error. This tends to happen more than you would expect. An application might show products A and B first, but on the next loop, it might show products C and D. If you attempt to make A and B not visible before making C and D visible, no products will be visible along the pivot field, which causes an error. To correct this, always loop through all pivot items and make sure to turn them back to visible before the second pass through the loop.

This process is easy in VBA. After building the table with `Product` in the page field, loop through to change the `Visible` property to show only the total of certain products:

```
' Make sure all PivotItems along line are visible
For Each PivItem In _
    PT.PivotFields("Product").PivotItems
    PivItem.Visible = True
Next PivItem

' Now - loop through and keep only certain items visible
For Each PivItem In _
    PT.PivotFields("Product").PivotItems
    Select Case PivItem.Name
        Case "Landscaping/Grounds Care", _
            "Green Plants and Foliage Care"
            PivItem.Visible = True
        Case Else
            PivItem.Visible = False
    End Select
Next PivItem
```

Using the conceptual filters

Beginning with Excel 2007, conceptual filters for date fields, numeric fields, and text fields are provided. In the PivotTable Fields list, hover the mouse cursor over any active field in the field list portion of the pane. In the dropdown that appears, you can choose Label Filters, Date Filters, or Value Filters.

To apply a label filter in VBA, use the `PivotFilters.Add` method. The following code filters to the customers that start with 1:

```
PT.PivotFields("Customer").PivotFilters.Add _
    Type:=xlCaptionBeginsWith, Value1:="1"
```

To clear the filter from the Customer field, use the `ClearAllFilters` method:

```
PT.PivotFields("Customer").ClearAllFilters
```

To apply a date filter to the date field to find records from this week, use this code:

```
PT.PivotFields("Date").PivotFilters.Add Type:=xlThisWeek
```

A value filter allows you to filter one field based on the value of another field. For example, to find all the markets where the total revenue is more than $100,000, you would use this code:

```
PT.PivotFields("Market").PivotFilters.Add _
    Type:=xlValueIsGreaterThan, _
    DataField:=PT.PivotFields("Sum of Revenue"), _
    Value1:=100000
```

Other value filters might allow you to specify that you want branches where the revenue is between $50,000 and $100,000. In this case, you would specify one limit as `Value1` and the second limit as `Value2`:

```
PT.PivotFields("Market").PivotFilters.Add _
    Type:=xlValueIsBetween, _
        DataField:=PT.PivotFields("Sum of Revenue"), _
        Value1:=50000, Value2:=100000
```

Table 13-2 lists all the possible filter types.

TABLE 13-2 Filter types in VBA

Filter Type	Description
xlBefore	Filters for all dates before a specified date.
xlBeforeOrEqualTo	Filters for all dates on or before a specified date.
xlAfter	Filters for all dates after a specified date.
xlAfterOrEqualTo	Filters for all dates on or after a specified date.
xlAllDatesInPeriodJanuary	Filters for all dates in January.
xlAllDatesInPeriodFebruary	Filters for all dates in February.
xlAllDatesInPeriodMarch	Filters for all dates in March.
xlAllDatesInPeriodApril	Filters for all dates in April.
xlAllDatesInPeriodMay	Filters for all dates in May.
xlAllDatesInPeriodJune	Filters for all dates in June.
xlAllDatesInPeriodJuly	Filters for all dates in July.
xlAllDatesInPeriodAugust	Filters for all dates in August.
xlAllDatesInPeriodSeptember	Filters for all dates in September.
xlAllDatesInPeriodOctober	Filters for all dates in October.
xlAllDatesInPeriodNovember	Filters for all dates in November.

TABLE 13-2 *(continued)*

Filter Type	Description
xlAllDatesInPeriodDecember	Filters for all dates in December.
xlAllDatesInPeriodQuarter1	Filters for all dates in Quarter 1.
xlAllDatesInPeriodQuarter2	Filters for all dates in Quarter 2.
xlAllDatesInPeriodQuarter3	Filters for all dates in Quarter 3.
xlAllDatesInPeriodQuarter4	Filters for all dates in Quarter 4.
xlBottomCount	Filters for the specified number of values from the bottom of a list.
xlBottomPercent	Filters for the specified percentage of values from the bottom of a list.
xlBottomSum	Sums the values from the bottom of the list.
xlCaptionBeginsWith	Filters for all captions beginning with the specified string.
xlCaptionContains	Filters for all captions that contain the specified string.
xlCaptionDoesNotBeginWith	Filters for all captions that do not begin with the specified string.
xlCaptionDoesNotContain	Filters for all captions that do not contain the specified string.
xlCaptionDoesNotEndWith	Filters for all captions that do not end with the specified string.
xlCaptionDoesNotEqual	Filters for all captions that do not match the specified string.
xlCaptionEndsWith	Filters for all captions that end with the specified string.
xlCaptionEquals	Filters for all captions that match the specified string.
xlCaptionIsBetween	Filters for all captions that are between a specified range of values.
xlCaptionIsGreaterThan	Filters for all captions that are greater than the specified value.
xlCaptionIsGreaterThanOrEqualTo	Filters for all captions that are greater than or match the specified value.
xlCaptionIsLessThan	Filters for all captions that are less than the specified value.
xlCaptionIsLessThanOrEqualTo	Filters for all captions that are less than or match the specified value.
xlCaptionIsNotBetween	Filters for all captions that are not between a specified range of values.
xlDateBetween	Filters for all dates that are between a specified range of dates.
xlDateLastMonth	Filters for all dates that apply to the previous month.
xlDateLastQuarter	Filters for all dates that apply to the previous quarter.
xlDateLastWeek	Filters for all dates that apply to the previous week.
xlDateLastYear	Filters for all dates that apply to the previous year.
xlDateNextMonth	Filters for all dates that apply to the next month.
xlDateNextQuarter	Filters for all dates that apply to the next quarter.
xlDateNextWeek	Filters for all dates that apply to the next week.
xlDateNextYear	Filters for all dates that apply to the next year.

TABLE 13-2 *(continued)*

Filter Type	Description
xlDateThisMonth	Filters for all dates that apply to the current month.
xlDateThisQuarter	Filters for all dates that apply to the current quarter.
xlDateThisWeek	Filters for all dates that apply to the current week.
xlDateThisYear	Filters for all dates that apply to the current year.
xlDateToday	Filters for all dates that apply to the current date.
xlDateTomorrow	Filters for all dates that apply to the next day.
xlDateYesterday	Filters for all dates that apply to the previous day.
xlNotSpecificDate	Filters for all dates that do not match a specified date.
xlSpecificDate	Filters for all dates that match a specified date.
xlTopCount	Filters for the specified number of values from the top of a list.
xlTopPercent	Sums the values from the top of the list.
xlTopSum	Filters for all values that do not match the specified value.
xlValueDoesNotEqual	Filters for all values that do not match the specified value.
xlValueEquals	Filters for all values that match the specified value.
xlValueIsBetween	Filters for all values that are between a specified range of values.
xlValueIsGreaterThan	Filters for all values that are greater than the specified value.
xlValueIsGreaterThanOrEqualTo	Filters for all values that are greater than or match the specified value.
xlValueIsLessThan	Filters for all values that are less than the specified value.
xlValueIsLessThanOrEqualTo	Filters for all values that are less than or match the specified value.
xlValueIsNotBetween	Filters for all values that are not between a specified range of values.
xlYearToDate	Filters for all values that are within one year of a specified date.

Using the search filter

Excel 2010 added a search box to the filter dropdown. Although this is a slick feature in the Excel interface, there is no equivalent magic in VBA. Figure 13-29 shows the (Select All Search Results) checkbox
selected after the search for "be. " Using the macro recorder during this process creates a 5,876-line
macro that goes through and turns all customers without "be" invisible:

```
With ActiveSheet.PivotTables("PivotTable3").PivotFields("Customer")
    .PivotItems("ACASCO Corp.").Visible = False
    .PivotItems("ACECUL Corp.").Visible = False
    .PivotItems("ACEHUA Corp.").Visible = False
' snipped 5870_ similar lines
    .PivotItems("ZUQHYR Corp.").Visible = False
    .PivotItems("ZUSOEA Corp.").Visible = False
    .PivotItems("ZYLSTR Corp.").Visible = False
End With
```

There is nothing new in Excel VBA to emulate the search box. To achieve the same results in VBA, you use the `xlCaptionContains` filter described in Table 13-2.

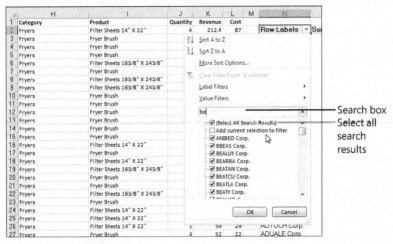

FIGURE 13-29 The Excel interface offers a search box. In VBA, you can emulate this by using the old `xlCaptionContains` filter.

Setting up slicers to filter a pivot table

Excel 2010 introduced the concept of slicers for filtering pivot tables. A slicer is a visual filter. You can resize and reposition slicers, control the color of the slicer, and control the number of columns in a slicer. Also, you can select or clear items from a slicer by using VBA.

Figure 13-30 shows a pivot table with two slicers. The State slicer has been modified to have five columns. The slicer with the caption "Territory" is actually based on the Region field. You can give slicers friendlier captions, which might be helpful when the underlying field is called `IDKTxtReg` or some other bizarre name invented by the IT department.

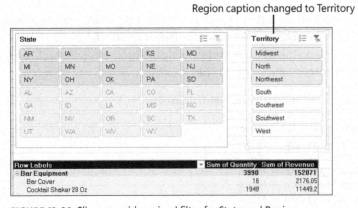

FIGURE 13-30 Slicers provide a visual filter for State and Region.

A slicer is composed of `SlicerCache` and `Slicer`. To define a slicer cache, you need to specify a pivot table as the source and a field name as `SourceField`. `SlicerCache` is defined at the workbook level. This enables you to have the slicer on a different worksheet than the actual pivot table. Here's the code to do all this:

```
Dim SCS as SlicerCache
Dim SCR as SlicerCache
Set SCS = ActiveWorkbook.SlicerCaches.Add2(Source:=PT, SourceField:="State")
Set SCR = ActiveWorkbook.SlicerCaches.Add2(Source:=PT, SourceField:="Region")
```

After you have defined `SlicerCache`, you can add `Slicer`, which is defined as an object of the slicer cache. Specify a worksheet as the destination. The `Name` argument controls the internal name for the slicer. The `Caption` argument is the heading that will be visible in the slicer. Specify the size of the slicer using `height` and `width` in points. Specify the location using `top` and `left` in points. In the following code, the values for `top`, `left`, `height`, and `width` are assigned to be equal to the location or size of certain cell ranges:

```
Dim SLS as Slicer
Set SLS = SCS.Slicers.Add(SlicerDestination:=WSD, Name:="State", _
    Caption:="State", _
    Top:=WSD.Range("O2").Top, _
    Left:=WSD.Range("O2").Left, _
    Width:=WSR.Range("O2:U2").Width, _
    Height:=WSD.Range("O2:O17").Height)
' Format the color and number of columns
```

Every slicer starts out as one column. You can change the style and number of columns with this code:

```
With SLS
    .Style = "SlicerStyleLight6"
    .NumberOfColumns = 5
End With
```

> **Note** I find that when I create slicers in the Excel interface, I spend many mouse clicks making adjustments to them. After adding two or three slicers, Excel positions them in an overlapping tile arrangement. I always tweak the location, size, number of columns, and so on. For many years in my seminars, I bragged that I could create a pivot table in six mouse clicks. That was before slicers were introduced. Slicers are admittedly powerful, but they seem to take 20 mouse clicks before they look right. Having a macro make all these adjustments at once is a timesaver.

After a slicer is defined, you can use VBA to choose which items are activated in the slicer. It seems counterintuitive, but to choose items in the slicer, you have to change `SlicerItem`, which is a member of `SlicerCache`, not a member of `Slicer`:

```
With SCR
    .SlicerItems("Midwest").Selected = True
    .SlicerItems("North").Selected = True
    .SlicerItems("Northeast").Selected = True
    .SlicerItems("South").Selected = False
    .SlicerItems("Southeast").Selected = False
    .SlicerItems("Southwest").Selected = False
    .SlicerItems("West").Selected = False
End With
```

You might need to deal with slicers that already exist. If a slicer is created for the State field, the slicer cache is named "Slicer_State". The following code is used to format the slicers shown in Figure 13-30:

```
Sub MoveAndFormatSlicer()
 Dim SCS As SlicerCache
 Dim SLS As Slicer
 Dim SCR As SlicerCache
 Dim SLR As Slicer
 Dim WSD As Worksheet
 Set WSD = ActiveSheet

 Set SCS = ActiveWorkbook.SlicerCaches("Slicer_State")
 Set SLS = SCS.Slicers("State")
 With SLS
     .Style = "SlicerStyleLight6"
     .NumberOfColumns = 5
     .Top = WSD.Range("A1").Top + 5
     .Left = WSD.Range("A1").Left + 5
     .Width = WSD.Range("A1:B14").Width - 60
     .Height = WSD.Range("A1:B14").Height
 End With

 Set SCR = ActiveWorkbook.SlicerCaches("Slicer_Region")
 Set SLR = SCR.Slicers("Region")
 With SLR
     .Style = "SlicerStyleLight3"
     .NumberOfColumns = 1
     .Top = WSD.Range("C1").Top + 5
     .Left = WSD.Range("C1").Left - 20
     .Width = WSD.Range("C1").Width
     .Height = WSD.Range("C1:C14").Height
     .Caption = "Territory"
 End With

 ' Choose three regions
 With SCR
     .SlicerItems("Midwest").Selected = True
     .SlicerItems("North").Selected = True
```

```
      .SlicerItems("Northeast").Selected = True
      .SlicerItems("South").Selected = False
      .SlicerItems("Southeast").Selected = False
      .SlicerItems("Southwest").Selected = False
      .SlicerItems("West").Selected = False
  End With

  End Sub
```

Using the Data Model in Excel

Excel incorporates Power Pivot into the core Excel product. This means you can add two tables to the Data Model, create a relationship, add a measure, and then build a pivot table from the Data Model.

To follow along with the example in this section, open the `13-BeforeDataModel.xlsm` file from the sample download files. This workbook has two tables: Sales and Sector. Sector is a lookup table that is related to the Sales table via a customer field. To build the pivot table, you follow these general steps in the macro:

1. Add the main table to the model.

2. Add the lookup table to the model.

3. Link the two tables with a relationship.

4. Create a pivot cache from `ThisWorkbookDataModel`.

5. Create a pivot table from the cache.

6. Add row fields.

7. Define a measure.

8. Add the measure to the pivot table.

Adding both tables to the Data Model

You should already have a data set in the workbook that has been converted to a table using the Ctrl+T shortcut. On the Table Tools Design tab, change the table name (`TableName`) to `Sales`. To link this table to the Data Model, use this code:

```
' Build Connection to the main Sales table
Set WBT = ActiveWorkbook
TableName = "Sales"
WBT.Connections.Add2 Name:="LinkedTable_" & TableName, _
    Description:="", _
    ConnectionString:="WORKSHEET;" & WBT.FullName, _
    CommandText:=WBT.Name & "!" & TableName, _
    lCmdType:=7, _
    CreateModelConnection:=True, _
    ImportRelationships:=False
```

Several variables in this code use the table name, the workbook path, and/or the workbook name. By storing the table name in a variable at the top of the code, you can build the connection name, connection string, and command text using the variables.

Then, adapting the preceding code to link to the lookup table requires only changing the TableName variable:

```
TableName = "Sector"
WBT.Connections.Add2 Name:="LinkedTable_" & TableName, _
    Description:="", _
    ConnectionString:="WORKSHEET;" & WBT.FullName, _
    CommandText:=WBT.Name & "!" & TableName, _
    lCmdType:=7, _
    CreateModelConnection:=True, _
    ImportRelationships:=False
```

Creating a relationship between the two tables

When you create a relationship in the Excel interface, you specify the following four items in the Create Relationship dialog (see Figure 13-31):

- Table 1 is Sector.

- Columns is Customer.

- Table 2 is Sales.

- Columns is Customer.

The code to create the relationship is more streamlined. There can be only one Data Model per workbook. Set an object variable named MO to refer to the model in this workbook. Use the ModelRelationships.Add method and specify the two linked fields.

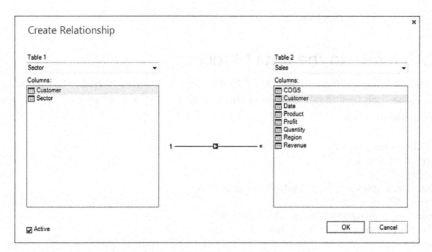

FIGURE 13-31 To create a relationship, specify a field in both tables.

```
' Relate the two tables
Dim MO As Model
Set MO = ActiveWorkbook.Model
MO.ModelRelationships.Add _
    ForeignKeyColumn:=MO.ModelTables("Sales").ModelTableColumns("Customer"),
PrimaryKeyColumn:= _
    MO.ModelTables("Sector").ModelTableColumns("Customer")
```

Defining the pivot cache and building the pivot table

The code to define the pivot cache specifies that the data is external. Even though the linked tables are in your workbook and the Data Model is stored as a large binary object in the workbook, this is still considered an external data connection. The connection is always called ThisWorkbookDataModel. Here's the code for defining the pivot cache and building the pivot table:

```
' Define the PivotCache
Set PTCache = WBT.PivotCaches.Create(SourceType:=xlExternal, _
    SourceData:=WBT.Connections("ThisWorkbookDataModel"), _
    Version:=xlPivotTableVersion15)

' Create the Pivot Table from the Pivot Cache
Set PT = PTCache.CreatePivotTable( _
    TableDestination:=WSD.Cells(1, 1), TableName:="PivotTable1")
```

Adding model fields to the pivot table

You need to add two types of fields to the pivot table. Text fields such as Customer, Sector, and Product are simply fields that can be added to the row or column area of the pivot table. No calculation has to happen for these fields. The code for adding text fields is shown in this section. When you add a numeric field to the Values area in the Excel interface, you are actually implicitly defining a new calculated field. To do this in VBA, you have to explicitly define the field and then add it.

Let's look at the simpler example of adding a text field to the row area. The VBA code generically looks like this:

```
With PT.CubeFields("[TableName].[FieldName]")
    .Orientation = xlRowField
    .Position = 1
End With
```

In the current example, add the Sector field from the Sector table by using this code:

```
With PT.CubeFields("[Sector].[Sector]")
    .Orientation = xlRowField
    .Position = 1
End With
```

Adding numeric fields to the Values area

In Excel 2010, Power Pivot calculated fields were called *measures*. In Excel today, the Excel interface calls them *calculations*. However, the underlying VBA code still calls them *measures*.

If you have a Data Model pivot table and you check the Revenue field, you see the Revenue field move to the Values area. Behind the scenes, though, Excel is implicitly defining a new measure called Sum Of Revenue. (You can see the implicit measures in the Power Pivot window.) In VBA, the first step is to define a new measure for Sum Of Revenue. To make referring to this measure later easier, assign the new measure to an object variable:

```
' Before you can add Revenue to the pivot table,
' you have to define the measure.
' This happens using the GetMeasure method.
' Assign the cube field to CFRevenue object
Dim CFRevenue As CubeField
Set CFRevenue = PT.CubeFields.GetMeasure( _
    AttributeHierarchy:="[Sales].[Revenue]", _
    Function:=xlSum, _
    Caption:="Sum of Revenue")
' Add the newly created cube field to the pivot table
PT.AddDataField Field:=CFRevenue, _
    Caption:="Total Revenue"
PT.PivotFields("[Measures].[Sum of Revenue]").NumberFormat = "$#,##0,K"
```

You can use the sample code to create a new measure. The following measure uses the Distinct Count function to count the number of unique customers in each sector:

```
' Add Distinct Count of Customer as a Cube Field
Dim CFCustCount As CubeField
Set CFCustCount = PT.CubeFields.GetMeasure( _
    AttributeHierarchy:="[Sales].[Customer]", _
    Function:=xlDistinctCount, _
    Caption:="Customer Count")
' Add the newly created cube field to the pivot table
PT.AddDataField Field:=CFCustCount, _
    Caption:="Customer Count"
```

Now that Power Pivot ships with every copy of Excel, you can use DAX formulas to create new measures. The following code adds a field for Median Sales:

```
' Add Median Sales using DAX
ActiveWorkbook.Model.ModelMeasures.Add _
    MeasureName:="Median Sales", _
    AssociatedTable:=ActiveWorkbook.Model.ModelTables("Sales"), _
    Formula:="Median([Revenue])", _
    FormatInformation:=ActiveWorkbook.Model.ModelFormatCurrency("Default", 2)
    PT.AddDataField PT.CubeFields("[Measures].[Median Sales]")
```

Putting it all together

Figure 13-32 shows the Data Model pivot table created using the code in Listing 13-7.

▲	A	B	C	D
1	**Sector**	▼ **Total Revenue**	**Customer Count**	**Median Sales**
2	Apparel	$758K	2	$10,752.50
3	Chemical	$569K	1	$10,137.50
4	Consumer	$2,195K	7	$12,756.00
5	Electronics	$222K	4	$14,554.00
6	Food	$750K	1	$12,743.50
7	Hardware	$2,179K	11	$11,547.50
8	Textiles	$35K	1	$8,908.00
9	**Grand Total ***	**$6,708K**	**27**	**$11,858.00**
10				

FIGURE 13-32 Two tables linked with a pivot table and two measures, all via a macro.

LISTING 13-7   Code to create the Data Model pivot table in Figure 13-32

```
Sub BuildModelPivotTable()
 Dim WBT As Workbook
 Dim WC As WorkbookConnection
 Dim MO As Model
 Dim PTCache As PivotCache
 Dim PT As PivotTable
 Dim WSD As Worksheet
 Dim CFRevenue As CubeField
 Dim CFCustCount As CubeField

 Set WBT = ActiveWorkbook
 Set WSD = WBT.Worksheets("Report")

 ' Build Connection to the main Sales table
 TableName = "Sales"
 WBT.Connections.Add2 Name:="LinkedTable_" & TableName, _
     Description:="MainTable", _
     ConnectionString:="WORKSHEET;" & WBT.FullName, _
     CommandText:=WBT.Name & "!" & TableName, _
     lCmdType:=7, _
     CreateModelConnection:=True, _
     ImportRelationships:=False

 ' Build Connection to the Sector lookup table
 TableName = "Sector"
 WBT.Connections.Add2 Name:="LinkedTable_" & TableName, _
     Description:="LookupTable", _
     ConnectionString:="WORKSHEET;" & WBT.FullName, _
     CommandText:=WBT.Name & "!" & TableName, _
     lCmdType:=7, _
     CreateModelConnection:=True, _
     ImportRelationships:=False

 ' Relate the two tables
 Set MO = ActiveWorkbook.Model
 MO.ModelRelationships.Add ForeignKeyColumn:= _
   MO.ModelTables("Sales").ModelTableColumns("Customer"), _
```

```
        PrimaryKeyColumn:=MO.ModelTables("Sector"). _
        ModelTableColumns("Customer")

    ' Delete any prior pivot tables
    For Each PT In WSD.PivotTables
        PT.TableRange2.Clear
    Next PT

    ' Define the PivotCache
    Set PTCache = WBT.PivotCaches.Create(SourceType:=xlExternal, _
    SourceData:=WBT.Connections("ThisWorkbookDataModel"), _
    Version:=xlPivotTableVersion15)

    ' Create the Pivot Table from the Pivot Cache
    Set PT = PTCache.CreatePivotTable( _
        TableDestination:=WSD.Cells(1, 1), TableName:="PivotTable1")

    ' Add the Sector field from the Sector table to the Row areas
    With PT.CubeFields("[Sector].[Sector]")
        .Orientation = xlRowField
        .Position = 1
    End With

    ' Before you can add Revenue to the pivot table,
    ' you have to define the measure.
    ' This happens using the GetMeasure method
    ' Assign the cube field to CFRevenue object
    Set CFRevenue = PT.CubeFields.GetMeasure( _
        AttributeHierarchy:="[Sales].[Revenue]", _
        Function:=xlSum, _
        Caption:="Sum of Revenue")
    ' Add the newly created cube field to the pivot table
    PT.AddDataField Field:=CFRevenue, _
        Caption:="Total Revenue"
        PT.PivotFields("[Measures].[Sum of Revenue]"). _
        NumberFormat = "$#,##0,K"
    ' Add Distinct Count of Customer as a Cube Field
    Set CFCustCount = PT.CubeFields.GetMeasure( _
        AttributeHierarchy:="[Sales].[Customer]", _
        Function:=xlDistinctCount, _
        Caption:="Customer Count")
    ' Add the newly created cube field to the pivot table
    PT.AddDataField Field:=CFCustCount, _
        Caption:="Customer Count"

' Add Median Sales using DAX
ActiveWorkbook.Model.ModelMeasures.Add _
    MeasureName:="Median Sales", _
    AssociatedTable:=ActiveWorkbook.Model.ModelTables("Sales"), _
    Formula:="Median([Revenue])", _
    FormatInformation:=ActiveWorkbook.Model.ModelFormatCurrency("Default", 2)
PT.AddDataField PT.CubeFields("[Measures].[Median Sales]")
End Sub
```

Using TypeScript in Excel Online to create pivot tables

Microsoft is investing heavily in Excel Online to try to make the Excel Online experience equivalent to the Windows Excel experience. They now support the creation of pivot tables in Excel Online. And, while Excel Online will never support VBA, there is a scripting language called TypeScript for Excel Online.

Currently, TypeScript is limited to Microsoft 365 customers with a commercial or educational license. That excludes everyone with a Home license. Also, you will need to head to the local Krispy Kreme donut shop because you need your administrator to enable the licenses for the company. For the latest rules, open a browser and search for "Introduction to Office Scripts in Excel."

The TypeScript macros are still in beta. You will be pleased that TypeScript and the macro recorder can successfully record these actions:

- Add a new pivot table to the right of your data set

- Add Product to the Rows area

- Add Revenue to the Values area

- Add Region to the Columns area

The recorded script is short, relatively easy to understand, and runs successfully.

On the downside, the script recorder does not (yet) support:

- Changing the number format of a numeric field

- Replacing blanks in the Values area with zero

- Using the suggested pivot tables from the Ideas feature

Figure 13-33 shows the recorded TypeScript code.

```
Script 4
1    function main(workbook: ExcelScript.Workbook) {
2        let selectedSheet = workbook.getActiveWorksheet();
3        // Add a new pivot table on selectedSheet
4        let newPivotTable = workbook.addPivotTable("PivotTable1", selectedSheet.
           getRange("A1:L564"), selectedSheet.getRange("N4"));
5        // Add pivot field to a hierarchy in newPivotTable
6        newPivotTable.addRowHierarchy(newPivotTable.getHierarchy("Product"));
7        // Add pivot field to a hierarchy in newPivotTable
8        newPivotTable.addDataHierarchy(newPivotTable.getHierarchy("Revenue"));
9        // Add pivot field to a hierarchy in newPivotTable
10       newPivotTable.addColumnHierarchy(newPivotTable.getHierarchy("Region"));
11       // Change pivot position in a hierarchy in newPivotTable
12       newPivotTable.getColumnHierarchy("Region").setPosition(0);
13   }
```

FIGURE 13-33 A 13-line script adds Product to the Rows, Revenue to Values, and Region to Columns in a new pivot table in Excel Online.

Here is an analysis of the recorded code with suggested changes.

- The script is named `Script 4`. In the Script Details, click the name and type a better name, such as `CreatePTBySectorAndRegion`.

- Comment lines start with `//` instead of an apostrophe in VBA.

- It appears that `selectSheet` is an object variable where VBA would do the following:

  ```
  Set selectedSheet = ActiveSheet
  ```

  TypeScript does:

  ```
  let selectedSheet = workbook.getActiveWorksheet()
  ```

- The code is case-sensitive. You have to use `getActiveWorksheet` and not `getactiveworksheet` nor `GetActiveWorksheet`. If you don't use the case correctly, the editor will flag it as an error but then coyly suggests that you *could* change the spelling to `getActiveWorksheet`. As a VBA fan, you will likely agree that it is a bit jerkish for the editor to know the spelling and not automatically correct it.

- When the script recorder creates the pivot table using `.addPivotTable`, it specifies a name, source data, and destination data. Hard-coding A1:L564 is not a good practice. TypeScript's equivalent of `.CurrentRegion` is `.getSurroundingRegion()` used as follows:

  ```
  selectedSheet.getRange("A1").getSurroundingRegion()
  ```

- The modified code to create a pivot table called PTOne, based on `A:L` and starting in cell N2, is shown below. Note that the results are stored in an object variable called `newPivotTable` for easy reference later in the script:

  ```
  let newPivotTable = workbook.addPivotTable("PTOne",
  selectedSheet.getRange("A1").getSurroundingRegion(), selectedSheet.getRange("N2"));
  ```

- Once the pivot table is created, you can add fields to the Rows area with:

  ```
  newPivotTable.addRowHierarchy(newPivotTable.getHierarchy("Sector"));
  ```

- For a column field, change `.addRowHierachy` to `.addColumnHierarchy`. For a Values field, use `.AddDataHierarchy`.

- Near the end of the script, the macro recorder added a stray line:

  ```
  newPivotTable.getColumnHierarchy("Region").setPosition(0);
  ```

- This would have been needed if you had multiple fields in the columns area, but with only one field in the Columns area, that line can be deleted.

- Documentation for everything shows up when you hover over any word in the script. This is better than VBA, where you have to press F1 and then wait for a web page to load.

After seeing the recorded code, it should be relatively easy to edit the recorded code. The following code in Listing 13-8 creates a pivot table with Sector in rows, Region in columns, and Revenue in Values.

LISTING 13-8   TypeScript code to create a pivot table in Excel Online

```
function main(workbook: ExcelScript.Workbook) {
let selectedSheet = workbook.getActiveWorksheet();
// Add a new pivot table on selectedSheet
let newPivotTable = workbook.addPivotTable("PTOne", selectedSheet.getRange("A1").
getSurroundingRegion(), selectedSheet.getRange("N2"));
// Add Sector to Rows
newPivotTable.addRowHierarchy(newPivotTable.getHierarchy("Sector"));
// Add Revenue to Data
newPivotTable.addDataHierarchy(newPivotTable.getHierarchy("Revenue"));
// Add Region to Columns
newPivotTable.addColumnHierarchy(newPivotTable.getHierarchy("Region"));
}
```

The resulting pivot table is shown in Figure 13-34.

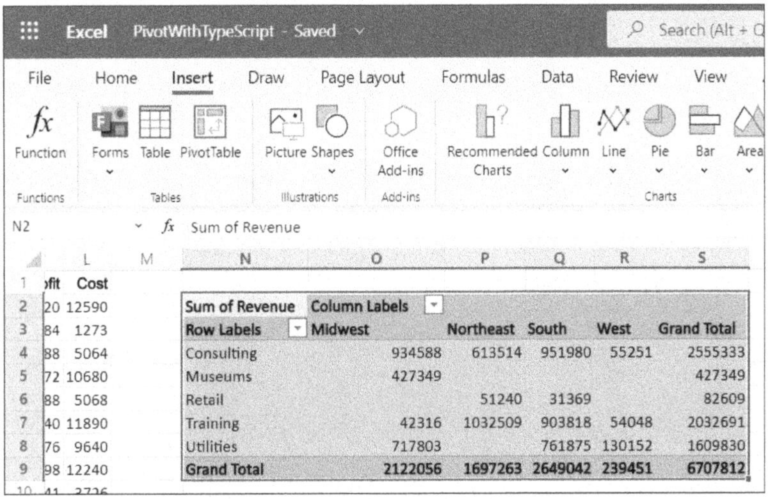

FIGURE 13-34 A pivot table created in Excel Online from a TypeScript macro.

It was back in 2018, in the pages of the sixth edition of this book, that I wrote, "Excel Online will never support the creation of pivot tables." So—this is amazing—just six years later, you are creating pivot tables in Excel Online and creating them with a script.

The script recorder is not perfect, but neither is the VBA macro recorder.

People who care a lot about speed note that the TypeScript macros are slower than VBA, but for this simple example, it does not matter.

There are still gaps. When you look at Figure 13-34, you might want to change "For Empty Cells, Show" to zero. There is a setting in Excel Online for this, but when you try to record a script for how to make that change, the macro recorder tells you that this is not yet supported in TypeScript:

```
// Unsupported event received: PivotTable.nullStringChanged
```

I am writing this in 2024. Within a few years, these gaps will eventually be filled.

Next steps

In Chapter 14, "Advanced pivot table tips and techniques," you'll learn many techniques for handling common questions and issues related to pivot tables.

Advanced pivot table tips and techniques

In this chapter, you will learn 23 pivot table tricks and techniques:

- Tip 1: Force pivot tables to refresh automatically

- Tip 2: Refresh all pivot tables in a workbook at the same time

- Tip 3: Sort data items in a unique order, not ascending or descending

- Tip 4: Use (or prevent using) a custom list for sorting your pivot table

- Tip 5: Use pivot table defaults to change the behavior of all future pivot tables

- Tip 6: Turn pivot tables into hard data

- Tip 7: Fill the empty cells left by row fields

- Tip 8: Add a rank number field to a pivot table

- Tip 9: Reduce the size of pivot table reports

- Tip 10: Create an automatically expanding data range

- Tip 11: Compare tables using a pivot table

- Tip 12: AutoFilter a pivot table

- Tip 13: Force two number formats in a pivot table

- Tip 14: Format individual values in a pivot table

- Tip 15: Format sections of a pivot table

- Tip 16: Create a frequency distribution with a pivot table

- Tip 17: Use a pivot table to explode a data set to different tabs

- Tip 18: Apply restrictions on pivot tables and pivot fields

- Tip 19: Use a pivot table to explode a data set to different workbooks

- Tip 20: Use percentage change from previous for year-over-year

- Tip 21: Do a two-way VLOOKUP with Power Query

- Tip 22: Create a slicer to control data from two different data sets

- Tip 23: Format your slicers

In this chapter, you'll discover some techniques that provide unique solutions to some of the most common pivot table problems. Take some time to glance at the topics covered here. Who knows? You might find a few unique tips that can help you tackle some of your pivot table conundrums!

Tip 1: Force pivot tables to refresh automatically

In some situations, you might need to have pivot tables refresh themselves automatically. For instance, suppose you create a pivot table report for your manager. You might not be able to trust that he will refresh the pivot table when needed.

You can force each pivot table to automatically refresh when the workbook opens by following these steps:

1. Right-click the pivot table and select PivotTable Options.

2. In the PivotTable Options dialog that appears, select the Data tab.

3. Select the Refresh Data When Opening The File Property checkbox.

When this property is activated, the pivot table refreshes itself each time the workbook in which it's located is opened.

> **Tip** The Refresh Data When Opening The File property must be set for each pivot table individually.

Tip 2: Refresh all pivot tables in a workbook at the same time

When you have multiple pivot tables in a workbook, refreshing all of them can be bothersome. Excel has a great way to refresh all pivot tables at one time. Click the Refresh All button on the Data tab, as shown in Figure 14-1. The downside to this method is that it also refreshes an external data connection, which can be a lengthy process. But if you do not have any external data connections, this is an easy way to refresh all of the tables.

FIGURE 14-1 The Refresh All button in the Data tab will refresh all pivot tables and external data connections.

Tip 3: Sort data items in a unique order, not ascending or descending

The region headings across the top of Figure 14-2 show the default sequence of regions in a pivot table report. Alphabetically, the regions are shown in the sequence Midwest, North, South, and West. If your company is based in California, company tradition might dictate that the West region be shown first, followed by Midwest, North, and South. Unfortunately, neither an ascending sort order nor a descending sort order can help you with this.

	A	B	C	D	E	F
3	Sum of Sales_Amount	Region				
4	Product_Description	MIDWEST	NORTH	SOUTH	WEST	Grand Total
5	Cleaning & Housekeeping Services	$174,518	$534,282	$283,170	$146,623	$1,138,593
6	Facility Maintenance and Repair	$463,077	$606,747	$846,515	$444,820	$2,361,158
7	Fleet Maintenance	$448,800	$610,791	$1,046,231	$521,976	$2,627,798
8	Green Plants and Foliage Care	$93,562	$155,021	$157,821	$870,379	$1,276,783
9	Landscaping/Grounds Care	$190,003	$299,309	$335,676	$365,928	$1,190,915
10	Predictive Maintenance/Preventative Maintenance	$478,928	$572,860	$472,045	$655,092	$2,178,925
11	Grand Total	$1,848,887	$2,779,009	$3,141,458	$3,004,818	$10,774,172
12						

FIGURE 14-2 Company tradition dictates that the Region field should be in West–Midwest–North–South sequence.

You can rearrange data items in your pivot table manually by simply typing the exact name of the data item where you would like to see its data. You can also drag the data item where you want it.

To solve the problem in this example, you simply type **WEST** in cell B4 and then press Enter. The pivot table responds by resequencing the regions. The West region's $3 million in sales automatically moves from column E to column B, as shown in Figure 14-3. The remaining regions move over to the next three columns.

	A	B	C	D	E	F
3	Sum of Sales_Amount	Region				
4	Product_Description	WEST	MIDWEST	NORTH	SOUTH	Grand Total
5	Cleaning & Housekeeping Services	$146,623	$174,518	$534,282	$283,170	$1,138,593
6	Facility Maintenance and Repair	$444,820	$463,077	$606,747	$846,515	$2,361,158
7	Fleet Maintenance	$521,976	$448,800	$610,791	$1,046,231	$2,627,798
8	Green Plants and Foliage Care	$870,379	$93,562	$155,021	$157,821	$1,276,783
9	Landscaping/Grounds Care	$365,928	$190,003	$299,309	$335,676	$1,190,915
10	Predictive Maintenance/Preventative Maintenance	$655,092	$478,928	$572,860	$472,045	$2,178,925
11	Grand Total	$3,004,818	$1,848,887	$2,779,009	$3,141,458	$10,774,172
12						

FIGURE 14-3 After typing WEST in B4, the numbers for West move from column E to column B.

Tip 4: Using (or prevent using) a custom list for sorting your pivot table

The technique of typing **WEST** in cell B4 in the previous tip is a great way to impress your friends at a bar, but it would be tedious to do this over and over. If your source data is stored in a worksheet and not in the data model or external data, you can permanently have all future pivot tables appear in the order of West, Midwest, North, and South by creating a custom list.

Type the regions in consecutive vertical cells in the proper sequence. Select the cells, and choose Go To File | Options | Advanced. Scroll all the way to the bottom and click Edit Custom Lists.

Excel opens the Custom Lists dialog, which is where Excel stores lists such as January, February, March, and Monday, Tuesday, Wednesday.

If you remembered to select your list before opening the dialog, simply click the Import button to add a new list (see Figure 14-4).

Custom lists are specific to one computer and one version of Excel. If you create a custom list in Excel 2016, it will not be available in Excel 2019. However, if you are only using one version of Excel, all future pivot tables will be sequenced using the custom list.

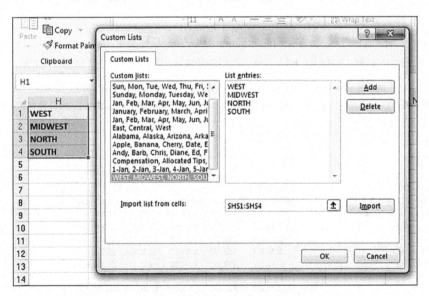

FIGURE 14-4 Add a new custom list with regions in the proper sequence.

Note   What if you later add regions for Canada and Mexico? Items that are in the custom list will appear first, followed by items missing from the custom list in alphabetical sequence. Your report will show West, Midwest, North, South, Canada, and Mexico. The solution, in this case, is to open the Custom Lists dialog, edit the list, and click Add to memorize the new list.

Note in Figure 14-4 that two lists contain "West." If there is a tie, the list nearest the bottom of the Custom Lists wins.

Sometimes, you might have the opposite problem. Say that your company is really chummy, and all the team members are reported by their first names. For some reason, Jan, May, or Friday keeps showing up before Andy, Barb, and Chris (see Figure 14-5).

	A	B	C	D	E
1	Team Member	Sales			
2	Andy	87.04			
3	Barb	50.85		Team Member ▾	Sum of Sales
4	Chris	29.99		Jan	67.53
5	Friday	54.88		Friday	171.06
6	Jan	67.53		May	225.31
7	May	80.03		Andy	121.49
8	Diane	69.81		Barb	50.85
9	Ed	14.28		Chris	51.73
10	Gary	86.35		Diane	147.44

FIGURE 14-5 Jan keeps showing up at the top of your pivot table reports.

Notice in Figure 14-4 that the third list already includes Jan and May. You can't see it, but the second list includes Friday. Because those people appear in a custom list, they get sorted before all of the people "missing" from the custom list.

I did ask the Pivot Table team at Microsoft why they split Jan and May with Friday. It is not alphabetical. It is not arranged by list from the bottom of the dialog to the top. The apparent answer is that no one knows anymore or that they don't have time to research a question that is only of interest to a few people.

One solution: Stop hiring people named May, Jan, or Friday. A less stressful solution: Display the Options dialog for a pivot table. On the Totals & Filters tab, clear the entry for Use Custom Lists When Sorting (see Figure 14-6).

If Jan or May will be a permanent problem, you can turn this setting off for all future pivot tables. See Tip 5.

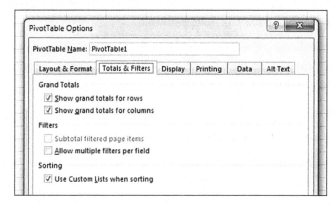

FIGURE 14-6 You can stop the sorting by custom lists using this setting.

Tip 5: Use pivot table defaults to change the behavior of all future pivot tables

Do you have a couple of pivot table default behaviors that you always turn off? I always want empty cells to show 0 and start in Tabular layout with Repeat All Item Labels turned on. Maybe you need to turn off Use Custom Lists When Sorting.

In the summer of 2017, Excel added the Edit Default Layout button for pivot tables. Go to File | Options | Data to find the Edit Default Layout button.

Initially, the Edit Default Layout dialog only offers a few settings, but if you click the PivotTable Options button, as shown in Figure 14-7, you can permanently change all the settings in PivotTable Options.

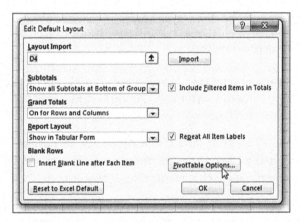

FIGURE 14-7 Change defaults for future pivot tables.

Tip 6: Turn pivot tables into hard data

Say that you created a pivot table in order to summarize and shape data. You do not want to keep the source data, nor do you want to keep the pivot table with all its overhead.

Turning a pivot table into hard data enables you to use the pivot table results without having to deal with the source data or a pivot cache. How you turn the pivot table into hard data depends on how much of the pivot table you are going to copy.

If you are copying just a portion of a pivot table, do the following:

1. Select the data you want to copy from the pivot table, right-click, and select Copy.

2. Right-click anywhere on a spreadsheet and select Paste.

If you are copying an entire pivot table, follow these steps:

1. Select the entire pivot table using the mouse or choose PivotTable Analyze | Select | Entire PivotTable. Copy with Ctrl+C.

2. Right-click anywhere on a spreadsheet and press Ctrl+Shift+V to Paste Values.

Tip You might want to consider removing any subtotals before turning a pivot table into hard data. Subtotals typically aren't very useful when you are creating a stand-alone data set.

To remove the subtotals from a pivot table, select "Do Not Show Subtotals" from the Subtotals dropdown on the left side of the Design tab in the ribbon.

Tip 7: Fill the empty cells left by row fields

When you turn a pivot table into hard data, you are left with the values created by the pivot table, as well as the pivot table's data structure. For example, the data in Figure 14-8 came from a pivot table that had a Tabular layout.

	A	B	C	D
3	Region	Market	Product_Description	Sum of Sales_Amount
4	⊟MIDWEST	⊟DENVER	Cleaning & Housekeeping Services	$12,564
5			Facility Maintenance and Repair	$160,324
6			Fleet Maintenance	$170,190
7			Green Plants and Foliage Care	$42,409
8			Landscaping/Grounds Care	$73,622
9			Predictive Maintenance/Preventative Maintenance	$186,475
10		DENVER Total		$645,583
11		⊟KANSASCITY	Cleaning & Housekeeping Services	$65,439
12			Facility Maintenance and Repair	$132,120
13			Fleet Maintenance	$133,170
14			Green Plants and Foliage Care	$35,315
15			Landscaping/Grounds Care	$52,442
16			Predictive Maintenance/Preventative Maintenance	$156,412
17		KANSASCITY Total		$574,899
18		⊟TULSA	Cleaning & Housekeeping Services	$96,515
19			Facility Maintenance and Repair	$170,632
20			Fleet Maintenance	$145,440
21			Green Plants and Foliage Care	$15,838
22			Landscaping/Grounds Care	$63,939
23			Predictive Maintenance/Preventative Maintenance	$136,041
24		TULSA Total		$628,405
25	MIDWEST Total			$1,848,887

FIGURE 14-8 It would be impractical to use this data anywhere else without filling in the empty cells left by the row field.

Notice that the Market field kept the same row structure it had when this data was in the row area of the pivot table. It would be unwise to use this table anywhere else without filling in the empty cells left by the row field, but how do you easily fill these empty cells?

The next sections discuss two options provided by Excel to fix this problem effectively.

Option 1: Implement the Repeat All Item Labels feature

The first option for easily filling the empty cells left by row fields is to apply the Repeat All Item Labels functionality. This feature ensures that all item labels are repeated to create a solid block of contiguous cells. To implement this feature, place your cursor anywhere in your pivot table. Then go to the ribbon and select Design | Report Layout | Repeat All Item Labels (see Figure 14-9).

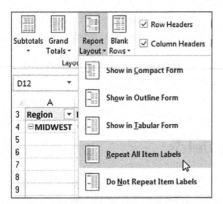

FIGURE 14-9 The Repeat All Item Labels option enables you to show your pivot data in one contiguous block of data.

Figure 14-10 shows what a pivot table with this feature applied looks like.

Now, you can turn this pivot table into hard values, and you will end up with a contiguous table of data without gaps.

	A	B	C	D
3	Region	Market	Product_Description	Sum of Sales_Amount
4	MIDWEST	DENVER	Cleaning & Housekeeping Services	$12,564
5	MIDWEST	DENVER	Facility Maintenance and Repair	$160,324
6	MIDWEST	DENVER	Fleet Maintenance	$170,190
7	MIDWEST	DENVER	Green Plants and Foliage Care	$42,409
8	MIDWEST	DENVER	Landscaping/Grounds Care	$73,622
9	MIDWEST	DENVER	Predictive Maintenance/Preventative Maintenance	$186,475
10	MIDWEST	DENVER Total		$645,583
11	MIDWEST	KANSASCITY	Cleaning & Housekeeping Services	$65,439
12	MIDWEST	KANSASCITY	Facility Maintenance and Repair	$132,120
13	MIDWEST	KANSASCITY	Fleet Maintenance	$133,170
14	MIDWEST	KANSASCITY	Green Plants and Foliage Care	$35,315
15	MIDWEST	KANSASCITY	Landscaping/Grounds Care	$52,442
16	MIDWEST	KANSASCITY	Predictive Maintenance/Preventative Maintenance	$156,412
17	MIDWEST	KANSASCITY Total		$574,899
18	MIDWEST	TULSA	Cleaning & Housekeeping Services	$96,515
19	MIDWEST	TULSA	Facility Maintenance and Repair	$170,632
20	MIDWEST	TULSA	Fleet Maintenance	$145,440
21	MIDWEST	TULSA	Green Plants and Foliage Care	$15,838
22	MIDWEST	TULSA	Landscaping/Grounds Care	$63,939
23	MIDWEST	TULSA	Predictive Maintenance/Preventative Maintenance	$136,041
24	MIDWEST	TULSA Total		$628,405
25	MIDWEST Total			$1,848,887

FIGURE 14-10 The Repeat All Item Labels option fills all cells with data items.

Option 2: Use Excel's Go To Special functionality

The other way to easily fill the empty cells left by row fields involves using Excel's Go To Special functionality.

You start by converting your pivot table into hard data, as explained in Tip 6. Next, select the range in columns A and B that extends from the first row with blanks to the row just above the grand total. In the present example, this is A4:B100. Choose Home | Find & Select | Go To Special. (Alternatively, use Ctrl+G or F5 to open the Go To dialog and then press the Special button.) This activates the Go To Special dialog, which is a powerful feature that enables you to modify your selection based on various conditions (see Figure 14-11). In this dialog, choose the Blanks option and click OK. Now, only the blank cells in the selection are selected.

FIGURE 14-11 Using the Go To Special dialog enables you to select all the blank cells to be filled.

Enter a formula to copy the pivot item values from the cell above to the blank cells. With four keystrokes, you can do this: Type an equal sign, press the up arrow key, and hold down the Ctrl key while pressing Enter. The equal sign tells Excel that you are entering a formula in the active cell. Pressing the up arrow key points to the cell above the active cell. Pressing Ctrl+Enter tells Excel to enter a similar formula in all the selected cells instead of just the active cell. As Figure 14-12 shows, you enter a formula to fill in all the blank cells at once with these few keystrokes.

At this point, there is no need for the formulas. You will want to convert those formulas to values. Reselect the original range A4:B100. You can then press Ctrl+C to copy and Ctrl+Shift+V to convert the formulas to values. This method provides a quick way to easily fill in the Outline view provided by the pivot table.

	A	B	C	D
3	Region	Market	Product_Description	Sum of Sales_Amount
4	MIDWEST	DENVER	Cleaning & Housekeeping Services	$12,564
5	MIDWEST	DENVER	Facility Maintenance and Repair	$160,324
6	MIDWEST	DENVER	Fleet Maintenance	$170,190
7	MIDWEST	DENVER	Green Plants and Foliage Care	$42,409
8	MIDWEST	DENVER	Landscaping/Grounds Care	$73,622
9	MIDWEST	DENVER	Predictive Maintenance/Preventative Maintenance	$186,475
10	MIDWEST	DENVER Total		$645,583
11	MIDWEST	KANSASCITY	Cleaning & Housekeeping Services	$65,439
12	MIDWEST	KANSASCITY	Facility Maintenance and Repair	$132,120
13	MIDWEST	KANSASCITY	Fleet Maintenance	$133,170
14	MIDWEST	KANSASCITY	Green Plants and Foliage Care	$35,315
15	MIDWEST	KANSASCITY	Landscaping/Grounds Care	$52,442
16	MIDWEST	KANSASCITY	Predictive Maintenance/Preventative Maintenance	$156,412
17	MIDWEST	KANSASCITY Total		$574,899
18	MIDWEST	TULSA	Cleaning & Housekeeping Services	$96,515
19	MIDWEST	TULSA	Facility Maintenance and Repair	$170,632
20	MIDWEST	TULSA	Fleet Maintenance	$145,440
21	MIDWEST	TULSA	Green Plants and Foliage Care	$15,838
22	MIDWEST	TULSA	Landscaping/Grounds Care	$63,939
23	MIDWEST	TULSA	Predictive Maintenance/Preventative Maintenance	$136,041
24	MIDWEST	TULSA Total		$628,405

FIGURE 14-12 Pressing Ctrl+Enter enters the formula in all selected cells.

Tip 8: Add a rank number field to a pivot table

When you are sorting and ranking a field with many data items, it can be difficult to determine the number ranking of the data item you are currently analyzing. Furthermore, you might want to turn your pivot table into hard values for further analysis. An integer field that contains the actual rank number of each data item could be helpful in analysis outside the pivot table.

Start with a pivot table like the one shown in Figure 14-13. Notice that the same data measure, Sum of Sales_Amount, is shown twice.

	A	B	C
1			
2			
3	Market	Sum of Sales_Amount	Sum of Sales_Amount2
4	BUFFALO	450478.27	450478.27
5	CALIFORNIA	2254735.38	2254735.38
6	CANADA	776245.27	776245.27
7	CHARLOTTE	890522.49	890522.49
8	DALLAS	467089.47	467089.47
9	DENVER	645583.29	645583.29
10	FLORIDA	1450392	1450392
11	KANSASCITY	574898.97	574898.97
12	MICHIGAN	678704.95	678704.95
13	NEWORLEANS	333453.65	333453.65
14	NEWYORK	873580.91	873580.91
15	PHOENIX	570255.09	570255.09
16	SEATTLE	179827.21	179827.21
17	TULSA	628404.83	628404.83
18	Grand Total	10774171.78	10774171.78

FIGURE 14-13 Start with a pivot table where the data value is listed twice.

Right-click the second instance of the data measure and select Show Values As | Rank Largest To Smallest (see Figure 14-14).

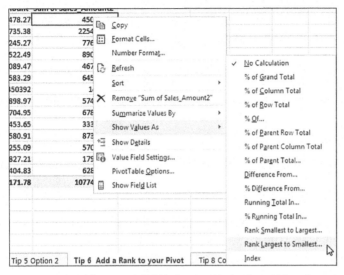

FIGURE 14-14 Adding a rank field is simple with the Show Values As option.

When your ranking is applied, you can adjust the labels and formatting to look as shown in Figure 14-15. This gives you a clean-looking ranking report.

Market	Sum of Sales_Amount	Rank
BUFFALO	$450,478	12
CALIFORNIA	$2,254,735	1
CANADA	$776,245	5
CHARLOTTE	$890,522	3
DALLAS	$467,089	11
DENVER	$645,583	7
FLORIDA	$1,450,392	2
KANSASCITY	$574,899	9
MICHIGAN	$678,705	6
NEWORLEANS	$333,454	13
NEWYORK	$873,581	4
PHOENIX	$570,255	10
SEATTLE	$179,827	14
TULSA	$628,405	8
Grand Total	$10,774,172	

FIGURE 14-15 Your final pivot table, with ranking applied.

Tip 9: Reduce the size of pivot table reports

When you initiate the creation of a pivot table report, Excel takes a snapshot of your data set and stores it in a *pivot cache*, which is a special memory subsystem in which your data source is duplicated for quick access. That is to say, Excel literally makes a copy of your data and then stores it in a cache that is attached to your workbook.

Of course, the benefit you get from a pivot cache is optimization. Any changes you make to the pivot table report, such as rearranging fields, adding new fields, and hiding items, are made rapidly and with minimal overhead.

The downside of the pivot cache is that it basically doubles the size of a workbook. So, every time you make a new pivot table from scratch, you essentially add to the file size of your workbook.

Delete the source data worksheet

If your workbooks have both your pivot table and your source data worksheet, you are wasting space. That is, you are essentially distributing two copies of the same data.

You can delete your source data, and your pivot table will function just fine. After you delete the source data, when you save the pivot table, the file shrinks. Your clients can use the pivot table as normal, and your workbook is half as big. The only functionality you lose is the ability to refresh the pivot data because the source data is not there.

What happens if your clients need to see the source data? Well, they can simply double-click the intersection of the row and column grand totals. This tells Excel to output the contents of the pivot table's cache into a new worksheet. So, with one double-click, your clients can re-create the source data that makes up the pivot table!

Tip 10: Create an automatically expanding data range

You will undoubtedly encounter situations in which you have pivot table reports that are updated daily (that is, records are constantly being added to the source data). When records are added to a pivot table's source data set, you must redefine the range that is captured before the new records are brought into the pivot table. Redefining the source range for a pivot table once in a while is no sweat, but when the source data is changed daily or weekly, it can start to get bothersome.

The solution is to turn your source data table into an Excel table using Ctrl+T. This works even if you convert the table after the pivot table has been built. Again, Excel tables enable you to create a defined range that automatically shrinks or expands with the data. This means that any component, chart, pivot table, or formula tied to that range can keep up with changes in your data.

To implement this trick, simply highlight one cell in your source data and then click the Table icon on the Insert tab (see Figure 14-16). Confirm the range to include in your table, and then click OK.

After your source data has been converted to an Excel table, any pivot table you build on top of it automatically includes all records when your source data expands or shrinks.

FIGURE 14-16 Convert your source data into an Excel table.

What if the data for your pivot table is the result of a complex dynamic array? As of 2024, it is still illegal to use a dynamic array inside of a Ctrl+T table.

For example, say that cell M1 contains a formula such as =VSTACK(A1:I1,FILTER(A2:I564,D2:D564=K1)). That formula in M1 might currently return data to cells M1:U82 but would return a different number of rows if the sector entered in K1 changes. Ideally, you would want the pivot table to show the new size of the data.

If you select this data and use Insert, PivotTable, the dialog box would show source data of Data!$M$1:$U$82. If you want this pivot table to resize with the dynamic array, change the source data in the dialog to Data!$M$1#.

Tip Keep in mind that although you won't have to redefine the source range anymore, you will still need to trigger a Refresh in order to have your pivot table show the current data.

Tip 11: Compare tables using a pivot table

If you've been an analyst for more than a week, you've been asked to compare two separate tables to come up with some brilliant analysis of the differences between them. This is a common scenario where leveraging a pivot table can save you some time.

Say that you have two tables that show customers in 2029 and in 2030. Figure 14-17 shows that these are two separate tables. For this example, the tables were made small for instructional purposes, but imagine that you're working with something bigger here.

	A	B	C	D	E
1	2029 Customers			2030 Customers	
2	Customer	Revenue		Customer	Revenue
3	PHALCO Corp.	$456.27		PHALSM Corp.	$1,902.25
4	PHALLA Corp.	$3,974.07		PHALTA Corp.	$2,095.01
5	PHALSE Corp.	$565.34		PHALWH Corp.	$1,740.27
6	PHALSM Corp.	$1,902.25		PHMAN Corp.	$3,228.33
7	POMTRA Corp.	$2,201.90		POPPIT Corp.	$604.18
8	POPAUS Corp.	$1,891.73		POPUSL Corp.	$870.28
9	POPCOA Corp.	$1,284.61		POPUSP Corp.	$2,421.01
10	PORADA Corp.	$10,131.22		PORADA Corp.	$10,131.22
11	PORCFA Corp.	$1,187.71		PORADY Corp.	$1,012.94
12				PORCFA Corp.	$1,187.71

FIGURE 14-17 You need to compare these two tables.

The idea is to create one table that combines both table. Add a Year column to tag which data comes from which table as shown in Figure 14-18.

Customer	Revenue	Year
PHALCO Corp.	$456.27	2029
PHALLA Corp.	$3,974.07	2029
PHALSE Corp.	$565.34	2029
PHALSM Corp.	$1,902.25	2029
POMTRA Corp.	$2,201.90	2029
POPAUS Corp.	$1,891.73	2029
POPCOA Corp.	$1,284.61	2029
PORADA Corp.	$10,131.22	2029
PORCFA Corp.	$1,187.71	2029
PHALSM Corp.	$1,902.25	2030
PHALTA Corp.	$2,095.01	2030
PHALWH Corp.	$1,740.27	2030
PHMAN Corp.	$3,228.33	2030
POPPIT Corp.	$604.18	2030
POPUSL Corp.	$870.28	2030
POPUSP Corp.	$2,421.01	2030
PORADA Corp.	$10,131.22	2030
PORADY Corp.	$1,012.94	2030
PORCFA Corp.	$1,187.71	2030

FIGURE 14-18 Combine your tables into one table.

After you have combined the tables, use the combined data set to create a new pivot table. Format the pivot table so that the table tag (the identifier that tells which table the data came from) is in the column area of the pivot table. In Figure 14-19, years are in the column area, and customers are in the row area. The data area contains the revenue for each customer name.

As you can see in Figure 14-19, you instantly get a visual indication of which customers are only in the prior year table, which are in the current year table, and which are in both tables.

Sum of Revenue Year			
Customer	2029	2030	Grand Total
PHALCO Corp.	456.27	0	456.27
PHALLA Corp.	3974.07	0	3974.07
PHALSE Corp.	565.34	0	565.34
PHALSM Corp.	1902.25	1902.25	3804.5
PHALTA Corp.	0	2095.01	2095.01
PHALWH Corp.	0	1740.27	1740.27
PHMAN Corp.	0	3228.33	3228.33
POMTRA Corp.	2201.9	0	2201.9
POPAUS Corp.	1891.73	0	1891.73
POPCOA Corp.	1284.61	0	1284.61
POPPIT Corp.	0	604.18	604.18
POPUSL Corp.	0	870.28	870.28
POPUSP Corp.	0	2421.01	2421.01
PORADA Corp.	10131.22	10131.22	20262.44
PORADY Corp.	0	1012.94	1012.94
PORCFA Corp.	1187.71	1187.71	2375.42
Grand Total	23595.1	25193.2	48788.3

FIGURE 14-19 Create a pivot table to get an easy-to-read visual comparison of the two data sets.

Instead of Count Of Customer, you could add Revenue to the Values area and see a comparison of this year's and last year's revenues.

Tip 12: AutoFilter a pivot table

The conventional wisdom is that you can't apply the Filter found on the Data tab to a pivot table. Technically, that's true. But there is a way to trick Excel into making it happen.

The trick is to place your cursor directly adjacent to the last title in the pivot table, as shown in Figure 14-20. (You can actually use any empty cell immediately to the right of your pivot table.) Once you have it there, you can go to the ribbon, select Data, and then select Filter.

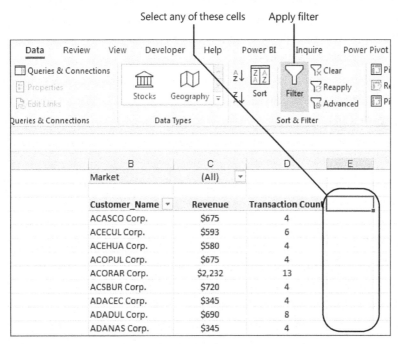

FIGURE 14-20 Place your cursor just outside your pivot table.

At this point, you have filter dropdown arrows added to C3 and D3! You can now do cool things like apply a custom filter to find all customers with above-average transaction counts (see Figure 14-21).

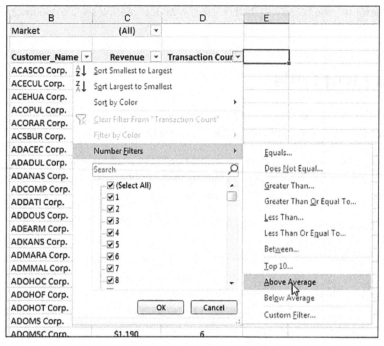

FIGURE 14-21 With a Data filter implemented, you can take advantage of custom filtering that's not normally available with pivot tables.

If you have product lines stretching across the top of your report, you might filter to show the top ten customers for one specific product (see Figure 14-22).

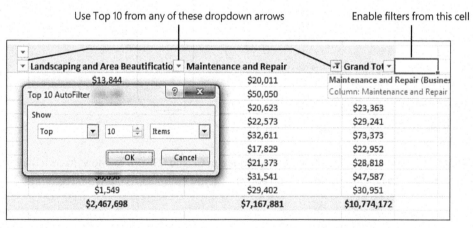

Use Top 10 from any of these dropdown arrows

Enable filters from this cell

	Landscaping and Area Beautificatio	Maintenance and Repair	Grand Tot
	$13,844	$20,011	Maintenance and Repair (Busines
		$50,050	Column: Maintenance and Repair
		$20,623	$23,363
		$22,573	$29,241
		$32,611	$73,373
		$17,829	$22,952
		$21,373	$28,818
		$31,541	$47,587
	$1,549	$29,402	$30,951
	$2,467,698	$7,167,881	$10,774,172

Top 10 AutoFilter

Show

Top [▼] 10 [⬍] Items [▼]

OK   Cancel

FIGURE 14-22 Choose a Top 10 filter from one column by using the filter trick.

Another use is to create a Top 10 report using the Top 10 filter but ask for the Top 11 values, as shown in Figure 14-23. To the Data filter, the largest "customer" is the Grand Total row. Asking for customers 2 through 11 will show the customers ranked 1 through 10. The advantage of this method is that the Percentage Of Total column will be as a percentage of the Grand Total instead of the percentage of only 10 customers. Note that the grand total is the total of all records and not just the top ten.

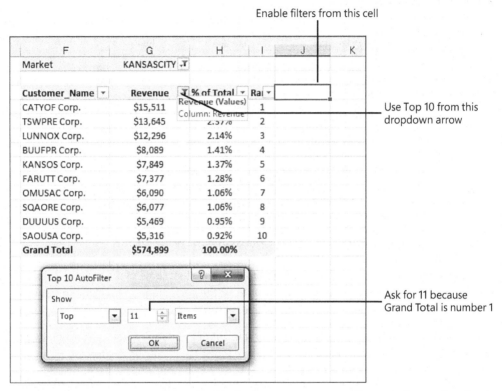

FIGURE 14-23 Using the Filter option and asking for the Top 11 customers will get you the grand total and 10 customers.

 Caution Using the filter from the Data tab is not supported by Microsoft. If you refresh or change the shape of your pivot table, expect to have to reapply any filters created with this method.

Also, to turn off the filters, you have to select a cell immediately to the right of your pivot table.

This is a fantastic way to add an extra layer of analytical capabilities to pivot table reports.

Tip 13: Force two number formats in a pivot table

Every now and then, you have to deal with a situation where a normalized data set makes it difficult to build an appropriate pivot table. For example, the data set shown in Figure 14-24 contains metrics information for each Market. Notice that there is a column that identifies the Measure and another that specifies the corresponding Value.

	A	B	C	D	E
1	Region	Market	Product_Description	Measure	Value
2	MIDWEST	DENVER	Cleaning & Housekeeping Services	Revenue	12563.91
3	MIDWEST	DENVER	Cleaning & Housekeeping Services	Conversion Rate	0.62
4	MIDWEST	DENVER	Facility Maintenance and Repair	Revenue	160324.22
5	MIDWEST	DENVER	Facility Maintenance and Repair	Conversion Rate	0.64
6	MIDWEST	DENVER	Fleet Maintenance	Revenue	170190.26
7	MIDWEST	DENVER	Fleet Maintenance	Conversion Rate	0.20
8	MIDWEST	DENVER	Green Plants and Foliage Care	Revenue	42408.61
9	MIDWEST	DENVER	Green Plants and Foliage Care	Conversion Rate	0.88
10	MIDWEST	DENVER	Landscaping/Grounds Care	Revenue	73621.62
11	MIDWEST	DENVER	Landscaping/Grounds Care	Conversion Rate	0.92
12	MIDWEST	DENVER	Predictive Maintenance/Preventative	Revenue	186474.67
13	MIDWEST	DENVER	Predictive Maintenance/Preventative	Conversion Rate	0.93
14	MIDWEST	KANSASCITY	Cleaning & Housekeeping Services	Revenue	65439.14
15	MIDWEST	KANSASCITY	Cleaning & Housekeeping Services	Conversion Rate	0.61

FIGURE 14-24 This metric table has many different data types in one Value field.

Although this is generally a nicely formatted table, notice that some of the measures are meant to be the number format, whereas others are meant to be the percentage. In the database where this data set originated, the Value field is a double data type, so this works.

The problem is that when you create a pivot table out of this data set, you can't assign two different number formats for the Value field. After all, the rule is one field, one number format.

As you can see in Figure 14-25, trying to set the number format for the percentage measures also changes the Format for the measures that are supposed to be straight numbers.

	A	B	C
1	Market	BUFFALO	
2			
3	Sum of Value	Measure	
4	Product_Description	Conversion Rate	Revenue
5	Cleaning & Housekeeping Services	27.08%	6684485.00%
6	Facility Maintenance and Repair	99.53%	6956962.00%
7	Fleet Maintenance	75.26%	8646011.00%
8	Green Plants and Foliage Care	0.36%	3483113.00%
9	Landscaping/Grounds Care	5.38%	6546546.00%
10	Predictive Maintenance/Preventative Maintenanc	31.58%	12730710.00%

FIGURE 14-25 You can have only one number format assigned to each data measure.

The solution is to apply a custom number format that formats any value greater than 1.5 as a number and any value less than 1.5 as a percentage. In the Format Cells dialog, click Custom and then enter the following syntax in the Type input box (see Figure 14-26):

    [>=1.5]$#,##0;[<1.5]0.0%

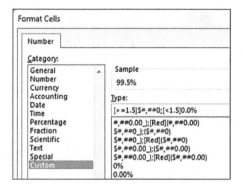

FIGURE 14-26 Apply a custom number format, telling Excel to format any number less than 1.5 as a percentage.

The result, shown in Figure 14-27, is that each Measure is now formatted appropriately. Obviously, you have to get a little lucky with the parameters of the situation you're working in. Although this technique doesn't work in all scenarios, it does open up some interesting options.

	A	B	C
1	Market	BUFFALO ⊤	
2			
3	**Sum of Value**	**Measure** ▾	
4	**Product_Description** ▾	**Conversion Rate**	**Revenue**
5	Cleaning & Housekeeping Services	27.1%	$66,845
6	Facility Maintenance and Repair	99.5%	$69,570
7	Fleet Maintenance	75.3%	$86,460
8	Green Plants and Foliage Care	0.4%	$34,831
9	Landscaping/Grounds Care	5.4%	$65,465
10	Predictive Maintenance/Preventative Maintenance	31.6%	$127,307

FIGURE 14-27 Two formats in one data field. Amazing!

Tip 14: Format individual values in a pivot table

If you have Microsoft 365 or Office 2021 or later, a feature lets you format certain values in a pivot table, and that formatting will stick even after pivoting or refreshing the pivot table.

For example, in Figure 14-28, right-click the cell containing East sales of Cherry and choose Format Cells. Apply a red fill to that cell.

When you pivot the data, the red formatting sticks with that cell (see Figure 14-29). Move Product from columns to rows. Move Region from rows to columns. After each move, the red cell moves with the $13,036 value.

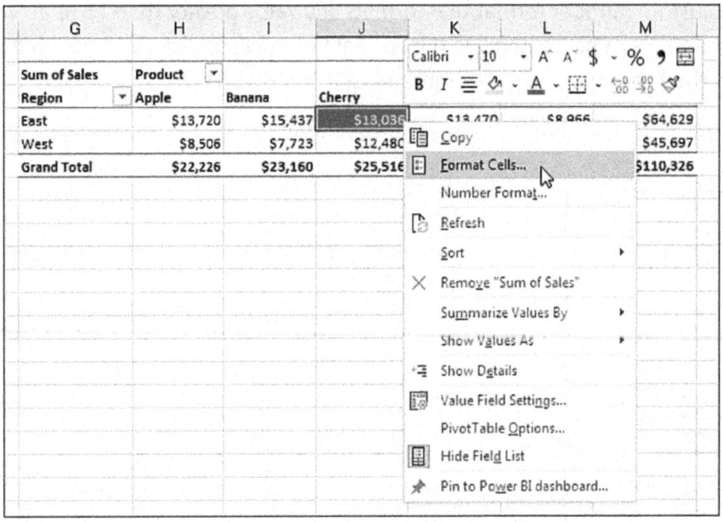

FIGURE 14-28 Use Format Cells in the right-click menu to format one or more cells in the Values area of a pivot table.

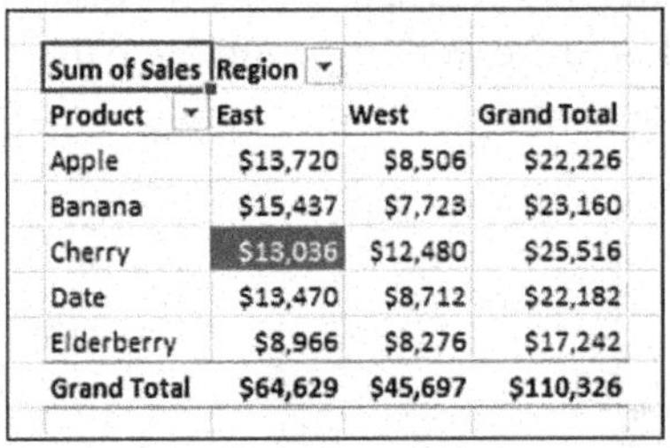

Sum of Sales	Region		
Product	East	West	Grand Total
Apple	$13,720	$8,506	$22,226
Banana	$15,437	$7,723	$23,160
Cherry	$13,036	$12,480	$25,516
Date	$13,470	$8,712	$22,182
Elderberry	$8,966	$8,276	$17,242
Grand Total	$64,629	$45,697	$110,326

FIGURE 14-29 After pivoting, the formatting sticks with that value.

Even more amazing: Add a new row field so that the East Cherry values occupy more cells. The red fill, which was previously only in one cell, expands to include all four cells that show East Cherry revenue. On the other hand, I am not sure why the total row for East Cherry is not also red see (Figure 14-30).

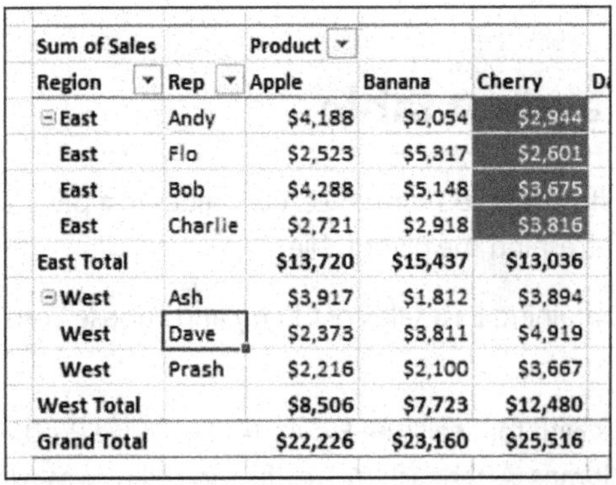

Sum of Sales		Product			
Region	Rep	Apple	Banana	Cherry	D
⊟East	Andy	$4,188	$2,054	$2,944	
East	Flo	$2,523	$5,317	$2,601	
East	Bob	$4,288	$5,148	$3,675	
East	Charlie	$2,721	$2,918	$3,816	
East Total		$13,720	$15,437	$13,036	
⊟West	Ash	$3,917	$1,812	$3,894	
West	Dave	$2,373	$3,811	$4,919	
West	Prash	$2,216	$2,100	$3,667	
West Total		$8,506	$7,723	$12,480	
Grand Total		$22,226	$23,160	$25,516	

FIGURE 14-30 Even if the pivot table expands, the red formatting stays with East Cherry.

The red formatting will stick if East is removed because of a filter or slicer, but the formatting will be lost if you completely remove Product or Region from the pivot table.

This new formatting trick in Office 365 would make the Tip 13 solution simpler. Rather than using a custom number format of $[>=1.5]\$\#,\#\#0;[<1.5]0.0\%$, you can simply select all of the cells in the Revenue column. Right-click. It is tempting to choose Number Format, but that will not work. Instead, choose Format Cells (see Figure 14-31). Apply a currency format.

Format Cells...applies to selected cells

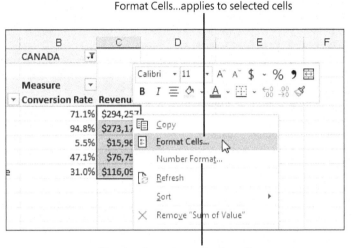

Number Format...applies to entire measure

FIGURE 14-31 To change all of the number formats for Revenue values, select those cells, right-click, and select Format Cells.

Tip 15: Format sections of a pivot table

While the new formatting trick in Tip 14 is great for Office 365, there is another legacy way to format areas of a pivot table available in all versions of Office.

To enable the method, open the Select dropdown on the PivotTable Analyze tab and choose Enable Selection (see Figure 14-32).

Once you have enabled selection, hover the mouse over the left portion of any cell in a pivot table. Watch for the mouse cursor to change to a right-facing black arrow. In Figure 14-33, hovering over the left quarter of cell H5 will select all Rep total rows.

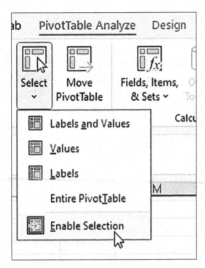

FIGURE 14-32 The legacy Selection feature is turned off by default.

	G	H	I	J
2	Region ▼	Rep ▼	Product ▾	Sum of Sales
3	⊟East	⊟Andy	Apple	$4,188
4	East	Andy	Cherry	$2,944
5	East	Andy Total		$7,132
6	East	⊟Flo	Apple	$2,523
7	East	Flo	Cherry	$2,601
8	East	Flo Total		$5,124

Cursor changes to black arrow when
over the left portion of H5

FIGURE 14-33 Hover over the left edge of a cell until you see the black arrow.

Click the left side of Andy Total, and all similar-level rows in the pivot table are selected. Apply a fill color, and you've effectively formatted all of the sales rep subtotal rows, as shown in Figure 14-34.

	G	H	I	J
2	Region ▼	Rep ▼	Product ▾	Sum of Sales
3	⊟East	⊟Andy	Apple	$4,188
4	East	Andy	Cherry	$2,944
5	East	Andy Total		$7,132
6	East	⊟Flo	Apple	$2,523
7	East	Flo	Cherry	$2,601
8	East	Flo Total		$5,124
9	East	⊟Bob	Apple	$4,288
10	East	Bob	Cherry	$3,675
11	East	Bob Total		$7,963
12	East	⊟Charlie	Apple	$2,721

FIGURE 14-34 When you click on the left side of Andy Total, all the cells at a similar level are selected.

There are many ways to select matching cells. If you hover over a Cherry cell in column I of Figure 14-35, all the Cherry cells will be selected.

	G	H	I	J
2	Region	Rep	Product	Sum of Sales
3	East	Andy	Apple	$4,188
4	East	Andy	Cherry	$2,944
5	East	Andy Total		$7,132
6	East	Flo	Apple	$2,523
7	East	Flo	Cherry	$2,601
8	East	Flo Total		$5,124
9	East	Bob	Apple	$4,288
10	East	Bob	Cherry	$3,675
11	East	Bob Total		$7,963

FIGURE 14-35 Click on the left edge of one Cherry cell to select all the Cherry cells and their associated sales.

Tip 16: Create a frequency distribution with a pivot table

If you've created a frequency distribution with the FREQUENCY function, you know it can quickly devolve into a confusing mess. Then there's the Histogram functionality you find in the Analysis ToolPak, which doesn't make life much better. Each time you have to change your bin ranges, you have to restart the entire process again.

In this tip, you'll learn how to use a pivot table to quickly implement a simple frequency distribution.

1. First, you need to create a pivot table where the data values are plotted in the Rows area (not the Values area). Notice that in Figure 14-36, the Sales_Amount field is placed in the Rows area.

FIGURE 14-36 Place your data measure in the Rows area.

2. Next, right-click any value in the Rows area and select Group. In the Grouping dialog (shown in Figure 14-37), set the Starting At and Ending At values, and then set the intervals. Essentially, this creates the frequency distribution.

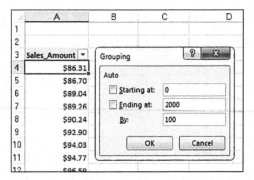

FIGURE 14-37 Use the Grouping dialog to create your frequency intervals.

3. After you click the OK button, you can leverage the result to create a distribution view of your data.

In Figure 14-38, you can see that Customer_Name has been added to get a frequency distribution of the number of customer transactions by dollar amount. Note that a sale amount of, say, exactly $400, would fall in the 400–500 range.

The obvious benefit of this technique is you can use the pivot table's report filter to interactively filter the data based on other dimensions, such as Region and Market. Also, unlike the Analysis ToolPak Histogram tool, you can quickly adjust your frequency intervals by simply right-clicking any number in the Rows area and selecting Group.

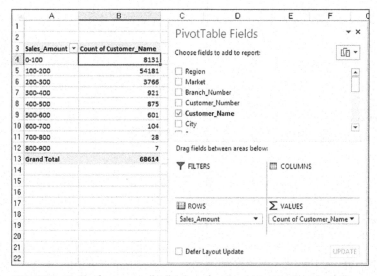

FIGURE 14-38 The frequency distribution of customer transactions by dollar amount.

Tip 17: Use a pivot table to explode a data set to different tabs

One of the most common requests an analyst gets is to create a separate pivot table report for each region, market, manager, or whatever. These types of requests usually lead to a painful manual process in which you copy a pivot table onto a new worksheet and then change the filter field to the appropriate region or manager. You then repeat this process as many times as you need to get through each selection.

Creating separate pivot table reports is one area where Excel really comes to the rescue. Excel has a function called Show Report Filter Pages that automatically creates a separate pivot table for each item in the filter fields. To use this function, simply create a pivot table with a filter field, as shown in Figure 14-39.

Place your cursor anywhere on the pivot table, and then go up to the ribbon to select the Analyze tab. On the Analyze tab, go to the PivotTable group, click the Options dropdown, and then select Show Report Filter Pages, as shown in Figure 14-40.

	A	B	C	D
1	Market	(All)		
2				
3	Sum of Sales_Amount	Sales_Period		
4	Product_Description	P01	P02	P03
5	Cleaning & Housekeeping Services	$80,083	$89,750	$78,182
6	Facility Maintenance and Repair	$121,304	$305,832	$115,232
7	Fleet Maintenance	$148,565	$297,315	$145,821
8	Green Plants and Foliage Care	$75,716	$135,529	$72,293
9	Landscaping/Grounds Care	$92,353	$99,173	$87,138
10	Predictive Maintenance/Preventative	$163,844	$189,317	$158,946
11	Grand Total	$681,865	$1,116,916	$657,611

FIGURE 14-39 Start with a pivot table that contains a filter field.

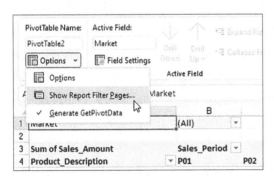

FIGURE 14-40 Click the Show Report Filter Pages button.

A dialog opens, enabling you to choose the filter field for which you would like to create separate pivot tables. Select the appropriate filter field and click OK.

Your reward is a sheet for each item in the filter field, with each one containing its own pivot table. Figure 14-41 illustrates the result. Note that the newly created tabs are named to correspond with the filter item shown in the pivot table.

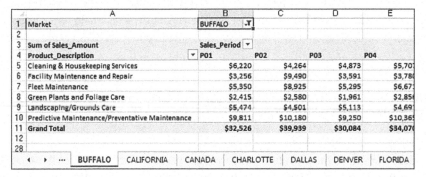

FIGURE 14-41 With just a few clicks, you can have a separate pivot table for each market!

Note Be aware that you can use Show Report Filter Pages on only one filter field at a time. This feature will not automatically replicate any pivot charts.

Tip 18: Apply restrictions on pivot tables and pivot fields

I often send pivot tables to clients, coworkers, managers, and other groups of people. In some cases, I'd like to restrict the types of actions users can take on the pivot table reports I send them. The macros outlined in this section demonstrate some of the protection settings available via VBA.

Pivot table restrictions

The PivotTable object exposes several properties that allow you, as a developer, to restrict different features and components of a pivot table:

- **EnableWizard**—Setting this property to False disables the PivotTable tabs in the ribbon.

- **EnableDrilldown**—Setting this property to False prevents users from seeing detailed data by double-clicking a data field.

- **EnableFieldList**—Setting this property to False prevents users from activating the field list or moving pivot fields around.

- **EnableFieldDialog**—Setting this property to False disables the users' ability to alter the pivot field via the Value Field Settings dialog.

- **PivotCache.EnableRefresh**—Setting this property to False disables the ability to refresh the pivot table.

You can independently set any or all these properties to either True or False. The following macro applies all the restrictions to the target pivot table:

```
Sub ApplyPivotTableRestrictions ()
'Step 1: Declare your Variables
 Dim pt As PivotTable
'Step 2: Point to the PivotTable in the activecell
 On Error Resume Next
 Set pt = ActiveSheet.PivotTables(ActiveCell.PivotTable.Name)
'Step 3: Exit if active cell is not in a PivotTable
 If pt Is Nothing Then
 MsgBox "You must place your cursor inside of a PivotTable."
 Exit Sub
 End If
'Step 4: Apply Pivot Table Restrictions
 With pt
 .EnableWizard = False
 .EnableDrilldown = False
 .EnableFieldList = False
 .EnableFieldDialog = False
 .PivotCache.EnableRefresh = False
 End With
End Sub
```

In this macro

- Step 1 declares the pt pivot table object variable that serves as the memory container for the pivot table.

- Step 2 sets the pt variable to the name of the pivot table on which the active cell is found. It does this by using the ActiveCell.PivotTable.Name property to get the name of the target pivot table.

- Step 3 checks to see whether the pt variable is filled with a pivot table object. If the pt variable is set to Nothing, the active cell was not on a pivot table, and thus, no pivot table could be assigned to the variable. If this is the case, the macro says this to the user in a message box and then it exits the procedure.

- Step 4 applies the pivot table restrictions.

Once your chosen features have been restricted, Excel disables the menu commands for the features you turned off. You can see in Figure 14-42 that the Refresh, Pivot Table Options, and Show Field List commands are unavailable.

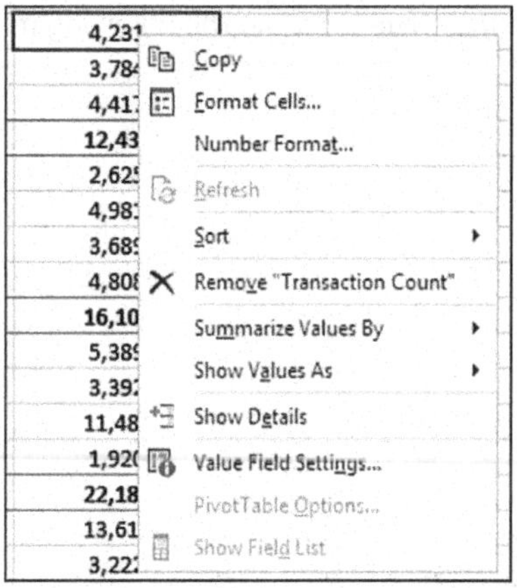

FIGURE 14-42 The commands for restricted features will be unavailable in all menus.

Pivot field restrictions

Like pivot table restrictions, pivot field restrictions enable you to restrict the types of actions users can take on the pivot fields in a pivot table. The macro shown in this section demonstrates some of the protection settings available via VBA.

The `PivotField` object exposes several properties that allow you, as a developer, to restrict different features and components of a pivot table:

- **DragToPage**—Setting this property to `False` prevents users from dragging any pivot field into the filters area of the pivot table.

- **DragToRow**—Setting this property to `False` prevents users from dragging any pivot field into the row area of the pivot table.

- **DragToColumn**—Setting this property to `False` prevents users from dragging any pivot field into the column area of the pivot table.

- **DragToData**—Setting this property to `False` prevents users from dragging any pivot field into the data area of the pivot table.

- **DragToHide**—Setting this property to `False` prevents users from dragging pivot fields off the pivot table. It also prevents the use of the right-click menu to hide or remove pivot fields.

- **EnableItemSelection**—Setting this property to `False` disables the dropdowns on each pivot field.

You can independently set any or all these properties to either `True` or `False`. The following macro applies all the restrictions to the target pivot table:

```
Sub ApplyPivotFieldRestrictions()
'Step 1: Declare your Variables
```

```
    Dim pt As PivotTable
    Dim pf As PivotField
    'Step 2: Point to the PivotTable in the activecell
    On Error Resume Next
    Set pt = ActiveSheet.PivotTables(ActiveCell.PivotTable.Name)
    'Step 3: Exit if active cell is not in a PivotTable
    If pt Is Nothing Then
    MsgBox "You must place your cursor inside of a PivotTable."
    Exit Sub
    End If
    'Step 4: Apply Pivot Field Restrictions
    For Each pf In pt.PivotFields
    pf.EnableItemSelection = False
    pf.DragToPage = False
    pf.DragToRow = False
    pf.DragToColumn = False
    pf.DragToData = False
    pf.DragToHide = False
    Next pf
End Sub
```

In this macro

- Step 1 declares two object variables, using pt as the memory container for the pivot table and pf as a memory container for the pivot fields. This allows looping through all the pivot fields in the pivot table.

- Step 2 sets the pt variable to the name of the pivot table on which the active cell is found. It does this by using the ActiveCell.PivotTable.Name property to get the name of the target pivot.

- Step 3 checks whether the pt variable is filled with a PivotTable object. If the pt variable is set to Nothing, the active cell was not on a pivot table, and thus, no pivot table could be assigned to the variable. If this is the case, the macro notifies the user via a message box and then exits the procedure.

- Step 4 of the macro uses a For Each statement to iterate through each pivot field and apply all the specified pivot field restrictions.

Once your chosen features have been restricted, Excel disables the menu commands for the features you set to False.

Tip 19: Use a pivot table to explode a data set to different workbooks

Imagine that you have a data set with 50,000+ rows of data. You have been asked to create a separate workbook for each market in this data set. In this tip, you'll discover how you can accomplish this task by using a pivot table and a little VBA.

Place the field you need to use as the group dimension (in this case, Market) into the filter field. Place the count of Market into the data field. Your pivot table should look like the one shown in Figure 14-43.

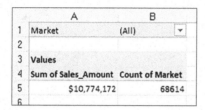

FIGURE 14-43 Create a simple pivot table with two values fields and a filter.

As you know, you can manually select a market in the page/filter field and then double-click Sum of Sales_Amount. This gives you a new tab containing all the records that make up the number you double-clicked. Imagine how you could do this for every market in the Market field and save the resulting tabs to their own workbook.

Using this same concept, you can implement the following VBA that goes through each item in the chosen page field and essentially calls the ShowDetail method for you, creating a raw data tab. The procedure then saves that raw data tab to a new workbook:

```
Sub ExplodeTable()
Dim PvtItem As PivotItem
Dim PvtTable As PivotTable
Dim Fname as variant
'Change variables to suit your scenario
 Const strFieldName = "Market" '<-Change Field Name
 Const strTriggerRange = "B4" '<-Change Trigger Range
'Set the pivot table name if needed
 Set PvtTable = ActiveSheet.PivotTables("PivotTable1") '<-Change Name if Needed
'Start looping through each item in the selected field
 For Each PvtItem In PvtTable.PivotFields(strFieldName).PivotItems
 PvtTable.PivotFields(strFieldName).CurrentPage = PvtItem.Name
 Range(strTriggerRange).ShowDetail = True
```

```
'Name the temp sheet for easy cleanup later
ActiveSheet.Name = "TempSheet"
'copy data to new workbook and delete the temp sheet
ActiveSheet.Cells.Copy
Workbooks.Add
ActiveSheet.Paste
Cells.EntireColumn.AutoFit
Application.DisplayAlerts = False
Fname = ThisWorkbook.Path & "\" & PvtItem.Name & ".xlsx"
ActiveWorkbook.SaveAs Filename:=Fname, FileFormat:=xlOpenXMLWorkbook
ActiveWorkbook.Close
Sheets("Tempsheet").Delete
Application.DisplayAlerts = True
Next PvtItem
End Sub
```

To implement this technique, enter this code into a new VBA module. Be sure to change the following constants as appropriate for your scenario:

- **Const strFieldName**—This is the name of the field you want to separate the data by (that is, the field you put in the page/filter area of the pivot table).

- **Const strTriggerRange**—This is essentially the range that holds the one number in the pivot table's data area.

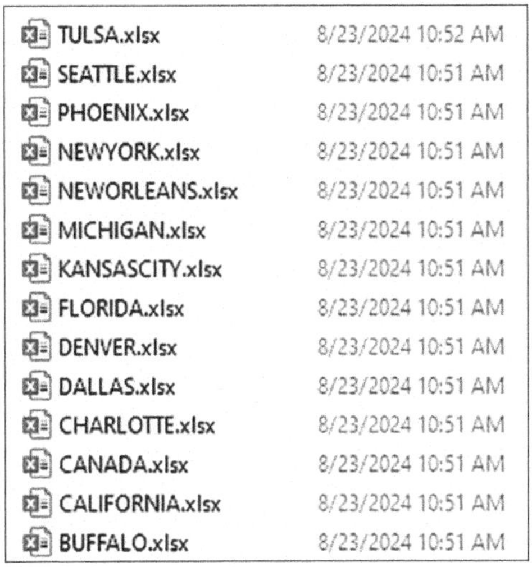

TULSA.xlsx	8/23/2024 10:52 AM	
SEATTLE.xlsx	8/23/2024 10:51 AM	
PHOENIX.xlsx	8/23/2024 10:51 AM	
NEWYORK.xlsx	8/23/2024 10:51 AM	
NEWORLEANS.xlsx	8/23/2024 10:51 AM	
MICHIGAN.xlsx	8/23/2024 10:51 AM	
KANSASCITY.xlsx	8/23/2024 10:51 AM	
FLORIDA.xlsx	8/23/2024 10:51 AM	
DENVER.xlsx	8/23/2024 10:51 AM	
DALLAS.xlsx	8/23/2024 10:51 AM	
CHARLOTTE.xlsx	8/23/2024 10:51 AM	
CANADA.xlsx	8/23/2024 10:51 AM	
CALIFORNIA.xlsx	8/23/2024 10:51 AM	
BUFFALO.xlsx	8/23/2024 10:51 AM	

FIGURE 14-44 After running the macro, you will have a separate workbook for each filtered dimension.

As you can see in Figure 14-44, running this macro procedure outputs data for each market into its own workbook.

Tip 20: Use percentage change from previous for year-over-year

If you have grouped daily dates to years, you are not allowed to add calculated fields or calculated items. With the pivot table in Figure 14-45, you have the revenue from the previous and current years in columns B and C, respectively. You would like to show a % change in column D.

One hack is to remove the grand total that normally appears in column D and build formulas outside the pivot table, such as =C6/B6-1. This is not the best method because you have to recopy the formula if the size of your pivot table changes.

Instead, use this method:

1. Drag Revenue to the Values area a second time.

2. In the Columns area, move the new Σ Values tile above the Date tile. This will produce the report shown in Figure 14-45.

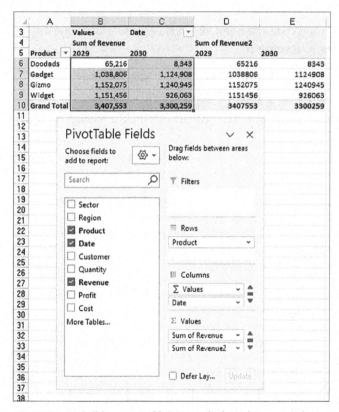

FIGURE 14-45 Build a report with Revenue in the Values area twice.

3. Change the calculation for the second Revenue field. Double-click cell D4 in Figure 14-45 to open the Value Field Settings.

4. In the Value Field Settings, type a new name such as **% Change**.

5. Choose the Show Values As tab.

6. Open the Show Values As dropdown and select Choose % Difference From.

7. For the Base Field, choose Date.

8. For the Base Item, choose (previous). The settings from steps 4 through 8 are shown in Figure 14-46.

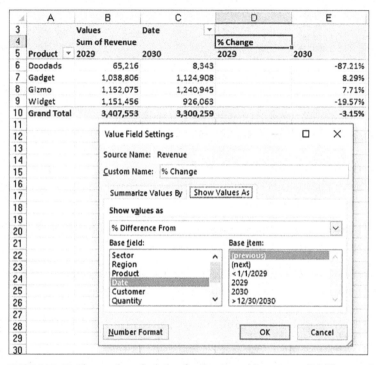

FIGURE 14-46 Change the calculation for the second Revenue to % Difference From.

9. The results are correct, but column D will be blank. Select one cell in column D and change the column width to 0.1. This will allow the % Change heading from D4 to show up in the pivot table (see Figure 14-47).

	A	B	C	E
3		Values	Date	
4		Sum of Revenue		% Change
5	Product	2029	2030	2030
6	Doodads	65,216	8,343	-87.21%
7	Gadget	1,038,806	1,124,908	8.29%
8	Gizmo	1,152,075	1,240,945	7.71%
9	Widget	1,151,456	926,063	-19.57%
10	Grand Total	3,407,553	3,300,259	-3.15%

FIGURE 14-47 The percentage change column is natively part of the pivot table.

10. Before you swap any fields in the row area, right-click the pivot table and choose PivotTable Options. On the Layout & Format tab, clear the Autofit Column Widths On Update checkbox.

11. You can now quickly change the report. Unselect Product. Choose Sector. You can repeat to show year-over-year data for Region or Customer (see Figure 14-48).

	A	B	C	E
3		Values	Date	▼
4		Sum of Revenue		% Change
5	Region ▼	2029	2030	2030
6	West	127,340	112,111	-11.96%
7	Midwest	763,873	977,551	27.97%
8	Northeast	1,130,172	994,440	-12.01%
9	South	1,386,168	1,216,157	-12.26%
10	Grand Total	3,407,553	3,300,259	-3.15%

FIGURE 14-48 Change the row field to produce a different year-over-year report.

Tip 21: Do a two-way VLOOKUP with Power Query

A note in Chapter 10, "Unlocking features with the Data Model and Power Pivot," mentioned that you could do a VLOOKUP while importing data with Power Query. This example will show you how to do a two-way VLOOKUP while importing with Power Query.

The source data in Figure 14-49 is a large sales database in columns F through H. For each sale, you have a Region and a Product. You need to report sales by product manager.

The product manager matrix is shown in A1:D6. Sometimes, a manager handles one product across all regions (such as Johnny for Apples), but other assignments are not straightforward.

	A	B	C	D	E	F	G	H
1	Product ▼	East ▼	Central ▼	West ▼		Region ▼	Product ▼	Sales ▼
2	Apple	Johnny	Johnny	Johnny		East	Banana	9633
3	Banana	Mikey	Mikey	Mae		Central	Banana	6297
4	Cherry	Mikey	Mikey	Mae		West	Cherry	4574
5	Date	Drew	Drew	Drew		East	Cherry	5146
6	Fig	Eve	Mikey	Mae		Central	Banana	5150
7						West	Fig	4369
8						East	Apple	8408
9						Central	Fig	4426
10						West	Fig	1867
11						East	Apple	6790

FIGURE 14-49 The table to assign product managers is shown in A1:D6.

The strategy is to process the lookup table first using Power Query and leave it as a connection-only query. You will then move the Sales data quickly through Power Query to create a second connection. Finally, you will use a Merge query to join the two of them:

1. Select A1 and choose Data | From Table/Range. The Power Query Editor opens. The Product column is selected by default.

2. In Power Query, choose Transform | Unpivot | Unpivot Other Columns.

3. Double-click the Attribute column and rename it to **Region**.

4. In the Query Settings pane on the right side, change the query name from Table1 to **ProductManagers**.

5. Go to the Home tab in Power Query. Be very careful not to click Close & Load. Instead, open the dropdown at the bottom of Close & Load and choose Close & Load To (see Figure 14-50).

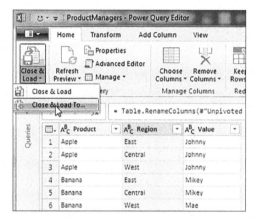

FIGURE 14-50 Unpivot the data. Choose Close & Load To.

6. The Import Data dialog appears. Choose Only Create Connection and click OK (see Figure 14-51). When you return to Excel, the Queries & Connections panel appears. A single query of ProductManagers is listed in the panel.

FIGURE 14-51 Only Create Connection.

Steps 6 and 7 are similar to steps 1 through 5, so there will be no figures.

7. Select one cell in the Sales table. Select Data | From Table/Range.

8. When Power Query opens, there are no changes needed. Select Home | Close & Load To.

9. In the Import Data dialog, choose Only Create Connection. Click OK. You should now see two queries in the Queries & Connections panel (see Figure 14-52).

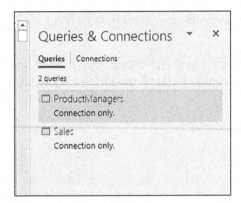

FIGURE 14-52 You've created connections to the data and the lookup table.

10. Select Data | Get Data | Combine Queries | Merge, as shown in Figure 14-53.

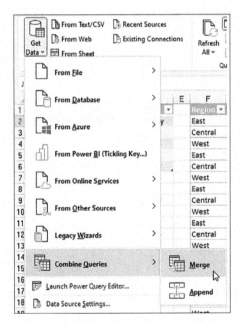

FIGURE 14-53 Choose to merge the two queries.

Note A Merge query is used to join two data sets with different fields. An Append query is used to join two data sets with the same fields.

11. The Merge dialog is confusing. Make sure to follow steps 11 through 17 and then compare to Figure 14-54 before clicking OK. In the top dropdown, choose the Sales table.

12. In the bottom dropdown, choose the ProductManagers table. The next steps are not obvious, and there are no instructions in the dialog.

13. In the data preview for Sales, click the Region heading.

14. In the data preview for Sales, Ctrl+click the Product heading.

15. In the data preview for ProductManagers, click the Region heading (even though it is listed second).

16. In the data preview for ProductManagers, Ctrl+click the Product heading.

17. Note the small "1" and "2" in each heading.

18. For the Join Kind, choose Left Outer Join. The dialog reports that all 1,535 rows have been matched (see Figure 14-54).

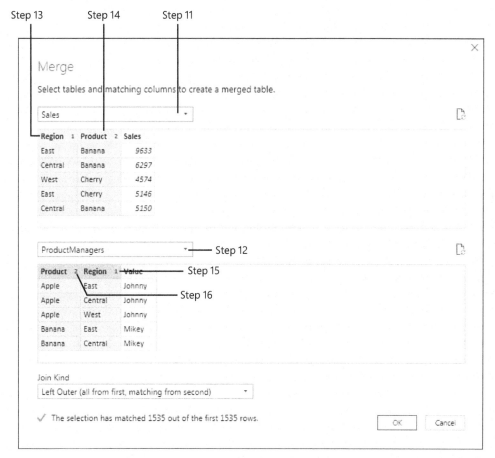

FIGURE 14-54 Choose the two tables and the key fields in common between them.

19. Click OK. The Power Query Editor opens. Where you expect to see the Product Manager, you see a column containing repeated "Table" entries (see Figure 14-55).

Expand

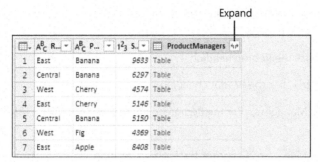

FIGURE 14-55 The appended query is loaded as a table.

20. Click the Expand icon next to the ProductManagers heading. Clear the fields that are duplicates: Product and Region. Clear the Use Original Column Name As Prefix checkbox (see Figure 14-56).

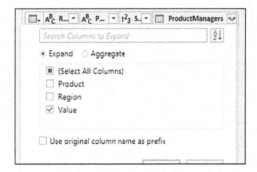

FIGURE 14-56 Choose which fields from the lookup table to show.

21. Rename the Value column to **Product Manager**. Drag that column to the left of Sales (see Figure 14-57).

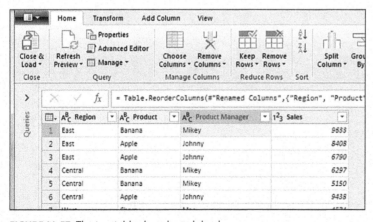

FIGURE 14-57 The two tables have been joined.

22. Choose Home | Close & Load. Your data will be returned to a new worksheet.

23. Build a pivot table to report sales by Product Manager (see Figure 14-58).

	A	B	C	D	E	F	G
1	Region	Product	Product Manager	Sales			
2	East	Banana	Mikey	9633			
3	East	Apple	Johnny	8408			
4	East	Apple	Johnny	6790		Product Manager	Sum of Sales
5	Central	Banana	Mikey	6297		Drew	$1,612,795
6	Central	Banana	Mikey	5150		Eve	$544,846
7	Central	Apple	Johnny	9438		Johnny	$1,758,253
8	West	Cherry	Mae	4574		Mae	$1,660,524
9	West	Cherry	Mae	3489		Mikey	$2,944,322
10	East	Cherry	Mikey	5146		Grand Total	$8,520,740
11	West	Fig	Mae	4369			
12	West	Fig	Mae	1867			

FIGURE 14-58 The final pivot table shows sales by Product Manager. Recall that this data started out in different tables.

In this example, it would have been very easy to replace the Sales table by choosing Data | Get Data | From File | From Workbook. Every time the underlying data changed, choosing Data | Refresh All would refresh all three queries. You will have to refresh the pivot table after the Refresh All, but it will be two steps to update instead of many steps.

Also, it would have been possible in Power Query to group by Product Manager and calculate the Sum of Sales to produce a finished query that had all the same data as F4:G9 in Figure 14-58.

Power Query is the real game-changer in Excel. This book about pivot tables has made significant use of Power Query in several locations:

- Power Query was used in Chapter 2 while cleaning data before pivoting.

- Power Query was used in Chapter 5 to create a calculated column.

- Power Query was used extensively in Chapter 7.

- Power Query was used in Chapter 10 for dealing with more than 1,048,576 rows of data.

- Power Query was mentioned as a way to get two data sets into 3D Map in Chapter 11.

- Chapter 12 proposed Power Query as an alternative to the VBA Macro Recorder.

- This chapter used Power Query as the lucky twenty-first tip to do a two-way VLOOKUP before pivoting.

Bottom line: You should really take a look at Power Query.

Tip 22: Create a slicer to control data from two different data sets

Back in Chapter 4, you learned how to drive multiple pivot tables from one set of slicers. That example required all the pivot tables to come from the same data source.

What if you have two different tables that have a field in common? Figure 14-59 shows a Sales table on the left and a Prospects table on the right. Both tables have the Sector field in common. If you build a pivot table from each data set, could one Sector slicer control both pivot tables?

	A	B	C	D	E	F	G	H	I	J	K	L	M	N
1	Region	Market	Date	Customer	Sector	Quant	Reven				Prospect	Sector	Period	Forecast
2	West	NoCal	1/1/2025	www.ExcelTricks.de	Training	1000	22810				Access Analytic	Consulting	3Q2028	495000
3	South	Houston	1/2/2025	Wilde XL Solutions Ltd.	Consulting	100	2257				adaept information management	Consulting	3Q2027	174000
4	Northeast	New York	1/4/2025	Harlem Globetrotters	Services	400	9152				All Systems Go Consulting	Consulting	2Q2028	241000
5	Midwest	Cleveland	1/4/2025	Tennessee Moon	Retail	800	18552				Analytic Minds	Consulting	3Q2028	491000
6	Northeast	New York	1/7/2025	Reports Wand	Applications	400	8456				Areef Ali & Associates	Consulting	1Q2027	209000
7	Northeast	New York	1/7/2025	Reports Wand	Applications	1000	21730				Association for Computers & Taxation	Associations	4Q2027	334000
8	Midwest	Cincinnati	1/9/2025	Serving Brevard Realty	Services	800	16416				Berghaus Corporation	Consulting	3Q2027	34500
9	South	Arkla	1/10/2025	JEVS Human Services	Services	900	21438				Bits of Confetti	Retail	3Q2028	75400

FIGURE 14-59 If you build a pivot table from each data set, can a single slicer control both pivot tables?

To solve the problem, create a third table with the superset of Sectors. Follow these steps:

1. Copy the Sector column from column E to column I.

2. Copy the sectors from L2:L82 to the bottom of the data in column I.

3. Select all the data in column I.

4. Choose Data | Remove Duplicates | OK.

5. Sort the short list in column I.

6. Press Ctrl+T to create a table in column I.

7. Rename the table from Table3 to **Sectors** using the Table Name field on the Table Design tab.

You should now have a third table, as shown in Figure 14-60.

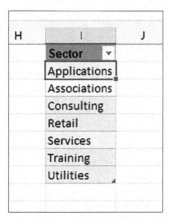

FIGURE 14-60 This third table will be used to drive the Slicer.

Build a data model with all three tables and two relationships. Follow these steps:

1. If you don't see the Power Pivot tab in the ribbon, go to the Data tab and select Manage Data Model. Switch back to Excel, and the Power Pivot tab will be visible.

2. Select one cell in the Sales table. On the Power Pivot tab, choose Add To Data Model. Switch back to Excel.

3. Select one cell in the Sectors table, and then choose Power Pivot | Add To Data Model. Switch back to Excel.

4. Select one cell in the Prospects table, and then choose Power Pivot | Add to Data Model. This time, stay in the Power Pivot window.

5. On the right side of the Home tab in Power Pivot, choose Diagram View.

6. Click the Sector field in the Sales table. Drag from that field to the Sector field in the Sectors table to create the first relationship.

7. Click the Sector field in the Prospect table and drag to the Sector field in the Sectors table to create the second relationship. At this point, the Data Model should appear, as shown in Figure 14-61.

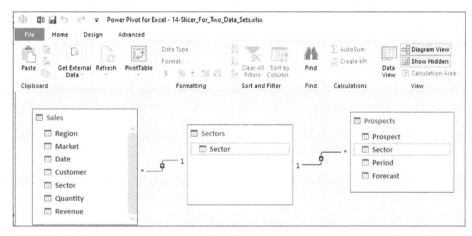

FIGURE 14-61 The Data Model connects both of the tables to the newly created Sectors table.

8. Once the Data Model is set up, you can create your pivot tables. From a blank cell, select Insert | PivotTable | From Data Model. Create as many pivot tables as you need, ideally some from the Sales table and some from the Prospects table. If you use Sector in any pivot table, it should come from the Sectors table.

9. From a blank cell in your workbook, select Insert Slicer. Excel will show the Existing Connections dialog. Choose the second tab, Data Model. Click Tables In Workbook Data Model and click Open.

10. The Insert Slicers dialog offers a list of fields. Although Sector appears in the Prospects table and the Sales table, you need to select the Sector field from the Sectors table (see Figure 14-62).

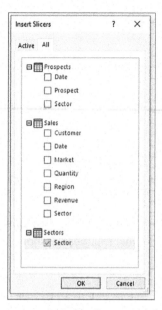

FIGURE 14-62 The Sectors table is connected to both of the other tables. Be sure to create the slicer from the Sector field in this table.

11. With the newly created slicer selected, go to the Slicer tab in the ribbon and choose Report Connections. In the Report Connections dialog, choose all existing pivot tables (see Figure 14-63).

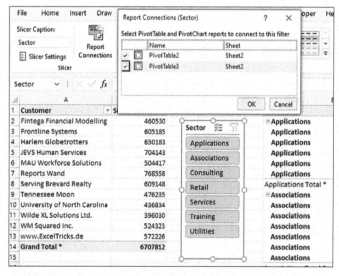

FIGURE 14-63 Connect the Sector slicer to each pivot table.

Tip 23: Format your slicers

Mike Alexander discovered that slicers don't have to look like slicers. He had a great blog post once that showed a whole series of slicers that did not look like slicers. This section covers some of his tricks.

When a slicer is selected, go to the Slicer tab in the ribbon and choose Slicer Settings. You can change the caption that appears at the top of the slicer. In Figure 14-64, the Sector slicer on the top has a caption reading "Industry." The Product slicer below has no caption because the Display Header setting in the Slicer Settings dialog has been deselected.

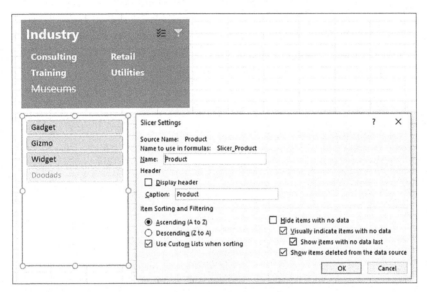

FIGURE 14-64 Change or eliminate the caption in the header.

Most of the coolness of Mike's slicers came from customizing the slicer style. With a slicer selected, choose a color from the Slicer Styles gallery. Right-click that style and choose Duplicate, as shown in Figure 14-65.

FIGURE 14-65 Duplicate an existing style.

Excel will duplicate the slicer and open the Modify Slicer Style dialog. While there are 11 elements that you can format, they follow an inheritance structure. For example, if you choose Whole Slicer and change the font to Segoe UI, everything in the slicer will be Segoe UI unless you choose a lower item and override the font.

In Figure 14-66, the Whole Slicer is set to an orange fill with no borders. The font is set to white, Segoe UI bold, 11-point. Choose each of the remaining 10 items and click the Clear button. This will remove all borders throughout the slicer.

To make the Industry caption larger, choose the Header element and click Format. The only thing you need to change is to set the font size to 18-point.

For the Selected Item With No Data option, choose Format. In the Format dialog, choose Strikethrough and change Regular to Bold. Repeat this process for the Unselected Item With No Data option. The result: a slicer that does not look like a typical slicer (see Figure 14-66).

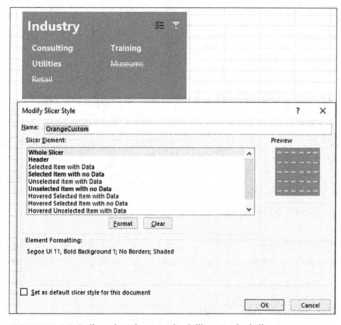

FIGURE 14-66 A slicer that does not look like a typical slicer.

 Caution After modifying the slicer style and clicking OK, nothing will change in the selected slicer because it is still using the original style. You have to keep the slicer selected and go back to the Slicer Styles gallery to choose the newly created custom slicer style, as shown in Figure 14-67.

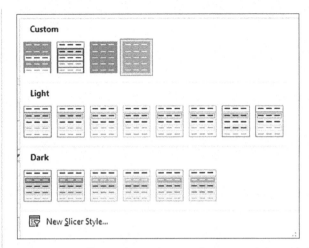

FIGURE 14-67 Choose the newly created custom style to apply to the slicer.

Tip Unfortunately, any custom slicer styles are only available in the workbook where you create them. To make the slicer available in a new workbook, follow these steps:

1. Open both the source and target workbooks.

2. In the source workbook, click the slicer and press Ctrl+C to copy it.

3. Switch to the target workbook.

4. Select a blank cell and press Ctrl+V to paste the slicer. The custom slicer style will be added to the Slicer Styles gallery in the target workbook.

5. Delete the pasted slicer. The style will remain and can be applied to slicers in the new workbook.

Next steps

In Chapter 15, "Dr. Jekyll and Mr. GetPivotData," you'll learn about one of the most hated pivot table features: the GetPivotData function. However, you'll also learn how to use this function to create refreshable reports month after month.

Dr. Jekyll and Mr. GetPivotData

In this chapter, you will:

- Avoid the aggravating GetPivotData problem

- Use GetPivotData to solve pivot table annoyances

This chapter shows you a technique that solves many annoying pivot table problems. If you have been using pivot tables for a while, you might have run into the following problems:

- Formatting tends to be destroyed when you refresh a pivot table. Numeric formats are lost. Column widths go away.

- There is no easy way to build an asymmetric pivot table. Using named sets is one way, but they are available only in a pivot table model, not in a regular pivot cache pivot table.

- Excel cannot remember a template. If you frequently have to re-create a pivot table, you must redo the groupings, calculated fields, calculated items, and so on.

The technique shown in this chapter solves all these problems. It is not new. In fact, it has been around since Excel 2002. I have taught Power Excel seminars to thousands of accountants who use Excel 40–60 hours a week. Out of those thousands of people, I have had only three people say that they use this technique.

Ironically, far more than 0.3 percent of people know of this feature. One common question I get at seminars is: "Why did this feature show up in Excel 2002, and how the heck can you turn it off?" This same feature, which most Excellers revile, is the key to creating reusable pivot table templates.

The credit for this chapter must go to Rob Collie, who spent years on the Excel project management team. He spent the Excel 2010 development cycle working on the PowerPivot product. Rob happened to relocate to Cleveland, Ohio. Because Cleveland is not a hotbed of Microsoft developers, Dave Gainer gave me a heads-up that Rob was moving to my area, and we started having lunch.

Rob and I talked about Excel and had some great conversations. During our second lunch, Rob said something that threw me for a loop. He said, "We find that our internal customers use GetPivotData all the time to build their reports, and we are not sure they will like the way PowerPivot interacts with GetPivotData."

I stopped Rob to ask if he was crazy. I told him that in my experience with about 15,000 accountants, very few of them had ever admitted to liking GetPivotData. What did he mean that he finds customers actually using GetPivotData?

Rob explained the key word in his statement: He was talking about *internal* customers, which are the people inside Microsoft who use Excel to do their jobs. Those people had become incredibly reliant on GetPivotData. He agreed that outside Microsoft, hardly anyone ever uses GetPivotData. In fact, the only question he ever gets outside Microsoft is how to turn off the stupid feature.

I had to know more, so I asked Rob to explain how the irritating GetPivotData could ever be used for good purposes. Rob explained it to me, and I used this chapter to explain it to you. However, I know that 99 percent of you are reading this chapter because of the following reasons:

- You ran into the unexpected GetPivotData.

- You turned to the index of this book to find information on GetPivotData.

- You are expecting me to tell you how to turn off GetPivotData.

So, let's start there.

Avoiding the evil GetPivotData problem

GetPivotData has been the cause of many headaches since around the time of Excel 2002 when suddenly, without any fanfare, pivot table behavior changed slightly. Any time you build formulas outside a pivot table that point back inside the pivot table, you run into the GetPivotData problem.

For example, say you build the pivot table shown in Figure 15-1. Those years across the top are built by grouping daily dates into years. You would like to compare this year versus last year. Unfortunately, you are not allowed to add calculated items to a grouped field. If you did, you'd get the error shown in Figure 15-1. So, you follow these steps:

1. Add a **% Growth** heading in cell D4.

2. Copy the formatting from C4 over to D4.

3. In cell D5, press Ctrl+1 to open the Format Cells dialog.

4. In the Format Cells dialog, choose the Number tab. Click the Custom format and type **+0.0%;-0.0%;0.0%**. Click OK.

5. In cell D5, type = (an equal sign).

6. Click cell C5.

7. Type **/** (a slash) for division.

8. Click B5.

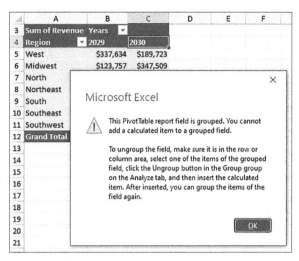

FIGURE 15-1 You want to add a formula to show the percentage of growth year after year.

9. Type **-1** and press Ctrl+Enter to stay in the same cell. Format the result as a percentage. You see that the West region dropped by 43.8 percent (see Figure 15-2).

D5   *fx* =GETPIVOTDATA("Revenue",$A$3,"Region","West","Years",
2030)/GETPIVOTDATA("Revenue",$A$3,"Region","West",
"Years",2029)-1

	A	B	C	D	E	F	G	H	I
3	Sum of Revenue	Years							
4	Region	2029	2030	% Growth					
5	West	$337,634	$189,723	-43.8%					
6	Midwest	$123,757	$347,509						
7	North	$16,457	$52,767						
8	Northeast	$122,611	$152,341						
9	South	$2,189,994	$3,192,255						
10	Southeast	$359,782	$801,992						
11	Southwest	$141,861	$191,353						
12	Grand Total	$3,292,095	$4,927,939						

FIGURE 15-2 Build the formula in D5 using the mouse or the arrow keys.

Note If you started using spreadsheets back in the days of Lotus 1-2-3, you might like to use this alternative method to build the formula in D5: Type **=** (an equal sign) and press the left arrow once. Type **/** (for division). Press the left arrow twice. Type **-1**. Press Enter. As you see, the GetPivotData problem strikes no matter which method you use.

10. After entering your first formula, select cell D5.

11. Double-click the tiny square dot in the lower-right corner of the cell. This is the fill handle, and it copies the formula down to the end of the report.

Immediately, you notice that something is wrong because every region happened to fall by 43.8 percent since last year (see Figure 15-3). There is no way this happens in real life. The data must be fabricated.

	A	B	C	D
3	Sum of Revenue	Years		
4	Region	2029	2030	% Growth
5	West	$337,634	$189,723	-43.8%
6	Midwest	$123,757	$347,509	-43.8%
7	North	$16,457	$52,767	-43.8%
8	Northeast	$122,611	$152,341	-43.8%
9	South	$2,189,994	$3,192,255	-43.8%
10	Southeast	$359,782	$801,992	-43.8%
11	Southwest	$141,861	$191,353	-43.8%
12	Grand Total	$3,292,095	$4,927,939	-43.8%

FIGURE 15-3 When the formula is copied down, somehow, the growth is −43.8% for every region.

Think about the formula you built: 2030 data divided by 2029 data minus 1. You probably could create that formula with your eyes closed (that is, if you use arrow keys to create formulas instead of your mouse).

This is what makes you not notice something completely insidious when you are building the formula. When you went through the steps to build the formula, as a rational person, you would expect Excel to create a formula such as =C5/B5-1. However, go back to cell D5 and press the F2 key to look at the formula (see Figure 15-4). Something unanticipated has happened. The simple formula =C5/B5-1 is not there. Instead, Excel generated some GetPivotData nonsense. Although the formula works in D5, it does not work when you copy the formula down.

	A	B	C	D	E	F	G	H	I	J
3	Sum of Revenue	Years								
4	Region	2029	2030	% Growth						
5	West	$337,634	$189,723	=GETPIVOTDATA("Revenue",$A$3,"Region","West","Years",2030)/						
6	Midwest	$123,757	$347,509	GETPIVOTDATA("Revenue",$A$3,"Region","West","Years",2029)-1						
7	North	$16,457	$52,767	-43.8%						
8	Northeast	$122,611	$152,341	-43.8%						
9	South	$2,189,994	$3,192,255	-43.8%						
10	Southeast	$359,782	$801,992	-43.8%						
11	Southwest	$141,861	$191,353	-43.8%						
12	Grand Total	$3,292,095	$4,927,939	-43.8%						

FIGURE 15-4 Where did GetPivotData come from?

When this occurs, your reaction is something like, "What is GetPivotData, and why is it messing up my report?" Your next reaction is, "How can I turn it off?" You might even wonder, "Why would Microsoft put this thing in there?"

Excel started inserting GetPivotData in Excel 2002. After being stung by GetPivotData repeatedly, I grew to hate it. I was thrown for a loop in one of the Power Analyst Boot Camps when someone asked me how it could possibly be used. I had never considered that question. In my mind, and in most other people's minds, GetPivotData was no good.

If you are one of those users who would just like to avoid GetPivotData, I've got great news: There are two ways to do so, as presented in the following two sections.

Preventing GetPivotData by typing the formula

The simple method for avoiding GetPivotData is to create your formula without touching the mouse or the arrow keys. To do this, follow these steps:

1. Go to cell D5; type =.

2. Type **C5**.

3. Type **/**.

4. Type **B5**.

5. Type **-1**.

6. Press Enter.

You have now built a regular Excel formula that you can copy to produce real results, as shown in Figure 15-5. Note that column D is formatted as a percentage with one decimal place using the formatting tools on the Home tab.

D5		f_x	=C5/B5-1	
	A	B	C	D
3	Sum of Revenue	Years		
4	Region	2029	2030	% Growth
5	West	$337,634	$189,723	-43.8%
6	Midwest	$123,757	$347,509	+180.8%
7	North	$16,457	$52,767	+220.6%
8	Northeast	$122,611	$152,341	+24.2%
9	South	$2,189,994	$3,192,255	+45.8%
10	Southeast	$359,782	$801,992	+122.9%
11	Southwest	$141,861	$191,353	+34.9%
12	Grand Total	$3,292,095	$4,927,939	+49.7%

FIGURE 15-5 Type =C5/B5-1, and the formula works as expected.

It is a relief to see that you can still build formulas outside pivot tables that point into a pivot table. I have run into people who simply thought this could not be done.

You might be a bit annoyed that you have to abandon your normal way of entering formulas. If so, the next section offers an alternative.

Simply turning off GetPivotData

If you do not plan to read the second half of this chapter, you can simply turn off GetPivotData forever. Who needs it? It is bothersome, so just turn it off.

In Excel, follow these steps:

1. Move the cell pointer back inside a pivot table so that the PivotTable Tools tabs appear.

2. Click the PivotTable Analyze tab.

3. Notice the Options icon on the left side of the ribbon (see Figure 15-6). Do not click the icon; rather, next to the Options icon, click the dropdown arrow.

FIGURE 15-6 Don't click the large Options icon. Click the tiny dropdown arrow next to the icon.

4. Inside the Options dropdown is the Generate GetPivotData choice (see Figure 15-7). By default, this option is selected. Click that item to clear this checkbox.

FIGURE 15-7 Select Generate GetPivotData to turn off the feature.

The previous steps assume that you have a pivot table in the workbook that you can select in order to access the PivotTable Tool tabs. If you don't have a pivot table in the current workbook, you can use File | Options. In the Formulas category, clear the checkbox for Use GetPivotData Functions For PivotTable References.

Speculating on why Microsoft forced GetPivotData on us

If GetPivotData is so universally hated, why did the fine people at Microsoft turn on the feature by default? Everyone simply wants to turn it off. Why would they bother to leave it on? Are they trying to make sure that there is a market for my Power Excel videos?

I have a theory about this that I came up with during the Excel 2007 launch. I had written many books about Excel 2007—somewhere around 1,800 pages of content. When the Office 2007 launch events were happening around the country, I was given an opportunity to work at the event. I watched with interest when the presenter talked about the new features in Excel 2007.

There were at least 15 amazing features in Excel 2007. The presenter took three minutes and glossed over perhaps three of the features.

I was perplexed. How could Microsoft marketing do such a horrible job of showing what was new in Excel? Then I realized that this must always happen. Marketing asks the development team what is new. The project manager gives them a list of 15 items. The marketing guy says something like, "There is no room for 15 items in the presentation. Can you cut 80 percent of those items from the list and give me just the ones with glitz and sizzle?"

The folks who worked on GetPivotData certainly knew that GetPivotData would never have enough sizzle to make it into the marketing news about Excel 2002. So, by making it the default, they hoped someone would notice GetPivotData and try to figure out how it could be used. Instead, most people, including me, just turned it off and thought it was another step in the Microsoft plot to make our lives miserable by making it harder to work in Excel.

Using GetPivotData to solve pivot table annoyances

You would not be reading this book if you hadn't realized that pivot tables are the greatest invention ever. Six clicks can create a pivot table that obsoletes the arcane process of using Advanced Filter, =DSUM, and data tables. Pivot tables enable you to produce one-page summaries of massive data sets. So what if the formatting is ugly? And so, what if you usually end up converting most pivot tables to values so you can delete the columns you do not need but cannot turn off?

Figure 15-8 illustrates a typical pivot table experience: You start with raw data. You then produce a pivot table and use all sorts of advanced pivot table tricks to get it close. You conclude by converting the pivot table to values and performing the final formatting in regular Excel.

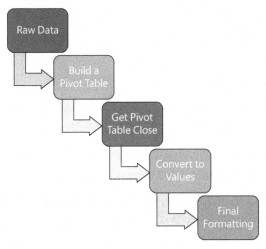

FIGURE 15-8 A typical pivot table process.

Note I rarely get to refresh a pivot table because I never let pivot tables live long enough to have new data. The next time I get data, I start creating the pivot table all over again. If it is a long process, I write a macro that lets me fly through the five steps in Figure 15-8 in a couple of keystrokes.

The new method introduced by Rob Collie and described in the rest of this chapter puts a different spin on the pivot table experience. In this new method, which people inside Microsoft tend to use, you build an ugly pivot table. You do not care about the formatting of this pivot table. You then go through a one-time, relatively painful process of building a nicely formatted shell to hold your final report. Finally, you use GetPivotData to populate the shell report quickly.

From then on, when you get new data, you simply put it on the data sheet, refresh the ugly pivot table, and print the shell report. Figure 15-9 illustrates this process.

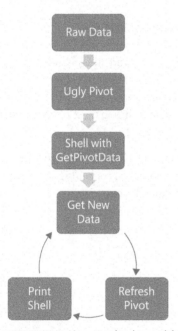

FIGURE 15-9 How people who work in the accounting department at Microsoft use pivot tables.

There are huge advantages to this method. For example, you do not have to worry about formatting the report after the first time. It comes much closer to an automated process.

The rest of this chapter walks you through the steps to build a dynamic report that shows actuals for months that have been completed and a forecast for future months.

Building an ugly pivot table

Say that you have transactional data showing the budget and actuals for each region of a company. The budget data is at a monthly level. The actuals data is at a daily level. Budget data exists for the entire year. Actuals exist only for the months that have been completed. Figure 15-10 shows the original data set.

Because you will be updating this report every month, it makes the process easier if you have a pivot table data source that grows as you add new data to the bottom. Whereas legacy versions of Excel would achieve this through a named dynamic range using the OFFSET function, you can do this in Excel by selecting one cell in your data and pressing Ctrl+T to make the range a table. Click OK to confirm that your data has headers.

You now have a formatted data set, as shown in Figure 15-10.

	A	B	C	D
1	Region	Date	Measure	Revenue
2	Midwest	1/1/2030	Budget	248000
3	North	1/1/2030	Budget	90000
4	Northeast	1/1/2030	Budget	266000
5	South	1/1/2030	Budget	360000
6	Southeast	1/1/2030	Budget	675000
7	Southwest	1/1/2030	Budget	293000
8	West	1/1/2030	Budget	563000
9	Midwest	2/1/2030	Budget	248000
10	North	2/1/2030	Budget	90000
11	Northeast	2/1/2030	Budget	266000
12	South	2/1/2030	Budget	360000

FIGURE 15-10 The original data includes budget and actuals.

Your next step is to create a pivot table that has every possible value needed in your final report. GetPivotData is powerful, but it can only return values that are visible in the actual pivot table. It cannot reach through to the pivot cache to calculate items that are not in the pivot table.

Create the pivot table by following these steps:

1. Select Insert | PivotTable | OK.

2. In the PivotTable Fields list, select the Date field. You will see daily dates in the first column (see Figure 15-11).

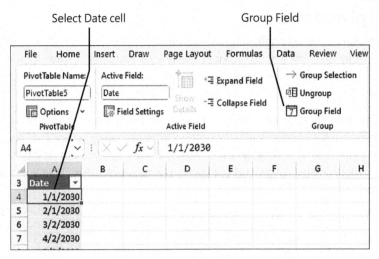

Select Date cell   Group Field

FIGURE 15-11 Start with daily dates down the left.

3. Select the first date cell in A4. From the PivotTable Options tab, select Group Field. Select Months and Years, as shown in Figure 15-12. Click OK. You now have actual month names in the Rows area, as shown in Figure 15-13.

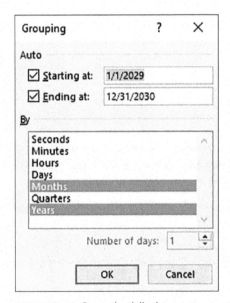

FIGURE 15-12 Group the daily dates up to months and years.

	A	B
3	Years (Date) ▾	Months (Date) ▾
4	⊟ 2030	Jan
5	2030	Feb
6	2030	Mar
7	2030	Apr
8	2030	May
9	2030	Jun
10	2030	Jul
11	2030	Aug
12	2030	Sep
13	2030	Oct
14	2030	Nov
15	2030	Dec
16	2030 Total	
17	Grand Total	

FIGURE 15-13 You have month names instead of dates.

4. Drag the Years (Date) and Months (Date) fields to the Columns area in the PivotTable Fields list.

5. Drag Measure to the Columns area.

6. Select Region to have it appear along the left column of the pivot table.

7. Select Revenue to have it appear in the Values area of the pivot table.

As shown in Figure 15-14, you now have one ugly pivot table. Having a total of January Actuals plus the January Budget in column D is completely pointless. This is ugly, but for once, you do not care because no one other than you will ever see this pivot table.

	A	B	C	D	E	F
3	Sum of Revenue	Years (Date) ▾	Months (Date) ▾	Measure ▾		
4		⊟ 2030	2030	2030	2030	2030
5		⊟ Jan	Jan	Jan Total	⊟ Feb	Feb
6	Region ▾	Actuals	Budget		Actuals	Budget
7	West	578379	563000	1141379	596267	563000
8	Midwest	312387	248000	560387	266949	248000
9	North	100742	90000	190742	95197	90000
10	Northeast	277435	266000	543435	336005	266000
11	South	4182773	360000	4542773	4182773	360000
12	Southeast	926977	675000	1601977	789647	675000
13	Southwest	361686	293000	654686	329772	293000
14	Grand Total	6740379	2495000	9235379	6596610	2495000

FIGURE 15-14 The world's ugliest pivot table. Summing Actuals and Budget in column D is completely meaningless.

At this point, the goal is to have a pivot table with every possible data point you could ever need in your final report. It is okay if the pivot table has extra data you will never need in the report.

Building the shell report

Now, it's time to put away your pivot table hat and take out your straight Excel hat. You will use basic Excel formulas and formatting to create a nicely formatted report suitable for giving to your manager.

Insert a blank worksheet in your workbook and then follow these steps:

1. Put a report title in cell A1.

2. Use the Cell Styles dropdown on the Home tab to format cell A1 as a title.

3. Put a date in cell B1 by using the formula =FOMONTH(TODAY(),-1). This enters the serial number of the last day of the previous month in cell B1. If you want to see how the formula is working, you can format the cell as a date. If you are reading this on July 14, 2030, the date that appears in cell B1 is June 30, 2030.

4. Select cell B1. Press Ctrl+1 to go to the Format Cells dialog. On the Number tab, click Custom. Type the custom number format **"Actuals Through" mmmm, yyyy**. This causes the calculated date to appear as text.

5. Because there is a chance that the text in cell A2 will be wider than you want column A to be, select both cells A2 and B2. Press Ctrl+1 to format the cells. On the Alignment tab, select Merge Cells. This allows the formula in cell A2 to spill over into B2 if necessary. Choose Align Left from the Home tab of the ribbon.

6. Type a Region heading in cell A5.

7. Down the rest of column A, type your region names. These names should match the names in the pivot table.

8. Where appropriate, add labels in column A for Division totals.

9. Add a line for Total Company at the bottom of the report.

10. Month names stretch from cells B4 to M4. Enter this formula in cell B4: =DATE(YEAR ($A$2),COLUMN(A1),1).

11. Select cell B4. Press Ctrl+1 to format the cells. On the Number tab, select Custom and type the custom number format **MMM**.

12. Right-justify cell B4. Use the Cell Styles dropdown to select Heading 4.

13. Copy cell B4 to cells C4:M4. You now have true dates across the top that appear as month labels.

14. Enter this formula in cell B5: =IF(MONTH(B4)<=MONTH($A$2),"Actuals","Budget"). Right-justify cell B5. Copy across to cells C5:M5. This should provide the word "Actuals" for past months and the word "Budget" for future months.

15. Add a Total column heading in cell N5. Add a Total Budget column in cell O5. Enter **Var %** in cell P5.

16. Fill in the regular Excel formulas needed to provide division totals, the total company row, the grand total column, and the variance % column. For example:

- Enter **=SUM(B6:B7)** in cell B8, and copy across.
- Enter **=SUM(B6:M6)** in cell N6, and copy down.
- Enter **=IFERROR((N6/O6)-1,0)** in cell P6, and copy down.
- Enter **=SUM(B10:B12)** in cell B13, and copy across.
- Enter **=SUM(B15:B16)** in cell B17, and copy across.
- Enter **=SUM(B6:B18)/2** in cell B19, and copy across.

17. Apply the Heading 4 cell style to the labels in column A and the headings in rows 4:5.

18. Apply the #,##0 number format to cells B6:O19.

19. Apply the 0.0% number format to column P.

20. Clear the formulas in rows 9, 14, and 18 for columns N and P.

> **Note** If the names in the pivot table are region codes, you can hide the codes in a new hidden column A and put friendly region names in column B.

You now have a completed shell report, as shown in Figure 15-15. This report has all the necessary formatting your manager might desire. It has totals that add up the numbers that eventually come from the pivot table.

In the next section, you'll use GetPivotData to complete the report.

	A	B	C	D	E	F	G	H	I	J	K	L	M	N	O	P
1	Actuals & Budget By Region															
2	Actuals Through July, 2030															
3		2030	2030													
4		Jan	Feb	Mar	Apr	May	Jun	Jul	Aug	Sep	Oct	Nov	Dec		Total	
5	Region	Actuals	Actuals	Actuals	Actuals	Actuals	Actuals	Actuals	Budget	Budget	Budget	Budget	Budget	Total	Budget	Var. %
6	Northeast															0.0%
7	Southeast															0.0%
8	East Division Total	0	0	0	0	0	0	0	0	0	0	0	0	0	0	0.0%
9																
10	Midwest															0.0%
11	North															0.0%
12	South															0.0%
13	Central Division Total	0	0	0	0	0	0	0	0	0	0	0	0	0	0	0.0%
14																
15	West															0.0%
16	Southwest															0.0%
17	West Division Total	0	0	0	0	0	0	0	0	0	0	0	0	0	0	0.0%
18																
19	Total Company	0	0	0	0	0	0	0	0	0	0	0	0	0	0	0.0%

FIGURE 15-15 The shell report before the GetPivotData formulas are added.

Using GetPivotData to populate the shell report

At this point, you are ready to take advantage of the thing that has been driving you crazy for years—that Generate `GetPivotData` setting. If you cleared the setting back in Figure 15-7, go in and select it again. When it is selected, you see a checkmark next to Generate `GetPivotData`.

Go to cell B6 on the shell report (this is the cell for Northeast region, January, Actuals), and then follow these steps:

1. Type = to start a formula (see Figure 15-16).

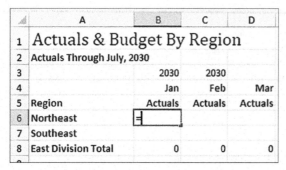

⊿	A	B	C	D
1	Actuals & Budget By Region			
2	Actuals Through July, 2030			
3		2030	2030	
4		Jan	Feb	Mar
5	Region	Actuals	Actuals	Actuals
6	Northeast	=		
7	Southeast			
8	East Division Total	0	0	0

FIGURE 15-16 Start a formula on the shell report.

2. Move to the pivot table worksheet and click the cell for Northeast, January, Actuals. In Figure 15-17, this is cell B10.

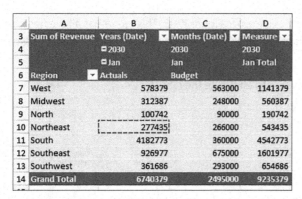

⊿	A	B	C	D
3	Sum of Revenue	Years (Date) ▼	Months (Date) ▼	Measure ▼
4		⊟ 2030	2030	2030
5		⊟ Jan	Jan	Jan Total
6	Region ▼	Actuals	Budget	
7	West	578379	563000	1141379
8	Midwest	312387	248000	560387
9	North	100742	90000	190742
10	Northeast	277435	266000	543435
11	South	4182773	360000	4542773
12	Southeast	926977	675000	1601977
13	Southwest	361686	293000	654686
14	Grand Total	6740379	2495000	9235379

FIGURE 15-17 Using the mouse, click the correct cell in the pivot table.

3. Press Enter to return to the shell report and complete the formula. Excel adds a `GetPivotData` function in cell B6.

The formula says that the Northeast region actuals are $277,435.

Tip Jot down this number because you will want to compare it to the result of the formula that you later edit.

The initial formula is as follows:

```
=GETPIVOTDATA("Revenue",UglyPivotTable!$A$3,"Region","Northeast","Measure","Actuals",
"Months (Date)",1,"Years (Date)",2030)
```

After years of ignoring the GetPivotData formula, you need to look at this monster formula closely to understand what it is doing. Figure 15-18 shows the formula in the Formula Bar.

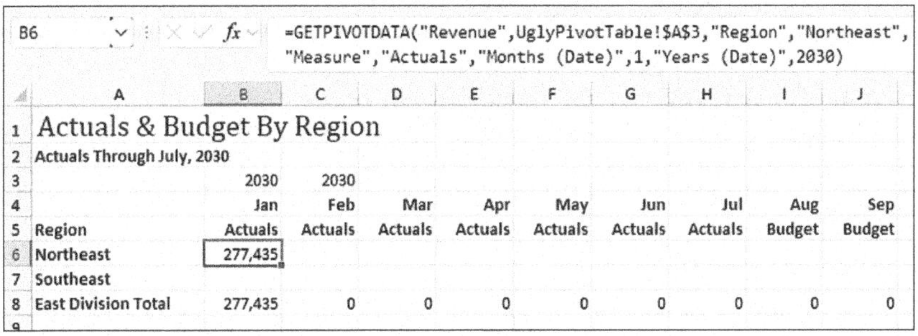

B6				fx	=GETPIVOTDATA("Revenue",UglyPivotTable!$A$3,"Region","Northeast", "Measure","Actuals","Months (Date)",1,"Years (Date)",2030)					
	A	B	C	D	E	F	G	H	I	J
1	Actuals & Budget By Region									
2	Actuals Through July, 2030									
3		2030	2030							
4		Jan	Feb	Mar	Apr	May	Jun	Jul	Aug	Sep
5	Region	Actuals	Actuals	Actuals	Actuals	Actuals	Actuals	Actuals	Budget	Budget
6	Northeast	277,435								
7	Southeast									
8	East Division Total	277,435	0	0	0	0	0	0	0	0

FIGURE 15-18 The GetPivotData formula generated by Microsoft.

The syntax for the function is =GetPivotData(data_field, pivot_table, [field1, item1], ...). In this case, there are four pairs of field*n*, item*n* arguments. Here are the arguments in the formula:

- **Data_field**—This is the field in the Values area of the pivot table. Note that you use Revenue, not Sum Of Revenue.

- **Pivot_table**—This is Microsoft's way of asking, "Which pivot table do you mean?" All you have to do here is point to one single cell within the pivot table. The UglyPivotTable!$A$3 entry is the first populated cell in the pivot table. You are free to choose any cell in the pivot table you want. However, because it does not matter which cell you choose, don't worry about getting clever here. Leave the formula pointing to $A$3, and you will be fine.

- **Field1, item1**—The formula generated by Microsoft shows Region as the field name and Northeast as the item value. Aha! So, this is why the GetPivotData formulas that Microsoft generates cannot be copied. They are essentially hard-coded to point to one specific value. You want your formula to change as you copy it through your report. Edit the formula to change Northeast to $A6. By using only a single dollar sign ($) before **A**, you are enabling the row portion of the reference to vary as you copy the formula down.

- **Field2, item2**— The field name is Measure, and the item is Actuals. This happens to be correct for January, but when you get to future months, you want the Measure to switch to Budget. Change the hard-coded Actuals to point to B$5.

- **Field3, item3**— The next two pairs of arguments specify that the Months (Date) field should be 1. The value for the month is 1, which means January. You probably thought I was insane to build that outrageous formula and custom number format in cell B4. That formula becomes useful now. Instead of hard-coding a 1, use MONTH(B$4). The single dollar sign before row 4 indicates that the formula can get data from other months as it is copied across, but it should always reach back up to row 4 as it is copied down.

- **Field4, item4**—This is Years (Date) and 2030. I nearly left this one alone because it would be months before we have a new year. However, why not change 2030 to YEAR($A$2)?

The new formula is shown in Figure 15-19. Rather than a formula that is hard-coded to work with only one value, you have created a formula that can be copied throughout the data set. The formula is:

```
=GETPIVOTDATA("Revenue",UglyPivotTable!$A$3,"Region",$A6,"Measure",B$5,
"Months (Date)",MONTH(B$4),"Years (Date)",YEAR($A$2))
```

	A	B	C	D	E	F	G	H	I	J	K	L	M	N
1	Actuals & Budget By Region													
2	Actuals Through July, 2030													
3		2030	2030											
4		Jan	Feb	Mar	Apr	May	Jun	Jul	Aug	Sep	Oct	Nov	Dec	
5	Region	Actuals	Actuals	Actuals	Actuals	Actuals	Actuals	Actuals	Budget	Budget	Budget	Budget	Budget	Total
6	Northeast	=GETPIVOTDATA("Revenue",UglyPivotTable!$A$3,"Region",$A6,"Measure",B$5,"Months (Date)",MONTH(B$4),"Years (Date)",YEAR($A$2))												
7	Southeast													
8	East Division Total	277,435	0	0	0	0	0	0	0	0	0	0	0	0
9														

FIGURE 15-19 After being edited, the GetPivotData formula is ready for copying.

When you press Enter, you have exactly the same answer that you had before editing the formula. Compare this with the number you jotted down earlier to make sure.

Copy this formula to all the blank calculation cells in columns B:M. Do not copy the formula to column O yet. Now that you have real numbers in the report, you might have to adjust some column widths.

You can tweak the GetPivotData formula for the months to get the total budget. If you copy one formula to cell O6, you get a #REF! error because the word *Total* in cell O4 does not evaluate to a month. Edit the formula to the pairs of arguments for Month and Years. You still have an error.

Caution For GetPivotData to work, the number you are looking for must be visible somewhere in the pivot table.

Because the original pivot table had Measure as the third column field, there is no actual column for Budget total. Move the Measure field so that it is the first Column field, as shown in Figure 15-20.

When you return to the shell report, you find that the Total Budget formula in cell O6 is now working fine. Copy that formula down to the other blank data cells in column O (see Figure 15-21). Note with amazement that all the other formulas work, even though everything in the underlying pivot table moved.

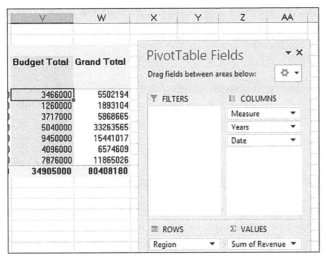

FIGURE 15-20 Tweak the layout of the Column Labels fields so you have a Budget Total column.

	Total	
tal	**Budget**	**Var. %**
665	3,717,000	3.1%
017	3,717,000	176.2%
682	7,434,000	89.7%

FIGURE 15-21 After rearranging the pivot table, you have a working formula for Total Budget.

The formula in O6 is as follows:

```
=GETPIVOTDATA("Revenue",UglyPivotTable!$A$3,"Region",$A6,"Measure",O$5)
```

You now have a nicely formatted shell report that grabs values from a live pivot table. It certainly takes more time to set up this report for the first month that you have to produce it, but it will be a breeze to update the report in future months.

Updating the report in future months

In future months, you can update your report by following these steps:

1. Paste actuals for the new month just below the original data set. Because the original data set is a table, the table formatting automatically extends to the new rows. The pivot table source definition also extends.

2. Go to the pivot table. Click the Refresh button on the PivotTable Analyze tab. The shape of the pivot table changes, but you do not care.

3. Go to the shell report. In real life, you are done, but to test it, enter a date in cell B2, such as **8/30/2030**. You will initially see a #REF error, but it will disappear after adding August actuals to the real data and refreshing the pivot table.

> **Note** Every month, these three steps are the payoff to this chapter. The first time you update, the data for July changes from Budget to Actuals. Formulas throughout recalculate. You do not have to worry about re-creating formats, formulas, and so on.

This process is so simple that you will probably forget about the pain that you used to endure to create these monthly reports. The one risk is that a company reorganization will add new regions to the pivot table.

To be sure that your formulas are still working, add a small check section outside of the print range of the report. This formula in cell A22 checks to see if the budget total calculated in cell O19 matches the budget total back in the pivot table. Here is the formula:

```
=IF(GETPIVOTDATA("Revenue ",UglyPivotTable!$A$3, "Measure ", "Budget ")=$O$19, "", _
"Caution!!! It appears that new regions have been added to the pivot table "&. _
"You might have to add new rows to this report for those regions. "
```

In case the new region comes from a misspelling in the actuals, this formula checks the YTD actuals against the pivot table. Enter the following formula in cell A23:

```
=IF(SUMIF(B5:M5, "Actuals ",B19:M19)=GETPIVOTDATA("Revenue ",UglyPivotTable!$A$3, _
"Measure ", "Actuals"), ", "Caution!!! It appears that new regions have been "& _
"added to the pivot table. You might have to add new rows to this report for "& _
"those regions. ")
```

Change the font color of both these cells to red. You do not even notice them down there until something goes wrong.

At one time, I thought that I would never write these words: GetPivotData is the greatest thing ever. How could we ever live without it?

Next steps

Chapter 16 shows how to create a pivot table in Excel Online.

Creating pivot tables in Excel Online

In this chapter, you will learn:

- How to sign in to Excel Online
- How to create a pivot table in Excel Online
- How to change pivot table options in Excel Online
- Where the rest of the features are

The employees at Microsoft—from CEO Satya Nadella on down—believe that Excel Online is the future. They figure that if all the people using Google Sheets can live in an online environment, Excel customers will follow suit.

Here is the difference: The customers using Google Sheets can't choose to work in a desktop version of the spreadsheet! Instead, they are forced to use an online product.

Excel customers, who have a choice, are still using Windows and Mac versions of Excel almost exclusively. Microsoft loves to cite the percentage of Excel customers who have opened Excel Online in the last year. Excel MVP Wyn Hopkins has an interesting theory on that: He runs into people who click a link in Outlook and are inadvertently taken to Excel Online. Those people promptly click Open in desktop Excel. So, one theory is that many of the people that Microsoft cites as "using" Excel Online might have arrived there accidentally.

When your CEO is a champion for Excel Online, it drives a lot of behavior with Microsoft. The Excel team is working feverishly to make Excel Online as close to the Windows versions of Excel as possible. Even though I have rarely met anyone who is using Excel Online on purpose, it stands to reason that because Excel Online now supports the creation of pivot tables, this book should cover that functionality as well.

In my seminars, I usually mention that Excel Online might be a life-saver if you are visiting your grandmother and your boss calls to say that he needs a pivot table created immediately. It is possible that your grandmother's computer won't have a Windows version of Excel, and you can save the day using Excel Online. So, this chapter could be re-titled as "Creating pivot tables at your grandmother's house."

How to sign in to Excel Online

I've talked to a fair number of people who have never ventured into Excel Online, so here is the quick start guide. The first thing you should do is open Excel on your desktop and go to File, Account. You should see that you are signed in to Excel with an e-mail address, and I am guessing you know the password because Microsoft forces you to change the password every few months.

Think about where you usually store your Excel workbooks. Do you store them on a local hard drive? Your company's network drive? Or do you save to OneDrive, SharePoint Online, or OneDrive for Business? If you don't have any workbooks already in OneDrive or SharePoint Online, you can upload one of your locally stored workbooks to Excel Online.

Armed with a user ID and password, open your favorite modern web browser (for example, Microsoft Edge or Google Chrome). In the address bar, type **Excel.New** and press Enter (see Figure 16-1).

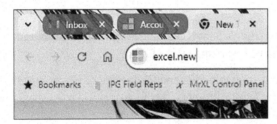

FIGURE 16-1 Excel.New is a shortcut to get to Excel Online.

The next step varies. You might be asked to log in, or your browser might already know that you are logged in to Microsoft and take you directly to a webpage that looks like the File, Home tab in desktop Excel.

I find that I have too many Microsoft logins. I have a couple of different logins for the Teams application. I have a very old login that was used for MSDN subscriptions. I attended Microsoft Ignite in 2019, and my login for that event matches the Gmail account I was using at the time. Finally, when Microsoft 365 came around, I was assigned a login from my company tenant. That means there are five different ways I can be signed in to Microsoft. You might have a similar situation.

You want to make sure that your Excel Online credentials match those in the File | Account screen in desktop Excel. Click your picture in the top right corner to make sure that you are logged in with the same credentials. If not, the same profile panel will let you log out and then log in again.

Finally, you are ready to start using Excel Online. The top section of the Home screen offers to create a New Blank Workbook. Below that, choose Open Files From This Device, as shown in Figure 16-2.

FIGURE 16-2 Choose to open files from this device.

A Browse dialog will appear. Browse to the workbook that you want to open on your computer. Microsoft will upload the workbook to your OneDrive and open it in Excel Online.

Note Going forward, you can use File | Save As from Desktop Excel to save your work-books to your OneDrive account. Provided the sign-ins for Desktop Excel and Excel Online match, the newly saved workbook should appear in the Recent Files section of Excel Online.

In Excel Online, across the top, you will see a ribbon with tabs for Home, Insert, Draw, Page Layout, Formulas, Data, Review, View, Automate, and Help (see Figure 16-3); You are now free to edit your workbook in Excel Online.

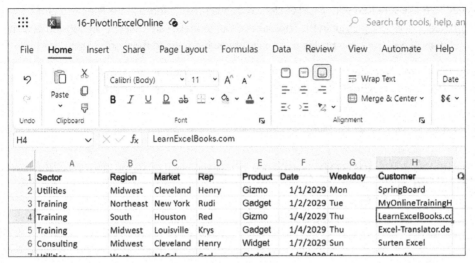

FIGURE 16-3 You are ready to edit this workbook in Excel Online.

Creating a pivot table in Excel Online

The rules for preparing your data in Excel Online for a pivot table are the same as on the desktop: one row of headings above each column and a contiguous block of data with no blank rows or blank columns. Select one cell in your data, as shown in Figure 16-4. On the Insert tab, choose PivotTable.

FIGURE 16-4 Select one cell in your data and choose Insert, PivotTable.

As shown in Figure 16-5, a new task pane opens on the right side of Excel Online. The assumed range for the data source is shown at the top, and you can edit it if necessary.

The Create Your Own PivotTable tile lets you build your own pivot table by dragging and dropping fields in the Fields pane. This is the choice that this chapter will focus on.

Note The rest of the task pane is filled with suggestions of possible pivot tables suggested by the Artificial Intelligence engine that is behind the Analyze Data feature in desktop Excel. The AI suggestions are pretty good, and you might get lucky. It makes sense to scroll through and see if one of the suggested pivot tables will work for you.

The Build Your Own and Start From An AI Suggestion links at the bottom of the Create Your Own PivotTable dialog allow you to choose whether you want the pivot table on a new worksheet or an existing worksheet. If you choose the Start From An AI Suggestion option, a small dialog asks you to specify the location for the pivot table.

FIGURE 16-5 This new task pane covers most of the options in the Insert PivotTable dialog in Excel for the desktop.

After specifying the location for the pivot table, the PivotTable Fields task pane appears, as shown in Figure 16-6. There are several things to note:

- The task pane shows the fields on the left and the areas where you can drop those fields on the right. This was Howie Dickerman's favorite arrangement and the only arrangement available today in Excel Online. After Howie suggested it to me, I switched to this arrangement, which is the only one I use now. There is no tiny dropdown menu to change to any of the other arrangements of the task pane.

- The Columns and Rows icons have been reinvented. They show that if you drop a field in the Columns area, the items from that field will appear at the top of the report. If you drop a field in the Rows area, the items from that field will appear on the left side of the report.

- Just like in Excel for the desktop, if you choose a numeric field, it will move to the Values area. If you choose a field that contains text or dates, it will move to the Rows area. If you want something in the Columns area, you should drag that field from the field—well, to the Columns area. You can also drag fields from one area to the other.

- Tiny dropdown arrows are visible to the right of each field when you hover over the field. The other choices allow you to rearrange the order of the fields, which can be done by dragging and dropping. You will also note that the Filter options that appear here in desktop Excel are replaced by an Add To Filters option, which is a nice way of saying that you cannot filter this field in its current location.

Figure 16-6 shows the PivotTable Fields for a pivot table with Market in Rows, Product in Columns, and Revenue in Values.

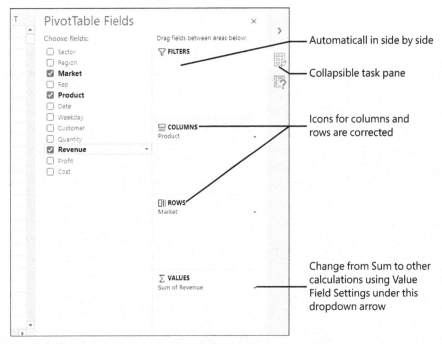

FIGURE 16-6 The PivotTable Fields pane feels similar to desktop Excel.

Figure 16-7 shows the pivot table created from the PivotTable Fields in Figure 16-6. Even though my desktop Excel specifies that all future pivot tables should start in Tabular Form, Excel Online is creating the pivot table in Compact Form, signified by the presence of the cells labeled "Column Labels" and "Row Labels." You will see how to change to tabular form in Figure 16-10.

Also, note that empty cells are showing up as blank instead of zero. It is clear that any PivotTable Defaults that you created in desktop Excel are not present here in Excel Online. You will see how to replace the blank cells with zero later in Figure 16-13.

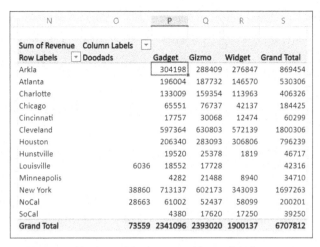

| Sum of Revenue | Column Labels | | | | |
Row Labels	Doodads	Gadget	Gizmo	Widget	Grand Total
Arkla		304198	288409	276847	869454
Atlanta		196004	187732	146570	530306
Charlotte		133009	159354	113963	406326
Chicago		65551	76737	42137	184425
Cincinnati		17757	30068	12474	60299
Cleveland		597364	630803	572139	1800306
Houston		206340	283093	306806	796239
Hunstville		19520	25378	1819	46717
Louisville	6036	18552	17728		42316
Minneapolis		4282	21488	8940	34710
New York	38860	713137	602173	343093	1697263
NoCal	28663	61002	52437	58099	200201
SoCal		4380	17620	17250	39250
Grand Total	73559	2341096	2393020	1900137	6707812

FIGURE 16-7 This pivot table was created in Excel Online.

Changing pivot table options in Excel Online

The two PivotTable ribbon tabs in desktop Excel are replaced by a single PivotTable ribbon tab in Excel Online, as shown in Figure 16-8. From left to right, the icons are:

- **PivotTable Name**—Type a new name for your pivot table here.

- **Refresh All**—If any changes happen in the source data, click this icon to reload the grid data to the pivot cache.

- **Change Data Source**—If you need to add more rows to the source data, you can respecify the source data range using this icon.

- **Insert Slicer / Insert Timeline**—Add a slicer to filter the current pivot table.

- **Move PivotTable**—Move the pivot table to a new place or to a new worksheet.

- **Show Details**—Select any number in the Values area of a pivot table and click Show Details to insert a new worksheet with all the rows that make up the number.

- **PivotTable Style Options**—The next two groups mirror the pivot table styles groups from desktop Excel and start with the four checkboxes for Row Headers, Column Headers, Banded Rows, and Banded Columns. Next is the gallery with 85 pivot table styles from desktop Excel.

- **Field List**—This button toggles (shows or hides) the PivotTable Fields pane. Now that the pane can be collapsed into the dock on the right side of the screen, this option seems less important.

- **Settings**—Initially, this is set to Off. Toggling it back on allows you to find the options for controlling your pivot table.

- **+/- buttons**—If your pivot table is in Compact Form and you have multiple Row fields, a series of expand and collapse buttons is available. If you don't plan on expanding and collapsing columns, turn this off.

Access pivot table options with the Settings button

FIGURE 16-8 Excel Online offers a simplified ribbon tab.

Click the Settings icon in the PivotTable tab of the ribbon to access a PivotTable Settings task pane. The various settings on this task pane are described in the rest of this chapter. At the top of the Settings dialog, you can type a new name for your pivot table.

The next section lets you toggle the Grand Total for Rows and/or Columns. Subtotals can be hidden, shown on top of each section, or shown at the bottom. Figure 16-9 shows these first settings in the task pane.

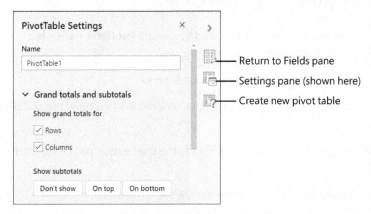

FIGURE 16-9 The top of the PivotTable Settings task pane.

Scroll down in the PivotTable Settings pane as shown in Figure 16-10. You will arrive at a setting that I will change in every pivot table that I ever create in Excel Online. In desktop Excel, the names are Compact Form, Outline Form, and Tabular Form with additional settings to Repeat All Item Labels.

In Excel Online, I like that the question has been reframed as "Do you want the fields from the Row area to be placed in separate columns or a single column?" If you choose Single Column, you can choose how many characters to indent the inner row fields.

Choosing Single Column is the same as choosing Compact Form in desktop Excel. Changing to Separate Columns is like choosing Outline Form in desktop Excel. Examples of Compact Form and Outline Form are shown in Figures 16-11 and 16-12.

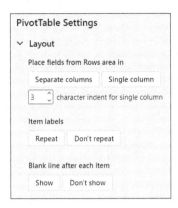

FIGURE 16-10 The desktop Excel settings for Compact, Outline, and Tabular are presented more intuitively in Excel Online.

Figure 16-11 shows the pivot table in Compact Form with a 3-character indent for the inner row field.

FIGURE 16-11 A pivot table in Compact Form.

Figure 16-12 shows the pivot table after choosing Separate Columns for Row Fields. Note that the Row Labels and Column Labels headings are replaced by these useful headings: Region and Market. The Item Labels are set to Repeat, which causes the word "Midwest" to appear on each row instead of just the first row.

A sign that this is actually an Outline Form and not a Tabular Form is when the row at the top of each region appears with just the word "Midwest," "Northeast," or "South." Unfortunately, there is no good way to get rid of those rows in Excel Online.

Tip   If you aren't *actually* at your grandmother's house and are just trying Excel Online as an experiment, there is a way to convert the pivot table in Figure 16-12 to Tabular Form: Open the workbook in desktop Excel. Change to Tabular Form and save. In a few seconds, the changes will sync to Excel Online, and your pivot table will be in Tabular Form.

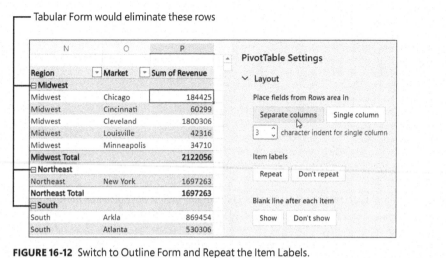

Tabular Form would eliminate these rows

Region	Market	Sum of Revenue
⊟Midwest		
Midwest	Chicago	184425
Midwest	Cincinnati	60299
Midwest	Cleveland	1800306
Midwest	Louisville	42316
Midwest	Minneapolis	34710
Midwest Total		**2122056**
⊟Northeast		
Northeast	New York	1697263
Northeast Total		**1697263**
⊟South		
South	Arkla	869454
South	Atlanta	530306

PivotTable Settings

∨ Layout

Place fields from Rows area in

Separate columns   Single column

3   character indent for single column

Item labels

Repeat   Don't repeat

Blank line after each item

Show   Don't show

FIGURE 16-12 Switch to Outline Form and Repeat the Item Labels.

Scroll down further in the PivotTable Settings pane. Under the misleading Sort And Display heading, you have these options as shown in Figure 16-13:

- **Toggle Autofit Columns Widths On Refresh**—This is one of the most popular options in the PivotTable Options dialog in desktop Excel. Most people turn this off.

- **Toggle the Expand/Collapse buttons**—This is a duplicate of the option in the PivotTable Analyze tab in the ribbon.

- **Control what shows for error values**—Replace error cells with "N.A." or any text of your choosing.

- **Control what shows for empty cells**—Replace empty cells with 0 or any text of your choosing (see Figure 16-13).

Under the Refresh And Save heading, you have these options:

- **Save Source Data With File**—This seems to foreshadow that future versions of Excel Online will be able to create pivot tables from external data.

- **Refresh Data On File Open**—This also foreshadows that Microsoft expects Power Query to become available in Excel Online.

The final settings are to specify Alt Text (alternative text) for the pivot table, as shown in Figure 16-14. This description is for someone who is visually impaired. In theory, this information will appear in the new Navigation pane designed to help someone using a screen reader to navigate the workbook (see Figure 16-14).

FIGURE 16-13 Specify that empty cells should show zero instead of being blank.

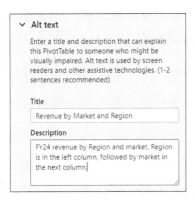

FIGURE 16-14 Specify Alt Text to assist someone who is using a screen reader to navigate the workbook.

Where are the rest of the features?

Creating pivot tables in Excel Online is a big step forward. The process is streamlined, and some of the ideas introduced in Excel Online might make it to desktop Excel one day.

People who would buy a book with "Pivot Table Data Crunching" in the title might be the kind of people who would, at this point, be asking, "What about all the other features?"

Some of those features simply don't apply. Excel Online does not support the Data Model, so there is no ability to convert the pivot table to cube formulas or to add a DAX measure.

Other features, such as grouping daily dates up to months, quarters, and years simply aren't available yet as I write this chapter in August 2024. However, by the time you read this chapter, more features will be added to Excel Online.

Note In all seriousness, a shout-out goes to the retired Excel Project Manager, Howie Dickerman. Howie was always willing to listen and often agreed with the MVPs. Howie was not afraid to say that pivot tables were confusing, with myriad options hidden in many different menus. Howie believed that the PivotTable Fields pane should start with the Fields Section and Areas Section side by side. Howie admitted that the Compact Form is not what most people want. He even agreed that the tiny icons next to Columns and Rows in the task pane were confusing and possibly reversed.

As I look at pivot tables in Excel Online, I can see Howie's fingerprints all over the new design. The task pane starts in Howie's favorite arrangement. The ability to change from Compact Form to Tabular Form is near the top of the settings and is labeled as "Place Fields From Rows Area In: Same Column | Separate Columns." He streamlined the Excel options to one task pane and one ribbon tab. And he redesigned the icons for columns and rows to be less confusing.

Howie was an architect of Power Pivot and DAX. He managed pivot tables on the Excel team for the last several years. I appreciate his foresight in designing pivot tables for Excel Online.

Enjoy your retirement, Howie!

Next steps

Chapter 17 takes a look at new ways to create a cross-tabular report without using pivot tables. From Dynamic Array Formulas to Python to Power Query, there are other options for creating a report that normally requires a pivot table.

Pivoting without a pivot table using formulas, Python, or Power Query

In this chapter, you will learn

- How to create cross-tabular reports without using a pivot table
- Use the new PIVOTBY or GROUPBY dynamic array functions
- Use the Pivot command in Power Query
- Using the pivot_table Python function in Excel

Before Microsoft called them pivot tables, the type of report with headings down the side and across the top was called a "cross-tabular report" or simply a "cross-tab report."

Cross-tab reports existed before pivot tables. I regularly created them as part of my job in finance and accounting. After a couple of Advanced Filters, a transpose, a DSUM, and a Data Table, you were done. Pivot tables made all that simpler.

But today, 35 years after the invention of the pivot table, there are new ways to create cross-tab reports. The new PIVOTBY and GROUPBY functions allow you to create most pivot tables with a formula. Python in Excel offers the pivot_table function. Power Query allows you to create cross-tab reports in a few clicks.

This chapter takes a look at the ways to create cross-tab reports without using pivot tables.

Creating cross-tabs using GROUPBY or PIVOTBY functions

In 2023, the Excel team added PIVOTBY and GROUPBY functions. While PIVOTBY is the obvious way to replace a pivot table, it is easier to learn about the various options in the function by using GROUPBY. Once you are comfortable with GROUPBY, then it is simple to move on to PIVOTBY.

Why would you want to replace a pivot table with a formula? Automatic refresh is one reason. With a regular pivot table, if the underlying data changes, the pivot table does not update until someone clicks Refresh. If that "someone" is your manager's manager's manager, it is easy to imagine a person who would not be comfortable navigating to the Data tab to click a Refresh icon. With a formula, the pivot table can be updated with every calculation of the workbook.

The data used for the GROUPBY examples are shown in Figure 17-1.

⊿	A	B	C	D	E
1	Sector	Region	Market	Customer	Revenue
2	Retail	South	Atlanta	Mike's Dog Store, San Antonio	4158
3	Consulting	Midwest	Cleveland	Surten Excel	8456
4	Training	Northeast	New York	IMSU Home of the Bulls	21708
5	Utilities	Midwest	Cleveland	SpringBoard	22810
6	Consulting	South	Hunstville	Spain Enterprises	19520
7	Utilities	West	SoCal	Ribbon Commander Framework	17250
8	Utilities	South	Houston	Resource Optimizer	18264
9	Consulting	South	Charlotte	Calleia Company	14580
10	Utilities	South	Houston	SkyWire, Inc.	11124
11	Training	South	Arkla	MySpreadsheetLab	6714

FIGURE 17-1 You want to create summaries from this data set.

The GROUPBY syntax

The function arguments for GROUPBY are:

```
=GROUPBY(row_fields,values,function,
field_headers,total_depth,sort_order,
filter_array,field_relationship)
```

You can create a useful summary by specifying a row field, a values field, and a function. All of the other arguments let you tweak the basic result.

Creating a simple summary with GROUPBY

For example, let's say you want to see the total Revenue by Sector:

- The Row_fields argument would be A1:A564.

- The Values argument is E1:E564.

- The Function argument is the word SUM.

The summary report in Figure 17-2 is created from this formula: =GROUPBY(A1:A564,E1:E564,SUM).

◢	G	H	I
3	=GROUPBY(A1:A564,E1:E564,SUM)		
4	Consulting	2,555,333	
5	Museums	427,349	
6	Retail	82,609	
7	Training	2,032,691	
8	Utilities	1,609,830	
9	Total	6,707,812	
10			
11	Field Headers: Default		
12	Total Depth: Default		
13	Sort Order: Default		
14	Filter Array: None		

FIGURE 17-2 A short GROUPBY formula produces a summary showing all of the Sectors in the data and the Revenue per Sector.

Here are some things to note about the default report shown above.

- The Sectors are sorted alphabetically in column A. You can override this by using the Sort_Order argument.

- No headings appear above the data. You can change this using the Field_Headers argument.

- A Total row appears at the bottom. Use the Total_Depth argument to suppress the totals, move the totals to the top, or to add additional subtotals when you have multiple row fields.

- The word SUM in the Function argument is a fancy thing called an "Eta-Lambda". Think of it as a very friendly shorthand way to write =LAMBDA(x,SUM(x)). You will agree that the word SUM is far easier than the alternative.

- Other Eta-Lambdas available include Sum, PercentOf, Average, Median, Count, CountA, Max, Min, Product, ArrayToText, Concat, Stdev.s, Stdev.p, Var.s, Var.p, Mode.sngl, or any function that you can write using a LAMBDA function. The concept of Median in a pivot table is hard to do. (See "Creating Median in a pivot table using DAX measures" in Chapter 10), but the GROUPBY and PIVOTBY not only includes Median but also the ability to write any function logic inside of the LAMBDA function.

- The example above has a single field for row fields. You can specify multiple row fields, as you will see in a future example. You can also specify multiple values fields, perhaps Quantity, Revenue, and Profit.

- The Filter_Array allows you to remove rows from the original data set. Perhaps you want everything where the Market is not "Inside Sales". You would specify C1:C564<>"Inside Sales" as the Filter_Array.

- The Field_Relationship is used when there are multiple Row_fields. If those fields form a hierarchy, then subtotals are available. If you specify that the data does not form a hierarchy, then you will not get subtotals.

Sorting the results of GROUPBY and PIVOTBY

The GROUPBY formula in this example returns two columns: Sector and Revenue. By default, the data is sorted alphabetically by the first column. You can override this default. Specify a Sort_Order of 1 to sort by the first column ascending or a Sort_Order of -2 to sort by the second column descending. Both 1 and 2 would sort ascending. How do you specify a descending sort? It is easy—make the argument negative.

In Figure 17-3, a Sort_Order of -2 makes sure that the result is sorted descending by the second column, which, in this case, is the Revenue column.

	G	H	I	J
3	=GROUPBY(A1:A564,E1:E564,SUM,3,1,-2)			
4	Sector	Revenue		
5	Consulting	2,555,333		
6	Training	2,032,691		
7	Utilities	1,609,830		
8	Museums	427,349		
9	Retail	82,609		
10	Total	6,707,812		
11				
12	Field Headers: 3 - Yes and Show			
13	Total Depth: 1 - Grand Total			
14	Sort Order: -2 - second column descending			
15	Filter Array: None			

FIGURE 17-3 Sort the report using a column number in the Sort_Order argument.

Note that headings have been added to the report above by using a Field_Headers argument of 3. Note that headings and totals are not impacted by the Sort_Order argument.

Moving totals to the top of the report

The Total_Depth argument controls if you have totals in the report:

- Use 0 (zero) for no totals.

- Use 1 for a single total row.

- Use 2 for a total row and subtotals when there are multiple row fields.

For many years, Excel MVP Roger Govier argued that there should be an option to move Pivot Table totals to the top of the report. Roger finally gets his feature with GROUPBY and PIVOTBY. Specify -1 for a Grand Total at the top and -2 for Grand Total and Subtotals above each section.

Figure 17-4 shows a report with a PERCENT OF function and totals at the top. Note that the sort order is based on the second column, but because the 2 is a positive, the data is sorted ascending.

◢	G	H	I	J
3	=GROUPBY(A1:A564,E1:E564,PERCENTOF,3,-1,2)			
4	Sector	Revenue		
5	Total	100.0%		
6	Retail	1.2%		
7	Museums	6.4%		
8	Utilities	24.0%		
9	Training	30.3%		
10	Consulting	38.1%		
11				
12	Field Headers: 3 - Yes and Show			
13	Total Depth: -1 - Grand Total at the top			
14	Sort Order: 2 - second column ascending			
15	Filter Array: None			
16				

FIGURE 17-4 This report shows the percentage of totals instead of sum. The total row is moved to the top, thanks to the negative 1 in the Total_depth argument.

Showing subtotals for multiple row fields using GROUPBY

One of the more exciting variations for GROUPBY and PIVOTBY is to specify multiple row fields. In the example below, the two columns that you want in the row fields are adjacent to each other. In this easier case, you can specify the row field as B1:C564. If your Row_Fields columns are not adjacent to each other, you could use HSTACK(A1:A564,C1:C564) to specify the row fields.

Figure 17-5 shows a report with Region and Market in the row fields. Some things to note:

- Region and Market occupy columns 1 and 2 of the report, moving Revenue from column 2 to column 3. If you want to sort by Revenue, you will have to change the Sort_Order from -2 to -3.

- The report is sorted descending by column 3, which is the Revenue column. This means that the South Region appears first because it has the lowest Revenue, followed by Midwest, Northeast, and West. Within each Region, the markets appear with descending Revenue.

- The bold formatting in the figure happens because of a conditional formatting rule. To chance columns G, H, and I to bold, use this conditional formatting formula =LEN($H5)=0.

▲	G	H	I	J
3	=GROUPBY(B1:C564,E1:E564,SUM,3,2,-3)			
4	Region	Market	Revenue	
5	South	Arkla	869,454	
6	South	Houston	796,239	
7	South	Atlanta	530,306	
8	South	Charlotte	406,326	
9	South	Hunstville	46,717	
10	**South**		**2,649,042**	
11	Midwest	Cleveland	1,800,306	
12	Midwest	Chicago	184,425	
13	Midwest	Cincinnati	60,299	
14	Midwest	Louisville	42,316	
15	Midwest	Minneapolis	34,710	
16	**Midwest**		**2,122,056**	
17	Northeast	New York	1,697,263	
18	**Northeast**		**1,697,263**	
19	West	NoCal	200,201	
20	West	SoCal	39,250	
21	**West**		**239,451**	
22	**Grand Total**		**6,707,812**	
23				
24	Field Headers: 3 - Yes and Show			
25	Total Depth: 2 - Grand Total and Subtotals			
26	Sort Order: -3 - third column descending			
27	Filter Array: None			

FIGURE 17-5 Specify multiple row fields, and you can get a report showing subtotals for each Region and a grand total overall.

I was excited to see the new PIVOTBY function arrive, but in reality, I find that I use GROUPBY far more frequently. Getting a Count of records by a field, a Percent of Totals, or Sums is great for ad-hoc reports. It seems that I need the column fields of the cross-tab report far less frequently.

Moving from GROUPBY to PIVOTBY functions

If you've followed along with the GROUPBY discussion above, you will be able to quickly understand the PIVOTBY function. Here is the function syntax:

```
'=PIVOTBY(row_fields, col_fields, values,function,
field_headers, row_total_depth, row_sort_order,
col_total_depth, col_sort_order,
filter_array, relative_to)
```

PIVOTBY and GROUPBY operate similarly. GROUPBY and PIVOTBY offer the same arguments for specifying row fields, how to subtotal, and how to sort the rows. Then, PIVOTBY adds arguments for column fields, then arguments for column total depth and column sort order.

In Figure 17-6, Sector is the row field, and Region is the column field. The values field is Revenue, and the function is SUM.

	G	H	I	J	K	L
4	=PIVOTBY(A1:A564,B1:B564,E1:E564,SUM)					
5		Midwest	Northeast	South	West	Total
6	Consulting	934,588	613,514	951,980	55,251	2,555,333
7	Museums	427,349				427,349
8	Retail		51,240	31,369		82,609
9	Training	42,316	1,032,509	903,818	54,048	2,032,691
10	Utilities	717,803		761,875	130,152	1,609,830
11	Total	2,122,056	1,697,263	2,649,042	239,451	6,707,812

FIGURE 17-6 This cross-tab report is created by the PIVOTBY function.

While the report generated in Figure 17-6 is great, it is not as flexible as a pivot table. There are no options to replace the blank cells in the values area with zeroes. There are no fancy pivot table formats available. But there will be times when getting the results from PIVOTBY and GROUPBY is enough for the task.

What are the pros and cons of GROUPBY and PIVOTBY?

Pros:

- Any changes to the underlying data will immediately be reflected in your summary reports.

- This is the only good way to display totals at the top of the report.

- The syntax allows you to control sort order and subtotals.

- If you have to create medians in your pivot table, this is an easy way to do it without resorting to DAX Measures.

- The LAMBDA function is available for doing other calculations in the values area.

Cons:

- There are several customizations available in pivot tables that are not available in these functions.

- One global problem with array functions is the inability to properly format the results. You will find yourself having to apply the right alignment to the Values area and apply bold to headings.

Creating a cross-tab using Power Query

Pivot tables are great if you have less than 1,048,575 rows of data. When you get more rows than that, you will have to use Power Pivot or Power Query to load that data and summarize it before the data lands in the grid.

Power Query offers many transformations that have been discussed in this book. This section will use two new transforms: Grouping and Pivot.

Getting your data into Power Query

Power Query wants to load data that is a named range or a table. Select one cell in your data and choose Ctrl+T to convert the data to a table.

By default, this table will be called Table1. Normally, if you are going to have a lot of tables, you would rename the table. But for this example, Table1 is fine.

On the Data tab in the Get & Transform Data group, select From Table/Range, as shown in Figure 17-7.

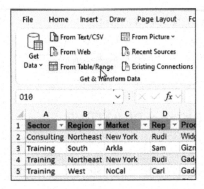

FIGURE 17-7 Start Power Query by clicking From Sheet on the Data tab.

Summarizing Revenue by Sector and Region in Power Query

You need to summarize the Revenue for each combination of Region and Sector. This is easy using the Group By command in Power Query:

1. In the Power Query editor, click the Sector heading. Ctrl+click the Region heading, so both Sector and Region are selected.

2. On the Transform tab, choose Group By, as shown in Figure 17-8.

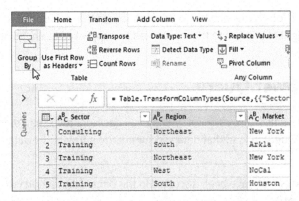

FIGURE 17-8 Preselect Sector and Region before starting the Group By operation.

3. Because you preselected Region and Sector in Figure 17-12, the Group By dialog starts with both Region and Sector as fields in the Group By dialog. You will have to change all three fields at the bottom of the dialog.

4. For New Column Name, type **Total Revenue**.

5. For the Operation, change Sum to Count.

6. For the Column, select Revenue. The Grouping dialog is shown in Figure 17-9.

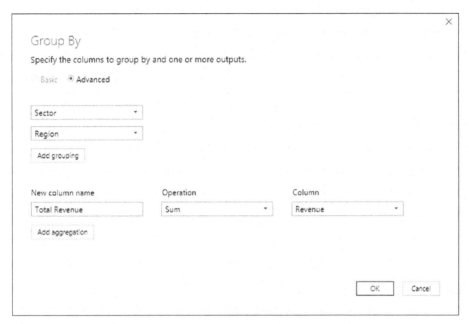

FIGURE 17-9 Grouping will reduce the 563 rows down to 1 row for each combination of Sector and Region.

Sorting and pivoting in Power Query

If you want the Regions across the top of your report to be sorted, now is the time to do it. Select the Region column by clicking the Region heading in Power Query. Use the AZ sort button on the Home tab, as shown in Figure 17-10.

You are now ready to pivot the Region field to go across. Click the Region heading in the Power Query Editor to select the Region field. From the Transform tab, click the Pivot Column icon (see Figure 17-11).

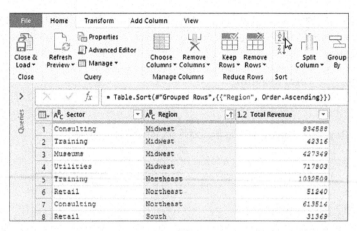

FIGURE 17-10 Sorting Regions while they are vertical is easier than dragging their locations once they are columns.

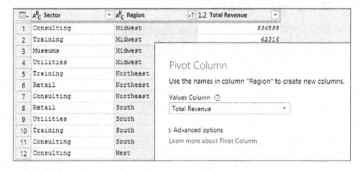

FIGURE 17-11 Select the Region column and then choose Pivot Column.

The Pivot Column dialog is fairly simple. Specify which numeric field should be used for the Values Column. Choose Total Revenue, as shown in Figure 17-12.

	A^B_C Sector	A^B_C Region	1.2 Total Revenue
1	Consulting	Midwest	934588
2	Training	Midwest	42316
3	Museums	Midwest	
4	Utilities	Midwest	
5	Training	Northeast	
6	Retail	Northeast	
7	Consulting	Northeast	
8	Retail	South	
9	Utilities	South	
10	Training	South	
11	Consulting	South	
12	Consulting	West	

Pivot Column

Use the names in column "Region" to create new columns.

Values Column ⓘ

Total Revenue

▷ Advanced options

Learn more about Pivot Column

FIGURE 17-12 Specify which column to use in the values area.

Cleaning final steps

Sort the data by Sector by choosing the Sector column and clicking AZ on the Home tab.

The last problem is that empty cells contain the word null instead of zeroes. Select all the Region columns in your result. On the Home tab, choose Replace Values.

In the Replace Values dialog, type **null** in lowercase for the Value To Find. In Replace With, type **0** (zero) and click OK (see Figure 17-13).

FIGURE 17-13 Replace null with a zero.

Once the query is built, you need to return the results to Excel. On the Home tab in Power Query, the Close & Load icon will return the results to a new worksheet. Instead of clicking the Close & Load icon, open the dropdown below Close & Load and choose Close & Load To. This opens the Import Data dialog, as shown in Figure 17-14.

FIGURE 17-14 Rather than sending the results to a new worksheet, use Close & Load To and select a cell on an existing worksheet.

Figure 17-15 shows the results in M2.

J	K	L	M	N	O	P	Q	R
Pr▼	C▼							
5082	6546		Sector ▼	Midwest ▼	Northeast ▼	South ▼	West ▼	
9198	12240		Consulting	934,588	613,514	951,980	55,251	
984	1273		Museums	427,349	0	0	0	
8856	11754		Retail	0	51,240	31,369	0	
4088	5064		Training	42,316	1,032,509	903,818	54,048	
7872	11472		Utilities	717,803	0	761,875	130,152	
1968	2314							
10220	12310							
2952	3288							

FIGURE 17-15 The results of the Power Query solution are a cross-tab table returned to the Excel grid.

What are the pros and cons of Power Query?

Pros:

- Adding or removing a Sector or Region will automatically be reflected in the results after you refresh the query.

- If you are loading data from an external database or file and it won't fit in the 1,048,576 rows of Excel, Power Query can process the extra rows in memory and return the result.

Cons:

- The report is not automatically updated if the underlying data changes. You either need to click Data | Refresh All or select the results of the query, show the Queries And Connections pane, and choose Refresh.

- The numbers are not formatted. In Figure 17-15, I had to format the numbers.

- There are no totals.

- This is probably the most complex to set up.

The big advantages of Power Query are the ability to point to an external data source—even one that is more than 1 million rows—and the ability to produce a pivot-like result in Excel.

Creating a cross-tab using Python in Excel

As of September, Microsoft has a version of Python running in its beta versions of Excel. Microsoft is expecting corporate customers who want to use Python frequently to pay an additional $24 per month for a Python license. Note that if your edition of Excel is eligible for a Python subscription, the Python tools will appear, and you can use a few Python calls each month for free. After the free quota is used, the speed of Python will slow, and Microsoft will nudge you to subscribe to restore Python to full speed.

To start writing Python code in a cell, use the Insert Python icon on the Formulas tab. You will see a green PY indicator to the left of the Formula Bar, so you know that you are writing Python code.

By default, Python code will return a data frame object to the cell. This is rarely what you want. There is a new dropdown to the left of the Formula Bar. Open this dropdown and choose the "123" icon to return Excel values.

As you are typing your Python code in the Formula Bar, pressing Enter will go to a new line in the Formula Bar. When you are done with the code, press Ctrl+Enter to commit the code and run it.

If you have Python code in multiple cells, the code is evaluated in row-wise order:

1. Code in cell A1 runs first, then cell B1, C1, and so on out to cell XFD1.

2. Calculation then moves on to row 2.

3. Any variables defined in an earlier cell are available to the later cells.

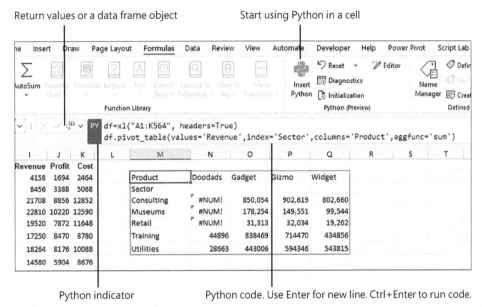

FIGURE 17-16 Python code is written in the Excel formula bar, and the results spill to the Excel grid.

Getting your data into a Python data frame

In Excel, you often refer to a range of data. Headings in row 1 and data starting in row 2 with 11 columns is referred to as the range A1:K564. In Python, this same table is called a Data Frame. The typical Python code will use a variable name of df to store a data frame.

The Excel team wrote a new Python function called x1 to be used to load an Excel range into a Python data frame. Here are the easy steps for loading a range into a data frame.

1. From an empty cell, start Python by clicking Insert Python or use the Ctrl+Alt+Shift+P shortcut key.

2. Type **df=**.

3. Using your mouse, highlight the data in the Excel grid.

4. Press Enter. Excel will write this line of code for you:

```
df=xl("A1:K564", headers=True)
```

The variable df is a Python data frame; you can use Python functions to operate on the data frame.

Using the Python pivot_table function

To create a pivot table from your data frame, use the `pivot_table` function. Some of the argument names will make sense to people using Excel. For example, the `Values` argument is used to specify fields in the values area. Same for columns. But what Excel calls row fields are specified using the index field in Python.

In Excel, the default aggregation is a sum. In Python, the default aggregation is a mean. Excel defaults to showing Grand Totals. In Python, they are off by default. Turn them on with `margins='True'`. The newly added total row and total column will default to a heading of All unless you specify a different heading using margins_name.

Excel pivot tables will default sort by any custom lists. There is no way to have this happen in Python. Sorting in Python seems quite limited—your only choice is to show the data in the original sequence or ascending alphabetically by the row fields. (I mean, index fields.)

Python offers an amazing variety of ways to group daily dates. However, when you use any of these, you cannot show the margins or grand totals.

In Excel, empty cells show as empty, and many people will use Excel Options to override the empty cell with a zero. In Python, empty cells show as a `#NUM!` error, and you would use the `fill_value` argument to specify zero or anything else to appear there.

Python stacks the headings in a way that will seem unusual to people who are used to Excel.

In Python, any Boolean settings must be set to `True` or `False`. Attempting to use `TRUE`, `FALSE`, "TRUE", 'false', "True", or "False" true, or false will result in an error.

For the `index` and `column` values, you can specify column names in single or double quotes. "Revenue" or 'Revenue' works. If you want two fields in the rows area, use square brackets like this: `index=['Region', 'Market']`.

For multiple aggregation functions, use curly braces. You can specify a different aggregation function for each value field: `aggfunc={'Revenue': 'sum', 'Profit': 'mean'}`

These are the arguments available:

- values Fields in the Values area. You can specify `'Revenue'` or `"Revenue"`.

- index Fields in the Rows area

- columns Fields in the Columns area

- **aggfunc** Summarize value field by (defaults to 'mean'). Valid choices include sum, mean, median, min, max, count, std, var, or a custom function defined using a LAMBDA function in Python.

- **fill_value** For empty/error cells, show this fill_value instead of a #NUM! error.

- **margins** Show grand totals (defaults to False).

- **dropna** Ignore any data rows that have non-numbers in a numeric column (defaults to True).

- **margins_name** Heading for Grand Totals (defaults to 'All').

- **observed** Set to False for show items with no data (defaults to False).

- **sort** Should the result be sorted? (Defaults to True.).

The Python code shown previously in Figure 17-16 produces a pivot table with Sectors down the side, Products in the columns, and Sum of Revenue in the values area:

```
df=xl("A1:K564", headers=True)
df.pivot_table(values='Revenue',index='Sector', columns='Product',aggfunc='sum')
```

Examine Figure 17-17 to compare the Python pivot table and an Excel pivot table. The Python pivot table appears in M2:Q8. The Excel pivot table appears in M11:R18.

Note that the backslash character is the line continuation character in Python. The code in Figure 17-17 uses backslash characters to keep the screenshot narrow.

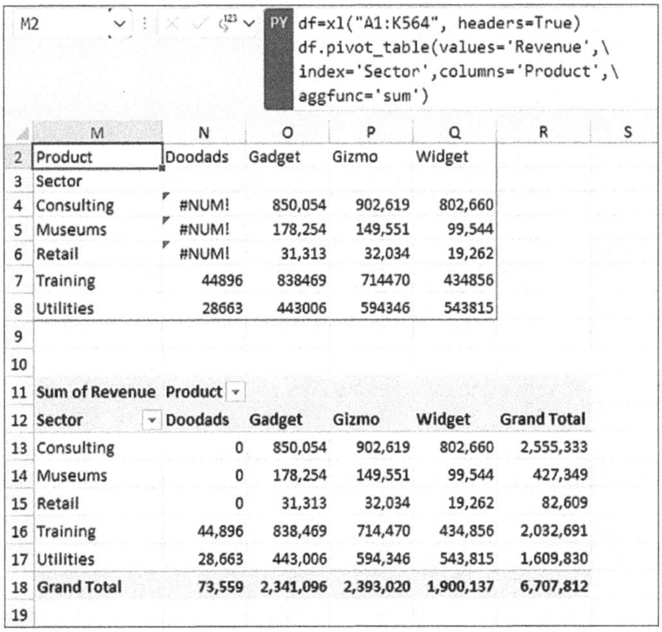

FIGURE 17-17 The Python pivot table shown at the top has a different layout than the pivot tables that Excellers would be used to.

By default, Grand Totals are missing from the Python pivot table. Add these arguments to show grand totals:

```
Margins='True',margins_name='Total'
```

Empty cells are shown with #NUM! errors in Python. Use the `fill_value` argument to replace the #NUM! errors with something else, such as a zero:

```
Fill_value=0
```

The number formatting and column alignment need to be manually applied using tools on the Home tab of the ribbon.

Putting this all together yields the Python pivot table shown in Figure 17-18, which is fairly close to the equivalent Excel pivot table.

M2	PY	df=xl("A1:K564", headers=True) df.pivot_table(values='Revenue',\ index='Sector',columns='Product',\ aggfunc='sum',\ margins='True',margins_name='Total',\ fill_value=0)						
	M	N	O	P	Q	R	S
2	Product	Doodads	Gadget	Gizmo	Widget	Total	
3	Sector						
4	Consulting	0	850,054	902,619	802,660	2,555,333	
5	Museums	0	178,254	149,551	99,544	427,349	
6	Retail	0	31,313	32,034	19,262	82,609	
7	Training	44,896	838,469	714,470	434,856	2,032,691	
8	Utilities	28,663	443,006	594,346	543,815	1,609,830	
9	Total	73,559	2,341,096	2,393,020	1,900,137	6,707,812	
10							
11	Sum of Revenue	Product					
12	Sector	Doodads	Gadget	Gizmo	Widget	Grand Total	
13	Consulting	0	850,054	902,619	802,660	2,555,333	
14	Museums	0	178,254	149,551	99,544	427,349	
15	Retail	0	31,313	32,034	19,262	82,609	
16	Training	44,896	838,469	714,470	434,856	2,032,691	
17	Utilities	28,663	443,006	594,346	543,815	1,609,830	
18	Grand Total	73,559	2,341,096	2,393,020	1,900,137	6,707,812	

FIGURE 17-18 The Python pivot table in M2:R9 is almost the same as the Excel pivot table in M11:R18.

The last remaining issue is the arrangement of the headings in the pivot table. Excel puts the word Sum of Revenue and the Product field name in row 1 and the actual Product names in row 2. Python puts the field name Product in the top-left cell and the Product names in the rest of Row 1. This leaves a strange row 2 with the Sector field name and three blank cells.

There is not a good solution to this. The pivot table returned by Python in cell M2 is referred to as M2#. You could use TAKE, DROP, CHOOSEROWS, HSTACK, and VSTACK to take the Python pivot table apart and put it back together in the correct arrangement. The formula in Figure 17-19 is

```
=VSTACK(HSTACK(TAKE(CHOOSEROWS(M2#,2),,1),DROP(TAKE(M2#,1),,1)),DROP(M2#,2))
```

	M	N	O	P	Q	R
20	Sector	Doodads	Gadget	Gizmo	Widget	Total
21	Consulting	0	850,054	902,619	802,660	2,555,333
22	Museums	0	178,254	149,551	99,544	427,349
23	Retail	0	31,313	32,034	19,262	82,609
24	Training	44,896	838,469	714,470	434,856	2,032,691
25	Utilities	28,663	443,006	594,346	543,815	1,609,830
26	Total	73,559	2,341,096	2,393,020	1,900,137	6,707,812

FIGURE 17-19 This rearrangement of the Python pivot table feels more like the results in Excel. But is the complex formula worth the time?

Caution It would be great if you could combine the Python code from cell M2 with the formula in cell M20. You could envision a LET function where you assign OrigPT to the Python code in M2 and then refer to OrigPT instead of M2# for the formula in Figure 17-19. But this approach won't work. A cell can contain Python code or Excel formulas but not a mix of both. That means you would have to display the Python pivot table in the grid and then use the formula in Figure 17-19 in another spot in the grid. That means every pivot table would be shown twice just to fix the arrangement of the headings. It might be easier to get used to the arrangement of the Python headings.

Grouping dates in Python pivot tables

The main problem with grouping dates is that you can no longer display the grand total row or column in your Python pivot table. That is a big limitation. If you can get past that limitation, then the variety of date grouping available in Python is amazing.

Start with a Python pivot table with daily dates down the left side, as shown in Figure 17-20.

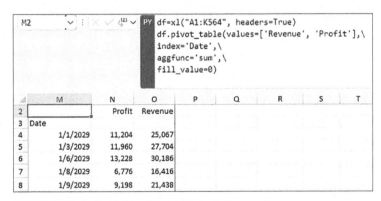

FIGURE 17-20 A pivot table with daily dates in the row field.

To convert the daily dates to months, use the following code:

```
index=pd.Grouper(key = 'Date', freq='M')
```

Figure 17-21 shows the result.

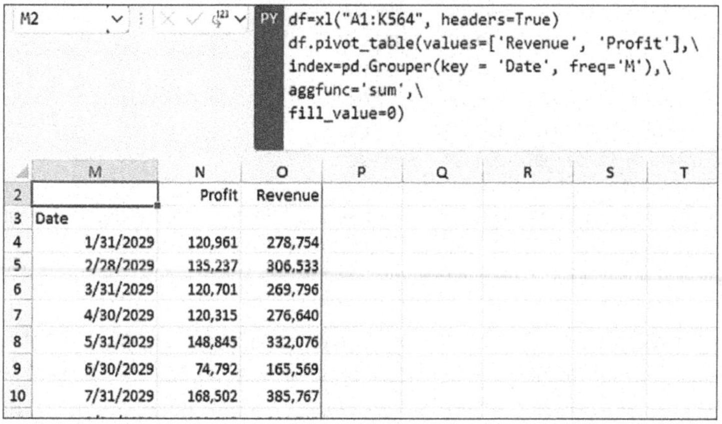

```
M2                    PY  df=xl("A1:K564", headers=True)
                          df.pivot_table(values=['Revenue', 'Profit'],\
                          index=pd.Grouper(key = 'Date', freq='M'),\
                          aggfunc='sum',\
                          fill_value=0)
```

	M	N	O	P	Q	R	S	T
2		Profit	Revenue					
3	Date							
4	1/31/2029	120,961	278,754					
5	2/28/2029	135,237	306,533					
6	3/31/2029	120,701	269,796					
7	4/30/2029	120,315	276,640					
8	5/31/2029	148,845	332,076					
9	6/30/2029	74,792	165,569					
10	7/31/2029	168,502	385,767					

FIGURE 17-21 Python rolls the daily dates up to months.

There is an astounding variety of codes that you can use for the Frequency in the pd.Grouper function. Table 17-1 lists all of the codes, but you can modify each of these codes by prefixing the code with a digit. So, while a Frequency of D means daily, you can specify 3D for three-day periods or 2W for two-week periods.

TABLE 17-1 Codes for Frequency in PD.Grouper

Alias	Description
B	business day frequency
C	custom business day frequency
D	calendar day frequency
W	weekly frequency
ME	month end frequency
SME	semi-month end frequency (15th and end of month)
BME	business month end frequency
CBME	custom business month end frequency
MS	month start frequency
SMS	semi-month start frequency (1st and 15th)
BMS	business month start frequency
CBMS	custom business month start frequency
QE	quarter end frequency
BQE	business quarter end frequency
QS	quarter start frequency
BQS	business quarter start frequency

TABLE 17-1 *(continued)*

Alias	Description
YE	year end frequency
BYE	business year end frequency
YS	year start frequency
BYS	business year start frequency
h	hourly frequency
bh	business hour frequency
cbh	custom business hour frequency
min	minutely frequency
s	secondly frequency
ms	Milliseconds
us	Microseconds
ns	Nanoseconds

Pros and cons of Python

Pros:

- The date grouping is far more flexible than Excel.

- Python code will automatically recalculate when the underlying data changes.

Cons:

- Microsoft has not announced if Python will be available in all versions of Excel or if there is an extra fee.

- The headings are slightly different than regular pivot tables in Excel.

- There are not many sorting options.

- When you have multiple row fields, there are no subtotals at each change in the outer row field.

The big advantage of Python is that you can be geekier than your coworkers. As Copilot makes everyone into a pivot table guru, you need a way to continue to feel superior in your tech skills. Python will up your cred with the data pros out there.

Next steps

Chapter 18 will take a look at using artificial intelligence and Copilot when creating Excel pivot tables.

Using Artificial Intelligence and Copilot for building pivot tables

In this chapter, you will learn how to use Artificial Intelligence in Excel:

- Using AI to add a column to your data before pivoting

- Using Analyze Data to find trends and ask questions

- Using Copilot in Excel to create pivot tables or pivot charts

- Using Copilot in Excel to generate formula columns

- Using Advanced Copilot in Excel with Python

- Using Copilot in OneDrive to analyze financial statements in Excel

- Using AI to find and summarize Excel YouTube videos

- Using Copilot to write VBA, Python, RegEx, or Power Query M Code

- Fun: Using Copilot to write Excel poetry or songs

In 2023 and 2024, Artificial Intelligence began moving at the speed of light. There are so many large language models (LLMs) coming to market right now. OpenAI is offering ChatGPT. Microsoft incorporates some of that functionality in its Copilot product.

Normally, if you start searching on YouTube for a solution to an Excel problem, a video from ten years ago would be as valid as a video from last week. But the videos about Copilot have a very short shelf life. Requests that failed two months ago probably are not failing today.

This chapter is about using Copilot in Excel for creating pivot tables, but it's more than that. You will also see how to write Excel formulas that get their answer from a large language model. You will also see the feature that has been freely available in Excel for more than three years, which is more reliable than Copilot for creating pivot tables.

In September 2024, as Microsoft's Satya Nadella was announcing Copilot had reached General Availability, the Excel team introduced an even better version of Copilot that generates Python as part of the task.

> **Note** This chapter is the least likely chapter in this book to age well. Things that are cutting edge in the fall of 2024, as I write this, will be replaced by more advanced features in six months or a year.

Using AI to add a column to your data before pivoting

Let's say you have a list of 2,500 songs stored in Excel. The data includes a category, the artist who recorded the song, and a song title. The categories were created by someone who was trying to be clever. For example, there are three categories that all seem to be similar: "Hip Hop You Don't Stop," "Rapattack," and "Rap-ture."

You decide that a pivot table organizing each category by year or decade would help to define the type of music in each category. This is fine, except there is no year information available in the data. What are you going to do? Visit Google 2,500 times? (See Figure 18-1.)

	B	C	D	F
1	Category	Artist	Song	Year??
2	Rapattack	Ice Spice	Bikini Bottom	
3	Break Stuff	Rob Zombie	Burn	
4	Rock Boom Baby	The Coasters	Charlie Brown	
5	Got Soul	The Supremes	Come See About Me	
6	Time Warp	Foreigner	Feels like the First Time	
7	Rap-ture	Busta Rhymes & T-Pain	Hustler's Anthem 09	
8	Rapattack	City Girls & Quavo & Lil Wayne &	Kitty Talk	
9	Rap-ture	Tinie Tempah	Pass Out	

FIGURE 18-1 The first step in creating the pivot table is to add a non-existent Year field to 2,500 rows of data.

This task is a perfect task to be solved by ChatGPT. First, ChatGPT can solve the problem in relatively little time. Second, even if it gets the answer wrong now and then, it is not a life-and-death scenario. No one will have to restate numbers to the US Securities and Exchange Commission (SEC) if the data is wrong.

Install and configure the Excel Labs add-in

A free add-in developed by Microsoft Labs in Cambridge, England will allow you to query ChatGPT through an Excel formula. The add-in adds a new function called LABS.GENERATIVEAI. Follow these steps to install and configure the Excel Labs add-in.

1. Find the Add-Ins icon in Excel. The Add-In Store icon was originally on the Insert tab from 2007 through 2023. In late 2024, the icon was moved to the Home tab, just to the left of the Analyze Data icon. It also appears on the left side of the File menu as Get Add-Ins.

2. Click the Add-Ins icon and search for Excel Labs.

3. Choose the Excel Labs add-in and install it in your Excel. An Excel Labs icon will appear on the right side of the Home tab.

4. In the Excel ribbon, click the Excel Labs icon. A new task pane will appear on the right side. As I am writing this, there are three tools available in the add-in: Advanced Formula Environment, LABS.GENERATIVEAI Function, and a Python Editor. Click the green Open button to expand the LABS.GENERATIVEAI section of the pane.

5. There are four sections: Keep In Mind, Configure API Key, Beginner's Guide, and Settings. You need to start with Configure API Key. Expand the section about the API Key and follow the link to Get Your API Key Here.

6. You will create a user ID and sign in at *https://platform.openai.com/api-keys*. Each call to the API costs a tiny fraction of a cent, although the calls during a trial period are free. Enter your credit card information, generate an API Key, and copy it to the clipboard.

7. Go back to Excel and paste the API Key in the task pane.

8. The next section in the pane is Beginner's Guide. Read those examples.

9. I recommend also visiting the Settings section because you can use the function by simply passing a question as an argument to the function. For example:

```
=LABS.GENERATIVEAI("Write a song about Excel in Reggae Dancehall style"
```

There are optional arguments where you can tweak the results:

```
LABS.GENERATIVEAI(prompt, [temperature], [max_tokens], [model])
```

10. Instead of repeating these optional arguments in each formula, you can change the settings using the Settings section of the task pane.

    - In the Settings section, lower the Temperature to 0. This limits the randomness of the answers. Given the current task of figuring out what year a song was recorded, you want the same answer every time.

    - Change the Maximum Output Length to 4 since you want a year. By default, ChatGPT is chatty, explaining "The song XYZ by artist ABC was recorded in the year 1995." You don't need all of that. You just want the year.

    - After changing these settings, click Save Settings (see Figure 18-2).

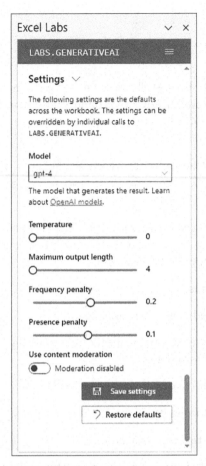

FIGURE 18-2 The first step in creating the pivot table is to add a non-existent Year field to 2,500 rows of data.

You are ready to begin querying ChatGPT through a formula.

Creating a prompt using a formula

Your data has Artist in C2 and Song Title in D2. Your goal is to build a question that can be sent to Chat-GPT. This formula would write a simple prompt:

=In what year did "&C2&" record the song "&D2&"?

I prefer to build the prompts in their own column. Enter the formula above in E2, which will give you a chance to see your question before sending it to ChatGPT. For row 2, the question will look like this:

In what year did Ice Spice record the song Bikini Bottom?

When I first tried this example, the results from ChatGPT were chatty. The formula would return an answer such as this:

The artist Ice Spice recorded the song Bikini Bottom in 1995.

But then, you need to parse to get the year out of 2,500 responses. It is easier to make your prompt to ChatGPT more precise. This formula generates a prompt that asks for just a four-digit year:

="In what year did "&C2&" record the song "&D2&"? Return the answer as a four digit year with no additional words."

This creates a prompt that asks for just the year. Double-click the Fill Handle in E2 to copy the question down to all rows of your data.

Prevent multiple calculations of each formula

Once you get past the preview period, you will start paying actual money for each call to ChatGPT. This 2,500-question project will cost somewhere around 50 cents. But you don't want to pay 50 cents every time the spreadsheet recalculates.

Go to the Formulas tab in the ribbon, open the Calculation Options dropdown, and change the setting to Manual.

Use the LABS.GENERATIVEAI function to retrieve answers

In cell F2, enter the formula =LABS.GENERATIVEAI(E2). When you press Enter, the cell will show a green circle and the #BUSY! Error for a few seconds. Soon, an answer will appear. This is a great time to save the workbook. The next steps might take 30 minutes or more.

Double-click the Fill Handle in cell F2 to copy the formula to all rows. Because Recalculation is set to Manual, the answer will be repeated, but all the answers will have the strikethrough format applied to indicate that you need to press Calculate Now.

On the Formulas tab, press Calculate Now. You will see the green circles appear, followed by new answers. If you really have 2,500 rows of data, this might be a great time to go to lunch while the formulas recalculate.

When you get back from lunch, the formulas should have finished calculating. The results are mostly filled in. There will be some instances where the formula does not know the answer, such as when a song is too new. Figure 18-3 shows a small subset of the results.

	C	D	E	F
E2	fx	="In what year did "&C2&" record the song "&D2&"? Return the answer as a		

	C	D	E	F
1	Artist	Song	Question	Year??
2	Ice Spice	Bikini Bottom	In what y	Sorry, but there's no available information about a song called "Bikini Bottom" by Ice Spice.
3	Rob Zombie	Burn	In what y	2013
4	The Coasters	Charlie Brown	In what y	1958
5	The Supremes	Come See About Me	In what y	1964
6	Foreigner	Feels like the First Time	In what y	1976
7	Busta Rhymes & T-Pain	Hustler's Anthem 09	In what y	2009
8	City Girls & Quavo & Lil Wayne	Kitty Talk	In what y	2020
9	Tinie Tempah	Pass Out	In what y	2009
10	Priya Ragu	Adalam Val	In what y	2021

FIGURE 18-3 The LABS.GENERATIVEAI function filled in the Year column for most of the records.

Once you have the solution, you want to change the formulas in column F to values. Copy column F and choose Paste As Values to prevent any future charges from OpenAI for this project.

Now that you have the new column with years filled in, you can carry on with normal Excel skills. Convert years to a decade with =LEFT(F2,3)*10. Build a pivot table with Decade in columns, Category in rows, and Song Count in values. Add some conditional formatting and a slicer. Figure 18-4 shows a portion of the report showing how the Hip Hop You Don't Stop category is mostly from the 90s, with Rapattack from the 2000–2010s and Rap-ture firmly in the 2010s.

	A	B	C	D	E	F	G	H
1								
2								
3	% of Workouts	Decade						
4	Category	1970	1980	1990	2000	2010	2020	Grand Total
5	Hip Hop You Don't Stop	1%	13%	67%	12%	6%	1%	100%
6	Rapattack	0%	0%	5%	26%	57%	12%	100%
7	Rap-ture	0%	0%	0%	10%	82%	8%	100%
8	Grand Total	0%	3%	18%	18%	53%	8%	100%
9								

Category			
Gratitude	Guilty Pleasures	Hair Brained	
Halloworkit	Heat	Hip Hop You Don'...	
Hoedown Throwdown	Ignite	Imagine Dragons	

FIGURE 18-4 After using LABS.GENERATIVEAI to fill in the missing data about years, a further summary can be created.

To me, this is a perfect use of ChatGPT:

- Do I care if there are some random wrong answers? No.

- Does it materially change the result? No.

- Am I reporting these numbers to the SEC? No.

Note For the last 10 months, I've been donning a Meta VR headset every morning and joining a virtual workout crew playing the game Supernatural Fitness. I've lost 40 pounds so far and am healthier than I've been in a long time. Some of you who are fans of Supernatural Fitness might recognize those categories. If so, find me in your leaderboard and hit me up. The morning crew has some great Excel discussions while working out!

Using Analyze Data to find trends and ask questions

In 2024, Copilot is all the rage. As you will read in the next section, there are a number of roadblocks to using Copilot in Excel. One of the best features of Copilot is the ability to analyze a data set to look for trends and build pivot tables and pivot charts. All of that functionality from Copilot in Excel has been in Excel for several years. Before you pay $360 per person per year, you should test out the version included for free in Microsoft 365.

One reason that the existing feature never caught on is that Microsoft kept moving the icon and renaming the feature. At various times, it was called Ideas, then Insights, then A|B testing of Data Ideas and Data Insights. The icon changed from a magnifying glass to a blue lightning bolt then back to a magnifying glass over a grid looking at a column chart. At this point, Microsoft has used the same icon and name for more than two years, so it seems like the name of the feature is set.

The Analyze Data icon will read up to 250,000 cells and look for 11 types of patterns in the data:

- **Rank**—Ranks and highlights the item that is significantly larger than the other items.

- **Trend**—Highlights when there is a steady trend pattern over a time series of data.

- **Outlier**—Highlights outliers in a time series.

- **Majority**—Finds cases where a majority of a total value can be attributed to a single factor.

- **Evenness**—A measure of how evenly distributed something is.

- **Composite Signal**—Can refer to a single time series that represents a combination of several underlying time series.

- **Attribution**—The process of determining the causes or contributors to an observed effect.

- **Outstanding Top Two**—Typically refers to the top two items in a ranked list that stand out significantly from the rest.

- **Monotonicity**—The property of a function or sequence to be either entirely non-increasing or non-decreasing. A monotonic function consistently moves in one direction without reversing.

- **Unimodality**—A distribution that has a single peak or mode.

Here are some important differences between Analyze Data and Copilot, both of which require an active Internet connection:

- Analyze Data can work with data stored on your local computer. There is no need to store the data in OneDrive and no need to enable the AutoSave feature. Copilot requires both to be true.

- For Analyze Data, you need an active Microsoft 365 subscription. You do not need to pay an extra $20 a month for Copilot Pro or an extra $360 a year for Copilot 365.

- The results from Analyze Data are going to be identical every time you run it with the same data set. The results will be 100 percent accurate, with no hallucinations. Currently, most AI Bots like ChatGPT and Copilot have the annoying trait of reaching a conclusion based on other facts, but the conclusion is something that never happened. People call these "hallucinations". Copilot will hallucinate; Analyze Data will not.

To try Analyze Data, select any one cell in a data set, as shown in Figure 18-5.

	A	B	C	D	E	F	G	H	I	J	K
1	Sector	Region	Product	Color	Date	Rep	Customer	Quantity	Revenue	Profit	Cost
2	Training	Midwest	Gizmo	Blue	1/1/2029	Kim	599CD.com	1000	22810	10220	12590
3	Software	Northeast	Gadget	Red	1/2/2029	Angela	F-Keys Ltd.	100	2257	984	1273
4	Associations	South	Gizmo	Blue	1/4/2029	Kellie	Association for Computer	400	9152	4088	5064
5	Consultants	Midwest	Gadget	Red	1/4/2029	Wendy	Construction Intelligence	800	18552	7872	10680
6	Consultants	West	Gadget	Green	1/7/2029	Nellie	Data2Impact	1000	21730	9840	11890
7	Software	Midwest	Widget	Green	1/7/2029	Kim	More4Apps	400	8456	3388	5068

FIGURE 18-5 Select one cell in your data set.

Click the Analyze Data icon, which is found toward the right side of the Home tab. In a few seconds, Excel will display the Analyze Data pane, as shown in Figure 18-6. Here are a few things to note about the Analyze Data pane:

- The pane starts with a text box where you can type a question about your data.

- There are a couple of suggested questions based on the fields in your data that you can try.

- The Discover Insights section shows a small number of possible analyses that Excel can perform. Each tile gives you an idea of what the analysis could look like a title, a button to Insert the analysis as a pivot table, a pivot chart, or a table. There is also a link to mark a thumbnail as helpful or not.

- A Settings icon at the top of the Discover Insights section takes you to a list of all fields and how Excel thinks those fields should be reported. In general, Excel will want to include all fields in the potential analyses. Text fields will be categorized as Not A Value. Numeric fields will be categorized as Sum. If you have a numeric field such as Sales Rep Number, you might want to change Sum to Not A Value. You can have numeric fields reported as Averages instead of Sums, or you can uncheck fields you don't think will be valuable. For example, a free-form comment field that rarely repeats would be something you could remove from the results (see Figure 18-7).

- If you scroll to the bottom of the tiles, a link to show an additional 20–30 tiles often appears. Excel attempts to show a small number of tiles quickly. If you spend 30 seconds scrolling through the first results, Excel works in the background to create more suggested tiles.

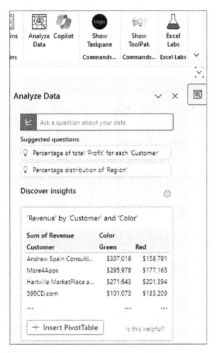

FIGURE 18-6 The first insights tile is a pivot table with customers in the rows area and colors in the columns area.

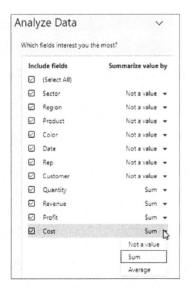

FIGURE 18-7 If Excel is attempting to summarize a field like Sales Rep Number, you can use this panel to prevent Excel from summing the ID number.

Caution New in 2024: If you click away from the original data set into a new data set, Excel will update the Analyze Data pane. In the past, this would only happen if you clicked the Analyze Data icon again.

How does the Analyze Data feature decide what tiles to show? Back in Figure 18-6, the pivot table shows Revenue with Customers down the side and Colors across the top.

Why did they choose Revenue by Customer and Color? The statistics in Figure 18-8 show the number of unique labels in each text field and the total of each numeric field. Revenue is the highest total of the numeric fields, so Excel thinks it must be the most important field for the first pivot table. Excel can see that the 457 date values are formatted as a date. Of the 6 other text fields, Customer has the most unique values with 27, so Excel offers this as the row field in the pivot table. For the column fields, you have a choice between Region with 4 unique values, Product with 4 unique values, Color with 5 unique values, Sector with 6 unique values, and Rep with 8 unique values. Excel chooses one in the middle for the columns field.

Field Name	Unique Text Values	Total Numeric Values
Sector	6	
Region	4	
Product	4	
Color	5	
Date	457	
Rep	8	
Customer	27	
Quantity		313,900
Revenue		6,707,812
Profit		2,978,394
Cost		3,729,418

FIGURE 18-8 If you are trying to figure out why Excel chose a certain combination of fields, statistics like these are likely part of the algorithm.

Here is a list of 23 suggested tiles for the data set in the sample data, which are variations on six main themes.

- Revenue by Customer and Color

- Cost has 5 outlier dates

- Revenue has 4 outlier dates

- Quantity has 6 outlier dates

- Profit has 6 outlier dates

- Sector Training has noticeably higher Profit

- Sector Training has noticeably higher Cost

- Sector Training has noticeably higher Revenue

- Sector Training has noticeably higher Quantity

- Rep Kim and Stacie have noticeably higher Revenue

- Rep Kim and Stacie have noticeably higher Quantity

- Rep Kim and Stacie have noticeably higher Profit

- Rep Kim and Stacie have noticeably higher Cost

- Frequency of Cost

- Frequency of Revenue

- Frequency of Profit

- Frequency of Quantity

- Field Quantity and Field Cost appear highly correlated

- Field Profit and Field Cost appear highly correlated

- Field Quantity and Field Revenue appear highly correlated

- Field Quantity and Field Profit appear highly correlated

- Field Revenue and Field Cost appear highly correlated

- Field Revenue and Field Profit appear highly correlated

Figure 18-9 shows 6 of the 23 suggested tiles.

Here are some observations on some of the tiles shown in Figure 18-9.

- The top right tile shows that there have been five outlier dates in two years of data. If you choose to insert this pivot chart, the five dates have an orange data point. There is no good way to create this chart with the outliers in a different point color. I appreciate that Analyze Data provides this formatting, but if the underlying data changes and some other dates are outliers, the Refresh command in the Pivot Table tab of the ribbon won't format the new outlier dates.

- The bottom right chart says there is a correlation between quantity and revenue. I am never impressed with this. It shows that as you sell more quantity, the revenue tends to increase. This is how business works. Sell more quantity, and the revenue would go up. When Analyze Data debuted in 2018, I started marking this chart as Not Helpful every time I encountered it. The original plan is that the machine learning algorithm would learn from customer feedback and start to offer more useful charts. However, Google and Microsoft are in a battle for dominance. Google will use your data to show you better ads. Microsoft has taken the position that it won't use your data to market to you. Anything that gets generated by Analyze Data is deleted and will not be tied to your identity. With this new corporate focus on privacy, there is no way for the machine learning algorithm to learn from the Is This Helpful? signal. Thus, I have stopped answering the question.

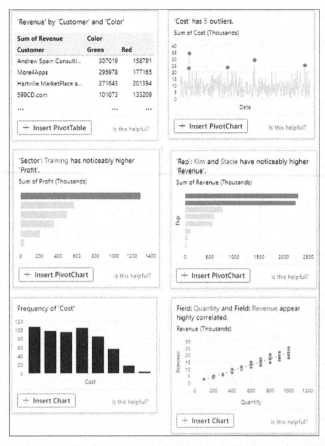

FIGURE 18-9 Six of the typical analyses suggested by the Analyze Data feature.

Each of the tiles is a small subset of the full report. When you see a tile that looks interesting, click the + Insert button. Excel inserts a new worksheet at the end of the workbook and builds the complete pivot table or pivot chart or a table of formulas.

While the first tile shown in Figure 18-6 shows 4 customers and 2 colors, the full pivot table shows 27 customers and 5 colors (see Figure 18-10).

	A	B	C	D	E	F	G
2	Sum of Revenue	Color ↴					
3	Customer	↴ Green	Red	Blue	Orange	Yellow	Grand Total
4	Andrew Spain Consulting	307019	158791	222968	122138	58538	869454
5	More4Apps	295978	177165	197443	65198	14379	750163
6	Hartville MarketPlace and Flea Market	271643	201394	144862	52400	34060	704359
7	599CD.com	101073	133209	153251	102964	132297	622794
8	MySpreadsheetLab	176573	104260	107336	77026	148319	613514
28	Association for Computers & Taxation	18076	0	16288	0	0	34364
29	Juliet Babcock-Hyde CPA, PLLC	15991	4158	11220	0	0	31369
30	Bits of Confetti	7306	0	23715	0	0	31021
31	Grand Total	1977239	1918406	1476302	704736	631129	6707812

FIGURE 18-10 Excel inserts the full report as a pivot table on a new worksheet.

When this feature debuted in 2018, I would often demo the feature in my live Power Excel seminars. The reaction was mixed. People who knew their data well were not surprised by the results. One common thought was that it might be useful to analyze data from other companies. If a vendor sends you a new price list, you could look for trends in that data. However, once you tried the feature a few times, it generally was ignored as a strange party trick instead of foreshadowing what would come five years later with ChatGPT.

The feature described above was released in early 2018 and is now more than six years old and very stable. By October 2019, Microsoft had released Version 2 of the feature with an important improvement—the ability to ask a question about your data.

Asking questions to Analyze Data

The Ask a Question feature debuted around 2014 in the Power BI product. During 2019, the Excel team in Redmond worked with the Power BI team to take the Ask a Question feature and add it to the Analyze Data feature in Excel.

While the Excel version reuses some of the code from the Power BI feature, there were improvements made specific to Excel.

The sample data set included with this book's downloads has these fields: Sector, Region, Product, Color, Date, Rep, Customer, Quantity, Revenue, Profit, and Cost. The natural language parser recognizes that Customers and Customer are the same. It understands that "this year" or "last year" refers to the Date field. It even understands that "quantities" refers to the "Quantity" column.

Unlike the Power BI version, there is no method for specifying a synonyms table. The feature won't understand that Sales is another word for Revenue.

For a sample of the types of questions you can ask, click in the Ask A Question text box. A dropdown will appear with suggestions based on your data (see Figure 18-11).

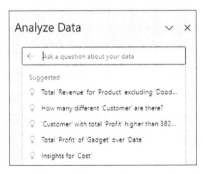

FIGURE 18-11 The sample questions are designed to show the types of questions that you can ask.

When you ask how many different customers are there, the result is a two-cell answer (see Figure 18-12).

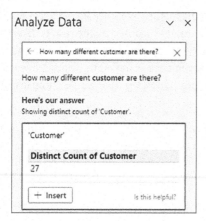

FIGURE 18-12 This looks like a pivot table based on the Data Model but since the button is simply offering Insert, it will likely return a formula.

Click the Insert button to see a new worksheet with two headings and a fairly impressive formula to calculate the distinct number of customers (see Figure 18-13).

```
=IF(SUM(ISERROR(AskAQuestion!$A$2:$K$564)*1)>0,NA(),
COUNTA(UNIQUE(AskAQuestion!$G$2:$G$564)))
```

The `first` part of this formula looks for any error cells in A2:K564. If an error cell is found, then the formula will return #N/A. Otherwise, the formula uses COUNTA of UNIQUE of the customer data.

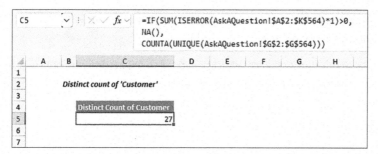

FIGURE 18-13 Excel chooses to use a fairly complex formula instead of a Data Model pivot table.

If your question includes the phrase "over time," then you are likely to get a time series line chart. Notice in Figure 18-14 that the task pane restates your question and bolds words that are either field names or items in those fields. For the "Total Revenue of Red over Time?" question, the task pane bolds Revenue, Red, and Time.

When you ask the questions, you can use modifiers to control whether the results appear as a table, chart, line chart, or pie chart (see Figure 18-15).

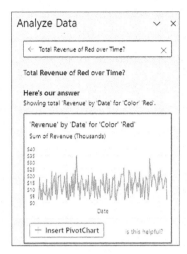

FIGURE 18-14 "Over time" will cause you to get a line chart with dates on the horizontal axis.

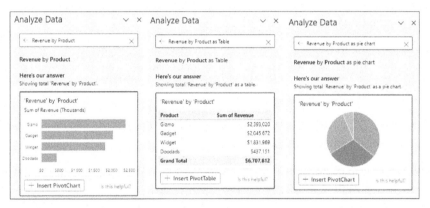

FIGURE 18-15 Specify if you want the result as a table, chart, or pie chart.

You can ask for the top N items for each person. Figure 18-16 shows the final pivot table when asked for "Top 2 Revenue Customers for each Rep". Notice the Filter dropdown on the Customer heading in D2. Open this dropdown to see that Excel has used the Top 10 Filter, but it is set to Top 2 customers.

Rep	Customer	Sum of Revenue
Top 2 in 'Customer' by total 'Revenue' for each 'Rep'		
⊟ Angela	F-Keys Ltd.	$390,978
Angela	Cambia Factor	$57,516
Angela Total		**$448,494**
⊟ Kelly	MySpreadsheetLab	$613,514
Kelly	ExcelTricks.de	$71,651
Kelly Total		**$685,165**
⊟ Kim	More4Apps	$750,163
Kim	599CD.com	$622,794
Kim Total		**$1,372,957**
⊟ Michelle	Fintega Financial Modelling	$55,251

FIGURE 18-16 Analyze Data can set up a pivot table to use the Top N filter.

I am a big fan of Analyze Data in Excel. The feature is mature, stable, and reliable, and it is included for free with your Microsoft 365 subscription. It will give the same answers every time.

However, in late 2024, all the buzz surrounds the new Copilot offering from Microsoft, which is included in every product in the Microsoft 365 suite. Copilot features are found in Word, PowerPoint, Excel, and OneDrive. As of September 2024, the features in Copilot for Excel include a feature very similar to Analyze Data, plus the ability to create formulas, sort, filter, and add conditional formatting.

The following sections provide some sample questions and their answers.

Using Copilot in Excel to create pivot tables or pivot charts

The features described in this section require a license for either Copilot Pro at $20 a month or Copilot for Office 365 at $360 a year. Copilot Pro is targeted at home and student customers. Copilot for Office 365 is targeted at enterprise customers who already have a license for Office 365 at the E3 or E5 level.

I am using Copilot for 365. If you are using Copilot Pro, your results from inside Excel should be the same as the results I am showing here.

In a corporate environment, someone in the IT department likely manages the Admin panel for your Microsoft 365 subscription. That person will have a category for Copilot and can choose which people are allowed to use Copilot.

Given that Copilot doubles the cost of Microsoft 365, I suspect that the IT department might be slow to offer licenses. Or, if they run out of licenses, they will check to see if someone is not making frequent use of Copilot and will assign that license to someone else.

If you are the first in your company to use Copilot, find the person who manages the Microsoft 365 admin panel, have them go to *admin.microsoft.com*, and look for Copilot in the left navigation bar. If you don't see Copilot there yet, click the Show All link at the bottom of the panel. Doing so will either offer you the chance to buy more licenses or manage existing licenses (see Figure 18-17). The admin can assign a license to your email address.

Click Manage Licenses. On the next screen, click Copilot For Microsoft 365. You will then be at a panel similar to Figure 18-18, where your admin can choose Assign A License to assign a license to you.

It is always odd to me that changes to the Microsoft 365 admin panel take some time to propagate. I immediately ran back to my computer and was disappointed that Copilot was not there yet.

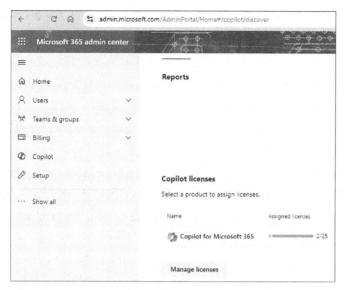

FIGURE 18-17 Use Manage Licenses and get your email address added to the Copilot license list.

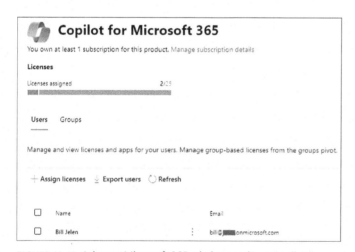

FIGURE 18-18 Ask your Microsoft 365 admin to assign a Copilot license to your email address.

These steps seem fairly nebulous, but it is what worked for me.

1. Find a data set that you want to analyze with Copilot.

2. Use File | Save As to save that data set to your OneDrive account. Make sure to save it to the same OneDrive email address that appears in Figure 18-18.

3. In the Quick Access Toolbar, enable AutoSave for the workbook. As of September 2024, Copilot will only work when the workbook is in AutoSave.

4. Click the icon in the top-right corner that has your face or initials. Make sure that you are signed in with the same account, as shown in Figure 18-18.

5. Open the File, Account screen. At the middle right, click the Update Account. You will have to sign in again.

6. Close and reopen Excel.

7. Reopen the workbook that has AutoSave turned on.

8. At some point, a large pop-up appears that asks if you want to Try Copilot. It warns you that results might be wrong. It might mention that your data will be shared with the Copilot server. Choosing to try Copilot places a Copilot icon on Excel's Home tab.

9. Copilot is also available for Word, PowerPoint, and Outlook. Even once Copilot is running in Excel, you might have to go through similar steps to get Copilot to appear in the other apps.

Look for the Copilot icon next to Analyze Data on the right side of the Home tab in Excel. When you click the Copilot icon, a Copilot task pane will appear on the right side of the screen.

Copilot will tell you that your data has to be stored in OneDrive and that AutoSave must be enabled. Once you comply with both of these requirements, then four choices should appear, along with a text box where you can ask a question (see Figure 18-19).

FIGURE 18-19 You are ready to ask Copilot your first question about the data.

Type a prompt such as

Show Total Revenue by Sales Rep.

Click the Send icon. The answer does not appear immediately. While you are waiting, an animated progress bar shows various messages:

- Analyzing your question

- Understanding the data in A1:K564

- Working on the results

Eventually, Excel will come back with a preview of the results. The results preview says that it analyzed the data in A1:K564 and then offers a pivot bar chart of Revenue by Rep. The chart preview does not include names but shows that the top 2 sales reps are way ahead of the next three who are ahead of the bottom four (see Figure 18-20). The chart also shows the following:

- At the bottom of the preview is the +Add To A New Sheet button.

- A warning that AI-generated content may be incorrect.

- You can provide feedback using the thumbs-up and thumbs-down icons.

In the next result bubble, words appear that you might want to email to someone. The total revenue by sales rep is as follows: Kim $2,227,917 and Stacie $2,252,446. See the PivotChart above for more details. Use the Copy button in this result to copy those words to the clipboard. A second warning reminds you that AI-generated content may be incorrect.

Copilot then suggests some additional prompts (only one of which is shown in Figure 18-20):

- Which sales rep generated the highest revenue?

- Show total profit by sales rep.

What if you wanted a pivot table instead? Copilot is waiting for a follow-up question.

You might provide this prompt:

That's close. Can you show the result as a table instead?

Copilot changes the result to a pivot table, but the data is not sorted from high to low. On the third follow-up, Copilot gets confused. Your prompt:

Can you sort the results from highest revenue to lowest?

At this point, it appears that Copilot wants to change the original data. Its response:

OK! Looking at A1:K564, here are 2 changes to review and apply:
Apply a custom sort on the column at index 5 in table A1:K564.
Apply a custom sort on the column at index 8 in table A1:K564.

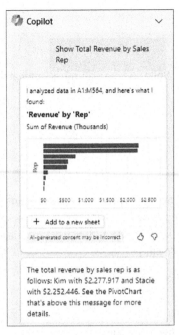

FIGURE 18-20 Copilot offers to insert a bar chart on a new worksheet.

At this point, you might find it faster to start over. This time, make your prompt more explicit like this:

Summarize total sales by sales rep. Return the results as a pivot table with the data arranged in descending revenue.

Figure 18-21 shows the results. In the preview pane, Copilot shows the correct pivot table, with People correctly sorted by descending revenue, but in the text result, Copilot says that it cannot sort and lay out the data as requested. This is a bizarre answer because the pivot table in the preview is exactly what you requested. I've seen this happen frequently—where the preview is correct, but the explanatory text says it cannot be done. If you choose Add To A New Sheet, the pivot table is, in fact, sorted correctly.

Note Right now, I am chalking this up to "It is a new feature, and Microsoft is still working on it." However, the accountant in me wants to know why we are paying $360 per year per person for something that is not really working all the way.

Caution Interestingly, Microsoft has a tough cancellation policy. If you cancel in the first seven days, you receive a pro-rated refund, but if you haven't canceled by day eight, then there are no refunds.

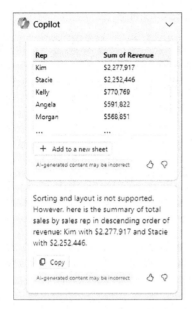

FIGURE 18-21 Copilot got the pivot table right, but the explanation says it cannot do what it just did.

If you read the previous section about Analyze Data, you might remember that Analyze Data happily created Line Charts, Pie Charts, and Bar Charts. When you asked Copilot to do the following:

Calculate Total Revenue by Region as a Pie Chart.

the first answer is a preview of a pie chart, but then the explanatory text says that Copilot is unable to create pie charts (see Figure 18-22).

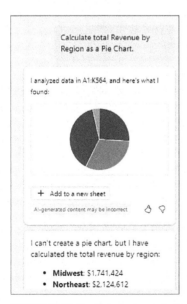

FIGURE 18-22 Copilot creates a pie chart but then says that it cannot create pie charts.

There are some interesting contrasts between Analyze Data and Copilot.

- Copilot seems to understand that a question about "Sales" means to analyze the column called Revenue. Analyze Data cannot do this.

- Copilot works with one follow-up question but seems to get confused with multiple follow-up questions. It might be easiest to start over with a new question. Analyze Data always requires new questions.

- Copilot requires AutoSave to be on. Analyze Data does not care.

- Copilot requires the data to be stored in OneDrive. Analyze Data does not care.

- Analyze Data can definitely create pie charts. Copilot actually creates them but then says that it cannot.

- Copilot constantly warns that AI Generated Content Might Be Wrong. Analyze Data is from an era when nothing would get added to Excel if there was the possibility of a wrong result. That is back when the Excel team proudly displayed a flag with the Prime Directive of "Recalc or Die."

At this point—especially if you are less than seven days into your Copilot journey—you might be thinking that the free Analyze Data runs circles around this feature in Excel Copilot, and you are correct.

However, Copilot is so much more than this one feature in Excel. The other features to create calculated columns are amazing. Read about those in the next section. And Copilot's ability to analyze Excel workbooks in OneDrive is even more amazing. Read about those later in this chapter.

Using Copilot in Excel to generate formula columns

Copilot can generate new formula columns for you. Here's a very simple example:

Add a column with GP%.

Copilot understands that "GP%" means "Gross Profit Percent," which is calculated as Profit divided by Revenue.

Normally, I would have written this formula as =J2/I2. Today, Copilot added an extra check to the formula to prevent a division by zero error. Figure 18-23 shows the formula generated by Copilot: =IF($I2=0,0,$J2/$I2). In the Copilot task pane is this explanation:

Calculates the gross profit percentage for each transaction by dividing the profit by the revenue, ensuring that if the revenue is zero, the result is zero.

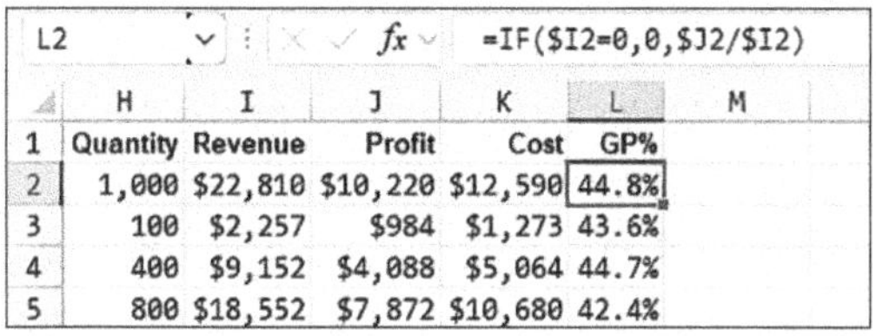

	H	I	J	K	L	M
1	Quantity	Revenue	Profit	Cost	GP%	
2	1,000	$22,810	$10,220	$12,590	44.8%	
3	100	$2,257	$984	$1,273	43.6%	
4	400	$9,152	$4,088	$5,064	44.7%	
5	800	$18,552	$7,872	$10,680	42.4%	

L2   fx   =IF($I2=0,0,$J2/$I2)

FIGURE 18-23 Copilot understands that GP% requires dividing profit by revenue.

Here is a more complicated example. I provided Copilot with this prompt:

Calculate a bonus that is 2% of revenue when GP% is in the top 20%.

Copilot's response was

$0.00

and then offered this formula, which is correct.

```
=IF($L2>=PERCENTILE.INC($L$2:$L$167,0.8),$I2*0.02,0)
```

But here's an unfair question. With a new data set, ask Copilot to detect if the quantity is a prime number. This is pretty tough to calculate in Excel. Copilot has a couple of different approaches. In Figure 18-24, it suggests this formula:

```
=IF(AND($B2>1,ISNA(MATCH(TRUE,$B2/ROW(INDIRECT("2:"&INT(SQRT($B2))))=INT($B2/ROW
(INDIRECT("2:"&INT(SQRT($B2)))))),0))),"Yes","No")
```

That formula looks complicated, and when you test it, you find that Copilot is getting the Is Prime wrong for 2, 3, 4, and 6.

So, you follow up with this response:

That formula is not working for quantity of 2, 3, 4, or 6.

Copilot then switches to embedding a lookup table in the formula:

```
=IF(AND($B2>1,ISNUMBER(MATCH ($B2,{2,3,5,7,11,13,17,19,23,29,31,37,41 43,47,53,59,61,
67,71,73,79,83,89,97,101,103,107,109,113,127,131,137,139,149,151,157,163,167,173,179,181,191,
193,197,199},0))),"Yes","No")
```

This works for prime numbers up to 199, but, as Copilot previously reported, the maximum quantity in the data set is 1,610. This formula works correctly for low quantities but misses all of the prime numbers of 211 and above.

	A	B	C	D	E	F	G	H	I	J
1	Invoice Number	Quantity	Price	Is Prime	Checking	Right	Wrong	Is Prime	Quantity Right	Wrong
2	1001	2	3.99	No	Yes		0	1 Yes	1	0
3	1002	3	6.99	No	Yes		0	1 Yes	1	0
4	1003	4	8.99	Yes	No		0	1 No	1	0
5	1004	5	3.99	Yes	Yes	1	0	Yes	1	0
6	1005	5	7.99	Yes	Yes	1	0	Yes	1	0
7	1006	6	4.99	Yes	No		0	1 No	1	0
8	1007	6	8.99	Yes	No		0	1 No	1	0
9	1008	7	8.99	Yes	Yes	1	0	Yes	1	0
10	1009	11	5.99	Yes	Yes	1	0	Yes	1	0
92	1091	199	7.99	Yes	Yes	1	0	Yes	1	0
94	1093	211	6.99	Yes	Yes	1	0	No	0	1
95	1094	212	8.99	No	No	1	0	No	1	0
507	1506	1609	4.99	Yes	Yes	1	0	No	0	1
508	1507	1609	3.99	Yes	Yes	1	0	No	0	1
509	1508	1610	3.99	No	No	1	0	No	1	0
510	E2:=IFNA(IF(SIGN(MATCH(B2,$L$2:$L$255,0))=1,"Yes","No"),"No")									
511	H2:=IF(AND($B2>1,ISNUMBER(MATCH($B2,{2,3,5,7,11,13,17,19,23,29,31,37,41,43,47,53,59,61,67,71,73,79,83,89,97,101,103,107,109,1									
512						Right	Wrong		Right	Wrong
513						503	5		286	222

FIGURE 18-24 Column E is the author's manual filling of prime numbers. Columns D and H are generated by Copilot. The Copilot formulas are wrong 5 times in column D and 222 times in column H.

In Figure 18-25, there are six rows with journeys. The data in columns B and C are geography data types that include a latitude and longitude for each city. I frequently have to calculate the distance between two cities, and I have to look up the calculation each time. It would actually be useful if Copilot could help with this calculation.

	A	B	C
1	Name	FromCity	ToCity
2	Bill	⅏ Cleveland	⅏ Merritt Island, Florida
3	Route 66	⅏ Chicago	⅏ Santa Monica, California
4	Thelma & Louise	⅏ Little Rock, Arkansas	⅏ Grand Canyon
5	Jack Kerouak	⅏ New York City	⅏ San Francisco
6	Easy Rider	⅏ Los Angeles	⅏ New Orleans
7	Lewis & Clark	⅏ St. Louis	⅏ Astoria, Oregon

FIGURE 18-25 Does Copilot understand that each data type cell contains latitude and longitude?

Copilot does not seem to understand about data types, even after spelling it out for Copilot with this prompt:

> Add a new formula to the data in A2:C7. Calculate the distance in miles between the FromCity column and the ToCity column. The data in the FromCity column is a geography data type. Use B2.Latitude and B2.Longitude as the starting points in the calculation. The data in the ToCity column is a geography data type. Use C2.Latitude and C2.Longitude as the ending points in the calculation. Use the Great Circle method for calculating distance.

Copilot says it needs more information:

> I need more information to start working on your request. Use these tips to write a new request: Mention specific columns or tables you want me to use. State specific calculations you want me to do.

Perhaps the problem is that Copilot does not understand Geography data types. However, Figure 18-26 shows that Copilot understands how to get the latitude out of the data type.

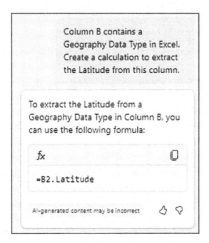

FIGURE 18-26 Copilot understands how to get data out of the Geography Data Type.

To calculate the distance, add four new columns to the data to extract latitude and longitude from the city pairs. With that data visible in the grid, ask Copilot:

> *Add a column that calculates the distance in miles between the Start Latitude and Start Longitude and the To Latitude and To Longitude.*

This works great. Copilot explains that it is using the Haversine formula and inserts this formula:

```
=3959 * 2 * ASIN(SQRT(POWER(SIN((RADIANS($F2) - RADIANS($D2)) / 2), 2) +
COS(RADIANS($D2)) * COS(RADIANS($F2)) * POWER(SIN((RADIANS($G2) - RADIANS($E2)) / 2),
2)))
```

Figure 18-27 shows the distance in miles.

H2	fx	=3959 * 2 * ASIN(SQRT(POWER(SIN((RADIANS($F2) - RADIANS($D2)) / 2), 2) + COS(RADIANS($D2)) * COS(RADIANS($F2)) * POWER(SIN((RADIANS($G2) - RADIANS($E2)) / 2), 2)))						

	B	C	D	E	F	G	H	I	J
1	FromCity	ToCity	Start Latitude	Start Longitude	To Latitude	To Longitude	Distance (miles)		
2	Cleveland	Merritt Island, Florida	41.48	-81.67	28.36	-80.68	908.56		
3	Chicago	Santa Monica, California	41.85	-87.65	34.02	-118.48	1,754.18		
4	Little Rock, Arkansas	Grand Canyon	34.74	-92.33	36.10	-112.10	1,114.99		
5	New York City	San Francisco	40.70	-74.00	37.78	-122.42	2,566.12		
6	Los Angeles	New Orleans	34.05	-118.24	29.98	-90.08	1,668.61		
7	East St. Louis, Illinc	Astoria, Oregon	38.63	-90.16	46.18	-123.83	1,780.75		

FIGURE 18-27 If you use formulas to bring starting and ending coordinates to the grid, Copilot understands how to calculate distance.

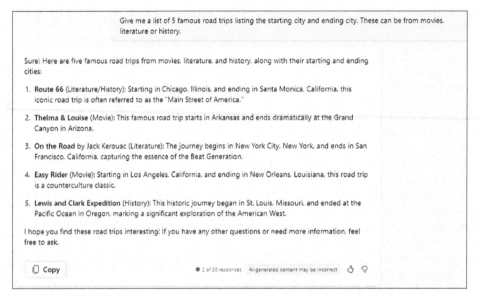

Give me a list of 5 famous road trips listing the starting city and ending city. These can be from movies, literature or history.

Sure! Here are five famous road trips from movies, literature, and history, along with their starting and ending cities:

1. **Route 66** (Literature/History): Starting in Chicago, Illinois, and ending in Santa Monica, California, this iconic road trip is often referred to as the "Main Street of America."

2. **Thelma & Louise** (Movie): This famous road trip starts in Arkansas and ends dramatically at the Grand Canyon in Arizona.

3. **On the Road** by Jack Kerouac (Literature): The journey begins in New York City, New York, and ends in San Francisco, California, capturing the essence of the Beat Generation.

4. **Easy Rider** (Movie): Starting in Los Angeles, California, and ending in New Orleans, Louisiana, this road trip is a counterculture classic.

5. **Lewis and Clark Expedition** (History): This historic journey began in St. Louis, Missouri, and ended at the Pacific Ocean in Oregon, marking a significant exploration of the American West.

I hope you find these road trips interesting! If you have any other questions or need more information, feel free to ask.

Copy   ● 2 of 30 responses   AI-generated content may be incorrect

FIGURE 18-28 Copilot Search did a great job of suggesting road trips for the last example.

Using Copilot in Excel for highlighting, sorting, or filtering

Copilot can be used in Excel to apply conditional formatting, sorting, or filtering. In Figure 18-29, Copilot applies a tricky conditional formatting that highlights the entire row if the bonus is greater than zero. Copilot suggests a solution. Click Apply, and the conditional formatting is added to the sheet.

FIGURE 18-29 Using conditional formatting to highlight the entire row requires a tricky formula-based condition with a single dollar sign.

Copilot can also sort data. Copilot understands the requirement if you ask the following:

Sort the data by Customer within Rep.

The reply is badly worded:

OK! Looking at A1:M564, here are 2 changes to review and apply
Apply a custom sort on the column at index 5 in table A1:M564.
Apply a custom sort on the column at index 6 in table A1:M564.

I am not sure why Copilot refers to this as a "custom sort." However, after you click Apply, the data is correctly sorted, as shown in Figure 18-30.

	E	F	G
1	Date	Rep	Customer
53	11/25/2030	Angela	WM Squared Inc.
54	5/28/2029	Katie	LearnExcelBooks.com
55	5/24/2029	Katie	More4Apps
56	1/4/2029	Kelly	Association for Computers & Taxation
57	1/29/2029	Kelly	Association for Computers & Taxation
58	1/7/2030	Kelly	Association for Computers & Taxation
59	8/16/2030	Kelly	Association for Computers & Taxation
60	2/16/2029	Kelly	ExcelTricks.de
61	5/14/2029	Kelly	ExcelTricks.de

FIGURE 18-30 Typing a short sentence might be faster than opening the Sort dialog.

If you had to sort by a single column, it would be easier to select one cell in the column and then use the AZ or ZA icon on the Data tab. However, for a multi-level sort such as the one above, using Copilot might require fewer steps.

In Figure 18-31, you asked Copilot to filter to show Kim's sales above $15000. You did not specify which column contained the word Kim and you did not specify which column contains sales. However, Copilot figured out that the Kim filter applied to F1:F564 and that the sales filter should apply to column I.

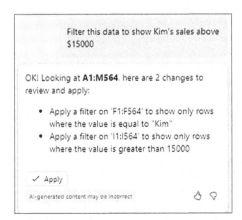

FIGURE 18-31 Copilot understands how to filter based on a simple sentence.

The results of the filter are great. For the Rep column, Copilot selected Kim using a checkbox. But for the Revenue column, Copilot switched to using a Number Filter or Greater Than. This way, the filter will continue to work if numbers change, as shown in Figure 18-32.

	E	F	G	H	I	J	K	L	M
1	Date ▼	Rep ☑	Customer	Quant ▼	Reven ☑	Pr(▼	C(▼	Gf ▼	Bon ▼
116	1/1/2029	Kim	599	Sort Smallest to Largest		$10,220	$12,590	44.8%	$0.00
119	2/27/2029	Kim	599			$7,623	$8,586	47.0%	$0.00
120	3/26/2029	Kim	599	Sort Largest to Smallest		$10,220	$12,870	44.3%	$0.00
122	4/28/2029	Kim	599	Sort by Color >		$10,220	$14,840	40.8%	$0.00
126	7/15/2029	Kim	599			$7,154	$8,722	45.1%	$0.00
133	12/6/2029	Kim	599	Sheet View >		$6,776	$10,080	40.2%	$0.00
137	2/26/2030	Kim	599	Clear Filter From "Revenue"		$10,220	$12,460	45.1%	$0.00
144	4/10/2030	Kim	599			$8,176	$10,168	44.6%	$0.00
147	4/29/2030	Kim	599	Filter by Color >		$8,856	$10,134	46.6%	$0.00
152	5/28/2030	Kim	599	Number Filters >	Equals...			5.28
154	6/26/2030	Kim	599					0.00
155	7/16/2030	Kim	599	Search	Does Not Equal...			0.00
163	8/26/2030	Kim	599	(Select All)	✓ Greater Than...			0.00
166	10/20/2030	Kim	599	$1,704				0.00
167	11/14/2030	Kim	599	$1,819	Greater Than Or Equal To...			0.00

FIGURE 18-32 Copilot correctly applied the filter using a Greater Than number filter.

Back in Excel 2013, the Excel team introduced the Quick Analysis options that appear when you select multiple cells. You might have turned these off using File, Options, Home, Show Quick Analysis Options On Selection.

Someone at Microsoft deemed that these features might feel like artificial intelligence. If you are signed in to an account that has Copilot, you will see the indicator for this feature is now a Copilot logo. Other than a Get More Suggestions From Copilot link, this feature is the same as it has been since 2013 (see Figure 18-33).

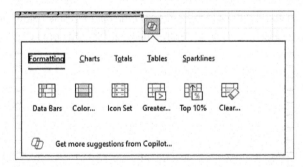

FIGURE 18-33 Rebranding Quick Analysis as Copilot might encourage more people to try it.

Using Advanced Copilot in Excel with Python

When Copilot was in preview, most of the Copilot tasks were completed by using core Excel functionality. You would ask for the top three customers by sector, and Copilot would use a regular pivot table with rarely-used settings to provide the answer.

However, after Microsoft added Python to Excel, an entirely new avenue became available for solving problems. In September 2024, the Excel team released a beta preview of an "Advanced Analysis Using Python" option to Copilot. These solutions are using Python in Excel to generate the answers.

On the one hand, this simplifies the task of "Use Copilot to Create Python Code" discussed later in this chapter. But on the other hand, it brings a whole new series of visualizations and solutions to Excel, all from writing a simple prompt or two.

As I've mentioned before, Copilot is evolving quickly. But after a year of testing Copilot in Excel and a few weeks of testing Copilot with Python in Excel, the latter has been far more reliable and less prone to silly mistakes.

In this section, you will see five tasks that Copilot with Python make easier:

- Join data from two tables and create a pivot table
- Create a word cloud chart from text
- Create a basketball shot chart in Excel
- Perform sentiment analysis from text
- Figure out which combinations of invoice amounts add up to equal the check received from a vendor (also known as the Knapsack Problem)

Join data from two tables and create a pivot table

In Chapter 10, "Replacing XLOOKUP with the Data Model" in Chapter 10," you joined two tables and created a pivot table using the Data Model. This can also be done with Python.

Figure 18-34 shows a data set and a lookup table.

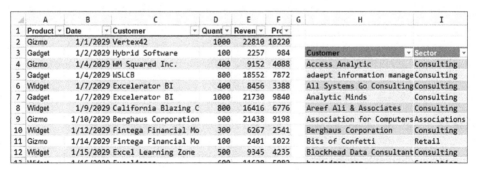

FIGURE 18-34 You want to create total revenue by sector.

With a cell in the left table selected, start Copilot and use this prompt:

Create a DataFrame from the Data table. Create another DataFrame from the Sectors table. Perform an Outer Join to create a third DataFrame with the Sector from the Sectors table added to the DataFrame from the Data table.

Copilot tells you how it will solve this problem, as shown in Figure 18-35.

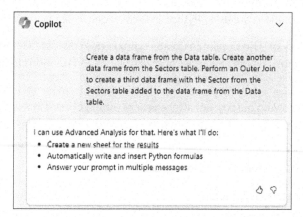

FIGURE 18-35 Copilot tells you that it will insert a new worksheet with Python formulas.

After a few seconds, you have a new worksheet with a DataFrame for the original Data and a second DataFrame after the outer join with the lookup table.

Now that you have a DataFrame with both Sector and Revenue, send a second prompt:

Analyze the revenue by sector.

Copilot returns a report with total revenue by sector, as shown in Figure 18-36.

A39		PY	revenue_by_sector = merged_df.groupby('Sector')['Revenue'].sum().reset_index()						
	A		B	C	D	E	F	G	H
37									
38	Calculate total revenue by sector								
39	[▾] DataFrame								
40									
41	Preview								
42			Sector	Revenue					
43			0 Applications	482074					
44			1 Associations	418988					
45			2 Consulting	2904312					
46			3 Retail	570426					
47			4 Services	877055					
48			5 Training	935397					
49			6 Utilities	519560					

FIGURE 18-36 Copilot uses Python to join the tables and summarizes the Revenue by sector.

At this point, you might be wondering if there is any value in this example. You could have easily created a new worksheet with similar data by using XLOOKUP next to the Data table and then created a better-looking pivot table using Excel's built-in data tools.

Some of the value is in learning how to write Python code. Copilot built the answer using four Python formulas that contain the code shown here. Many people using Excel will be new to Python—having Copilot generate the following code prevents a lot of watching YouTube tutorials or searching for Python examples.

```
Data_df=xl("Data[#All]", headers=True)
Sectors_df = xl("Sectors[#All]", headers=True)
merged_df = pd.merge(Data_df, Sectors_df, on='Customer', how='outer')
revenue_by_sector = merged_df.groupby('Sector')['Revenue'].sum().reset_index()
```

The next two examples use Python to create a visualization that is not already built in to Excel.

Create a word cloud from text

For this example, I used Copilot in OneDrive to extract all headings from the Word documents that represent this book. Pasting the results into Excel, I have a set of 300+ headings in a column. I added columns for ID and Chapter Number. I've noticed that Python prefers data with an ID field and will add it if the data does not have an ID field.

One important technique with word clouds is to exclude the database of Stop Words. These are insignificant words such as "The," "A," "An," and hundreds of others. The size of each word is based on the number of times it is used in the text. If you left the Stop Words in the analysis, most word clouds would have a really large "The", "An", "A", and other small words that would tell you nothing about the data.

Databases of Stop Words are available online, but you can simply ask Copilot to exclude Stop Words.

Open the Copilot pane. Start the Advanced analysis and use this prompt:

Create a word cloud from the Text column. Exclude Stop Words.

Copilot uses Python to generate the image shown in Figure 18-37.

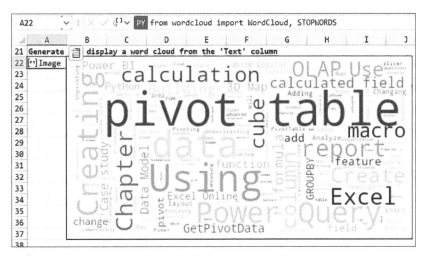

FIGURE 18-37 Python includes the ability to create many charts that are not available in regular Excel.

The chart shown above is generated with the following Python formula:

```
from wordcloud import WordCloud, STOPWORDS
# Combine all text entries into a single string
text_combined = ' '.join(Sheet1_A1_C259_df['Text'])
```

```
# Define stop words
stopwords = set(STOPWORDS)
# Generate the word cloud
wordcloud = WordCloud(stopwords=stopwords, background_color='white').generate(text_combined)
# Display the word cloud
plt.figure(figsize=(10, 6))
plt.imshow(wordcloud, interpolation='bilinear')
plt.axis('off')
plt.show()
```

There is some gee-wiz factor about creating a word cloud natively in Excel. I've done these before, but it is complicated. You have to find the database of stop words and remove all of the stop words from your text. You also have to get rid of some punctuation. Then, split the text into words using TEXTSPLIT. Then, get a unique list of words and how many times they are used. Any time that I've done this in the past, the result is not worth the effort.

However, now, with Copilot, it is easier to create the word cloud chart. It might be tempting to create a bunch of word clouds—one for each product category. In this case, I started with the Python code generated by Copilot but then was able to add additional code to make it easier to have a parameter field that would change the word cloud.

Case study: Enhancing the generated Python code

My goal is to start with a database of descriptions for 3,000 products that fall into 40 categories. This table has fields for ID, Category, and Description. I want to be able to choose a Category from the list, filter the data to only the descriptions for the products in that Category, and update the word cloud.

As a bonus, you can add a Title to the word cloud to identify the Category.

In Figure 18-38, the table in columns A:C is called WordCloudData. The table in E1:E2 is called Chosen. Cell E2 is the Category to be used in the word cloud.

	A	B	C	D	E
1	ID	Category	Description		Category
2	1001	A Call To Arms	Get ready to sculpt an		Jazz It Up
3	1002	A Call To Arms	Put the FUN in funky as you focus		
4	1003	A Call To Arms	Coach Dwana leads a Quick Hit made		
5	1004	A Call To Arms	Get your arms burning with Coach D		
6	1005	A Call To Arms	Get dancing—and bobbing and weavin		

FIGURE 18-38 Set up a way to select one chosen category for the word cloud.

Following is the Python code used to filter the word cloud Data to just the chosen category and then generate a word cloud using the chosen category as the title.
First, create a DataFrame for the word cloud data:

```
WordCloudData_df=xl("WordCloudData[#All]", headers=True)
```

Use Copilot to create a DataFrame for Chosen:

```
Chosen_df=xl("Chosen[#All]", headers=True)
```

Filter the word cloud Data to only records where the category is the chosen category:

```
chosen_categories = Chosen_df['Category'].tolist()
filtered_df = WordCloudData_df[WordCloudData_df['Category'].isin(chosen_
categories)]
```

Finally, this longer section of Python generates the word cloud and includes a title:

```
from wordcloud import STOPWORDS, WordCloud
import matplotlib.pyplot as plt
title = Chosen_df['Category'].iloc[0]

# Combine all descriptions into a single string
text = ' '.join(filtered_df['Description'].tolist())

# Define stop words
stopwords = set(STOPWORDS)

# Generate the word cloud
wordcloud = WordCloud(width=800, height=400, background_color='white',
stopwords=stopwords).generate(text)

# Plot the word cloud
plt.figure(figsize=(10, 5))
plt.imshow(wordcloud, interpolation='bilinear')
plt.axis('off')
plt.title(title, fontsize=16)
plt.show()
```

Any time you paste a new category into cell E2, Python will update the word cloud. Figure 18-39 shows the word cloud with a title.

FIGURE 18-39 After changing the Category, the word cloud updates.

At this point, it would almost be perfect to have some VBA to loop through each Category and print the resulting word cloud. Actually, it would be better to export the word cloud as a picture, but the VBA to export the shape as a picture is not available yet.

Create a basketball shot chart in Excel

Python is not as popular as Excel. Current estimates are 800 million people using Excel and 8.2 million people using Python. But the people using Python have already solved a lot of interesting data problems and those solutions are available in Copilot. This example shows the breadth of available Python analyses.

Ever since 2013, the National Basketball Association (NBA) has installed sensors in all of their arenas that track the X and Y location of the basketball at every moment of every NBA game. The NBA has extensive data for every basketball shot since the 2013 season. Figure 18-40 shows a small portion of the NBA data. The larger workbook has every shot taken by Lebron James during the Cleveland Cavaliers' 2016 playoff run.

	E	H		L	R	S	T	U	V	W	X
1	PLAYER NA	PER	ACTION TYPE		LOC X	LOC Y	SHOT ATTEMPTED FLAG	SHOT MADE FLAG	GAME DAT	HTN	VTN
9690	LeBron James	1	Running Layup Shot		-4	-6	1	1	20160417	CLE	DET
9691	LeBron James	1	Running Finger Roll Layup Shot		1	-5	1	1	20160417	CLE	DET
9692	LeBron James	1	Driving Layup Shot		-2	-6	1	1	20160417	CLE	DET
9693	LeBron James	1	Fadeaway Jump Shot		1	77	1	0	20160417	CLE	DET
9694	LeBron James	1	Driving Reverse Layup Shot		-1	-1	1	1	20160417	CLE	DET
9695	LeBron James	1	Floating Jump shot		-38	67	1	0	20160417	CLE	DET
9696	LeBron James	1	Cutting Layup Shot		-6	2	1	1	20160417	CLE	DET

FIGURE 18-40 A small segment of the NBA data available.

Open Copilot and use this prompt:

Create a Basketball Shot Chart.

Copilot springs into action and delivers the chart shown in Figure 18-41.

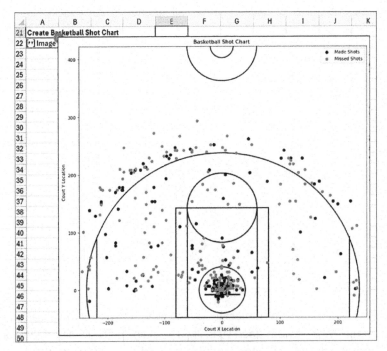

FIGURE 18-41 Python knows how to create a basketball shot chart.

Rather than copy the entire Python code here, you can examine the code in the sample file. But I want to show that the code includes all of the lines, rectangles, and arcs needed to render an image of a basketball court, as shown in Figure 18-42.

```
def draw_court(ax=None, color='black', lw=2, outer_lines=False):
    if ax is None:
        ax = plt.gca()

    # Create the various parts of an NBA basketball court
    hoop = plt.Circle((0, 0), radius=7.5, linewidth=lw, color=color, fill=False)
    backboard = plt.Rectangle((-30, -7.5), 60, -1, linewidth=lw, color=color)
    outer_box = plt.Rectangle((-80, -47.5), 160, 190, linewidth=lw, color=color, fill=False)
    inner_box = plt.Rectangle((-60, -47.5), 120, 190, linewidth=lw, color=color, fill=False)
    top_free_throw = plt.Circle((0, 142.5), radius=60, linewidth=lw, color=color, fill=False)
    bottom_free_throw = plt.Circle((0, 142.5), radius=60, linewidth=lw, color=color, fill=False)
    restricted = plt.Circle((0, 0), radius=40, linewidth=lw, color=color, fill=False)
    corner_three_a = plt.Rectangle((-220, -47.5), 0, 140, linewidth=lw, color=color)
    corner_three_b = plt.Rectangle((220, -47.5), 0, 140, linewidth=lw, color=color)
    three_arc = plt.Circle((0, 0), radius=237.5, linewidth=lw, color=color, fill=False)
    center_outer_arc = plt.Circle((0, 422.5), radius=60, linewidth=lw, color=color, fill=False)
    center_inner_arc = plt.Circle((0, 422.5), radius=20, linewidth=lw, color=color, fill=False)
```

FIGURE 18-42 Someone took the time to figure out the elements for a basketball court, and now that chart is available in Excel.

The point here is that the Excel team would never have the engineering resources to create a native basketball chart in Excel. But, thanks to the 8.2 million people using Python, you have a rich variety of visualizations available in Excel.

Perform sentiment analysis from text

Copilot with Python is able to evaluate text comments and decide if the comment is positive or negative. You could ask for the results to be presented as "positive" or "negative." Or, you can ask for a numerical scale, where a 100% score is very positive, and a –100% score is very negative.

The starting data contains a Category and Description. Open Copilot, choose Advanced Analysis to create a DataFrame from the data, and then use this prompt:

Perform sentiment analysis on the Description. Assign a numerical score for positivity.

It is strange that Copilot first explains that it would prefer to do text analysis using the TextBlob library but that Python in Excel does not support that library yet. But, it rebounds with an idea to use the Vader library instead. I am not sure why Excel is telling me that there might be a better library available if I left Excel and installed Python instead.

Figure 18-43 shows the initial results. Each record now has a Sentiment score.

| A22 | | ∨ ⋮ × ✓ ⟨⟩∨ | PY | from nltk.sentiment.vader import SentimentIntensityAnalyzer |

	A	B	C	D	E	F	G	H	I	J
22	[▾]DataFr⬚									
23										
24	Preview									
25		ID	Category	Descripti	Sentiment_Score					
26	0	0 A		Hello, I'	0.508					
27	1	1 B		OK, so it	0.9008					
28	2	2 C		Hi all, 1	0.8271					
29	3	3 A		hi, woulc	0.8834					
30	4	4 B		Hi, I r	-0.3818					
31	...	...	...	...	...					
32	94	94 B		I get the	-0.6249					
33	95	95 C		I am on t	0.9771					
34	96	96 A		Hi, I'm F	0.7717					
35	97	97 B		Hi, I ha	0.9175					
36	98	98 C		Hi, I ha	0.9175					
37										

FIGURE 18-43 The Sentiment Intensity Analyzer library assigns a numerical score to each comment.

Note that the preview shown in Figure 18-43 is only the first five and last five records. This is typical of a Python preview. To visualize the data, submit this follow-up prompt:

Visualize the distribution of sentiment scores across different categories.

Copilot generates a box plot showing the distribution of comments for each category, as shown in Figure 18-44.

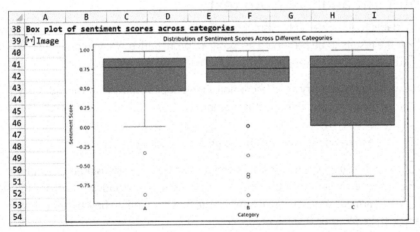

FIGURE 18-44 Python creates a chart showing the distribution of comments from high to low sentiment. While the bulk of comments are positive, there are negative outliers for Formula, Pivot Table, and Power Query.

Sentiment analysis is helpful in categorizing the comment fields in a survey.

Solve the knapsack problem

Say that you work in accounts receivable for a company. You receive a check for $74,366.37 from a customer. On the one hand, you are happy to finally receive a payment from this customer. On the other hand, there is no remittance advice saying which invoices are being paid with this check.

Figure 18-45 shows the open invoices from the customer. Your job is to figure out which of the amounts shown in H7:H21 exactly add up to $74,366.37.

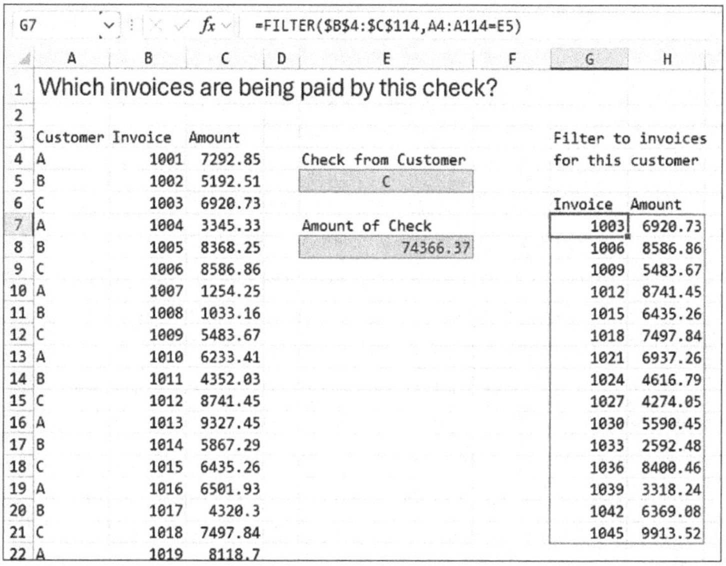
G7 =FILTER($B$4:$C$114,A4:A114=E5)

	A	B	C	D	E	F	G	H
1	Which invoices are being paid by this check?							
2								
3	Customer	Invoice	Amount				Filter to invoices	
4	A	1001	7292.85		Check from Customer		for this customer	
5	B	1002	5192.51		C			
6	C	1003	6920.73				Invoice	Amount
7	A	1004	3345.33		Amount of Check		1003	6920.73
8	B	1005	8368.25		74366.37		1006	8586.86
9	C	1006	8586.86				1009	5483.67
10	A	1007	1254.25				1012	8741.45
11	B	1008	1033.16				1015	6435.26
12	C	1009	5483.67				1018	7497.84
13	A	1010	6233.41				1021	6937.26
14	B	1011	4352.03				1024	4616.79
15	C	1012	8741.45				1027	4274.05
16	A	1013	9327.45				1030	5590.45
17	B	1014	5867.29				1033	2592.48
18	C	1015	6435.26				1036	8400.46
19	A	1016	6501.93				1039	3318.24
20	B	1017	4320.3				1042	6369.08
21	C	1018	7497.84				1045	9913.52
22	A	1019	8118.7					

FIGURE 18-45 Which of the invoices in H7:H22 are being paid with this check?

In the past, you might try to use Solver to figure this out. However, the free Solver that comes with Excel failed at this task. There are other convoluted methods using What-If Data Tables that will successfully solve this example in which you have 15 open invoices. But those methods fail when you have 20 open invoices because the number of combinations increases exponentially.

Open Copilot and start the Advanced Analysis. Use this prompt:

Find combinations of amounts that add up to 74366.37.

In less than 60 seconds, the result shows the only combination of invoices that can produce that result (see Figure 18-46).

Note that the combination shown in row 22 of the above figure matches the order of the invoices in the original worksheet. To test the results, enter a **1** next to the chosen invoices. Multiply the 1s by the amounts and total them. Figure 18-47 shows the result matches.

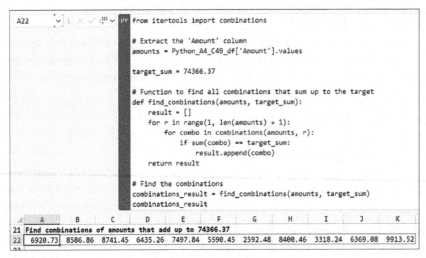

```
A22                    PY  from itertools import combinations

                           # Extract the 'Amount' column
                           amounts = Python_A4_C49_df['Amount'].values

                           target_sum = 74366.37

                           # Function to find all combinations that sum up to the target
                           def find_combinations(amounts, target_sum):
                               result = []
                               for r in range(1, len(amounts) + 1):
                                   for combo in combinations(amounts, r):
                                       if sum(combo) == target_sum:
                                           result.append(combo)
                               return result

                           # Find the combinations
                           combinations_result = find_combinations(amounts, target_sum)
                           combinations_result
```

	A	B	C	D	E	F	G	H	I	J	K
21	Find combinations of amounts that add up to 74366.37										
22	6920.73	8586.86	8741.45	6435.26	7497.84	5590.45	2592.48	8400.46	3318.24	6369.08	9913.52

FIGURE 18-46 Python quickly finds the invoices that add up to the amount of the check.

	E	C	F	G	H	I	J
5		C					
6				Invoice	Amount	Use?	H*I
7	Amount of Check			1003	6920.73	1	6920.73
8		74366.37		1006	8586.86	1	8586.86
9				1009	5483.67		0
10				1012	8741.45	1	8741.45
11				1015	6435.26	1	6435.26
12				1018	7497.84	1	7497.84
13				1021	6937.26		0
14				1024	4616.79		0
15				1027	4274.05		0
16				1030	5590.45	1	5590.45
17				1033	2592.48	1	2592.48
18				1036	8400.46	1	8400.46
19				1039	3318.24	1	3318.24
20				1042	6369.08	1	6369.08
21				1045	9913.52	1	9913.52
22					Total		74366.37 ✅

FIGURE 18-47 A quick check shows that the selected invoices do add up to the $74,366.37 check.

Problems like this one are generally referred to as a knapsack problem. Solving them has always been very difficult. The Copilot with Python solution makes this dramatically easier.

Overall impressions of Copilot in Excel

The Data Analysis parts of Copilot in Excel are very similar to the Analyze Data feature that was added to Excel six years ago. It works slightly better in understanding that Sales and Revenue mean the same thing.

Create Formulas is impressive, although sometimes the formulas are wrong. This sort of means you have to know what you are doing in order to judge if the formula is correct.

Highlighting data using conditional formatting is good. Sorting and filtering might be slightly faster than the equivalent commands.

Advanced Analysis with Python is the feature that shows the most promise, as it brings functionality that is actually new to Excel.

To me, it seems like Excel Copilot is trying very hard to be impressive, but I don't think I would pay $360 a year for it. However, the Copilot in Excel is only a tiny piece of the Copilot environment—you are getting more than just Copilot in Excel.

The next section shows a jaw-dropping example of using Copilot to analyze an Excel workbook.

Using Copilot in OneDrive to analyze financial statements in Excel

The following example is one of the more impressive uses of Copilot. I originally saw this demo from Excel MVP Dr. Nitin Paranjape. Anyone interested in Excel and Copilot should subscribe to his YouTube channel. Search YouTube for "Efficiency 365 by Dr Nitin."

The Excel workbook called 18-CocaColaFinancialStatements.xlsx is a worksheet from Coca-Cola's 2023 10K filing that I copied from the SEC Edgar website. To be transparent, there were several extra columns caused by merged cells. I removed all merged cells and did some manual clean-up to produce the file in the downloadable files included with this book.

The workbook has an Income Statement in A1:D37 with the current year and two years of history. Next is a Balance Sheet in A38:C81, which has the current and prior year. Finally, a Consolidated Statement of Cash Flows is in A83:D125 that includes the current year and two years of history. Figure 18-48 shows a portion of the income statement.

I saved the workbook to my OneDrive for Business folder. Use Chrome or Edge to open your OneDrive folder by navigating to *https://www.microsoft365.com/onedrive/?auth=2&home=1*.

When you hover over the Financial Statements workbook, a Copilot icon will appear. Click it to open the Copilot pane in your browser (see Figure 18-49).

	A	B	C	D
1	THE COCA-COLA COMPANY AND SUBSIDIARIES			
2	CONSOLIDATED STATEMENTS OF INCOME			
3	(In millions except per share data)			
4				
5	Year Ended December 31,	2023	2022	2021
6	Net Operating Revenues	45,754	43,004	38,655
7	Cost of goods sold	18,520	18,000	15,357
8	Gross Profit	27,234	25,004	23,298
9	Selling, general and administrative expenses	13,972	12,880	12,144
10	Other operating charges	1,951	1,215	846
11	Operating Income	11,311	10,909	10,308
12	Interest income	907	449	276
13	Interest expense	1,527	882	1,597
14	Equity income (loss) — net	1,691	1,472	1,438
15	Other income (loss) — net	570	-262	2,000
16	Income Before Income Taxes	12,952	11,686	12,425
17	Income taxes	2,249	2,115	2,621
18	Consolidated Net Income	10,703	9,571	9,804
19	Less: Net income (loss) attributable to noncontrolling interests	-11	29	33
20	Net Income Attributable to Shareowners of The Coca-Cola Company	10,714	9,542	9,771
21	Basic Net Income Per Share	2.48	2.20	2.26

FIGURE 18-48 Three financial statements copied from the SEC Edgar website.

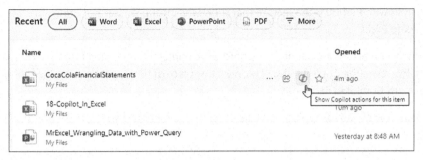

FIGURE 18-49 Hover over an Excel workbook in OneDrive to reveal the Copilot icon.

When you hover over the Copilot icon, there are four choices:

- Summarize This File

- Create An FAQ From This file

- Suggest Next Steps From This File

- Ask a Question About This File

Choose Ask A Question. A Copilot task pane opens with the same choices. Click in the text box at the bottom and ask

> *How is the financial stability of this company based on these financial statements?*

In a few seconds, Copilot returns the following answer:

> *Based on the financial statements of Coca-Cola, here is an overview of the company's financial stability:*
>
> ***Income Statement***
>
> ***Net Operating Revenues*** *have increased from $38,655 million in 2021 to $45,754 million in 2023.*
>
> ***Gross Profit*** *has also increased from $23,298 million in 2021 to $27,234 million in 2023.*
>
> ***Operating Income*** *has shown a steady increase from $10,308 million in 2021 to $11,311 million in 2023.*
>
> ***Net Income Attributable to Shareowners*** *has increased from $9,771 million in 2021 to $10,714 million in 2023.*
>
> ***Balance Sheet***
>
> ***Total Assets*** *have increased from $92,763 million in 2022 to $97,703 million in 2023.*
>
> ***Total Current Assets*** *have increased from $22,591 million in 2022 to $26,732 million in 2023.*
>
> ***Total Liabilities*** *have increased from $66,937 million in 2022 to $70,223 million in 2023.*
>
> ***Total Equity*** *has increased from $25,826 million in 2022 to $27,480 million in 2023.*
>
> ***Cash Flow Statement***

Net Cash Provided by Operating Activities has decreased slightly from $12,625 million in 2021 to $11,599 million in 2023.

Net Cash Used in Investing Activities has increased from -$2,765 million in 2021 to -$3,349 million in 2023.

Net Cash Used in Financing Activities has increased from -$6,786 million in 2021 to -$8,310 million in 2023.

Overall, Coca-Cola appears to be financially stable with increasing revenues, gross profit, and net income. The company has also shown growth in total assets and equity, although there has been an increase in liabilities and cash used in investing and financing activities.

Now, ask another question:

Please calculate key financial ratios from these financial statements.

Copilot returns this answer:

Here are some key financial ratios calculated from the financial statements of Coca-Cola:

Liquidity Ratios

Current Ratio: [{Current Ratio} = {{Total Current Assets}}{{Total Current Liabilities}} = {26,732} {23,571} 1.13]

Quick Ratio: [{Quick Ratio} = {{Total Current Assets} - {Inventories}}{{Total Current Liabilities}} = {26,732 - 4,424}{23,571} 0.95]

Profitability Ratios

Gross Profit Margin: [{Gross Profit Margin} = {{Gross Profit}}{{Net Operating Revenues}}\times 100 = {27,234}{45,754} \ times 100 59.52%]

Net Profit Margin: [{Net Profit Margin} = {{Net Income Attributable to Shareowners}}{{Net Operating Revenues}} \times 100 = {10,714}{45,754} \times 100 23.42%]

Return on Assets (ROA): [{ROA} = {{Net Income Attributable to Shareowners}}{{Total Assets}} \ times 100 = {10,714}{97,703} \times 100 10.97%]

Return on Equity (ROE): [{ROE} = {{Net Income Attributable to Shareowners}}{{Total Equity}}\ times 100 = {10,714}{27,480} \times 100 39.00%]

Leverage Ratios

Debt to Equity Ratio: [{Debt to Equity Ratio} = {{Total Liabilities}}{{Total Equity}} = {70,223} {27,480} 2.56]

Interest Coverage Ratio: [{Interest Coverage Ratio} = {{Operating Income}}{{Interest Expense}} = {11,311}{1,527} 7.41]

These ratios provide insights into Coca-Cola's liquidity, profitability, and leverage, indicating a strong financial position with good profitability and manageable debt levels.

Wow! This analysis of an Excel file is amazing. It seems far more useful than most of the analyses available from inside Excel.

Using AI to find and summarize Excel YouTube videos

One of the cool things about Copilot 365 is the Copilot Studio, where you can train your own bot. But those bots aren't going to be public. In 2023, I teamed up with Twinbox.AI to create a publicly available bot that was trained on every word I said in 2600+ YouTube videos.

To search this Excel knowledge base, navigate to https://mrx.cl/gpt. Type any question and the bot will provide links to the videos that talk about that topic (see Figure 18-50).

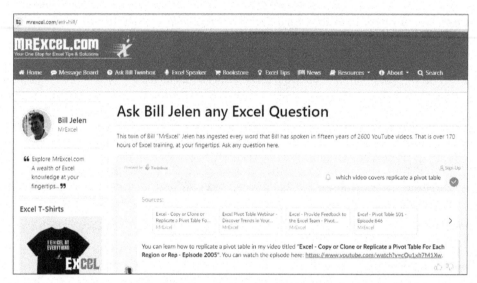

FIGURE 18-50 Twinbox.AI trained a bot on every word spoken in 2,600 of my Excel videos.

It hurts to admit this, but even though I have recorded hundreds of hours of Excel videos on YouTube, finding a video in your search results never seems like a fast way to get an answer. You often waste a couple of minutes with the YouTube Creator talking about their kids or why they didn't make a video last week before you ever get to the answer.

> **TIP** Back in 2015, Microsoft Press instituted a policy of providing alt text for every image in all of their books. This initiative made me look at accessibility across *MrExcel.com*, and I ended up hiring a team to transcribe 2,000 videos so they would have accurate subtitles.

The following technique only works with videos where the creator has invested the time to provide a transcript for their video. This is an amazing benefit of using Copilot in combination with Microsoft Edge.

1. Open the Microsoft Edge browser.

2. Make sure you are signed in using the same email as your Copilot account.

3. Browse to any YouTube video that has subtitles. (In the YouTube search results, a "CC" indicator appears below the video.)

4. Click the Copilot icon in the top right of the browser (see Figure 18-51).

5. Type the "Generate Video Highlights" prompt and press Enter. Edge sends the entire video transcript to Copilot, which returns a summary of the video, including time stamps.

Copilot Icon

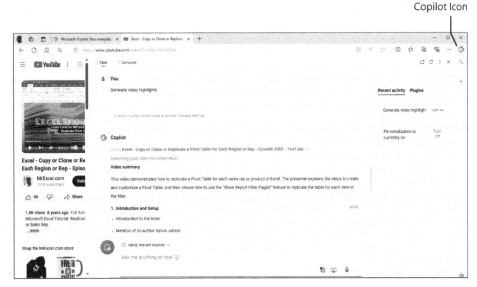

FIGURE 18-51 A Copilot 365 subscription, coupled with the Edge browser will prevent you from having to watch the entire YouTube video.

For example, here is the summary provided by Copilot for this video:

1. Introduction and Setup (Timestamp 0:00)

Introduction to the topic

Mention of co-author Szylvia Juhasz

Initial setup of the Pivot Table

2. Customizing the Pivot Table (Timestamp 0:32)

Changing row labels to "Customer"

Formatting revenue as currency

Applying banded rows and color

3. Replicating the Pivot Table (Timestamp 01:33)

Adding items to the filter

Using the "Show Report Filter Pages" feature

Replicating the table for each sales rep

4. Final Tips and Recap (Timestamp 2:22)

Ensuring correct formatting before replication

Recap of the steps

Mention of Szylvia Juhasz for Excel training

Feel free to ask if you need more details on any specific part!

After skimming this summary, the actual technique for replicating a pivot table is in section 3. Click the heading for that section to jump to 1:33 in the video. By 2:04 in the video, you've found the relevant instructions in 30 seconds instead of 3 minutes.

Thanks to Copilot 365 and the Edge browser, I will never have to watch a complete YouTube video again.

Using Copilot to write VBA, Python, RegEx, or Power Query M Code

I have written 69 books about Microsoft Excel. A lot of those books go into great detail about writing VBA code or Python or Power Query M code. With Copilot or ChatGPT, you can generate a lot of that code by asking the AI bot.

Right now, in late 2024, the results are mixed. The code will be 90 percent correct, but you will still have to search out a human expert to fix the errors.

Generating a pivot table using VBA from Copilot

Here is a prompt that you can send to *Copilot.Microsoft.com*:

Write some Excel VBA code to create a pivot table from the current region. The customers field is in the rows area. The products field is in the Columns area. Sum of Revenue is in the Values area. Add a slicer for Region.

Copilot returns the following code, which gets you pretty close to the result.

```
Sub CreatePivotTable()
    Dim ws As Worksheet
    Dim pvtCache As PivotCache
    Dim pvtTable As PivotTable
    Dim pvtField As PivotField
    Dim rng As Range

    ' Set the worksheet
```

```
Set ws = ActiveSheet

' Set the range for the pivot table
Set rng = ws.UsedRange

' Create the pivot cache
Set pvtCache = ActiveWorkbook.PivotCaches.Create( _
    SourceType:=xlDatabase, _
    SourceData:=rng)

' Create the pivot table
Set pvtTable = pvtCache.CreatePivotTable( _
    TableDestination:=ws.Cells(1, rng.Columns.Count + 2), _
    TableName:="PivotTable1")

' Add fields to the pivot table
With pvtTable
    .PivotFields("Customers").Orientation = xlRowField
    .PivotFields("Products").Orientation = xlColumnField
    .PivotFields("Revenue").Orientation = xlDataField
    .PivotFields("Revenue").Function = xlSum
End With

' Add slicer for Region
ActiveWorkbook.SlicerCaches.Add(pvtTable, "Region").Slicers.Add ws, , "Region", "Region", ws.Cells(2, rng.
Columns.Count + 5)

End Sub
```

The Copilot code refers to the `.UsedRange` property. It is too easy for extra blank columns and rows to get activated and these will be included in the `.UsedRange`. You would have to make sure to delete all the blank rows and columns before running the code. It would have been better for the code to refer to `Set rng = Range("A1").CurrentRegion`.

When Copilot tries to change the Revenue field to a Sum, that code fails. The line is not necessary since the pivot table will already default to a sum. You can comment out this line of code.

Finally, the position of the slicer is not working, so the slicer never gets created. The problem is solved by using the Excel macro recorder to figure out the correct arguments for the position of the slicer.

I used the same prompt at ChatGPT to generate this code:

```
Sub CreatePivotTableWithSlicerChatGPT()

Dim ws As Worksheet
Dim wsPivot As Worksheet
Dim dataRange As Range
Dim pivotTable As pivotTable
Dim pivotCache As pivotCache
Dim pivotTableRange As Range
Dim slicerCache As slicerCache
```

```
' Set the source data range
Set ws = ActiveSheet
Set dataRange = ws.Cells.CurrentRegion

' Add a new worksheet for the Pivot Table
Set wsPivot = Worksheets.Add
wsPivot.Name = "PivotTableSheet"

' Create a Pivot Cache
Set pivotCache = ThisWorkbook.PivotCaches.Create( _
    SourceType:=xlDatabase, SourceData:=dataRange)

' Set the location for the Pivot Table
Set pivotTableRange = wsPivot.Range("A3")

' Create the Pivot Table
Set pivotTable = pivotCache.CreatePivotTable( _
    TableDestination:=pivotTableRange, TableName:="MyPivotTable")

' Add fields to the Pivot Table
With pivotTable
    .PivotFields("Customers").Orientation = xlRowField
    .PivotFields("Products").Orientation = xlColumnField
    .PivotFields("Revenue").Orientation = xlDataField
    .PivotFields("Revenue").Function = xlSum
End With

' Add a slicer for the "Region" field
Set slicerCache = wsPivot.Slicers.Add(pivotTable:=pivotTable, _
    slicerCache:=pivotTable.pivotCache.SlicerCaches.Add( _
    SourceField:="Region", Name:="RegionSlicer"), _
    Top:=wsPivot.Cells(2, 6).Top, _
    Left:=wsPivot.Cells(2, 6).Left, _
    Width:=100)

End Sub
```

This code is also close. It attempts to add the Slicer to a worksheet object, but it needs to be added to the ActiveWorkbook instead. Just like the Copilot code, this code generates errors when setting the Revenue function to XLSum and when generating the slicer.

Generating a pivot table using Python Code generated by Copilot

As I am writing this in 2024, Python in Excel is still in preview, so I don't expect AI to know about the XL function in Python. My plan is to start the Python code like so:

```
df = xl("A1:K564", headers=True)
```

Then, I ask *Copilot.Microsoft.com* using this prompt:

Create Python code to generate a pivot table from the DataFrame called df. Customers should be in the rows area. Products in the columns area. Sum of Revenue in the values area.

The Python code is perfect, using the `pivot_table` function. At the end of the code, however, Copilot prints the pivot table to the Python console. I changed the last line of this code from print(pivot_table) to simply a line that says pivot_table and then used the dropdown to the left of the formula bar to ask for the results as Excel values.

The following code worked really well, with minimal adjustments:

```
df = xl("A1:K564", headers=True)
pivot_table = pd.pivot_table(
    df,
    values='Revenue',
    index='Customers',
    columns='Products',
    aggfunc='sum',
    fill_value=0  # Optional: Replace NaN with 0
)
pivot_table
```

Generating Power Query M code using Copilot

In this example, you have converted the data set to a Table by choosing Home | Format As Table. Then, on the Table Tools tab, change the table name to MyData.

Use the following prompt at Copilot.Microsoft.com:

Write Power Query M code to read from the Excel table called MyData. The Power Query should group by Customer. It should pivot the Product field with a Sum of the Revenue field.

Copilot returns the following M code:

```
let
    // Load the Excel table named "MyData"
    Source = Excel.CurrentWorkbook(){[Name="MyData"]}[Content],

    // Group by "Customer"
    GroupedData = Table.Group(
        Source,
        {"Customer"},
        {{"AllData", each _, type table [Customer=nullable text, Product=nullable text, Revenue=nullable number]}}
    ),

    // Pivot the "Product" field and aggregate using the sum of "Revenue"
    PivotedData = Table.TransformColumns(
        GroupedData,
        {"AllData", each Table.Pivot(
            Table.TransformColumnTypes(_, {{"Product", type text}, {"Revenue", type number}}),
            List.Distinct(Table.Column(_, "Product")),
```

```
        "Product",
        "Revenue",
        List.Sum
    )}
),

// Expand the pivoted columns back into the main table
ExpandedPivot = Table.ExpandTableColumn(
    PivotedData,
    "AllData",
    {"Customer"} & List.Distinct(Table.Column(Source, "Product"))
)

in
    ExpandedPivot
```

This code has a couple of problems:

- It doesn't group the data by customer.

- In the ExpandedPivot section, it tries to add a second field called Customer, which generates an error.

The good news is that your favorite Power Query author, such as Mike Girvin, Ken Puls, Miguel Escobar, or Chandeep Chhabra won't be replaced by Copilot just yet.

Generating RegEx with Copilot

In 2024, Microsoft released new functions to work with Regular Expressions or RegEx. The syntax for RegEx patterns is complicated to learn.

In this example, I have a column of prospects. The data is comma-separated. Fields can be missing. A comma will follow a name, and a comma might also follow a company name. Line 1 of the street address is almost always present, followed by a comma. Line 2 of the street address might be there in a few cases, followed by a comma. The final line of the address is almost always the city, a comma, state, a comma, and then zip code. If your goal is to get the city name, one strategy is to isolate everything from the second-to-the-last comma back to the third-to-the-last comma.

Asking both Copilot and ChatGPT for the RegEx code produced three different patterns, none of which work in Excel:

```
(?:[^,]*,){2}([^,]*)(?=,[^,]*$)
(?:[^,]*,){2}([^,]*),[^,]*$
(?:[^,]*,){2}([^,]*),[^,]*,[^,]*$
```

Figure 18-52 shows the incorrect result.

One solution is to abandon RegEx and use two new Excel functions:

```
=TEXTBEFORE(TEXTAFTER(A2,", ",-3),", ")
```

B2 =REGEXEXTRACT(A2,"(?:[^,]*,){2}([^,]*)(?=,[^,]*$)")

	A	B
1	Contact	RegEx to Get City
2	Lamar Brenin, Flowserve, 291 Receipt Boulevard NW, Floor 18, Anchorage, AK, 90210	Floor 18, Anchorage, AK
3	Myles Beckett, Monsanto, 6693 Dime Ln NE, Glendale, AZ, 64928	6693 Dime Ln NE, Glendale, AZ
4	Phoebe Lindsey, 3M Company, 3627 Tramp Blvd, Glendale, AZ, 81954	3627 Tramp Blvd, Glendale, AZ
5	Angélique Ludlow, 4435 Hat Blvd S, Daly City, CA, 60710	4435 Hat Blvd S, Daly City, CA
6	Willow Sellick, Ingersoll-Rand PLC, 950 Payment Boulevard NE, Room 101, Corona, CA, 39815	Room 101, Corona, CA
7	Asia Reynolds, Lowe's Cos., 827 Stop Avenue E, Rialto, CA, 36534	827 Stop Avenue E, Rialto, CA
8	Wilson Marchi, 3M Company, 3120 Pancake Blvd W, Chula Vista, CA, 83695	3120 Pancake Blvd W, Chula Vista, CA
9	Juliana Kilburne, Kraft Heinz Co, 765 Beggar St, Palmdale, CA, 29231	765 Beggar St, Palmdale, CA
10	Lee Bingham, Starbucks, 496 Chin St, Jurupa Valley, CA, 49232	496 Chin St, Jurupa Valley, CA
11	Nehemiah Ribeiro, BlackRock, 5256 Bear Ave SE, Sunnyvale, CA, 17720	5256 Bear Ave SE, Sunnyvale, CA
12	Christopher Doyle, Clorox, 9792 Smoke Avenue NW, Apt 2, Waterbury, CT, 69694	Apt 2, Waterbury, CT

FIGURE 18-52 Even after three tries to generate the correct RegEx, it is not working.

Or, you could find a human who is comfortable with RegEx and can provide a working pattern, like I did. (Thanks to Suat Ozgur for the 4 AM consult!)

```
(?:\s([^,]*),){1}[^,]*(?=,[^,]*$)
```

For those afraid that AI is going to take all of our jobs, there is still a need for humans in the workflow!

Fun: Using Copilot to write Excel poetry or songs

One of the early strengths of ChatGPT or Copilot is the ability to write songs or poems. If you are looking for some fun, you can have Copilot write some lyrics or poetry for you.

Prompt:

Write a haiku about the joy of pivot tables.

Return:

Numbers dance and spin,

Data's story comes alive,

Pivot tables win.

Prompt:

Write a Limerick about using the Excel Data Model to create a pivot table from millions of rows of data.

Return:

In Excel, the data's so grand,

With millions of rows close at hand.

The Data Model's the key,

For a pivot, you see,

To slice, dice, and truly command!

Prompt:

Write a Shakespearean sonnet about using an Excel pivot table to discover amazing trends in data.

Return:

Upon the grid where numbers oft confound,
A pivot table's magic doth appear,
To twist and turn the data all around,
And from the chaos, patterns become clear.

With simple clicks, the fields begin to dance,
Dimensions shift, and measures intertwine,
What seemed like noise now blooms into a chance,
For hidden trends and insights to align.

Like stars that dot the dark and endless night,
These charts reveal what eyes could not before,
A sales spike here, a cost that's taking flight,
A newfound path to profit and explore.

Oh, Excel's art, thy pivot's noble role,
Doth guide our minds to reach a greater goal.

Prompt:

Write a Country Music love song about pivot tables in Microsoft Excel in the style of Garth Brooks.

Return:

(Verse 1)
I was stuck in a rut, with my data in a bind,
Rows and rows of numbers, almost lost my mind.
But then I found the answer, like a light shinin' bright,
In a pivot table, everything turned out right.

(Chorus)
Oh, pivot table, you turned my world around,
You took my data blues and laid them down.

From the boardroom to the bar, I know I can depend,

On a pivot table, my new best friend.

(Verse 2)

Now I'm slicin' and dicin', with just a simple click,

Seeing trends in the data, it all makes sense so quick.

Ain't no need for worry, I got you by my side,

With Excel and a pivot, I'm on a data ride.

(Bridge)

Like a cowboy needs a horse, or a farmer needs the rain,

I need my pivot table to make it through the pain.

It shows me where I'm goin', where I've been before,

I'm lovin' every minute, and I'm always findin' more.

(Chorus)

Oh, pivot table, you turned my world around,

You took my data blues and laid them down.

From the boardroom to the bar, I know I can depend,

On a pivot table, my new best friend.

(Outro)

So here's to Excel, and here's to you,

My pivot table love, forever true.

In 2023, for Spreadsheet Day, I went out to Cameo to find famous singers who were willing to sing in the Cameo and found Roy Stride, frontman for the UK band Scouting for Girls. At this point in time, Copilot had not arrived on the scene. I used Chat-GPT and asked for a song about Excel in the style of Scouting for Girls.

See Stride singing about Excel on Cameo at *https://www.youtube.com/watch?v=2POYY7pM1ko*.

Following are the lyrics produced by the Excel LABS.GENERATIVEAI function:

Oh, Excel you're my number one!

My data has never been so fun.

With your formulas and your charts,

You make spreadsheets a work of art.

I wasn't really familiar with Jamaican dancehall music, but the artist D'Angel is apparently huge in Jamaica. It took her a second take to get the lyrics flowing, but you can find the world's leading dancehall song about Excel here: https://www.youtube.com/watch?v=M9yyvrKXoU0. Following are the lyrics:

Microsoft Excel Oh What a Tool

It keeps me organized, it keeps me cool.

Columns and rows, formulas galore

Makes my data dance like never before!

The next time you are at work and need to toast your CFO for his 30 years of Excel prowess, remember to turn to Copilot or ChatGPT to help write a poem or song for them. You can also use *Suno.com* to have the lyrics sung in any particular style.

Next steps

Chapter 19 will take a look at undoing this entire book (e.g., how to unpivot data that is already pivoted).

Unpivoting in Power Query

In this chapter, you will:

- Learn why data in headings creates bad pivot tables

- Use Unpivot in Power Query to transform the data

- Unpivot data with two rows of headings

- Unpivot data from a delimited cell to new rows

You've spent the previous 18 chapters learning how to pivot your data to create summary reports. What happens if your source data is already pivoted? It creates pivot tables that are difficult to work with. In this chapter, you will see how the Power Query tools in Excel can be used to unpivot data.

Data in headings creates bad pivot tables

The data in Figure 19-1 is in a common format. There are three columns of labels on the left and 12 columns of monthly data going across the top.

⊿	A	B	C	D	E	F	G	H	I	J	K	L	M	N	O
1	Product	Rep	Region	Jan	Feb	Mar	Apr	May	Jun	Jul	Aug	Sep	Oct	Nov	Dec
2	Apple	Andy	East	81	22	59	94	74	23	54	33	63	57	27	38
3	Apple	Barb	Central	37	95	71	52	18	14	68	64	21	40	49	38
4	Apple	Chris	West	52	43	33	91	44	52	98	30	17	83	11	48
5	Apple	Diane	East	92	38	60	91	33	27	57	70	60	70	49	69
6	Apple	Ed	Central	39	57	78	64	59	76	65	83	54	24	54	44
7	Apple	Flo	West	67	37	46	95	13	84	40	39	25	14	29	44
8	Apple	Gary	East	54	94	79	48	33	31	85	47	51	91	48	72
9	Apple	Hank	Central	70	76	57	83	14	86	30	56	27	24	29	65

FIGURE 19-1 Placing the months in column heading is a common format.

However, starting with source data that looks like this creates horrible pivot tables. If you wanted to show all 12 months, you would have to drag 12 fields to the Values area. Figure 19-2 shows the pivot table with just the first three months.

Once you get the months into the pivot table, adding a grand total will require a calculated field. Select PivotTable Analyze | Fields Items And Sets | Calculated Field, and then build the formula, as shown in Figure 19-3.

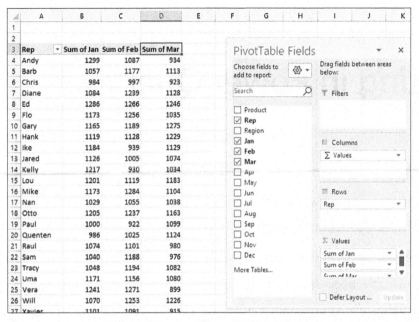

FIGURE 19-2 You would have to choose all 12 months to get the whole year in the pivot table.

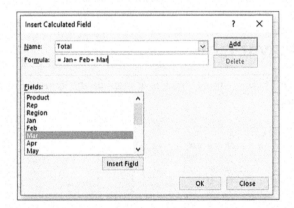

FIGURE 19-3 By the end of the year, you will have edited this formula to add all 12 months.

Figure 19-4 shows the Total column for January through March. As you continue adding more months, you will have to edit the Total formula for each month.

Rep	Sum of Jan	Sum of Feb	Sum of Mar	Sum of Total
Andy	1299	1087	934	3320
Barb	1057	1177	1113	3347
Chris	984	997	923	2904
Diane	1084	1239	1128	3451

FIGURE 19-4 While it is possible to get a total of all the months, doing so is unwieldy.

Using Unpivot in Power Query to transform the data

As a general rule, you are looking for narrow and tall data sets instead of wide data sets. Instead of having 12 columns of sales data, you would want five columns in the original data: Product, Rep, Region, Month, and Sales. This causes the data set to get taller. If you had 500 rows of the data from Figure 19-1, you would need 6,000 rows of data in the new format, but the pivot tables would work better.

The Get And Transform Data tools on the Data tab offer many ways to transform data, including a command called Unpivot. These tools are called the Power Query tools. Power Query will keep your original data set intact, perform transformations in memory, and then load the transformed data to a new worksheet or directly to the workbook data model. Follow these steps:

1. To get started, you should format the data as a table. Select any one cell in your data and press Ctrl+T. Make sure that Excel chooses My Table Has Headers. The data will be formatted, and filter dropdowns will appear on the heading row.

2. Go to the Table Design tab in the ribbon and change the Table Name from `Table1` to something meaningful. In Figure 19-5, the Table Name is `FormattedData`.

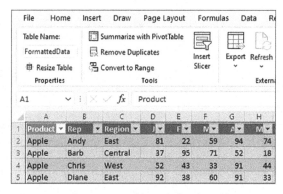

FIGURE 19-5 Format as a table and give the table a name.

3. On the Data tab, look in the Get And Transform Data group and choose From Sheet. (In earlier versions of Excel, this was called From Table/Range.) The Power Query editor will open.

4. Select the Product column by clicking the Product heading. Ctrl+click the Region heading to select all the label columns.

5. In Power Query, on the Transform tab, open the Unpivot Columns dropdown and choose Unpivot Other Columns (see Figure 19-6).

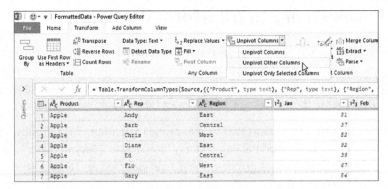

FIGURE 19-6 A single Unpivot operation in Power Query replaces a dozen time-consuming steps in Excel.

6. After choosing Unpivot Other Columns, the 12 columns of monthly data are replaced by two new columns. These columns are always initially called Attribute and Value. As shown in Figure 19-7, the former column headings of Jan, Feb, Mar, and so on are now arranged vertically in the Attribute column. The former sales figures are now arranged vertically in the Values column.

	Product	Rep	Region	Attribute	Value
1	Apple	Andy	East	Jan	81
2	Apple	Andy	East	Feb	22
3	Apple	Andy	East	Mar	59
4	Apple	Andy	East	Apr	94
5	Apple	Andy	East	May	74

= Table.UnpivotOtherColumns(#"Changed Type", {"Product", "Rep", "Region"}, "Attribute", "Value")

FIGURE 19-7 The wide data set is now narrow but 12 times taller.

There is a formula bar in Power Query that is not shown by default. If you select View | Formula Bar, you can see that the previous step of unpivoting is recorded in the formula bar as this line of code:

```
= Table.UnpivotOtherColumns(#"Changed Type", {"Product", "Rep", "Region"},
"Attribute", "Value")
```

A quick way to rename the Attribute and Value columns is to click in the formula bar and change Attribute to Month and Value to Sales, as shown in Figure 19-8.

	Product	Rep	Region	Month	Sales
1	Apple	Andy	East	Jan	81
2	Apple	Andy	East	Feb	22
3	Apple	Andy	East	Mar	59
4	Apple	Andy	East	Apr	94

= Table.UnpivotOtherColumns(#"Changed Type", {"Product", "Rep", "Region"}, "Month", "Sales")

FIGURE 19-8 Edit the previous step in the formula bar to clean up the generic headings used by Unpivot.

Tip The code shown in the formula bar is a bit of the M programming language. When you perform actions using the ribbon commands in Power Query, those commands get translated to M code and are shown in the formula bar and in the Advanced Editor available on the View tab.

M is a very rich language with many options. Only a fraction of those options are revealed in the Power Query ribbon. When you choose Unpivot Other Columns, the results appear. The Power Query team could have decided to show another dialog asking for the new name for `Attribute` and `Value` columns, but they figured it would be easier to quickly give you the amazing results of the unpivot and then let you use existing methods to rename the columns if that is important to you.

There are other ways to rename the columns using the Power Query ribbon. You could double-click each heading to put the heading in edit mode: Type a new value, or right-click each heading and choose Rename.

I've met people who never use the Power Query ribbon. They create a blank query and type all the M code from scratch. I am not that hardcore, but I will look for opportunities to consolidate a few steps into a single step by editing the formula bar.

You are done in Power Query. From the Home tab, click Close & Load. Your transformed data is inserted in a new sheet to the left of the original sheet.

Figure 19-9 shows the results of Power Query in columns A through E and then in a new pivot table starting in G2. With the pivot table, drag Month to Rows, Region to Columns, and Sales to Values.

Product	Rep	Region	Month	Sales
Apple	Andy	East	Jan	81
Apple	Andy	East	Feb	22
Apple	Andy	East	Mar	59
Apple	Andy	East	Apr	94
Apple	Andy	East	May	74
Apple	Andy	East	Jun	23
Apple	Andy	East	Jul	54
Apple	Andy	East	Aug	33
Apple	Andy	East	Sep	63
Apple	Andy	East	Oct	57
Apple	Andy	East	Nov	27
Apple	Andy	East	Dec	38
Apple	Barb	Central	Jan	37
Apple	Barb	Central	Feb	95
Apple	Barb	Central	Mar	71
Apple	Barb	Central	Apr	52
Apple	Barb	Central	May	18
Apple	Barb	Central	Jun	14
Apple	Barb	Central	Jul	68
Apple	Barb	Central	Aug	64
Apple	Barb	Central	Sep	21
Apple	Barb	Central	Oct	40
Apple	Barb	Central	Nov	49
Apple	Barb	Central	Dec	38
Apple	Chris	West	Jan	52
Apple	Chris	West	Feb	43
Apple	Chris	West	Mar	33
Apple	Chris	West	Apr	91
Apple	Chris	West	May	44
Apple	Chris	West	Jun	52
Apple	Chris	West	Jul	98
Apple	Chris	West	Aug	30
Apple	Chris	West	Sep	17
Apple	Chris	West	Oct	83
Apple	Chris	West	Nov	11
Apple	Chris	West	Dec	48

Sum of Sales	Region			
Month	East	Central	West	Grand Total
Jan	10219	9922	9093	29234
Feb	10253	9915	8896	29064
Mar	9559	10362	8408	28329
Apr	9894	9663	9075	28632
May	10580	9742	8701	29023
Jun	9566	9589	8449	27604
Jul	10114	10313	9068	29495
Aug	10547	9690	8143	28380
Sep	10566	9959	8551	29076
Oct	9121	9223	8601	26945
Nov	9935	9846	8428	28209
Dec	9339	10339	9062	28740
Grand Total	119693	118563	104475	342731

FIGURE 19-9 It is far easier to create more pivot tables using the data in this tall and narrow format.

Unpivoting from two rows of headings

The previous example was simple: A single unpivot transformed your data. The example shown in Figure 19-10 might be more like what you will see in the real world. The data in column A is shown in outline form, where the word East in A3 applies to the blank A4:A11 rows. The year 2029 in C1 applies to all the blank columns from D1 to N1. The year 2030 in O1 applies to the blank columns to its right.

Power Query makes it very easy to fill in the blanks in column A, but it is more complex to fill across row 1.

	A	B	C	D	E	F	G	H	I	J	K	L	M	N	O	P
1			2029												2030	
2	Region	Rep	Jan	Feb	Mar	Apr	May	Jun	Jul	Aug	Sep	Oct	Nov	Dec	Jan	Feb
3	East	Andy	1299	1087	934	1173	1073	1120	1077	849	1190	954	1156	1183	1559	1304
4		Diane	1084	1239	1128	1105	1136	1239	1096	1116	1318	1284	1021	1244	1301	1487
5		Gary	1165	1189	1275	984	1027	1082	1114	1127	1237	1007	988	993	1398	1427
6		Jared	1126	1005	1074	1069	1327	998	1150	1226	1139	1020	1156	1018	1351	1206
7		Michelle	1173	1284	1104	1068	1358	1047	1269	1287	1297	1114	1259	971	1408	1541
8		Paul	1000	922	1099	1234	981	954	1246	1265	1052	1024	1089	805	1200	1106
9		Stacie	1040	1188	976	906	1211	1073	1210	1145	1071	871	1224	938	1248	1426
10		Vera	1241	1271	899	1140	1251	1064	891	1260	1175	885	963	1101	1489	1525
11		Yazmin	1091	1068	1070	1215	1216	989	1061	1272	1087	962	1079	1086	1309	1282
12	East Total		10219	10253	9559	9894	10580	9566	10114	10547	10566	9121	9935	9339	12263	12304
13	Central	Barb	1057	1177	1113	1087	1066	1138	1193	1098	1037	965	1186	964	1268	1412
14		Ed	1286	1266	1246	942	1119	1115	1181	829	1005	1034	1028	1062	1543	1519

FIGURE 19-10 You can transform this data using Power Query.

Power Query loves to work on tables, but tables require a heading above every column. The data in Figure 19-10 does not have headings that can be used in a table. Most of row 1 is blank. The monthly headings in row 2 are not unique. So, in this case, rather than using a table, you should use a named range:

1. Select all the data from A1:Z32. Click in the Name Box (located to the left of the formula bar), type **MyData**, and press Enter.

2. With the entire MyData range selected, go to Data | From Table/Range. Power Query will understand that you are using a named range and will not try to add headings to your data.

3. Fill in the blanks in column A. Select the Column1 heading. On the Transform tab, open the Fill dropdown and choose Down, as shown in Figure 19-11.

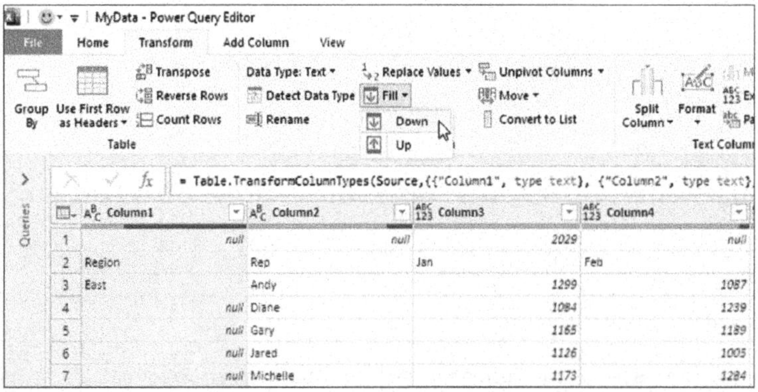

FIGURE 19-11 Your days of using Go To Special Blanks in Excel are over.

4. Amazingly, choosing Fill | Down fills each blank cell with the value shown in Figure 19-12.

FIGURE 19-12 The blanks in column A are filled in with the region from above.

5. This is the point where I always wish that I could select row 1 and choose Fill | Right, but Power Query does not offer a Fill, Right command. Because Microsoft doesn't offer Fill | Right, you will have to transpose the data, choose Fill | Down, and then transpose back. All of the steps from Figures 19-13 through 19-17 could be replaced if Power Query would offer a Fill | Right command.

6. Look carefully back at Figure 19-12. The ribbon shows the Transpose command on the Transform tab. Choose Transpose to temporarily turn the data sideways so you can choose Fill | Down.

7. As shown in Figure 19-13, choose the column that has years 2029 and 2030. Choose Transform | Fill | Down.

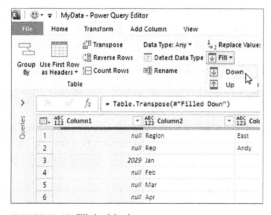

FIGURE 19-13 Fill the blank years.

After filling down, you have two columns on the left that represented column headings in the original data. The year is in Column1, and the month abbreviation is in Column2. You need to combine these into a single column. In Excel, you might use =B2&" "&A2 and copy that formula to the other rows.

The equivalent command in Power Query is called Merge Columns. Because you want the month from Column2 before the Year from Column1, you need to follow these instructions very carefully:

1. Click the Column2 heading to select the months first.

2. Ctrl+Click the Column1 heading to select the years second.

3. On the Transform tab, choose Merge Columns (Figure 19-14).

Caution If you are not carefully reading the steps above, you will tend to select the columns in the wrong sequence. It feels natural to click the left column (with years) and then Ctrl+click (or Shift+click) month. Selecting the columns in the wrong sequence will not produce the correct results.

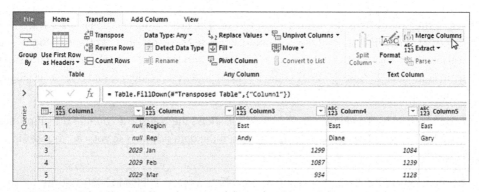

FIGURE 19-14 Select the months and years, and then select Merge Columns.

In the Merge Columns dialog, you get to choose a separator to be used between the columns and then supply a new name for the column. By selecting a space as the separator, you should get Jan 2029, which will make the results look enough like a date for Power Query to transform it as a date (see Figure 19-15).

I have a small rant about the results of the merge. In the previous example, you were merging Column2 and Column1. You might have expected Power Query to put the new column to the left of Column1 or to the right of Column2 (or even to the left of Column2). However, Power Query always adds the new column to the right of the last column. Scroll all the way out beyond Column32 to find the new month and year data.

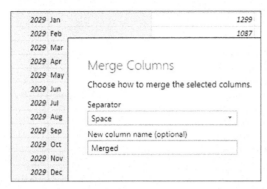

2029	Jan		1299
2029	Feb		1087
2029	Mar	
2029	Apr	Merge Columns
2029	May	
2029	Jun	Choose how to merge the selected columns.
2029	Jul	
2029	Aug	Separator
2029	Sep	Space
2029	Oct	New column name (optional)
2029	Nov	Merged
2029	Dec	

FIGURE 19-15 Change the separator to a space before merging the month and year.

Right-click the heading for the new column and choose Move | To Beginning, as shown in Figure 19-16.

FIGURE 19-16 Move the merged column back to the beginning.

It is not shown in the figures, but now that you have month and year as the first column, you can delete Column1 and Column2.

Because you have successfully combined the two rows of headings into a single value, you are ready to transpose the data back to the original structure. From the Transform tab, choose Transpose (see Figure 19-17).

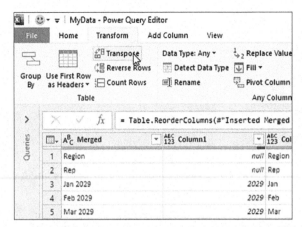

FIGURE 19-17 Transpose the data back to the original orientation.

After transposing the data back to its original orientation, you have column headings appearing in row 1 of the data. On the Home tab, choose Use First Row As Headers (see Figure 19-18).

Column1	Column2	Column3	Column4	Column5
Region	Rep	Jan 2029	Feb 2029	Mar 2029
East	Andy		1299	1087
East	Diane		1084	1239
East	Gary		1165	1189
East	Jared		1126	1005
East	Michelle		1173	1284
East	Paul		1000	922
East	Stacie		1040	1188

FIGURE 19-18 Row 1 is really a column header. Use First Row As Headers to move them above your data.

There is one more bit of clean-up before you unpivot. It seems pretty likely that the original data set was the result of a pivot table. Before sending this report to you, someone created a pivot table, copied it, and pasted it as hard values. If you could find this person, you would likely ask them to send you the source data instead. However, at the very least, you could have asked them to turn off Subtotals for the Region field.

You don't need the East Total shown in row 10 of Figure 19-19. You also don't need the Central Total shown in row 20. Further down in the data, but not shown in the figure, you will also find rows containing West Total and Grand Total. You don't need those either.

One easy way to get rid of the total rows is to open the Filter dropdown for the Rep field and remove any null values.

FIGURE 19-19 If you filter to remove the null values in the Rep column, you will get rid of all the total rows.

You are finally ready for the Unpivot. Select Region and Rep. Right-click the Rep heading and choose Unpivot Other Columns (see Figure 19-20).

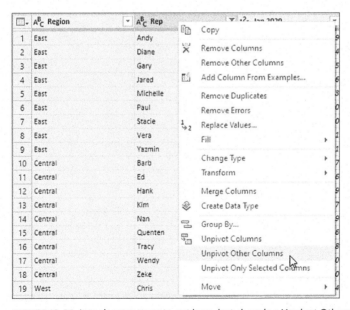

FIGURE 19-20 It took extra steps to get here, but choosing Unpivot Other Columns is still the important step.

The month and year values that made up the column headings are transposed to the Attribute column, but they are showing as text. Select the column containing those values. On the Transform tab, open the Data Type dropdown and choose Date. The "Jan 2029" text will be converted to the date of 1/1/2029 (see Figure 19-21).

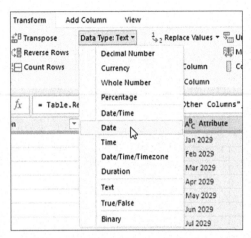

FIGURE 19-21 Convert the text "Jan 2029" to a real date.

This is pretty good, but the sales for January did not all happen on January 1. You might prefer to convert January 1, 2029, to January 31, 2029. Once you have real dates in the column, this is easy to do.

Select the dates. On the right side of the Home tab, open the large Date dropdown. Choose Month | End Of Month, as shown in Figure 19-22.

FIGURE 19-22 As I look at those five options and start thinking of the equivalent Excel formula to do each transform, I appreciate the simplicity of Power Query.

Note You might prefer to have the date column broken out into two or three columns, such as Year, Month Name, and Month Number. You can right-click the Attribute column and choose Duplicate Column twice. Then, use the Date dropdown shown in Figure 19-22 to choose Year for the original column, Month Name for the first duplicated column, and Month Number for the second duplicated column.

Rename a couple of columns, and you are ready to close and load. Figure 19-23 shows the transformed data set.

	A	B	C	D
1	Region ▾	Rep ▾	Date ▾	Sales ▾
2	East	Andy	1/31/2029	1299
3	East	Andy	2/28/2029	1087
4	East	Andy	3/31/2029	934
5	East	Andy	4/30/2029	1173
6	East	Andy	5/31/2029	1073
7	East	Andy	6/30/2029	1120

FIGURE 19-23 Flip back and compare this to the source date shown in Figure 19-10.

With a simple Refresh, you can quickly convert any data from the old format to this useful format.

Unpivoting from a delimited cell to new rows

A few times a year, I see data where many data values are concatenated into a single cell with a delimiter in between. One extreme example is shown in Figure 19-24. Column C contains many pairs of values. The two values in each pair are separated by a comma, but then each subsequent pair of values is separated by a pipe character (|). Each cell in column C contained about 1,000 pairs of data, all in one cell.

You need to split the data by delimiter and then unpivot those results to new rows. In this particular data set, the delimiters are nested. Each pipe character (|) signifies a new row, and each comma signifies a new column.

Power Query makes transforming this data a snap:

1. Format the data as a table.

2. On the Data tab, choose From Sheet to get the data into Power Query.

3. Select column C. On the Power Query Home tab, choose Split Column By Delimiter.

4. As shown in Figure 19-25, change the Delimiter to Custom, and type the pipe character (|).

5. Open the Advanced Options and choose Split Into Rows. When you split column C into new rows, the data from column A and column B are copied down into the new rows. This is perfect and incredibly useful.

	A	B	C	D
1	Product	Manager	Combinations	
2	AAA	Andy	134,AFA|134,ASD|134,AUJ|134,E	
3	BBB	Bob	277,AHR|277,AIK|277,ANQ|277,	
4	CCC	Andy	150,ACF|150,ARP|150,AUK|150,	
5	DDD	Bob	159,AAB|159,AER|159,AHF|159,	
6	EEE	Charlie	135,AQN|135,ASQ|135,BQO|135	
7	FFF	Charlie	150,AAP|150,AJP|150,AKI|150,A	
8	GGG	Dave	102,AKC|102,AKK|102,BAD|102,	
9	HHH	Dave	115,AGJ|115,AOT|115,AQH|115,	
10	III	Dave	123,ACS|123,AEM|123,AGQ|123	
11	JJJ	Andy	100,AEI|100,AKC|100,AUM|100,	
12	LLL	Charlie	142,AAQ|142,AKP|142,ALM|142	
13	MMM	Dave	168,ACE|168,BFQ|168,DJH|168,E	
14	NNN	Andy	142,ACC|142,AIO|142,BID|142,B	
15	OOO	Bob	141,AGF|141,AHA|141,AHH|141,	
16				

FIGURE 19-24 Each cell in column C contains a large array of data.

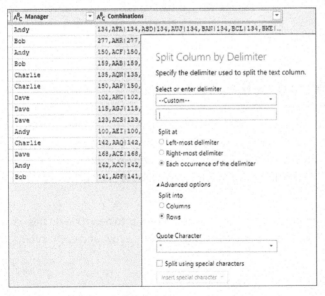

FIGURE 19-25 Split each delimiter into a new row.

6. The last step is to break the third column at the comma, as shown in Figure 19-26.

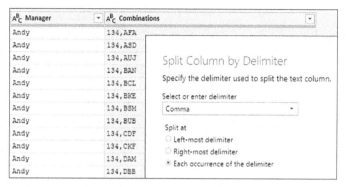

FIGURE 19-26 Split at the comma to create two columns from this data.

The results are shown in Figure 19-27. The data from the 14 cells in Figure 19-24 are quickly transformed into more than 16,000 rows of data.

	Product	Manager	Combinations.1	Combinations.2	E
16338	OOO	Bob	976	TEO	
16339	OOO	Bob	976	TNK	
16340	OOO	Bob	976	TPC	
16341	OOO	Bob	976	TPN	
16342	OOO	Bob	976	TRK	
16343	OOO	Bob	976	UDL	
16344					

FIGURE 19-27 The data quickly unwound into many rows.

Do you notice the "bad" column names in columns C and D above? If this was really your data and you were going to refresh this every day for the rest of your career, you would take the time to rename the column in Power Query.

I remember the day that this question was sent to me. My first attempt at a solution was a convoluted collection of Dynamic Arrays, but it turns out that the tools in Power Query made the solution much easier.

Conclusion

There you have it—everything that I know about pivot tables. You should have all the tools you need to turn ugly, detailed data into beautiful summary reports.

Afterword

This is the eighth edition of this book. When Mike Alexander and I originally wrote a book dedicated to pivot tables back in 2005, it quickly shot up the charts. (The first edition of the book was the number-one best-selling computer book on Amazon.com, for one hour, at four in the morning, on a cold January morning.)

The brand new Copilot feature discussed in Chapter 18 could be the new feature that changes everything. Right now, the feature is very new and not as reliable as most Excel customers will need. However, those limitations will be fixed over time.

Chapter 17 shows how the new PIVOTBY and GROUPBY dynamic arrays can be used to create something that looks like a pivot table without using a pivot table.

But I think the big story theme is Power Query, especially for the 99 percent of Excellers who are still using Windows. It is amazing how many times the data cleansing tools in Power Query become an important part of creating pivot tables. Power Query shows up in 8 of the 18 chapters of the book.

Most people—even those using Excel 40+ hours a week—don't realize that the icons on the Data tab that serve as the entry point for Power Query are special. Those icons, added in 2016, replaced a bunch of very similar legacy icons from Excel 2013. It would be easy to think nothing significant has changed.

For the people using Excel all day, every day, if you have not discovered Power Query, go back and check out these examples in the book:

- Case study: Cleaning up data for pivot table analysis in Chapter 2

- Case study: Using DAX measures instead of calculated fields in Chapter 5

- Leveraging Power Query to extract and transform data in the last 75 percent of Chapter 7

- Processing big data with Power Query in Chapter 10

- Combining all files from a folder using Power Query in Chapter 12 (see Creating a Macro with Power Query).

- Tip 21: Do a two-way VLOOKUP with Power Query in Chapter 14

- Pivoting without a pivot table using Power Query in Chapter 17

- Unpivoting with Power Query in Chapter 19

Index

S